# THE DOC'S
# DEVILS

## MANCHESTER UNITED
### 1972-1977

# THE DOC'S DEVILS

## MANCHESTER UNITED
### 1972-1977

## SEAN EGAN

First published in Great Britain in 2010 by

Cherry Red Books
Power Road Studios
114 Power Road
Chiswick
London W4 5PY
England

ISBN: 978 1 901447 37 8

Cover image and photographs courtesy of Getty Images

# Contents

# Acknowledgments

My grateful thanks to the people who agreed to be interviewed for this book: Frank Blunstone, Laurie Brown, Martin Buchan, Peter Coyne, Gerry Daly, Mick Docherty, Peter Fletcher, Alex Forsyth, Brian Greenhoff, Gordon Hill, Stewart Houston, Ted MacDougall, Jim McCalliog, David McCreery, Sammy McIlroy, Mick Martin, David Meek, Jimmy Nicholl and Colin Waldron.

All of the above gave their time generously, but I am particularly indebted to Frank Blunstone, Martin Buchan, Gordon Hill, Mick Martin and David Meek, who fielded multiple queries with probably unwarranted patience.

My thanks too to Michael Crick, not only for his foreword, but for employing his superior expertise about Manchester United to correct various factual mistakes throughout the original typescript – as well as his superior mathematical expertise to work out teams' average ages...

Additional grateful thanks for assistance go to Claire Burrows of the Professional Footballers Association, David Sadler of the Association of Former Manchester United Players, Iain McCartney of Reds Research and Joseph Tedesco of the Manchester United Supporters Club of Malta. Apologies to anyone who provided assistance whom I have inadvertently omitted.

# Foreword

This is an extraordinary book. Sean Egan describes in great detail for the first time a remarkable, rollercoaster period for Manchester United, an era generally neglected by other club historians. It's the product of years of painstaking and dedicated research.

I lived through the Tommy Docherty years as a teenager. Every tiny move at Manchester United in those days dominated my daily thoughts. I calculate that I attended around 80 per of the games for which TD was in charge, travelling to away fixtures on football specials from Manchester, then later hitch-hiking thousands of miles up and down England's motorways.

I endured the agony of the 5-0 defeat at Crystal Palace which secured the dismissal of Frank O'Farrell in 1972. Later came the curious novelty of visiting new grounds in the Second Division – clubs such as Orient, Cardiff City and York City, during what was a surprisingly enjoyable season of rebuilding. This was quickly followed by the exhilaration of 1975-76 when we roared back to Division One in style, and very nearly won an FA Cup and League double

Sean Egan's account of events during these four and a half years rings astonishingly true with my own fond and vivid memories. His book brings back the noise and the colour of being in Docherty's Red Army following the team home and away, the smells and physical experience of the mid-Seventies on the Stretford End. The euphoria and the fear, the joy and despair, all come back.

Following Manchester United is rarely dull. This period bears that out. During every season in this book, United spent some time either bottom of the league, or on top. The start of the

Docherty era saw some of the most defensive and negative football in the whole of United's history. But then, within only a year or two, we experienced some of the most dramatic, swashbuckling play ever performed by the Reds. These years saw the sad departures of all three of the Holy Trinity who made United so popular in the 1960s – Bobby Charlton, Denis Law and George Best. Instead, the Docherty period will forever be associated with a new generation of dazzling young Reds – among them Steve Coppell, Gerry Daly and Gordon Hill. The Docherty team was never a world-class side to compare with the legendary Manchester United teams of 1958, 1968 or 1999. But for sheer entertainment, great goals and attacking wing play, the Docherty XI of 1974-77 was on a par, I'd say, with any team of the Ferguson years. As crowd-pleasers they may even have matched the great Busby Babes.

Sean Egan has tracked down and interviewed many of the players from the Docherty era. And he's talked to them at length. He's not assembled the usual collection of dull retired footballer cliches – though there's the odd one – but genuine revelations about what happened at Old Trafford between 1972 and 1977. And why it happened.

The Doc's Devils is an impressive, comprehensive chronicle of Tommy Docherty's time at Old Trafford. It will be years, I suspect, before anyone will improve on it.

Michael Crick
Co-author, *Manchester United: The Betrayal of a Legend*
Author, *The Boss: The Many Sides of Alex Ferguson*

# Introduction

**I**n May 1993, after a 26-year title drought, Manchester United won the First Division championship, or, rather, the Premier League as it had recently been renamed.

Despite being arguably the most legendary name in world football, it was generally agreed that since the retirement of Matt Busby as manager in June 1969 after a quarter of a century in the post, the club had spent another quarter-century trading on past glories. As one fan articulately lamented prior to that 1993 title, "We've got a history, but that's all we've got." Naturally, following the 1993 triumph, much celebration ensued, with manager Alex Ferguson being hailed as a saviour who had rescued a great club from mediocrity and restored it to its true place in the hierarchy. Since then, United have barely looked back. When Ferguson took charge of the club in November 1986, United had won the First Division championship seven times in their 108-year history. By June 2010, they had won it a further 11 times.

Yet many who have memories stretching back a little longer than Ferguson, or Dave Sexton and Ron Atkinson, his alternately dull and flamboyant predecessors in the manager's hot seat, are convinced that United could have started that run of modern-day championships a long time before they did had they not taken the decision to sack manager Tommy Docherty for non-football reasons in 1977, just 44 days after he had secured the club the FA Cup. As Gordon Hill – probably the player who epitomised the Docherty era at Manchester United in both his youthful brashness and swashbuckling, sometimes reckless, playing style – says, "What really ticks me off about United, they don't really play the Doc era up much ... From when we won the FA Cup right the way through, they haven't looked back, and yet no one recognises [that]. It's all Fergie, Fergie, Fergie." While one can dispute the idea of unalloyed success from Docherty through to the modern age, Hill has a point about the unjustified neglect of Tommy Docherty's legacy.

Docherty – affectionately nicknamed 'The Doc' by a press he had a knack for buttering up – was brought into Old Trafford in the closing days of 1972 in what were the worst times for United in living memory. Their nickname The Red Devils – evocative of their traditionally dashing and adventurous approach to football – was a sick joke. Winners of the European Cup (in 1992 rechristened the Champions League) as recently as 1968 (and at the time still the only English team to have taken that trophy), they were now in the middle of a relegation struggle. Initially, Docherty – who had given up the Scotland manager's job to take up a role that had been his lifelong ambition – did seem a saviour, yanking United out of the relegation zone sufficiently to ensure that they would be starting the next season still in the top flight. He then persuaded the iconic George Best out of retirement (albeit briefly). However, collapse followed salvation: the following season United seemed unable to win, unable to score and far too busy dealing with the exigencies of an ageing squad and relegation worries to occupy themselves with thoughts of good football. The unthinkable trauma of dropping into the Second Division was the consequence.

It's possible that only the thought of the embarrassment involved for the United board in dismissing a third manager in less than four years saved Docherty from the sack. Whatever the reason for United's faith in the Scotsman, he more than repaid their loyalty in the following three seasons. In the Second Division, he started rebuilding the side. When United re-entered the First Division in August 1975, they were unrecognisable from the team that had so ignominiously gone down. One football pundit described the new Manchester United as a "revelation" for their youthfulness and boldness. Docherty's signing of Gordon Hill a few months into the 1975/76 campaign enabled him to finally adopt the 4-2-4 system he had long wanted. For the remainder of the season and the whole of the next, Manchester United were the most exciting side in English soccer. They were not the most successful, yet their *joie de vive* seemed almost a moral victory over Liverpool, who were the dominant club of the age due to an undeniably efficient but ultimately sterile low-risk possession football. United's attractiveness made them omnipresent. Though football coverage on television in those days was severely rationed, the impressionistic memory of that era (no doubt inaccurate but in one sense revealing) is of United being represented on the box every single week, said coverage always augmented by the amusing sight of Docherty in his black raincoat giving a post-match analysis around a mouthful of gum. The broadcasters risked alienating viewers who wanted their local side given their fair share of the limited TV slots because Docherty's side were in demand. The Doc's Devils were liked by neutrals – admired – in a way that Alex Ferguson's teams can only dream of.

As gates at Old Trafford boomed, the stage was set for Manchester United's young lions to overtake Liverpool and become the dominant force in the land. In an alternate universe, Tommy Docherty would have been allowed to build on the success he brought to the club, effecting the eclipse of possession football by a brand of soccer that thrilled the masses in the way only risk-taking and flair can.

It was not to be. In June 1977, Docherty's affair with a colleague's wife hit the newspapers. We will probably now never know whether, as rumoured, the club used this as a pretext to rid themselves of a manager whose flamboyance, avarice and tempestuousness made some board members consider him an embarrassment. One thing, however, cannot be disputed: Docherty's dismissal led to the squandering of a team on the brink of greatness. Subsequent managers altered and ultimately dismantled the Docherty side in a vain quest for improvement and it took the cub – through the efforts of Alex Ferguson – more than a decade-and-a-half to pick up the thread of flair and success once again.

This work is not a hagiography that overlooks either Docherty's personal or professional flaws, nor does it seek to exaggerate the quality of the team he created. However, what it does do, with the assistance of many of the players from the time, is analyse in depth the four-and-a-half remarkable years The Doc spent at the club – probably for the very first time – and in so doing seek finally to give The Doc's Devils their due.

# PART ONE

# 1972/73: Rescue

**D**ecember 16 1972. Manchester United were just about to hit their lowest ebb since 1939, a time when they were – unthinkably by now – a club in the second tier of the English Football League.

They were playing Crystal Palace at the latter's Selhurst Park ground. Palace were a rather unprepossessing club. Currently bottom of the First Division – then the top flight of English football – not only would they be relegated this season, they would be relegated to the Third Division the season afterwards. As recently as April 1971, United had put five past Palace at this ground (even if the home side had replied with three). This fact, however, only told part of the story, for Manchester United were no strangers to the lower depths of the First Division themselves at this juncture and were hovering above the relegation zone (which then constituted just two places). Even the extent of Palace's 5-0 trouncing of United this day did not fully explain why the result was so cataclysmic.

Yes, losing 5-0 was humiliating, but the result had a symbolic quality far and away above the realities of current form, squad weakness and League positions. The club that Palace took apart were a legend. Not for nothing was the 39,484 gate that day the biggest at Selhurst Park so far that season, as well as the largest in the four divisions of the Football League that day. Manchester United, then as now, were the most famous club name in English, nay British, possibly – even then – world football. As with many legends, tragedy – in this case, the Munich air disaster of 1958 which had taken the lives of eight members of United's young team – played its part, but the legend was based far more on achievement than sympathy. This achievement was as much to do with conduct as honours. During the 60s, United had won the FA Cup and two League championships and had become the first English team to win the European Cup. However, it was the style with which they had taken those trophies that endeared them to the public in a way that others who won similar honours with more prosaic soccer could never hope to match. Under manager Matt Busby, the Red Devils – as they were nicknamed from the early 60s – put the emphasis on swashbuckling, attacking football. Busby's nose for players who would fit this vision had ensured that United's name was attached to those of a string of iconic footballing figures, Duncan Edwards, Bobby Charlton, Denis Law and George Best amongst them. In short, Manchester United was a name synonymous with quality. To see United succumbing to a sub-standard side like Palace as both teams attempted to keep their feet off the relegation trapdoor was tragic.

Asked if the 5-0 scoreline accurately reflected the run of the play, Martin Buchan, a central defender for United that day, says, "Oh aye. We were lucky to get nil. I remember Don Rogers running riot. They thoroughly outplayed us." Striker Ted MacDougall agrees, and says, "We basically as a team knew that the manager was going to get canned and it was a feeling of insecurity."

So how is it that things had come to this, just four-and-a-half years since United had achieved that European Cup milestone? The resignation of Matt Busby as manager in 1969 was perhaps inevitable. Mentally, Busby had been rendered an old, old man by Munich, a sense of responsibility for the deaths of his beloved young charges weighing heavily on his shoulders because he had insisted on taking part in European competition when the Football League had made their opposition to it explicit. He had no reason to feel guilty: if it hadn't been for a petty rule dreamed up by League secretary Alan Hardaker as a sulking response to Busby ignoring officialdom's opposition, the Munich tragedy would not have happened. The rule – which dictated that any team taking part in European competition must be back in their home country a full 24 hours before their next domestic fixture – prevented the club from simply abandoning their journey until the next day when the conditions might have been more conducive to air flight. The tried to take off in terrible weather conditions with horrific consequences. Nonetheless, Busby blamed himself and many got the sense that he had only held on to a job for a further decade that he would have gladly relinquished in 1958 because had he not won the European Cup it would almost be as though the deaths of the members of the 'Busby Babes' were for nothing. With that European Holy Grail finally secured, Busby – knighted shortly after it – could settle into the retirement he had long desired. He quit his post on April 26 1969 after 24 years as manager. At the time of writing it appears that Sir Alex Ferguson will at least equal that record, but he will never be able to claim – as Busby was too modest to but many of his fans are happy to testify – that he built the cub in his own image. Ferguson inherited a legend. Busby inherited a team whose last glories were a generation in the past and whose Old Trafford ground was a World War II bomb-site and *built* it into a legend.

Busby's successor was a surprise. Managers like Johnny Carey (a member of Busby's first great United team, the 1948 FA Cup winners), Ron Greenwood and Don Revie were all spoken of for the role but instead it went to somebody most of the public had never heard of. Wilf McGuinness had been a Busby Babe himself before injury cut short his career and led him to turn to coaching, a career move that had made him not only a United youth and reserves coach but put him in charge of the England under-23s and additionally ensured his involvement in England's 1966 World Cup triumph. The journey from the position of coach to manager is not uncommon in football (although he was actually given the title of 'Chief Coach', while Busby remained 'General Manager', even if selection, coaching, training and tactics were exclusively McGuinness' preserve). However, what complicated this appointment was the fact that McGuinness was a contemporary of many of the current United team. At 31, he was the youngest-ever chief coach/manager of a First Division side. Additionally, his tender years were compounded by a familiarity that would not have applied had he been an outside appointment. Busby had an effortless authority about him (illustrated by the fact that every single player interviewed for this book who spoke of him referred to him as "Sir Matt"). McGuinness was just one of the lads. Perhaps this is why McGuinness sometimes seemed to be trying too hard in the disciplinary stakes. United winger Willie Morgan – one of the few rays of hope in this period in United's history – has related with disgust how a McGuinness rule that anybody caught with his hands in his pockets would be required to execute press-ups led to Bobby Charlton – a figure of infinitely greater gravitas and dignity than McGuinness – having to humiliatingly drop down to the mud of the club's training ground dressed in a smart suit.

McGuinness' United won only one of their first eight League games. A match in August 1969 against Everton saw five players dropped, including – shockingly – Law and Charlton. The match resulted in a 3-0 defeat and, according to Busby, a visit to him by McGuinness seeking his advice. At McGuinness' request, Busby told him what team he personally would select, one that included Law and Charlton. McGuinness picked it and stuck to it, resulting in a 10-match unbeaten run. Though at the end of the season, McGuinness could point to the fact that he had taken United to FA and League Cup semi-finals and a position in the League of eighth – better than Busby's final season – for those within the club *au fait* with the fact of the counsel given, his status must have been utterly undermined. McGuinness formally became team manager in the summer of 1970 but by Christmas of the 1970/71 season, he couldn't even point to respectable results: United were flirting with relegation. McGuinness taking United to the semi-final of the League Cup no more swayed the United board than his two semi-finals the previous season. That record was deemed not good enough given that he had inherited a European Cup-winning side and that he had at his disposal players of significant calibre among them Bobby Charlton, Denis Law and George Best, the latter a man many to this day consider the greatest footballer of all time. On December 28 1970, McGuiness was fired.

United then advertised their vacant manger's position for the first time in their history. United's legendary defender Pat Crerand (one of the European Cup team) has said that the idea of making an appointment from inside was a prescient one (Liverpool would later turn it into an art-form for a spell) but that McGuinness came to the job too young: another three or four years would have seen a new influx of players to whom he was more of a figure of authority. One could add that it should be remembered that Busby's last season in charge was not exactly spectacular. Though United reached the semi-final of the European Cup – and many contend would have reached the final had it not been for some criminally dubious refereeing – they had only qualified for that competition as holders. Their League form that season was mediocre and their gates had actually halved. In March 1969, a team with the European Cup on their sideboard were as low as 17th in the table. They recovered a little but could only manage a final position of 11th. Crerand later said, "We didn't become bad players, but maybe subconsciously we were like Matt. What else was there for us to achieve?" There was also another reason for the precipitous decline: the fact that 31-year-old McGuinness was a contemporary of many of his new charges doesn't only show how young he was for a manager but cuts the other way, giving an indication of the ageing nature of the United team, a side to whom Crerand admitted Busby had probably been too loyal that season. McGuinness was anxious to replenish the side even if Busby hadn't been but the receipts emanating from (usually) the highest attendances in the land did not translate into a readiness to make big money transfers, nor to pay wages commensurate with United's stature – a situation that would prevail well beyond the reigns of McGuinness and his two successors.

The first of those two successors – after a period between December 1970 and the end of that season during which Busby took the helm again and engineered a final League position of eighth – was Frank O' Farrell. This appointment came after Busby had a secret meeting with legendary Celtic manager Jock Stein about the vacant post, engineered by Stein's former charge Pat Crerand. Stein's ultimate record with Celtic would be breathtaking: in

13 seasons, he won them 10 League titles, eight Scottish Cups and six League Cups. Stein turned down the United manager's job and an unamused Busby was convinced that he had simply exploited United's interest to get a pay rise from Celtic, though Crerand has claimed that opposition from Stein's wife was the deciding factor. Future United manager Alex Ferguson later revealed, "I recall the late Jock Stein once telling me that the biggest mistake he made was to turn down United."

Frank O'Farrell was an austere Irishman who had been making a name for himself by guiding Leicester City to the Second Division championship and securing them an FA Cup final appearance. O'Farrell made some good signings, including the long-term rock of defence Martin Buchan, the prolific goalscorer Ted MacDougall and the silky-skilled winger Ian Storey-Moore. He also made a thrilling start to his first season in charge. At the end of 1971, United led the table by five points, at a time when a win was only worth two points. Denis Law had already scored 12 goals and George Best had racked up 14. Best – despite recent bad boy behaviour that had led many to diagnose him a liability whatever his talents – was not only playing brilliantly but scoring with such exquisite skill that his strikes from that period have become a staple of goals videos and DVDs whose titles are usually preceded by a number and whose second word is usually 'great' or 'classic'. However, this form, on the parts of both Best and the club, was a flame that quickly expired due to the underlying decay at the club. Martin Buchan joined from Aberdeen in March 1972, playing the last two months of that season. He was perplexed by what he was confronted by. "I think the squad was a curious mixture, ranging from … Law and Charlton to players who wouldn't have got a game in Aberdeen's reserve team," he recalls. "It was really strange. There were some good pros there, lads like Tony Dunne, but it was a team of contrasts."

United finished the season eighth, a position respectable enough for most other clubs but disappointing for the Reds, especially after that great start. Ditto their sixth-round FA Cup ejection. The next season, however, was more than disappointing, a yardstick of which is the fact that Bobby Charlton was the club's top scorer in that campaign. Several of those goals were in the blistering long-range tradition for which he was loved by both United fans and – as until recently a long-term fixture of the England team – the nation. However, his League tally was a paltry six goals. MacDougall was signed two months into this season and he recalls of the club's situation: "Frank O'Farrell alienated himself from the players and he became distant. Unfortunately, he wasn't a great communicator and he certainly wasn't very good when it comes to tactics or trying to put the team right. Where had he been before? Leicester. Torquay. When you look at Manchester United, if you're an actor, it's like being in a play in the provinces and then suddenly going on the West End. It's a bit of a difference. It's a goldfish bowl and you know that everything you do is under the microscope as a player and as a manager and some people can handle it and some people can't handle it."

The players saw a lot more of Malcolm Musgrove – whose official position was trainer in an era where 'coach' wasn't common in UK football parlance – but MacDougall wasn't much more impressed with him: "Malcolm was a lovely lad, but Malcolm would insist somebody like Willie Morgan, who was different class with his feet, head the ball. Why would you spend all hours trying to teach Willie Morgan to head a ball when Willie couldn't head a ball and didn't want to? If you've got great players, let them be great at what they've got. That's why they became great." There were, according to MacDougall, other problems at the club. The striker later said, "Old Trafford was not the happiest dressing room back then … Frank O'Farrell was a lovely man, but United were an ageing side in decline … Sir Matt Busby … never spoke a word to me in the five months I was there. Clique is too strong a word, but there was a definite 'them and us' mentality between the older players and the new guys … I never thought to ask why, but at training we always got changed in the reserves' dressing room." Striker Sammy McIlroy had been given his debut by O'Farrell when things were going swimmingly for the club. "They were having a great run at the time and everything was going great," he says. "But in football things change and the results started going the other way and things started happening. There were players coming to the end of their career, all the great names … and that's a big hell of a re-building to do. The players then didn't believe in Frank. Frank really couldn't handle the media side of things." He adds, "And the George thing got him down as well."

Completing the sense of decay, even chaos, around United at that time was the behaviour of George Best. The Belfast man's own personal triumph had coincided with United's: 1968 was the year he was voted European Footballer of the Year. He had then tumbled into a decline as precipitous as his club's (and in some ways, as their star player, the two things were intertwined). Just 22 at the time of the Reds' 1968 victory over Benfica at Wembley, Best found himself having to deal with the anti-climax of being a world-class player in a side that sometimes struggled to defeat mediocre teams. His bitterness at the way Manchester United and hence his own career had gone into decline was recounted in Michael Parkinson's book *Best: An Intimate Biography*, as was his frustration at the way Busby continued basing the side around the ageing Charlton rather than him. He didn't even have the consolation that some of his colleagues had in the form of possible glory in international football: as a Northern Ireland native, the most he could hope for was helping to upset England in the annual Home Championship. He remains without question the greatest player never to participate in the World Cup finals. A death threat from the IRA (a sympathiser was suspected of being responsible for shooting Best's sister in the leg) had additional adverse – and possibly underrated – consequences for his peace of mind and confidence. He increasingly turned to drink to bury his problems, with the inevitable detrimental results for his form. 1972 was littered with news stories of his being fined and dropped for missing training. Though he finished the club's top scorer that season with 26 from 53 appearances in all competitions (a tally double that of the second-placed player in the United goals chart, Denis Law), in the close season he announced his retirement from the game two days before his 26th birthday. After a meeting with O'Farrell, he changed his mind. However, come the new season, the problems with his missing training got so bad that on December 5th he was transfer listed and suspended for two weeks. Manchester United chairman Louis Edwards had announced that Best would resume training – the implication being that he was now off the transfer list – the day before the Crystal Palace game, something that some interpreted as a deliberate piece of undermining by Edwards designed to provoke O'Farrell's resignation.

Best didn't play in the Palace match. The side that took the field at Selhurst Park that miserable day – from which Charlton (presumably injured) was also absent – comprised a mixture of European Cup-winning veterans (quality, unfussy goalkeeper Alex Stepney, dependable defenders Tony Dunne and David Sadler, fine forward Brian Kidd), new or new-ish, promising kids on the block (Martin Buchan and Ian Storey-Moore), signings whose tenures were so brief that history and the Stretford End – Old Trafford's West stand, which bulged with the club's most fanatical supporters – weren't quite able to adjudge them (Ted MacDougall, towering centre-forward Wyn Davies, full-back Tommy O'Neil and Tony Young, who alternated between midfield and defence). Betwixt-and-between these categories was a man who was too young to be an establishment player but, as someone who had made his first team debut as far back as 1968, was hardly a novice: Willie Morgan, a classy and much-loved right-sided winger. The substitute that day was a man who didn't play against Benfica in 1968 through injury but whose performances in the campaign made him unquestionably part of the European Cup-winning team, fiery forward Denis Law, one of the most beloved players ever to pull on a red shirt.

No fewer than 10 of those 12 players had been or would be capped for their country. The men on the teamsheet of the Crystal Palace side, on the other hand, were for the most part not even household names in their own households. Yet the lack of camaraderie brought about by O'Farrell's aloofness and the snowball diminution in confidence engendered by bad form resulted in what Alex Stepney – who as a native Londoner had many of his relatives sitting in the stands – later described as "the most humiliating experience of my entire career."

Palace's Paddy Mulligan put the home side in front after 10 minutes. It was at that point that Tony Dunne had to hobble off through injury. Almost indicative of the chaos surrounding the United team was the fact that it took the United bench 10 minutes to put a man on in his place. By the time Law did make an appearance, the United goal had been so battered that Palace could have been four up. Miraculously the deficit was still only one goal when 'The Lawman' entered the fray. Three minutes before half-time, Mulligan got his second. Rogers scored a minute into the second half and three minutes before full-time. Also on the scoresheet was Whittle. The assertion by some that the score could easily have been 10-0 doesn't seem too much of an exaggeration. Only the efforts of Stepney (who, amazingly considering the score-line, had a good game) and good luck prevented the humiliation being greater.

It was an horrendous spectacle for the travelling Red Army. "Frank O'Failure" screamed one tabloid headline. Another newspaper, the broadsheet *Guardian*, took a more measured but no less critical view of the match. Under the headline "One of the saddest days for United", Albert Barham said, "It is with the greatest sadness that one records not only the result of this match but the humiliating manner of defeat." United were "disunited and disillusioned" and defensively "calamitous". In any event, for Barham the match had been lost before kick-off: he ventured that a meeting between Edwards and Busby the previous week about the George Best problem – by implication the one that led to Best being taken off the transfer list – had pulled the rug out from under O'Farrell and that he might resign over the issue.

As the man who had let in five, Stepney could be said to have a vested interest in his comment: "I have never played in a team that was so lacking in spirit and fighting quality." But then Palace's chairman – hardly the holder of the most envy-making job in football – remarked to the press after the match that United were the most unimpressive visitors to Selhurst Park for a long while. The result left United in 21st position in the First Division, which in those days meant they were one from bottom in the top flight of the English Football League.

Sitting in the stands that day was Tommy Docherty. The reason for Docherty's presence was his position as manager of the Scottish national side. United, as they almost always did, had a sprinkling of Scots on the pitch but according to the man nicknamed 'The Doc' it wasn't their form he had come to observe but – at the suggestion of Palace manager Bert Head – that of Crystal Palace defender Tony Taylor. Docherty was also pleased at the chance of attending because it so happened that he was a friend of O'Farrell, with whom he had played at Preston North End and who was godfather to one of his sons, Peter.

\*\*\*

Thomas Henderson Docherty was born in the Gorbals in Glasgow on August 24 1928. His sickly father – an iron-factory worker – died when he was nine, leaving Docherty, his two sisters and his mother to live a life that Docherty has described as "grim" and "pitiful". So much so, that National Service seemed to Docherty a form of salvation. As of course did professional football. Docherty's career after his demobilisation began at the very top for a Glaswegian: with Celtic. As well as Celtic, Docherty's playing career encompassed Preston North End, Arsenal and Chelsea. Good enough to win 25 Scottish caps and to captain his country, he was described by the legendary Sir Stanley Matthews as "a stylish wing-half" and by the almost as legendary Sir Tom Finney as a "top quality player". One of his managers when he turned out for the national side was Matt Busby, who helmed two games for Scotland as their temporary manager in 1958. Docherty played two matches in the 1954 World Cup finals in Switzerland. Despite this highly respectable career, Docherty won no major honours as a player. His only Cup Final appearance came for Preston against West Bromwich Albion in 1954, a 2-3 defeat in which Docherty laid on one of his team's goals but gave away a penalty (unjustly, he averred).

Docherty would become famous for (amongst other things) quipping that as a manager he had had more clubs than golfer Jack Nicklaus. By December 1972, he was about halfway toward the tally of 13 teams whose footballing affairs he would oversee (not counting those clubs he managed for more than one term). His first managerial post was at Chelsea. Docherty had originally been appointed by Chelsea as coach in February 1961, although quickly turned into a player-coach when it was decided the struggling London team could use his talents on the field. Frank Blunstone was an outside-left at Stamford Bridge at the time. He recalls, "He was a good-hearted player, hundred per cent, very physical. Good player." Chelsea manager Ted Drake was sacked in September that year, and Docherty was asked to act as caretaker manager until a replacement could be found. Come January however, the board told Docherty they would like him to continue in the manager's post. "We didn't know him all that well, he'd only just come," Blunstone explains. "There were two factions at the club. There was a bit of a split: one were for Ted Drake and one for Tommy ... The older players had been brought up with Ted Drake ... But he proved he was right: he did a fantastic job."

Blunstone also says, "Tommy was a very strong manager. He wouldn't have any nonsense, Tommy ... If you upset him in any way, God help you." A theme that will emerge in this book is that if a player was not in The Doc's good books or was considered by him superfluous to requirements, Docherty was apt to treat him almost like a leper. Was that Blunstone's experience? "Oh yes. No doubt about it. He'd have you on your way if he got the opportunity." However, another theme that will emerge is the way Docherty could be as considerate and good-natured as he could spiteful. Blunstone says, "He was very fair and I got on well with him. If you did your job and you worked hard and you were dedicated, he'd do anything for you … When I was at Chelsea and he became manager and the maximum wage was taken off, one day he called me to one side. He said, 'What are your wages?' I said, 'I'm on 40 pound a week.' He said, 'Right from next week, you're going on 45.' I said to him, 'I've signed a contract, I'm not bothered, I'm happy. I haven't asked for a rise.' He said, 'You are giving 100 per cent, far better than some of these blokes who are on 45 pound a week here.' That's the type of bloke he was."

Chelsea were bottom of the First Division at the time of Docherty's appointment, so no one blamed him when the club were relegated. The Doc began rebuilding his ageing team in the Second Division and a new, zestful, young Chelsea team won promotion at the first attempt. Recalls Chelsea's midfielder Jim McCalliog, "The oldest player in the team was Frank Blunstone, who was 29. There was John Mortimer, he was 26. And the rest of the squad was 23 and under. There was a fantastic spirit there, laughing and joking." This story of reuvenation of a fallen giant with fresh blood will be familiar to the followers of Manchester United under Docherty. Less familiar is the wheeling and dealing in the transfer market in which The Doc engaged. Docherty famously became Chelsea's first 'transfer millionaire', a rather confusing tabloid term which in fact means a manager whose total outlay exceeds £1m. Of course, this dubious accolade is essentially meaningless, dictated just as much by inflation as profligacy. As with just about every club he helmed, Docherty managed to balance the books, in this case receiving £116,000 more in transfer fees than he ever spent. Nonetheless, in those days Docherty was happy to opt for the (ostensibly) instant solution to an under-performing side by plunging into the transfer market for a big-name signing (an option of course reliant on a club with a cash surplus and an amenable board, circumstances in which he would not always be happy enough to find himself). By the time he had been in the Manchester United hot seat for a couple of years (although certainly not from the moment he took up the post), Docherty had completely changed his mind about the managerial philosophy that led him to break Chelsea's transfer record four times.

Every player questioned for this book – while not disputing Docherty's footballing intelligence – states that his main strength as a boss was on the psychological side: getting the players he selected to go out and play to the best of their ability. "He was a great motivator," says Blunstone, who became Docherty's youth coach, then his assistant manager at Old Trafford. "Probably the best motivator I've ever seen. But he wasn't a great coach." Asked if that is a deficiency in a manager, he says, "No, no, no. Because if you've got somebody with you who does know it, it's alright. He was like Bill Shankly in a way. Typical Scotchman. Even when you're struggling, he'd have a little laugh and a joke, and he was great." The "somebody who does know it" that Docherty appointed at Chelsea was Dave Sexton, in whose company he had won his coaching badge at Lilleshall, the Football Association's academy. Sexton became his assistant trainer in February 1962. "Dave was brilliant," says Blunstone. "He knew the game inside out." Sexton – a man whose intellectualism and taciturnity was an almost parodic contrast to Docherty's blunt-speaking and loquaciousness – would ultimately become a manager himself, and a weird intertwining of the two's careers in the game would ensue over the following decades.

Not that Docherty was uninterested in tactics and preparation. As his son Mick – who served his football apprenticeship under his dad at Chelsea – points out, "Dad was very innovative in his training methods. He went abroad a lot to watch foreign opposition train and come back and [would] try and integrate that into the training at whichever club he was at. He certainly built a very good side at Chelsea, although never realised the fruition of it. And the same at United. He instigated a lot of fast, free-flowing, attacking play and that was very indicative of his sides. They were always exciting to watch." Colin Waldron, one of Docherty's purchases at Stamford Bridge, says of The Doc's tenure there, "Chelsea were playing different systems that were unheard of in English football, playing a sweeper ..."

Docherty's transformation of Chelsea was impressive. Once back in the First Division, under him Chelsea always finished the season in the upper heights: fifth, third, fifth and ninth. They also secured good cup runs, winning the League Cup in 1965, reaching the FA Cup semi-final in 1965 and 1966 and the FA Cup final in 1967. They were semi-finalists in the Inter-Cities Fairs Cup (precursor to the UEFA Cup), also in 1966. Docherty has said that had phenomenal goalscorer Jimmy Greaves not been sold to AC Milan shortly after his arrival, Chelsea would have won a First Division championship without a doubt. Many people think Chelsea would have actually won that championship in 1965 had it not been for a disciplinary measure taken by The Doc that seemed to amount to cutting his nose off to spite his face. With the League Cup having been secured and with 10 League games to go, the club were sitting on top of the table with a three-point advantage over Leeds United and a five-point lead over Manchester United. Though they began to falter from here, they still had more than a chance of being champions by the time they booked into a hotel in Blackpool to prepare for their last two games, against Burnley and Blackpool. However, when eight players broke Docherty's 10.30pm curfew by means of a fire escape and stuck to their false story that they had not left their rooms all evening – even when Docherty took the step of whipping back the bedsheets of a couple of them to reveal them, almost farcically, dressed in street clothes beneath – Docherty took drastic steps to assert his authority. The eight players whom he suspected of breaking the curfew were given rail tickets home. The exiled eight included great talents like Terry Venables, Eddie MacCreadie and John Hollins. Reserves were hurriedly drafted into their places. Chelsea were slaughtered 6-2 at Burney and lost 3-2 at Blackpool. Manchester United won the League title by goal average, having finished, like Leeds, on 61 points. Had Chelsea won their last two games, they would have finished on 62 points. Writing in his 2006 autobiography *My Story*, Docherty said, "I suppose one could say that I forsook what chance we had of winning the championship on a matter of principle. However, I felt I had to take a stand, discipline the players who had overstepped the mark and did not regret my action in the least."

Many, perhaps most, people with the hindsight of 40-plus years would have rued that they had gone too far and admitted that their naiveté in their first managerial job had backfired on them. Docherty, however, seemed to be clinging stubbornly to the position that "I was right". Or perhaps desperately would be the more appropriate adjective, for what would it do to Docherty's peace of mind to accept that a club fine would have been the more suitable response to the indiscipline when he then had to contemplate the fact that the First Division championship was an honour he never secured in his long management career?

That note of undiminished defiance in his autobiography more than four decades after the incident will be to some minds something that sums up Docherty. Yet there would seem to be a marked difference between the private and the public Docherty personas, judging by the recollection of Blunstone. The latter reveals, "He admitted after, he made a mistake to the senior players. 'Cos we weren't involved in that. It's the young lads that went out nightclubbing. We said to him, 'You were unfair because you made us suffer.' He admitted it after: he should have made them play and punish them after."

McCalliog disputes that Docherty threw away the championship, saying, "I don't think it would have absolutely happened … I don't think we'd have quite been there. I would have thought in the next few years it was certainly on the cards." Right or wrong, Docherty's actions are no particular surprise to Waldron, who says, "If you gave him everything you had got, then he'd stay loyal to you through thick and thin. But if you crossed him, then it was like black and white – you're gone."

Despite the incident, Blunstone still had a lot of time for his boss. "I finished playing when Tommy was there and again he was wonderful," he recalls. "I had to pack in because I'd ruptured my Achilles tendon and he gave me a job straightaway as youth team coach. I was lost for words, 'cos when you're finished, what you gonna do?" Others weren't so lucky. Terry

Venables was despatched to Tottenham Hotspur. Recalls McCalliog, "Terry Venables was the captain and Terry was a good organiser and he liked to be the boss and be in charge and I think there was a problem there when we had the wee Blackpool night out thing and Terry Venables was one of the guys that actually went down the fire escape. I think it goes on from there. The boys that went out, they all bonded together and I thought that Tommy thought Terry Venables was a wee bit of threat to his authority." It has even been suggested that Venables was not averse to changing Chelsea's tactics after kick-off without Docherty's authorisation, but though this would be inexcusable mutiny Docherty in any case seemed throughout his managerial career to have a quasi-irrational distrust of older players. McCalliog: "I found he was better when I was younger with him. I think he was always a wee bit – not particularly myself – wary of experienced players. He liked to give young players a chance. Whether it's because he got given a chance when he was younger, I don't know, but Tommy Docherty loved for younger players to be coming up. When me and [Peter] Osgood was at Chelsea, he was kind of raving about the pair of us – 'Wait till the pair of them come along.' I think the experienced players get a wee bit cheesed off with it as well."

Docherty's decision to break up Chelsea's promising team in 1966 following their second successive FA Cup semi-final defeat amazed many. Docherty told the press after that second defeat, "This team is just not up to the standards we want to set at Chelsea." Chelsea did finally make it to Wembley the following year, even despite the transfer of assets like Venables. They were beaten by Tottenham Hotspur in the FA Cup final, one of several Wembley heartbreaks for The Doc as both player and manager. However, many remained bewildered by the restructuring and wondered whether things would have been better if he had stuck with the team he had.

One of Docherty's new signings turned out to be particularly disastrous and crucial to a sudden collapse in results. The close season before Docherty's final campaign at Chelsea saw the purchase from Bury of 18-year-old centre-half Colin Waldron, who turned down the chance of joining Bill Shankly's Liverpool to go south. Recalls Waldron, "Tommy Docherty was just larger-than-life at that particular time and Chelsea were the new team." One of Waldron's first direct tastes of Docherty's larger-than-life nature came when the pair did a joint interview to discuss the way The Doc had snatched his services from under Shankly's nose. To give some sort of context to Waldron's following anecdote, it should be noted that this was an era when football managers – as with anybody else talking to the media – tended to couch their words in euphemism, refrain from blunt-speaking and studiously avoid controversy (which itself was then defined in far broader terms). "We had to do a TV thing which was like me walking into a different world in those days," Waldron says. "You're talking 1967, when TV sport was in its infancy. He goes and does it and I sit and I watch him be interviewed and it's a good interview that'll go down great anyway and the producer comes and says, 'Tommy great interview, fantastic, honestly, brilliant, but you haven't mentioned Shankly, you haven't done this', all the points that were really sensational. So he said, 'We'll re-do it.' So he re-does the interview and just to placate the producer brings out this white-hot sensational interview, which brings in the Shankly thing. I drove home that night thinking, 'Well, this is going to be unbelievable', and they showed it and of course it's in the papers, and all it is is Tommy Doc has helped this producer out and by doing it allowed him to be sucked in and courted controversy again." Waldron retained a certain awe, as well as bemusement, about Docherty even when a grizzled veteran. He reveals, "I've been at nine clubs. I must have had 15 or 16 managers and he was totally different to any of 'em. He was a manager but he really was one of the players. He was always laughing and joking, he would socialise with the players. He always had the ability to mock himself." Not that he found Docherty all sweetness and light: "Wherever Doc went, there would be people who didn't like him, because he rubbed people up the wrong way, because he just did what he wanted and didn't give a shit."

Waldron, who had turned 19 just before the season started, had made something of a name for himself at Bury and Docherty put him straight into the Chelsea first team. Says Waldron, "I just thought he were bullshitting me, but lo and behold, I'm playing … " Yet thrilled as he was to be taking to the field in a team riddled with household names like Peter Bonetti, Charlie Cooke, Ron Harris and Peter Osgood, Waldron says putting him amongst them was "a huge mistake." He explains, "I wasn't ready. I was thrown in the deep end and I sank, and I nearly sank the club. I was dire. We conceded six at home in one game, five away in another. Now, that wasn't entirely down to me, but obviously, I was a major, major factor. I was still learning my position, daft as it sounds, because I'd switched from a centre-forward, and I'd only been in the position two years … For me you are not going to be a top-notch centre-half until you're 25. The unfortunate thing with a centre-half, you make a mistake and it ends up in the back of the net. I really was like a fish out of water. I'd only played I think 20 League games for Bury in the Second Division … " As for Chelsea, "I played nine games. I were lucky to last nine and I've never been as thankful in my life when he dropped me." His thankfulness seems to be wrapped up in the way he was treated by his manager. As will be seen, Docherty could be callous beyond belief when dispensing with players deemed surplus to requirements, but as will also be seen, he could just as easily be quite extraordinarily kind-hearted. Trying to work out what prompts either approach in the man can be confusing, even unfathomable, but suffice it to say that on this occasion an angel, not a devil, was sitting on The Doc's shoulder. Waldron: "I knew I were going to get dropped and I went in and the way he spoke to me, I came out feeling 10-feet tall. I'll always remember it. A great man-motivator. I loved the guy from the minute I met him signing to the minute I left." This testimony is made more impressive by the fact that Waldron is not one of the puzzlingly numerous uncomplicated souls who in their time serving under The Doc mysteriously failed to observe the fact that he had a dark side. Says Waldron, "I know some friends of mine who detest him with a passion. Willie Morgan's one … If he treated Denis Law and Willie like I've heard, then maybe they've got a right. But for me I can only speak highly of the guy. "

Docherty resigned from Chelsea in October 1967 but this doesn't necessarily seem to be down to what most people would assume: the club's tumble down the First Division table. Docherty's first wife Agnes later claimed that Docherty's decision to resign was down as much as anything to what he felt was a lack of support from the Chelsea board over an allegedly racist remark he had made to a black match official on a visit by the club to Bermuda. (Agnes denied Docherty was racist, and at the point she did so had no vested interest in lying for the man who had left her for his mistress.) Docherty himself, though, said the new chairman was the major problem: "I chucked it in for a basic reason – I just didn't get on with Mr [Charles] Pratt." Stewart Houston, a defender who was a recent Stamford Bridge signing by Docherty, confirms the impression of some that Docherty never felt as comfortable at Stamford Bridge again after the death of chairman Joe Mears in June 1966. "I know he was very, very, very close to the chairman," says Houston. "He always spoke very, very highly of the chairman and Tommy lost a dear friend. What I'm led to believe is he, because he had a big affiliation with the man, lost a lot of hunger and desire and momentum."

Gordon Hill, one of Docherty's future charges, says of Docherty, "Unfortunately, the Boss, as I call him, had a self-destruct button every three or four years, and done something that got him the sack." This comment, it should be pointed out, comes from somebody who in the love-him-or-loathe-him Docherty stakes (few seem to feel neutral about The Doc) is firmly in the former category. Journalist Albert Sewell, writing in 1972, seemed to be halfway endorsing Hill's comments on Docherty's mercurial mentality when he said, "Docherty was near to building the greatest Chelsea side in the club's history. Only his impatience stopped him. When it did not come, he broke up the side and as older players became disillusioned – those who were not transferred – the club went into decline, and when Docherty resigned in October 1967, they were third from the bottom in Division One."

Docherty's next port of call was Second Division Rotherham, a club battling relegation when he became gaffer in November 1967. By now, he had become known as a true character, a manager whose quips and capacity for soundbites (before that phrase existed) got his club into the newspapers and piqued the interest of the paying public. When he was appointed at Rotherham, it was therefore not a surprise that this and his good (if lately faltering) track record more than doubled the gates overnight. However, neither Docherty's force of personality nor his transfer dealings could stop the rot and Rotherham shortly became the second club he had taken down a tier of English football, even if he did steer them to an impressive FA Cup quarter-final appearance. History is not able to adjudge whether he would have engineered the same bounce-back the following season as he had when Chelsea went down – which he would have had to do with a side he had made one of the youngest in the League – for in November 1968 First Division London club Queens Park Rangers swooped for his services. Unfortunately, history is left even less able to adjudge what kind of job he would have done at Loftus Road, for Docherty's time there ended after just 28 days when, Docherty claimed, QPR chairman Jim Gregory refused to agree either to the fee necessary to purchase Rotheram's Brian Tiler or to refrain from interfering in team selection. Aston Villa took Docherty up north in December 1968. As before, the man able to deliver hilarious comments to the media with a deadpan face inspired confidence that he would also be able to deliver results. The Second Division club saw their gates treble and, at first, their on-field fortunes improve too. But ultimately Villa beat the drop by only three places. They went down the next season, but Docherty had departed before they did so, sacked in January 1970 with Villa bottom of the table. Docherty blamed a group of heavy drinkers in the team whom the board would not let him sell for the club's poor performances.

By now the magic The Doc had worked for several seasons at Chelsea was looking severely tarnished. Perhaps it was the knowledge of this fact and the attendant disinclination of English clubs to be interested in his services that led him in February 1970 to take up the post of manager at Portuguese club Oporto. He did well there – the club finished runners-up in their league by two points – and studiously learnt the language, but in April 1971 he spurned a new contract to return to the family and the British football that he missed. He was assistant manager to Terry Neill at Hull City for a few months before – somewhat surprisingly – the Scottish Football Association decided to overlook his lately less-than-spectacular record by making him national team manager in November 1971.

The Doc lived up to his nickname during the 13 months he presided over his national team, turning an ailing patient into a robust figure. Docherty later said of being a national manager, "Having the pick of the players was like being a millionaire and being able to afford anything." However, previous managers had had the same luxury and produced risible results. Scotland legend Denis Law has gone as far as to say that the Scotland team before Docherty's tenure was a "pathetic joke". Docherty lost only three of his 12 matches in charge, and those all by a single goal. A nation that had – notwithstanding the many great players it had bequeathed the English League – always been lightweight on the football stages was transformed into a formidable opponent. Though Docherty did not technically ensure qualification for the World Cup finals, it was only left for his successor as manager, Willie Ormond, to keep the ship steady to book their place in West Germany in 1974, their first qualification since 1958. Martin Buchan, who played under Docherty for both Scotland and Manchester United, says, "He did a lot of the spade work, and I don't think he really got enough credit for the part he played in helping the team qualify." Docherty's win rate during his tenure remains among the best of all Scotland managers.

Docherty's appointment as Scotland boss was of course, as it would be for any patriotic, football-minded Caledonian, a dream job. However, he would later admit that the post of international manager didn't involve enough work for his liking. Journalist David Meek – who has been covering Manchester United for four decades-plus – recalls a man unfulfilled by the Scotland gig. He also recollects an incident that shows that Docherty was agitating for the position of Manchester United manager even then. "Although initially honoured and proud to be manager of Scotland, it didn't suit him and he admitted it didn't suit him because he didn't have that day-to-day involvement with players which is one thing that makes a character like Tommy Docherty tick," says Meek. "I remember him standing on the steps of Hampden Park after one Scotland international and saying – 'cos he knew I was covering Manchester United – 'This isn't for me. I just hope that somebody invites me to be manager of Manchester United.' It was towards the end of Tommy's time as Scotland manager. I guess it would be in 1972 when Frank O'Farrell was ... coming towards the end of his time at Old Trafford. I am sure Tom knew exactly what he was saying and that it would get back to Louis Edwards." As is the way of these things, Meek informed the United board of Docherty's interest via a circuitous route: "I just did a story in the *[Manchester] Evening News* but without direct quotes from Tommy so as not to get him in trouble with the Scottish FA. It was one of those 'People say etc'." We will probably never know whether it was Docherty's planting of this seed in the United board's collective mind that led to him being offered the job of Manchester United manager following the Crystal Palace catastrophe, but it says much about the allure of Manchester United that Docherty gave up the chance of overseeing Scotland's campaign in the biggest tournament in soccer to supervise a grim relegation dogfight in the rain-sodden north of England.

\*\*\*

There seem to be different recollections about when and how Docherty was offered the job of United manager at Old Trafford: some accounts say that it was at half-time during the Crystal Palace game, others (and Docherty's own recollection) at full-time; others that Busby merely vaguely asked him on the day of that match if he would be interested in the post if anything "happened" over the next few days. Alex Stepney has said that the United players understood that Docherty was only there in the first place because he wanted to see the team before deciding whether to become manager, which of course suggests that he had been sounded out for the job prior to the day of the Palace match. Whatever the truth, O'Farrell was summoned to appear before the United board on December 19 and dismissed.

O'Farrell later recalled of his sacking, "The night before it happened I went to a Bobby Charlton testimonial dance with my wife, Anne. The directors were there, it was all quite friendly, and we didn't leave until after midnight. I was totally unprepared when Louis Edwards called me to his meat factory the following morning. The entire board were there and I was told my contract was being terminated. When I asked why, the chairman replied there was 'no reason.' I laughed and said they couldn't sack me without a reason. Mr Edwards finally said it was because United were bottom of the First Division." No doubt Edwards was also painfully aware of the fact that United had been knocked out of the League Cup in the third round in October by Third Division Bristol Rovers, after having been taken to a replay by Oxford United of Division Two in the second round (the tournament's first round for top-flight clubs). Of his record at the club, O'Farrell said, "It wasn't a bad performance considering that everybody knew the team was in decline … I was neither a bad manager or a novice."

United not only dismissed O'Farrell but his coach Malcolm Musgrove and – somewhat unfairly in some people's opinions, as he was not part of the O'Farrell regime – chief scout John Aston Sr. As if to emphasise that the club were determined to instigate a new era, they also announced, "Furthermore, George Best will remain on the transfer list and will not be again selected for Manchester United as it is felt it is in the best interest of the club and the player that he leaves Old Trafford." The statement did acknowledge though that Best had quit before he could be sacked: after preparing the announcement of their decision to not allow Best to be selected, the board received a letter from the Irishman telling them he was retiring from the game.

David Meek says, "I think Frank O'Farrell's problem is that it wasn't his team. There were some experienced, very good quality players there, but their best days were behind them and there were too many of them. You need some older players but he had too many like that and you need some youth in the team. [The older players] each individually had some more football left in them but collectively as a team it was a bit of a tall order for them to gel. I remember Frank O'Farrell telling me one day, 'I need time. I can't really do anything until Matt Busby's players have moved on and I can't just move them all out overnight. Until they've gone though it won't be my team and I can't really create anything important ...' I thought they should have stuck with O'Farrell and I wrote so at the time when they were thinking of sacking him and got booted off the team coach for criticising the board in that respect."

From his ground-level perspective, Buchan was able to see other problems. He says, "There was still this philosophy in the dressing room: 'Sir Matt used to tell us to go out and enjoy ourselves', but after 1966 everybody was playing organised football. Sir Alf Ramsey won the World Cup playing 4-3-3, which he felt was the best use of the players available to him, and all of a sudden every coach in the country was playing 4-3-3. They weren't tailoring their systems to suit their players, they were making players adapt to the system. If you have a very tall front man, it makes sense to take advantage of his height by playing a percentage of long balls from the back, and also making sure he gets a good service into the penalty area from both wings. Everybody was trying to be more organised and there was a lot of resistance from some of the players to Frank O'Farrell and Malcolm Musgrove's attempts to combine the flair that United was famous for with organisation ... Coaching was quite a relatively new invention before Sir Alf Ramsey came up with his 4-3-3 system. Coaching was a more individual thing before then. But that's why nowadays teams from little countries – dare I say Scotland – can go to World Cups and get draws with teams like Brazil, because good organisation cancels out a lot of the superior individual ability of opponents." The "resistance" Buchan talks about, "... manifests itself in all sorts of ways. For example, we signed a goal machine called Ted MacDougall from Bournemouth. He never got the service he needed to score the goals."

Perhaps the reason O'Farrell talked of fortunes turning around after a process of natural attrition is because he did not have the option of buying players to replace the veterans, or at least as many as he wanted. O'Farrell's signing of Buchan had – incredibly – been only the third time United had paid money for a player since Stepney's purchase in 1966, the others being Willie Morgan (1968) and Ian Ure (1969). Although the board did allow O'Farrell to dip into the bank for Ian Storey-Moore, Wyn Davies, Ted MacDougall and Trevor Anderson, rumour has it that Alan Ball, David Nish and Colin Todd were three other players he wanted to bring to Old Trafford – more than one source has suggested that Ball virtually proffered himself to United on a plate – only to find the moves vetoed, apparently by Busby. McGuinness is also rumoured to have wanted Todd, as well as Ipswich's Mick Mills, but was stymied too.

In her posthumously published account of her marriage, Agnes Docherty recalled that Matt Busby telephoned Docherty on Tuesday December 19 to offer her husband the job of United manager and that Docherty accepted over the phone. Though Agnes was sad for their friend O'Farrell, she said, "As soon as he hung up, Tommy and I shrieked and danced around the lounge like demented teenagers." Docherty would later claim that he didn't apply for the job ("I have too much pride for that"), adding that in any case there was a manager *in situ*. "Frank O'Farrell was also a friend", he said. One could argue that, as Docherty has himself admitted that he began speaking with Matt Busby about the United manager's job before O'Farrell was officially dismissed, he was showing little loyalty to his friend. Alternatively, you could take the view that managers know the score about their dispensability, and that as O'Farrell's demise was inevitable, it would have been silly for Docherty to refrain from speaking to the club. Certainly, O'Farrell and Docherty remained friends after the events of December 1972.

Though a national hero in Scotland through his spectacular stewardship of the country's side, Docherty was conscious of the fact that he had never racked up the honours commensurate with the way he tended to talk up himself and his teams. Speaking in 1977, he said, "If I'd had a little bit of luck, my honours list would be frightening. I won the League Cup with Chelsea and we could have been in the finals in three years. I took Scotland to the World Cup finals, or at least to within one game of qualifying." A précis of a career so hemmed in with qualifications, one might think, as to be laughable. It should also be pointed out that when Docherty won the League Cup, it was not considered a substantial competition, with several top clubs declining to participate. In fact, Chelsea themselves refused to take part the season after they'd won it, with Docherty preferring to concentrate on the Fairs Cup. But that big mouth of Docherty's also gave him a presence in the game, one that could persuade others to accept his point of view that his sideboard would be groaning with trophies if only his undeniably classy football had been complemented by something beyond his control: Lady Luck, the rub of the green, fate, etc. Perhaps this is what persuaded the United board to ignore that paucity of achievement. For his part, Meek wasn't surprised by the appointment: "The previous manager was rather staid, slow-moving, and Manchester United needed a stick of dynamite, so they went for somebody whose track record was probably not as good as Frank O'Farrell's but could be guaranteed to let off a few fireworks. And indeed he did. The place needed waking up." Did he get the impression that on his appointment to Old Trafford Docherty toned down his flamboyant, even arrogant act? "No, I don't think he did, because Tommy Docherty's a character who can't pretend," says Meek. "What you see is what you get. You like him or hate him. I don't think he paid any great deference to Manchester United. He wasn't frightened of the job. He sailed in." Frank Blunstone also didn't find anything too remarkable about The Doc being given the United job: "He was a great character and he's full of life and I think someone like that at United, that's what they want. He'd been manager of Scotland, manager of Chelsea, so they weren't talking too big a risk. [They would] if they'd taken somebody from the Third Division or a young kid. They took a chance with Wilf. Wilf had never been a manager. Tommy was high-profile."

At the time, David Meek wrote that he felt that Docherty had briefly been a candidate for the job after the dismissal of McGuinness. Judging by a recollection of Docherty, his appointment at Old Trafford was in the wind at that time: he has recalled a phone call from a journalist friend informing him of a poll in Manchester that revealed he was the first choice of fans to be installed as the new manager. Meek said that The Doc's controversial reputation had made the United board lose their nerve then. However, his impressive stewardship of Scotland in the interim had swung it for him this time around. There was also the fact that some of that Scotland team were singing Docherty's praises to the powers-that-be at United. Law and Morgan both told Busby and/or other members of the board that he would be a good manager for United. In fact, it was Morgan – according to Michael Crick and David Smith in *Manchester United: Betrayal of a Legend* – who furnished Busby with Docherty's telephone number during a game of golf after the Palace match.

Law had been impressed by Docherty ever since he had first encountered him in 1958 when as an 18-year-old Scotland debutant he had been made to feel very welcome by Docherty. The Doc – a senior player – was clearly aware of how awkward it would be for a youngster entering the team, especially in a day and age when the mass media did not serve to effectively introduce players to one another before they had formally met. A fortnight later, Law was again struck by Docherty's thoughtfulness when Docherty – then an Arsenal player – became aware that Law was in the capital for a visit by his club Huddersfield Town. The two were due to meet in midweek anyway for another Scotland match but Docherty invited Law out to dinner with a group of his friends and later travelled up to the Scotland match with him. Then there was the happy experience Law had had when Docherty became Scotland manager. In April 1972, Law had last played for Scotland almost three years previously and he had assumed his international career was over. Docherty recalled him to the team and in his first game back made him captain. Law repaid him by scoring two goals. Law was also impressed by Docherty's relaxed and humanitarian approach to the job of manager. Law has said that United's decision to appoint Docherty was "in no small way" due to the testimonials provided by him and Morgan. In time, both he and Morgan would have bitter cause to regret those testimonials.

At 23, Martin Buchan was too young to be sounded out by the United top brass about his international manager (although advice had flowed the other way according to Docherty: he says it was he who recommended Buchan to O'Farrell). His feelings about the Docherty appointment were mixed, as he felt a loyalty to O'Farrell. He now says, "It's always disappointing when someone loses a job, but life goes on and Tommy Docherty gave me my first Scottish cap. You don't tend to analyse it too much. I mean, it's not your decision. It's the board that appoints the manager and you just get on with it. I didn't have any problems personally with him joining as a manager, because I knew he was good with the players in the Scotland squad."

According to Docherty, when he was picked up from Manchester Airport by Louis Edwards on Friday December 22 1972, the recruiting process consisted of the United chairman asking whether he wanted the job, to which the answer was a one-word affirmative. This was followed by the question, "When can you start?", to which The Doc replied, "I've already started!" This version of events has the smack of a coat of gloss being applied, and it doesn't chime with Agnes Docherty's recollection of terms being agreed over the telephone. However, both Dochertys agree on the annual salary: £15,000 (plus a car, according to Tommy). "It is a privilege to be asked to join a club like Manchester United," Docherty told the press. Later, Docherty and Edwards joined the United players at a Cheshire hotel at which they were staying in preparation for the home match against Leeds the following day.

Docherty's appointment led to many potted précis of his career appearing in print, as well as summaries of his abilities and qualities. Eric Todd wrote of his long list of clubs, "He left some of them in disarray and tears, gave others hope where none existed, but wherever he went, they knew he'd been there." John Rafferty said of his time as Scotland boss, "He was not just the manager – he was a supporter. When he bubbled with enthusiasm and glorified Scottish players and Scottish skills, that was the supporter talking. The manager showed only in private, when he was subdued and technical." Rafferty also noted how Docherty made sure he was popular with Scottish journalists, "… firstly because he was quotable and produced results, and secondly because he studied how reporters worked and knew their problems and tried seriously to cooperate with them." He also noted that Docherty, when he didn't have an audience, dispensed with his Glaswegian vocabulary and "assessed players with sharp, technical phrases. He was shrewd in his assessments and showed a tremendous memory for detail." On a personal note, he said, "His enthusiasm and gregariousness are startling. He came to my home one night when there was a crowd in and the piano was going, and before introductions had been made he had on a funny hat and was leading the singing."

Forgotten by history is the fact that after his appointment by United, Docherty initially harboured hopes of continuing to manage the Scottish national team. "I would like to see the Scottish team through the World Cup qualifying rounds and I hope that something can be worked out," he said. In a sense, it was natural for Docherty to desire this arrangement, for originally he had been caretaker manager of Scotland while retaining his position at

Hull. However, the idea was nixed by the International and Selection Committee of the Scottish Football Association. The Committee's Jimmy Aitken said, "I feel strongly that we must employ a manager full-time. When the Manchester United chairman, Louis Edwards, phoned me in the first instance asking for permission to approach Tommy Docherty, he said that he would like him to continue as Scotland manager and that his club would co-operate in this. I do not see how this would be possible, for too many embarrassing and invidious situations could arise. What, for instance, would Tommy Docherty do if Manchester United were involved in a desperate relegation game and he as Scotland manager wanted the release of one of his own key players? He would be in an impossible position."

\*\*\*

It's one of the hazards and ironies of football that any manager taking over a new post is liable to find on his payroll a player – or even several of them – whom he had discarded when the boss of a different club. For Docherty, there was just such a player on United's books in the shape of Alex Stepney. The two had a brief but curious history together. As Chelsea boss, Docherty bought Stepney in May 1966 for £50,000, a world record fee for a goalkeeper. 112 days later, he sold him to Manchester United for another world record fee, this time £55,000.

None of this necessarily meant that Docherty and Stepney were not going to get along. Nor did it mean that Docherty was not cognizant of the keeper's abilities. But as events unfolded many would have been assuming that Stepney's days in Manchester were numbered. As far as Docherty was concerned, "I had been called in to be the unpopular guy whose job it was to clear the decks for the future." Part of that job involved getting rid of players whose ageing status had come to seem irrelevant by some at the club next to the fact that they were fan favourites, even national institutions. "Perhaps because he had retired from playing himself at the age of 32, TD couldn't understand the reluctance of others to similarly call it a day," opined his wife Agnes. Moreover, many would come to suspect from the business-like, even brutal, manner in which he ended the Manchester United careers of several of the veterans on the club's payroll that Docherty's actions were informed not merely by impatience with those who couldn't see that their best days were behind them but by the fact that he was obsessed with making clear that this was now his club, not Matt Busby's. Aside from Stepney, the remaining members of the team that played in the 1968 European Cup campaign were Bobby Charlton, Tony Dunne, Brian Kidd, Denis Law and David Sadler. One could also add two other names who were players in that era in the form of squad member and occasional first-teamer John Fitzpatrick and reserve goalie Jimmy Rimmer. By August 1974, all of those players bar Stepney were gone from Old Trafford. Pat Crerand – a 1968 veteran who Docherty made his assistant manager at the suggestion, Crerand has theorised, of Busby – would quit in extremely acrimonious circumstances in 1976. His European Cup team-mate Bill Foulkes was currently also a member of United's backroom staff and he too would have a falling-out with Docherty. Admittedly, Charlton and Fitzpatrick departed the stage through retirement (age and injury the respective reasons) and Docherty did seem at one point to genuinely want Kidd as part of his new set-up, plus there is the fact that Docherty would eventually agree to take back another of the 1968 side, George Best. Nonetheless, a pattern of out-with-the-old, in-with-the-new was clearly and, to some, painfully apparent in Docherty's first months at United. Some have suggested that Docherty was determined not to be undone by the player power that was alleged to have seen off his two predecessors and to build a team whose members would feel loyalty only for him. Docherty himself would give credence to that idea – or more accurately confirm it – when he said in 1976, "Some men had to go because they were cheats and bad professionals. There were cliques that had to be smashed. If I hadn't got rid of those players, they would have got rid of me … After all, two managers had gone before me in quick time." George Graham, Docherty's first United signing and a man whom Docherty evidently knew to be a keen gardener, has recalled Docherty saying to him that he had a lot of "weeding out" to do.

Though he was 29 when Docherty came to Old Trafford, Stepney, it transpired, was initially immune to this new broom. Over the next few seasons, stints between the sticks by first Rimmer, then Paddy Roche occurred only because Stepney was injured. Stepney returned to the first team as soon as he was fit again pretty much regardless of results in his absence. Stepney repaid this faith with performances that made him one of the only plusses at United at this juncture. Only in the 1975/76 season did Docherty seem to come to the opinion that Stepney's best days were behind him and that it was time to ease him out in order to avoid conceding those few precious goals per season that could make all the difference between being also-rans and champions. Almost comically, though, the plan never quite worked due to a combination of the board refusing Docherty the money to attract the keeper he had in mind as Stepney's successor and the disastrous performances of Roche between the sticks. In the end, Stepney would out-last Docherty at Manchester United.

Stepney was born on September 18 1942 in Mitcham, which is technically in Surrey but culturally in south London. His career had started with non-Leaguers Tooting & Mitcham United. He joined Millwall in 1963, and attracted the attention of bigger clubs with his performances in the Fourth and Third Divisions. Stepney played just one match for Chelsea, an away game against Southampton. Before the match, Chelsea's regular goalkeeper Peter Bonetti approached him and wished him luck. Stepney thought there was something peculiar about an earnestness in Bonetti's tone that went beyond mere politeness. It transpired that Bonetti had an interest in Stepney giving a good account of himself – it would help facilitate his own hoped-for transfer. (Like many players, he had fallen out with The Doc.) Stepney did in fact do well, keeping a clean sheet as Chelsea knocked in three.

However, Stepney was in for a shock. Having only agreed to the move from Millwall after being assured that Bonetti was on the way out and that he would be first-choice goalkeeper at the club, Stepney was then told that that Bonetti would be staying. This turn of events occurred when in the wake of chairman Joe Mears' death the remaining members of the board decided that they wanted to hold the keeper nicknamed The Cat to his contract. This of course was not Docherty's fault, but his solution to the problem of suddenly having at his disposal a goalie who was an England international and another who had just arrived on a goalkeeper's world-record transfer fee was one Stepney found "bordering on the absurd". The two men, Docherty announced, would play in alternate matches. Stepney found this to be in keeping with the impulsive, extravagant gestures of a man who when he had been about to sign the forms taking him to Stamford Bridge suddenly and completely unnecessarily announced that Chelsea would pay Millwall an additional £10,000 if Stepney made the England team. However, before Stepney could even grapple with this strange situation, his life was in upheaval yet again. Ten days after his Chelsea debut, he was told that Matt Busby and his assistant manager Jimmy Murphy were on their way down from Manchester to meet him. Such presumptuousness was not uncommon in football then. Technically, Stepney could hold Chelsea to his contract, but of course might find himself marooned in the 'B' team as punishment, so the likelihood of his refusing to counternanace a move was slim. In any case, Stepney was hardly going to take umbrage at the prospect of playing alongside men like Best, Law, Charlton and Crerand and the offer of £100 a week plus £20 per League point – handsome remuneration for the era whatever United's traditional stinginess. He agreed to sign for the Northerners.

Stepney realised pretty quickly he had made the right decision in becoming a Red Devil. In his first season with the club, they won the League Championship. Or perhaps that should be, he won the League Championship for them. Matt Busby said at the time, "The key to our success was the form of Alex Stepney in goal. He never let us down."

Stepney managed to keep the ball out of the net more often than most keepers in the country without making a big deal of it. He was no showman: the spectacular dives were few and far between, courtesy of his acute positioning sense. Future United colleague Steve Coppell – an England international – said of Stepney, "His anticipation was better than any other goalkeeper's I have played with or against." A classic 'line' keeper, Stepney disdained tearing out of the goal to claim a ball. He perhaps didn't need to come off his line much simply because of the way he bossed his penalty area. Brian Greenhoff, who would be his first-team colleague from the 1973/74 season onwards, recalls Stepney continually alerting his team-mates to danger: "Big Alec was always talking, telling you where to go, pulling you here, pulling you there."

Even better was to come for Stepney after that 1967 championship when the following season he became one of the 11 players who wrote their names in the history books by becoming the first English team to lay claim to the European Cup. United almost experienced the unbearable sensation of missing out once again on the trophy whose pursuit had cost so many lives in 1958. In the dying minutes of normal time in the final, with the scores level, the great Portuguese striker Eusebio was one-on-one with Stepney. Bobby Charlton has opined that Eusebio would have scored had he not decided to do something spectacular by hitting a powerful shot instead of executing something more subtle. Nonetheless, Stepney did brilliantly by holding his nerve and throwing himself down to block. In extra-time, United romped to victory.

It seems logical that such a fine goalkeeper was capped, but Stepney himself thinks that the only reason he did get to play a solitary game for England was because national team manager Alf Ramsey was doing United a favour: his international debut came against Sweden a week before the Benfica match and took place at Wembley, where the European Cup final happened to be staged that year. It was Ramsey's way of giving Stepney the perfect preparation for the latter fixture. Nonetheless, the fact that Stepney never got to pull on an England shirt again surely had less to do with this than the fact that in his time he was competing for a place with the stellar likes of Gordon Banks, Peter Shilton, Ray Clemence and – indeed – Peter Bonetti.

After those glory days, Stepney saw a slow decline in the football he observed from the back of the pitch, culminating in that bleak day when Crystal Palace put five past him. When Docherty was named as the man the club had decided would try to pull them out of the mire, Stepney was sceptical. His experience at Chelsea had taught him that Docherty was capable of "juvenile" behaviour. He also felt that Docherty's flamboyant and outrageous personality was not in keeping with the dignity surrounding Manchester United, nor likely to co-exist happily with the personalities of Louis Edwards and Matt Busby. However, he found Docherty a "changed man", fun to be around and prepared to listen to players.

\*\*\*

Docherty had the good fortune that his first match in charge of United – on Saturday December 23 1972 – was at their own ground, enabling him to be introduced to a 46,382-strong home crowd before kick-off. Supporters providing the traditional welcoming ovation may not seem particularly important but psychologically it must provide some sort of fillip to both crowd and players, as well as the new boss himself. A fillip was what was needed, for his first match was going to be something of a baptism of fire. Leeds United were in the peak years of the reign of manager Don Revie. They were the FA Cup holders and would be the following season's League champions. Not only did their teamsheet boast great players like Jack Charlton (Bobby's older brother), Peter Lorimer, Allan Clarke and Johnny Giles, but the side gave no quarter, in all senses of the phrase. The historical Yorkshire-Lancashire rivalry bound up in the clash – football's War of the Roses – only added to the fixture's intensity. The Reds could only count themselves lucky that Leeds' midfield firebrand Billy Bremner was absent.

Crerand had been put temporarily in charge of the United team in the brief hiatus between O'Farrell's dismissal and Docherty's arrival so it may have been his hand more than The Doc's in the selection of the starting XI chosen to combat Leeds' formidable combination of great skill and low gamesmanship. The line-up was: Alex Stepney, Tommy O'Neil, Tony Dunne, Denis Law, David Sadler, Martin Buchan, Willie Morgan, Ted MacDougall, Bobby Charlton, Wyn Davies and Ian-Storey Moore. Docherty might ultimately prove to have misgivings about the presence of Law and Charlton at Old Trafford because of declining abilities and a venerated status that had the potential to undermine his management, but even he wasn't going to turn his nose up at the idea of fielding Charlton, nor did he let what he felt was Law's lacklustre performance in the Selhurst Park match as substitute (he later said Law seemed to have lost his spark – an enthusiasm that was one of his greatest assets – against Palace) prevent him from including him in the starting line-up. Young and Kidd were the players making way for the legendary veterans.

United impressed with some early moves, and when Law fed MacDougall, only a challenge from Trevor Cherry that left the latter on the deck and many in the crowd wondering at its legality stopped him going one-on-one with Harvey. Additionally, it was the Reds who scored first when Morgan's low cross found MacDougall hovering for the type of simple knock-in in which he specialised. The second half saw Docherty replace Law with Brian Kidd.

A triumphant debut win two days before Christmas would have been a great Yuletide gift for The Doc and the Old Trafford faithful, but the proceedings had a faintly sickening denouement. The 88th minute saw Clarke pounce on a high ball to whack it past Stepney. The goal looked offside but it stood – a scenario that many would attest would not occur today in an age where so many referees seem intimidated by the atmosphere of Old Trafford and the power of Manchester United. Despite the gloss being taken off the match by that turn of events, the most important thing was that United had looked convincing whereas just seven days before they had been profoundly less than the sum of their parts. *The Observer* went so far as to say, even at this early stage, "If Manchester can produce this form, relegation will certainly be avoided." For the time being, they remained in 21st place.

After the Leeds match, grim reality came crashing down on United and their supporters with their Boxing Day visit to the Baseball Ground. Though they had been going through a bad patch until recently, Derby County were the reigning League champions and therefore something of a litmus test for the issue of whether the performance on Saturday had been down to Docherty's tactical nous or something more akin to the euphoria of regime change. Docherty of course could not turn a club around instantly, nor could he be blamed for the team he had inherited. However, he couldn't claim that a rather threadbare performance was nothing to do with him.

United were unchanged from Saturday with the exception that Kidd came in for Law. (Tony Young replaced an injured Dunne a minute into the second half.) They were two down within 18 minutes. Derby captain Colin McFarland was completely unmarked for the first goal, but it wasn't just United's defence that were lacking. Of the players further up the park, only Morgan and Storey-Moore were impressive. On 57 minutes, a McFarland header hit the underside of the bar before thumping behind the goal-line. United actually pulled one back via a Storey-Moore header soon enough to have feasibly set their sights on a draw, but it was the Reds' only goal of the game. The score left United bottom of the League and, as journalist Denis Lowe observed, cognizant of "the size of the task now facing Tommy Docherty".

Docherty set about that task by diving head-first into the transfer market. Meek: "I remember Tommy Docherty saying, 'Well, Wilf McGuinness and Frank O'Farrell have made my job much easier than it might have been. I've come at the right time because it's clear now that these players will have to go. They've had that extra year or two after their triumph in the European Cup in '68 and everybody accepts, including the players themselves, that it's time to move on, so half my job has been done for me.' He appreciated that he was starting with virtually a clean slate, and my word he made up for lost time, didn't he? Players were coming and going. He had a terrific hire-and-fire policy. He brought so many people in that to a certain extent he was stabbing in the dark. Some came off brilliantly, but there were a few others who didn't." Was he overlooking the merits of some of the players already there? Meek: "No, I think he needed to shake up the place. Of course,

The Doc doesn't do things by halves. Many managers would have recognised the need to bring in new players but might not have brought in quite so many quite so quickly, but that was his style and he just got on with it."

Within five days of becoming manager, Docherty made the first of a flurry of purchases to bolster United's team: George Graham. Born in Bargeddie, near Glasgow, on November 30 1944, Graham was a well-known figure, having displayed his elegant, laid-back skills in Arsenal's midfield since 1966, after previously turning out for Aston Villa and Chelsea. The Gunners let him go for a fee of £125,000 or £130,000 (the reported figured, as often the case for football transfers, varied). Graham – who seemed intended for the role once occupied by Crerand – had been bought before by Docherty at Chelsea. It had also been Docherty who had sold him at Chelsea. Nonetheless, Docherty had latterly been placing faith in him by selecting him for Scotland, despite the fact that though he was only 28 he was no longer an automatic first-team choice at Arsenal. Accompanying Docherty to London to talk about the proposed deal with Graham was Sir Matt Busby, even though he was retired and merely a board member (albeit influential in that he could veto signings). Docherty claimed that it was his idea that Busby accompany him ("I wanted his vast experience behind me"). However, if it wasn't then it seems to have soon become club policy for Busby to speak to every player that United wanted to sign. It was certainly a wise procedure: the closest thing English football had to a saint, Busby's presence in a room must have affected many a prospective signing's emotions. Certainly Graham – who was from a background similar to Busby's Lanarkshire village childhood – himself later admitted, "... meeting the incomparable Sir Matt helped sway my decision to sign for United."

Graham recalled the first time he had come across Docherty: "I first met Tommy nearly 10 years ago, at a refreshment bar in Gatwick Airport. I was just on my way to a holiday in Spain, having agreed to sign for Southampton. Then out of the blue, and with typical breathless flourish, up sped The Doc. He talked to me for just 10 minutes ... At the end of that time I was a Chelsea player! He never promised the moon. He simply said that he had seen me play for Scotland Youth, thought I had a lot of promise and he would very much like the chance to work with me. It was my first experience of his winning way with players and, believe me, nothing has changed." Graham said that he had forgiven Docherty for selling him when he was at Stamford Bridge and that when he had heard he had been given the job of manager at Old Trafford he was hoping he would make a bid for him. He also pointed out that as Docherty had given him his first full international cap when manager of Scotland, this felt like it was the third time he had been signed by him. "In the times I have been under his control, especially during those Chelsea days, I wouldn't like to recall the number of times we've had words," said Graham. "But that's what I like about the man – he doesn't hold any grudges. The Doc is essentially an honest man. He's blunt, outspoken and he says what he thinks, sometimes irrespective of the cost." Said Docherty, "United have always had great players ... George Graham is a great player and if I go for any other players they will have to have quality."

Within 20 hours, Docherty had indeed gone for another player and made another big-money signing of a Scotland international. 20-year-old full-back Alex Forsyth was born in Swinton, Berwickshire, on February 5 1952. He was a purchase from Partick Thistle and as such was considerably less well-known down south than his compatriot Graham. However, he would actually turn out to be the more successful of the two signings. Some might have predicted that greater success beforehand, for whereas Graham's nuanced skills (which had earned him the nickname Stroller) didn't strike many as the requirements for a relegation dogfight, Forsyth's hard-tackling prowess did. However, Forsyth was handily equipped for sections of the field other than defence too, possessing unusual dribbling skills for a full-back and a fearsome shot useful in dead-ball scenarios.

Docherty had capped Forsyth four times for his country so far. Forsyth recalls, "After the 71/72 Cup Final when we beat Celtic 4-1, I think six of the Partick Thistle players were capped. After that we went to the Mini-World Cup in Brazil." Forsyth was thrilled about being thrust into the big-time by The Doc: "He was brilliant, 'cos I was only at a small club, Partick Thistle, and you're away [with the] international team and you're playing with players like Billy Bremner, Lorimer, Harvey, George Graham, Denis Law. Big, big stars. Martin Buchan was playing. They were all good, good players and me playing with a smaller club, it wasn't sort of known ..." Forsyth recalls Docherty being "an all-out attacking" Scotland manager: "... overlapping full-backs. He liked me to get forward and get shots in and get crosses in. He wasn't too much worried about defending."

Forsyth remembers the circumstances of him becoming Docherty's second Manchester United signing: "I went into training at Partick. The trainer says to me, 'Look, the manager says Tommy Docherty has been on the phone for you. Are you interested in going to United?' I says, 'Of course I'm going to United.' I didn't even talk about it. 10 minutes later, I'm out to see my dad at his work. (My mum wasn't in the house.) My dad said, 'What are you doing away from the football?' I said, 'I'm going down to sign with Man United.' He says, 'You're kidding me'." Forsyth says that United's lowly position at the time didn't give him pause for thought: "Not really. When somebody's saying it's a club like United, there's no way you can turn that down, especially after you've been in Scotland. I was over the moon. I couldnae turn that move down."

United's £100,000 signing of Forsyth almost didn't happen. Docherty agreed the fee with Partick on December 27 1972. Forsyth – upon being told of the deal the next morning – jumped in a car with Partick manager Dave McParland and drove 230 miles to sign his contract. The drive down was one which presumably involved pushing the speed limit as far as legally possible, for the Football League's signing deadline for Saturday's matches was that day. Forsyth took five minutes to sign his United contract and the club then – in times prior to fax machines – sent a telegram to the Football League. They beat the deadline by 13 minutes. "He is an ambitious boy and we did not need to talk long to close the deal," said Docherty. "He is a great full-back on the right or left side. In fact, we've got three players for the price of one."

Graham and Forsyth were playing for United the following day in a home friendly against Hull City. No doubt in that match, Forsyth followed his meticulous pre-match preparation procedures that would so amuse his colleagues. The defender was almost religious in the way he equipped himself for battle. Forsyth: "Always went out third on the park. Always liked carrying a ball on. All these wee silly things that players do. Put your boots on last, your shirt was last on, put the Vick's [VapoRub decongestant] on, up your nose, put your Vaseline on your right eye first, on your left eye second, then your cheeks and a wee bit on your chin. And the last thing you do is go and wash your hands." And Forsyth hasn't even mentioned other elements of his pre-match routine that others observed: placing plasters around his shinpads to keep them in place and specific requirements about the way the tie-ups around his socks were arranged, the laces on his boots tied and the way his shirt was tucked into his shorts.

A home friendly against Second Division opposition gave Docherty an opportunity to try out his new signings in a reasonably pressure-free environment. MacDougall and Davies were dropped. Kidd was in the starting line-up, as was Law. Ironically, Docherty got an unexpected but ultimately fruitful chance to observe the talent and form of someone not in his own team, when Hull's diminutive but powerful young striker Stuart Pearson had an early if unsuccessful attempt to put the visitors ahead. Pearson would eventually become a key part of Docherty's United set-up. A second irony was provided by the fact that the two scorers for the Reds were men whose age precluded them being part of the new United Docherty was seeking to build, Law and Charlton. Hull scored once. In a game characterised by a relaxed attitude, both Graham and Forsyth did what they had to do reasonably well.

That a lowly club like Hull should obtain a lucrative friendly fixture against Manchester United was probably a compensatory matter, for Docherty had enticed their trainer Tommy Cavanagh to come and serve under him as coach at Old Trafford. The two had known each other as players at Preston, although Cavanagh had not become a first-team regular. Scouser

Cavanagh subsequently played for Preston North End, Stockport County, Huddersfield Town, Doncaster Rovers, Bristol City and Carlisle United. He first managerial post was in 1961 at Cheltenham. He lost his job after four games, and those who later observed him in action as a coach won't be too surprised to learn that his dismissable offence was bad language. Following this, Cavanagh served as coach for Brentford and Nottingham Forest. It was Docherty who recommended Cavanagh to Hull's Terry Neill. Cavanagh had also helped Docherty on a voluntary basis when the latter was Scotland manager.

Shortly after Docherty took up his post at United, a story appeared in a tabloid about the first training session of the Docherty-Cavanagh regime. Willie Morgan was described as staggering off a pitch at the club's Cliff training ground exclaiming, "Hey, Tommy, have you got a spade handy? I feel like digging my grave." Ian Storey-Moore, who knew Cavanagh's methods from their days together at Nottingham Forest, said, "I don't think any of the other lads have ever been through a training session like it before." Cavanagh's future colleague Frank Blunstone says of him, "Old-fashioned sergeant-major. He wasn't everybody's favourite. He could be a bit harsh at times." Cavanagh certainly didn't believe in modifying his approach to accommodate different personalities. Blunstone: "He'd treat them all the same. Give them all a bollocking." Mick Martin, a Docherty United signing, recalls, "He was a pal of The Doc's. He was important in as much as he was a character. A character you could either like or dislike a lot. Tommy [Cavanagh] could change from one minute to another from being a nice person to being a person you would like to punch. But he was full of enthusiasm."

Cavanagh's attitude as a coach can probably be summed up by his quote, "People have said I'm a hard man but you don't get the players complaining how I treat them. Of course I want my players to fight and play hard but I have yet to see a player killed while playing soccer." Some aspects of his behaviour, however, were plainly and simply a form of bullying, as this anecdote from Gordon Hill, a latter-day Docherty signing, illustrates: "We had a training tracksuit which was nice but it was nylon and I couldn't wear nylon on my legs because I broke out in a rash. He said to me, 'If you don't wear these at the start of the season, I'm going to take 'em off you and you're not going to wear 'em all season.' And I couldn't wear them all year, so I had to go out with flipping shorts on in the middle of winter at The Cliff." Says Gerry Daly, another future United signing, "Not an awful lot of people got on very well with Tommy Cavanagh. Not an awful lot of people liked him. He was [a] very abusive, aggressive type of a chap." In mitigation, his sergeant-major routine was at least tempered by a belief in elevated soccer values. "I cannot stand negative football where you go three passes backwards to go one forward," Cavanagh said. "The one thing we will not do is turn the United players into robots. They will be encouraged to play football at all times."

Says Buchan, "If I'm being honest, I don't believe that Frank O'Farrell gave Malcolm Musgrove as much authority as he might have done, because whether it was Doc or Cav taking a training session, it didn't matter. It was all done properly, there was no messing about. You never thought, 'This is the second-in-command taking the session today, we don't have to be on our toes so much.' In fact, if anything, it was the other way around." Mick Martin remembers Cavanagh being more visible – or perhaps audible – than Docherty in the dressing room before matches: "Tommy Cavanagh was the one who came in and was all the hype and the shouting and all that stuff, 'Let's get into them and play it down here, keep it tight ...' Wasn't the greatest coach in the world but had a great way of geeing players up and getting players to react and probably to perform." Gerry Daly seems to perceive the Docherty-Cavanagh axis as operating on almost a nice-cop/nasty-cop level. "Cavanagh was more of a mouth than anything else," he says. "He was just a ranter and a raver. Cavanagh was the sort of aggressive one where Docherty would be the one that would calm things down." Brian Greenhoff, a youth player when Cavanagh was appointed but who would graduate to the first team the following season, says, "If he had something to say, Cav would say it, and if it upset you, it didn't bother him." However, he didn't have a big problem with Cavanagh's unsubtle methods: "He did it with me a few times, but afterwards if you'd reacted to it, he'd be the first one to come up and put his arm round you and say 'well done'. It's like we're all in it together and [all] he wanted to do was get the best out of his players. But a bully? I would say no."

Martin Buchan cannot speak too highly of the man whom the players came to know as "TC" to distinguish him from Docherty, known to them as "TD". "Tommy Cavanagh was a wonderful man to have in your corner," he says. "As a coach, very straightforward, nothing too complicated. I worked under Cav for eight years and when I got the chance to go into management at Burnley I took him up there to help me. So I think that says it all. You don't do that if you don't have the utmost respect for someone."

Docherty's other main staff appointment was one very familiar to United fans. Pat Crerand had been the midfield general of the European Cup winning team, continuously spraying long elegant passes from the back of the field. When he had been a Celtic player, Crerand claims that Docherty rang him and offered him a five-fold salary rise to come and play for Chelsea, an offer Crerand declined because he was as much Celtic supporter as player. Matt Busby turned out to have greater powers of persuasion than Docherty and took him to United in 1963. A genial and humorous man, Crerand was also incongruously, to quote George Best, a "case-hardened Scots nut where it came to bother" and it was to him that Best looked for protection if, as he frequently was, he was threatened with physical assault by opponents. Like many of that 1968 side, Crerand was now getting long in the tooth. O'Farrell appointed him youth team coach in August 1971, although Crerand didn't formally retire as a player until July 1972. Docherty promoted him to assistant manager on January 2 1973, although Crerand also had reserve-team duties. One of Crerand's colleagues from the 1968 team – imposing centre-half Bill Foulkes, a Munich survivor – was given more responsibilities by Docherty in his job of reserve team coach, being allowed to select the team for the Central League in which the reserves then played, a contrast to most other clubs where the first-team manager took responsibility for all team tiers. Upon his appointment, Docherty contacted his old Chelsea colleague Frank Blunstone with a view to him looking after the youth set-up at Old Trafford. Blunstone: "He asked me to go there because he thought I did a good job. We had Alan Hudson and Butch Wilkins and all that lot who I brought through." Blunstone turned the job down: "I wouldn't go because I was manager at Brentford then. I was a manager in my own right and I wanted to have a go at managing."

***

That both Ted MacDougall and Wyn Davies were left out of the friendly against Hull City was a harbinger of the way United's existing strike force would be quickly consigned to history by the club's new manager. The goal MacDougall had scored in the Leeds match that marked the inauguration of Docherty's United tenure was his fourth in seven starts. Many managers would have been impressed by such a strike rate but it seemed to cut no ice with Docherty, nor did the fact that MacDougall and Davies had been at Old Trafford for three months and had scored nine goals in 15 games between them.

MacDougall had never had too happy a time at United. He was signed from Bournemouth in September 1972 and said he was informed by Frank O'Farrell, "The kings are abdicating. I hope you'll be one in the future." He was something of a goalscoring sensation. Among the 126 strikes he made for Bournemouth in his 165 appearances for the club were, famously, nine in an 11-0 slaughter of Margate in the FA Cup in November 1971. "I didn't even know it was a record till I got home," MacDougall recalls. "The BBC called up and said it was a record." Though the thought of breaking records hadn't entered his mind during the match, he remains proud of his achievement: "That record stood since 1928 and I broke it in 1971, which [is] 40 years on."

However, some remained unimpressed. After all, Bournemouth were a Third Division side (and Margate resided beyond the lowest tier of the Football League in the Southern League). Meanwhile, though MacDougall could net them, by his own admission, that was about all he could do. "My job was to finish and to try and score goals and to complete everybody else's stuff," he says. "That's what I tried to do: just an out-and-out goalscorer." Nonetheless, though he may have been an uncomplicated player, his high conversion rate was something many players of greater all-round skill would have loved to be able to boast. Asked what his secret was, he says, "I think one is a desire and one is that you've got certain instincts. A lot of people haven't got those instincts and a lot of people haven't got the desire because you can get hurt. You've got to be brave. Bravery comes in different forms but certainly you know you're going to get hurt and people are going to close you down and there's a lack of space. What I used to work on was I'd try and understand about space and movement."

Though moving to Old Trafford constituted two big steps upwards, MacDougall says he at no time worried that scoring prolifically in the lower divisions would not translate into a high strike-rate in the top flight. "I always thought the goals were the same size. Same dimensions in the First Division as they were in the Fourth Division." As for Division One defenders, "I thought they were sharper because the game is quicker but I still think they made the same mistakes. I still think they ball-watched when they shouldn't ball-watch, they didn't cover when they should have covered, and I think if you made enough runs inside the box and enough angles inside the box, you can still lose defenders." However, what he did not envisage was that his new colleagues would not be as enthusiastic about helping him score as his previous ones had been: "When I was playing for Bournemouth and Norwich and other teams, it was about me and they were crossing balls and making stuff for me. Where if you go to Manchester United, they don't give a toss about me so it was very difficult. I wasn't a George Best or a Bobby Charlton or a Denis Law or whatever. I needed other people ..."

MacDougall was born on January 8 1947 in Inverness. He says there were "a few" clubs who expressed interest in him after the Margate match, "... but I'd supported Man U when I was a kid so I went there. I got an extra 10 pound a week." Perhaps if the financial gap between being a Third Division player and a top-flight footballer had been greater, he might have found it easier to bear the disdain that he has long claimed he encountered from his new colleagues at Old Trafford. MacDougall would later complain that the established United players seemed resentful of the massive price tag he had come with and that when he would fail to do something well in training, it would lead to sarcastic comments. MacDougall recalled trying to give as good as he got when George Best also failed to do something well in training. The retort to this sarcasm from the Irishman was that he hadn't cost the club £200,000. MacDougall was also unimpressed by the attitude of Bobby Charlton. He recalls, "Bobby Charlton spoke to me when he was my roommate. I think he said to me, 'Can you turn the light off?' That was the last time he spoke to me." He has also said in the past that he had once asked Charlton the best way to the training ground and had never received an answer. It seems peculiar that

MacDougall doesn't seem to have observed something that just about everybody at the club had noticed in this period: Charlton's usual taciturnity had hardened into an almost complete uncommunicativeness that was the manifestation of his utter despair at the straits the club for which he had played football his entire adult life – usually in an atmosphere of glory and achievement – had found themselves in. Says Buchan, "I think he was disappointed and upset to see the team he'd won the European Cup Final with four or five seasons previously being in such, by the standards of his career, a dire position. I think it almost broke Bobby's heart." As to the training ground sarcasm, it's difficult to adjudge whether what MacDougall experienced was the normal mickey-taking that goes on within a football team – especially a British football team – or whether it was something more sinister, but it being the case that Best, whatever his faults, was a generally good-natured fellow, it does seem that MacDougall was being over-sensitive to the aforementioned remark.

Certainly, Mick Martin remembers MacDougall as a man with a thin skin: "He was a volatile character who you could fall out with very easy and you could finish up arguing with him. No wonder him and Tommy may not have got on at the end. He had an ability Ted, but he could be moody." MacDougall concedes the point. "I'm not putting myself up as everybody was wrong and I was right," he says. "I was a moody player – because I wanted to score goals. I would do anything to score a goal. Some people can't handle that. For example, if Willie Morgan made the angle to cross the ball, I made my run to the near post. If Willie takes an extra touch, what does that mean then? It means I'm in too early. I've got to come out of it again. Now, that would upset me because he should play the ball in when he should play it, but he didn't because he took an extra touch. Now the crowd don't see that because they're watching Willie or whoever."

As previously noted, Buchan seems to confirm MacDougall's suspicions about something sinister being afoot. "I played against Ted when he was at Bournemouth," says Buchan. "I knew exactly what he and his striking partner Phil Boyer were doing, the runs they were making and the positions they were taking up, because of the education I'd had at Aberdeen. A lot of the players around me didn't have a clue what was going on, because they'd never been coached at that level. There was a certain amount of derision that he couldnae do tricks with the ball, but his trick was putting the ball in the back of the net if he got the right service and a lot of them didn't like that. They certainly didn't go out of their way to help him." MacDougall: "Everybody was in survival mode. Manchester United were still getting 58, 60,000 and we were struggling. We were near the bottom of the League. It's like a sinking ship. Everybody's looking after themselves. They're not interested in me, they're interested in themselves. These people were doing the things that made them great. When Bobby Charlton is looking to knock 40-yard diagonal balls and, say, a simple ball to play me in, what do you think he's going to play? If George Best is going to beat two and three players because he can and he sees something else that may be a better opportunity for me, what do you think he's going to do? Would Wyn Davies be a classic Manchester United player? That's debatable. Was I? Obviously not. Could I do something that they couldn't do? Yeah. Was I allowed to do that? No. In a different setting, when your team is doing well, I think anybody would embrace a goalscorer. I don't think anybody would say, 'Oh no, all he does is score goals'."

MacDougall recalls instant dismay as his reaction to Docherty being given the manager's job at United: "I heard in the car park by Willie Morgan 'cos I was in his car and he said, 'Oh great news. You know who's going to get the job? Tommy Docherty.' I said, 'Oh my, that's me gone then. I'll be gone by deadline', which was round about March the 12th." The paths of MacDougall and Docherty had crossed before. MacDougall appeared in an all-star team against West Ham United in Geoff Hurst's testimonial immediately after he had achieved that nine-goal record against Margate. Docherty was acting as manager for MacDougall's side. MacDougall: "That's the first time I had anything to do with Tommy Doc. I scored and he took me off at half-time." MacDougall was the only substitution The Doc made on the night. For MacDougall, Docherty simply resumed that irrational dismissive behaviour at United. Docherty later claimed MacDougall made it known that he wasn't happy at Old Trafford and wanted a move down south. MacDougall's version was completely different. "I never wanted to leave the club I'd idolised as a kid," he insisted. "I never asked for a transfer." Docherty, he claimed, "... pre-judged me. He didn't rate me at all." MacDougall now says, "It was obvious to everybody that I was surplus. I'd go in and see him on a semi-regular basis in his office and say, 'What's going on? Have you heard anything?' He was taking the piss. Let's be honest, that's what Tommy Doc's all about, that's the humour. I didn't do a transfer request and he didn't formally put me on the transfer list. [It was clear] that it was probably right if I move on. I just knew it was a hopeless cause, because just the atmosphere and the way it was."

MacDougall himself said that Docherty never told him to his face that he thought he couldn't play but judging by the recollections of others he wasn't the victim of paranoia. "He didn't rate Ted MacDougall," recalls Meek. Asked if The Doc gave MacDougall a fair chance, Meek says, "No, I don't think he did actually. They told the story that the team photograph at the beginning [sic] of the season, Ted MacDougall was lined up somewhere in the middle and he said, 'Ted, do you mind just moving out of there and standing on the end, because when you leave it'll be easier to clip you off the team picture?'" Macari also later recalled the incident, and said, "Typical of the Doc. Quite funny and even Ted had to chuckle at it." Forsyth says of MacDougall, "Never got a chance because The Doc didnae like him. He just didn't like him. I remember one day at training he said, 'That boy, in the box he's fine, but outside the box he's absolutely hopeless'."

MacDougall said that within a week of Docherty's arrival, he was informed that he didn't fit into his plans. Though the information was relayed in a somewhat more civilised manner than would attend the departure of other players under the Docherty regime like Denis Law and Willie Morgan ("... we didn't have slanging matches"), this was little consolation for a man who had been in his new house with his wife and baby for only two weeks and who had been in his previous house in Bournemouth for just five weeks. The upheavals of moving are part and parcel of football – albeit not usually so extreme – but MacDougall's feelings were heightened by a sense of injustice.

Though MacDougall could take some consolation from the fact that he was still young and an attractive proposition on the transfer market, the future seemed bleaker for Wyn Davies, who had already turned 30 when O'Farrell bought him from Manchester City in September. "If Pele had been born in Prestatyn, Tommy would have dropped him for not scoring enough goals ... As far as he was concerned, the Welsh were worthy of nothing more than contempt," wrote Docherty's ex-wife Agnes in her autobiography. Those who assume this provides an explanation for why Docherty so quickly dispensed with Davies's services would probably be barking up the wrong tree: The Doc's record reveals no profound aversion to employing Welshmen. More convincing is that Docherty just didn't like Davies's type of player, for he was another uncomplicated goalscorer, albeit one with the additional attribute of an imposing physique. "Wyn, big centre-forward, but he needed the right service," summarises Buchan of the man born on March 20 1942 in Caernarvon. Welsh international Davies would seem to have had the right service for the bulk of his career so far, having scored 66 goals in 155 League matches for Bolton Wanderers, 40 in 180 for Newcastle United (winning the Fairs Cup with them in 1969) and eight in 45 for Manchester City. His preternatural ability to head goals led to Newcastle fans nicknaming him 'The Leap'. When he signed for Manchester United in September 1972, he became the first player to move between the Manchester clubs since 1934. Yet Docherty would give the Welshman one last first-team game before consigning him to the sidelines.

MacDougall would be sold to West Ham United in March 1973 for £170,000 – just before that transfer deadline he had been put in mind of by The Doc's appointment – while Davies moved to Blackpool in June 1973 for £14,000.

\*\*\*

Forsyth and Graham made their debuts proper on Saturday January 6 against Arsenal at Highbury. (The long gap between fixtures was the result of the postponement of the Reds' home match against Everton, which rather made Forsyth's mad dash to sign a waste of time.) By coincidence, Arsenal were the club Forsyth had been with as a boy before returning north of the border. O'Neill, Dunne, MacDougall and Davies were missing from the previous match's teamsheet, with Young and Law included.

"The game was very, very frantic," Forsyth says of his United and English League debut in front of a whopping 56,194 crowd. "Arsenal were always a very, very good side." He recalls of the match, "Hundred mile an hour. You hadnae a lot of time on the ball. Players were all marked very, very tight and you hadnae time to do things that you liked to: take a bit of time, pick out players and play up to feet."

Docherty's tactics were ultra-cautious today, but it did him little good, with the Gunners running rampant in the first half. Arsenal's first two goals came via cruel strokes of fate, Stepney sent the wrong way by a rebound for one and for the second unable to deal with a cross because his sight was blocked. Arsenal then began contemptuously rolling the ball around, although their third goal – an Alan Ball header on 68 minutes – was both deserved and well executed. United obtained a token reply on 84 minutes with a Kidd effort. Once again, the result saw United propping up the First Division.

Though this match was amongst the hardest of English League fixtures, this level of football was something Forsyth would have to get used to south of the border. "There's no comparison," he says. "You get down to the English League, every game's a hard one. You very, very rarely get an easy game. [At] Old Trafford you get a couple of goals up and all that, you can maybe [pull] your foot off the pedal a bit, but away from home everywhere you went, everybody wanted to beat Man United." One consolation for the harder work was that the industrious Forsyth quickly became an Old Trafford favourite. Forsyth: "I think they liked a good honest guy who tried their heart out, got near the goals, had a go. Maybe not the best defender but tackled hard and put good crosses in. Just a good working hard Scottish guy [who] enjoyed his football. I loved playing football – and how can you not with that crowd every week?"

\*\*\*

Docherty was given a bit of headache at this juncture when United lost the services for much of the rest of the season of a player whose uncommon skills might have gone a long way to easing the club's relegation worries. Ian Storey-Moore, bought by O'Farrell in March 1972, was a player firmly in United's exhilarating tradition. He not only provided goals by crossing from the byline after making his way to it by weaving past defenders but could also score them: his 105 strikes for Nottingham Forest in 236 League appearances was a staggeringly high ratio for a winger. Unfortunately, he would now play only twice more this season, and even then was substituted each time. This was frustrating for Docherty, for it stymied his ambition to utilise a 4-2-4 formation. "I have always believed in wingers," Docherty said at the time. "I played with two in the Scottish international team, Willie Morgan and Peter Lorimer, and as soon as possible I want to do the same at Old Trafford …"

Another strong element of the United squad, although not currently a member of the first team, was also put out of action that January. On the third day of the first month of 1973, Sammy McIlroy and his wife were involved in a road collision in Manchester so serious that it took the fire brigade to free them. Though his wife was able to return home after her hospital treatment, McIlroy's injuries required a stay of eight days in hospital, during which time he lost half a stone. McIlroy revealed that he was later told that only his fitness had saved his life. "I had a punctured lung and something like four broken ribs," McIlroy recalls. Although the doctors were able to shortly tell him that his footballing functions were not impaired in the long term, the Irishman points out, "This car crash set me back six months … I couldn't rush the injury back."

McIlroy had been the final player signed by Busby and had poetically lived up to his status as the last Busby Babe via a spectacular start to his United career – albeit under Frank O'Farrell – by scoring on his debut in November 1971. McIlroy would score three times in his first five starts. By the end of the season, McIlroy had made 11 starts in the first team and been brought on a further 10 times as substitute. He had also been selected by Northern Ireland, making him at 17 years and 198 days the second-youngest British player to turn out for his country behind Norman Kernoghan (whose record was set in 1936). However, in the 1972/73 season, McIlroy had fallen back slightly. Though frequently coming on as substitute, he had only made four first-team starts by the time Docherty took over in December and hadn't made the field for more than a month. Because of his reserve status, McIlroy hadn't actually met the new manager by the time he was hospitalised. Their introduction came in less than ideal circumstances, even if those circumstances displayed a thoughtfulness and compassion on the part of Docherty that – whatever his detractors might say – were just as much hallmarks of his management style at Manchester United as the undeniable callousness and cruelty he was also wont to show. The Doc introduced himself to McIlroy by coming to see him in hospital, Paddy Crerand in tow. "I was still a little bit groggy," says McIlroy. "He did say that he'd give me every chance to make my mark in the team again and that gave me a boost, because obviously when you're out of it and you read the papers about him buying players, players leaving [you think] 'would I be one that he discards right away without having a look at?'"

McIlroy – born in Belfast on August 2 1954 – not only shared a Belfast heritage with George Best, but the two had been discovered by the same scout, Bob Bishop. "He started looking after me since I was nine years old, so the United connection was always there from an early age," says McIlroy. "He used to tell us the stories all about George when George was playing for a local club and that's when Bob first seen him and he used to tell us the stories about this scrawny little kid too small, too thin, but what an unbelievable ability and skill. Bob was the only one then who had faith and belief that he was going to be a world-class player." Bishop informed United that he had another prospect in his patch in the shape of McIlroy: "When I was 14, I went over for a trial. Then they signed me when I was 15 in August '69. They'd just won the European Cup the year before so the place was absolutely buzzing. It was a great place to be around even though I was very, very homesick at that time. The scouting staff – Johnny Aston and Joe Armstrong at the time – used to send the boys home once a month so they could get over their homesickness. I started playing in the reserves when I was 16 and I went on a trip to Dublin under Sir Matt Busby with the first team when I was 16 and had a run out for the first team against Bohemians in Dublin."

Of his debut, aged 17, against Manchester City, McIlroy says, "It was unbelievable. Manchester City had a fantastic side in them days: Bell, Lee, Summerbee, fantastic forward line, and United with their forward line of Best, Charlton, Law. I stepped in for Denis Law that day because Denis was injured and failed a fitness test. Which was a fantastic honour for me to replace Denis Law, but I didn't find out until 11 o'clock that morning." McIlroy was nervous but George Best put his fellow Belfast boy at ease that morning before the team went for a pre-match meeting at a golf club. Best, McIlroy, reports, "just said, 'There'll be a bottle of champagne for you if you score today. Just go out and enjoy yourself, no problem.' And that sort of settled me down, but on the way to the ground you see the massive crowd and when you run out in front of 63,000 people at Maine Road ... I've never heard noise like it before and obviously the butterflies were starting to float round there and I was more concerned really about letting people down than actually me own performance. But once the game started, there was Bobby Charlton, there was George, there was Brian Kidd, Willie Morgan, they all helped me settle down. Getting the goal as well settled me down ... I can remember picking the ball up deep in our own half and I passed it inside to George and I just kept going. George started running with the ball and I just kept going towards Manchester City's box and George played the ball out to Brian Kidd and ran into the box and I followed in behind George. When Brian Kidd put the ball in, [City defender] Tony Book actually was tugging away at George's shirt so George couldn't control the ball. It actually came away from George and as I was following George into the box, the ball fell to me and I just slid it past Joe Corrigan. The place erupted and I could have ran out of the ground and ran back in again with the feeling I had, to score a goal on my debut, especially against your arch rivals." The match ended 3-3: "It's fantastic memories of that game still. It's one of the best derbies I think ever played and six goals, 63,000 people – a fantastic experience." McIlroy's spectacular start in a red shirt didn't end there: "I knew the score with Frank: when Denis was fit, Denis would come back in. But when Denis came back in, Brian Kidd was injured so I stayed in then. I remember playing Tottenham Hotspur at Old Trafford. That was my second League game against a great Spurs side and we beat them 3-1. I scored and Denis got two. That was another fantastic memory."

Though he may have had reservations about O'Farrell's dismissal, McIlroy approved of the new manager. "He came with the reputation of a bubbly manager," he says of Docherty. "He liked to play football. He was doing well with Scotland and I obviously remember his Chelsea days as well, when I was a youngster. He had a great side at Chelsea. He always liked to crack a joke and I always thought the way he handled the press and everything that he would turn it around."

***

Saturday January 13 saw United begin their FA Cup campaign with their third-round match against Wolverhampton Wanderers at Molineux in front of a crowd of 40,005. Davies replaced the injured Storey-Moore in an otherwise unchanged starting XI. Docherty played a two-man attacking line of Davies and Kidd. The latter had to be substituted 15 minutes into the second half, replaced by Dunne (later sent off). In an uninspiring match, the important action was all over by the second minute when a Wolves free-kick inspired panic in the United defence and Bailey scored with a high, powerful shot from the edge of the penalty area. United had fallen at what was for top-flight teams the FA Cup's first hurdle.

***

By the time of United's next game the following Saturday there would be two more new names on the teamsheet courtesy of Docherty once again exploiting the club's newfound largesse with the cheque book.

Docherty, deciding he needed a centre-half, reportedly offered £50,000 for Stephen Deere of Third Division Scunthorpe United. His approach was rebuffed by Scunthorpe's manager Ron Ashman, who said Deere was unavailable in the immediate future. "Two First Division clubs want Deere but he'll stay here until after the Cup," said Ashman. On such attitudes do players' entire careers hinge. Deere never did get to play in the top flight. He did get to play with George Best, but it wasn't until he was on loan to Stockport County in 1975 and the Irishman made some appearances for that lowly club at the fag-end of his career. Had Ashman been more accommodating, Deere (who turned out more than 300 times for Scunthorpe). might have enjoyed the terrace-darling status accorded the man Docherty signed in his stead, Jim Holton. Yet another Scot, Holton was a £70,000–£80,000 purchase from Third Division Shrewsbury Town. Though just 21, Holton's fearsome playing style and hulking physical presence somehow made him seem older. Crerand has recalled he had gone to Shrewsbury to watch another player but been enchanted by Holton's ability in the air and capacity for intimidating forwards. Crerand recommended Holton to The Doc, who bought him on recommendation alone (although maybe not just Crerand's for it has also been said that O'Farrell had had Holton watched). Crerand reckoned that Shrewsbury manager Harry Gregg – a former United team-mate – made Docherty pay double Holton's market value. United fans would aver he turned out to be a good buy regardless. Holton – born on April 11 1951 in Lesmahagow, Lanarkshire – became a favourite of the Stretford End, acquiring a fan club and a terrace chant: "Six foot two/Eyes of blue/Big Jim Holton's after you". Holton (eyes actually brown) only endeared himself to the fans more when their cries of appreciation would be met by the sight of him raising his clenched fist in their direction. Holton, though, was by no means beloved by every United supporter. The only player close to a traditional hard man that Docherty played during his United tenure, many was the long-term Reds follower who felt Holton's methods brought dishonour to the club.

Forward Lou Macari was also a Scot and would also become a huge favourite at Old Trafford. A buy from Celtic on January 18, Luigi Macari was born in Edinburgh on June 4 1949. Naturally with a name like that, he has Italian ancestry, although both parents were Scottish born and bred. Which is more than can be said for Macari himself, who had moved with his family to the south of England at the age of six months as a consequence of his father owning a café in London. In England, Macari's father played for amateur soccer team Leytonstone. Macari's family returned to Scotland when he was nearly 10. Though nobody would know from his thick Scots brogue as an adult, he has reported that as a child he had "the full Cockney accent." By the time he had just turned 14, Celtic were sufficiently interested in acquiring his talents to invite him to train with them a couple of nights a week. This of course was an incredible privilege, if no less than his budding exquisite talent deserved. By August 1970, he was in the first team.

Macari had come to Celtic without a settled position, although felt that he was roughly an inside-left. Though his scoring an inordinately high number of goals in schoolboy football was what first attracted Celtic's attention and though Celtic's captain Billy McNeill publicly declared him "the hottest scoring property in the country", Macari was never formally cast as a striker at Celtic. He would later say of Stein, "He would tell 10 players where to play and how to play. But he just gave me a shirt and told me to go out and enjoy myself. He didn't try to tie me down because he knew I would lose my enthusiasm."

Macari got a reputation in Scotland for ostentatiously taking pride in his on-field triumphs. "I loved showing off to the crowd," he said. "They pay their money and they are entitled to a bit of showmanship ... At Celtic I was a marked man by the opposition fans because I used to say my piece and score goals. They really hated me, but I didn't mind." Yet though temperamental and prone to preening, Macari was no brainless egotist. His interest in football, for instance, was limited to his time at work. He prided himself on his professionalism and his 100% commitment in training and matches, but, he said, "Afterwards, I go home as far as possible from football and I relax ... There are people like Jock Stein and Tommy Docherty who can't get enough football. They talk about it all day, go to training, plan the tactics for next week, go to watch another game at night. Then they want to talk football again. That's not me. Once the game's over, I don't want to know." Macari's lack of ego is illustrated by a comment he made to a newspaper shortly after his free-roving remit had made him the darling of the Celtic Park faithful: "If I had gone to any other club but Celtic straight from school, no one would ever have heard of me. I don't claim to be a great player. I'm certainly not a dedicated player. But anywhere other than Parkhead and I would have been an almost unknown player."

Though he wasn't one of the so-called Lisbon Lions Celtic team that in 1967 became the first British club to win European Cup, Macari had won everything there was to win in Scottish soccer, usually more than once. By 1972, he was also – courtesy of one Tommy Docherty – a Scottish international. As Macari's five-year contract with Celtic was coming to an end and the necessity to sign a new one loomed, Macari decided that he did not want to compete for Celtic in a two-horse race against Rangers season after season, something that Scottish football then ultimately constituted. "When you've done just about everything in your own country ... and you're still only 22, the prospect of another 10 years doing the same thing begins to lose its excitement," he later said. However, one month after requesting a transfer and being told he would be sold only if a 'suitable' offer was received – this was in the days before freedom of contract let alone the Bosman ruling – Macari withdrew his transfer request and signed a new five-year deal. Over the next couple of years, starting with the Scottish Cup Final in April 1971, which secured his club the League and Cup double, Macari won another slew of honours. However, quite by coincidence in the same month as Tommy Docherty was appointed Manchester United manager, Macari handed in another transfer request. With his wife expecting their first baby, he had decided the time was right to begin a family life elsewhere.

Initially, he seemed destined for Liverpool. However the fact that Celtic did not inform anybody other than Bill Shankly that he was available for transfer before the meeting they arranged with the Liverpool boss at Anfield on January 16 '73 implied that Celtic felt that his move there was a mere formality. This rankled with a man with a "stubborn streak" (his own words). He also wondered whether joining a Liverpool team that was sweeping everything before it was not that much different to playing for a club that didn't really have any competition in the Scottish First Division. Docherty, Crerand and United director Bill Young were also at Anfield that day. (Liverpool's opponents were Burnley, whose line-up included Docherty's son Mick.) Crerand offered to sit in the stand when he found there were only two director's box seats and found himself next to Celtic assistant manager Sean Fallon and Macari. Crerand has recalled that when he found out from Macari that he was here to discuss terms with Shankly, he took him aside and asked him if he would be interested in signing for United. Crerand told Docherty of the conversation in the car after the game. Within 24 hours United had matched Liverpool's transfer offer and Macari was given permission to speak to Docherty. Macari and Docherty by now knew each other well. Not only had Docherty given the player his first full Scotland cap, but the two had been near neighbours in Scotland and Docherty would visit the player's home frequently. Macari was informed by a person he didn't identify in his 1976 autobiography that Docherty was on the point of selling Ted MacDougall to West Ham, thus freeing up a place for him in the first team. Even so, it's to Macari's credit that he found the challenge of joining a club near the bottom of the First Division more interesting than signing for a club with the winning habit. Macari's terms with his new club were £200 per week plus a signing-on fee of £10,000 (approximately £1800 and £100,000 in today's money), a deal that to Macari "seemed an absolute fortune at the time."

Macari, Docherty and Crerand travelled down to register the player's transfer with the relevant football authorites in Docherty's car. They almost didn't make it due to another instance of a phenomenon that would speckle Docherty's time at Old Trafford – a car crash. In foggy conditions near Gretna, a lorry hit the boot and tore the side as it kept going.

Considerable damage was done to Docherty's three-day-old Mercedes, but there was no harm done to the occupants. "We were very lucky," said Docherty. "It could have been a really nasty one – particularly for Lou there in the back. There was fog about and this lorry following us had evidently been hit from behind … Lou got quite a jolt. He's okay. He'll pass the medical in the morning but I shudder to think what could have happened." Said Crerand, "It's fortunate we were using this car. The one Tommy had been using until Monday was much lighter and I don't think it could have taken that kind of impact."

Of Macari himself, Docherty said, "He's a tremendous player. He's terrific at taking the half-chance and though he's only five feet, five inches, he's also pretty useful in the air." Indeed, match reports during his time with United are littered with references to the pint-sized Macari winning aerial challenges. This apparent mystery is explained by Frank Blunstone: "His timing. And also, you've got to realise little fellas are good jumpers because when they're young they've had to learn to jump. Now you get big fellas, kids, they're six foot, they don't have to jump when they're playing against the same age group, so they never learn to jump." His heading wasn't the only thing remarkable for an individual of Macari's physique. It's difficult to talk about the bravery and power shown by the diminutive on the football stage without sounding patronising, but the tenacity Macari habitually displayed as he bobbed and weaved through ranks of defenders to whose brick outhouses he was a mere commode was quite remarkable and fully deserving of that cliché "Little man with a heart like a lion". Macari's (contrary to his modesty) exquisite skills cost United £190,000–£200,000, a fee that was not only Docherty's biggest outlay of his managerial career so far but broke the record between English and Scottish clubs that had been set by Joe Harper when he moved from Aberdeen to Everton the previous month.

Curiously, considering subsequent developments and Macari's memory of being told MacDougall was on his way out, Docherty spoke of Macari not as a replacement for MacDougall but as a future striking partner for him. "I feel that Macari and MacDougall will form a very good spearhead," he said. MacDougall is bewildered by the comment: "I never saw a quote like that. Was never privy to him pulling me to the side and saying this, this and this or I was part of his plan." In fact, Docherty quickly thereafter decided that his strike force would be comprised of Macari and Brian Kidd.

\*\*\*

The chanted nickname "Kiddo" had been ringing around the terraces from appreciative fans for a long while, Brian Kidd having made his debut in 1967 and having sealed his place in

Old Trafford mythology a year later when this Manchester local lad scored United's third goal in the European Cup final, a fixture that – for added poetic poignancy – coincided with his 19th birthday. That performance promised much, as did the fact that in his first season, Kidd scored 15 times in 38 League matches. Some are of the opinion that Kidd never really lived up to that early promise. Certainly his dribbling skills – which existed but went only so far as a dropped shoulder – never progressed beyond the merely serviceable. Kidd could of course defend himself by pointing out that Stanley Matthews – the archetypal Wizard of the Dribble – was also a one-dummy pony. He could also invoke bad service in a declining team for the fact that his goal tally – which would ultimately amount to 70 in 266 games – was fairly low for someone in a striker's position. There was, though, no doubting the skills he did have. His pace, powerful left foot and natural strength had already earned him over 200 appearances for United by the time of Docherty's arrival, as well as two England caps.

While the sight of Kidd celebrating a goal in his amusingly boyish manner – both hands balled over his head, both feet in the air, a grin spread across his face beneath his mop of brown hair – may not have been as regular an occurrence as it should have been for some, Docherty was convinced that there was untapped potential in a man who had lately begun to fall from favour. A combination of injuries and bad form had reduced Kidd's scoring rate to such an extent that O'Farrell had become reluctant to field him. It should be pointed out though that Kiddo had even had his ups-and-downs with Busby. When dropped by him in April 1971 during his caretaker manager period, Kidd fulminated in the press, "Is Sir Matt trying to humiliate me altogether? ... Everyone knows that he doesn't want me at Old Trafford ... Sir Matt has completely washed all my feelings for Manchester United out of me ..." Docherty said in his first season, "It was a disgrace the way Brian Kidd had been buried at Old Trafford. He is a great player and given the right encouragement, I think he can do a fine job for Manchester United." Kidd spoke quite emotionally of what a difference the appointment of the new manager had made to him. "Tommy Docherty brought me back from the dead," he said. "He has given me my appetite for the game back. The very first time I met him he was great, the way he talked to me and explained what he wanted me to do." Kidd's renewed appetite was manifested in the fact that of the four goals he scored that season, all came after Docherty was made manager.

\*\*\*

Signed just before Macari was Mick Martin, who came from Bohemians for £25,000. Docherty's transfer dealings meant that he had now spent £520,000 in less than a month, an eyebrow-raising sum in those days, and not just for a club known for both its parsimony and its spurning of big-name signings in favour of nurturing of young players. Responding to this, The Doc said, "The one concern of the directors is the progress of Manchester United and they have proved it in the amount of money they have been prepared to spend." Docherty also said, "We need at least 18 top-class players in our squad", adding that his signings did not necessarily mean that he would unload players.

It should be noted that concern about transfer inflation was not only down to an irrational feeling that a mere sport couldn't be worth such amounts of money. On the same day that Macari's transfer hit the headlines, Alan Hardaker – secretary of the Football League, which in those days was the body that controlled top-flight football in England – spoke of a crisis in soccer engendered by its apparently declining popularity. "If gates continue at their present level they will be the lowest since League attendances were first recorded in 1938," he said. "The way things are developing, football is going to be put out of business lock, stock and barrel in five years." Even United were not immune to the downwards trend. Their average gate of 45,980 so far this season was nearly 2,000 down on the previous season. They had now spent £1,115,000 in the last 11 months despite having to inform their shareholders the previous September that they were down £245,958 on the previous season, their biggest-ever deficit. Not only had the club spent £825,000 since then on players, they had also had to pay an undisclosed sum to Frank O'Farrell, who had still had three-and-a-half years remaining on his contract when he was dismissed, while there was still a balance of £75,000 outstanding to Bournemouth for MacDougall. Their only income from the transfer market subsequently had been the £80,000 they had received from Huddersfield for Alan Gowling, the £40,000 received from Southampton for Francis Burns and the £30,000 Luton Town had paid for John Aston. Also revealed in the balance sheet was the fact that the club paid out £342,027 in wages and bonuses, a figure that was only £140,000 more than their net gate receipts, which then provided the vast bulk of a club's income. That wage bill would have gone up significantly with their latest star signings. Just to complete the gloomy picture, an early exit from the FA Cup this season closed off a potential source of considerable revenue.

*\*\**

For the match against West Ham United at Old Trafford on Saturday January 20, Macari displaced Davies (who was substitute) and fellow debutant Holton displaced Sadler. The other change from the last game was MacDougall replacing Kidd. The fact that United's team featured eight Scotsmen indicated a trend that the Reds' fans had clearly picked up on: several supporters in the 50,878 crowd were seen to be sporting Tam O'Shanters and at least one Scottish flag was seen flying in the Stretford End. Such did Docherty seem to have a predilection for players from Scotland that the joke going around was that he still thought he was the manager of his national side. For a brief period, United fans started wearing Tartan scarves in wry acknowledgement of this Caledonian bias.

The wisdom of Docherty's purchases (of any nationality) and his tactics must have been severely doubted by the 25th minute, when the away team were two goals up. On the half-hour mark, though, United got a rare stroke of luck with a dubious penalty award. Charlton converted. Charlton distributed well today but fellow veteran Law had a poor game full of back passes and gave way to Davies after 55 minutes. United were the superior team for the last half-hour and few could begrudge them the goal they nabbed 10 minutes from time when the tireless Morgan beat a defender and hit over a ball for Macari to cap an irrepressible debut by sticking out a leg to turn in his first goal in a red shirt. United may have been left still bottom of the League, but today's fight-back revealed definite signs of improved team spirit.

"Who put the ball in the West Ham net?" the United fans sang when Macari scored. "Skip to me Lou Macari!" It would take Macari a while to obtain the position in the United team in which he felt most comfortable – and indeed his results in an unfamiliar position would make his love affair with the Old Trafford faithful touch-and-go for a while – but today they were overjoyed: Macari's goal got United above one goal for the first time since December 2.

*\*\**

United's home League match against Everton on Wednesday January 24 saw the debut of Mick Martin. Martin was odd man out in the quintet of new arrivals, hailing not from Scotland but the Republic of Ireland, or Eire as the maps called it in those days. He was born in Dublin on July 9 1951.

Recalls Martin, "Tommy Docherty was interested in a couple of players that we had in our side, both me and Gerry Daly in particular, and he came across one Sunday to watch Bohemians play another team called Shelbourne, a local derby in Dublin. Him and Paddy Crerand were over and he contacted us the following day. My father was an ex-professional footballer who played for Leeds United and Aston Villa. On the Monday morning my father came up. He woke me up fairly early (which wouldn't have appealed to me too much because I was out the night before) to say, 'Get yourself up and get washed and changed, we're going down to the Gresham Hotel in Dublin' – which was a very, very well-known hotel worldwide – to meet Tommy Docherty, Paddy Crerand and indeed Sir Matt Busby. So I took this as a jest and I said, 'Do us a favour dad. I've had a late night.' Eventually it registered that it might have been possible because I'd heard that they were at the game, I'd played quite well, we'd won three-nil. So I went along with him and lo and behold met Tommy Docherty – who would have played against me da – Paddy Crerand and Sir Matt. I had a chat. They said they wanted to sign me, no trials involved: 'We saw enough to suggest that you're going to be a good player'." That The Doc was prepared to make up his mind so quickly was refreshing for Martin, who had turned down overtures from other English clubs because they were so embedded with caveats: "I was an international player before coming across to England. I had a variety of football clubs ringing me at home because they had got my number from contacts I had played with at international level in England who would say, 'Listen there's a kid over there who's a good player, you should get him across'. I had phone calls from Glasgow Celtic, I had phone calls from Tottenham Hotspur, I had phone calls from Wolverhampton Wanderers, and they all wanted [me] to go across on a trial 'So we could have a look'. And I says, 'Well look, I'm an international player, you've been recommended me. I'm not prepared to go on trial. I've got a full-time job, I'm a part-time professional footballer. If you want to make a commitment, you sort of take me on recommendations. I'm not prepared to go anywhere so you can look at me'."

He continues, "I managed a sports shop in Dublin. I went away on the Monday, contacted my boss in the sports shop and we went back and tickets were booked for us to fly to Manchester the following morning. It was as quick as that." Docherty apparently was not so instantly impressed by Martin's colleague Gerry Daly, although Daly would eventually become one of The Doc's Devils. Recalls Daly, "He was supposed to be coming to see me but he signed Mick Martin instead and then he said he'd be back for me." Was he worried he'd missed his chance? "No. I think I was a bit too young then to realise anything."

Though clearly a level-headed fellow not easily overwhelmed by the allure of top-flight clubs, Martin admits that it was impressive to be joining the company of living legends: "It was certainly humbling to think that you're the training ground at The Cliff changing beside Bobby Charlton and Denis Law." He was also impressed by the attitude of at least one of the legends: "The Tuesday morning we had a bit of a practice match up at the training ground. It was the first time I was introduced to people, and I was just standing around and Denis Law came up to me. He was the very, very first to come to me, and he said, 'Is this the new Irish boy? Listen I wish you all the best son, welcome to Manchester United', which I felt was very nice and very good of him. We went out and we played the first team against the second team and I was in the second team and we won two-nothing." So privileged did Martin feel to be playing for a club like United that he was unconcerned with whether there was currently a sense of decline about them. Martin: "I was only too happy to be at the club and savouring the thought of training with these great players on a daily basis took my mind completely off whether the team was good enough or bad enough."

Martin was also glad to be part of a sudden influx at Old Trafford. "I was fortunate in as much as Tommy Docherty had signed four or five players in the same week: me, my great, great pal Jim Holton, Alec Forsyth, George Graham and Lou Macari. We all stayed in the same hotel, we all got in the same cars to go to training and we all socialised together. That was a very, very big help for me in as much as coming from being a part-time professional. It just made [it] a little bit easier to gel and to get together and do training together as opposed to going in on your own and walking into a dressing room on your own when you kind of knew everybody but knew nobody." He struck up particular friendships with Holton, Macari ("We'd go to the horse racing, we'd go to the dogs when we had our free time because there was nothing else for us to do") and Brian Kidd: "I stayed with Brian a lot when I came over, with him and his wife Margaret, and then I went into digs with his mother in-law Mrs. Kellard for a year-and-a-half."

The crowd of 58,970 for the Everton game was amazing for a midweek match, and MacDougall adds, "There was about 10,000 locked outside." The Old Trafford faithful's loyalty in the midst of a relegation battle was partly rewarded today by a United team who were now clearly making incremental progress back toward respectability, even if once again Docherty cautiously opted for a two-man attack. Law was absent, the only change from Saturday aside from Kidd taking the place of Davies on the sub's bench, which in those days consisted of one person. Everton dominated for the final 20 minutes but once again United could boast, if that's not too strong a word for a 0-0 draw at home, that things were getting just a little bit better, not least in the fact that they were finally off the bottom of the table, which position was now occupied by their old friends Crystal Palace.

Recalls Martin, "I thought I'd played quite well in a position that I would never play in normally, which was outside-left, because I wasn't as good on my left side as I was on my right side. But it was a great experience: 58,000 and I enjoyed the night … When we came in, I was told to pop up and see Mr Docherty and Sir Matt and when I went in my mam and dad were there, so it was nice to see them after a hard night's work." Playing in an unfamiliar role would be par for the course for Martin during his time at Old Trafford, as Docherty would use him in a variety of positions. Martin: "When I came over from Bohemians to Manchester United, I was playing in the position where Martin Buchan would be playing. I was playing alongside the centre-half." Not long after signing him, Docherty said that he felt Martin's pace and creativity meant he had "too much football in him to play as a sweeper". Said The Doc, "I would describe him best as a Liverpool kind of footballer – a player's player. He never tries anything awkward, but prefers the simple thing. He picks out the easy tasks where the chances of breaking down are less. I don't mean he is a negative player, because he is aware of situations and uses space well." "I was very adaptable," says Martin. "I could play at the back. I could play full-back. I could play wide right. I could play centre midfield."

MacDougall was said to be so displeased by the 56th-minute decision to substitute him this day that he stormed out of the ground. MacDougall: "I came off early and there was a bit of a hoo-hah over that one because Denis wasn't playing and Denis said, 'Do you fancy going away early before the [crowd] and we'll go and have a pint?' So I left and that was construed as me going off in a huff, but it wasn't really like that." Asked about the fact that he hadn't shaken hands with Brian Kidd when he went off, he says, "I don't have any problem with Brian." Did he have a problem being substituted? MacDougall: "Well obviously I wasn't too enamoured when they took me off. He couldn't leave me out because of the money [I'd cost] but if he had an opportunity to sub me then obviously that would be the way he would go."

Not long afterwards, MacDougall reported that Docherty had spoken to him about the fact that the Stretford End had expressed their disapproval over his substitution, "… he said I was popular with a section of the crowd … and he would have to do something about it." MacDougall described this as "the climax in our relationship."

Some might posit the fact that MacDougall was actually failing to do the job he'd done so well hitherto as a legitimate cause for Docherty wanting him off the park, but MacDougall says, "I don't think he was ever going to get the best out of me. If you're feeling not part of it and not wanted, there's a feeling, 'Well okay, maybe I should go somewhere where I am wanted. I don't have to be with Manchester United.' I think my game just started to degenerate because there's a certain amount of confidence you need to be a player at any position but certainly a goalscorer." For the record, though he had scored in the Leeds game, it was the only time MacDougall hit the back of the net when Docherty was his manager at United: his Manchester United goals-per-game ratio under Docherty was one in seven; pre-Docherty it had been one in two.

***

United were unchanged for the match against Coventry at Highfield Road on Saturday January 27. In his debut against West Ham on January 20, Holton had had a fairly quiet game. The same was so in his second appearance, the 0-0 draw against Everton. Today, however, Holton – to use a euphemism – made his presence felt, executing some ground-shuddering tackles – three of them in the first 15 minutes – that might have been technically legal for the most part but which ran the risk, if slightly mistimed, of inflicting severe damage. Surprisingly, though, it was Holton who opened the scoring, and with a not half-bad goal. On 34 minutes, he threw his head impressively at a free-kick to provide the Reds with the novel sensation of being in the lead. The euphoria didn't last long. Within two minutes, Stepney was beaten with a low shot. Dismayingly, the Reds then proceeded to time-waste in the worst Leeds United style and the 1-1 draw saw the teams booed off the field at full-time by the 42,767 crowd. The Guardian's David Lacey was no less critical, opining, "While Manchester United are sorting out their problems at the bottom of the First Division, their friends would best do them service by coughing politely and turning away. Whether they will have many friends left outside Old Trafford once the ungainly exercise has been completed is open to question."

The man most responsible for this disapproval was Holton. United had had famous hard-men before, of course, particularly Nobby Stiles, but the latter possessed some form of an alibi: he (and his colleagues) could always claim that his atrocious eyesight explained the instances were he went in 'over the top'. David Meek seemed almost to be making a different kind of excuse in his report on the match. "Manchester United's fight for their First Division lives is going to be a rugged one," he said. "It's going to upset the purists and there was much head-shaking at Coventry about the way the Reds got stuck in. But desperate situations call for desperate remedies ..." As a United loyalist, Meek could be expected to be inclined to give the benefit of the doubt to Holton and his team-mates in this way, but he was absolutely correct in his prediction that the 'purists' would become ever more discomforted as the season progressed at the way the elevated football values of their team were giving way to a stay-up-at-all-costs approach.

Even the one consolation from this best forgotten match – a climb to the giddy heights of 19th in the table – wasn't all it seemed: the three clubs below the Reds all had a game in hand on them.

There were no English League domestic fixtures on February 3, it being a Saturday reserved for FA Cup fixtures. As United were no longer involved in that competition, they took the opportunity for a friendly match against Docherty's former club Oporto in Portugal on the Sunday. In a dreary 0-0 draw, Jim Holton managed to get himself sent off for the first but by no means last time when playing for United. Also going for an early bath was Oporto forward Abel who objected to what Holton described as – in what would become a familiar protestation over the coming seasons – a "fair tackle".

No doubt a man who was building for the future – and expensively so – would have preferred the two goals that United put past Wolverhampton Wanderers at Old Trafford on Saturday February 10 to have come from one of his signings, but the fact that veteran Charlton got both for United (one a penalty, the other one of his long-range specials) mattered less than the fact that after five weeks in the job and in his eighth match in charge, Docherty finally gave Manchester United (unchanged from the last official fixture) a victory. Stepney was later beaten by a lob but this time United neither threw away their two-goal lead, nor engaged in shabby time-wasting. The final whistle generated such a response from the home fans in the 52,089 crowd that it was as if United had won the Cup Final. Not quite, but they had climbed one more rung up the ladder of First Division survival, lying now in 18th position.

Asked if he was surprised that it took the club he reported on so long to rack up their first win under The Doc, David Meek says, "I obviously recognised that it was a slow start but I felt that that was a reflection of the low state that the club had sunk to and that it was going to be more difficult than some people assumed to get the team resurrected, so to speak. I wasn't unduly surprised." MacDougall says there wasn't much in the way of team talks or strategy from the new regime: "I can't remember anything apart from his mickey-taking. No tactics. Give it to Bobby Charlton, who'll knock a 40-yard ball after he's done his hairstyle, and go and play. I don't think that Tommy Doc was any better than Frank was at particular facets of the game. I just think you just go out and play and if it comes off for you it's great, you look like a genius, if it doesn't come off, well we got beat." Buchan's memory of those early days of The Doc's reign are hazy – he needed to be reminded that it took The Doc so long to secure his first win – but he does recall a significant change in the managerial style upon Docherty's arrival: "He was a larger-than-life character and he did his very best to send us out as well-prepared as we could be for the games. He didn't have a standard team talk. Sometimes he could be very entertaining." By way of an example, Buchan invokes a team talk from a Sunderland match (clearly not from this particular season, as Sunderland were not in the top flight then): "He went through the team one by one. It was almost like one of Bill Shankly's famous team talks ending with, 'If you cannae beat that lot, you shouldn't be playing football for a living.' He just, in a lighthearted way, got his point across. Some of the managers at that time were handing round dossiers on the opposition and players were almost frightened to go out on the pitch because they'd read how good their opponents were before the game. He made us aware of the strengths and threats of the opposition, but in such a way we went out knowing what to expect but not dreading playing against them."

\*\*\*

United may have been a team battling relegation but they were stuffed to the gills with internationals, most of them of course Scottish. This may have actually worked against them when they attempted to consolidate that inaugural Docherty victory in their match against Ipswich Town at Portman Road on Saturday February 17. United's line-up was Stepney, Forsyth, Dunne, Graham, Holton, Buchan, Martin, MacDougall, Charlton, Macari and Kidd. Midweek had seen a Scotland Centenary celebration fixture at Hampden Park that ended in a 5-0 victory for England. Docherty's Scottish management successor Willie Ormond had played Forsyth, Buchan, Macari, Graham and Morgan and there certainly seemed to be fatigue in the air in a performance by United that journalist Alan Road described as "depleted and dejected". The result was a shocking comedown in the space of seven days. Macari pounced enterprisingly on a weak back pass but in the context of a catastrophic 4-1 defeat it barely even merited the description consolation goal. He and his team must have been rattled by the chants of "What a load of rubbish" that drifted from their supporters in the 31,918-strong crowd. It was a loss that sent United tumbling back into the relegation zone, leaving only West Bromwich Albion below them in the table.

With their League position left so precarious by the switchback in fortunes, it could be argued that the last thing the Reds needed was the distraction of playing in an utterly meaningless tournament, specifically the Anglo-Italian Cup. Nonetheless, Wednesday February 21 saw United battle Florentina at home in this competition, which was started as a sort of second-rate version of the hardly prestigious Fairs Cup. This was the last of the four seasons the tournament in its original incarnation existed. That this competition was the closest United could come to European glory these days might have been thought by some in their ranks to be a humiliation that compounded the fact of the whole enterprise being a waste of time. Buchan, though, considered such fixtures, whatever the juncture played, just part of "a way of life". He says, "You just get on with it. You're employed to play football and you do what the club tells you. You don't pick and chose what games you play in." He adds, "In those days you were happy to play twice a week. If you were on the international scene, you had quite a lot of mid-week trips and then of course the League Cup was always played mid-week. If you were playing twice a week, it meant your team was having a reasonable time and, of course, United were always in demand anyway for friendly games if they didn't have official fixtures. We made a lot of trips to Ireland, where we got a lot of our young players, sort of PR trips to the clubs that we signed our young players from. You played twice a week, lived out your childhood dream. I had quite a lot of experience against foreign opposition. Aberdeen were very go-ahead and we used to go to Germany and Holland every pre-season and I enjoyed pitting myself against other styles of play and learning about how other forwards went about their business, so it was a big adventure for me." Mick Martin agrees: "I never thought of anything as a distraction playing Italian teams. I thought it was all good experience and if you were to win the game and enjoy the game, you would be feeling confident going out on Saturday." Forsyth: "Of course they're meaningless but you use these games to get your fitness levels up and get your team sorted out."

Nonetheless, Docherty's heart, for one, didn't seem to be in the match. He used the fixture to give one Paul Jones, aged 19, a run-out and although the centre-half was impressive, he was never seen again in a red shirt. Holton got on the Reds' scoresheet with a good header on 26 minutes. Florentina – whose football was the more impressive throughout – replied in the 59th minute. The crowd of just 23,951 was already thinning out before the referee blew for full-time.

The Coventry caution carried Holton (already booked three times at Shrewsbury) over 12 disciplinary points and made him ineligible to play in the visit to Old Trafford of West Bromwich Albion on Saturday March 3. He was replaced by James in a fixture that, as West Brom were also relegation candidates, was a 'four-pointer.' Other changes to the team that had lost to Ipswich were the omissions of Dunne, MacDougall, and Martin, with Young, Morgan and Storey-Moore appearing. (Forsyth switched flanks.)

As though determined to make up for the spineless submission to Ipswich, United attacked from the off and it was a shock to the 46,735 crowd when in the 40th minute, the first goal came from the visitors via a powerful Jeff Astle shot. The groans and the tuts of a Stretford End who had become weary of such dissipated promise in recent times turned into more positive noises when it took Kidd just 30 seconds to reply. And within seven minutes of that Astle goal, United were in the lead, Macari, taking the ball round West Brom keeper Latchford. United climbed to 19th as a consequence of the 2-1 victory.

Though not quite as crucial as the West Brom game had been, United's visit to Birmingham City on Saturday March 10 was another bottom-of-the-table tussle. St. Andrews bulged with a crowd of near-Old Trafford proportions of 51,278. There was an unfamiliar figure between the sticks for United this day, the only change in United's line-up from the previous fixture. (Mick Martin replaced Storey-Moore in the second half.) Stepney was out injured, so in came Jimmy Rimmer. Born in Southport on February 10 1948, Rimmer at this stage had only racked up a few dozen appearances in United's first team despite being one of the current squad who had been on the club's books the longest. He was familiar to United aficionados as the other green-jerseyed man in the team photos taken at the beginnings of seasons, but broadly unknown to the wider public. Joining United in 1963, he had had to wait nearly five years to make his first-team debut. Since then, he had remained in Stepney's shadows, occasionally emerging for brief runs before being consigned to the half-life of a reserve-team keeper once more. His only extended period of activity had been toward the end of McGuinness' reign, in which he was made first-choice goalie. However, Stepney was reinstated when Busby became caretaker manager following McGuinness' dismissal. Despite his paucity of first-team appearances, Rimmer had picked up the admiring nickname, 'The Cat', one he shared with Chelsea's Peter Bonetti.

Though Rimmer saw three go past him this day, he doesn't seem to have been responsible for the defeat. Journalist Mike Beddow instead pinned the blame on what he termed United's "expensive misfits in the alien atmosphere of the relegation issue". Macari was United's scorer in a loss that left the Reds 20th.

Holton may have been suspended for this game but that didn't keep him out of trouble. Unhappy at the treatment meted out to Macari by Birmingham's John Roberts, Holton approached Roberts after the match and – according to David Meek – informed him, "I'll break you in two when you come to Old Trafford for what you did to the wee dwarf today." If Roberts thought this was an idle threat, he must have been quaking in his boots when he heard reports of Holton's behaviour in United's next fixture, a home game against Newcastle United on Saturday March 17.

Though Holton was reinstated now that his suspension was over, his stand-in James wasn't dropped but instead displaced Forsyth. The only other change to the line-up was Martin stepping in for Storey-Moore. The gate was 48,426. Holton played well and scored United's first goal just before half-time with a powerful left-foot shot. However, he was sent off just before full-time for headbutting the Magpies' rampaging, sideburned forward Malcolm 'Supermac' Macdonald in the back of the head. It generated yet more concern over the unfamiliar physicality of United's game. While no apologist for Holton, journalist Ted Macauley suggested that Macdonald made the most of it, lying as though unconscious. Either way, the screaming and even wrestling between elements in the two dug-outs that followed the incident was unseemly indeed.

Eight minutes after the interval, Mick Martin put United two up. Recalls Martin of his first goal for the Reds, "I took up position at the edge of the box and I think it was a corner kick or a free-kick had gone in and it came out to me sort of on the 'D'. I side-footed it with a bit of curve on it past the goalkeeper." Although Newcastle replied when Nattrass beat Rimmer within three minutes, it was United's day. Whatever that was worth, beyond a climb to 18th. Opined Macauley, "Like cornered men, they are fighting fiercely for every chance of escape and inevitably, somebody, something is going to get hurt. I feel it will be United's reputation."

"People seem to have made up their minds that Manchester United are going down, and perhaps they don't like it when we show them that it is not going to happen," responded Docherty to such complaints. "We have taken nine points from the last six home games. Part of the trouble against Newcastle was that Malcolm Macdonald hardly had a kick at the ball, thanks to Jim Holton … It's nonsense talking about United kicking their way out of trouble. Look at our midfield 'killers' – Bobby Charlton, Willie Morgan and George Graham. Those vicious Charlton tackles make me laugh. Old Trafford is becoming a hard place once more for visiting teams to get away with points. That is the way I want it to be, but I resent these accusations that we are a dirty team." Matt Busby also stepped into the debate. "I don't think the criticisms were deserved," he said. "The first half at Birmingham the previous week produced far more heavy tackling against us than was experienced in the whole game with Newcastle. Yet we did not come away screaming … If I felt something was happening in our style of play that could destroy our image, I would say something. It is just not there."

Were Docherty and Busby right and everybody else wrong? It seems implausible, despite the fact that Holton was ultimately cleared by a disciplinary hearing after appealing against the dismissal. Even George 'Stroller' Graham has admitted of this period, "I have to admit that I was getting more physically involved than ever before. It was desperate stuff and not at all pretty to watch." But David Meek opines, "I don't agree that they were a dirty side and I don't think Doc deliberately set out to encourage the team to play in that way. It's always true that a club that's in desperate straits and fighting relegation is going to commit more fouls and therefore have more cards and more people sent off than people cruising it at the top. I don't accept that Docherty brought a brand of roughhouse football at all. Later on, when he was able to, he had the team winning the Fair Play League so it wasn't in his nature to encourage the team to play a dirty style of play and I don't believe they did."

Every United player questioned for this book insists that United were never told by Docherty to go out and play dirty. Though McIlroy says, "When you're fighting for your life you're fighting for survival. It's not all about being pretty," he adds, "Tommy Docherty always wanted just to play football." Buchan points out that his own disciplinary record gives the lie to the idea that The Doc told the Reds to play dirty: "I think I only ever got booked five times in 20 years. I know some of the Leeds players of the time didn't rate me because I didn't go around kicking people but you cannae put something in there that's not …" As for United's controversial play at this point he says, "Do you not think maybe desperate would be a better word than dirty?" Offers Peter Fletcher, soon to make his United debut, "When things are not going well, you out of desperation want to win the ball and you go in a bit harder. 'Cos things are not going well for you, you think it'll come that way, if you get stuck in more. Frustration brings things on like that."

However, it should be noted that Docherty himself had been a player in Holton's roughhouse mould in his own playing days. It was also not the first time Docherty had been accused of strong-arm tactics to avoid a divisional drop. When attempting to prevent a descent by Aston Villa into the Third Division, The Doc had come in for strong criticism over the way his players were behaving, with Bob Stokoe – then manager of Carlisle United – accusing the club of using "diabolical tactics".

The man responsible for much of this furore often gave the impression of being bewildered by what he had stirred up. Certainly nobody seems to dispute the fact that away from the game Jim Holton was the archetypal gentle giant. At the season's end, Holton admitted that he was concerned about the reputation his sendings-off were bringing him. "If I was the sort of player who went over the top, then I'd deserve to be out of the game, but I'm not," he said. "I'm not a ball player or anything like that. I'm a winner of the ball and good in the air … You've got to be physical … But I'm not a dirty player. I may have a few rough edges but it would be ridiculous to say I'm crude." MacDougall says, "I thought he was a terrific character, Jim. I think he was one who lacked a lot of confidence but I think that Tommy give him confidence. He started to believe in him and Jim started to respond to it. At times he was a bit clumsy but I don't think he was dirty."

A crowd of 52,834 attended United's Anglo-Italian Cup match in Lazio on Wednesday March 21. They certainly saw a spectacle in this 0-0 draw, but not really a football one. Ironically, the match saw United being given a taste of the medicine that they had been accused of dishing out lately. Lazio's tackling was violent in the extreme and their behaviour, as was not uncommon for Latin teams of the period, provocative. United refused to rise to the bait, however. Referee Gordon Hill – who shared his name with a man who was to become a centrepiece of Docherty's United in the next few years – was full of praise for the good example set by senior United players like Charlton and Graham in walking away from trouble, although Lazio's Maestrelli allegedly got his jaw broken by Kidd when the ball wasn't within 20 yards of either. However, the fact that a Rome newspaper conceded that four Lazio players would have been sent off had this been a 'proper' match and the fact that Lazio's general (as opposed to team) manager was so angry with his captain that he wanted to demote him probably indicates who was more the sinner and who the more sinned against.

The trip to Rome brought about something that at least two of the United players were profoundly affected by: a meeting with the Pope. Willie Morgan has said it is the one thing for which he remains grateful to Docherty. Pope Paul made such an impression on Graham (who thinks that in fact it was Busby, a devout Catholic, who arranged the meeting) that he wrote down his words of wisdom, which he retains to this day: "Never cease to be conscious of the influence for good that you can exercise. Always seek to live up to the finest ideals, both of sport and right living. Always strive to give an example of manliness, honesty and courtesy both on the field of sport and in your daily lives. Be worthy of imitation by those whose eyes are constantly upon you."

Following their unpleasant experiences in Italy in midweek, let alone the advice of his Holiness, one might have thought United would temper the dubious aspects of their own play in their game against Tottenham Hotspur at White Hart Lane on Saturday March 24. However, this was to be yet another match in which United – their line-up unchanged from the Newcastle fixture – were involved in some unsavoury incidents and tactics.

United went ahead after six minutes, Graham thumping in a rebound from a free-kick for his first United goal. However, going ahead so early disguised United's mediocrity – and many were puzzled that they had been given a free-kick at all. In the 84th minute, Martin Chivers salvaged a point for his side. At full-time, the United players were booed off by their own fans in the 49,751 crowd. They maintained their position of 18th.

Brian Glanville was given the task of reviewing the match for *The Sunday Times*. The excellent Glanville (whose *Puffin Book of Football* could be found in many a school library at the time) tended to write about the game in a far more nuanced way than most reporters. He made some interesting points in his article, which dared to question the saintly image Matt Busby had acquired of late. He pointed out that a Joe Kinnear assault on Kidd in this match was in fact possibly retaliation for a punch Kidd threw at Kinnear on this same ground in 1968, when Docherty had never been near Old Trafford except as a spectator. Invoking the fact that Busby's post-Munich team were in 1958 referred to by one disgusted chairman as "Teddy Boys", the fact that sending-offs were not uncommon under Busby and that Busby had failed to condemn an incident in 1969 at Old Trafford when an opposition goalkeeper was left unconscious after a missile was thrown from the crowd, Glanville stated that a couple of factors had worked to disguise the reality that United could get physical in the Busby era: "... the calm reassuring presence of Busby and the fact that they were so gifted and attractive. United's present team are neither, so that, unable to play their way out of trouble, there is an evident temptation to try to kick their way out."

Such intelligent analysis cut no ice with either the average newspaper reporter – for whom scandal is synonymous with better copy – nor with the 'purists' on the terrace, whose impressionistic memory of the Busby era was going to be exclusively that of the sumptuous skill that was so sorely lacking in the present team. In any case, it would have been dishonest for reporters not to mention what was happening to United. As Glanville himself conceded, the Reds were a "very difficult team to love these days".

United's visit to The Dell on the last day of March marked their third match in a row with an unchanged line-up. Southampton were surprisingly cautious against a team with a solitary away win and whose goalkeeper was briefly knocked out in the first half. Charlton scored one and provided the second for Holton. "They call us cloggers, but we didn't clog today, did we?" said Docherty after the 2-0 victory. The United fans in the 23,161 crowd had their happiness tempered by the fact that the result actually left United one place lower than had their last fixture.

\*\*\*

If Mick Martin had felt the odd man out amongst the new signings, it was not to last long. Docherty felt that the League of Ireland had been badly neglected by English clubs, finding that the standard of play in that league, part-time or no, was a lot higher than many of his fellow managers appreciated. He opined that he had seen many players in their mid-20s in the Emerald Isle who could easily have been English Third or Fourth Division players. Docherty himself was more interested in players in a younger age group, men in their teens or early 20s with whom he could help build United's future. To this end, not too long after the Mick Martin signing, Docherty was back in Dublin to agree terms with Martin's former Bohemians colleague Gerry Daly, an 18-year-old midfielder whose stick-thin frame disguised an impressive stamina and depth of skill. His purchase in April 1973 for £22,000 was followed swiftly by that of Ray O'Brien, 21, a full-back for Shelbourne, for £20,000. Of this Irish triumvirate, it was Daly who would be by far the most successful at Old Trafford.

Daly would not make his competitive debut for the club until the following season but it so happened that Wednesday April 4 was the date of United's home fixture in the Anglo-Italian Cup against Bari. The Irishman was rapidly, if briefly, given a taste of the limelight in a match in which Docherty was hardly going to risk regular first-team players who might prove invaluable in the relegation fight, demonstrated by the fact that the game saw Docherty rest Buchan, Charlton and Graham. Though this was a sensible precaution, it left Docherty with the conundrum of who would step into Charlton's shoes as captain. His choice was a surprise but making Steve James skipper for the Bari match confirmed how impressed The Doc had been by the way the player had latterly made the best of an unexpected opportunity.

James was born November 29 1949 in Coseley, Staffordshire. He had been at United since 1965 and had made his debut in 1968. Until recently, though, he hadn't even been second choice for the centre-half position. He was rescued from what seemed like impending oblivion because David Sadler – the man in front of him for Jim Holton's place – was injured for the West Brom and Birmingham games for which Holton was suspended. James stepped into the breach so impressively that Docherty kept him in the team when Holton returned. This of course necessitated a casualty. To Docherty's credit, he had the courage to acknowledge that though Alex Forsyth had cost the club a good deal of money, sticking with a formula that was working was more important than saving face. Forsyth didn't even appear as substitute for the rest of the season, while James kept his place for the remainder, apart from the final two 'dead rubbers' when Arnold Sidebottom was given a try-out.

Ian Storey-Moore was in the starting line-up against Bari. However, despite scoring United's second with a close-range shot, he had to be replaced for the second-half after a recurrence of problems with his right foot that had been plaguing him for the previous three months. Law had opened the proceedings by pouncing when the Italian goalkeeper dropped a cross. Though Bari's Martin pulled one back after 70 minutes, four minutes later Mick Martin (presumably no relation) settled things for the home side. "It was a big shock to me," Daly says of the experience. "When Tommy Docherty was driving me to Old Trafford to sign my contract and he asked me would I like to play in the game the following night, I said, 'Ooh, yeah, of course.' It was a big shock to walk into the dressing room and there's all these famous great players getting dressed in the same room. Bit nerve-wracking, but you managed to steady your nerves and get over it and get on with it. It was very easy for me in the fact that Law scored two or three goals in the first 10 or 15 minutes [sic]. I done alright. There wasn't an awful lot for me to do. All I had told to do was just run around, pick the ball up, give it to somebody who could play. [Laughs]." Thrilled though Martin and Daly naturally were over their part in the 3-1 victory, the game attracted a paltry gate of 14,303.

United's home match against Norwich City on Saturday April 7 saw the return of Stepney to the side. Rimmer may have had cause to feel a little aggrieved by the recall of the man to whom he had been understudy his entire professional life thus far. Though he had let in three in his first match, his confidence had evidentially blossomed throughout his three-week run, manifested in an incrementally decreasing number of goals conceded: two against Newcastle, one against Tottenham and finally a clean sheet against Southampton. His giving away six goals in four games didn't compare unfavourably with Stepney's record up to that point that season: 57 goals conceded in 36 matches. Brian Greenhoff: "Jimmy was a good goalkeeper. I used to train a lot with Jimmy, I used to go back in the afternoons with him sometimes. He was very, very dedicated but when he come into the first team, something happened ... I think sometimes things just don't go right for you and I think Jimmy was one of them ... He never could sustain it long enough to keep Alex out, so Alex, if he got left out, he'd always get back in." Whether Docherty was agreeing with Greenhoff's analysis of Rimmer as someone prone to bad luck or whether he was just taking the lazy option of bringing back the more experienced man, it was a stark contrast to the way in coming seasons The Doc would seem to tolerate Stepney's presence under sufferance.

The only other change to the United team from the Southampton match was a, these days, rare first-team appearance for Denis Law. This was due to Macari having been involved in a car crash the day before the Bari match. (Kidd, injured, had to make way for Trevor Anderson in the 56th minute.) Norwich had gone 18 successive games without a win but United put on a poor performance for the 48,593 who braved the dreary weather and little happened until the 81st minute, when Mick Martin got his head on the end of a Morgan cross. "I just got enough on it to keep it away from Kevin Keelan," Martin recalls, referring to the Norwich keeper whose name's appearance in print in the 70s would so often be misread as 'Kevin Keegan' and who was the only top-flight Asian footballer that anybody was aware of.

Norwich manager Ron Saunders could be heard saying after the match that 32 points virtually guaranteed a club First Division survival. His team were six points short of that figure, but United were now on 31 points and holding steady in 19th position. If Saunders' 32-points-and-you're-safe theory might have been debatable, those Reds celebrating a home win on Wednesday April 11 that saw United go past that mark and up to 18th in the table were probably inclined to go with it, not least because in an example of neat poetry their opponents were Crystal Palace. A crowd of 46,895 saw a match that one could posit as a litmus test for United's recovery under Docherty from that Palace-inspired post-War nadir the previous December. United were unchanged from the last game with the exception of Macari reclaiming his spot from Law. Palace were without Don Rogers, one of the architects of that 5-0 massacre, and United were hardly stunning, but the solidity of the Reds' play made the tactical and motivational shambles of the Selhurst Park defeat seem like ancient history. Kidd scored with a neat lob in the 27th minute. He also created United's second, centering low for Morgan, who evaded a defender and executed a good shot inside the far post. The 2-0 victory virtually assured First Division safety. It was sweet revenge.

United visited Stoke City's Victoria Ground on Saturday April 14. The Reds were unchanged bar for Anderson taking Kidd's place. Striker sub Peter Fletcher obtained his first United appearance when he replaced Anderson, who clearly failed to make the most of Kidd's injury. Like United, Stoke had – barring improbable-to-impossible results elsewhere – secured their continued Division One status. One might think that this would lead to the sides being in a sufficiently relaxed state to provide an entertaining, positive game of football for the 37,051 spectators. Instead something "Straight from the League of Rubbish" was offered according to journalist James Mossop (or his headline writer). After a 2-2 draw in which Macari and Smith (o.g.) scored for the Reds, United were left 16th in the table but Mossop warned of their now assured Division One future, "I saw not a solitary sign to offer encouragement for next season."

United exhibited more vitality for their visit to Elland Road on Wednesday April 18. Leeds had been third in the League the previous Saturday but few who didn't know would have been able to tell the championship contenders from the recent relegation dodgers. The Reds' starting line-up was the same as for the previous match, and this time Trevor Anderson did make the most of his opportunity, heading home the game's only goal. (Strangely, Anderson was replaced by Fletcher immediately afterwards.) United and Docherty might have been forgiven for incurring nosebleeds after the final whistle, not just at the heady feeling from what was an impressive victory but by a dizzyingly high League position of 12th.

Anderson was yet another Irish import, although this time from north of the contentious border. He had been bought earlier that season from Portadown for £18,000 (or £20,000 depending whom you believe), the final O'Farrell signing. Born on March 3 1951 in Belfast, he'd secured his place in the first team via a reserve-team run that saw him score seven in six appearances. His first-team gradient began with the Anglo-Irish Cup, continued with three appearances as a substitute in League matches and culminated in his full starting debut in the April 14 Stoke game. Anderson by his own admission was too like a rabbit in the headlights to be of much use in that match but was retained for the following fixture. This time he enjoyed himself and the cherry on the icing of course was securing the winner. For a brief moment, Anderson was spoken of as the new George Best. His Belfast origins made it an easy cliché to reach for, as did his silky skills, even though they weren't in the same universe as that of Georgie's. He was also a bit of a looker, his shoulder-length black hair and thin moustache giving him a passing resemblance to contemporaneous television secret agent Jason King. This match though was about as good as it was going to get for Anderson. Despite 18 further United appearances (six as sub), he only hit the back of the net one more time. It took a step down the League for him to find his true level and thrive. After Docherty released him to Swindon Town for £25,000 in November 1974, Anderson scored on his debut and was the club's top scorer the following season. 22 Northern Ireland caps and the Northern Ireland Football Writers' Player of the Year award in 1986 can also be added to the list of his soccer-based achievements.

Kidd replaced Anderson in an otherwise unchanged team for the local derby at Old Trafford on Saturday April 21. Anderson came on for an injured Young in the second half and his speedy runs inspired cheers from the United fans but there was no miracle goal from him this time round, nor a goal of any variety from anyone else in an uninspired match. Although they dropped a place in the table, the fixture brought United's unbeaten League run to eight matches, with the 61,676 bearing witness the highest attendance in the Football League that season.

\*\*\*

It was out with the old and in with the new in United's final home game of the season, against Sheffield United on Monday April 23, which 57,280 attended. 19-year-old Arnold Sidebottom made his debut appearance, playing at full-back – he replaced James in the sole line-up change – and did very well. Bobby Charlton, meanwhile, was making his Old Trafford farewell in a career that had started before Sidebottom was born. He also did well. Though nobody was pretending that his pace or velocity of shot were what they had been five years ago, let alone 15, Charlton's footballing intelligence and classy touch were frequently on parade, both in the midfield position in which he started the game and the forward position in which he finished it. A goal in front of the fans who had adored him for 17 years would of course have been the perfect capstone to his career but such poetic incidents usually took place only in 'Roy of the Rovers'. That famous strip had begun appearing in the boys' weekly comic *Tiger* two years before Charlton made his 1956 professional debut after signing terms in 1953. The exploits of Roy Race (who would get his own comic in 1976) had already therefore thrilled two generations or more of British boys, some of whom were now grown up and worked in the media and used his name in their copy as a byword for unlikely soccer-based brilliance. Charlton might indeed have the gentlemanly mien, great sportsmanship and cannon-like shot of Race, but inspiring his team to a victory in his home farewell proved beyond him, let alone scoring. However, he did set up the United goal in a 2-1 defeat, putting through Morgan on 12 minutes.

United were in 15th place after the match. Their earlier escape from relegation had made Charlton's decision to retire easier. "If the club had gone down, I would most certainly have carried on," he said at the press conference he had reluctantly called to announce his retirement. ("I always thought press conferences were for Prime Ministers and other such peoples ... But I have been under so much pressure recently that I thought it would be the simple and easiest thing to do if I told you all together in an official manner.") Before the match, the two teams lined up to form a guard of honour for Charlton. It was a moving ceremony that celebrated the remarkable career of a one-club man. Born in Ashington, Northumberland, on October 11 1937, he had made his debut in October 1956 (against, of all clubs, Charlton Athletic). His final stats, including the following fixture against Chelsea, would be 759 appearances and 249 goals, both club records. (His appearance tally would many years later be recalculated as 758.) Charlton was famed for his ferocious long-range shots from either foot and contrasting delicate touch, loved for the sportsmanship that saw him booked only once in domestic competition (a caution the referee decided not to make official by reporting it) and visually iconic through the way he disguised his baldness with what would come to be known in later years as a 'comb-over'. Add the mythology entwined in both being a survivor of the Munich air crash who had clawed his way back from that psychological hell to professional triumph and being a key figure of the national team that had given England its greatest glory in 1966 and it's easy to see why Charlton had long ago passed into the ranks of living legends. Buchan even says, "I always felt he could have played another year. He kept himself very fit." Buchan is not talking of Charlton taking up a sweeper's position either: "He'd too much to offer with his shooting and his passing to be moved too far back. He's the only truly two-footed player I've ever seen. I cannot speak too highly of him because he did try to help me settle in Manchester when I first joined. He took me to his home. I've got a great deal of respect for Bob."

However, the thought must have been running through the heads of at least two of the 57,000-plus in the stadium that Charlton's retirement was coming not a moment too soon. Charlton himself has since admitted that he played too long, although he also conceded that he only truly realised this in retrospect when he recalled remarks about his declining abilities. Finishing that season as the club's top scorer might have disguised the loss of pace and reflex to which any 36-year-old is susceptible, no matter how industrious on the training pitch, but Charlton was a big fish in a small pond: that seven strikes (all competitions) could make him king of the goalscorers merely illustrates how unproductive his colleagues had been in front of the net. Additionally, as remarked earlier by Buchan, football for Charlton can't have been much fun at this point. No doubt he was intelligent enough to appreciate that no sportsman is entitled to untrammelled glory, but there must also have been a sadness about the fact that the twilight of his career had been spent a universe away from the joy he had known as one of the brilliant Busby Babes, an FA Cup winner in 1963, a League championship medal winner in 1957, 1965 and 1967, a European Cup winner in 1968, Footballer of the Year and European Footballer of the Year in 1966 and, of course, World Cup winner, also in 1966. Such achievement was now a long time gone at United. Charlton truly did look like a man from a different era alongside the likes of Jim Holton and Lou Macari.

One person pleased at the prospect of Charlton's retirement was Tommy Docherty. History has shown that Docherty wasn't even keen on O'Farrell's signings, so veterans of an era well before it would have been even further up the danger list. Will McGuinness had attracted opprobrium for daring to drop both Law and Charlton for a game a few years back and though Docherty would have theoretically found it easy to deny a first-team place to a man past the halfway mark on his three-score-and-ten, Charlton – along with 1966 World Cup captain Bobby Moore – was the closest thing in English football to a national institution. Docherty has publicly admitted that Charlton's retirement did him a favour by saving him from the grisly necessity of dispensing with his services – and as Denis Law would shortly find out, Docherty's method of dispensing with one's services could be grisly indeed.

There was another guard of honour for Charlton in United's last League game of the season, a visit to Stamford Bridge on Saturday April 28. United were unchanged. Charlton's farewell to competitive football didn't produce anything as pleasing as a Charlton-assisted goal, let alone a final strike for Bobby. In fact, it didn't produce anything much pleasing at all, although a game in which Buchan got one of his rare bookings and Holton mysteriously failed to pick up one of his frequent ones despite knocking lumps out of Peter Osgood wouldn't appear to be one about whose outcome neither side cared. The United fans in the 44,184 gate who'd taken the time and expense to travel for the match were letting their displeasure known in the kind of language not heard much at football grounds when Charlton made his debut all those years ago. Osgood got the only goal of the game.

It meant two losses in two games for the Reds and saw them tumbling to a final League position of 18th after being 12th just 10 days ago, but at this stage of the season few cared. United finished with a tally of 37 points. In winning 12 League fixtures, drawing 13 and losing 17, they had beaten relegation by seven points, a fairly healthy margin in the days of two points for a win. For the second year in succession, Willie Morgan won the Manchester

United Supporters Club Player of the Year award, which had in fact been inaugurated the previous season. Though his opinion would soon change, Willie Morgan at this point was thanking the gods that United had heeded his advice and obtained Docherty's services. Speaking in the 1990s to Jim White, despite everything that had happened between him and Docherty in the meantime, Morgan had to concede that, "He was a breath of fresh air after Frank. Very outgoing, very positive. He was wonderful. I think his attitude alone saved us from relegation that year."

Meek admits that the relegation battle had been something he had been pessimistic about: "It was a close call. He'd been making some good signings, he was getting them to play in the pattern that he wanted, but until the very end I thought that it was an uphill battle that he would lose." Buchan took a different view: "It's the old saying: you think you're too good to go down. It was ... a case of 'What are we doing down here? We're better than this'." Asked whether this mentality was kind of what the problem was at United at the time, Buchan replies, "It wasn't arrogant. I don't think we could really understand quite why we weren't getting the results that we thought our play deserved."

***

At lunchtime on the day of the match against Chelsea that marked Charlton's farewell, the media reported that Denis Law, another Old Trafford legend, would never be playing for the club again. In some senses, it wasn't a complete shock. Law was just coming up to his 33rd birthday. Moreover, both the number of his appearances and his strike rate had declined noticeably in recent years. The past season had seen him take to the pitch only 14 times, including two substitute appearances. Docherty's memory of Law when he took over was that he was rarely on the training ground and usually on the treatment table. While the hint of reproach in Docherty's observation might be unreasonable – a man can't help it if he's injured – there was no getting around the fact that Law was at an age when recovering from knocks takes an inordinate amount of time. Nor was there any avoiding the fact that his tally of two goals this season was hardly awe-inspiring, especially for a player whose final stats for United showed that he hit the back of the net 237 times in 404 appearances – and that's not even counting his unfairly disallowed goal in the 1969 European Cup semi-final that would have enabled him to try to gain the winner's medal he had cruelly been denied by injury the year before. Of course, one could make the point that Charlton was top scorer this season with a tally of just five more than Law, and that from a total of four times as many games as Law had played. But Tommy Docherty was a new manager who was building for the future and it was perfectly reasonable that he should remove ageing players from the wages bill to make way for youth. As Forsyth points out, "He had to get rid of all the older players and it was a very, very tough job to say to them all, 'Find other clubs' because obviously there wasnae jobs at United for everybody. He couldn't give every one of them a job because there were far too many of them."

What was not reasonable was the manner in which this long-standing servant was despatched. Law knew on the Friday before the Chelsea match that he wasn't in the team, but had come into The Cliff to do some light training. Docherty called him into his office where he informed Law that he was giving him a 'free'. The free transfer was a new concept in football. Once a player was 33, he was entitled to switch clubs without money changing hands, something that prevented a move being frustrated by haggling and which also enabled a last big pay-day insofar as a club which might be put off engaging the services of an undeniably skilful but ageing player by a transfer fee would be more amenable to signing him if all they were risking was a signing-on fee and/or his weekly wages. Law, though, was immediately resistant. One of his reasons was that old footballing cliché: he still felt he had a couple of years of quality football in him. It's a cliché because all footballers think that, and perhaps it would be worrying if they didn't thusly rage against the dying of the light. However, there were other more rational reasons for his instantaneous distress. One was that Docherty had told him in front of witnesses that he had a job for life at Old Trafford – that once his playing days were over he would be able to ease into the sort of backroom position to which Forsyth refers above. Another was that he had recently arranged to buy a new house for his family, who were settled in Manchester and who included a five-month pregnant wife. Unless the unthinkable happened and he moved across to rivals Manchester City, a transfer to another top-flight club would mean leaving town. Then there was the fact that as well as the year remaining on his contract, he was due a lucrative testimonial against Ajax in the first week of the new season. Finally, he was dismayed at the undignified scenario of being offloaded as unwanted goods by the club where he had been a crowd favourite for 11 years. For all these reasons, Law told Docherty that he would rather simply retire from the game than accept the free move. He generously offered to announce his retirement directly after the August testimonial and thus free United from the obligation of fulfilling the remainder of his contract. Docherty acquiesced to this and Law, with Docherty's permission, departed for his native Scotland to pick up his children, who had been spending Easter there. That is Law's version of events, and Docherty later broadly verified it in his evidence in a libel case he brought against Willie Morgan.

Recalls David Meek, "I wasn't aware of promises that Docherty had made to Denis. All I know is that towards the end of the season, as was the habit in those days, the local reporter would get the Retained List and the list of players that were put on the transfer list and those who were given a free transfer. So it was one Saturday I approached The Doc and said, 'Are you ready to give me the Retained List?', etc. He gave me it in the normal routine and Denis was there with a free transfer." Referring to the *Manchester Evening News*, he continues, "So I did the story for the football Pink that Saturday and that got picked up by radio or television – both maybe."

On the list of those players not being retained that The Doc provided Meek were six names. Those of Tommy O'Neil, Paul Jones, Danny Healey and Ian Donald were no surprise: they were men with just 74 appearances between them, with Jones and Healey never having played in a competitive match. A mild surprise for some was the presence of the name of full-back Tony Dunne, one of the elite eleven who had carried off the European Cup in 1968 and still only 31. Though he was nearly two years older than Dunne, Denis Law's living legend status made his presence on that list a bigger surprise for many. For Law himself, it was a real shocker. Sitting in a pub with friends in Aberdeen that Saturday, he was startled when a presenter on the establishment's television announced that he and Dunne had been given free transfers by Manchester United. When contacted by the media, Dunne said, "Tommy Docherty has treated me well. He told me there was no hope of getting back in the first team with three players fighting for the job. I didn't want to hang around until the end of my contract. I had the choice, but I want to get involved in the game." Law was less equanimous. He was horrified, mortified and upset. He was also instantly resigned, knowing the process was in motion. "It was not very good management by The Doc," says Meek. "He should have had the courtesy to have told Denis before he told me, or at least at the same time. He didn't, but then he was a bit ham-fisted and blunt and not very sensitive when it came to dealing with players."

There seems absolutely nothing for Docherty to gain by not sticking to the agreement Law had struck with him. In fact, the very opposite. Even if he felt that by his actions he was acquiring for himself a useful reputation as a man who was not going to be daunted by Manchester United's history and legend in his task of rebuilding the club, surely he must have known that his actions would rebound on him if the full truth about them became known? Luckily for Docherty, Law – as gentlemanly a man off the pitch as he could be occasionally spiteful on it – kept mum about the betrayal and the truth only became public because of the aforementioned libel action. It was a court case in which Morgan naturally used everything he could to defend himself, including the ill-treatment of his former colleague. By then, though, Law was long retired. Had Docherty's betrayal of Law become public knowledge at the time, The Doc's career at United might have been over as soon as it had begun, for few were as loved by both the Stretford End and the employees at Old Trafford as the man they called The King. A backlash that the board might have found difficult to resist could have followed.

Law, born on February 24 1940 in Aberdeen, had been bought by United from Italian club Torino in 1962 for £115,000. He had played for Huddersfield Town and Manchester City before becoming one of the first British footballers to move abroad. Matt Busby converted him from a midfielder to a striker. Law didn't enjoy this front-man role as much – standing with one's back to the opposition goal for most of the match is not fulfilling to everyone – but he certainly enjoyed scoring and showed this fact by saluting the crowd when he did, a gesture which he pioneered. Law struck in United's 1963 FA Cup final victory and was a key component in their 1965 and 1967 championships. He was already iconic through the quiff of blonde hair that back in 1958, when he made his debut for Huddersfield, had made him look like the first rock 'n' roll footballer, and through his habit of clutching his sleeves waifishly in his palms. He became adored by the Stretford Enders for his thumping headers, his spectacular overhead kicks and his amazingly high strike rate (in the 1963/64 season, he scored a mind-boggling 46 goals in 42 matches). He could dribble a bit as well and had two good feet. The youngest Scottish international of the 20th century, Law would win 55 caps for his country. In 1964, he was voted European Footballer of the Year.

None of which mattered to Docherty. To a certain extent, that was reasonable, but only a psychiatrist would be able to explain why someone who is a warm and generous friend and mentor to people currently in his favour should – as in the Law case – seek to put a distance between himself and people he has decided have outlived their usefulness with a completely unnecessary degree of cruelty.

This chain of events did not mark the first time that the Law and Docherty families had crossed swords. During a United-Burnley fixture on April 19 1969, an incident between Law and Docherty's eldest son Mick – a Burnley half-back – left the latter writhing in pain on the deck. Law had a well-known penchant for taking revenge when treated harshly by an opponent. Mick Docherty recalls of the incident, "Denis sparked me when nobody was looking. He just threw a right hook and knocked me out. That's part of learning. I was only 19 and I learnt from it very, very quickly. Never happened again. We had many a run-in, Denis and I, in the following seasons but that was Denis. It's how he was: very physical, aggressive, a wonderful, great player, great goalscorer and a lovely man. You can ask Denis now: I get on very well with Denis Law." For those who might conclude that Docherty Sr.'s harsh treatment of Law might have something to do with bearing a grudge over that incident (then only four seasons previous), Mick asserts, "No. Not in a million years. That would never have come into the equation. Because dad was a hard man." The latter is a reference to the fact that Docherty had not been averse to sticking the boot in during his own playing days.

Whatever the motive, Docherty's decision to dispense with Law would come back to haunt him, not just through revelations in the libel trial about the circumstances surrounding the free transfer but in the sense of firepower Law might have provided United at a time when they sorely needed it in the 1973/74 season.

That jettisoning of Law, combined with Charlton's retirement and Best's (pre-Docherty) walk-out meant that Docherty's first season in charge had marked the complete departure of the Holy Trinity, whose aura belonged to an age that was Busby's, not his. Some might be inclined to suggest that this would have made Docherty happy. That is speculation, but what is not is the talismanic nature of those three players, individually and in conjunction. Not for nothing did pop group Herman's Hermits sing of Charlton, Best and Law in the 1968 song 'It's Nice To Be Out In The Morning' (written by Graham Gouldman, like the Hermits a Mancunian), "It's a most fantastic day when they play." Denis Law once observed that because of injury he, Charlton and Best rarely played together. Law's twinkle-eyed sense of humour seems to be at work here. The trio played together no fewer than 287 times and their names almost became synonyms. For three such magnificent players to play for one club was remarkable enough, but for them to be contemporaries was little short of a miracle. This combination of genius-level skill and magical happenstance was something that no manager could replicate and indicated the task Docherty was up against in carving his own niche at United.

\*\*\*

Wednesday May 2 saw United play Verona in an Anglo-Italian Cup fixture, and if we can forget that this was not a competitive match – it was part of what was considered an exhibition tournament by football's authorities – we can posit that it provided Bobby Charlton with the fairytale ending to his career so many had been willing. It wasn't in front of his home fans and the crowd in Italy was a paltry 8,168 but the old sensations of pleasure and pride can't have been absent in Charlton as he nabbed a brace. Fletcher and Olney were his team's other scorers in a 4-1 victory that, unfortunately, wasn't enough to take United through to the next round of the tournament.

The match saw George Graham pull on the captain's armband for United for the first but by no means the last time. Docherty made it clear before the match that Graham was to be the club's skipper in the long term. "You ask yourself who can really replace Bobby as captain and the answer has to be George Graham," he said. "He has the ability, the respect and most important the experience." Docherty's predecessor as manager had promised that Buchan would actually succeed Charlton as captain, Buchan having fulfilled that role with Aberdeen, although of course Graham wasn't at the club during O'Farrell's tenure. "Martin is ready for the job, but George Graham is more ready," reasoned Docherty. "Buchan will become captain in time and I think he understands the position." Graham himself later stated that Docherty's feeling was that Buchan wasn't experienced enough yet in English football.

The close season following the end of the 1972/73 campaign saw Docherty release 13 players in all. Though this is a deceptively high number – many of those people will have been non-regulars and reserves the public had barely heard of – it constituted a statement of intent. Docherty later said, "As far as I was concerned, I had only made a start in changing the personnel at the club."

The close season also saw Docherty appoint Frank Blunstone as his youth-team coach. "Tommy had been onto me quite a few times," Blunstone recalls. Docherty's persistence in the face of rejection paid off, for Blunstone, despite achieving a certain amount of success as Brentford manager, had had enough of the Third Division club: "I fell out with the chairman at Brentford. We had got promotion but I just went to him and said, 'Look are we going to be a bit more ambitious?' He said, 'What do you mean?' I said, 'Well it's time we started a youth team, a reserve team, started bringing some kids through.' He said, 'We can't do that, Frank', so I said, 'Okay then, I'm leaving. I've been offered another job and I'm off'." Unfortunately, his appointment would be slightly delayed. Recalls Blunstone, "I went and spoke to Tommy and agreed the terms. On the way back, I ... had a terrible crash. It was a lovely night. 70 miles an hour. I wasn't racing or anything, in the middle lane, and a bloody lorry come through the central reservation coming the other way. His wheels overheated and locked and pulled him right across and I ran into him. The car caught fire but they managed to get me out quick. Fortunately, in them days, you didn't have to have seatbelts so I wasn't locked in or anything. The door jammed. They smashed the door and pulled me out. I had a broken femur and broken ribs, broke all me face. Me chin, the whole lot had to be restructured." Though Blunstone estimates that this happened in July 1973, there was no question of him being ready to take up his post at the start of the season. Blunstone: "I had to wait till I was really 100% but Manchester United were fantastic. They kept it open for me and told me to take me time and they would continue the contract as soon as I was ready to start. End of October, I came in and started work then."

Meanwhile, Docherty was publicly looking forward to a chance to resurrect his dreams of a United with two wingers. "I think it makes for exciting football and pleases the crowd," he said of 4-2-4. "I am really looking forward to seeing Ian Moore in action again. I think he is a tremendous player. Willie Morgan has been in top form." Predicting that Lou Macari would be a big success and stating that Brian Kidd had more than justified the faith he had shown in him, Docherty said, "I would really like to see the four of them in action together."

From the sound of it, McIlroy, despite his youth, was not getting carried away with a belief that avoiding relegation in itself heralded a new dawn for the club. "I knew he thought the job wasn't completed when we stayed up," McIlroy says. "He knew there was work to do that following season to turn it round and get what he wanted. He believed in getting his own side there. There was players who were coming to the end of their career, there was players bought by Frank O'Farrell that Tommy Docherty I don't think fancied, so they all had to go, so this rebuilding was still going on." McIlroy himself got the chance to prove to Docherty that he could play a part in this rebuilding process in the close season. United's youngsters were due to play a youth tournament in Switzerland. Though a seasoned first-team player and an international, Sammy McIlroy certainly still answered to the description of youth and was therefore eligible to play in a competition that would be a useful test of the footballing abilities he hadn't been able to display since his January car crash. Docherty told McIlroy that he was accompanying the kids on the trip and would be watching him, thereby communicating to him that it would be a trial. Though he was less than 100% fit and still experiencing breathing difficulties, McIlroy played in all the matches on the tour and performed well enough for Docherty to inform him at its end, McIlroy reports, "I'm keeping you on, I'll give you a chance."

During this trip, McIlroy saw a dubious side to Docherty when the manager slipped a Mickey Finn into his drink when the players were enjoying some leisure time in the bar of their hotel. Though no harm was done, this sort of prank was the kind of action which those around the peripheries of United would begin to mutter – increasingly loudly over the coming years – was not the sort of thing that went with the dignity of the office of manager of Manchester United.

# PART TWO
# 1973/74: Relegation

A few weeks before the start of the 1973/74 campaign, Docherty faced the new season with optimism, almost euphoria. "I'm manager of the biggest club in the world," he told journalist John Sadler. "It's marvellous ... I always wanted to be manager of Manchester United and, within me, I believed it might happen one day ... I just love it here."

Docherty said he didn't realise just how enormous an institution was United until he took up his post and that sometimes he would want to go somewhere in casual clothes but would put on a collar and tie because to do otherwise was not befitting the post he had. He also said he had learned from his intemperate comments in previous jobs and that he would now watch younger managers making the same mistakes and think to himself, "You'll learn." Yet, even as he attempted not to make the kind of grandiose pronouncements that had rendered him a laughing stock in some quarters in the past, Docherty couldn't resist letting his ambitions gleam though. "People want success quickly but I know it can take time," he said of the coming season. "We need a good start and I want us to be in things right to the finish ... Like Leeds – in everything until the end. And in Europe." As for his current, expensively assembled squad, he said, "I think we are just one player away from completing the side. But even if we don't make that signing, I'm confident the present squad can do well. I didn't buy only to survive last season. I bought players for the future."

Docherty's words must have turned to ashes in his mouth on Saturday August 25 when United kicked off their campaign at Highbury. His club's start to the season could not have been more terrible. Macari got the ball in the net at one point and some felt he was unlucky to be adjudged offside, but had the goal stood it would hardly have made a difference on a day when United were utterly outclassed, embarrassingly so during the first half.

Anderson was in the starting line-up, Docherty clearly having decided to give the Irishman a chance to prove he was worthy of the fan's favourite status he had made strides toward being: he would start the following eight games. Another new-ish arrival, Gerry Daly also started, making his debut proper, although he gave way to McIlroy at half-time. Martin Buchan was in an unfamiliar left-back position, his full-back bookend being Tony Young. Mick Martin's good form in the last stages of the previous season was also rewarded with a place in the starting XI. The rest of the team was made up by Stepney, Holton, James, Morgan, Macari and Graham. "It wasn't a vintage Manchester United line up was it?" says Buchan. "You don't like to name names, but there were some average players in that line-up. Possibly a bit better than some of the team that I made that remark about who wouldn't get a game in Aberdeen reserves, but if you're talking about Man United as one of the top clubs in the country, we were still a bit short." Still a lot of work to do? Buchan: "Oh there was, aye." Despite this, Buchan says of escaping relegation the previous season, "We thought we'd got through the worst of it." He was to be proven sadly wrong.

Veteran or newcomer, United's men wilted in the day's blistering heat. That Arsenal's players bloomed shouldn't have been too much of a surprise – they had finished runners-up in the previous campaign – but that United were so patently simply not in their metaphorical league was disquieting. Three minutes from time, Alan Ball put the tin hat on the 3-0 humiliation of a club he would have been a member of if they hadn't been so stingy/slow off the mark.

Mick Martin seems to question the wisdom of Docherty's team selection on this day. "Arsenal were an extremely good side, a lot of very, very good and experienced players," he says. "Tommy was tinkering and he was bringing players in: Gerry's first game, I hadn't had an awful lot of games, and you've got Trevor Anderson, again a novice. To go down to Highbury and expect to do something would have been a tall order." Daly: "It was a very daunting experience. Couldn't get into the game whatsoever. Roasting hot day. Things didn't go well at all. It's a bit of a reality check when you're playing against such fine players as Charlie George and all them players. Also the disappointment of Docherty taking me off at half- time. I didn't blame him at all."

League tables don't mean much at this stage of the season – in fact, newspapers, didn't even bother printing them until the third group of fixtures in those days – but, for the record, the opening day's drubbing in front of a crowd of 51,501 left United 17th. One reporter, Mike Langely, while acknowledging that it was a bit early to be talking about relegation, said of the Reds' two Tommys, Docherty and Cavanagh, "A chill of fear must have touched them. The realisation that United's new season could be just as desperate as the last one."

Meanwhile, back in Manchester, City were playing Birmingham. They ran out 3-1 winners. The scorer of two of City's goals was Denis Law. The King had opted to take that unthinkable move across Manchester when, less than a week after his free transfer was announced the previous season, he had met the new Manchester City manager Johnny Hart at the Football Writers' Association dinner. Hart asked whether he was interested in returning to his old club. Law had already had a couple of offers of work from clubs wanting to take advantage of his freebie status but had turned them down. He clearly found the reality of a return to City intrigued him where its notional status had previously repulsed him and the two men shook hands on the offer there and then. In his first stint with City from 1959 to 1961, Law had netted 21 times in 44 games, and that's not including six goals he scored in an FA Cup fourth-round tie against Luton which were wiped from the official record books when the match was abandoned due to bad weather. Law was clearly back in his old City groove. A week after the Birmingham match, he scored for City again in a 1-1 draw at Stoke. The Lawman would hit the back of the net 12 times in 26 appearances for the club this season, a return to form that saw him recalled to the Scotland squad. Those disgruntled people at United and its peripheries who disagreed for sentimental reasons with Law being jettisoned by Docherty now had cause to believe that Docherty's actions were wrong on a footballing level too.

Buchan found cause to doubt Docherty's footballing nous as well: his new position was sprung on him and would inexplicably be maintained for the next five-and-a-half months. "I just got told I was playing full-back," he says. "I wasn't happy about it. He had me playing at left-back for reasons best known to himself. Defensively I like to think I was more than competent in that left-back position, but going forward Ryan Giggs or Gordon Hill I was not. I just didn't have the confidence to take people on and cross the ball with my left foot, although I could use my left foot when required. I did say, 'Look if you're going to play me at full-back, play me at right-back'." Meanwhile Mick Martin would find himself shuffled around the pitch over the next few weeks. "It was anywhere across the middle of the park whether it was wide right, centre midfield or wherever," Martin recalls. "Because of the fact that we got well beaten at Arsenal, he might have had a look at me closer and said, 'Well, he might be struggling a little bit', even though you tend to forget that you were playing against an extremely good side. If you chop and change that early in the season, you're not going to get any sort of consistency. If you played me in one game and then you don't play in the next game and you're not sure about the following game, you become indecisive yourself."

After that atrocious start, the following Wednesday – August 29 – saw United at least make a respectable showing in their first home game of the season, though visitors Stoke City were less than scintillating. Sammy McIlroy had declared himself fit at the start of the season and Docherty evidently felt that his display as sub against Arsenal showed he had recovered sufficiently from his car crash to merit inclusion in the starting XI today. Daly was dropped for the match, with Martin shuffled across to take his place. United were otherwise unchanged. The sole scorer in the game – played in the rain in front of 43,614 – was something of a surprise, Steve James getting his first strike for two seasons when he trotted up for a corner and got his head to a McIlroy centre. United were left in 15th place.

United's first Saturday home fixture of the season came on September 1 in front of 44,156. Newly promoted Queens Park Rangers were the opposition. Sidebottom got a game in place of James in an otherwise unchanged team. QPR scored first but Holton headed an equaliser, by which time Martin had made way for Fletcher, who had also come on as sub in the previous match. Six minutes from time, the ball found McIlroy unmarked in front of goal. His shot was shaky, but it crossed the line.

Rangers' Stanley Bowles was left severely disappointed that United's 2-1 victory didn't reflect the run of play. "It was a scandal," he said afterwards. "This United team are just not in the same street as the old lot. They're the worst team we have met." Even Docherty conceded, "We were terrible." He said, "The only thing we can take credit from is that we kept going and there were also some good individual performances. But collectively I'm being kind when I say we were very disappointing." The result left the Reds in seventh place in the table and, despite their mediocrity, Macari has opined that the United players at this point were even beginning to think about being involved in a championship battle this season. They were, after all, currently five spots above title holders Liverpool.

Wednesday September 5 saw United visit Leicester City at Filbert Street for a match in which they were disjointed and narky. With Macari injured, Kidd made his first appearance of the season. Sadler, replacing Sidebottom, surfaced for the first time since January. Daly started at the expense of Martin. The gate was 29,152. The only goal of the game was scored by Leicester City's Frank Worthington. United were left in 13th position.

***

With a charismatic new manager and the retention of the First Division status that had so inconceivably been in peril the previous season, all that the Old Trafford faithful needed to make them conclude that happy days were if not here again then on the horizon was the return to the club of the prodigal genius George Best. They were shortly to see their fantasy come true.

The man who many felt was the greatest footballer to ever pull on a United – or indeed any other – shirt was born in Belfast on May 22 1946. Someone who was still just 26 obviously had many years to offer football if he wanted to. He had recently publicly spoken of returning to playing, albeit only for Northern Ireland. Docherty had talked to Best in August and the two had agreed to meet on September 6. Best later said that his decision to return to football had been prompted by Matt Busby, who came to see him when he was in hospital with a blood clot in a leg and asked him when he was returning to the game. It's not known whether Docherty's August conversation with Best occurred before or after this. For his part, Meek feels that The Doc did all the running: "Busby had had his fingers burnt with criticism of Wilf and Frank O'Farrell and I think he let The Doc get on with it. Whatever he wanted: if he wanted Best, fine, but it was up to him." Agnes Docherty's recollections chimed with Meek's. Her husband was "... in the invidious position of having one of the greatest players who ever lived still contracted to his desperately struggling club, and he couldn't even select him."

"Out of the blue," says McIlroy of the news of the return of the man to whom he had been closer than many at Old Trafford. "Just in the press. I didn't know anything about it until I seen them in the paper at Manchester Airport: The Doc with George and Tommy Cavanagh. [They] decided to give George another go and try and get him fit. It was an awkward one because George was such a fantastic player, but his lifestyle had gone a little bit by then. I loved the feel of him coming back because he was my idol, he was a fantastic player. He was a lovely man. When I came through, George was always fantastic with me. George was always great company."

Some will have been surprised that Best would deign to return to United when the 72/73 season – before he walked out – had seen him say of the relegation that seemed to be a possibility at the time, "If that happens, I will ask for a transfer. If United said no, then I would quit." Though Docherty had saved United from that fate in Best's absence, they were still hardly an illustrious side compared to the ones in which the Irishman had played and certainly not yet in a position to compete for the kind of honours Best had been achieving almost as soon as his professional career began. However, it should also be noted that a move to a club capable of vying for trophies was probably not really an option. When United put

Best on the transfer list during that 72/73 season, so well-known was his dilettantism that not one significant club had come in with a serious offer for arguably the greatest player on earth.

The upshot of the September 6 meeting was that four days later Best reported for training at The Cliff. Genius or no, he was not in a position to be simply thrown into the first team. Docherty said he told him in training that he was a month away from being match-fit. This seems no exaggeration. Even after that month – during which time nobody seems to dispute that the Irishman worked like a Trojan – Best was notably thick-set. Meek recalls, "Docherty always said that providing you could get George Best to the ground for training, he was no problem because he always had this natural love and appetite to train. He said the problem is getting him there and getting him there on time. Once there, Docherty was full of admiration for the way that Best trained. That was the saving grace and why he persevered and kept trying to persuade him to continue."

\*\*\*

United visited Ipswich's Portman Road on Saturday September 8. Holton was out injured for a match in which United's starting line-up was otherwise unchanged. The surname of the man drafted in to plug the gap no doubt caused some amongst the 22,023 spectators to wrinkle their foreheads in puzzlement when it came over the stadium's public address system. Had Docherty splashed out yet again and gone and bought Stoke City's striker Jimmy Greenhoff?

22-year-old Brian Greenhoff had been at United since August 1968. More than five years after signing as a schoolboy, he was getting his chance in the first team. Greenhoff recalls, "I was just told that I was travelling and I thought, 'Oh, I'm 13th man, so I have to get the skips in and that', thinking I'm not going to do anything. So when they took the food order, I ordered a steak, and suddenly, boomp, you're playing, which was a bit of a shock." When Docherty announced that Sadler was moving into Holton's position and Greenhoff would be taking Sadler's role, Greenhoff – suddenly facing the thought of making his debut in the toughest league in the world for the most famous name in soccer – found his appetite gone.

Brian was Jimmy's kid brother and, though he had a less glamorous role than marksman Jimmy, had shown promise way back. Anybody reading extensively about football will sooner or later come to the conclusion that it represents a sort of vast family tree. A perfect example is the fact that though Greenhoff was a player whom Docherty inherited when he took over the United management the two were already familiar with each other. Not long before Greenhoff had signed on the dotted line for United, the 15-year-old was taken to lunch by Docherty, who wanted him to sign for the club he was then managing, Rotherham. Greenhoff: "He invited three from the Barnsley Boys team. We all went with our dads and had a meal in Rotherham: Trevor Phillips and a guy called Jeff English ... Barnsley always had a good reputation. He was desperate to sign us. He wanted all three of us. He was like he always was: he always had a joke for you, he always wanted to have a bit of a laugh, he made everybody feel welcome. We enjoyed it. Trevor Phillips signed there, whereas Jeff went to Arsenal."

Born on April 28 1953, Greenhoff was a Barnsley native. His father James was originally a miner but took over the running of the local pub when Brian was 10. Football was in the blood. His father had played for Lincoln City and of course Brian's childhood was spent watching the progress of seven-years-older brother Jimmy – a man Brian admitted that he idolised – in the sport. By the time Brian was nine, Jimmy had signed for the soon-to-be-mighty Leeds United. Brian also showed some promise as a cricketer but says, "I don't think I was good enough, so I just played a bit of local cricket, that was all." A kid in his school football team actually managed to balance those two passions: Arnold Sidebottom would not only sign terms at Old Trafford but would run a parallel career by turning out for Yorkshire in county cricket in the summer.

It's an indication of Brian Greenhoff's down-to-earth nature that he in no way dismissed Docherty's overtures to join Rotherham, despite that club's lowly position in the world and the fact that one of the other clubs seeking his signature was Manchester United. Barnsley was the third club wooing him at that stage. "Me dad left it up to me who I wanted to sign for," he says. "All he did, he told me who'd made the offers, what would be happening to me when I went there and all that. I went on holiday with friends, me auntie and me uncle, and came back, and he just said, 'Right, you've got to make a decision'. And I'd already made it and I decided it had to be United." His decision to make his future at Old Trafford was made partly because the waiter in his holiday Spanish hotel prattled incessantly about United (who had only just won the European Cup) and partly because he felt that they had the most impressive set-up and had treated him best. Docherty took it well: "When told him I were going to United, he said, 'You made a good choice, son.'" When Docherty arrived at Old Trafford in 1972, Greenhoff was recovering from a broken leg: "I think at that time I was actually playing for either the 'A' team or the 'B' team and he was at The Cliff and he came out and he got introduced to me and he remembered me, which was nice. A week later or two weeks later, I was in the reserves."

Brian was a different type of player to Jimmy. "That was never me," he says of his brother's striker position. Brian had alternated between centre-half and centre-forward in his school team, "But with the town team, I basically played midfield all the time. It never bothered me where I played as long as I played, but I was stuck in midfield and that sort of seemed to be my position. I got picked for Yorkshire Boys in that position and it seemed a logical thing that's where I finished up." Though Docherty initially tended to use him in midfield, he would eventually settle him into a defender's role (albeit one more likely than normal to make his way into the opposition half courtesy of Docherty's attacking style). However, Greenhoff was nothing if not versatile and was used as a striker on a few occasions, and even in one memorable match as a goalkeeper.

The Ipswich match ended 2-1 to the home club and was somewhat one-sided. Ipswich scored after only six minutes when a ball from Kevin Beattie travelled 40 yards through a motionless United defence and found Lambert. Johnson headed the second two minutes before the interval. Trevor Anderson had a good game and deserved the goal he flicked in from Morgan's free-kick in the 86th minute. Docherty asked Young to switch flanks with Buchan at half-time after the latter had proved unequal to the task of dealing with Lambert. Another Docherty manoeuvre was impenetrable to Ipswich's young John Peddelty, who said of Kidd's replacement by Macari in the 55th minute, "I was astonished. Kidd was the only one worrying us." United were now lying 16th.

Greenhoff later said of his debut performance, "It was really nerve-wracking but the rest of the team were marvellous ... All I was worried about was that I had done okay. I knew of some players who had appeared once for a team and never again and I was a bit jumpy." He now adds, "I thought I did alright. I felt quite comfortable. At that early part of the season, I'd been playing really, really well for the reserves and I'd had a really good pre-season which was the first one I'd had for a couple of years, because I broke my leg [when] I was 19. It was only a year and four months after breaking my leg. When you have a pre-season, it makes a big difference. If you miss it you never seem to get your fitness back. It just felt natural. It's something that you aim for. It didn't faze me out." Greenhoff's competitiveness, ball-winning, intelligent distribution and general consistency is what made him for some United's player of the season. England manager Alf Ramsey would take the trouble to see him play and by the end of the campaign Greenhoff was in the England under-23 squad. Docherty had taken note of the extent of Greenhoff's potential long before Ramsey: a few months into the season, Docherty was in discussion with Derby County about purchasing Archie Gemmill – a Scottish international – to help shore up the United team. No doubt if Derby hadn't cited a fee of £225,000, Docherty would have been more inclined to buy the player who would achieve immortality in 1978 with an unforgettable goal for Scotland against Holland in the World Cup in which he dribbled past three players before slotting the ball past the keeper. However, the fact that Greenhoff was showing such promise seems to have been the thing that gave Docherty the courage to keep the United cheque book that he had made such heavy use of closed on this occasion.

Martin Buchan had had a less happy time of it than the debutant. Perhaps it was the humiliation of the rebuke implicit in being made to switch roles that made Buchan's patience snap today at the fact of Doherty continuing to insist he play full-back instead of his preferred role in central defence. "We actually had a bit of an up-and-downer in the dressing room at Ipswich," says Buchan, "and I was asked was I unhappy, did I want to move. I said, 'Yeah, I'm quite happy to get a move'."

United were much changed for the home match against Leicester on Wednesday September 12. McIlroy was dropped and wouldn't reappear until December. Despite his goal against QPR, the Irishman wasn't surprised by his exclusion. "I think I came back too soon," McIlroy later said. "It wasn't until later in the season that I felt properly recovered." With Holton available again, Greenhoff also made way, though it was James, not Sadler, who was the other central defender. Daly and Kidd were also absent, with Martin, Macari and Storey-Moore returning. To complete the air of wholesale change, Buchan and Young switched flanks, at least judging by the official teamsheet. Much good did any of this tinkering do. The Reds were 2-0 down by the 53rd minute. Some of the United fans in the 40,793 crowd started chanting for George Best.

A handball decision in the Ipswich penalty area led to a strange occurrence in the 67th minute. When United were awarded the spot-kick, the stadium watched in puzzlement as Alex Stepney trotted up the field from his penalty area. A buzz began around the crowd as he placed the ball on the spot. Surely they weren't about to see the United keeper take a penalty kick for his team? But as Stepney started walking backwards, it was clear that the unthinkable was indeed about to take place before their very eyes. Ever the professional, Leicester keeper Peter Shilton betrayed no emotion as he watched his counterpart go about the process he would normally expect anybody but a fellow goalie to engage in. Stepney trotted forward and beat one of the best goalkeepers in the country quite easily, placing the ball low to the right while Shilton dived left.

Docherty had taken note of the fact that Stepney had scored a penalty in a shoot-out with South American side Penarol during a pre-season visit to Spain and when discussion turned just before the start of the season to who would take the spot-kicks, the manager suddenly announced that it would be Alex. Stepney's willingness to take on this almost unprecedented task for a goalkeeper may have been an adjunct of his propensity to play – rather effectively from the testimony of team-mates – in an outfield position in training. He also later admitted that a certain arrogance had led him to thrust aside misgivings such as his fear that he might be caught stranded should he hit the post or the opposition goalie save his effort. The misgiving was a valid one and Stepney later decided that the decision to give him the role was "crazy" and an indictment of Docherty as a manager. Journalist Paul Wilcox was equally apalled, but, unlike Stepney, didn't wait for a passage of several years to pass before making the fact known. In his match report he said, "Tommy Docherty has enough problems without accepting that his outfield players are no-hopers as far as shooting is concerned. To judge from the catalogue of chances created and missed last night they are; but when the manager condones the fact, football has gone mad."

United failed to add to Stepney's goal and finished the match in 20th position. This was an alarming development. Up until now, the relegation zone had consisted of two places, but this season a new three-up, three-down system had been introduced by the Football League. Though it was early days, it can't have done United much psychological good to be standing on the expanded trapdoor leading into the Second Division. (It should also be noted that this was an era in which the safety net of play-offs didn't exist.)

Nonetheless, Stepney felt that that eccentric decision by Docherty was actually the exception to the rule regarding his conduct that season. United may have had a torrid time of it from day one, but Stepney found Docherty a perennially encouraging figure, smiles and optimistic words always on his lips even when inside he must have been bitterly disappointed at the way things were developing.

Saturday September 15 saw the highlight of United's season. Though they would register wins as good as their 3-1 home victory over West Ham, they would be ones that took place when they were fighting for their First Division lives. After this match, United climbed to 14th in the table. While Macari (whose absence today made him the only change) may have been in a small minority in thinking of the club as championship contenders, what with the fact that a certain recalled Old Trafford favourite provided the tabloid writers the handy headline-friendly label the Comeback Kidd with a pair of spectacular, long-range goals, plus the fact that Ian Storey-Moore seemed to have put his injury troubles behind him via a strike of his own, it would seem that happy-ish days were here again. The only goal United conceded was from a penalty.

Sadly, Storey-Moore's sumptuous skills were never to be seen in serious football again. He would retire in December, finally conceding defeat to the ankle injury that had been hounding him for so long. He was just 27. Says Martin Buchan of the man born in Ipswich on January 17 1945, "It was a shame. Ian Storey-Moore actually had a dickey ankle when he joined us. On his day he was a devastating winger and a great guy, too." Docherty's winger dream – a plan to play Morgan on the right flank and Storey-Moore on the left – was scuppered.

Potentially, though, United now had a player who could fill that vanacy. In the West Ham match, Holton had to go off injured after a collision with ex-United man Ted MacDougall (making his return to Old Trafford). The gap in the team was made up by George Buchan, younger brother of Martin by one year, recently signed from Aberdeen after the Scottish club had granted him a free transfer following 29 league games and two goals for them. George was a wide player who was predominately right-sided but who could use his left foot. He was born in Aberdeen on May 2 1950. Explains Martin Buchan of his brother's arrival, "George called me at the end of season 72/73. He was due a benefit payment of £750 from Aberdeen after five years' service. In a typical gesture of Aberdonian generosity, he was told he could have the payment and go on the transfer list, or he could choose to waive the payment and have a free transfer. He chose the free and there was some interest from Bury FC. I told him that I would try to find out what the wage structure was at Bury so he didn't sign for less than the going rate. When he left United, Frank O'Farrell had said to give him a ring if I ever needed any advice so I went in past the ground late one afternoon to see if I could get a number for him from Kath on reception. I bumped into The Doc in the doorway and asked him if he knew what they were paying at Gigg Lane. When he asked why, I explained that George had been released by Aberdeen and had had some interest from Bury. Right away he said, 'Tell him to come down here, I'll give him a year.' I asked him in jest if he'd been drinking, but he said that he'd seen George playing while watching me and some of my team-mates at Aberdeen when he was Scotland manager and had been impressed with his pace and work rate. He also said that he had signed a player, Pat McMahon, on a free transfer from Celtic when he was boss at Aston Villa and that Pat had done a good job for him."

\*\*\*

When Docherty read out the team sheet for the match on Saturday September 22, Brian Greenhoff knew that – regardless of what happened to him from hereon – he was at least not going to be a one-game wonder. For United's visit to Leeds United at Elland Road, he was wearing the number four shirt, displacing Mick Martin. That was the good news. The news that some might have interpreted as bad was that Greenhoff's task today was to mark Billy

Bremner. The other change from the West Ham match was that Storey-Moore was missing and Macari made a comeback.

The fixture was one of the toughest in football. Clubs hated playing away to Leeds, despising the gamesmanship and the negative football of Don Revie's side, even while grudgingly having to admit that it was stuffed to the gills with quality players. Leeds at this point in the season had a 100% win rate and talk was in the air of them overhauling Tottenham Hotspur's record of 11 consecutive top-flight victories. Docherty decided to deal with the situation by beating Leeds at their own game. The Reds effectively played with a nine-man defence and Docherty's comment after the match that "I wasn't concerned with providing a spectacle" could be said to describe Revie's entire footballing philosophy. In fact, the roles of the two Uniteds were almost reversed. Holton got booked for a crash tackle on Mick Jones as early as the third minute. One reporter – Rodger Baillie – considered Greenhoff's ultra-tight marking of Bremner to be "a campaign of blatant provocation", while another, John Sadler, accused Greenhoff of "tripping, pushing and shirt-pulling the Leeds skipper". What we now know about Greenhoff's nature and his good career disciplinary record suggests that the shocking spectacle this conjures up was entirely at the behest of his manager. The referee admonished the United team for time-wasting in the first-half and, with five minutes still to go in the second, United players were telling the referee to blow for time in finest intimidatory Leeds fashion. Interestingly, at least twice during the season Docherty publicly expressed his admiration for Leeds, cooing over their football while failing to mention or condemn their gamesmanship, even if strides had been taken by Revie of late to improve their disciplinary record.

Greenhoff pleads innocence to the accusation of intimidation and says The Doc issued no sinister edict. Greenhoff: "He said just follow him wherever he goes. Billy and Johnny Giles both turned round to me in one little break and they said, 'We're going to break your legs, son.' If I provoked them, I provoked them but I don't think a 20-year-old lad could provoke them two." Little of note happened in a grim 0-0 draw watched by 47,058 spectators, unless you count George Buchan coming on for Macari in the second-half. Still, Docherty had achieved his objectives, however modest they were: not conceding a goal to the table-toppers at their own intimidating ground. In making Leeds drop their first point of the season, United obtained a respectable table position at close of play of 13th.

Because of the hatred felt for Leeds United outside their home city, few were going to feel pity for them but John Sadler was writing in sorrow for United's fall from grace when he said, "There is something pathetic, not to say sickening, in the spectacle of once dignified Manchester United resorting to the behaviour of the hooligan simply to avoid defeat."

Reasoned Docherty, "What's the point in coming here and having a good open game and losing 6-2? We get relegated and I get the sack. Leeds are a world-class side and we have to defend because we are not yet equipped to go to them." Docherty's comments displayed his footballing intelligence, but many a long-term United fan could be forgiven for wishing he sounded a bit more regretful about his realism.

The following Saturday – September 29 – saw another goalless game that once again constituted a good result for United in light of the strength of the opposition. In happier times, perhaps a 0-0 draw at Old Trafford against Bill Shankly's Liverpool would not be considered so noteworthy but the fact that the squad Docherty had inherited and augmented was not humiliated by the likes of Kevin Keegan and Steve Heighway in front of their home crowd was tantamount to a real improvement. United were unchanged (Macari was replaced by George Buchan on 75 minutes). Though negative tactics abounded, the 53,882 crowd at least weren't subjected to the kind of nastiness that had enveloped Elland Road the previous weekend. United were now 14th in the League.

The Wednesday after the Liverpool game saw Denis Law's testimonial at Old Trafford. That he was now a City player clearly mattered little to the approximately 45,156 who attended the ground to see a Manchester United team that included George Best take on European Cup holders Ajax. United won 1-0, Forsyth the scorer. Disappointingly for both Law and the fans, the great Johan Cruyff did not appear as had been anticipated because the Dutch club had recently sold him to Barcelona. Even more disappointingly, Law couldn't take part through injury. Nonetheless, the rapturous send-off Law received from the Old Trafford faithful whom he had given so much pleasure for more than a decade was a refreshing contrast for The King to the empty ground he had encountered when he had gone back a few months before to clear out his locker.

\*\*\*

George Graham had not exactly distinguished himself since becoming Tommy Docherty's first purchase for United, but on Saturday October 6 during the Reds' visit to Molineux, he had a veritable nightmare. United's line-up was unchanged for the confrontation with Wolverhampton Wanderers in front of a gate of 32,962. Trevor Anderson had to go off with a bruised muscle in the 16th minute, replaced by McIlroy. Seven minutes after the interval, the Reds' captain found himself trapped in his own penalty area with the imposing figure of Derek Dougan bearing down on him. Graham panicked and his desperate ball found only Wolves' Jim McCalliog, who gleefully fired past Stepney. Graham was caught bungling again 10 minutes later. The ball bobbed up off Graham's foot and found Dougan, who managed to head into the back of the net even as he was falling backwards. United pulled one back late on via McIlroy. United dropped to an ominous 17th in the table.

\*\*\*

Upon their simultaneous retirements, both Charlton brothers had gone into management. Bobby had become the gaffer at Second Division Preston North End. (He would take David Sadler there in November.) Jackie (as he was commonly referred to then; it became Jack as the world seemed to become embarrassed at how feminine the other sounded) took over the reins at Middlesbrough. As managers, the brothers' respective achievements were almost the reverse of their playing careers. Though both had been England internationals, Jack had always been the unglamorous and physically ungainly defender to Bobby's midfield/striker superstar. The fact that this season Middlesbrough would be promoted to Division One, while Preston would plummet into Division Three was not a fluke. Bobby's managerial career was brief and inauspicious, Jack's long and illustrious. Knowing that now, it is less of a shock that Middlesbrough should beat United at their own ground on Monday October 8 and send them crashing out of the League Cup. Daly replaced Anderson for this game. Neither he nor any of his colleagues in an otherwise unchanged starting line-up could effect a recovery after conceding the game's only goal after two minutes. For some in the 23,906 crowd, alarm bells may have been faintly starting to ring.

George Buchan's appearance as a substitute in this match – his fourth – was his last in a United shirt. Following the year he had promised George at Old Trafford, Docherty sold him in August 1974. Says Mick Martin, "It wasn't his level of football. I think the next club he went to was a good level for George." George's brother is of a different opinion. Says Martin Buchan, "I never quite forgave The Doc for not starting him at least once before moving him on, because he picked a number of lads to start games that season who, in my opinion, were not as good as George. In fact, I'm sure one of them sat down to pee. The punchline is, of course, that The Doc sold George to Bury for £11,000, recouping his wages for his season at Old Trafford and making a tidy profit to boot."

\*\*\*

The following Thursday, the papers contained the shock news that Lou Macari was on the transfer list. Docherty told the press that the player had refused to play in a friendly the previous night and that as a consequence he was fining him two weeks' wages and selling him.

The fact that the friendly was an insalubrious fixture between United reserve and youth players against non-League side Mossley in a testimonial match for Kevin Burke may have been part of the reason for Macari's reluctance to participate: the contrast to this and his £200,000 price tag was bound to be brought up by some of the press. Docherty's only informing Macari on the afternoon of the Mossley game is also something likely to have provoked his ire, plus the fact that this would be his fourth game in seven days. However, when one also reads in Docherty's book *My Story* that he suspected Macari "was not even trying to make a go" of the striker's position he had, to the player's reluctance, put him in at United, one begins to suspect that Macari's attitude might have been informed by something far more significant. "Perhaps unfairly" is Docherty's view now of his suspicions about Macari's failure to shine leading the attack. If we give Macari the benefit of the doubt – and as a teetotaller, hard trainer, diet-watcher and all-round 'model pro' it seems unlikely that Macari would have been shirking – and then put ourselves in his shoes, we can only imagine the depth of his fury. Macari had had a miserable time of it since joining United, and misery was a state of mind utterly alien to a man whom all his colleagues remember as a perennial practical joker.

Although it was partly the shooting-fish-in-a-barrel ease of winning in Scotland that motivated Macari's move down south, and although he knew perfectly well the position United were in when he agreed terms with them, it was a shock for Macari to find himself in a mediocre-cum-awful team, one for whose misfortune he was bearing a large part of the blame from the media and the terraces: as the centre-forward, he was the player charged with winning games. His five strikes in 16 fixtures in his first season was below par. He had failed to score in his eight starts thus far of the 1973/74 season. "Nothing went right," he later said of his and his club's jointly dwindling fortunes. "When you are in trouble you never get a break." Other forwards were also not scoring but this fact was not brought up as much because their lack of goals had not come at the expense of £200,000.

Macari had taken advice about the friendly from the Professional Footballers' Association, who had told him that it would not be wise to refuse to play. Accordingly, he drove to the match and got changed. Docherty came down to watch it along with Crerand and United director Denzil Haroun. Following their *contretemps*, he was surprised to find Macari there. Macari in fact felt that Docherty was "shaken". This may have been something to do with the fact that Docherty seems to have decided to engineer a scandal in the press: Macari has claimed that upon his arrival, journalists one after another asked him what he was doing here and informed him that they had been told he wasn't coming and to get there to do a story about it. Macari was instructed not to get changed by Docherty as he wouldn't be playing. There followed another *contretemps* between the two men.

"Everyone not with us is against us," Docherty told the papers as he announced the fine and transfer listing. "Every player's attitude must be right, not just when they are playing in the first team but when they are in the reserves and in the dressing room ... There is a place in the first team if he can earn it better than anyone else. The ball is now in Lou Macari's court." Docherty also wrote in his weekly tabloid newspaper column that, "Things could possibly change once Macari recaptures the form we know he's capable of. It's entirely up to him. One way or another, I'm not particularly bothered."

Macari was dropped for United's home League encounter with Brian Clough's Derby County on Saturday October 13, while Young occupied the position Daly had in the previous match, enabling the return of Forsyth after seven months. Anderson also got a recall. The Scotsman's reappearance in front of 43,724 was not a happy affair: it was his bad back-pass in the first-half that gave Kevin Hector the opportunity to score for the visitors, the game's only strike.

The position of 18th the Reds occupied that evening and the sobering fact that they had scored a solitary goal in their last five matches must have been playing on a few minds, including Docherty's. However, according to Agnes Docherty, it was after this match that Matt Busby paid a visit to their home and informed Docherty that even if United were relegated, "... it wouldn't matter in the slightest" and would be "... just part of the rebuilding process."

The Monday after the Derby game saw United travel to the Republic of Ireland for a friendly against Shamrock Rovers. Normally, this fixture would be at the most a distraction. Today though a very special person was going to be wearing one of United's red shirts. George Best had completed his month's hard labour on the training ground and Docherty was giving him his first test in the closest thing to a real match since his return to the club. The game gave Docherty great cause for optimism, with Best's play, in the manager's own words, "scintillating". The match must have also brought home to Docherty the aura of legend that hung over Best, one which even his most expensive or wise purchases for United could never hope to replicate. The club's ground was full to its 25,000 capacity, with thousands more locked out. With 80 minutes gone, play had to be abandoned when Best scored and fans invaded the pitch, all eager – as any football-loving Irishman, northern or southern, was in those days – to touch the hem of Best's metaphorical garment. United won the truncated match 2-1.

Docherty decided Best was now ready to return to Division One. Or rather, he decided, in his own words, "Even a half-fit Best is better than most in the First Division." Having lost three matches on the trot and tumbled 11 places in under six weeks, Docherty didn't have the luxury of waiting to field a player of Best's quality. Accordingly, he was selected for the home match against Birmingham City on Saturday October 20. Docherty said of the Irishman, "He recovered his timing almost immediately he returned to training. But he is still 3lb overweight and short of his old pace." Best himself said, "I am not completely match-fit. It is going to take five or six first-team games to regain my peak. If I find I am struggling against Birmingham I shall ask to come off. I don't anticipate making a fool of myself."

Docherty himself could be said to have come pretty close to having made a fool of himself when it emerged that lining up alongside Best against Birmingham would be Lou Macari. The man whom Docherty explicitly said he was not bothered about ever seeing in a red shirt again had been recalled after just 11 days in the wilderness into which Docherty had so ostentatiously cast him, presumably for the same reason as motivated the hurrying of Best into the side.

Docherty's story now is, "The fact that Lou turned up and played against Mossley broke the ice." (Macari's recollection is that, in fact, he didn't play.) "Having established my authority as manager and made my point, I was more inclined to discuss his role in the team." Perhaps Docherty did indeed assert his authority and then out of the kindness of his heart acquiesce to the midfielder's role Macari wanted – a switch that Docherty admitted reaped benefits. Then again, perhaps Macari had come perilously close to following in the footsteps of Ted MacDougall and Denis Law and preceding those of George Graham and Willie Morgan in being rubbed out of the picture, and only Docherty's inability to offload him had saved him from this fate. Macari's treatment by The Doc had been cruel. Observers have claimed that Macari had to train on his own in a secluded part of the training ground. It was presumably at this juncture that Macari became so disconsolate about the way he was treated by both club and fans that he seriously considered going to play in America, birthplace of his wife, only drawing back at the decision because he feared he might be sued. Looking at this situation and comparing it with the consistent *modus operandi* Docherty displayed with other out-of-favour players, it would seem that Docherty was preparing the ground for what he usually did when he felt a man wasn't performing: a personal distancing followed by a brutally executed exile. An apparent terror by Docherty of being tainted by failures – or people he perceived as such – led him to treat them like outcasts in the usually short time before he could dispense with them. Unfortunately for him, the pattern seems to have been disrupted this time by the fact that nobody came in to buy Macari. A man who has been hitting the headlines for being a costly error is not exactly going to have other managers beating a path to his club's door with their cheque books in their hands. Even at an asking price of £50,000 – a quarter of the money he had cost United – nobody was biting.

103

Docherty was big enough to publicly admit his error, stating later that the clash that led to Macari's initial refusal to play in the friendly may have been the climax of months of frustration on the player's part: "I'd been playing Lou wrongly. He'd made an impact for Celtic and for Scotland as a striker, but once I moved him to midfield he was a revelation." Nonetheless, Macari's misery would continue for a while longer: his goal tally at the end of this season, in which he made 37 starts and one substitute's appearance, was just six, a far lower figure than Macari would have found acceptable even now he had dropped back in the formation. His misery was completed by failing to be called up for Scotland's campaign in that summer's World Cup finals.

The other change for the Birmingham match was that Young dropped back in the formation, displacing Forsyth. When George Best took the field for the first time in a competitive match for 11 months, some in the 48,937 crowd at Old Trafford must have wiped away a tear at seeing their beloved superstar return to the scene of so many of his past triumphs. Others might have been more inclined to ask, "What's wrong with this picture?" The sight before them was not the whiplash-thin figure whose bravery, stamina and strength had always provided a surreal contrast to his almost shocking appearance of fragility. Admittedly, a luxuriant beard – all the rage in 1973, and Bestie had always been a man of fashion – created an optical illusion that probably made him seem a little heavier (and older) than he was. However, there was no disguising that he was overweight for any footballer, let alone for George Best.

Best did reasonably well but began to get tired in the second half and was pulled off in favour of Mick Martin after 75 minutes. The crowd – 5,000 up on the previous Saturday's gate, unquestionably not by coincidence – booed in disbelief, then gave Best a standing ovation. (Some sections began to drift out). Though Best was not yet what he had been, the same could be said for his club. Stepney's 68th-minute penalty conversion – which he took like a goal kick – embarrassingly left him, on two goals, United's joint top scorer. United climbed two places to 16th as a consequence of their 1-0 victory. "I found myself afraid to make mistakes early in the game," Best admitted afterwards. "Later I felt we were going to win, and the longer it went on the more relaxed I became. I enjoyed myself all the time I was out there … The crowd were tremendous – fabulous."

Of Best's comeback in general, Buchan says, "Although he was in relative decline because his mind wasn't on the game, he's still the best British player I've ever seen and he did things with the ball that we could only dream about. You would never guess if you were a fly on the wall looking down on the dressing room that he was the best player in that dressing room by a mile. He didnae strut about like certain other players did thinking they were top dogs. He was very down-to-earth, with a mischievous sense of humour." Mick Martin also found the most famous footballer in Europe – and probably second only to Pele as the most famous in the world at that time – tended to wear his celebrity easily: "When he come back to the club, he made it a point to come across and say hello to me and have a chat and he'd say, 'Come on, I'll take you to a bit of lunch' and that type of thing rather than just say 'Hey' and ignore you. Great character. He become a very good friend of mine." Did Martin think Best a bit nervous when he turned up to train for his comeback? "No, but I did get the opinion that he probably found it a little bit difficult because the team he was coming back into wasn't at the same level as the team that he had won the European Cup with."

*\*\**

United's 0-0 draw with Burnley at Turf Moor on Saturday October 27 – which kept them in 16th position – may not sound like a particularly impressive result but Burnley had been in second place after the previous Saturday's results. Nonetheless, Docherty was pushing it a bit when he pronounced himself "delighted" after the match because "Burnley only played as well as we let them." 18-year-old central defender Clive Griffiths – born in Pontypridd on January 22 1955 – was given his debut, playing in place of Holton in an otherwise unchanged starting line-up. Kidd had to go off injured, replaced by Sadler. A crowd of 31,796 attended.

United's home match against Chelsea on Saturday November 3 was seen by 48,036. The Reds – unchanged – actually climbed two places after this 2-2 draw, but there was no disguising the fact that it was a point obtained by the skin of their teeth. The visitors were 2-0 up by the eighth minute. Kidd was trying hard, as was Best. The latter though had picked up a couple of knocks that he would not have in the old days. Though as fast as anyone else on the pitch, his preternatural pace of yore was still absent and meant that he was being caught by men he would previously have left for dead. Nonetheless, Docherty moved Best to the centre as the match progressed, his possible thinking summed up by reporter Brian Crowther: "... a patched-up lifeboat is better than none".

United were handed a pair of strokes of fortune as many of their fans were streaming out of the ground. The first was that the highly effective Blues forward Chris Garland had to be taken off injured, replaced by a very young Butch Wilkins. Then in the dying moments, Chelsea were reduced to 10 men when Graham Watkins sustained a hairline fracture of the left leg. Racing against the clock, Greenhoff set up Young, who rifled in a shot from well outside the area. It was his first goal for the club. In injury time, it was Young's turn to set up Greenhoff for *his* inaugural United goal, an effort from close range. "I can remember just turning and whacking it in the far corner then wondering what to do to celebrate," says Greenhoff. "I just ran towards the halfway line." It could be said that United deserved the point (and blushes) they saved so late in the day because of their refusal to give up, but this was hardly the form of serious contenders for anything other than a competition to kill supporters through stress.

Tony Young's goal was the one and only strike in his name throughout his five-and-a-half-year playing career with United, which career was actually not far from its end. Born in Urmston, Lancashire, on Christmas Eve 1952, Young had signed with the Reds in May 1968 from junior football. A workhorse who was handy at tackling, from his debut against Ipswich Town in September 1970 onwards he never staked a position as his own. "Tony Young was a very prolific scorer as schoolboy, played inside-forward," reveals Martin Buchan. "He ended up playing at right-back for Manchester United." This season, he became even more of a – to use a somewhat ambiguous term – utility player. Docherty employed him at various stages as midfielder, right-back *and* left-back and though Young racked up 32 appearances in his various positions, Docherty himself felt that it affected the player's form. Come the end of the season, Docherty observed, "I messed Tony about a lot last season ... It was in the interest of the team of course, but I am not sure it was in Tony's interests."

\*\*\*

George Best once said that he was a selfish player, by which he explained that he meant that if his team had lost but he had played well personally, he still had a good feeling coming off the pitch. One wonders if this still applied after United's game against Tottenham Hotspur at White Hart Lane on Saturday November 10, in which the pleasure of scoring his first goal since his comeback had to be balanced against the fact that not only were his team defeated but that the defeat sent them tumbling to 18th position, a salutary reminder that this was not a loss that could be dismissed like they might have been in the glory days when the next victory was just around the corner and relegation battles weren't even in the equation.

Griffiths lost his place to the returning Holton in the only change. A gate of 42,756 saw an exciting match, if over-defensive and – on United's part – over-physical. With Chivers having just scored for Spurs, Best collected the ball and decided to have a go. One wonders whether the benevolence of a statistician pleased by the return of football's prodigal genius accounted for the fact that George received the credit for an effort that ended up in the opposition net courtesy of Spurs' Cyril Knowles. Not that it mattered once Knowles had curled a fine free-kick just inside United's left post.

The unchanged United's visit to St James's Park on Saturday November 17 produced a game with five goals but little else to remember it by. Greenhoff set up Macari's goal on 34 minutes, following a 12th-minute opener by Newcastle. Reporter John Dougray said of Best today that he was "playing deep and hopelessly short of pace" and that the goal he set up for Graham "was about his only contribution." That Stroller strike came just before half-time. Stepney, as so often lately, was having a good game, but in the 65th minute he was made to look a rank amateur as the ball went between his legs to put Newcastle level. Newcastle grabbed a winner on 71 minutes. The Reds fans in the gate of 40,252 had once again been put through a rollercoaster ride by their team. They took what consolation they could from the fact that United hadn't slipped any further down the table.

\*\*\*

The debate about three-up, three-down has now receded into the mists of time, as has the haemorrhage of spectators at football matches that no doubt motivated the Football League to introduce its supposed enhanced excitement to the sport, but it caused no little controversy in 1973/74. Witness this: "The wisdom of new regulations demanding the demotion of three clubs at the end of this season was once more [called] into question. These two clubs are too near the edge of the drawbridge to display the calmer, nobler arts … " Such was the verdict of reporter Tony Stevens on the visit by Norwich City to Old Trafford on Saturday November 24.

One figure stood dignified above the fray throughout. "Thank goodness for George Best," opined reporter Paul Doherty. Another journalist, Edward Giles, noted, "Best, even at his leisurely pace, was unrivalled for his ability to beat a man and deliver the wonderfully weighted pass of precision." The (Best excepted) unlovely spectacle ended 0-0 and left the Reds in the same League position – 18th – as the previous Saturday. The crowd of 36,338, incidentally, was the biggest First Division gate of the day, but United's lowest home League attendance of the season so far.

Following three games with the same line-up, Docherty rang in the changes for the visit by Southampton on Saturday December 8. Macari and Graham were dropped and McIlroy, Griffiths and Forsyth brought in, with Young moved upfront. Kidd replaced Anderson on the hour mark. (Holton was out injured.) All of this was to no avail. The paltry crowd of 31,648 were subjected to yet another goalless draw and a result that yet again left the club in 18th position. An unusually subdued Docherty said afterwards that the recent goal drought was "inexplicable", and indeed his team had manfully created multiple chances.

Kidd was dropped and Macari brought back in for the home game against Coventry City on Saturday December 15. If Red fans felt they had been made to suffer by goalless home matches lately, now they had to suffer seeing three goals put past the visitors and a feeling that was becoming increasingly more difficult to ignore that there was something terminally awry with the club. The fact that United didn't actually play badly and that the match was entertaining would have been very little consolation. Best scored a consolation goal which, alarmingly, made the season's Johnny-come-lately joint top United scorer on two goals. The goalkeeper, of course, was – even more alarmingly – one of the men with whom he shared that honour. Morgan also scored with a quality header. The 3-2 loss ensured United slipped to 19th in the table. The gate was a miserable 28,589.

Graham, Kidd and Sidebottom made re-appearances on Saturday December 22 for the traditionally difficult fixture against Liverpool at Anfield, Forsyth, James and McIlroy making way for them, though the latter did come on as substitute in the second-half when Kidd injured a knee. The fact that Kidd, of all players, had been operating as an extra full-back gives an idea of Docherty's tactics today in front of a 40,420 crowd. The siege mentality failed as comprehensively as it had succeeded at Elland Road, only the brilliance of Stepney preventing the scoreline being worse than 2-0. United remained 19th.

A different man was now wearing the United skipper's armband. How this came to pass provides another depressing insight into Docherty's inability to treat an out-of-form player with simple human compassion. Docherty wrote in a newspaper column later, "George Graham has been a disappointment this season. Probably he's been trying too hard. I relieved him of the captaincy hoping that the lack of responsibility would help him." However, it was later claimed that Docherty, far from showing Graham such thoughtfulness, relieved him of the captaincy in the most humiliating and public way possible: by making a performance of grabbing the ball off him before a match and handing it to Morgan. Additionally, according to the latter, Docherty told Morgan that he was going to make him captain because Graham had asked him to lighten him of the responsibility as it was adversely affecting his play. Morgan replied that he would be happy to be captain as long as it was okay with Stroller, who was a friend. However, after that humiliating ball-grabbing incident, Morgan found Graham wasn't speaking to him. When after a few days he demanded to know what his problem was, Graham said that Docherty had told him that Morgan had been agitating for the captaincy for some months and that he had given Morgan the job to shut him up. "I thought, 'This is incredible.' I couldn't work it out," Morgan later said.

Some might describe this kind of behaviour by Docherty as Machiavellian. This would be a mistake, for the man whose name gave rise to that adjective manipulated people for a purpose. In this and other instances in which Docherty was alleged to have acted deceitfully and played one person off against another, there seems to have been no objective in mind. We can of course reach an uncomplicated conclusion that in claiming to Graham that Morgan had been agitating for the skipper's role he was simply trying to get a grumbling George Graham off his back, but no player needs reminding that it is a manager's prerogative to award the captaincy to whom he pleases. If Docherty had simply come out with the same lack-of-responsibility-would-help-him reason for the switch that he had to the newspapers, it would surely have had the same effect of getting him off his back as the assertion of Morgan's treachery. As with so many other instances, Docherty seems to have engaged in devious behaviour to no point whatsoever, and incurred a considerable and unnecessary amount of resentment among his manipulated victims along the way.

\*\*\*

Recalls Blunstone, "Tommy said to me, 'Have Brentford got any good players?' I said, 'Yes, they have got a good player – Stewart Houston's a good player, do a good job'." Houston, born in Dunoon on August 24 1949, was actually a known commodity to The Doc, who signed him when he was Chelsea manager from Port Glasgow Rangers. Just before Christmas 1973, Manchester United paid Brentford £50,000 for the left-back after Docherty went to see him play for Brentford against Stockport County. Blunstone recalls of Docherty's response to his suggestion of Houston to bolster United's team, "'Phone 'em up and see what they want for him.' I said, 'You must be joking. You phone him. I've just packed in there, they aren't too pleased with me.' So he phoned him and he got him." Recalls Houston of his Stamford Bridge days with The Doc, "I was playing on the west coast of Scotland in the Paisley and District League, juvenile football. I got picked up by one of the scouts in the local area. Tommy Docherty was taking quite a few Scots boys down at that particular time. This was '67. They'd got to the FA Cup final that year, got beat by Tottenham. Things were definitely on the up. It was an exciting time." Stewart is one of those players who seemed to have cruised through his time under The Doc – in his case, times in the plural – cheerily oblivious of the profound shortcomings in Docherty's character that many others have cited. Stating that his first impression of Docherty as a man "didn't really change", he sums up that impression as, "He's a bubbly character, loves a joke, loves a chat, plenty of talk, he's one of them type of guys.

What you see is what you get with Tommy. He was a great one-liner. On the training ground and even in the dressing room, he could always see a funny side of things."

Not that Stewart's first acquaintanceship with Docherty was much more than fleeting. Houston: "Tommy signed me in '67 in August. He actually left the club in September and Dave Sexton took over. I just thought I was going back to Scotland, because a few boys went home from Scotland at that particular time. Some had a month's trial and went home." Though Sexton decided he showed enough promise to keep him on the books, Houston was struck by ill-fortune at Chelsea. "I made my debut in February '68, but I was in and out of the team and the squad 'cos that was a decent squad at the time and unfortunately I got a cartilage problem. It took me a whole season [to recover]. It was a double incision in them days." After making that debut as an 18-year-old, he had played only nine first-team League matches for the Londoners by the time he was 21 and was increasingly frustrated. When Blunstone, whom he had known in his first season at Chelsea as the youth-team coach, enquired in early 1972 about obtaining his services for Brentford, Stewart concedes with understatement, "I had a decision to make." Though only across town, Brentford were a world removed from the top-flight environs of Chelsea. Indeed, when Houston subsequently asked to be put on the transfer list at Brentford, they were 92nd of the 92 clubs in the Football League. Explains Houston, "At Chelsea at that time we had some decent players on show and it was hard to break into that team. There was internationals in the team."

Blunstone himself had been looking for a centre-forward because Brentford's striker was serving a four-week suspension. "I rung Dave Sexton up," he recalls. "He said, 'We haven't got any centre-forwards Frank, but I'll tell you what I'll do – you can have Stewart Houston. I've played him up the front in certain games and he could do well.' So I took Stewart on loan from Chelsea to Brentford, and then I bought him at the end of the season. His true position was left-back, but he could play left-back, centre-back or centre-forward. He's an all-round player, Stewart, give you 100% in any position. Fantastic character, lovely lad."

Though Houston now says of his transfer to Brentford, "On reflection, that proved the correct move," not long after joining United, he revealed that he had been regretting his move to Brentford (where he played 77 League games) and had been feeling trapped. "I always felt I could play at a higher standard than the Fourth Division, but as time went on I began to wonder just who was going to give me the chance," he said. Docherty and Frank Blunstone might make unlikely fairy godmothers, but it was they who decided that he would go to the top-flight ball. "Brilliant buy," says Blunstone. Greenhoff agrees, feeling it was a step toward Docherty creating a well-balanced team. "Because if you looked at how many players played left-back for United and were right-footed the year before … ", he says, adding that Buchan's deployment at left-back had been "crazy". Houston explains, "My natural position when I was playing as a young boy was the old left-half, which got basically transformed into left centre-back when it went to a standard back-four. That's where I was probably more natural, but I did play a lot of left full-back. I probably played [more] at left full-back when I went to Manchester United than I did at left centre-back. I was pushed over a little bit more 'cos of the balance. We did have a problem [with] left full-back at the time when I first went to Manchester United, so I can see why Frank had on reflection pushed [for me]."

Of course, Blunstone's formal role was not to assist in the purchase of players, but to bring up players through the youth system and thereby acquire the club talent for next to nothing. Recalls Blunstone of his United youth set-up, "We didn't get many through, but then they bought quite a few, so it's hard to buy players and bring kids though. You're not going to leave a player out. For instance, Alec Forsyth – 120,000 [sic] for a full-back. You're not gonna leave him out and put a kid in because they'll say, 'Why did you buy him if you've got a kid who's better than him?' We did manage to get three through at one stage: Arthur Albiston, Jimmy Nicholl and Dave McCreery. Them three came through from that group … The one that also did well – and he was one of my apprentices – was Andy Ritchie. He played in the first team and he got a few goals an' all." Was being head of the youth team an easier job at Old Trafford because young prospects were eager to join, dazzled by the name of Manchester United? Blunstone: "Not necessarily, because it can work against you, because some parents would say, 'Well if I send my kid there he's not got much chance of getting into the first team 'cos there's so many good players'."

Though financial inducement to join a club as a child was then – and is still – illegal, football is littered with stories of parents of young prospects finding wads of £5 notes (and notes of higher denominations) down the side of armchairs after the visits of scouts and even managers. A *World in Action* television documentary in 1980 alleged that parents were bribed by United to sign their teenage sons with the club, with Brian Greenhoff being cited as a specific example. If this was true, it would seem to have been done in such a surreptitious manner that it completely escaped the youth coach's attention. "Not while I was at United," Blunstone insists. "We were too big a club. We lost players because we didn't do that. I knew it for a fact that we lost a very good player 'cos his father was an ex-pro and he was looking for money and he got money from the club the boy went to. He wanted to come to us, but we wouldn't pay him. You've got to realise, we had a wonderful figurehead: Sir Matt Busby. You didn't want to buck the club into any disrepute so [we] went against that completely. We never paid a penny while I was there for any player at my knowledge." For his part, Brian

111

Greenhoff disputes the *World In Action* allegations. Though he says of illegal payments, "In them days it was rife anyway. I think every club was doing it," he also finds it implausible that his own family were paid money for his signing to United because of the complete lack of any pressure applied by his father when he was deciding with whom to pledge his future. He also points out that United's first-team wages were notoriously low in this era, raising the question of whether such a parsimonious operation would divert finances to untested youngsters. "They were very clever the way they did it 'cos my dad had died so that means we couldn't sue them," he says of the *World In Action* programme. "They'd no proof. I did get offered money from other clubs. I didn't receive any money [from United]. No pressure with me dad. If I'd have gone for money, I'd have gone to other clubs."

Blunstone was no authoritarian like Cavanagh and the pastoral care he introduced into the United set-up over the course of his tenure as youth coach was remarkable. "We decided to send 'em to college," he says of the Old Trafford kids. "You got 15 apprentices in them days. Roughly two out of 15 would make the grade. It didn't mean the other players went out of the game. Some of them were dropped down to Rochdale, Bury, Crewe and got a living out there. But I thought if we could get 'em to be educated and have another thing in the locker … So we sent them to Salford College. They didn't like it! They didn't like going." Additionally, Blunstone dispensed with the age-old football tradition of the juniors cleaning the boots of the seniors: "We tried to get 'em down the training ground as much as we could. Treat them like the pros. They're not there to clean boots, brush terraces. They're going to be professional footballers. I did all that, it didn't do me any harm, don't get me wrong, but we're growing up into a different era now aren't we? We all did that when we were apprentices, but you don't see any of the clubs now doing it."

Though these forward-thinking approaches were Blunstone's ideas and he sounds naturally proud of them, there is one grisly necessity in the job of a youth-team coach that cannot be modernised out of existence: telling a kid he isn't going to make the grade. The United kids' standard morning's training was augmented by afternoon sessions where special skills received attention, and two full-time coaches were ultimately looking after the boys, but none of this could magic away the statistical fact that some teenagers will have to be told they don't have what it takes to make the grade. "Not very nice," says Blunstone of the duty. Has he ever been wrong about a player? "No, not a lot. Can't say as I have. I've been very fortunate in that respect. They've gone on and played for little clubs. Some develop late, but you can't tell with them boys. Youth-team players, they say, 'Oh, he's a great player', but when they step up a class, it's a different thing. Unless they're world beaters. I was lucky enough to play with a world beater: Duncan Edwards. I played with him in the England team … His first game for England I played in, against Scotland. By the way, Tommy played in that. And by the way, we beat them 7-2! There are some you can tell. Osgood was another one. I had Ossie in the reserves at Chelsea. He was a certainty. You get them now and again."

Blunstone had responsibilities in addition to being youth-team coach. Blunstone: "I took the reserve team. I took the youth team Saturday mornings at The Cliff or wherever we were playing and then come back and take the reserves in the afternoon." Such was Docherty's hire-and-fire policy that very often the reserve team at United would be stuffed full of players that any other club would be pleased to have in their first team. "Some are resentful and won't give you anything and mope," says Blunstone of the attitude of reserves, "and you get others who come in and say, 'Right, I'll prove him he's wrong. I'm going to get back in the first team.' That was my job – to go back to Tommy and say, 'Well, he did well, he did well, and he give everything'."

Reserve-team matches took place on Saturdays, with a kick-off time of 2 o'clock. If the United first team were playing at Old Trafford, the reserve team would be playing away and vice versa. Home reserve-team matches would see Old Trafford look something less than the Theatre of Dreams it is nicknamed, as they were watched by no more than 3,000 spectators. "The youth team played at The Cliff," says Blunstone. "The only time the youth team played at Old Trafford was in the FA Youth Cup." He adds, "I only saw the first team if the reserves didn't have a game or midweek. I didn't see them play a lot." Ironically, now that television coverage has advanced to such a degree that a reserve-team coach could still catch up vicariously with the first team's progress if he wanted, the conflict no longer exists: "A lot of the reserve-team games [nowadays] are played midweek and they're not played at home. For instance, Chelsea, their reserves play at Brentford midweek so everybody can be with the first team Saturday."

\*\*\*

Boxing Day saw United play host to Sheffield United. A measure of their desperation was that Holton was recalled even though patently not fully fit. Sidebottom and Kidd were dropped, McIlroy brought back in and Griffiths moved to full-back. This latter switch meant that Buchan was now reinstated in the number 6 shirt, occupying his favoured centre-back position. Not long after the *contretemps* in the dressing room at Ipswich, Buchan recalls that Docherty told him that Chelsea had expressed interest in him. "The Doc told me that Dave Sexton wanted to buy me and was I interested?" says Buchan. "I said 'yes'. I wasn't interested, of course, but I wasn't going to back down. In fact I think he told me that the fee was to be £160,000. He said '[I'll] see what they've got to say.' I never heard another thing about it." We will probably never know why The Doc had this change of heart about Buchan's role in central defence – Docherty realising Buchan was too valuable a player to lose, Docherty fretting about United's losing streak or even the Chelsea overture being a lie – but it is interesting that Buchan had done what many players had so far failed to do or would fail to do in the future: successfully faced Docherty down. Buchan though comes across as someone disinclined to indulge in triumphalism in such circumstances or to bear any grudges. Asked about Docherty's insensitivity implicit in this incident, he shrugs, "Well, management style in those days wasn't touchy-feely. You just did what you were told and got on with it … We had a disagreement about where I was playing and eventually I was reinstated in my favourite position. At one time he was very close to Willie Morgan and then they ended up in court. I remember that he had a bit of a fall-out with George Graham. So maybe he felt he needed to show who was boss." Did he have to be as ruthless as he sometimes seemed to be? "Well, sometimes that's the way you've got to do it. There's no time for sentiment when you're trying to build a team and your job depends on it." It should be noted that for some the conflict between Buchan and Docherty was not as low level as Buchan seems to be recalling it as. Crerand has said that at one point Buchan was so tired of Docherty that after he had stormed out he, Crerand, had to follow Buchan to the car park and persuade him not to ask for a transfer.

The eighth minute of the Sheffield United match saw United go in front when Macari scored with a header. The visitors equalised against the run of play. The 38,653 crowd might have been able to reconcile themselves to merely a point, but they were to witness an incident that gave strength to a growing feeling that bad luck was dogging Manchester United. Blades' keeper John Connaughton (once United's third-choice goalie) punted the ball upfield in the second minute of injury time. The strapped-up Holton misjudged the flight of the ball and saw it bounce over his head. Alan Woodward raced onto it and beat Stepney. "Their winner was typical of the things that have been happening to us," said Docherty afterwards. The sickening twist of fate took United down to 20th.

*\*\**

It was now a year since Docherty had been given what he described as the best job in the world. He was asked to give a progress report by a tabloid newspaper. "Frankly, I'm disappointed with Manchester United's position," he said. "Another six points and we would be in a comfortable position. All our troubles have stemmed from the goal famine … I've chopped and changed searching for the successful formula – and because of injuries – but now I'm planning a more settled line-up which I expect to take us to a mid-table position by the end of the season. I can't promise anything more. We are going through a transitional period – 27 players have left the club since I took over a year ago – and I'm only £200,000 in the red on all my deals. I've not finished spending, but it will be only on the right players when they become available, although I would rather not spend at all. I'll be delving into the Third and Fourth Divisions if the occasion demands, but I don't expect to restore the flair that players like Pat Crerand, Bobby Charlton and Denis Law produced under Sir Matt Busby." Docherty threw in his own two-penn'orth about the negative effects of the season's new development: "The pressures these days are against all-out attack unless you are a great team like Leeds. The reason – the introduction of three-up and three-down. It makes managers cautious. If we drop into the danger zone then I'll not hesitate to tell my players: 'We've got to tighten up'." Docherty cited QPR and Burnley as teams he admired. He criticised Norwich and Southampton for their negativity. He also laid into Newcastle, calling for the authorities to clamp down on their gamesmanship. His criticism of them "constantly shouting what they'll do to the opposition" was somewhat undermined by the fact that twice in the article he went out of his way to express his admiration for Leeds United, who for so long, if not so much lately, had needed no lessons from anyone about intimidation.

An unchanged United hosted a visit by Ipswich Town on Saturday December 29 in front of a crowd of 36,365. The Reds' poor finishing plagued them again until late on. On 77 minutes, McIlroy scored. Three minutes later, Macari got another headed goal. United climbed a place in the table by virtue of the 2-0 victory.

New Year's Day 1974 saw United visit Loftus Road for a match that was probably the turning point in the decline of both the club and George Best. Although both would enjoy a resurrection of sorts, it would not be this season for either. For both, things would get worse before they got better. Though United tried hard against Queens Park Rangers – and none more so than Best – they were thrashed 3-0. Best's sad predicament was summed up by journalist David Lacey who, while acknowledging his effort, spoke of him "producing half-remembered tricks" and added, "Seldom can he have been caught in possession so often ..." Of course, even as a shadow of his former self, Best was probably the most able player on the pitch. New left-back Houston – making his debut – recalls a team almost dependent on Best: "He was playing on the left wing. My brief was, 'Win the ball and give it to George.' It was as simple as that. It was as easy as that. I never really got forward too much because George was doing it." Nor were many of Best's colleagues mediocre, let alone bad, and lack of application was not an issue. Yet United had no coordination and once again the spectre rose of a team that – like Frank O'Farrell's – simply could not translate decent players and hard work into results. The line-up was the same as for the previous match with the exception of Houston, who replaced Griffiths. That Stanley Bowles – who scored a brace – was the star of the match was perhaps symbolic. Though a wonderful entertainer, Bowles was a George Best manqué, right down to a dilettante approach that was Toytown (betting and missing training) compared to Best's epic excesses. Today though, his dribbling seemed like the real McCoy for those neutral observers disappointed by the absence of it from the past master.

As well as a thumping victory to celebrate, QPR were able to happily contemplate that the crowd of 32,339 was, lucratively, the largest so far at Loftus Road this season. In complete contrast, United were left miserably brooding over the fact that the result left them in 20th position. For the travelling United hordes and the 'Cockney Reds', it was an awful New Year's present, but in no way unrepresentative of what awaited them in 1974.

Mick Martin explains the glum psychology of a losing team: "When you get into a rut, when you start losing games and games become difficult for you to win, they become twice as difficult to win the following week. Expectation is high, particularly at home. You're sort of relieved to play away from home because you're not getting the stick that you might be getting when you're playing badly and things aren't going for you. I think that might have been exactly what was happening to Manchester United at the time. The team might have been changing too regularly to get any sort of continuity in it and when the results weren't coming [you] didn't mind being left out of the side because the pressure was off you." His new colleague Houston recalls, "They didn't really get started that season. They were slow out of the blocks and it seemed to drag into the autumn from the previous season. That's what it looked like to me. Results breed confidence and we weren't getting the results."

Midweek saw Best miss training. After having travelled home with the team, he, like his colleagues, had a day off the next day but failed to appear at The Cliff on the Thursday. The story made the newspapers on the Friday. Docherty was said by one paper to be reluctant to talk about the matter, although their story did carry a quote from him: "George Best's landlady told us that he had left for the ground at the normal time, but we haven't seen him or had any message. Obviously I am concerned, but I don't know whether he is ill and will not pre-judge the issue until I know the full facts ... If I don't hear from him I shall eventually have to put the matter before the directors." Saturday January 5th saw United start their FA Cup campaign with a third-round match at home to Third Division Plymouth Argyle. What happened before this match led to Best's permanent departure from top-flight football.

Best told his biographer Michael Parkinson that he was informed shortly before the match by Docherty that he wasn't going to play him because he had missed training. For Best, this constituted the manager reneging on a deal he had with him whereby if he did fail to turn up at The Cliff it would be forgotten if he tried twice as hard the next day. Docherty later claimed that it was Best's late arrival – 2:35pm, by which time Docherty had handed in the team sheet to the referee in preparation for the 3pm kick-off – that was the problem, as well as the player reeking of alcohol and being in the inappropriate company of a young blonde lady. These stories, as with so many surrounding *contretemps* between Docherty and players, contradict each other. The only witness to the exchange in question between Best and The Doc was Pat Crerand, who told Joe Lovejoy, another of Best's biographers, "All that stuff about him turning up half an hour before the kick-off with a girl being with him and dropped for that reason is bullshit. The teamsheet was ready before that, and his name wasn't on it." Crerand also said that Best was at the ground for the team's midday meal, something which Brian Kidd also told Lovejoy he was "pretty sure" of. Kidd said he "definitely" remembered Best told him he wasn't playing "well before" half-past two. Mick Martin bears out part of Docherty's story, recalling, "I've got a feeling that I came into the side because George wasn't there." Yet it should also be noted that Bob Greaves of the *Sunday Telegraph* stated in his match report on the Plymouth game that Docherty had dropped Best two hours before kick-off and that he gave as the reason "loss of form." Greaves indicated he felt the loss of form explanation a cover for Docherty's irritation at his having missed training, but more to the point is that the timing of the dropping and the reason given here contradict the he-was-late line Docherty was still giving in his 2006 autobiography. The loss-of-form line also seems to contradict comments Docherty made a few weeks later to journalist John Maddock, where he said in defence of Best's performances, "Even the two bad games he had at Liverpool and QPR were chalked down to a temporary lapse. After all, most of the United players ... have suffered from loss of form in successive matches."

Meek, though. says the he-said, she-saids are largely irrelevant: "It came to an inevitable conclusion. I didn't worry too much about the nuts and bolts of what was said and not said because it wasn't something that just happened that day. It had been building up to the sort of crisis and a decision. It was the pattern that was the key to it and the pattern was downhill and The Doc decided that enough's enough. He'd been late for training, he'd come in smelling of drink, there was a whole succession of ill-discipline. And of course the other players were getting restive as well because they felt there was one law for George Best and one for them. And The Doc would know this of course." Forsyth's recollection is similar: "The next day, George would never turn up. Nobody knew where he was. He would train and he would [play] and the next day he wouldnae turn up." As Forsyth hadn't been at the club during Best's previous tenure there, it can't be the case that he is inadvertently conflating Best's behaviour here with behaviour under a different manager. Additionally, Greenhoff says, "I think his fitness let him down and it was the first time when we'd really seen him drinking." Asked if he could smell drink on Best in the morning, Greenhoff says, "No, never once but you've seen him out a couple of times ..." Yet even if Best had become unreliable, according to both Best and Agnes Docherty, Docherty's behaviour in dropping him would constitute a breach of promise. Agnes said that her husband had managed to persuade Best to return to the club by informing him "... he didn't even have to turn up on time and train like other mere mortals." The fact that the attitude of Agnes towards Best and his wayward life in her autobiography was one of frosty disapproval gives credence to her comments. She added, "... the famous philanderer had made the mistake of taking the manager at his word."

Houston replaced Forsyth for the Plymouth match, while Kidd came in for McIlroy. Notwithstanding that Martin was a decent player, that he was the man who replaced Best might have made some inclined to guffaw. Of course Best's banishment would have backfired on Docherty quite spectacularly had United suffered a loss to lowly Plymouth. However, though Docherty substituted Martin for McIlroy on 60 minutes, United chalked up their expected victory, even if in less than overwhelming fashion. In the end, a solitary goal was the only thing that divided clubs usually separated by two divisions, Macari scoring – with his head again – in the 64th minute. A win is a win of course, but it's doubtful that many United fans were feeling like celebrating that weekend as they contemplated the depressing combination of a paltry 31,810 crowd, scraping a 1-0 home victory against less than illustrious opponents and a terrible sense of *deja vu* about the latest instalment in the George Best saga, which duly began to unfold across the newspapers.

\*\*\*

That instalment in the Best–United saga transpired to be the final one. Best later said that while the game went on, he sat and watched racing on television. He had a drink with the team after the match and once they had all gone walked around the empty stadium – "I knew I was never going back" – remembering the good times he'd had there. "He came to me in the players' lounge and said that he wasn't playing," recalls McIlroy, "and obviously I was shocked. I think that was the final straw for him. I knew then that when he had gone, that was the end of George. I could see it when he told me that day that he wasn't playing. By looking at him and the way he left the ground I knew. I said to one or two team-mates then, 'I don't think we'll see George again'." When Best didn't report back the next week for training, United suspended him and placed him on the transfer list again, but it was a measure akin to threatening the death penalty to somebody already intent on suicide.

Best's departure from football would seem to have been inevitable even without what he considered to be the injustice done to him. McIlroy says, "Obviously there's talk about he wasn't happy with the players that he was playing with, because he had fantastic players around him in his heyday." However, Best was just as unhappy with himself. In his 12 competitive games since his comeback, he had often been anonymous. Best claimed that in the game against Tottenham – his fourth, and the one in which he scored his first goal – he had felt his timing, balance and skills returning. However, it became clear to all, including Best, that his pace was lost irretrievably. This was something with which he could not come to terms. He could still send players the wrong way with a dip of the shoulder or subtle feint, but – fatally – once past them, instead of leaving them choking in his slipstream he found that they could catch him and try to dispossess him. This of course was something also apprehended with great relish by all the defenders Best had once humiliated. As time went on, Best was realising that he could not dismiss loss of speed as the result of ring-rustiness. A young man he might still have been, but he himself later admitted that in his time away from the game he had "punished" his body though alcohol. Says McIlroy, "When he came back and he couldn't actually perform to what he wanted to perform, I think that got to him. I think George felt, 'Well, I'm not entertaining', because he always wanted to entertain and I don't think he wanted to see people look at him the way he was when he came back."

McIlroy's apparent feeling that Best's melancholy over his loss of ability contributed more to his departure from Old Trafford than the dispute with Docherty is borne out by comments from Best himself. He said on television immediately after making known his final retirement from top-flight football, "I came back because I was missing the game. I thought if I didn't give it another try I might regret it in the future. I got fit enough, but that spark, that extra yard of pace, was not there. I felt I was still playing well, but I was not satisfied with myself." Asked why he had not simply told United this instead of disappearing, Best conceded, "This has always been my big failing. I've tended to run away from things instead of going to the club and telling them what I was doing." Additionally, Best told David Meek, "I know now that I have lost forever that certain spark that set me apart from other players and I also know that I can never get it back. I said when I returned to Manchester United that if I could not recapture my previous form I would call it a day. I am just sticking by that promise ... I could not face being just an average First Division player." As those comments appeared in one of David Meek's annual Manchester United books, which were family-oriented, they were probably either cleaned up or else made deliberately anodyne by Best himself. Their sentiments were genuine however, as illustrated by somewhat more embittered quotes Best later gave to his friend, the journalist and broadcaster Michael Parkinson: "I noticed people used to come up to me before a game and wish me well … They never used to do that before because they knew I was going to have a blinder … Now they felt sorry for me and that made me mad."

Intermingled with this, there may have been another reason for Best's retirement. Daly says, "I don't think he had any real respect for Tommy." He is not the only player to offer this observation. To some extent, it seems to have been mutual. Not long after his comeback, Best opened a club called Slack Alice. This was something that George Graham has recalled as Docherty not being pleased by at all, feeling it would distract him from football. Though one could make the argument that Best's failure to lay off the booze in this period was down to disappointment with himself, The Doc's misgivings about his proximity to alcohol engendered by Slack Alice were partially borne out.

Asked in that television interview if he would ever come back again, Best said in a comment that revealed he was far from the prima donna figure that he was being painted as in some quarters, "I don't think anybody would stand for it again."

Indeed. George Best had left Manchester United with egg on their face yet again, bearing out in the eyes of many the comment by one journalist when the announcement was made that Docherty had persuaded him back to the game, "United must be daft". Was it all worth it? Meek thinks so: "I think a manager's job is to manage and when you hit a problem you don't just say, 'Oh, I can't be doing with that' and wash your hands of it. You try as hard as you can to bring the player back into a positive attitude, and that's what he did. It's easy with hindsight. Looking back you could say it was a hopeless task, you should have just got rid of him straight away, but he had to try, he did try and it was worth the try … He put in some good performances and some not-so-good. I think he was still a good player, as he went on to prove when he went on to America. Okay, not such a high standard, but people forget that he had quite a long career in the States. I think he [made] nearly 300 League appearances in the States, so the boy still had football left in him and that's what Docherty of course was trying to bring out for Manchester United. There were moments when you thought, 'Yeah this could work out – we might see the old George again'." Buchan offers, "When he came back he wasn't half-hearted about it. Probably did as much as his condition would allow, in that he hadn't been training regularly, and I just cherished the fact that I got a chance to play with the guy. I don't blame him for Manchester United's demise. There are a lot more reasons for that than George."

Willie Morgan was less charitable. He said of Best, "George thought he was the James Bond of soccer. He had everything he wanted and he pleased himself. He had money, girls and tremendous publicity. He lived from day to day. Until right at the end, he got away with it when he missed training or ran away." Morgan complained that so inclined were people to make excuses for Best that he didn't even have to bother to do it himself. As for the pressures and depressions it was claimed Best was subject to, Morgan said, "It was rubbish. He just hadn't any responsibilities, nothing to worry about at all. All kinds of people covered up for him, even the press, and he was lucky to get away with it for so long."

Some will be inclined to attribute Morgan's unsympathetic attitude to jealousy. Few doubt that Morgan felt he was as talented as the Irishman and was resentful that this supposed fact wasn't widely acknowledged. Nonetheless, many shared Morgan's opinions about Best's behaviour. Best was a man who apparently had everything going for him, his blessing of sporting genius augmented by a generous Mother Nature with other advantages like looks, charm and (not widely known but cited by all those who knew him) great intelligence that would each be a recipe for happiness for most human beings. Yet he acted like he had nothing going for him, jeopardising his livelihood, his friendships and his health by his chaotic behaviour and intake of alcohol. It's little surprise that so many were bewildered by this and – contrasting his life to their own unhappy or unfulfilled lives – resentful. Yet though Best's decision to leave United for good was rather less to do with the clamouring crowd than the fact that he was now virtually embarrassing himself in front of them, the pressures that went with that clamouring crowd seem to a large part to have led to the self-abuse and wild behaviour which made him incapable of playing to his previous standard. Perhaps surprisingly, it was Docherty who provided one of the best and most succinct summings up of why Best behaved like he did. In *My Story*, he said, "Before him, football stars enjoyed a fame that never transmitted beyond the game itself." When his good looks, in-vogue Beatles hairstyle and preternatural talent gave Best the opportunity to become the first soccer player with the profile of a pop star, he – knowing no better – seized it. Several years later, announcing his first retirement, he was admitting that the image he had created – by which he clearly meant the unprecedented overlapping of soccer player and celebrity – had "backfired" on him. He had found out a sobering fact: you can go from obscurity to fame, but you can't make the return journey. Making it worse was the fact that Best was far less insulated than were 'real' celebrities from the clamouring crowd: footballers still made little money and even with his considerable off-field earnings, hiring the sort of human wall of employees favoured by movie stars and rock artists was beyond his means. McIlroy: "He was being hunted by the press, he was photographed getting out of cars, the media were on top of him and he was such a quiet lad and a lovely lad. Okay, people say why didn't he cry for help, but you don't really know what is going on until it's happening to yourself. George was absolutely followed everywhere and pressured everywhere."

One of the symbols of Best's downfall is a widely circulated photograph from 1973 showing staff members of famous London waxwork museum Madame Tussaud's removing Best's effigy from display and replacing it with one of Johan Cruyff. In 1974, Cruyff would go on to become even more famous than his exploits for Ajax had made him at the time of that Madame Tussaud's picture: his skills were the highlight of that year's World Cup finals. Just as Cruyff's star burnt the brightest of his career, Best had abandoned the upper reaches of the game. The two men were the same age.

\*\*\*

Saturday January 12 saw United visit Upton Park. In this match, Docherty paired Houston and Forsyth at the back for the first time and though things didn't go particularly well today, the two would in time develop a long-standing partnership that for a while would make their names synonymous. Houston seems to recall his new defensive bookend with fondness: "The two of us – that was like, Scottish full-backs – we got a partnership going. We used to call him 'Bruce'. He used to whack the ball like he used to do on the field first thing in the morning and we thought, 'You're going to pull a muscle.' He wouldnae listen, but that's the way he was." Houston enjoyed the overlapping full-back role required of him at his new club. "I was a fit enough player to cover the ground. The television programmes in them days had *The Six Million Dollar Man*. That's what the lads christened me. "

Young was moved upfront again for the West Ham match, with Mick Martin the man making way in the only change to the starting XI from the last time out. Martin was frustrated by his failure to command a regular first-team place. "This was when I thought that I should have been in the side because results weren't going so well," he says. "I thought, 'Well, why don't they play me?' Tommy was chopping and changing. He'd decided on Greenhoff and Tony Young. Tony Young was really a full-back, but he put him in the middle of the park because he was a greedy little player who got tackles in and got forward and tried to create chances."

The West Ham match – which attracted a gate of 34,147 – was a four-pointer: the Hammers had been in the bottom three since September. The encounter was your archetypal ugly relegation dogfight. Billy Bonds opened the Hammers' account with a nice half-volley. The Reds' goal – as if proving their raggedy, rhythmless path this season – came from their substitute. McIlroy, brought on for Kidd, equalised by pouncing on a poor clearance. At one point United looked as if they might take two points, but a half-expected sickener – for rare was a United game these days without a sickener – came in the 85th minute. A West Ham corner found the head of Holland and the strapping figure of Clyde Best intelligently ducked to allow it to beat Stepney. United were now one from bottom.

There was a hiccup in Buchan's return to his favourite position when he was made a full-back for the visit to Old Trafford by Arsenal on Saturday January 19. He wouldn't return to the centre of the defence for another three games. James, McIlroy and Martin came back into the starting line-up, with Forsyth, Kidd and Graham dropped. When James headed in a Morgan free-kick, United were clearly anxious to at least keep their one-goal cushion, but their hard work all came undone when just about the only moment of inspiration from the Londoners during the entire match secured an equaliser from Ray Kennedy. The crowd was a paltry 38,589 and United were still one from bottom.

In the week following the Arsenal game, the Old Trafford career of Bill Foulkes seemed to be as unequivocally over as George Best's after he was sent home following what was said to be a disagreement in training. Docherty said that Foulkes had not been sacked or suspended, but that he had been told to stay away from the ground for a period of time. The manager stated that he was going to discuss the matter with the directors. Foulkes had been at Manchester United half his life, first as an imposing defender who straddled two great championship winning teams – the Busby Babes and the 60s team – and, since his retirement in 1970, backroom staff member, first as youth-team coach, then upon the appointment of Frank Blunstone, reserve-team coach. Foulkes made 688 appearances for the club, second only to Bobby Charlton at that time.

For United's home FA Cup fourth-round tie on Saturday January 26, Forsyth, in the only change, replaced Houston, who was cup-tied, i.e. fell foul of the Football Association's rule that a player could not turn out for two different teams in the FA Cup in the same season. United's opposition was a team – Ipswich Town – who had recently lost 5-0. This must have given United fans in the 37,177 crowd some hope that their club could salvage some glory from the season. Some of them had memories that went back to United's last FA Cup final victory in 1963, one that had coincided with them narrowly avoiding relegation.

It wasn't true to state – as some journalists did in a lazy from of shorthand – that the present United team had nobody in their ranks of the quality of Foulkes' previous team-mates. Certainly, no one currently on their books approached the Holy Trinity in terms of skill, but that was true of every club in the world. Plenty of managers would have loved to have been able to put names like Stepney, Buchan, Morgan, Macari, McIlroy and Kidd (fielded today on 50 minutes for Martin) on their teamsheet. Against Ipswich, though, once again the talent didn't gel. Ipswich were in front by the seventh minute when Trevor Beattie's head beat Stepney to a high ball following a corner. An overly cautious approach didn't help the Reds. In the first-half, United's attack kept floundering through the lack of options available to Macari and McIlroy as their only two frontmen. There were no further goals and lo, Manchester United's season was reduced to nothing more than a struggle to stay in the top flight. What with the departure of Best, the possible departure of Foulkes and a season ahead of them in which they could only hope to attain the staving off of humiliation, the aura of decay and decline hung over Manchester United once more.

February would see the departure from Old Trafford of another member of the old guard when Jimmy Rimmer went on loan to Arsenal and then was formally transferred in April for £36,750–£40,000. Rimmer had been on loan to Fourth Division Swansea City for nearly three months and Arsenal had been sufficiently impressed by his form there to view him as a replacement for their ageing regular keeper, Bob Wilson. United also parted with Ray O'Brien at this juncture in a move to Notts County. The fact that Rimmer fetched the same approximate £40,000 fee as O'Brien hardly constituted good business sense. O'Brien had never made a start for United and would not play top-flight football until 1981. Rimmer, on the other hand, was a resounding success in London, thriving at one of the country's biggest clubs when given the opportunity to prove he could be something more than Alex Stepney's understudy. That role now went to Paddy Roche, a United signing in October 1973, when Docherty had raided the League of Ireland again. The spindly young keeper cost £15,000 from Shelbourne. Recalls Mick Martin, "Paddy funnily enough played in that game for Shelbourne when we beat them three-nothing in Dublin which got me the move across to Ireland. In actual fact there was four players there on that pitch who eventually finished up in Manchester United before the end of the season. There was me, Gerry Daly, Ray O'Brien and Paddy Roche." Roche was a respectable goalkeeper – he had already been capped by the Republic of Ireland – but certainly not in the same class as Rimmer and future events gave Docherty cause to bitterly regret not having Rimmer on hand.

\*\*\*

United's match on Saturday February 2 at Highfield Road saw Martin give way to Kidd in the starting line-up and Houston take over from Forsyth again. By now, Docherty, United players and the United fans in the 25,313 crowd knew what to expect: mediocre football, a single deciding goal and a delight by fate in spitting in the Reds' faces. Expectations were not defied on any count. In a boring match, the 35th-minute goal came as a consequence of an unlucky deflection. Coventry's Alderson got the credit. Forysth replaced an injured McIlroy for the last 10 minutes or so. Though the Scotsman played well in an unfamiliar midfield role, it goes without saying that when Coventry's goalie Glazier got a hand to a shot by him and the ball hit the woodwork, Lady Luck did not deign to deflect it into the net but sent it back out to safety. The only consolation for United was that they were still 21st in the table.

Meanwhile, Bill Foulkes was back at the club. A statement was issued by United which said, "The misunderstanding has been resolved and Bill Foulkes will resume his normal duties ... " Docherty said, "Personally I am very pleased that this problem has been solved in the best interests of the club." Nothing new about the incident that sparked the suspension-that-wasn't-a-suspension materialised from this statement other than that, surprisingly, the incident involved Pat Crerand and Alex Stepney, neither of whom were natural bedfellows of Docherty and both of whom, of course, had a history that went way back with Foulkes. One thing seems significant, though: Matt Busby had been on holiday at the time of the *contretemps* (whatever it was) and, reading between the anodyne lines on the matter, it seems to have been his influence that restored the equilibrium.

Old Trafford bulged with its highest attendance of the season – 60,025 – for the Saturday February 9 War of the Roses. The United team picked to take on the League leaders was unchanged from the last fixture, with the exception that Forsyth started, playing in midfield, displacing McIlroy. Recalls Forsyth of Docherty's reaction to his substitute appearance at Coventry, "He says, 'You looked quite good in the middle of the park left-side there. I'll have a look at you and maybe give you a wee run there'." Forsyth was glad of the opportunity, for he had never considered himself a defender: "I was trained and coached as a midfield player at Arsenal. When I was a boy at Thistle, 16, 17, 18, I was playing in the middle of the park and doing well. One day at Raith Rovers the left-back got injured and [they said], 'Away you go and play at left-back the last half-hour' and I played absolutely brilliant. I was overlapping, scored a goal. He said, 'That is your position now, you won't be moving from there again', and I played left-back, right-back ever since then. That was me sort of stuck at full-back then [when] I preferred the middle of the park."

Sadly, Forsyth had a miserable time of it today, finding himself all at sea against a Leeds midfield that could boast titanic talents like Terry Yorath and Billy Bremner. The Doc wasn't impressed by his performance: "After an hour, he says, 'You're just a wee bit lost'." It wasn't just Forsyth who struggled against Leeds though: they were not at the top of the table for nothing. To their credit, United rose to the occasion to the extent of keeping the game goalless through to the 57th minute, when a breakaway move saw Mick Jones beating Stepney. Though McIlroy replaced Forsyth, the Leeds substitution was the more successful one, Joe Jordan adroitly putting the ball between the post and the advancing figure of Stepney two minutes after his 85th-minute entrée.

The deafening support of the massive crowd and the eagerness of the United players had all been to no avail. The argument could be made that the same was true of all that had passed since O'Farrell's dismissal. Exactly one year and seven weeks after Docherty first took charge of a Manchester United match, the club were again in a worse position than they had been when he joined. They were bottom of the table.

Following the match, Morgan told the press, "The lads are sick at losing after playing so well against Leeds." Also after the match, Docherty and Morgan publicly stated that there would now be a change of strategy. "Away from home, we have had to play it a bit tight and go for a point," said Docherty. "Now we must go out to win every game." Morgan said, "We must attack. That will be the best policy." One wonders whether this new approach marked the point at which Docherty decided to heed the advice of Matt Busby over what approach the club should take on the pitch in the face of apparently inevitable relegation. The previous season, Busby had stepped into the row about United's allegedly dirty tactics by saying that if he felt that the club's image was in danger because of what was happening on the pitch, he would make his feelings known. We don't know whether or not it was the accusations of foul play that led to it, but at some stage during the 1973/74 season it is said that Busby approached Docherty and suggested that as the club looked doomed to relegation anyway, they may as well go down in style. The way they would do this would be by playing attacking football using a 4-2-4 system, a formation that Busby had helped to pioneer and which he had employed in the brief period between the sacking of McGuinness and the appointment of O'Farrell. Crerand, coincidentally, has said that he and Docherty frequently argued about formations during this season and that Docherty favoured 4-3-3, while he and Busby wanted a system with wingers, although 4-4-2 rather than 4-2-4. Crick & Smith state that Crerand says he was a witness to the conversation between Busby and Docherty in which Busby suggested the change in strategy. Busby himself told *The Sunday Times* in 1976 that he had said to the manager, "Let's go out with dignity, Tommy."

Says Buchan, "There wasn't any address to the troops in the dressing room: 'Right we're going to go down with all flags flying.' I can't remember that." Did he notice any change in tactics? "No, because we were trying to win every game. We didn't go out to lose or draw." Buchan is representative of his colleagues in that most of the players questioned for this book don't have a particular recollection of notification of a tactical change – although it should be pointed out that Buchan gets the wrong end of the stick to some extent: even if The Doc had decided attack was the best option, he would not have risked demoralising his players by linking it to an assumption of inevitable relegation. Forsyth at least does remember the change: "He just says, 'We're not getting anywhere. We'll just go all-out attack and attack'." Daly doesn't recall an address either, but does remember a change of style – one he recollects as bound up with a certain fatality: "It was way before we were actually relegated that I think Docherty had succumbed to the fact that that was going to happen and I think he'd made up his mind that we were going to go all out for it next year and then let people go out and express themselves." Greenhoff (who seems to possess a good memory) recalls a change in approach, saying, "It was after Christmas and suddenly we changed the way we played. We seemed to be more adventurous and we had a few good wins." However, he considers it somewhat belated: "The damage had been done. We were always playing catch-up."

According to Crerand, it wasn't a tactic about which Docherty was particularly enthusiastic. He later recalled that it took place after Docherty had had a request for transfer funds rebuffed. Docherty had wanted to buy another of the talents he had blooded at Stamford Bridge, in this instance Peter Osgood. Crerand was opposed because he thought Osgood had never been the same player since a broken leg and because Docherty was talking of agreeing to a transfer fee adjacent to £400,000, double the itself sizeable sum spent on Macari. Nonetheless, Crerand acquiesced to The Doc's request to approach Busby about the purchase. Sir Matt may have had no control over team selection and tactics, but he still held the purse-strings. Crerand has said that Busby "almost swallowed his pipe" when informed of the identity of the player and that he "nearly collapsed" when told how much money was involved. Busby vetoed the purchase on the grounds that he had made up his mind that the club were going down and that they needed to save money to rebuild in the Second Division. Crerand recalled a day, presumably shortly thereafter, when, sitting talking with The Doc and Cavanagh, he told them he thought the club ought to concentrate on creative midfield players. He said he was laughed at and told by Docherty, "You wouldn't get a kick in today's game." Enter Matt Busby, whom Crerand claims proceeded to attack the defensive approach United had latterly adopted. "Doc and Cavanagh were struck dumb," Crerand claimed, "but they took the hint. The style was changed and ... we produced our best football between then and the end of the season."

\*\*\*

There were now 15 matches remaining before that season's end, the first of which took place at the Baseball Ground on Saturday February 16. The Doc dropped James and Young, gave starting places to McIlroy and Fletcher, paired Forsyth and Stewart at the back again and relocated Buchan to central defence. Daly was named substitute and made an appearance. The attendance was 29,987.

Perhaps dropping Forsyth in the deep end in a midfield position against the table toppers had presented him a tall order, but in this desperate season Docherty couldn't afford to take unnecessary risks, least of all to accommodate one player's frustrations. Forsyth found himself once more wearing the number two shirt that as far as he was concerned may as well have been prison garb, albeit in a gilded cage. Forsyth: "He never really played me again [in midfield]. I think I was just unlucky that we happened to be playing Leeds." A few seasons later, Forsyth was publicly lamenting, "I am stuck at full-back. I don't feel involved enough, but I suppose there is not much I can do about it." Blunstone, though, says, "I wouldn't have fancied him in midfield. I don't think he was clever enough. He was a good defender and he was good getting forward, but whether he'd play in midfield I don't know." Buchan concurs: "I don't know if he would have had the engine or the discipline to do that job. You need to have an awareness of what's going on around you when you play in midfield because you're getting the ball from all angles. It's easier coming onto it as a defender. And you need stamina, too, because you're involved in every facet of the game if you're a midfield player. When your team's defending, a lot of the time you're trying to protect your back four as attackers are coming onto you and then, when you have possession, you're either trying to create something or you're trying to get up in support of your forwards." Forsyth begs to differ: "The only [manager] that ever put me in the middle of the park is when I was finishing with Hamilton Accies, John Lambie, and I tell you I thoroughly enjoyed it and I scored a lot of great goals for them. I played in the middle of the park for a year or two at Accies, but obviously it was too late in my career."

When United went two goals down within half an hour against championship contenders Derby, the situation seemed grimly predictable. United's defence were nowhere to be seen for the second goal, nor was their all-out attacking style in evidence in the first-half. However, the tenacity they showed in clawing their way back to a point was described by one journalist as "splendid". Greenhoff tried his luck with a 25-yard shot and – if he subscribed to the belief of those who felt that luck was spitefully refusing to play host to the Reds – must have been amazed to see it beat Rams keeper Boulton. United dominated the second half and when Houston made it two goals by Red defenders from speculative long-range shots, few could doubt the equaliser was justified. The 2-2 draw secured a climb of one place in the table.

The Derby match saw Holton, with his first tackle, booked yet again, an offence that took him over 12 disciplinary points and which therefore meant – once the disciplinary panel had adjudicated – he would miss two games through suspension. As he always did, Holton pleaded innocence, claiming that he slid in with the clear intention of going for the ball and the Derby player fell over his leg. Holton felt he was a marked man by now, saying that even the action of jumping for a ball was causing referees to tell him to calm down. It was not the first time that the bookings Holton accumulated meant that the Reds had to endure the absence of this important part of the defence in a season in which they desperately needed strength at the back.

The suspension once again raised the issue of whether Holton was besmirching his club's good name. Blunstone says of the party line that Holton didn't mean to hurt people and was merely clumsy, "No, I don't buy that. He's not going to tell referees he's going to kick people, is he? Or the press, 'cos they'll jump on it. He knew what he was doing." Demurs Jim McCalliog, soon to become a colleague of Holton, "Big Jim was clumsy more than dirty. In five-a-sides you could see it. We used to put him in goal because he would hurt us. He just looked menacing, but a lovelier guy you couldnae meet." Holton's partner in central defence, and a stranger to dirty play himself, also defends his colleague. "Jim was just a big up-and-at-'em centre-half, just a big honest lad trying to do his best to win the ball," says Buchan. "I didn't have any problems playing alongside him. I never felt, 'Oh, that's a bit too much.' He was no shrinking violet, but he wasn't a thug, and there's a lot of forwards I've played against were dirtier players than Jim Holton was."

Despite his tendency to cause upheaval by his suspensions, this was the season that United – following Holton's selection for the World Cup finals in Germany – decided to extend his contract so that theoretically he would be at Old Trafford until he was 32. Even though this was really a five-year deal with a five-year 'option' – the latter essentially an expression of goodwill in no way constituting a legal commitment – it was certainly a significant gesture, for United were emphatically showing whose side they were on in the Holton debate. It certainly wasn't the same side as the publishers of alternative football magazine *Foul*, who had nicknamed him the Big Bopper and had featured him in their sardonic Foul of the Month contest more than once. Bobby Charlton had noted that had it not been for Holton, his retirement from football could well have coincided with United's relegation. This respect for Holton was reflected by both Scotland manager Willie Ormond (who capped him after he'd played just 16 First Division games), his colleagues (all of whom continue to testify to this day to his good nature) and the fans. The devotion Holton inspired amongst the Old Trafford faithful was illustrated at the end of this current season when he won the Manchester United Supporters Club Player of the Year award.

\*\*\*

United remained unchanged – including Daly as sub – for the home match against Wolverhampton Wanderers on Saturday February 23. In a goalless draw in front of 39,260, Wolves' stand-in goalkeeper Gary Pierce was able to do something that two other keepers – including the esteemed Peter Shilton – hadn't this season: save an Alex Stepney penalty. In the 73rd minute, Pierce correctly predicted his counterpart would shoot to his left. There was little sign of United's supposed new attacking style in a fixture that left them once again in 21st position.

After the match, Docherty stated that Stepney would continue to be the club's penalty-taker, but this in fact proved to be his last spot-kick. Daly recalls of his miss, "Alex was getting on a wee bit then and he had to run all the way back the length of the pitch. I looked around and I thought, 'This is ridiculous this is.' And Alex turned around and said, 'That's the last one I'm taking because I'm too old to be running the length of that pitch.'" United shortly found outfield players adept at the art of the penalty kick. Even four seasons later, though, Stepney's brief spell in his unique dual role of goalkeeper-goalscorer lingered in the memories of the Old Trafford faithful and an award of a penalty to the side would sometimes be met with the half-sarcastic, half-fond chant, "Stepney, Stepney ..."

\*\*\*

For United's visit to Bramall Lane on Saturday March 2, Kidd and Fletcher were replaced by Daly and Martin. Sheffield United were lacklustre, but no credit could be taken away from the visitors, who finally exhibited evidence of attacking intent. Morgan was the standout, but Forsyth and Houston were overlapping with the forwards regularly. Macari's goal was the only one of the game. Even if United were still rooted to the 21st position, their supporters in the 29,203 crowd had seen their first win in two months and – astonishingly – their first away win of the season.

After today, Peter Fletcher would never be seen in a red shirt again. He remembers his time trying to make his mark at Old Trafford as a frustrating period. In a sense it was a culmination of the frustration he had felt over the previous few seasons as he had seen managers come and go. A Mancunian born on December 2 1953, he had joined the club in 1969 from junior football but had had to wait until April 1973 to make a first-team appearance. "You had to prove to somebody else coming in that you were ready for the chance and you could fill that position," he recalls of the period in which McGuinness, Busby, O'Farrell and Docherty occupied the managerial seat in quick succession. "It just seemed to be like that for three years." Even once Docherty did give him the opportunity in the first team he had long been hankering for, he never felt like he had an even chance: "You were coming into a team that was fighting [for] its life and it didn't help your performances. If you're coming into a really good settled team ... but you were being in and out and 'maybe this week, maybe next week' and playing other players and this, that and the other." Asked what kind of a striker he was, he says, "I tried to play football. I might not have been the quickest, but I was quite skilful for a big fella, being six foot two and not that heavy. I was quite all-round." However, he says, "As a striker, you need providers. Stuff wasn't being created. If anything went in, it was going to be an own goal or a 30-yarder. I shared a room a couple of times with Ted MacDougall and he felt the same. I think it was every man for himself and they played more regular and [they] thought, 'Well, I'll try and look after myself'. I think it was just those experienced players thought they could do it."

With no League matches played on Saturday March 9, United took the opportunity to play host that day to Glasgow Rangers in a friendly. Just how friendly things were can be judged by the fact that supporters – mostly Scottish – invaded the pitch before kick-off, Holton got booked and United players protested vehemently about a penalty decision as though it mattered a damn. Docherty clearly took the match somewhat less seriously: the United line-up was littered with unfamiliar names like that of reserve goalkeeper Paddy Roche, Mike Wardrop (who would never play a competitive game for the Reds) and teenagers Jimmy Nicholl and Paul Bielby. For the record, United lost 3-2 in front of a 22,215 crowd.

The Rangers match may have been a ridiculous distraction for United in this of all seasons, and at this of all stages of the season, but it at least gave Docherty the opportunity for a bit of experimentation. The willingness Brian Greenhoff had shown over the previous months to go forward and have a crack at goal is perhaps what prompted Docherty to try him out in a centre-forward's role in this match. Within seven minutes of kick-off, Greenhoff had put the ball in the back of the net. Throughout the rest of the match, Greenhoff displayed a keen understanding of the requirements of the striker's position, laying off the ball well and moving into space intelligently. However, though Greenhoff did occupy a forward position four times over the next few weeks, ultimately Docherty decided not to switch him permanently to a role up front, despite goalscorers being desperately needed. Based on his later comments about Tony Young, it might seem safe to surmise that Docherty was aware of the potential for unsettling Greenhoff by switching him around. However, a conclusion that would be equally plausible is that The Doc apprehended that weakening a back line that was currently one of United's few saving graces was too risky.

As seen by his earlier comment, Greenhoff didn't mind what his role was as long as he made the pitch. This may have been because – by common consent – Greenhoff was a pleasant and unassuming character. It may also have been the psychological legacy of a horrendous run of injuries that a religious person might have interpreted as a sign from on high that he wasn't meant to be a professional footballer. A sinus operation, an appendix operation, a broken leg and a damaged knee all afflicted Greenhoff at various points after his signing terms for United as a 15-year-old. The knee problem threatened his very future as a soccer player, not helped by the threadbare facilities common in football at the time. Greenhoff: "Treatment in them days wasn't anywhere like it is now. It was very difficult for me to get 100% fit. I never had what I would call top-class treatment to get it right. To build everything up, everything you had to do you had to do yourself, or in my case through the great help of Billy Foulkes. They didn't have a proper gym. I trained in the summer with Jimmy Rimmer and John Fitzpatrick (who'd had a knee operation) and we trained at Old Trafford and the old St John's room was our gym, which basically was like a pulley for building your muscles up, which looking back was not short of being useless. To build my muscles up I used to walk up the Stretford End paddock, which was quite high." While the course of weight training provided by Bill Foulkes eventually got him back to match fitness, there is little like the prospect of losing a childhood dream to make one grateful for the very fact of being able to step on a football field at all. Without being too harsh on George Best, one wonders whether misfortune like this might have tempered the disdain he seemed to come to feel for playing in a team that was not as great as the ones in which he had formerly played.

* * *

That United's players had unnecessarily decided to make a difficult match of the Glasgow Rangers encounter might have been brought home to them when they turned their attention to their next League fixture the following Wednesday, March 13, in which they faced yet another tricky obstacle on their long, grinding quest to avoid relegation: a local derby, away.

Either Bielby's performance against the Scots impressed Docherty or else the manager had intended to play him today anyway – after all, the 17-year-old had been playing well for the England youth team. Bielby displaced McIlroy in the only change from the Sheffield United match. Greenhoff started out in a striker's role but unfortunately had to beat a hasty retreat to Mick Martin's defensive position after 25 minutes when the Irishman sustained an injury to his right arm after Summerbee stuck his foot into it. Substitute George Graham took Martin's place. Summerbee had his name taken.

Manchester derbys are enthusiastically fought at the best of times, but this season both City and United were involved in relegation battles, even if City's predicament wasn't as dire as their rivals'. Quite quickly, Macari became annoyed at the treatment he was receiving from Mike Doyle. When Doyle felled him in the 30th minute, Macari wasn't to be mollified by a free-kick in his team's favour. He got up and threw the ball in the City man's face. The referee that day was Clive Thomas. Nicknamed 'the Book' for his zealousness in punishing infringements, Thomas was probably the most famous British official of the era. Perhaps not surprisingly, the disciplinarian immediately red-carded both men. Yet astonishingly both players refused to leave the field, walking away from Thomas after making a show of shaking hands. The 51,331 spectators proceeded to be witness to one of the most remarkable sights ever seen at a football ground. Thomas blew his whistle and waved all 22 players off the pitch. In the dressing rooms, the referee informed both managers that the match would not be re-starting with Macari or Doyle on the pitch. Doyle and Macari both later received two weeks' suspensions and fines of £100. The game's 45 official fouls illustrate that things weren't much calmer when the teams emerged again. Eric Todd described the 0-0 draw as "one of the most atrocious games ever played by Manchester City and Manchester United ... " After all the drama and the anguish, United were left in the same 21st place in the table they had occupied before the teams kicked off.

Before the next fixture, United obtained a new player in the form of Jim McCalliog, signed from Wolves for £60,000. Born on September 23 1946, midfielder McCalliog was not just a Glaswegian like Docherty but another player Docherty had groomed at Chelsea. McCalliog: "I first met [him] when I was playing for Scotland schoolboys against England. I got home from Ibrox and I was down playing with my ball after the match and my mum shouted there was somebody to see me. My mum and my dad weren't really football people so I went upstairs and I got in our front room and in the room was Tommy Docherty. I just recognised him because of him playing for Scotland and in the football books and what have you. He was trying to get me to go to Chelsea and I'd already made my mind up that I was going with Don Revie to Leeds. So I went to Leeds, but I left Leeds before I was a professional and Tommy Docherty come after me again and I signed for Chelsea when I was 17." Docherty's previously mentioned singing to all and sundry of the precocious McCalliog's praises may be what caused McCalliog to have such a high market value that Docherty was forced to let him leave Stamford Bridge – despite brusquely turning down previous transfer requests from the youngster. "The Doc put me in and dropped Terry Venables, he put me in and dropped George Graham and I felt that I was a wee bit in the middle of everything," McCalliog recalls. "I was young, I was only 18, 19. But I actually asked for a transfer three times before Chelsea would let me go. Tommy Docherty wasn't going to let me go. The first time I went in to see him to ask for my transfer, he told me to get out the room, that I would never get away from Chelsea. He kind of frightened me then, but I told my dad that and my dad just laughed. He said, 'Well, if a manager wants you that bad, then just you stick around and see if it changes.' Well, I stuck around and I felt, 'Well, it's not changing' and then I went in and asked for the second transfer. He said no again. Then the third time, it must have got around the grapevine that I was looking to move and the next thing I knew Sheffield Wednesday bid a British record transfer fee for a teenager."

McCalliog's reunion with Docherty at Old Trafford saw him entering a very different situation to the one he had known at Stamford Bridge. McCalliog: "The atmosphere wasn't how it should be at a club insofar as there was quite a few players there that weren't really pulling their weight and they were on the treatment table and they weren't actually going to get out on the pitch and try and keep the team up ... Brian Kidd had got a foot injury. I just thought if I was in that kind of position and we were needing players, I think I might have played in a game and had a padding on. I think if Kiddo might have done that for us, that might have helped as well, because he was obviously a feared name. I was a wee bit disappointed with Brian Kidd over that. I thought: a kick in the foot, you can put a padding on it. Just his presence out there would have been a good help ... I never played with Kiddo in the time I was there ... There was a few players that were swinging the lead a wee bit and I think that deep down hurt The Doc ... The atmosphere there, it wasn't terrific." McCalliog of course was also cognizant of United's perilous League position, but he had long wanted to go to United: "I was going with Sir Matt six years earlier. It was all earmarked for me to go to Old Trafford then. As far as I was concerned, I would have walked to Old Trafford. I could have gone to Aston Villa and got a lot more money. I wanted to go to Man United regardless of what atmosphere was there or anything else." However, he does add, "The Doc never got down, other than when we were in big trouble. And the dressing room was a happy place. He would come in and he'd laugh and he'd joke, and so would Tommy Cavanagh. It wasn't a dead place. There was fun in the place ... What Tommy Docherty was instilling into us in the dressing room was belief. All the time, he was still trying to lift the place."

McCalliog replaced Morgan in the United team that visited St Andrew's on Saturday March 16. Daly was replaced by Graham. Birmingham were also relegation candidates, so anybody in the 37,768 crowd hoping for an exhibition of the Beautiful Game rather than an example of soccer played on the brink of panic was going to be disappointed. United's attack once again had no teeth and it was easy to see why they had the worst away goals tally in the division. The single, deciding, crushing goal came in the 83rd minute from Birmingham substitute

Gallagher, who looped a ball over Stepney to the far post, possibly a mis-kick. A linesman indicated that Gallagher's colleague Hatton was offside well before the ball crossed the line, yet though the referee had a conflab with his fellow official, when play re-started, it was from the centre-spot. Greenhoff says of the season, "It just seemed nothing was going for us. When things are going well, you always seem to get the luck." Though still in 21st position, United's First Division status looked more precarious than ever.

After this miserable return to the team, George Graham would now watch his team's attempts to stay in the First Division from the sidelines. Graham has claimed that Docherty proceeded to give him the "leper treatment", demoting him to the reserves and trying to humiliate him by making him train with youth players, all designed – he felt – to force him into a transfer request, a move which would have cost the player a considerable amount of money.

The home fixture against Spurs on Saturday March 23 saw reshuffle and change in United's ranks. Greenhoff was moved back to defence, displacing Martin, James replaced the suspended Holton, and Macari, Graham and Bielby were usurped by Kidd, McIlroy and Daly. McCalliog couldn't wait to get out in front of the 36,278 present for his home debut but says, "The Doc wouldn't let us go out first. That was a change from when we were at Chelsea with him because we used to fly out of the tunnel. At Old Trafford he wanted to let the opponents hear the roar of our crowd. I remember us kicking our feet." More reshuffling and alteration occurred during the match, with Kidd replaced by Bielby in the second-half and Greenhoff moved upfront again. And the end result was yet another loss by a solitary goal. United were left bottom of the League.

United returned to the capital for a match against Chelsea on Saturday March 30. Martin replaced Kidd in the only line-up change. What followed in front of the crowd of 29,602 was the embodiment of Docherty's defiant words after the Birmingham game: "I would hate to be in a war with the people who are saying we are already down, for they have surrendered. We have not". Morgan scored his second goal of the season with a shot from close to 30 yards. Daly and McIlroy gave United a three-goal cushion (a phrase that nobody had been able to utter about the Reds all this season so far) and only a late goal from Gardner in the closing minutes took the gloss off a comprehensive victory that, though it couldn't lift United off the bottom of the table, indicated that preserving their First Division status in the season's final month and remaining eight matches wasn't necessarily a pipe dream.

The great victory did not come without casualty. As he went down to head the ball to safety, a boot connected with Steve James' mouth, knocking out several teeth and requiring eight

135

stitches. When Bielby replaced the unfortunate James, Brian Greenhoff was moved back to central defence and this reshuffling seemed to make the United team 'click'. It seems that this marked the moment when Docherty decided what Greenhoff's best position was. Greenhoff would with the exception of the next game remain in that central-defence position for the rest of the season – and the rest of his United career. Judging by what he says, it's the position in which he felt most comfortable. Greenhoff: "I always found it better when I had the ball coming from the back 'cos you can see the bigger picture. I didn't think I was the worst passer of the ball in the world and I could use my range of passing better playing from the back."

For Crick & Smith, the Chelsea match was the key to United's late-season recovery, and judging from what they say, they feel that this in fact was the juncture – not the home Leeds match – at which Busby successfully implored for an attacking style. From hereon, the crowds only saw Stepney boot the ball upfield either when taking a goal-kick or executing an emergency hoof. In keeping with United's newly positive approach to football, when he had possession Stepney would not take the traditional goalkeeper's option of tossing the ball up and volleying it as close to the opposition goal as he could physically manage. Instead, he would throw the ball out to the nearest unmarked colleague and the attack would be built from the back. Buchan: "A kick out from a goalkeeper's hands is a lottery, it's 50/50, and sometimes it's 60/40 for the opposition because the centre-half's coming onto it."

Holton was back for the home match against Burnley on Wednesday April 3, replacing James, but the team was otherwise unchanged. Burnley's Colin Waldron recalls the United fixture as something his team viewed almost as a potential catharsis: "On the Saturday we'd got beat in the semi-final of the FA Cup, which was an awful feeling, and we needed a game quickly to get over it." A yardstick of United's diminished status at the time is provided by the revelation that he recalls his team being glad of their opposition: "We went there confident."

United got their supporters in the 33,336 crowd in a hopeful mood after just 32 seconds when McIlroy scored a fine goal with a powerful shot, but Burnley were a class act – at times rolling the ball around quite majestically – and just 11 minutes later they equalised. Forsyth restored United's lead with a characteristically powerful free-kick. That lead was wiped out via two Burnley penalties. Holton scored an 87th minute equaliser. "The three-all draw flattered them," avers Waldron. "They were a disjointed side." This was going to matter little to Manchester United, who didn't have the luxury of concerning themselves with such things as getting "the crap of the semi-final out of our system" that Waldron says had been the potential benefit of the match for he and his colleagues. The Reds were now off the bottom of the table.

Come Saturday April 6 there was yet another tough game for Manchester United. Their visit to Carrow Road was to play Norwich, another team facing relegation. Macari replaced Martin. Stepney had to be on his toes throughout, as Norwich launched wave after wave at the Reds' goal. Some would consider it an injustice that after an hour of virtually one-way traffic, United should steal both points, but if any team deserved a reversal of fortune it was they. And both goals were well taken, Macari executing a sweet lob over Keelan and Greenhoff slotting home after a surge from the halfway line. The United contingent of the 28,223 gate were noisily ecstatic and Docherty ordered his men back from the tunnel to go and salute the wall of fluttering red-and-white scarves. Docherty spent the train journey home in the buffet car with some of the travelling Red supporters and made an emotional promise to them that if United did go down, they would bounce back up at the first attempt.

A feeling must have been growing in the United fans to whom he held court that he would not have to make good on this promise. Before this, it had always been possible to dismiss Docherty's gritted-teeth optimism as what you would expect of a manager who needed to maintain a brave face in public for his players' morale. Today, though, few could dispute that United genuinely did appear to have a hope of saving themselves in the dying throes of the season, even if they were still 21st. They had now taken eight points of a potential 10 from their last five away games. They had also scored eight goals in their last three fixtures, which was close on a third of their tally for the entire season before that. Moreover, even Lady Luck now seemed to be smiling on them. McCalliog recalls, "We really looked like we were going to get out of it."

For the visit by Newcastle United on Saturday April 13 (attendance 44,751), Docherty did something that he hadn't had much opportunity to this season: keep a winning team unchanged. Macari later mischievously described the method by which McCalliog scored his first United goal, the game's only strike, as a "misheader". McCalliog's version of events runs thus: "The ball didn't bounce the way I wanted it to bounce. I was going to kick it and then I just thought, 'No, I'm not kicking it' and went down and headed it." It should have been much more than a single-goal victory, but McFaul was excellent in the Newcastle goal. Though still 21st, United had now dropped only one point in four games. There was better to come. McCalliog says, "Then we went on a wee bit of a run."

In the press the next day, both Docherty and Stepney were cautiously optimistic. "I reckon that if you reach 36 points you are able to sit back and smile," said Docherty. "That means seven points from our remaining games. I think it will go right to the end of the season. We just have to keep battling away. It is never too late until statistics prove you wrong." "It could be too late," Stepney said, but he struck a note of optimism gained from his perspective at the back of the pitch: "... suddenly the lads are starting to play for each other. There is a chance. They are talking on the field, shouting to each other. Helping each other." Stepney said that some of the new signings had seemed overawed by the situation and by Manchester United, singling out Gerry Daly and Alex Forsyth as men who had taken an inordinately long time to settle down in the red shirt. Even more caustically, he said, "Sometimes I thought some of the younger players were more interested in their own personal problems – like playing for Scotland – than they were about the club." It being the case that United's squad was at the time packed to the gills with Scottish internationals, and not knowing what this elder statesman's criterion is for "younger", it's difficult to know who Stepney is talking about here, but few could dispute his right to state his opinion, it being the case that he had a virtually blot-free copybook by dint of the extraordinary few number of goals he had let in this season. "It's no good arguing that going down could be a blessing," he also said. "Every footballer wants to play in the First Division." Daly, incidentally, rejects Stepney's criticism: "What was I? 18, 19 years of age. If you're at a big club like Manchester United for God's sake, if you can get into the first team after what, six months or a year, you're not doing badly are you?"

The first of two fixtures United were due to play against Everton in the space of eight days took place on April 15. The side was unchanged except for the replacement of Forsyth by Young. A massive Old Trafford crowd for a Monday night of 48,424 were treated to United's most comprehensive victory of the season, an absolute rout that ended 3-0, but could easily have been five or six. McCalliog was always looking for the ball and scored twice, the first a wonderful free-kick that curved over Everton's wall. Sandwiched between the new boy's brace was one from Houston. The Six Million Dollar Man (also nicknamed Superman by his colleagues) used his height to head in a faultlessly flighted Morgan free-kick. The Stretford End thundered "Super-reds!" United were now in 20th position. They had scored 12 and conceded just four in five matches, amassing nine out of a possible 10 points. Had they played this way from the start, they would literally have been championship contenders.

An unchanged United visited the Dell on Saturday April 20. Southampton were just one place above United after the Everton result, so this was yet another clash with much at stake for both teams. Against all expectations, though, the diminishing number of fixtures and hence opportunities for salvation did not produce a nasty spectacle, even if this was not exactly a classic match. United played simple, tidy football and used space intelligently against a Southampton side that, though they had the exciting figure of Mick Channon tearing forward whenever humanly possible, was shambolic defensively.

United went ahead with a penalty conceded after Southampton keeper Martin rushed out of goal to bring down McIlroy with a tackle more suited to a rugby field. Instead of Stepney making the plod down from the opposite end, McCalliog stepped up. Although this was one of the jobs he had had at Wolves, he explains that it was a role rather thrust on him today: "Willie Morgan was a pal of mine before I went to Man U because we met on the Scotland round-the-world tour. I went to Willie's wedding. We were on the coach going to the Southampton game. I said, 'Who takes the penalties, anyway?' and Willie says, 'Oh, I'll take them.' When we got the penalty, all I could feel was this hand on my back saying, 'Go on Jim, you can do it' and it was Willie. I thought, 'Thanks very much, mate. That's really nice of you. You told me on the bus that I wouldn't be taking them 'cos I'd just arrived and then you drop me in it.' Maybe a wee attack of nerves. But it was never a problem for me taking penalties. I remember thinking, 'Christ, this could be one of the most important ever.' I just strode up. I used to always run up and do a wee stop and then I used to place them in the corners." McCalliog converted successfully.

The irrepressible Channon scored for the home side. A 1-1 draw after the euphoria of Monday may have been a mild disappointment for the Reds in the 30,789 crowd – especially as United dropped a place – but at least these days they had no need to be ashamed of their team. To quote from David Lacey's match report, "Manchester United are playing with much more composure now. Their football still has little of the individual excellence or the emotive, surging movement of previous Old Trafford teams, but at least they have shed, for good one hopes, the dour, desperate image which was so tarnishing the club's reputation."

There were now three games to go, away fixtures at Everton and Stoke sandwiching a local derby at Old Trafford. There were endless permutations of outcome to be deduced from those matches. United had a game in hand over three of the other clubs in the bottom six, and two games in hand over the other two. They were on 32 points. Norwich, below them, had 29. Birmingham, above them, had 33. Southampton, in 19th place, had 34 points and had played 40 games to United's 39. West Ham were 18th and had amassed 36 points in their 41 fixtures. One above the Hammers, Coventry had obtained 37 from 41. One of the campaign's final matches would be Norwich against Birmingham, which was not merely a four-pointer, but a match the consequence of whose result could ripple out in various ways for other teams, including United. Head-spinning mathematics aren't for many in a game in which the instinct is to do, not to contemplate. Docherty would appear to have decided to just thrust such numerical ponderings aside and concentrate on things that he – to a certain extent – could control. He predicted that United would "murder" Everton on Tuesday April 23 in the sequel to the April 15 match that had done so much to lift Old Trafford spirits.

Forsyth replaced Young for said visit to Goodison Park, a solitary switch from both the last game and the previous Everton encounter. Mysteriously, though, it was the other 10 players who seemed to have been replaced, substituted for imposters without any of the fighting spirit they had shown over the last few giddy weeks. Still, common-sense dictated that a relegation-threatened team were hardly going to sustain for too long a run in which they more closely resembled champions. Additionally, Everton had only incurred one home defeat in the League in this campaign. A crowd of 46,093 packed into the ground, but the high drama they might have been expecting was rarely to be seen. Stepney, Forsyth, Houston, Buchan and Greenhoff all played well for United, but the defence had never been the problem with the club in this campaign. Once again, the forwards – so admirable over the past few games – did not create or finish well enough. Experience had taught United this season that on the rare occasions when Morgan wasn't on song, the whole team suffered from the consequent loss of width and penetration and, unfortunately, today Morgan was being contained by Bernard, and – when he switched wings – Sergeant. In the 46th minute, the doubtful nature of the benefits of Holton's presence in United's ranks was raised yet again when – for the umpteenth time since he had joined the club – one of his infringements led to a goal, this time by Lyons.

For McCalliog, the fixture left a sour taste in the mouth above and beyond the disaster of the 1-0 scoreline. "They gave out scores over the Tannoy," he says. "I thought that was a wee bit classless. It come over just before the end of the game and it kind of rubbed it in a bit. I don't think it demoralized us but it was so unusual to hear an announcement while the game was on unless it was somebody perhaps had been hospitalised or a kid was missing." One of said scores was that of the Birmingham-QPR match taking place that day. To add to the blow of United's loss, they learned that, against all the odds, Birmingham had beaten QPR, which meant that the Blues now had three points more than they. It didn't take an Einstein to realise that the Reds, no matter how well they did in their remaining two fixtures, had been left at the mercy of other results, particularly the Norwich-Birmingham encounter on Saturday.

\*\*\*

On that last Saturday of the season – April 27 – Manchester United met Manchester City at Old Trafford. Poetry, irony and potential drama abounded. The possibility of City sending their local rivals down was, of course, part of the intoxicating mix. Another part of it was that the City player who might conceivably achieve that was Denis Law, who had enjoyed an Indian summer this season. Almost as if exulting in that drama, City manager Tony Book made Law his club's captain for the match. The King was given a warm welcome by many Reds in the 56,996 crowd, with some even chanting "Give us a goal!"

Should Norwich beat Birmingham today at the same time as United took the maximum two points from their game, then the Reds stood a good chance of staying up, something that could be confirmed with their match against Stoke on Monday. City meanwhile had no particular stake in the match against United – apart from the considerable stake that is the pride of winning a derby. Despite their taking part in the League Cup final, City were not necessarily a tough prospect. They had had a poor season in the League, with manager Ron Saunders being sacked with four games remaining. Under new manager Book, they had only secured their First Division status for the following season in their previous fixture.

"You're always hopeful when you play football right to the final nail in the coffin," says McIlroy of the United team's state of mind that day. "Manchester City weren't going to do us any favours. They had decent players: Bell, Doyle and all these people who loved beating Manchester United. So it was an uphill task, but you go out on that field thinking, 'Maybe there's a miracle there that might happen today'." Buchan says at no point in the season had he resigned himself to relegation: "I probably felt we'd scrape out of it like we did in the previous season. I never gave up hope." Surprisingly, Docherty retained the same team as for the Everton match, perhaps concluding that it was the opposition that had played well rather than United badly, or maybe even weary of the endless reshuffling and changing of the team that had characterised his *modus operandi* this season.

"Everything seemed to be a bit of a blur on that particular day," recalls Daly. Unlike in the Everton away fixture, United played like what they were, a team fighting for their very First Division lives. This time though, there was little of the nastiness of that last tumultuous local derby. McCalliog came close to scoring when Morgan magicked his way past two defenders (a common sight today) and centered, but City's keeper Joe Corrigan swooped it off the United man's head. On 13 minutes, Corrigan was less assured as a corner by Morgan found McIlroy on the far post. McIlroy lofted the ball back across the penalty area. Corrigan went for the ball, but dropped it. McCalliog was standing in attendance and headed toward the net, but as the United fans were throwing their arms aloft, Donachie headed off the line. Shortly, Corrigan was clumsy again when Macari fired a shot at goal, but gathered himself – and the ball – just as Daly came tearing in. Not that it was all one way: Stepney had had to use all his agility to pluck a fiendish cross by Summerbee out of the air. City's attacks increased, with Booth heading over the bar and Oakes shooting the wrong side of a post.

As United tussled with their local rivals, they and their fans were keen to hear about what was happening at Birmingham's ground. The news filtering through was good: Norwich had taken the lead. There was everything for United to play for. Unfortunately, Birmingham equalised and then went ahead before half-time. Nonetheless, when the teams trooped back out for the second half, United were not buried. If they could use their home advantage to beat City and if Norwich could score again and deny Birmingham at least a point, they could still ensure First Division safety with the Stoke game.

Four minutes into the second half, a shot by McIlroy was heading toward goal with Corrigan not in attendance. Agonisingly, Barrett was there to block the effort. United kept plugging away for a goal without success, but were at least managing not to concede one. That is until seven minutes from time, at which point Booth cut diagonally and to the right across the United penalty area. Denis Law had been moving into the United box. As he did so, he looked as eager as any striker would at the opposition's end. This was given the lie by what happened next. Booth side-footed the ball back across the goalmouth. Law, standing with his back to goal right on the six-yard line, stabbed at it with his right heel. Stepney was so bamboozled by the action that he remained frozen to the spot as the ball shot over the line. Forsyth: "I'll never forget, Denis just backheeled it as if to say, 'Well, I don't know where that ball's going', and it ended up in the back of the net. I was right beside it." Houston: "I think all of the defence was to be aware of him on that particular game. There was no specific marker. If you see it again, it's just a bit of genius from Denis."

The United defenders turned away from the goal, their body language indicating disgust or despair or both. What was remarkable about the tableau was that Law's body language was indistinguishable from theirs. The man who had single-handedly turned the celebration of a goal on a soccer pitch from a matter of a sober handshake to air-punching triumphalism did not rejoice in his strike in any way. As he realised what he had done, he froze, his mouth open in horror. He turned away. His team-mates congregated around him to congratulate him. He did not throw his arms around any of them, nor smile, but instead, looking shell-shocked, his shoulders slumped, walked slowly back to his own half. Team-mate Colin Bell, clearly puzzled, affectionately slapped his face twice. It brought no reaction. When City full-back Colin Barrett flung his arms around him, Law's response can only be described as passively weathering it.

Like Houston above, commentators would say afterwards that the goal resulted from a typical piece of Law impudence or improvisation, that it demonstrated his intact goalscoring genius. Others were, and are, not so sure. Goalscoring genius Law may still have been, but that kind of subtlety was not the sort of thing with which soccer crowds associated him. His penchant was for the empathic. A backheel was a curious thing to do for a man whose wont was to dramatically swing a leg and send the ball crashing into the net or to leap in the air and perform a scissor kick with his back to goal. It was this very uncharacteristicness that made some suspect that that backheel had in fact been a deliberate attempt to not score while giving the impression that he was at least trying to do his job. Further ammunition for this suspicion was provided not just by Law's crestfallen reaction, but by the fact that he subsequently admitted he had not wanted to play in the match. Daly says, "I wasn't too far away. I don't think he wanted to score. It was the way he done it and his reaction afterwards." To be clear, did he think that he was trying deliberately not to score? Daly: "That's the honest impression that I got."

Law, though, has never said that he deliberately didn't try to score and maintained his story long past the point where he had anything to lose – and perhaps something to gain in terms of greater book sales – by saying otherwise. In his *An Autobiography*, (1979) he said, "It was really no more than a reflex action which made me flick out my heel as it went past. I didn't realise until I saw the incident on television film, years later, how close I had been standing to the centre of the goalmouth." Law also said that more often than not he would have failed to make contact in such a situation. In his second autobiography, *The King* (2003), although he admitted he had been half-hoping that the match would end as a draw, he basically said the same thing about the goal. However, if one reads his comments carefully, it is noticeable that they don't actually quite deny that he was trying to miss.

Meek dismisses ideas that Law was trying to miss: "There weren't any thought processes by Denis: 'Oops, if I score it might send United down.' It was just an instinctive striker's reaction." Houston agrees: "At the end of the day he had to do what he had to do, otherwise it becomes a question why he's on the team. He obviously didn't enjoy doing what he did, but he had to do it as a professional." Peter Fletcher – who had graduated from child fan of Law (he had gripped his sleeves in his palms in emulation of Law in schoolyard matches) to colleague – also finds it difficult to believe the intended-to-miss idea. Fletcher: "I don't think it was in his make-up. Denis Law back-headed goals. I've seen Denis Law put goals in [with] his backside. Denis Law would have shot his granny to have scored in a game. That's why Denis Law was the top of the tree." Offers McCalliog, "Denis wasn't always flash. He could do that kind of thing."

Intended or not, the goal that sent such a sick feeling into Law's stomach was to be his last kick in club football. He was substituted immediately afterwards, and confusion and competing theories rage even over that. Docherty's then-wife Agnes was of the opinion that the change was made to prevent Law flicking a V-sign at his hated former manager. Daly offers, "I think he walked off the pitch. I think they wanted him to stay on, but I don't think Law wanted to stay on. He was so gutted about it. I can vaguely remember that they were waving from the bench, sort of saying, 'Stay on, stay on', and he wouldn't have any of it." Law though said, "Tony Book beckoned me off for my own safety." The reason the City manager had cause to be concerned about Law's safety was the pitch invasion that immediately followed the goal.

"I didn't really feel in any danger," says Buchan of suddenly being surrounded by supporters. "It was quite a common occurrence in those days, folk coming on the pitch." The police were clearly more agitated. Recalls Mick Martin, "I was on the substitute's bench and I was coming off the bench. The chief inspector had his baton out and he hit me with his baton because he thought I was one of the supporters! He tried to pull me back and hit me across the legs with it. I went, 'Hold on a minute' and he realised who I was then. He went, 'Oh, sorry about that'." The police managed to clear the pitch and play was resumed for another four minutes, but once again, the Red hordes took to the field and the referee felt compelled to usher everybody back to the dressing rooms again. This time, the crowd remained rooted. Matt Busby pleaded with them to vacate the pitch over the ground's public address system, but was largely ignored.

Just as the pitch invasion that attended Ronnie Radford's giant-killing Exocet shot for Hereford United against Newcastle United in the FA Cup third round in 1972 freezes for eternity fashions of the day – almost without exception, all the kids who erupted from the terraces were dressed in the original green parka coats with red linings – so the United v City pitch invasion amusingly captures sartorial youth concerns of its era: pictures of the incident feature boys (no girls) with shoulder-length hair with centre partings and feather cuts, red-and-white scarves tied around wrists (not a replica shirt in sight) and Oxford Bag trousers, also known as Birmingham Baggies but a hilarious flared, ridiculously low-pocketed and wide-waistbanded creation by any name. Those teens looked cool then, though, and perhaps it was just a desire to look cool – or hard – that motivated the pitch invasion, rather than an intention to cause the match's abandonment and hence ensure the score was struck from the records, thus gaining their team another chance to stay up.

It has always been assumed the latter was the cause, but even in the distant days of 1974, a means by which supporters on the terraces could keep track of the results elsewhere – transistor radios – existed. The fans with their ears pressed to their 'trannies' were perfectly *au fait* with the fact that likely defeat by City looked like being rendered irrelevant by the fact that Birmingham were beating Norwich (and Southampton beating Everton). (The players on the pitch also vaguely knew what was going on elsewhere. Buchan: "We sensed from the crowd that things weren't going well for us." Greenhoff agrees: "We guessed. You sort of know.") It should also be pointed out that there wasn't one pitch invasion that day, but four. Two occurred before kick-off, and there were still some kids on the pitch when the two teams came out. Added to this is the fact that by then it was a tradition at Old Trafford for supporters to swarm onto the pitch on the day of the last home game of the season, even if the custom was to wait until after the final whistle. With both the season and United's Division One status now apparently dead and buried, perhaps the supporters had simply decided that there was no reason to wait until full-time to take to the pitch again.

Referee Dave Smith – who may or may not have known that Joe Corrigan had been the target of missiles, including bottles, a dart and a smoke bomb – told both managers that he felt it would be unsafe to resume play. The match was formally abandoned. McCalliog: "I was quite shocked that the game never carried on. I couldnae understand that. Maybe we felt a wee bit cheated. If we'd have got a wee bit more time, you don't know, we might have gone up there and got another one." Getting another one, though, would have – it transpired – been futile. The fact that Birmingham beat Norwich 2-1 meant that United were definitely down. This was the final, most sick-making irony of the day: as Docherty later pointed out, even if United had won 10-0, they would have still been doomed. Upon finding that out, Denis Law probably didn't know whether to laugh or cry. Interestingly, whatever emotion he was feeling after the match, he was feeling it in United's dressing room, not City's. McCalliog: "When the game finished and I walked into our dressing room, who was in the corner? Denis, in his blue and white shirt. Denis was sat in the corner with his head in his hands."

Docherty – a man to whom dignity was not a word that easily attached – was unquestionably dignified on a day on which he must have been devastated beyond words. He ensured that champagne was delivered to the City dressing room and gave himself uncomplainingly to every one of the reporters clamouring for his post-match analysis. Only once did the façade of composure crack, when, bombarded with competing demands, he said, "Fellas, I can't tear myself in two." Docherty found himself not just having to field the usual questions about the match, but about facing life in the Second Division, about the transfer of Law coming back to haunt him and about the hooligan element who had provided an awful denouement to an already grim day.

The Football League subsequently ordered that the score before the referee finally gave up that day must stand. Considering the ramifications of the Birmingham-Norwich result, realistically few (least of all United) were going to want the Football League to order a replay. However, the order to let the score stand gave the football authorities the opportunity to flex their muscles and indulge in an ostentatious display of their determination that Hooliganism Must Not Prevail, something they may have been itching to do since March when an FA Cup tie between Newcastle United and Nottingham Forest was replayed from scratch following similar crowd troubles.

"I feel sick about it all," was Law's only comment to the press after the match. It was a terrible way for anyone to conclude his club career. At least Law could take some kind of consolation from the fact of his Wembley appearance earlier that year and acquire more with the remaining, non-club, matches it turned out he did have ahead of him. In March, he had been part of the City team that reached the League Cup final. Although City lost 2-1 to Wolves, it was entirely appropriate that a magnificent footballer like Law should play on the biggest soccer stage in Britain in his last season. It was also fitting that he should be selected for Scotland's trip to the World Cup finals. (He turned out for Scotland in the Home Championship beforehand.) He would only play one game in the German tournament and some suspect that even that was a sentimental gesture by the Scotland manager. Nobody though would begrudge the fact if this was indeed largesse on the part of Willie Ormond: as a footballer and as a person, Law was universally loved.

Following the devastating events of Saturday, there was one more insult that fate had to add to the Reds' collective injury. Rather than being able to crawl away and lick their wounds, United were required to drag their bodies to Stoke the following Monday, April 29, to fulfil their last fixture. For United, the match was utterly meaningless, not even possessing the opportunity to put on a show for their fans that a home fixture would offer. Stoke, though, had plenty to play for in the shape of a place in the following season's UEFA Cup. They were currently enjoying their highest League placing for nearly three decades, largely through the efforts of their maverick midfield maestro Alan Hudson, whom Tommy Docherty had nurtured as a youth at Chelsea but never gotten the chance to field.

"I've absolutely no memory of that match whatsoever," says Buchan. Few do. Amongst the minority who recall it is McCalliog, who says, "There's nothing you can do. You're professional. You're paid to play, so you got on with the game. The one thing that I can always recall about The Doc, although we went down, he didnae change his tune. He kept going and kept trying to be happy and cheerful with the guys. He still went though the same motions on the Stoke game he always did." The authorities were taking no chances today after the events of the weekend, with 250 policemen on duty, but the worst they had to deal with from the 27,392 crowd was a few fires on the terraces. Daly was replaced by Martin, but United were otherwise unchanged. On the first occasion on which Brian Greenhoff had faced his brother in competitive football, Docherty made him captain for the day. Jimmy was Stoke's skipper. Greenhoff: "Because the referee was Keith Stiles. He's from Barnsley, so I think Keith Stiles asked him 'cos I think he wanted a photo for his album." That Docherty should engineer the sight of the two Greenhoffs tossing up in the centre-circle before kick-off was an act of sentimentality that would have been in keeping with the feelings of the boys' mother but was hardly the sort of gesture for which The Doc had become known, yet as has been shown before, and as would be seen again, when the circumstances were right (a definition for which only Docherty knew, but you can hazard a guess that it did not involve a player who he felt was a declining force), The Doc could show Disney-level slushiness. "I know first-hand how nice a fella he can be," says Greenhoff. "He has a lot to say and he's quite vocal about it, but with his players I think he was very loyal." As for the match at hand, Greenhoff points out that there was a reason for it being an even more grisly experience than the futility of a meaningless fixture: the glee taken by the opposition supporters at how the mighty Manchester United had fallen. "It wasn't nice because you knew what was going to happen: Stoke fans are going to take the mickey all game."

Stoke dominated the match, though with one exception failed to translate their domination into goals courtesy of the good defending that had been United's saving grace all season. It was United's third 1-0 loss in a row. For the record, Stoke did indeed make it into the UEFA Cup. Manchester United finished 21st in the First Division table (where they had been after the City game), with a final tally of 32 points, generated by 10 wins, 12 draws and 20 losses. The contrast between their home and away form was demonstrated by the fact that there was a perfect symmetry to their results at Old Trafford: home wins, draws and losses were split evenly at seven apiece. Away, they had lost 13 and won just three. Going down with United were Southampton and bottom-placed Norwich City. Leeds United were the season's champions.

It is a football commentator's cliché that a side are in trouble if they are leaking goals. The fallacy of that received wisdom was illustrated by United's record this season, for the chief irony of United's relegation was the fact that their defence was actually one of the best in the First Division. They let in 48 League goals. This was 10 fewer than Ipswich, who wound up only just outside the top three. An interesting fact is that only twice before in the previous 23 years had United conceded fewer goals: seasons 64/65 and 66/67. They won the championship both times. Of course the crucial difference is that Ipswich scored 67 league goals in the 73/74 season. United managed 38. Their miserable scoring record was underlined by the fact that McIlroy was the club's top League scorer on a meagre six goals. (Macari got five in the League, six in all competitions.) "It wasn't through want of trying," says Buchan, refusing to blame his attacking colleagues for failing to do their job as well as the defence had undeniably done theirs. "It's a collective thing. You defend as a team and you attack as a team. That's the way I was brought up in the game."

***

For Willie Morgan, what made relegation particularly upsetting was that United's run of good form in the closing weeks of the season had meant that he had begun to dare to believe that they could beat the drop that had long seemed inevitable. When the fightback began, Morgan was "reconciled" to going down, but United's rediscovery of the habits of both scoring and winning meant that, "I thought the impossible was going to happen. But in the end we just couldn't make it and it was heart-breaking."

Matt Busby was also devastated, the hurt audible in his voice even in cold print as he pointed out, "In all my 40 years as player, manager and director, I've never been in the Second Division. It's a terrible disappointment. I can't tell you how much of a loss I feel, what it means to me and everyone in the club." Another Old Trafford legend threw in his two-penn'orth. Said Bobby Charlton, "It really hurts me to admit it, but it's not a shock. I've seen it coming for the last five or six years ... Highly talented players were not being replaced. I don't mean by buying – by breeding." Docherty blamed himself. Speaking in 1976, by which time he had turned attacking into a permanent philosophy, he observed that he had wrongly stuck to the defensive approach that had saved United from relegation the previous season. "Everything was geared for safety rather than gambling on attack," he lamented. "By the time I realised what was happening, it was too late. We were virtually down ... but once I changed the policy we had a tremendous run. We almost avoided the drop."

Many people were now expecting Docherty to be dismissed, not least – by his own admission, and apparently despite the assurances Agnes Docherty said were given him by Busby after the Derby County home fixture – Docherty himself. As the man who had become infamous for taking the mighty Manchester United down into Division Two, employment prospects for The Doc would not exactly be looking rosy should that happen. Considering that Docherty had given up the Scotland manager's job, and thereby participation in the World Cup finals that summer, to come to Manchester, it's little wonder that Docherty has admitted to feeling like an empty shell after the City game.

Yet Docherty kept his job, despite the previous dismissals of McGuinness and O'Farrell, neither of whom had presided over United dropping into the Second Division. No doubt McGuinness and O'Farrell felt to some extent aggrieved that they did not have such ostentatious faith shown in them by the United board in far less grievous circumstances. O'Farrell later observed, "Tommy Docherty was brought in to put things right ... Yet after 18 months, the same time I'd been allowed, United were relegated." Reasons David Meek, "They couldn't go on sacking managers every 18 months. It would have been ludicrous. Wilf got 18 months, O'Farrell got 18 months and it was obvious that the club were in poor shape and even the board accepted it was futile to keep sacking the manager. They'd got to stick with somebody and get on with it."

Docherty has said that Busby had, when offering him the United job in the first place, likened the long, mammoth task of reviving United's fortunes to turning around an oil tanker. After the relegation, Docherty says that Busby said to him, "I knew it would take time, so we are going to give you the time." Edwards and Busby indicated that support for him on the board was unanimous. In addition to – or intertwined with – this is the possibility that United may have wanted to sack Docherty but didn't feel they could afford to, because of the humiliation involved in their judgement of manager being effectively self-declared as wrong for the third time in less than four years and/or the financial cost of breaking Docherty's contract.

Forsyth was one of several signings attracted to Old Trafford by the allure of the club's name, an allure that was not consistent with playing Second Division football. Asked if the events made him think he had made an unwise choice, he says, "Never, ever one moment in my life did I ever regret going there." However, there was no disguising the magnitude of what had happened. "It was a catastrophe we went down," states Blunstone. McIlroy felt this as much as anyone, having been at Old Trafford since he was a boy and the club were the holders of the European Cup. "It was a feeling of numbness right round the place," he recalls. "But to be fair to Tommy Docherty, he was very, very upset as well, when we got relegated. I could see the determination in him, that if there was anyone going to get Manchester United back it would be Tommy Docherty."

# PART THREE

# 1974/75: Resurrection

**D**ocherty may have been devastated by relegation but he wasn't paralysed by it. Within days of realising the club were doomed to be spending the next season in Division Two, he was moving to obtain the on-field wherewithal to ensure they had a good chance of bouncing straight back up.

This did not involve casting around for defenders, as United's goals-against record in the relegation season proved none were needed. In the mission of obtaining a better goals-for, Docherty had had his eyes on three men: Mick Channon of Southampton, Duncan McKenzie of Nottingham Forest and Hull City's Stuart Pearson. Of the three, Pearson was perhaps the one whose arrival at Old Trafford was the least expected. McKenzie ended up at Leeds United, while Channon remained at Southampton, where he would later play a part in a grim day for Docherty's United. Both men's names were well-known. Pearson's was not quite in that category, although his strike rate for Hull – 31 goals in 67 matches – was certainly attention-grabbing.

Docherty knew the player already from his days as assistant manager at Hull. That club's loss of key striker Chris Chilton to Coventry City in August 1971 had occasioned some worry but a flurry of three goals in three games by Pearson – so long the centre-forward's understudy – led Docherty to declare, "We are not going to miss Chilton, even though he is a great player. We expect Pearson to be better. I have had a lot of great players under my wing, including Peter Osgood, and this lad Pearson will stand alongside them all one day. He goes out and runs like he never wants to stop. He will be the answer to our goalscoring worries." Cavanagh, of course, had also been at Hull, and more recently than The Doc. As Pearson began making his name there – joint top scorer in his first full season and selected for the England Under-23 squad – Cavanagh responded with a bit of banter that perhaps came easier to the rough-and-ready coach than praise. He told Pearson it was about time he got a hat-trick and said he would buy him a shirt if he did so. The comment came immediately before Hull beat Portsmouth 5-1. Pearson scored four.

Not long before Docherty swooped for Pearson, the striker was led to believe he was on his way to Maine Road. But a deal with United's great rivals – with a transfer fee of £200,000 agreed – was cancelled when a dependent transfer of Mike Summerbee to Leeds fell through. Pearson had been all psyched up for his move to a big club and was heartbroken by the turn of events. "I felt I was back to square one," he later said. Pearson did his best to put it out of his mind and concentrate on the job at hand at Hull. When he was told to meet Hull manager Terry Neill in London on the eve of the 1974 FA Cup final, Pearson assumed that a club in the capital had made a bid for him. This wasn't too logical, as many club representatives would have been in London for the Wembley match. He claimed that when it transpired that the club who wanted him were newly relegated Manchester United, he wasn't at all disappointed, as he considered them, "the greatest club in the country". Docherty said, "I have known for some time that I needed a striker but the right men just were not available. When the season ended I spoke to Terry and he told me to put in an offer. I am confident that this is the young man who will get us the goals."

Notwithstanding Docherty's canny raiding of the Irish league for undiscovered talent, a modest club like Hull was not exactly the sort of place at which Docherty had become known for splashing out transfer money. This, however, would set a precedent for the way Docherty would predominately operate when strengthening the team for the remainder of his time at United. Though this was originally born out of necessity – with United now nursing a £300,000 overdraft, the coffers were running as close to the status of empty as it's possible to be for a club with a huge box-office appeal and therefore a stream of guaranteed income – it soon became Docherty's preferred policy. To some extent this would create a greater intensity of loyalty amongst the already fanatical Old Trafford faithful, for an unforeseen by-product of The Doc's looking to the lower divisions for new talent was that in this era the United fans rarely experienced the awkwardness that comes with finding one is now expected to cheer players one had despised hitherto. When Docherty bought now, in almost all cases it was someone who the fans had barely – sometimes never – heard of.

Stuart Pearson was born on June 21 1949 in Hull. Apart from his first season with the Reds, he would not actually replicate his virtual one-in-two Hull strike-rate for Docherty, but this didn't actually turn out to matter in the long term, partly because the team Docherty continued to build from here had goalscoring ability across the board, partly because of how unusually multi-faceted Pearson was for a striker. Pearson had a powerful shot in both feet and the confidence to use such even when the angle was acute. Though only 5'10", he punched well above his weight. Not only was he muscular and sturdy and therefore well equipped to ride hard tackles and brush past attempts at body-checking, he also had a quality about him that Docherty was not alone in comparing with a similar attribute possessed by Denis Law in his prime. Just as footage of Law reveals he had an emphatic quality about him, so too Pearson seemed to do things with an *umph*, bustling and bristling in his movement and celebrating his goals by shaking his fist at the crowd at shoulder level in way that seemed deliberately designed to show off a healthy-looking bicep. Recalls McIlroy, "He took a hell of a lot of stick Stuart. A lot of people didn't know he worked on telegraph poles before he played football and he wasn't like the tallest of players, but he was built up." Martin: "He was a very good player. He struggled all through his career with injuries but he was strong. Good finisher. He wasn't a prolific goalscorer but a good player." Though he may not have been prolific by Martin's definition, Greenhoff seems to feel he was prolific enough: "We needed a centre-forward desperate to score goals. Stuart Pearson was perfect. It took a lot of pressure off people like Sammy."

Yet though Pearson was a rampaging figure and though his nickname of 'Pancho' was a bastardisation of 'Puncho' and therefore a reference to his physical nature, he was far from a traditional unsubtle English centre-forward. "His touch was unreal," says McIlroy. "We had this understanding, I knew when the ball used to come to Stuart, he would lay it off first time. He wasn't really known as that sort of touch player."

Pearson cost United £167,000 plus a player, namely Peter Fletcher, whose makeweight value was deemed to be £33,000. Fletcher was one of those players who experienced the barely imaginable thrill of being snapped up by mighty Manchester United as a boy but then had to endure a slow deflation of expectation and excitement. He didn't make his full debut until February 1974 after a substitute appearance the previous season but though it was Docherty who had given him that debut (and indeed a total of seven games, albeit five of them as substitute), within three months of that full debut The Doc was dispensing with his services. Those who saw Fletcher's appearances with United are of the opinion that he was a striker with potential and touches of skill. To be fair, however, though Fletcher subsequently had a respectable career, it was outside the top flight. "It was a big shock for me leaving the club,"

Fletcher admits. "You think you're going to go there right through the rest of your life." It wasn't just the fact of leaving but the manner in which it was done that upset him. "I don't think he had any other way," he says when asked if Docherty's manner was nasty. "That's how he was. Very blasé and spoke what he thought." He explains, "I had a year on my contract left and was told, 'You won't get any chances. You'll be played in the 'B' teams and 'A' team, and you'll languish more or less at that standard.' I was young. You didn't have anybody who could talk for you. There was no agents then or anything. That was the big thing. You had nobody to back you up. I only had my father and he just [did it] for the love of the game. He didn't know anything on that side of it about making money or you should be playing or stay for another year and try and fight your place out. You weren't wanted and that was it."

Though Pearson's arrival brought unhappiness for Fletcher, it was an important factor in the decision by Jim McCalliog to remain with the club. At the end of the 1973/74 season, the prospect of life in the Second Division did not appeal to him. "I went in and talked to the boss about it," McCalliog recalls. "I think that was the only time other than when I signed for Man U that I ever went in his office. I said, 'I'm going to think about this.' So he said, 'Okay fair enough, but I want you to stay here and there's no doubt about it, we'll come flying back next year.' I had the summer to think about it." By the time the next season rolled around, McCalliog had decided that he could bear Division Two: "We'd got Stuart Pearson in. We had a good young side. I thought there was quality in there. There was a good atmosphere when we went back to training. He was buzzing was The Doc, you could feel it. We went on a pre-season tour and everything was fine and I knew we were going to have a good season." Not necessarily related to his decision to stay, McCalliog had also been impressed by United's treatment of their players immediately following relegation: "The club showed to me how big they were and why they're the best. When the season had finished we went to [Spain]. It was just a week where everybody got a wee think about what had happened, because obviously when you're at home they've got families and different things and what have you. I thought that was fantastic because usually if you go down nobody's got the presence of mind to think, 'We'll go away, we'll get a bonding together and then we'll go for it next year'."

Also deemed superfluous to requirements at the end of the 1973/74 season were a trio who, respectively, were a pre-Docherty signing given his first game under The Doc, a big-money Docherty signing and an Old Trafford legend: Trevor Anderson, George Graham and Brian Kidd.

Though Anderson had earned his first international cap in the 1973/74 season, just one goal in 11 starts clearly made Docherty feel he could find somebody better, though some would cite Anderson as yet another *in situ* player about whom Docherty seemed to make up his mind before really giving him a chance. Anderson was sold to Swindon Town for £25,000 in November 1974. George Graham, meanwhile, was still declining to make a transfer request, so Docherty had no option but to keep him on the books, if not in the team.

Whereas most United fans could easily live with the jettisoning of Anderson and Graham, the departure of Kiddo was a different matter. Docherty had ostentatiously shown faith in the European Cup-winning veteran in the 1972/73 season and Kidd had been as effusive in his thanks as Docherty was in his praise for his neglected abilities. Kidd, however, morphed into yet another player whose effusions over Docherty became a hostage to fortune or a way to mock him in light of the way things subsequently developed. The four goals Kidd had netted in 16 weeks in his euphoria over the way he had been brought "back from the dead" by the newly installed manager was actually double the total that Kidd managed the following season in the course of no fewer than 23 starts and one substitute appearance. Both of those goals came in the home win against West Ham. As that match also saw the final top-flight goal ever scored by Ian Storey-Moore, it could be said to constitute a last hurrah for both players. The closing of Storey-Moore's scoring account, however, was due to his sad injury-enforced retirement. Kidd was still only 25 years old and as fit as the proverbial fiddle. Arsenal bought Kidd for a purported £85,000 (with some estimates as high as £110,000) in August 1974.

Docherty seemed slightly bewildered by the turn of events. "Brian Kidd should be in the England team," he said. "I should be picking up the phone saying ... there is not enough money in the game to buy him ... He is a player who has everything ... Brian shouldn't be challenging for a place ... He should be commanding one." Asked to explain why it was all couldas and shouldas with Kiddo, Docherty once again demonstrated a capacity for sharp analysis that has always marked his managerial career, even if that analytical brain hasn't always led to correspondingly rational decisions. Docherty stated that Kidd had strength, speed, skill and strong shooting skills but was weak in applying those abilities in a match. Docherty's frustration seemed to spill over when he said, "You have to motivate Brian, but there comes a stage when he should be doing that himself." Another possibility Docherty mentioned was that Kidd might have been spoiled by being nurtured in a team of superstars. Surrounded by men of the capability of Law, Best, Charlton and others, Kidd did not get the proper grounding in working hard that can come from compensating for deficiencies in those around him.

Kidd – born on May 29 1949 – hailed from nearby Collyhurst. Mick Martin, who was close to Kidd and his family, says, "I don't think Brian Kidd was all that keen to go to Arsenal ... He was a Manchester lad through and through with a great affinity and love for Manchester

United." McIlroy later opined that Kidd's departure from Old Trafford must have been one of the worst moments of his life. He now says, "Brian Kidd's been a fantastic player. I came through with Brian Kidd. Every manager has his opinion on players and it was a bit of a shock when Brian was transferred. Managers make these decisions and some work and some don't but Brian went on to still have a fantastic career." Indeed. Just as Denis Law seemed a man reborn at Maine Road, so Kidd found at Highbury the new lease of life he had mistakenly thought Docherty had conferred on him. Sporting a new, fashionable perm, he scored 30 goals in 77 League appearances for the Gunners. Though a certain restlessness seemed to mark the rest of his career – he played for Arsenal, Manchester City, Everton and Bolton Wanderers in the space of eight years, before (as many players did in those days) getting his pension by playing in America – he kept up a respectable goals-per-game ratio.

Some were shocked, many dismayed, at the departure of Kidd. His subsequent success begs the question of whether Docherty was wrong to let him go. An analysis of the situation would have to conclude that he wasn't. When the local lad made his way down to the metropolis, he left behind a scoring record of 70 goals in 264 games, or in other words just under one goal in four games. Ostensibly, those stats are just about respectable for a man whose main job it is to hit the net. But that's an averaged statistic ranging across the entirety of his United career. His ratio in the 1973/74 season – or that part of it in which he participated – was one in 12. Furthermore, he was playing in a side in which scoring was at a premium. We'll never know what went on behind the scenes between Kidd and Docherty and whether there was a personal or even psychological reason for Kidd not performing well under Docherty (in footballer's parlance, not going out and playing for the boss), and that being the case we can only judge things on bald statistics. Ditto for Docherty. The Doc had given Kidd a fair crack of the whip but come the end of March he was gone from the side, never to reappear. The case could be made of course that a player of Kidd's proven experience would be just what the club needed to help the task of guiding them out of the Second Division, plus there's the fact that in that miserable relegation season *nobody* at United was scoring prolifically – though top scorers McIlroy and Macari had a better goal-per-game ratio – but one can't blame Docherty (who always had to factor in players' wages when deciding who to keep on the books) for concluding that he would be better off cutting his losses and looking elsewhere for a goalscorer.

\*\*\*

Shortly before the start of the 1974/75 season, it was announced in the press that Manchester United players were to receive pay rises and large bonuses. Reported one paper, "Besides generous rises on basic salaries, United will share £30,000 among the first team if they achieve promotion. In addition, there will be £40 a point payment per man in every match … For a team that failed so consistently last season, this move underlines the desperate need to return to First Division football as soon as possible." In fairness, this apparent reward for failure was by no means restricted to the Reds. Chelsea, who had hardly had a glorious season, had just decided to pay players £45 a point, plus an additional £100 per point over a total of 50 at season's end.

As they prepared to face life in the Second Division, there was not necessarily any reason at all to believe that a resurgent United would bounce straight back up. Yes, with a squad packed with international players, they seemed rather out of place in the Second Division, but their plethora of caps had not made them immune from going down in the first place. Morgan, then just shy of 30, was facing the possibility of his career ending outside the top flight. It's possible that Morgan's intelligence made things look even grimmer for him, for he declined to engage in the sort of tribalistic optimism that characterises the approach of many footballers. Dismissing those assuming a climb-back at the first attempt, he stated that United had to come to terms with the fact that they were now a Second Division club and stated that any assumption by United players that the club had a right to be in the top flight might backfire on them. He also brought up the possibility that every team they met in the Second Division would treat the prospect of playing the mighty Manchester United as the equivalent of a cup tie in which they were the potential giant-killers and raise their game accordingly. "None of us at Old Trafford are really looking forward to this season," he glumly announced.

For the only United player who was his senior, things must have looked even grimmer. Though just a year older than Morgan, Alex Stepney had had the fortune to have been at the club a bit longer than him – long enough to have tasted the sort of glory that would be completely absent from Morgan's Old Trafford tenure. (A statistic that Morgan doesn't like to be reminded of is that he is the longest-serving post-War United player not to have a major honour to his name.) After having won the League Championship and the European Cup with his club and with the fact that he wasn't getting any younger staring him in the face (at a time when a goalkeeper's career arc was generally shorter than it is now), Stepney was looking at the possibility of ending his professional life in depths that he had never thought imaginable for United.

"I think the feeling among the playing staff was 'Let's get out of this division as quickly as we can'," says Buchan. Buchan could be forgiven for thinking it had been a huge mistake leaving

Aberdeen for United, but he says he didn't view it that way: "I remember thinking, 'Right, we're in a mess here.' There was a suggestion that some clubs were interested in me, but I said, 'No, I owe it to this club. I'm one of the squad that got them into the Second Division, I want to try and help them get out.' There was never any thought of deserting a sinking ship."

The season kicked off on Saturday August 17 1974. The first port of call for Manchester United in English football's second tier was London club Orient. The team played at Brisbane Road and until 1966 had been called 'Leyton Orient' but that was probably the extent of the knowledge of most United men about them. "We didn't even know their players," recalled Alex Stepney of the first stage of his club's plunge into what he termed "the unknown."

The United team who took the field that day was Stepney, Forsyth, Houston, Greenhoff, Holton, Buchan, Morgan, Daly, Pearson, Macari and McCalliog, with substitute McIlroy also making an appearance. With the exception of Stepney, Buchan, Morgan and McIlroy, all had either been signed by Docherty or blooded by him. Manchester United were now beginning to look like a new team for a new era. They certainly played like it. Just as United had gone down in style – or at least attempted to – so this season Docherty would appear to have been determined to regain First Division status via anything but a grim haul that took no account of the values that secured that ascension. Brian Greenhoff later said of the Reds' mentality in the Second Division, "The boss made it clear we would never play defensively again." From hereon, there would be no return to the kind of tactics that had besmirched the club's reputation in their two relegation dogfights. Docherty would say in his autobiography that the defensiveness that characterised many teams' approaches at this point in history had never been his style. Anybody who had seen United play from December 1972 through to all but the last months of the 1973/74 season is in a position to state that that simply isn't the case. However, few could argue that this description by Docherty of how United played under him applied from the closing stages of the 1973/74 season though to the end of his days there: "I placed the emphasis on attack and we played to a simple philosophy: when we had the ball we were all attackers, when the opposition had the ball we were all defenders." McIlroy recalls of The Doc's approach to life in the Second Division, "His attitude was, 'Let's go, play football, entertain, play the right way and let's get out of this league as quick as we can.' No matter whether it was home or away, we went to beat teams, and he gave us the confidence to beat teams." Forsyth: "Every game we attacked everybody, didn't matter who we were playing." Not only that, but a virtuous circle was achieved as the season went on because opposition teams found themselves in a Catch-22 situation at home. Under siege by red shirts, they still felt obliged to leave their own goal vulnerable because they dared not play defensively in front of their own supporters. This in turn made it even easier for United's players to put a premium on attack. McIlroy has said that because of this, some of the United players – including himself – began to actually prefer playing away.

Jack Charlton, manager of Middlesbrough, just promoted from Division Two, had recently said that football in the Second Division was "grisly". Greenhoff's recollection seems to confirm this: "I found it a bit hard to adjust to begin with because it's even more physical than the Premiership [sic.]" McIlroy was more struck by reduced circumstances. "Some of the dressing rooms, some of the grounds we went to, weren't up to scratch," he says. "Not what we were used to in the First Division. Some of the grounds were a little bit run down." McCalliog: "Some of the grounds in the Second Division then were obviously not fit for purpose."

Unfamiliar their opening day opponents may have been to the United players, but even last season Orient had theoretically not been separated from them in quality by an entire division. Orient had missed out on promotion by a solitary point. However, there was clearly a great gulf between the quality of the Reds today and their opposition, one that couldn't be fully explained by the fact that Orient were today without three of their first team regulars, or even by the incentive of an extra £80 in the United players' back pockets. Morgan scored with a rifled shot on 27 minutes. Not long after McIlroy replaced Macari on 75 minutes, the Irishman was taking an excellent free-kick which found Forsyth, who headed the second and last goal of the game.

After a match pocked by collisions, an apparently shocked Buchan said, "The tackling is so wild in the Second Division, we'll never get an easy game." Although Buchan could be said to have a clean conscience about the dirty play that had done so much to bring United into disrepute lately, there was, some might think, poetic justice here, not least in its out-of-their-depth element: the Reds, or some of them, may have thought they were playing dirty before, but the players in Division Two were masters of the black arts in a way First Division players could never hope (or, in the main, want) to be.

Alarm bells may have started ringing for some United fans when their second goal of the season came from a defender. However, this was no harbinger of a return to the mediocrity of the front line that had doomed United the previous season, but rather an indication of the breadth of the ability of the team, epitomised by the form of the other full-back, Stewart Houston. Docherty would later cite Houston as one of the team's most improved players this season. As well as the usual defender's skills of marking and tackling, the left-back had speed and good aerial skills to his advantage. A bonus was the fact that he was confident in the opposing team's penalty area, not just his own. That great Liverpool defender Alan Hansen once spoke of how his complete control in his own half dissolved when he found himself in front of the opposition goal and his elegant footwork suddenly transformed into leaden-footed incompetence that precluded scoring. That Houston was a very different creature is illustrated by the fact that he would knock in seven goals in total in this campaign. Though his bookend Alex Forsyth would only claim one goal, he also displayed a comfort in making sorties into the opposition half, often raising a cheer from the Stretford Enders with the sort of fast-clipped mazy dribbles that were more to be expected of a winger. That United's full-backs so frequently joined the attack only underlined the point that this was a club in a hurry to get back to what they felt was their rightful place.

The 2-0 victory left United – by virtue of the tortuous weighing up of goals scored and conceded and alphabeticisation that determined table placings this early in the season – fifth in the division. Sunderland and Norwich City were top.

The Reds' first match in the Second Division for 35 years marked two milestones, both to do with the crowd, one positive, the other negative, if intertwined. United's average home attendance for League games this season would be 48,388, higher by 6,000 over the 1973/74 season, and everywhere the team went they brought tens of thousands of fans with them. The attendance figure of 17,772 was Orient's highest gate of the season and that would be the norm for the vast majority of clubs United visited. Even when a ground's gate was the second highest of the season upon a United visit, this was only because the relevant clubs – Bristols City and Rovers and Nottingham Forest and Notts Country – had engaged in local derbies. In the case of only two clubs – Norwich City and Aston Villa – did the occasion of a visit by Manchester United fail to bulge the attendance to either the best or second best of 1974/75. In a sense, United barely knew the sensation of playing away in this campaign, for their fans outnumbered and/or out-sang the home supporters at away grounds almost every time. United fans showed true loyalty in this campaign in their support for the dream that a suddenly diminished club could be great again.

However, the thousands of extra pounds in revenue for the other clubs in the Second Division did not come without a price. Those who had predicted apocalypse after the pitch invasion in the home Manchester City match last season seemed to have a point when elements of the 10,000 travelling Red Army took to the grass at Orient an hour before kick-off. Vandalism on the terraces saw railings turned into javelins. Glass was thrown into the Orient goalmouth. Naturally, there was also some fisticuffs in an era where the thought of separating opposing supporters was still on its way from something perceived as hysterical overreaction to being acknowledged as the only practical option. Matt Busby – a man from an era in which such things simply didn't happen – pleaded for order over the ground's loudspeakers, but to little avail. It became a cliché over the course of this and subsequent seasons for both United and fair-minded journalists to point out that the hooligan element was very small and that the vast majority of United fans were law-abiding football lovers and violence spurners. Michael Crick – now an author and BBC journalist but then a teenaged member of the Red Army – disputes this, saying, "I don't think it was really true that the hooligan element was very small. As someone who went to almost every away game, I'd say it was pretty large, even perhaps a majority of away fans." Even had it been the truth, it would have been scant consolation to the traders in the streets near football clubs who began boarding up their windows on the day of United visits as the sound of shattered glass increasingly became the accompaniment to Stretford End chants, the opposition fans who either got beaten up or suffered the trauma of seeing violence done to others, the British Rail workers who had the unpleasant task of cleaning up carriages that had hosted the journeys of United fans between Manchester and the city of the away fixture, or the police, club stewards and other workers whose job it was to try to keep the Red Army calm and co-operative. Football hooliganism – a problem that had begun, or which at least had first been noticed by the media, in the late 60s – was entering what would be its worst phase and United fans were its blackest villains.

Orient's usually laid-back manager George Petchey could be heard after the match urging life bans from football grounds for those guilty of the type of behaviour seen at this match, of whom he said, "The sort of brutes the police were taking from the ground on Saturday nearly conquered the world 30 years ago. They're like the Hitlerites all over again – totally irresponsible, ruthless and unbalanced. If they're not stopped, they will destroy the game." Docherty himself revealed that his 18-year-old son was banned from attending United away fixtures. "I've refused to let him go, even though he says he'll steer clear of any trouble," he said. "Home games are different – he can be guaranteed a seat. But if he follows us away, there's just no guarantee of safety." Of the hooliganism itself, he said, "If there's anything I can say that will help, I'll do it today. We have the best supporters in the world, and probably the best club support in the world. The troublemakers are a minority. But because of the size of our following, that minority is larger than any other in football ... We believe the ultimate solution to the problem lies with the courts. But the maximum penalties laid down by the law for the offences these people are committing have simply got to be raised." Matt Busby echoed that last sentiment and added, "It has reached a stage where we on the board feel embarrassed as we enter an away ground because of the worry as to just what this minority will be doing next." It's disturbing to think just how bad the violence that season might have been if United had not thrived in the Second Division and supporters already feeling humiliated at having to visit unfamiliar grounds found their side being beaten by clubs whose existence had only previously impinged on their consciousnesses when flashing by on the *Grandstand* teleprinter as they waited to see how First Division sides had got on.

Buchan says of the hooliganism, "For most of the time we were insulated from it. At one time we used to go up and down on the train to London but by then we were starting to use coaches because they were fitted with microwaves and they could serve hot food on the coach. We didn't come in contact with the fans as we used to do on the way to and from the games. A lot of the incidents happened when we were either in the dressing rooms the hour before the game or afterwards. We saw more of it on television and the newspapers than we actually saw taking place in front of our eyes. We knew it existed. We weren't happy about it. The people were doing that in our name." He adds, "I don't think the Government tried very hard to deal with that, because I think they'd rather have them fighting outside or inside football grounds at three o'clock in the afternoon than in town centres or shopping precincts." McCalliog seems to feel the problems were exaggerated. He says, "The fans have proved themselves over the years to be fantastic... I thought in general, football fans were there to be shot at, because there was always something you could talk about. If the game weren't fantastic, you could always say the hooligans were out."

\*\*\*

United's first home match of the season on Saturday August 24 saw a lamentable but understandable breach with the past. With the supporters behind each goal now separated from the pitch by a red metal fence well over head height whose top was angled back, Manchester United fans (or the non-seated ones, anyway) had become the first soccer supporters who were effectively caged. It was punishment of course for the scenes at the City game at the end of the previous season.

McCalliog and Macari were missing today from the first match's line-up, McIlroy and Martin appearing in their stead. United were simply rampant against their opponents, Millwall, another London club. Some might suggest that their goal tally being doubled in the last five minutes by the awarding of two penalties flattered them, but United had plenty of other near misses, while the most Stepney had to do all afternoon was jump for a couple of crosses and block a shot. The first goal came in the fourth minute when a bad back-pass was seized on by Pearson, who smartly hoisted the ball over a defender and walked it around goalkeeper Bryan King. Pearson had scored three goals in two games in the close season tour of Denmark, as well as a goal against Hull in a friendly (the match was probably part of the deal involved in his transfer) but getting on the scoresheet less than five minutes into his first home game, by his own admission, took the pressure off him. Like many who came to Old Trafford, he had known nothing like the massive crowds who were now looking at him expectantly. The second goal also came in the first half, Daly pouncing on a rebound.

With McCalliog sidelined with an Achilles injury, a tripping of McIlroy in the opposition goal area required a replacment spot-kicker. Daly volunteered. He aimed his firm penalty to the bottom left-hand corner. Martin was the next United player infringed on and this time Daly placed his spot-kick to the right, with equally successful results.

Despite their 4-0 victory and their 100% record, United were still only sixth in the table that evening, with Fulham and Norwich top. Nonetheless, as early as this match, promotion predictions were being made. Journalist James Mossop said that from the moment of Pearson's opening goal, " … the feeling grew that Manchester United's stay in the Second Division will be brief." Millwall manager Barry Fenton acknowledged the importance of the Reds' vociferous support in the 44,756 crowd: "A lot of teams will come here to find such an atmosphere a completely new experience. It affects players. It can drain away all their energy. This crowd will certainly be working for United and against the opposition this season."

That two of Daly's goals were penalties does not diminish his hat-trick, and not just because he says, "I think one of them was scored with my left foot. I wasn't the best in the world with my left foot." The nerve and skill required to be a spot-kicker is considerable, as evidenced by the fact that even a genius like George Best had never shown any great keenness to volunteer for the role. The role was an important one this season and the remainder of Docherty's tenure, for United's attacking style, by the law of averages, ensured numerous fouls in the box as defences unsuccessfully struggled to cope with waves of red shirts. Daly would take nine in all this season. His deceptive run-up saw goalkeepers regularly diving the wrong way.

Daly has a firm philosophy about the art of taking a spot-kick. "Never, ever do I like to see a left-footer taking a penalty," he says, "because I'm always of the opinion that good left-footed players are great chippers of the ball – Liam Brady was a great chipper of the ball; Maradona for instance – but when they were stroking a ball around, they were always leaning back, and the amount of left-footers leaning back and blazing the ball over the bar is unbelievable." He also says, "I never formed the opinion which a lot of people do these days that you hit it as hard as you can. I hate to see the people just smashing the ball straight at the goalkeeper and hoping that the goalkeeper is going to move. To me, that's the worst penalty you could ever take because if they stand still you just smack it against them. I didn't agree with the fact also of this business of stopping and starting and then chipping it over the goalkeeper when he's lying on the ground. I always thought that was a bit risky." As for his own technique, Daly explains, "I'd always side-foot the ball. I never liked to see anybody running up straight onto the ball, because they have to contort their body. I always came at it from an angle. I always approached the ball from the left-hand side and that gave me the option then. I liked to side-foot the ball into the net, either side that I wanted to take him." Also integral to the process, he says, is "having the confidence". McCalliog certainly noticed this quality in the Irishman. Daly had claimed the spot-kicker's role for his own by the time McCalliog was back from injury, something which the latter took with equanimity. "When somebody's confident, let them keep taking them," McCalliog says.

It was yet another weapon in Daly's considerable armoury. Born in Dublin on April 30 1954, Gerry Daly goes to prove the philosophy that size doesn't matter in football – apprehension of which, of course, United obtained back when a little Irish lad by the name of Best spectacularly disproved all the club scouts who had turned up their noses at his scrawny frame. Daly wasn't quite in Best's class but he punched well above his 10st 6lb weight. This weight was actually half a stone more than Daly could boast when he first started training at United. Though Daly's smallness was to some extent a legitimate concern for his managers during his career – the rough going in English football fields during the winter tended to sap what strength he had – he more than compensated for that not just in his enthusiasm (even if his failure to measure out his effort properly could also make him tire too quickly) but in his wide array of skills. Daly offers, "Even though I looked fragile I was physically strong and I could run all day long. It was never a problem. If I didn't finish first in the cross-country runs, I knew there was something wrong with me. Lou Macari could run all day but he was happy to finish second to me." As for the rest of his game, he says, "I wouldn't say I was slow over ten yards but I wasn't the quickest either. Basically for a midfield role, it was what was needed. I was always a tidy passer of the ball. I could always score a few goals from midfield. I was always fairly confident when I was on the pitch."

Ragamuffin scamp he may have looked, but on the ball Daly had the mien of a soccer aristocrat. His colleagues found themselves the pleased recipients of flicks, chips and lay-offs boasting a beautiful touch. Although he had both the vision and feel to release his colleagues on a run, Daly could also beat men. Though his goal tally was ratcheted up by his penalties, he scored more than a few in non-deadball situations, often from great distances, courtesy of a thunderous shot. Despite dribbling skills that could have seen him operate successfully as a winger, Daly says he had no hankerings in that direction: "I was always a midfield player. There was no way I could have been stuck out on the wing. I always wanted to be in the thick of the action. Waiting for somebody to go and win the ball for me and wait there for them to pass it to me, I couldn't be doing with that."

The adding of role of penalty-taker supreme (Daly would only miss one of the 17 spot-kicks he took for the Reds) came about because he had performed well in that task in pre-season training. Perhaps Daly excelled at this task where better players had not even had the courage to give themselves the opportunity to do so because of a certain philosophy he brought to the job. "Nobody else wanted to take 'em," he says. "It was as simple as that. So I says, 'Well, I'll take it.' I came up with this idea: if I start taking penalties and I miss one or whatever, don't blame me because nobody else wants to take 'em. Somebody has to take the damn thing. I always took them for Ireland." Tied in with this was the psychological fall-out of an emotional incident from Daly's early days with the club. "We went over to play in a youth tournament in Zurich or Geneva," he says. "We got to the final and it went to extra-time and it went to penalties and I took one and I missed it. Obviously I was gutted. When I was out there, I got a call-up to get my first cap for Ireland over in Oslo. I went across and got my cap and then I had to fly back to Geneva, I think it was, to play in another tournament. As things have it, we went to the final again and we went to penalties. I wouldn't take one. Some other young lad went and took the penalty and missed it." Daly told David Meek that the boy was reduced to tears: "I was one of the oldest there and I felt I had let him down. So missing does not bother me now. Somebody has got to miss occasionally ... " He now elaborates, "I happened to be sitting in the dressing room afterwards and I was feeling a bit smug if you like in the fact that alright we've lost the tournament but at least I didn't miss a penalty. That was my initial reaction towards it, until Bill Foulkes gave me the biggest bollocking I ever got in my life. He says, 'You go across and you get your first cap for your country at senior level and you haven't got the balls to out there and take a penalty and you let this other young kid take it and you look really smug there now in the fact that you haven't taken it and we've lost the tournament. I hope you feel proud for yourself'."

Some felt that Daly became a better player in the Second Division, almost as if dribbling past defenders not quite up to the mark he had got used to in Division One was a good means for experimentation and confidence buttressing. Daly was aware that he was attracting approving attention but demurred from the belief that dropping a division was the key. "I think it is ... fair to say that I started to play better while we were in the First," he insisted. Daly was less devastated by relegation than some. "I'm a young lad there," he says now. "Obviously you want to play in the First Division, but it wasn't really that much of a great deal of difference to me because I still had to prove myself. My mentality was look after yourself. It was a case of

I have to prove not only to myself that I am capable of going out and playing this particular game but to the supporters."

"He certainly was an excellent player for us," says Buchan. "Bags of nervous energy, never stood still for a second. Just amazing reserves of stamina, could run all day although he was very slight. Good football brain as well." Mick Martin, who of course knew Daly from the League of Ireland, says, "He was frail but very good feet. Smashing little finisher." However, he adds a caveat: "In a flair side Gerry was ideal. If your backs were to the wall, you could take him off."

What is astonishing is that Daly had all of these attributes to his name despite the fact that his diet and habits resembled more those of a navvy than a professional footballer. While grilled chicken and pasta were still a decade or more from being the Football League player's choice of sustenance, even his fellow 70s professionals raised an eyebrow at Daly's heavy smoking habit. Docherty later recalled he would nag Daly about his nicotine addiction and that Daly would respond by pointing out that he was hardly a quitter on the field.

Having only turned 20 in April, Daly was – until the arrival of Steve Coppell in February – behind only Sammy McIlroy in being the baby amongst the regulars of Docherty's increasingly young side. Daly reveals that though he got on well with Docherty – and was grateful to him for giving him his chance on the big stage – it was Busby and United scout Jimmy Murphy (who had discovered him) who were more his mentors. Almost, in fact, in opposition to Docherty and Cavanagh. "I was a bit cocky in them days and I think that was the reason why I got on so well with Sir Matt Busby and Jimmy Murphy," he says. "I lived on Warwick Road North just beside the ground and I remember bumping into Jimmy Murphy one day and he said to me, 'We brought you over from Ireland [for] what you did. Don't change, no matter what anybody says to you' – and I'm taking this as Tommy Docherty and Cavanagh. This is what I thought that he meant, was that no matter what [they] say to you, just go out and play your own game. That's why you're here in the first place. You're playing at the best club in the world. Go out and express yourself. When you're on the ball, do whatever you want with it."

\*\*\*

The United players might have felt distant from terrace mayhem but nobody liked to hear horror stories about innocent people being caught up in violence or contemplate long-term fans drifting away in fear, nor did the club want a reputation as the pariahs of football. A new scheme was announced to try to prevent the wilder elements of the Reds' crowd mortifying them as they had at the City game at the end of last season and the Orient match at the beginning of this one. Credit for this scheme has usually been given to Docherty but journalist James Mossop stated at the time that Alex Stepney was the impetus. The veteran goalie asked Supporters Club secretary David Smith to invite both genuine supporters and 'naughty boys' to meet the players at Old Trafford one Sunday early in the season in a meeting that was the first of several between fans and supporters at Old Trafford on the Sabbath. "The players are as concerned as anyone that a few young lads are giving the club and its good supporters such a bad name," Stepney told Mossop. "We are prepared to meet them, show them round the ground and talk to them. We want to guide them and let them know that they are letting us all down. I believe they will listen to us and that we will be able to get through to them. They may change so much that they really can become the best-behaved supporters in the country. How much better, for instance, if they can take a real pride in their conduct and become famous for being completely well-ordered. They would surely get a bigger kick out of that than knocking in people's windows."

Reading those words gives an impression of a quality about Stepney that could almost be termed innocence. In his autobiography a few years later, he fulminated, "It is surely wrong that a Manchester United player flying with his club for a summer tour to Australia should need to be told by an official to watch his language. But that happened in one case." Somebody with an olde-worlde mentality like Stepney hardly strikes one as the kind of person who would be taken seriously by the generation responsible for the mayhem. And though Docherty had a way with the fans, banter and bonhomie in the odd buffet car was hardly going to sway the psychopaths into clean-cut behaviour. Though the hooliganism problem had to be addressed and though Docherty and the players' anguish over the problem seems genuine, to some extent the whole scheme smacks of posturing, scrabbling in the dark or both. Football hooligans themselves were hardly going to attend these workshops and the Supporters Association types who were (plus starstruck kids exploiting the opportunity to meet their idols) were hardly going to be in a position to offer solutions: grassing up people was not an option when so many of the hooligans were not even Manchester residents. As Buchan points out, "United supporters were drawn from all over the country." Not necessarily talking about hooligans, he adds, "I'll never forget playing at Newcastle one day and coming back on the team bus and being amazed by the variety of place names on the supporters' buses, from Devon, South Wales, the Southeast corner of England. To see where all the different coaches came from, as we travelled back down the A1 was an eye opener." On a related theme, Docherty subscribed to a form of conspiracy theory about the problem. "We never seemed to have any bother at Old Trafford," he said. " ... I'm sure that on occasions when we were travelling, fans at the other end put on red-and-white colours just to stir up trouble ... "

Football would have to wait upon a leap in technology – the introduction of affordable CCTV systems – before the blight could begin to be addressed. Until then United would have to resign themselves to having their club name tainted by association and Docherty and the players to having to field questions in interviews and at press conferences about something that had nothing to do with them and over which they had no control.

*\*\**

United's newfound attacking reputation would seem to have preceded them when they hosted a visit by Portsmouth on Wednesday August 28. Portsmouth produced a suffocatingly negative performance to deal with it. Ironically, the United team – unchanged from the Saturday game – turned out to be having an off day. Daly successfully converted his third penalty in two matches. McIlroy also got on the scoresheet. Portsmouth converted a last-minute penalty of their own. After this 2-1 victory – watched by a very healthy midweek gate of 42,547 – United were placed second, with Fulham at the top of the table.

After their visit to Ninian Park on Saturday August 31, an unchanged Manchester United – who beat Cardiff City by a single goal from yet another Daly penalty – were top of the Second Division, leading Fulham by a point. Though it was achieved without Pearson, who departed injured after 20 minutes, replaced by Young, United's performance was slightly complacent. Nonetheless, pole position was pole position. "We got off to a good start, started scoring goals and that breeds confidence," says Buchan of the campaign. "Self-belief started to come back. Some new players were bedded in and the likes of Gerry Daly was starting to blossom, and it was a much younger United team. A lot of the older players had moved on or retired … " Says Mick Martin, "Yes, the sides that you were playing weren't at the same level you were playing the year before, but it doesn't matter. They still needed to be beaten." Greenhoff says, "We were fit, we worked hard for each other and once you start enjoying the way you play you can't wait for the next game … Nearly every ground you went to, you're breaking the crowd record or they're having the highest gate of the season, so the atmospheres are always fantastic. If you can't get up for games like that then you shouldn't be playing the game."

McCalliog offers, "We had a good pre-season training. We were fit. Everybody was pulling the right way. There was no disharmony anywhere in the club. It was a good place to be …" He also says the purchase of Stuart Pearson resulted in the team playing "with a different style". He explains, "Pancho was a good target man. When you hit the ball at him, it stuck, and being a midfield player it always is nice to have a player where you played the ball at his feet and it would stay with his feet and gave everybody a chance to get up and support him. He made a hell of a difference." Daly says, "He was a focal point for us upfront. He was a bit of a leader." Another player who combined well with Pancho was Macari. "He liked to lead the line, leaving me to work the spaces just behind", said Macari. Macari of course did not like to lead the line and with the new striker, the days when The Doc might entertain playing him out of position in a centre-forward's role were over. Buchan: "There's no doubt that Lou was at his most valuable playing in that area between midfield and a striker. He could get up and down that field like a little machine."

McCalliog adds, "We were a better side from the back. They would tend to play willy-nilly, just play it off the cuff. When Greeny went in the back four, The Doc started from pre-season encouraging us to play from the back and even started working on Martin Buchan to go forward. 'Cos Martin Buchan stayed at the back all the time and he was probably one the fittest guys in the club and he could have done that. He pushed people forward … " McCalliog adds, "My position changed. I went more from being a free player, which was the way I'd played when I first arrived, and it was more that they were finding me with the ball towards the left-hand side of the park and people were running around me."

Daly: "It took off for everybody. Everybody seemed to be playing well. We were a young side. We were enthusiastic. Everybody wanted the ball. We had some cocky players in the team. It was a great time to be at the club. We were a very entertaining side because we were a young side with very little inhibitions." Daly rejects the suggestion that playing against slightly inferior position than they were used to was the main reason for United flying high this season: "How many people do you see turning around now and saying, 'When you drop down a division it's very difficult to get out?' They go up into the Premiership and then they get relegated and they can't get out of it. They're lucky if they didn't get relegated again. It's a downward spiral. The cynics will say 'Well, obviously [you're not] playing against the same type of player as in the First Division', but that's probably what the team needed at that time: young players, give them a bit of confidence, which it certainly did."

\*\*\*

Hamstring trouble saw Pearson give way to McCalliog for the home match against Nottingham Forest on Saturday September 7. United were otherwise unchanged except that Macari (who would come on for an injured Greenhoff) was sub. The match was closely fought. The Reds were playing some wonderful football in the first-half and their 26th-minute opening goal when Greenhoff ran onto a good through-ball from Martin was just rewards.

However, Forest began probing a United defence that, the assured Buchan excepted, was unusually shaky and scored six minutes before and after half-time.

The 40,671 gate weren't going to be satisfied with a loss, though. Afterwards, Forest manager Allan Brown said, "I think we would have won had not the crowd lifted United so much." McIlroy salvaged a point – and some justice – for the home side in the dying minutes, and he did so with some style. Receiving the ball 25 yards from goal, he set off on a run that saw him leave two defenders in his wake before driving the ball into the net from the edge of the penalty area. McIlroy, in fact, could conceivably have secured all the points for United when he subsequently went down in the box, but the referee resisted the howls for a penalty. Docherty suggested officials were reluctant to give United spot-kicks because the club had had so many awarded in recent games, a comment that would nowadays only be made in the context of Old Trafford with extreme sarcasm. United remained on top of the table.

Greenhoff's goal was one of the few glimmers of happiness for him in this early stage of the campaign, for the good form that had seen him gain an England Under-23 cap the previous season even though he was in a team hurtling toward relegation had been transformed into a strange mediocrity. It wasn't bad enough for his place to be threatened – he only failed to make an appearance in one League game – but he found himself only occasionally coming off the pitch with the glowing knowledge of having performed well. His struggling to come to terms with the contact lenses he was now wearing on the park may have been part of the problem. Greenhoff also suspected that he may have lost his edge through complacency about his place. However, he wasn't so complacent that he didn't seek the advice of Tommy Cavanagh, who gave him a refresher course in midfield play. Greenhoff worked harder in training and began to consciously apply himself more in matches and gradually began emerging from his fallow patch.

Docherty, ironically, considered Greenhoff such an asset that he said after the Forest game that he probably wouldn't risk Greenhoff in the home second-round League Cup tie against Charlton Athletic on Wednesday September 11 because he wanted to make certain he would be fit for the West Brom game the following Saturday. Accordingly, for the Charlton match Martin moved back in the formation to plug the gap, while Macari made a return to the starting XI. Third-Division Charlton shocked the 21,616 crowd, and probably themselves, by going ahead in the first minute. The United players may have been smarting with a sense of injustice at the Peter Hunt goal – some had frozen in anticipation of an offside flag – but that alone couldn't account for the way they proceeded to demolish their visitors over the following 89 minutes. By the 14th minute, a shell-shocked Charlton were 3-1 down, courtesy of a McIlroy header, a panic-stricken back-pass own goal and a Macari drive. Five minutes into the second half, Houston rose to head home a corner. In the 79th minute of a match that Charlton were barely in from the second minute onwards, Macari secured his comeback brace and a 5-1 victory.

Though Macari's two goals meant he was opening his scoring account for the season in impressive style, Docherty was not particularly looking for Lou to rack up a high tally this season. The fact that the pressure to score – and thereby justify the £200,000 outlay on him – was off his shoulders clearly left Macari a happier man. His form this season was exceptional. Paradoxically, it also led to him re-acquiring his goalscoring touch, particularly in the League Cup. His brace in this match was just the start of a campaign in which he emerged with seven goals, the highest number of any player in the competition that year. Meanwhile his overall total of 11 League goals would be a stark contrast to the dismal five he had scored the year before when he was frequently played as a striker. Having said all that, Macari made way for Pearson in the League match on Saturday September 14 against West Bromwich Albion. As it turned out, Greenhoff didn't make the starting line-up at the Hawthorns in front of a 28,666 crowd, though did come on for Martin on the hour.

West Brom were the better team and went ahead after six minutes. However, on 31 minutes, Pearson scored an opportunist's goal. Within seven minutes of coming on, Greenhoff was involved in a collision that saw him stretchered off. When he returned after touchline treatment, he seemed dazed. He wandered off again, but when he returned a few minutes later, he still didn't seem 100% there. There were no further goals. Despite the dropped point, United maintained their position at the top of the table over Norwich on goal average.

Such are the vagaries that the fixture list throws up that the following Monday, United and Millwall met for the second time in five weeks. Greenhoff had recovered from his dazed state sufficiently to make the starting line-up for the match at The Den. Martin was dropped, Sidebottom replaced the injured Holton and Macari the injured Pearson. Shortly after the interval King raced out to Macari, who had broken through on goal, and the Scotsman went down. The penalty award incurred the fury of the home fans amongst the 16,988 present. Daly stepped up to put a spot-kick past King for the third time in just over a month. It was the game's only goal, and this and other decisions that aroused the ire of the Millwall fans (notoriously, even bigger hard-nuts than the worst United supporters) saw referee Ray Toseland given a police escort off the pitch, which black shield King – still outraged – tried to get past after running the length of the field. These tumultuous events and narrow victory left United two points clear at the top of the table.

United's home match against Bristol Rovers on Saturday September 21 was Alex Stepney's 300th League appearance. The goalie didn't have much to do by way of celebrating his milestone, however, as United tormented Rovers, with captain Morgan particularly inspirational. Holton was back in for Sidebottom (the only change from the last fixture), although he wouldn't have time to get used to it because his two-match ban for going over 12 disciplinary points with a booking in the West Brom game was about to kick in. There were only two goals in the match – a Greenhoff header and an own-goal – but that did not tell the full story of United's dominance, which but for poor finishing would have translated into a 5-0 or 6-0 scoreline. United thrilled their fans in the 42,948 crowd by piling up an almost ridiculous number of near-misses, including a line clearance, three woodwork-rattlers and even a shot from Buchan.

The 2-0 victory meant United now led the table by four points. Afterwards, Docherty was urging caution. Referring to his time with Chelsea in the Second Division, he said, "We were once eight points ahead. Then look what happened. Bump! We ended up scraping promotion on goal average. It's great for the lads to be winning again but we mustn't get our heads in the clouds."

Docherty expressed concern leading up to the Reds' home match against Bolton Wanderers on Wednesday September 25 that the absence of Holton during that and the following match might be damaging. Well, a team unchanged from the Bristol Rovers match apart from Sidebottom donning Holton's shirt seemed to manage pretty well. Old Trafford hosted its biggest crowd of the season thus far – 47,084 – despite it being a midweek affair. Not that Bolton were allowing this to intimidate them in a spirited and by no means negative performance, but United were just too much for the visitors and it seemed a near miracle that it took 41 minutes for the Reds to score via a Macari volley. Houston then came forward to piledrive into the back of the Rovers net a free-kick that was given instead of an expected spot-kick, the second arguably valid penalty claim the Reds had had turned down. United continued to apply pressure in the second-half, albeit at a more stately pace. Bolton's spirit was finally broken when in the 62nd minute Morgan sent in a tantalisingly curving cross that McAllister found himself back-heading into his own net. Their 3-0 victory brought United's tally of games without a loss since the season's start to ten. A team who had found goals so hard to come by in all but the final month of the previous season had, including their League Cup match, scored 23 in 10 matches. They now led the table by five points.

*\*\**

Though Alex Stepney was naturally happy to be in a side that was winning again, in a way it was slightly detrimental to his technique. "During relegation, I was always in the game," the keeper noted. "I had plenty of practice and many a game seemed to revolve round me." Things changed as he found himself in a team who were taking the game to their opponents. He was a goalie who always liked to get an early feel of the ball but, as he observed, "Frequently I had to go the first 10 minutes of a match without touching the ball."

Meanwhile, Stepney was less than ecstatic with a change he claims he observed in Docherty. While the spirit of solidarity involved in fighting relegation had brought out the best in the manager, the ascension to the top of the Second Division had effected a change in The Doc that reminded him of what he had seen in his brief time at Chelsea. "He began to strut about with the aloofness of a game-cock," he recalled in 1978. "He seemed to step away from Sir Matt, whom he had previously courted avidly." Independently, and a few years earlier, Morgan said much the same thing: "He's humble in the bad times but prone to destroy when things are going right ... When he arrived at United he was terrific. We were under pressure from relegation and he handled everything right. But it seems he just could not cope with success. Once United hit the top of the Second Division things began to change. It was incredible."

This was behaviour on the low end of the disagreeable scale, but Stepney and his fellow senior team member Morgan were horrified by an incident this season that involved Docherty calling the pair into his office to talk about Tommy Cavanagh. Seemingly, things were not going too well between the manager and the man he had recruited to be his coach. Both Stepney and Morgan have subsequently and independently gone on record as saying that Docherty asked them in this meeting whether they thought he should sack Cavanagh. The reasons Docherty gave were Cavanagh's language and behaviour around younger players. Morgan said in a newspaper interview the following season that the logic of calling the two of them in was that he was captain and Stepney the senior pro. Morgan claimed Docherty said, "I want you and Alex, on behalf of the players, to say that you're not happy with him and that you want him away. This will give me the support I need to sack him." Both were appalled at being put in this position. Stepney responded that it was a matter for Docherty himself and that he should not ask him and Morgan to give him the backing to dismiss Cavanagh. Morgan later said, "We were astounded and both of us stuck up for Cav. We pointed out that he had faults but was ... 100% behind the players. Cavanagh stayed – he was lucky. But that gave me an insight into Tommy Docherty's methods."

\*\*\*

If we try to put ourselves into the mind of Docherty-discard Ted MacDougall before United's visit to Carrow Road on Saturday September 28, it's tempting to conclude that we might encounter a fermenting fantasy that involved him scoring both goals in a 2-0 victory for Norwich City – the club he had joined in 1973 after a few post-United months at West Ham – a victory that was furthermore of some importance both in the Second Division title race (Norwich lay third before the game started) and symbolically (Manchester United were the only unbeaten team in the four divisions of the English Football League).

If this was indeed MacDougall's fantasy – and it would be understandable if it was – it was one that came true. MacDougall provided yet another example of the way that Docherty's treatment of players he considered dispensable had a habit of coming back to haunt him, one already (sort of) demonstrated in Docherty's United tenure by the example of Denis Law. Some might read something eerie into this. Others might just point out that Docherty fell out with so many of his employees that the law of averages dictated that the fixture list would sooner or later provide some of them with the opportunity to deliver The Doc the footballing equivalent of an "up yours".

Of course, this was not entirely down to MacDougall. An unchanged United were simply outclassed by John Bond's all-out attacking team and this time round the absence of Holton did indeed seem to make a difference. Buchan was frequently having to abandon his own duties to help out an ungainly and uncertain Sidebottom. By the end of the first-half, United's defence – who had not experienced this sort of onslaught in this campaign – were losing their tempers with each other. MacDougall executed a textbook penalty low to a corner for a 24th-minute goal and in the 58th minute, puzzlingly unmarked. he sealed his theoretical fantasy by smartly spinning on his heel to send the ball under the bar.

If it's true that a manager's true test is in adversity, Docherty's graceless comments after the match ensured that he failed it. His discussion of Ted MacDougall was not too far in spirit from the cries of "reject" that the United fans in the 24,586 crowd had aimed at him. "Nothing that happened today has changed my opinion," he said. "I still think MacDougall can't play." Bond responded by pointing out that MacDougall had cost his club £140,000, £60,000 less than obtaining Lou Macari's services had cost United. "I am willing to bet right here and now that Ted will score twice as many goals this season as Macari," said Bonds. "Ted can be difficult to handle but I know how to cope with him and I wish people would stop taking it out on him just because they were unable to get the best out of him." (For the record, MacDougall notched up 24 strikes to Macari's 18.)

Perhaps Docherty was irritatedly mindful of the fact that the result ensured that Norwich leap-frogged Fulham in the table and were now just three points behind the Reds. United's next fixture was away to Fulham, who would be hopeful of making their own contribution to chipping away at their lead. The commanding position United had enjoyed now looked far from unassailable.

In the end, any trepidation about the Fulham match at Craven Cottage on Saturday October 5 turned out to be unfounded, though whether this was because Holton was back (replacing Sidebottom) or due to the return of Pearson (displacing Macari) is unclear. Certainly, United's defence did not look as shaky as it had the previous Saturday. Pearson scored both United's goals, each a poacher's strike. However, five minutes from the end of a second-half in which they mounted a bit of a fight back, the Cottagers scored from a corner, and the only thing that prevented the Reds from having to make the journey back to Manchester with a solitary point was a great Stepney save in the dying moments. The 26,513 crowd was treble Craven Cottage's usual gate. United still sat astride the table with a comfortable cushion of three points, even if Sunderland directly below them had a game in hand.

\*\*\*

October saw Frank Blunstone offered one of the most prestigious jobs in football: manager of Chelsea. The Blues had just parted company with the services of Dave Sexton. Remarkably, the United youth-team boss turned it down. Blunstone: "I went down to see the chairman of Chelsea. 'Could I start on the Monday?' I said to him, 'I'll think about it over the weekend.' So I told Tommy. He said, 'What's he offered you?' I said, 'He's offered me a bit more money.' 'We'll give you the same,' he said, 'and stay here.' So I said okay. I loved Chelsea but they were in financial trouble. They were in a bit of a mess, so I wasn't that keen to go at that time. Also, I loved United." Did he ever regret not taking the job? "No. Because they all went there, they all struggled. How many did they have? They had about five, six managers, didn't they?" Implicit in Blunstone's decision was the recognition of an *esprit de corps* at Old Trafford of the type which had been so lacking in recent years. Stepney and Morgan might disagree, but the club that had been a festering heap of grudges, grievances and cliques when Docherty arrived was now a place where people wanted to be.

That in dropping down into Division Two United had not been completely cut adrift from top-class football had been brought home to them when the draw was made for the third round of the League Cup. Their own name was pulled out first, which meant a home fixture. Gasps and smiles must have been the reaction when the next name enunciated was that of

Manchester City. A massive crowd for a midweek fixture – 55,159 – turned out on Wednesday October 9 for the unexpected derby. It was going to be an interesting test for the Reds: City were the first Division One opponents United had met in a competitive match since they had started playing in the second flight. Furthermore, City were currently nestled with Liverpool and Derby County at the top of the First Division. There was also an aura of expectation over the fixture, and not just for those who still mistakenly assumed (as some still do today) that City's vanquishing of United on the last day of the previous season had sent the Reds down: revenge for that humiliation would have been sweet in the eyes of many in the Stretford End.

The only change from the Fulham match was the debut of 17-year-old full-back Arthur Albiston, replacing an unfit Houston. Nobody who had not been informed beforehand would have known which was the Division Two side from what they saw. Even so, City's wonderful flair player Rodney Marsh was in the thick of the action. He twice had City fans thrusting their arms in the air in salute of a goal. The Blues froze in their celebrations both times when the strikes were disallowed for offside. Macari took over from an injured Pearson for the second half. A City handball gave United a 78th-minute penalty. Daly stepped up to do his usual meticulous job. It was the game's only goal.

Marsh's two goals-that-weren't, incidentally, were the result of a defensive strategy that United had – despite their penchant for attack – honed to perfection. Explains McCalliog: "It was the call from Martin. It had to be a decent clearance. Not like a short clearance. We wanted it to go about 30 yards, maybe 40 yards, and if everybody was right then Martin would push everybody up. You'd get a lazy forward who doesn't want to run back so you'd catch him offside. It was a thing that was practised and I thought it was as perfect as an offside could be." Forsyth's recollection is of an approach less dependent on Buchan and ultimately almost psychic. "You played with each other so often, the ball's coming through, you just stepped up that couple of steps," he says. "You just automatically knew what to do." Greenhoff disagrees with the nomenclature. "We used to break quick," is the distinction he makes. "People'd say it was an offside play but it never was. We used to call it attacking the ball. Them days, if they knocked it over the top, they were offside. So it worked for us, because if we did get the ball, we're away. We never played it as an offside. We did it to go and attack, not to stop the game."

This match was probably the Manchester derby at which Forsyth recalls being taught a valuable lesson by Mike Summerbee: "The ball came down the line. He just knocked it by me and I went over the top but I didnae mean it. A couple of minutes later we were going back the way, he says 'Look son, those sort of tackles, don't ever do that.' I says, 'What do you mean?' He says, 'You're over the top. I'm a wee bit older-fashioned than you. I can go over the top a lot easier than you. I can let you win a tackle and I'll leave my foot in and I'll break your leg. I don't mind a hard tackle but don't go over the top to me. Just watch laddie, you go over the top, the ones down here will sort you out.' I never forgot that and it was a good bit of advice and I've always thought the boy was good telling me that." Forsyth adds, "I was never a dirty player. My definition of a hard player, he'll go into a 50-50 tackle and win it. A lot of people will say hard players will go over the top and break legs. Anybody can do that. That's not being hard. That's just being dirty. There's a difference between a dirty player and a hard player." Having said that, Forsyth injects a bit of ambivalence when he says, "Then you could tackle from behind, where now you cannae do it, plus the fact that you'd only one camera, which was great for a player then, because you could do loads and loads of things: you could stand on people's toes after the ball was away and if the linesman didn't see it you were away. You got away with a lot of things then that you can't do now."

***

Pearson's triumphant comeback against Fulham turned out to be a false dawn in regard to the striker overcoming his hamstring problems. Sidelined once more, he only made a return to the starting line-up four matches later, and that would not be the end of his problems in this department. Indeed what is so remarkable about Pearson's high scoring rate this season is the fact that he barely got the chance to get into his stride. He had started the season feeling a little under par after taking the opportunity to have a tonsils operation in the close season. Only when he came out of hospital nine pounds lighter than he went in and began pre-season training feeling somewhat diminished in energy did he appreciate that an adult is not quite able to handle a tonsils operation as easily as a child. The hamstring 'niggle' – soccer parlance for an injury that keeps returning like a bad penny, inflicting a series of psychological blows as a footballer realises with a sinking heart that a malaise that he had thought he had gotten over is making its presence felt yet again – meant he had a rather bitty season and missed some important games. Moreover, several of the games in which he did participate were ones for which he wasn't match-fit. It makes his final goal tally of 18 from 36 starts and one substitute appearance all the more impressive.

Perhaps his impressive strike rate was down to the fact that he found there were boons to being in Manchester United's team that helped his game. At Hull, he had been not just the star player, but virtually the player on whom the entire side depended. The Hull defence was oriented around playing the ball straight up to him at every opportunity. At Old Trafford, suddenly surrounded by players of a higher calibre, he experienced the novel sensation of finding the ball making its leisurely way up the field amongst midfielders and wide players who were comfortable on it. "They make my life a lot easier," he said. "Everyone is working for each other."

Macari replaced Pearson and Houston replaced Albiston for United's home match against Notts County on Saturday October 12. United seemed to be still recovering from the euphoria of knocking City out of the League Cup. Either that or they were self-conscious in the face of the unusual presence at a Second Division fixture of the BBC's *Match of the Day* cameras. Docherty acknowledged afterwards that, "We can play so much better than that."

Though McIlroy powered the ball home in the 17th minute, at the other end Holton and Stepney were having to do sterling work to prevent the visitors replying. More than one journalist – in a synchronicity of opinion that showed how well Pancho had settled in – felt there was a Stuart Pearson-sized hole in United's team today. On the plus side, United were still top of the division, while the 46,565 gate was United's highest for a League match so far this season and a stark contrast to concerns about declining attendances at football matches elsewhere. "The only problem here is wear and tear on the hinges," Docherty laughingly told a reporter who asked him about the latter subject.

On Tuesday October 15, in the only starting XI change, Albiston got another chance to stand in for Houston. This time the affair in question was more sedate than the bearpit of a local Manchester derby, involving a visit to Fratton Park – although in some respects Portsmouth came closer to beating United than City had. However, despite making plenty of chances, the closest Portsmouth came to scoring was when Alex Forsyth was forced to make a goal-line clearance in the 75th minute. Though Macari was the characteristically hyperactive, ultra-creative figure United fans had now got pleasantly used to, he failed to convert a trio of chances. Despite a 0-0 draw and their second so-so performance in a row, United were still top of the table.

The match occasioned the first public sign of trouble to come between Docherty and Morgan when The Doc substituted the winger, giving David McCreery his senior debut. Morgan made his anger clear as he stalked from the pitch. This sight of disaffection can't have made things any easier for a 17-year-old already facing the daunting task of his first game. "It made me feel a bit concerned," admits McCreery, "but then at the same time when you're younger, your nerves and whatever just go out the window. I think there was a wee bit of tension at the time but I just got on with it. I think I did alright." Says Greenhoff of a substitution that would be so much a harbinger, "It was the biggest load of crap you've ever played in your life, they played man-for-man all over the pitch. If somebody had held my number up to go off, I'd have been, 'Thank God for that.' Willie was took off and went ballistic. They took us all out for a meal that night to the Playboy Club in Southsea. I sat by Willie and he just slagged The Doc off all night just 'cos he took him off."

For United's visit to Bloomfield Road on Saturday October 19, the line-up was Stepney, Forsyth, Houston, Greenhoff, Holton, Buchan, Morgan, McIlroy, Macari, McCalliog and Daly. It's worth listing all those names because apart from Stepney – who on this occasion was barely called upon to exercise his skills – all of them played a part in the demolition of Blackpool Football Club.

Docherty cast-off Wyn Davies was in the Blackpool side and, if he harboured the same revenge fantasies we have assumed on the part of Ted MacDougall, 90 seconds into the match, he must have thought that they had come true. However, his 'goal' was disallowed and in short order Blackpool simply didn't know what had hit them. Attendance for this game has been variously stated as 25,370 and 22,211. However many there were in the stadium, they were treated to a textbook example from United of how to take a side apart by endless slick passing and the unleashing of wave after wave of assaults on the opposition goalmouth involving at some point every single outfield player. Forsyth scored the first goal from a 23rd minute free-kick. On the hour mark, Macari got the second with a sweet flick. In the 71st minute, McCalliog – whose masterful midfield performance made him most people's man of the match – lofted the ball 18 yards over a couple of defenders, colleague McIlroy and towering Blackpool keeper George Wood. "I just wish it had been on the telly," laments McCalliog of his sumptuous strike.

"They paralysed us," said Blackpool defender Dave Hatton in the shell-shocked aftermath of his team's 3-0 loss. George Wood conceded, "United were so good that they were taking the mickey out of us in the last 20 minutes." Wyn Davies expressed a sentiment that matched that of more than one reporter when he said of United, who were, naturally, still top of the division afterwards, "They deserve to go up." He added, "It's all very well saying that we didn't play – United's pressure just wouldn't let us." Willie Morgan, so unhappy at his substitution against Portsmouth, seemed in a good mood after being another individual (of admittedly quite a bunch) who had performed well. "I really feel on top now that the midweek matches are coming to an end," he said. "I was finding two matches a week exhausting. But give praise to Blackpool. There were no kickers and they let us play football."

\*\*\*

In the week following the Blackpool match, Docherty was asked by one newspaper whether the winter would bring an end to United's winning streak. "It is a fallacy," Docherty said dismissively. "I just don't see heavier grounds as a danger. We are capable of varying our game to suit the conditions. We play it short and we play it long all the time anyway. Many of our players have just been though a period of playing two games in a week, occasionally four games in 10 days, and they are not tired. So I don't see how playing one match on the heaviest of grounds is suddenly going to make us run out of steam. We have one or two players on the slim side, but it certainly won't worry the defence. Jim Holton, Stewart Houston and Alex Forsyth will probably play better on heavy grounds and Martin Buchan is playing brilliantly on anything. Brian Greenhoff is a strong player and so also is Stuart Pearson." Of course, Docherty left out the physically slighter players against whom question marks could be put regarding their ability to cope in sodden conditions: Lou Macari, Jim McCalliog and – especially – Sammy McIlroy and Gerry Daly. However, though that winning streak – inevitably – didn't last, and though its end did coincide with the stage of the season when the going on the turf was rough, The Doc proved to be right, with none of those latter four players exhibiting any particular collapse in form.

Southampton visited Old Trafford on Saturday October 26. Macari played well but neither he nor any of his colleagues were able to break the impasse. Finally, Pearson, who had come on as substitute, sorted things out. On 78 minutes, he glanced Houston's cross adroitly into the far corner of the Southampton goal with his forehead. The 1-0 win wasn't exactly convincing but United maintained their unbeaten home record, as well as their pole position in the table.

There were a couple of Reds who were not happy campers today. Macari told reporters afterwards that he was tired of being Pearson's stand-in. "I'm not being conceited but I believe that I am playing well enough to be in the first team whether Pearson is fit or not," he complained. "If I find that I am still considered only for the first team as stand-in for him then I shall have to have a think about my situation. I'm ambitious like any other player who believes in his ability." He then revealed that the impression some may have got that differences between he and Docherty were now over following his transfer listing and subsequent rapid recall to the team last season was erroneous: "Let's face it, I wasn't left out of the first team in the first place this season because of my ability on the field. It was something behind the scenes, as the saying goes, and I don't want to talk about it."

Docherty was only saved from the impression being given of a club in turmoil by the fact that Willie Morgan didn't air his own complaints to reporters afterwards. His grievances revolved around his substitution. A chant had begun among the 48,724 spectators – the club's biggest

League gate of the season yet – for the appearance of Pearson, who was the substitute for a team whose starting line-up was unchanged since last weekend. It was an indication of just what a crowd favourite Pancho had become. However, when in the 57th minute the supporters got their wish, it turned out to be a poisoned chalice. When the identity of the man making way for Pearson became known, many in the stadium – according to reporter Don Hardisty – "gasped in surprise". His comment indicates that the crowd's unhappiness at Morgan being pulled off was down to something more than the fact that Willie was another crowd favourite and a much more long-standing one than Pancho. Though United had been repeatedly opening up the Southampton defence, so far they had also repeatedly failed to deliver the killer blow – despite Southampton being at the opposite end of the table – and Docherty had reasonably decided something needed to be done about it. But this was the second time in three games that the winger had been taken off. Morgan was even more furious this time than when McCreery replaced him against Portsmouth. That Pearson transpired to score the only goal of the match would have been for Morgan beside the point. Nor was it, for him, the point that all players get substituted at some stage. In his view, his substitutions were nothing to do with fluctuating form but part of a pattern of deliberate humiliation by his manager. "I was so sick that I got changed and went straight home without waiting for the end," said Morgan at the end of the season. "I didn't do it to cause any trouble. It was a spontaneous reaction and I apologised for it afterwards, even though there was nothing in the club rules at the time to say that you should not leave the ground as soon as you'd finished playing. From then on it seemed to me a matter of having a bet each game on the time I was going to be pulled off."

His humiliation was only going to get worse. In January, he was stripped of his captaincy, which was given to Buchan. (This symbolic move mirrored, of course, the way the out of form/favour George Graham lost that role to Morgan himself.) March saw the signing of Steve Coppell, who – like Morgan – was a right-sided winger and whose arrival could therefore be interpreted as a pointed message that Morgan's services were no longer required. Indeed, by the last two months of the season, Coppell had usurped Morgan's place in the side.

The minutes of the Manchester United board meetings for that October show that Docherty told the directors that Morgan had asked him for a transfer and that Docherty was recommending to the board that they reject his request. The only reason the world – and Morgan – knows this fact is that Morgan subpoenaed these minutes when he found himself sued for libel by Docherty in 1977. Morgan said he was astonished at this claim and that no transfer request had been made by him, not least because a lucrative testimonial for his long service was on the horizon. His conclusion as to why Docherty should make such an assertion, if true, does – this time – deserve the adjective Machiavellian: Docherty, he thought, was trying to make him look bad in the eyes of the board so as to make it easier to offload him. Docherty himself didn't deny that he was disenchanted with Morgan but attributed it to what would – if true – be something that would be perfectly reasonable. Morgan had picked up an injury in the close season after 1973/74, not from his exertions in that summer's World Cup in West Germany, but from a tennis match once he returned home. Hit in the eye by a tennis ball, he suffered a detached retina. Morgan had an operation and Docherty cut short his holiday to visit him. Despite this act of kindness – one Docherty claims he engaged in as a matter of policy with hospitalised players, something that does seem to be borne out by the facts – Docherty became of the opinion that Morgan's subsequent performances indicated that his capacity to shred defences with his dribbling skills had been significantly and permanently hampered by going under the knife. Yet Morgan claimed that having missed pre-season training because of his injury, Docherty had insisted he start the season in the first team despite not being fully fit: "I remember his words now: 'I'd like you to play because even if you aren't fit you'll take a lot of marking, you'll take a lot of players off other players.' He went on to say I would get fit as I went along. But despite all this and the fact that the team were winning and doing well, he started with remarks against me."

"I didnae see that coming," says Jim McCalliog of his friend's dispute with their manager. "It was a terrible injury and it was a very unusual injury, because to get a tennis ball in your eye, it doesnae seem possible, does it? You just think how can a big tennis ball go in somebody's eye? It was just kind of weird, and we didn't know about it for a wee while. It could have affected him. The boss was in training every day. Tommy Cav would take the training but he was watching all the time was The Doc. He was a good footballer himself, so he knew the score." McCalliog says he didn't notice whether Morgan's abilities had declined ("I wasn't that type of person. I just got on with my own thing"), but offers, "Your eye does affect your balance." Greenhoff doesn't recall a deterioration in Morgan's abilities. "I got on well with Willie, playing wise," he says. "We seemed to have a really good understanding." However, that doesn't mean he has sympathy for his point of view on Docherty: "Willie just doesn't see anything good in Doc. He doesn't see any good in anybody, Willie."

Some might suggest that Morgan's storming out of Old Trafford in fury at being pulled off when, as captain, he was supposed to set a more temperate example justified that position being taken away from him. No doubt though, Morgan – if he was inclined to quote anonymous ancient philosophers – would retort that those whom the gods wish to destroy, they first make mad.

\*\*\*

The following Saturday, November 2, Macari got his wish for a place in the starting line-up regardless of Pearson's fitness. This, though, meant Morgan was displaced and the winger sat – no doubt simmering – on the substitute's bench for much of the match. The other change was Sidebottom coming in for Holton. United's 4-0 home victory against Oxford United in front of a crowd of 41,909 was as convincing as the 1-0 win the previous week had been unconvincing. Pearson was rampant, hitting a hat-trick that took his tally to eight goals in seven games. As if proving a point, Macari got the other goal.

Afterwards, Pearson said, "This is easily the best Second Division side I have played in – a class above everything else. We have had poor games and still won, whereas last season United were apparently playing well and losing matches by the odd goal. It's tremendous playing in front of this crowd. How can any player fail to be motivated by it?" Pearson didn't even think his Second Division status would affect the possibility of him being considered for the England team, which selection was a notion in the air at the time. "My own international chances must be better here than anywhere else," he said. "And like all professionals, I'm ambitious in that direction." Pearson might be said to be biased, but Oxford manager Gerry Summers was no less complimentary about the Reds, if somewhat less ebullient. He commented, "We were taught a lesson today. We were geared up for this game and thought we would be okay if we could get over the first 20 minutes. But we didn't, and United punished us for some bad defensive play. They are a very good side who are putting everything together."

The Reds were now five points clear at the top of the table again, even if the four clubs below had a game in hand. United's wobble at Norwich, then, would now appear to be over. Yet Saturday November 9 saw a result that confirmed a slightly worrying pattern in the play of Manchester United this season: a tendency to follow an emphatic victory with a performance that was distinctly lacklustre. Just as with the underwhelming United performances in the fixtures following the Bolton, Manchester City and Blackpool games, so the Reds' display at Ashton Gate following the trouncing of Oxford left much to be desired. Usually, United got away with poor form, their extra class ensuring they could ride out the storms created by substandard play and convert more chances than their opponents. This time, as with the Norwich match, their luck ran out.

The Reds stroked the ball around with something approaching imperiousness in the first quarter of an hour, but soon Bristol City manager Ian Dicks' strategy of keeping United too preoccupied coping with striker Tom Ritchie to settle into their normal classy groove began paying off and the exact same United line-up that had taken Oxford apart began to look like impostors. The half-hour mark saw City's John Emanuel score. George Graham replaced Daly after the interval but still the Reds couldn't muster a serious attempt on goal, let alone a reply.

"We had a bad day," Docherty said afterwards of the humiliation in front of a 28,104 gate. "We did not play well, and suffered for it." Stepney blamed himself for the goal and apologised to Docherty afterwards for not cutting out the cross that led to it. "Alex was upset, but I sympathised with him," said The Doc. Referring to the fact that United – and Stepney – had conceded just eight goals in 17 League games, Docherty said, "We still have the best defence in the Second Division."

Of course, that success for Bristol City was measured in the fact that they had defeated the table leaders by a single goal where on a good day United gave clubs the hiding of their lives illustrated the relative nature of the Robins' triumph. Additionally, United's League status was left unaffected due to closest rivals Norwich losing their home match today. Asked about the promotion prospects of City – who now lay fourth – Docherty sniffed, "I doubt if they will be there at the end of the season, because they do not score enough goals. They are the most defensive team we have met so far. I was surprised to see them play with so much emphasis in defence in front of their own supporters." Though this might plausibly be posited as an example of Docherty once again not being able to be gracious in defeat, for the record, he was right: Bristol City ended up fifth, having scored 28 fewer goals than the team immediately above them.

Docherty kept faith in the starting line-up beaten by Bristol City for the League Cup fourth-round tie on Wednesday November 13 against First Division Burnley at home, although changed the substitute from Graham to Morgan. The 46,275 who once again provided an excellent midweek turnout were rewarded with a fine match, if maybe one a little too close for Docherty's comfort. *Match Of The Day* were once again filming a United fixture.

Though United scored a fine goal when Forsyth found Macari by chipping over the Burnley defence, the Reds went in for the interval 2-1 down. Willie Morgan's equalising goal four minutes into the second-half was straight out of 'Roy of the Rovers' on two levels. The first was its sheer, unfeasible skill. Receiving the ball far outside the Burnley penalty area, he walked with it for a few yards and then executed the most astonishing chip, leaving Stevenson helpless as it ballooned past him into the top corner of the goal. The second Roy of the Rovers quality was its timing, not in the match but in a wider sense. Morgan celebrated by facing the United dug-out, his arm raised, his face unsmiling. Morgan didn't score many goals – this was his second of the season, and one of only four from him in 1974/75 – but he could not have wished for a better moment (and manner) to confirm the fact of his intact skills, and indeed – considering the distance – eyesight, in the face of a sceptical manager. "What I was saying," Morgan later revealed of his gesture, "was 'up yours'."

Classic strikes don't win matches though, only the acquiring by a team of more goals than the opposition. On that count, the tie was still up for grabs. Three minutes from the end, Macari received the ball and slammed in a shot. It hit the post. He made no mistake with the rebound.

Burnley's Colin Waldron was unhappy about his team losing and was not convinced of the brilliance of Morgan's strike. "We had a full-back on the post," he recalls. "The full-back's six foot, and I felt that he should have jumped and he could have kept it out, but he didn't. He wasn't a good header of the ball. It's no good saying you're gutted to go out to Man United. You're gutted going out to a Second Division side. It was a game that we should have at least got a draw out of. In those days, the League Cup was a good cup, not like it is now, a peanut thing, and to go out to a Second Division side … " Though he says of Docherty's United, "They'd improved", he adds, "They weren't a great outfit. I felt that the 3-2 flattered them. Even if it's a Fourth Division side, if you deserve to get beat, you deserve to get beat, but I remember going out for a meal afterwards in Manchester with some friends of ours and being absolutely mortified that we got knocked out."

\*\*\*

Euphoria seems to have been the mood around Old Trafford now. So much so that though Docherty was still sticking to his refusal to predict promotion at the end of the campaign, it seemed perfectly clear from comments made to reporter Frank Clough that November that the club were contemplating life back in the top flight the following season. "We have had our bad times but the club is smiling again," said Busby. "You can feel the happiness in the dressing rooms and the corridors and right through the club there's this certain feeling that we're on the way back." With remarkable candour, Busby went on, "To be honest, the past few years have been like a nightmare. It was getting so bad that I even feared going to the ground. We seemed to have fallen into decay, good youngsters weren't coming through any more. We seemed unable to prevent things going wrong. But everyone is smiling now. And it's not just because we're top of the division. We are back on the right lines again and I've got this feeling deep down that we are going to be okay for a good few years. The team isn't just playing well, they are going out and entertaining, playing some marvellous football. And they must be the youngest side since before Munich. I'm delighted – not just for the club but for the fans. Their loyalty last season was fantastic ... and I'm delighted for Tommy Docherty. I think this chap is going to be one of the great managers."

That potential great manager was also in a candid mood. Docherty said, "I thought we'd worked a wee miracle when we stayed up in that first season I took over. I thought we'd won enough breathing space but I was wrong. Losing world-class players like Law, Charlton, Best and Ian Moore didn't help [but] in the end it was my fault. We played far too defensively for much of last season. When I finally gave the lads their heads and told them to attack, I was a month too late. They did superbly but ran out of time. But in that period Matt and I saw something that more than made up for going down. We saw youngsters starting to come through, starting to believe in themselves, starting to express themselves. We knew that if we could keep that momentum going this season we'd have a chance of jumping straight back. But I'll always feel that relegation was a black mark against me. I owe this club something and I'd love to start repaying them by winning promotion."

Saturday November 16 saw United take on Aston Villa at home. Morgan's and Greenhoff's roles were reversed from the previous match (the only change), although only Docherty knows whether this was because Morgan's brilliance last time made it impossible to justify putting him back on the sub's bench. Though currently fifth-placed, Villa would ultimately turn out to be United's closest rivals in the title race and their quality was on full display on a day where they refused to he intimidated by a massive Old Trafford gate of 55,615. More than one reporter noted how the usually rock-steady Stepney seemed shaken by what his team was up against. Villa were ahead after 12 minutes. With the loss of Pearson 10 minutes later with a knee injury, the stage seemed set for an upset.

Gradually though, United began to recover, no doubt with the assistance of some wise and/or profane words from The Doc and/or Cavanagh in the dressing room in the interval. Still, though, the Reds were having trouble in fulfilling their fans' vociferous exhortations to get the ball in the back of the net and things were looking bleak until the 68th minute. A Forsyth cross ran down Villa right-back Robson's chest and arm onto his hand. The ground naturally must have resounded with the age-old football spectators' cry of "ANDBALL!" Robson was known to have a habit of sticking out his arms to balance himself, and Villa boss Ron Saunders was adamant that it wasn't a deliberate handball. Much of the main stand seemed to agree, while Robson himself was furiously gesturing at his chest. However, the referee – at the risk of sounding like television commentator John Motson at his most obsequious – was perfectly placed to see it. Daly's spot-kick – which sent Villa goalie Cumbes the wrong way – was his seventh conversion this season.

The penalty proved crucial when in the 80th minute Houston sent in a low and powerful cross that Daly turned into his second goal and the game's last. Villa may have had good cause to be resentful but one thing couldn't be disputed: after the endless catalogue of decisions, flukes and accidents working against them last season, in this campaign, luck was on United's side. The Reds were now six points clear at the top.

Pearson's injury meant he missed the visit to Boothferry Park for a clash with his old club Hull City in front of a crowd of 23,287 on Saturday November 23. Greenhoff took his place in a side that was otherwise unchanged. United were rampant in the first quarter of an hour. Gradually though, Hull's containing tactics and some wince-making tackling began to tell, though Hull's opening strike – a deflection off Forsyth – was semi-farcical. In the 85th minute United's defeat was sealed in a rather sweet way for the home side: Hull veteran Ken Wagstaff – celebrating exactly 10 years at the club – poked in a cross.

"Some of the tackling was diabolical," Docherty fumed afterwards. "We were the better team and should have had at least one penalty. The way Hull played made this the worst match we've been involved in all season." Docherty may have been, as ever in the face of defeat lately, ungracious but there was some justification in his claims. The match saw four Hull players booked. However, Greenhoff was cautioned, too, and Alf Wood's offence was dissent after taking a bashing from Sidebottom. The match was so ill-tempered that hostilities between the players continued in the stadium's reception room afterwards. There was also fighting on the terraces, although admittedly the hooligan element of the travelling Red Army hardly needed an excuse for a tear-up. Hull's John Kaye preferred to focus on the positive aspects of his team's play: "We had ideas about stopping them, like making them play across the pitch. We worked at it and succeeded."

The cushion they had built up meant that United still had a four-point lead at the top. That said, that they had played a game more than their closest rivals and the fact that their next opponents were second-placed Sunderland gave supporters cause to fear that they were in danger of going into their second wobble of the season.

\*\*\*

It was in this month that the staring contest between Docherty and George Graham ended. Docherty blinked first. The Doc called the out-of-favour player into his office and asked how he fancied a move to Portsmouth. Even though Portsmouth were then bottom of the Second Division, Graham accepted.

Graham's tenure at United was like a dream, by which is meant not a fantasy but something that evaporates with almost no lingering impressions. Indeed, to this day some people who feel they know a little about football in general or Manchester United in particular are surprised to find out that George Graham ever donned the red shirt once, let alone 46 times. "I was at Chelsea with George," says Blunstone. "I thought he'd do a good job, but he didn't settle all that well. Mind you, some don't from London. Coming from London, it's always difficult." McIlroy later said that he felt sorry for Graham, who never seemed to hit it off with the Stretford End and had to endure some terrible stick. Mick Martin, who arrived at the club at the same time as Graham, says, "Why it didn't happen for George I couldn't tell you. Maybe because confidence was low in the side as opposed to coming from a side that was full of confidence at the Arsenal." Graham's failure to make an impression at Old Trafford may also have been because he was slightly bewildered at the situation he found himself in. Having won the FA Cup and League double with Arsenal as recently as 1971 – in the days when the double was so difficult to achieve that it had only been done once before that century – it must have been a shock to him to fetch up at a club engulfed by collective psychological crises and on-field mediocrity, if not outright awfulness. The days when his stately, elegant play was an integral part of the tactics of a winning side must have seemed a painfully distant memory as he tried vainly to make them useful to a team that very often didn't have time for such niceties as they fought for their First Division lives. Meanwhile, though he wasn't bought primarily to score, his final tally of two goals for United – as opposed to his strike rate of 77 in 308 for the Gunners – was pitiful. Forsyth offers, "I think maybe he just never had the pace The Doc liked. George liked to play a bit of football and kept it a wee bit slower. Other players around about him were all sort of attacking players, fiery players." Daly defends Graham: "In my opinion, he done alright. I played in the midfield with him." However, Graham himself later admitted, "I rarely managed to produce anything like my best at Old Trafford," adding, "There was too much tension and anxiety around and suddenly all the rhythm went out of my game and Stroller became something of a workhorse."

The transfer fee Portsmouth are reputed to have paid for Graham is £35,000, although there seems to be some confusion as to whether this is merely the valuation Portsmouth put on their striker Ron Davies, who left for Old Trafford as part of the deal. Davies was

32 – born on May 25 1942 in Holywell – and would only make a handful of substitute appearances for United before departing. However, United fans whose memories went back to August 16 1969 were under no illusions that Davies wasn't a centre-forward of some prowess: that was the day Davies scored all four goals for his team Southampton in their 4-1 humiliation of United at Old Trafford (after the home team had scored the first goal). Matt Busby had tried to purchase Davies in 1966 but had been rebuffed despite indicating a willingness to offer a record-breaking £200,000 for the man he considered the finest in his position in Europe.

\*\*\*

Pearson was back for the Sunderland match – at Old Trafford on Saturday November 30 – and the fact that The Doc dropped McCalliog so that he and Macari could share the starting line-up seems to indicate that Docherty now agreed that Macari should not be treated merely as Pancho's understudy. Holton was also back, displacing Sidebottom, and Greenhoff returned to his normal position.

This was the sort of clash that leads commentators to utter that deathless cliché, "One way or another, something's got to give." The teams occupied the first two places at the top of the division. Though United had a formidable win-loss ration. Sunderland had only lost twice in the preceding 16 months. Old Trafford bulged with 60,585 spectators (United's highest of the season, as it ultimately transpired). At a time when TV airspace for football was at a premium, United were playing host to the BBC's cameras yet again. How appropriate that the spectacle provided should be such a thrilling one. Normally, filleting 90 minutes' action to the 25 minutes allocated by *Match of the Day* for each of its two featured fixtures posed little problem but, explained the programme's presenter Jimmy Hill, such was the positive, attacking football played by both teams, and the plethora of exciting incidents that resulted, it had proved difficult deciding what to leave out.

The erstwhile rivals Macari and Pearson combined for the first goal, Pancho executing a superb shot after receiving the ball from the Scotsman on 11 minutes. However, the jubilant Red fans were reduced to stunned silence when the visitors took the lead within three minutes via two goals in quick succession. The energised Sunderland buffeted the United goal. After the interval, however, United – roared on by the biggest support in English football – showed why they had led the table since the second week of the season. On 55 minutes, Morgan guided the ball into the Sunderland net from a Pearson cross. Docherty gave Ron Davies his debut on 60 minutes, bringing off Greenhoff. Though the Portsmouth signing would not

189

have an illustrious career at Old Trafford, his time there couldn't have gotten off to a better start. A minute after having his studs checked by a linesman, he was feeding the ball through in a move that ended in McIlroy firing in the winning goal.

The teams were given a standing ovation at the match's end. To cap a perfect day for the Reds after a 3-2 victory that left them six points clear of both Sunderland and Norwich City, the hooliganism problem that had given them so many bad headlines recently was absent: there were no reported arrests.

The team were unchanged for the League Cup fifth-round tie at Ayresome Park attended by 36,005 on Wednesday December 4, a game watched by England manager Don Revie. Jack Charlton's Middlesbrough were thriving in Division One following their ascension the previous season. United dominated the first 15 minutes, but were soon stifled by a defensive approach normally used by Middlesbrough at away fixtures. Stepney made several good saves on the night, the most crucial one coming 14 minutes from time when Hickton volleyed from ten yards out. Stepney's out-thrust arm prevented United's ejection from the tournament and set up a return encounter back in Manchester.

Morgan later recalled Docherty being asked by pressmen about Stepney's fine performance today. The winger noted, "This was an ideal chance for a manager to praise one of his players. But because it was Alex, all Docherty said was, 'That's what he's paid for'."

United maintained the same starting line-up for their visit to Hillsborough on Saturday December 7th. A crowd of 35,067 saw a thrilling, see-sawing match. The match wasn't quite so thrilling for Jim Holton. Eight minutes after United had gone ahead with a seventh-minute Houston free-kick, Big Jim was stretchered off following a challenge by ex-Red Eric McMordie. Not only was the latter not penalised but Sheffield Wednesday took advantage of Holton's absence (for which Davies was brought on to compensate) to mount their first serious attack and scored from a corner. When Colin Harvey put Wednesday ahead on 24 minutes, pandemonium erupted on the terraces. Despite mounted police rushing to deal with it, the fighting spilled over onto a corner of the pitch. Referee Ken Baker cast several anxious glances in that direction but kept the game going. Battle was still being waged on the half-hour mark when Wednesday went 3-1 up.

Whereas the yobs vented their fury with their fists and boots, United proceeded to play like the champions they were hoping to be. Eight minutes after the interval, Macari pulled one back. By the 63rd minute, Pearson had equalised. Though the see-sawing wasn't over – five minutes later Wednesday were ahead once more – on 78 minutes, Macari scored the final goal of the game.

When the final whistle blew on a 4-4 draw whose thrills and switchbacks must have left the attendees drained, Docherty was so jubilant that he threw caution to the wind in his post-match analysis with the gentlemen of the press. There was no talk now from The Doc of being careful to not assume the club would bounce straight back. Instead he vaingloriously declared, "We needed character as well as skill to come back from that ... There is no other team in the League that would have come back against Sheffield Wednesday the way we did ... I haven't said it before but now I'm sure: we'll be in the First Division next season." United's lead at the top had narrowed, but they were still five points clear of second-placed Sunderland.

The diagnosis for Holton turned out to be a broken leg. Though Holton took Docherty's comment afterwards as the jocularity it was ("Of course it's a blow to us. It now means we're left with the second-best centre-half in the League – Arnie Sidebottom"), Big Jim was left contemplating the injury that any footballer most dreads. At the very least, it ruled Holton out for the rest of the season. That United had only recently given him a new five-to-ten-year contract must have made Holton feel a little better in terms of financial security, but he faced a long road to recovery. United, meanwhile, faced the problem of filling the vacuum in defence his loss created. In point of fact, though United did struggle for a while without Holton, in the end they managed. Ultimately, they managed very well. Without being unkind to Big Jim, it was for the best that he was displaced. His brand of football – whether brought about by malice or clumsiness – simply did not fit in with the team that Docherty was building. Though the process of cleaning up United's tactics had already started, with Holton remaining in the team, it is to be doubted that Manchester United would have won the *Daily Mail*'s Fair Play Award in the following two seasons.

\*\*\*

Daly replaced McCalliog and, of course, Sidebottom replaced Holton for United's home match against Orient on Saturday December 14. Orient clearly came to Manchester mindful of the suggestion of some that the massive, deafening support for the Reds – 41,200 today – was virtually worth a goal start. The London's club's cagey strategy frustrated United so effectively that for the first time this season, they failed to score at their home ground. Afterwards, Docherty slammed Orient's "pathetic tactics, which frankly I wouldn't pay to watch". Nothing The Doc did, including bringing on Davies for Greenhoff on the hour mark, had been able to overcome what he adjudged, "parasite football – trying to live off other teams." He added,

"They are so pleased with themselves, you'd think they had won the FA Cup." The dropped point meant United's lead at the top of the table narrowed from five to four points.

For the home replay of the Middlesbrough League Cup tie on Wednesday December 18, United made one change to the team, replacing Forsyth with Young. This meant that the United team was different to the one that had taken on Middlesbrough at their own ground a fortnight previously to the tune of two players (the other difference, of course, being Sidebottom for Holton). The outcome, however, couldn't have been more profoundly at odds with that of the previous match. Both sides were tentative during the first 15 minutes but in time such was United's onslaught that Middlesbrough began to plant themselves in their own half for safety. United obtained a free-kick in the 54th minute. Though Macari's effort curled over the wall, it didn't look dangerous until goalie Jim Platt failed to hold it. Pearson took advantage of his clumsiness to force the loose ball into the net. Middlesbrough realised that they had no option but to go forward as their Wembley dream began to recede.

One could argue that the fact that another Middlesbrough blunder led to United's second goal indicated that this match might have gone either way. The counter argument is that United were piling on so much pressure as to make the possibility of error greater. Graeme Souness was the culprit, hitting a careless pass that McIlroy intercepted. Having said which, the manner in which the Irishman dribbled with the ball and came out on top as he went one-on-one with Platt was cool-headed class. Macari closed the proceedings, volleying in a cross for a 3-0 victory. It later emerged that Martin Buchan had executed his creditable performance while suffering from a broken nose, the injury sustained in the Orient match. The club had kept it secret. The thumping good crowd of 49,501 were left pleased they had shrugged off their tiredness after a day's work and braved the weather for the trip to Old Trafford.

United knew already that their opponents in the semi-final were to be Norwich. Though Norwich had been one of the only sides to beat United this season, reporter Frank McGhee noted that this had been the Reds' third First Division scalp in succession in this tournament. "Only Norwich block their path to the League Cup final," said McGhee, "which on last night's replay form makes me feel slightly sorry for Norwich."

Once more, after the Red euphoria came the Red comedown. Their visit to Bootham Crescent to play York City on Saturday December 21 produced a so-so match and a narrow 1-0 victory, despite United boasting exactly the same starting line-up as on Wednesday. True, Sidebottom had to go off after an awkward fall onto his shoulder, with substitute Ron Davies playing upfront and Greenhoff falling back to replace Sidebottom, but all that happened on 50 minutes, by which time the humdrum tone of this match had been set. Morgan at least executed exciting wing work and his cross provided the 18th-minute goal, Pearson the scorer.

The crowd – 15,314 or 15,567, depending on whom you believe – was the lowest United would play to all season. Nonetheless, the stadium was full to capacity. The match was all-ticket and York did a then-novel thing in containing the travelling Reds (approximately 6,000 of them) in one area, behind an eight-foot-high metal fence to the rear of one goal. It proved a good idea, even if there was a minor ruckus when it turned out that some United fans had smuggled themselves in at the other end.

York City's manager was Wilf McGuinness, who had been deemed a failure as United manager but had never taken them down into this division. By interesting coincidence, the match took place on the eve of Docherty's two-year anniversary as Manchester United boss. Perhaps not a fantastic way to celebrate the occasion, but United had won and were still five points clear at the top of the table. And while it was true that that division was not the one in which they had been competing upon The Doc's arrival, their exhilarating football this season and the fact that they had beaten First Division opposition three times left few in any doubt that Docherty had effected a real turn-around at the club.

The Reds were unchanged for their home match against West Bromwich Albion on Thursday December 26. The fixture attracted a gate of 51,104, which was duly treated to the first Boxing Day victory of The Doc's tenure. It was not a great football spectacle and it took yet another Daly penalty to achieve, but it was far preferable to the Old Trafford faithful's previous two Boxing Days, which had seen them witnessing miserable losses that put them right off their turkey sandwiches.

McIlroy infused the United fans with Christmas cheer after only five minutes when he fired in a shot from an acute angle that cannoned in off the body of West Brom's keeper Osbourne, who had been expecting him to cross. The visitors got an equaliser directly before the interval. The incident that led to Daly's 62nd-minute penalty saw Pearson go down in the box from a challenge by Gordon Nisbet. While the consensus was that it was a harsh decision, the failure of the ref to award another penalty eight minutes later when McIlroy was brought down was generally considered equally as unjust.

Albiston replaced the injured Houston in an otherwise unchanged United team that visited Boundary Park on Saturday December 28. Oldham Athletic, engaged in a relegation struggle, were desperate men and played like it. Only luck prevented United going 1-0 down in the 12th minute when Oldham's Ronnie Blair came up with a header which many in the 26,356 crowd were convinced had hit a stanchion and bounced out again. The referee waved played on. Stepney conceded immediately after the game, "It definitely went in." United did their best to play football as the 'Latics tried, as one reporter put it, to "kick them out of their stride" but the only goal of the game came on 68 minutes when Sidebottom handled in the area. The resultant penalty was converted by Maurice Whittle. United were now only four points clear of Sunderland, who had a game in hand, as did third-placed Norwich, though the latter were adrift by six points.

Houston was fit again and Albiston therefore dropped for the FA Cup third-round match on Saturday January 4 1975 against Walsall at home. The team were otherwise unchanged. Third Division Walsall were not the type of team a club who had knocked three Division One sides out of the League Cup already this season were going to have sleepless nights over meeting, but the visitors came to the most intimidating ground in the Football League (containing 43,353 today) and – by virtue of a Black Hole Of Calcutta strategy in their own half – obtained a goalless draw and a replay in more comfortable surroundings. Docherty pulled off Morgan in favour of Davies in the 63rd minute but, if anything, Walsall subsequently looked the more likely to score.

Morgan lost his place to McCalliog for the replay at Fellows Park before 18,105 the following Tuesday in the only change. The first goal came in the 21st minute from Walsall's Bernie Wright. Eight minutes before half-time, United pulled one back when they obtained a penalty – Daly the taker, naturally – engendered by a possibly harsh handball decision.

Morgan later claimed that at half-time he tried to give some advice to Forsyth and that, when he did so, Docherty interjected, "You've got your own troubles without telling him how to play." Still, at least this time, Morgan remained on the park for the duration, with Daly maybe surprised to find himself being pulled off in the second-half in favour of Davies. Docherty explained afterwards, "Walsall by then were looking for another replay. I wasn't, so I decided to do something different." Considering the half was only eight minutes old when he did this, one wonders whether The Doc was anxiously mindful of the fact that a further replay would take place the next Monday – the same week as both United's League Cup semi-final and a highly important League match against second-placed Sunderland.

With the score still at 1-1 after 90 minutes, the match went to extra-time. In the 20th minute of the extended period, Stepney fumbled a cross and diminutive Walsall striker Alan Buckley headed it in. With five minutes to go, United's players may have been beginning to panic as well. The usually clean-cut Buchan tripped George Andrews in the penalty area. Buckley put the home side 3-1 up from the spot. McIlroy then managed a second for United, but it was implausible that they could recover in the time remaining.

After the first Walsall match, at least three reporters had claimed that Docherty didn't want the distraction of FA Cup replays in United's promotion campaign (although none gave exact quotes). Well – the sarcastic might aver – The Doc now had something even better: the club were not going to be distracted by that competition at all. In all seriousness, it was a rare disaster for United this season.

Morgan's status in Docherty's affections would seem to have been ambiguous at this point. Morgan later said of the half-time incident, "I went in to see the manager the following day to say that if that was the way things were going to be it was pointless me being captain. But next Saturday, in front of all the other players in the dressing room, he apologised. That was quite a gesture and shows how unpredictable he is." Yet the home match against Sheffield Wednesday on Saturday January 11 marked the point at which Martin Buchan became United skipper. Despite being stripped of his armband, though, Morgan was back in a significantly reshuffled team, even if he was pulled off in favour of Daly on 63 minutes. The starting line-up was Stepney, Forsyth, Houston, Greenhoff, James, Buchan, Morgan, McIlroy, Pearson, Macari and McCalliog. Attendance was 45,662.

Those hoping for a repetition of the eight-goal extravaganza these two teams had provided in the first week of December were to be disappointed. United were mostly lacklustre. Which is not to say that this was another United capitulation to inferior opposition such as had been witnessed midweek. Halfway through the first half, United won a penalty. With Daly sitting on the sub's bench, McCalliog temporarily resumed the penalty-taker's role, converting successfully. Five minutes after half-time, McCalliog made sure of United's victory and his own personal day of triumph by crashing the ball into the roof of the Wednesday net. Yet McCalliog was left with a nagging dissatisfaction. "I was dying to get a hat-trick at Old Trafford," he says. Worryingly, in light of Wednesday's League Cup semi-final, Pearson had to hobble off four minutes from time after an innocuous-looking challenge.

United might still be top of the table but reporter Douglas Peacock made an interesting point about the match and what it showed about United's see-sawing inconsistency. "Though they may not be marking time until their almost inevitable return to the First Division, Manchester United seem to have become bored by the flimsy challenge posed by such clubs as Sheffield Wednesday. They have shown often enough that they can rise to an occasion, but if the occasion itself does not arise, they are apt to be as ordinary as the next team … "

\*\*\*

Buchan would retain the skipper's armband for the rest of the season, apart from the home fixture against Fulham in the season's closing stages that constituted the one match Buchan missed. He would also be United's permanent skipper – barring injury – for the rest of Docherty's tenure at the club. Though there seems to be convincing evidence that taking the captaincy from Morgan was part of a campaign to undermine an out-of-favour player, few would dispute that Buchan had the mien of a captain. It could also be posited that he fitted the role more convincingly than Morgan. The first reason being that he was a defender. Though we all love wingers like Morgan, it is their self-consciously swashbuckling on-field nature that endears them to us and it somehow seems far more appropriate that a man concerned not with thrilling the crowds but with ensuring his team doesn't let in goals should be given authority over his colleagues. A second reason was Buchan's grooming. In an era where all footballers sported sweeping tresses, Buchan favoured a cut that showed his forehead and ears. Additionally, though not an unpleasant man, Buchan also had a certain pomposity about him, both on and off the field. Finally, he showed a consistency in form that implied a steady hand on the tiller: Docherty later observed that the important point to be made about the fact that Buchan was an almost ever-present this season was that he played well in all of his many games.

Not that any of these qualifications for the captaincy marked Buchan out as a staid character. Anything but. In a profession in which men tend to reserve their individual expression for their playing style, Buchan was one of those people whose ability to think for himself and propensity to display tastes and interests beyond the familiar and the lowest common denominator made him stick out like a sore thumb. Buchan was sort of the 70s equivalent of Graham Le Saux, although if anything his unusual qualities were even more pronounced in an era in which footballers were so shallow that the player profiles in the weekly kids' football magazine *Shoot!* saw them give comically identikit answers (Favourite music: ELO, The Eagles; Favourite food: steak and chips; Person you'd most like to meet: Muhammad Ali). For one thing, as Gordon Hill says, "Martin kept himself to himself." Says Buchan of this loner disposition, "I'd rather sit and read a book than play cards or get my face in the racing section of the paper. If that's being a loner, I love being a loner. I've got a mind of my own … You cannae help the way you are. When I was in the Scotland squad I was quite happy to sit in a corner and read a book, I didn't feel I had to worship at the feet of some of the senior players in the Scotland squad at the time." He adds, though, "I like to think I was my own man but I was still a team player."

Buchan's range of interests certainly indicate that he wouldn't have felt completely comfortable with the average soccer player: his United career coincided with him studying Spanish and French and honing his skills on guitar. Additionally, he spurned the betting shop culture which at that time was predominant in football. "Never had a bet in my life," he says. "I used to feel guilty putting a pound in the kitty for the Grand National draw." Yet another thing that marked Buchan out as different to his colleagues was his not being affected by where he was playing: "A lot of players have a mental barrier, and are happier playing at home as against playing away," he says. "To me the pitch is the same size, there are still 11 opponents whether you play at home or away. The rules of the game are the same. But there is no doubt certain players are often regarded as homers, performing better in front of their home crowds, but I don't really know there's any excuse for that."

When discussing his keener intellect, another unusual quality in a footballer – humility – shines through in Buchan's comment, "I was just fortunate enough to have a good education. Having an education doesn't make you more intelligent than other people." However, he points out he wasn't as unusual as has been suggested: "When I played at Aberdeen ... our local derby was at Dundee 67 miles away so we were used to travelling. In those days you had just one sub so your travelling party was 13 players: the first XI, the sub and an extra guy in case anybody fell ill, so you would be crammed into two six-seater [train] carriages. Well, the card school would be in one and we senior secondary lads would play all sorts of word games and the like for fun in the other rather than play cards for money ... " Referring to United's Alan Gowling, who divided his time between Old Trafford and obtaining a degree in economics, Buchan says, "Alan Gowling was a very intelligent lad. I think you're doing him a disservice if you don't mention him and you mention myself and Steve Coppell."

Though he might have a captain's mien, Buchan was not exactly the yes-man one would expect a person who did well in a position of authority to be, as manifested in several recent incidents. He was sent home before a friendly match against Hull just before the 1974/75 season started in a dispute over the club retaining his passport, which he considered to be a private piece of property that was to be held only by himself. Though he later changed his mind and travelled up by car to Hull to apologise, Docherty was to learn during a bitty practice match during the following season that an iconoclastic leopard does not change its spots. The Doc kept blowing on his whistle to stop proceedings when things were unsatisfactory. When Willie Morgan later spoke publicly about the incident, he said, "At training one morning,

Docherty was ranting and raving during the practice match and Buchan yelled, 'The way you're going you're not helping things.' Docherty sent him off and they've had repeated verbal clashes in the dressing room." According to Morgan, Docherty was not amused to find that Buchan was no yes-man. "He has … tried three times to transfer Martin Buchan," Morgan claimed after the 1974/75 season. "In the dressing room, in front of everybody, he has told Buchan that he'll have him on his way as quickly as he likes."

One wonders whether this stubborn and individualistic streak may have been partly why Docherty had taken so long to pass the captaincy to Buchan following Bobby Charlton's retirement. Even when he had taken it off George Graham, he had initially overlooked Buchan, despite having previously publicly spoken of him as Graham's successor. Buchan himself admits that his captaincy did not engender any closeness between he and the manager. "Some other players were part of Doc's 'inner circle' but I certainly wasn't," he says. Did he get the impression that some players were fairly close to Docherty? Buchan: "I knew that certain players were carrying tales to him."

His contrariness saw Buchan refuse to participate in a deal agreed by the rest of his colleagues with sportswear company Gola. Though it was worth around £300 for each player (approaching £2,500 in today's money), Buchan turned his nose up at the idea on the grounds that he was happy with his present make of football boot. The option existed, of course, for a judicious application of paint to pretend his normal boots were the sponsor's (such practices hit the headlines that season) but Buchan found such behaviour distasteful. Some no doubt found such attitudes superior but there was a very positive side to this iron morality. Steve Coppell has recalled a man who would frequently visit sick children in hospital and would ask (actually, more like demand) his colleagues sign autographs for kids who idolised them.

O'Farrell purchased Buchan from Aberdeen in February 1972 for £125,000. Born in Aberdeen on March 6 1949, Buchan says, "I started off as an inside-forward in my primary school team. By the time I was 11, I'd lost a bit of pace and they moved me back to number six. That's where I stayed." Of course, no little boy projects himself into the role of a defender when fantasising about being a professional footballer, so regardless of how highly respected he was as a centre-back, did it frustrate him that fate consigned him to that role? "I would have liked to have been an accomplished midfield player," he says. "Like Beckenbauer before he stepped back into the sweeper role. He was a very, very good midfield player and I would have liked to have played in that position the way that Beckenbauer did because you're involved in the game all the time." Buchan had a small dilemma as he came up to his 18th birthday. Though Aberdeen had expressed interest in him, his academic progress could clearly garner him a university place. However, football was in his blood: his father had also played for Aberdeen. Nonetheless, it's an indication of the mature head on his shoulders that he gave himself a deadline of the age of 21 to have made the grade in football, failing which he would return to academia. He made his debut while still 17 and by the following season was a semi-permanent fixture in the first team. There was a hiccup when Buchan was sidelined by a broken ankle suffered in a car crash, but his key-to-the-door age arrived in the same week Buchan played in the semi-final of the Scottish Cup. Aberdeen won their match against Kilmarnock and Buchan led out his team at Hampden Park to play Celtic, becoming the youngest-ever victorious Scottish Cup final captain at that venue. 1971 saw Buchan voted Player of the Year by Scottish football journalists. Scottish Under-23 and full caps followed shortly thereafter.

However, the achievement in revitalising the fortunes of Aberdeen of which Buchan was part – the Cup victory was only their second since their formation – was if not quite an ersatz accomplishment then something adjacent to it. Without wishing to be patronising to Scottish football – after all, Celtic took the gloss off Manchester United's European Cup victory by making their way into the history books as the first British club to win it in 1967, leaving United only with the first English winners accolade to lay claim to – there is no disputing the fact that many Scottish players of significance see the sport in their home country as merely a stepping stone to bigger things. Those bigger things, then and now with perhaps a brief hiatus in the 80s and 90s when continental European honours briefly had a greater cachet, are English football trophies. Buchan says, "It had always been my ambition to test myself in the English League, which even in those days was calling itself the best league in the world. I wanted to see how good it really was ...

"The time was probably right for me to leave Aberdeen, in that my mentor Eddie Turnbull, the manager who'd taught me virtually everything I knew about the game, had left the previous season to take over at his first love, Hibs. When I joined United on 29 of February, Aberdeen were second in the League, about 13 points adrift of Celtic ... Before I joined United I'd been told very fairly by my manager at Aberdeen, the late Jimmy Bonthrone, that Liverpool and Leeds were in the hunt but I was told that United wanted to sign me because they had concerns about David [Sadler]'s knees. I sensed there was an opportunity for me to play first-team football straight away, whereas if I'd gone to Liverpool or Leeds, there were a couple of obstacles in the way, namely Tommy Smith and Norman Hunter, in my position. People say to me, 'Well, if you'd gone to Leeds or Liverpool you could have won a few medals', but they could have been Central League medals. I might never had made the first team at either club. Anybody who has had a professional career will tell you that they were in the right place at the right time and had taken their chance when it presented itself." Additionally, "When we used to play in the street as kids, we'd give running commentaries of the game and it was always a Manchester United game you were voicing over as you were playing – 'And it's Charlton out to Law, to Best' – so possibly there was an attachment there, because we grew up thinking about Manchester United."

Buchan made his debut for United on Saturday March 4 1972 at White Hart Lane. He was joining a club that were not only the most legendary name in English football but – mathematically at least – title contenders. The last time United had played Spurs had been on November 13 the previous year. United won 3-1 then, which increased their lead at the top of the First Division to three points. United had still been league leaders eight Saturdays before Buchan's debut but had begun drifting down the table as they suffered a run of bad results, including a 5-1 hiding from Leeds at Elland Road on February 19. That season, Buchan played 15 matches and in the Manchester derby in April even scored one of only four goals he would nab for United in his decade there. But the closest the club would come to glory that season was finishing eighth in the League they had led for a long spell and reaching the sixth round of the FA Cup. Alex Stepney has said, "I think if O'Farrell had signed Buchan at the beginning of that season instead of the end, we might have won something that year and Frank might have been saved. He would have made that much difference."

Instead, by Christmas of the 1972/73 season Buchan's move down south would seem to be proving the wisdom of the adage about pride coming before a fall. From being a member of a cup-winning side to fighting relegation was hardly the career trajectory he had envisaged. The alarm bells ringing in Buchan's head must have begun to peal all the louder when, as part of his transfer deal, United played Aberdeen in a friendly. Aberdeen won 5-2. As rumours swirled that O'Farrell was facing the sack, Buchan was contemplating asking to be put on the transfer list. The manager thanked him for his loyalty but dissuaded him. Further apparent celestial disapproval of Buchan's hubris came in the form of United's relegation, even if Buchan could take some consolation that he was the general of a defence whose conscience was clean in the matter of United's calamitous form in that miserable season.

Fortunes had turned since, of course. Being made captain in the middle of the triumphant 1974/75 campaign was hardly an onerous job: it was already clear that United would be there or thereabouts at the close of the season, so 'steady as she goes' was generally the extent of the gee-up Buchan was required to give his colleagues. Nonetheless, the formal authority conferred on him seems, in retrospect, the logical conclusion of the clout he had always seemed to possess.

Another footballer with an effortless authority about him was the aforementioned Franz Beckenbauer, the West German nicknamed The Kaiser who captained his country to World Cup glory in 1974. Buchan and Beckenbauer shared something in common: The Kaiser's habit of calmly rolling the ball under his foot as he looked for options on the field was similar to the way Buchan would not be hurried when searching for a colleague to lay off to. When this author makes this comparison, Buchan squirms. "Our surnames begin with the same letter, that's about the only similarity," he scoffs. "He was a fantastic player." However, Jimmy Greenhoff paid Buchan just as great a compliment when he said that his "reading of the game was so superb that it reminded me of the great Bobby Moore."

***

A crowd of 58,010 packed into Old Trafford on Wednesday January 15 for the first leg of the League Cup semi-final against Norwich. In the absence of the injured Pearson, Daly was in the United starting line-up, with Young sitting on the sub's bench. Greenhoff formed a striking partnership with McIlroy.

With half-time three minutes away, Macari passed to Greenhoff, whose low shot beat Keelan. However, the miserable, drizzling weather had turned the pitch into a sponge and the velocity of the ball was so slow that Benson was able to squelch back and clear off the line. In the last minute of the half, Powell scored for the visitors. Once again, Lou Macari – playing upfront in the second half – was the man of the match in a League Cup tie. He claimed his sixth and seventh goals of the tournament, both of them special. On 50 minutes, he lobbed the goalkeeper when a packed penalty area seemed to prohibit a way through. He had his back to goal at the time. His second goal, which put the Reds into the lead 21 minutes later, saw him receive the ball from Houston, evade multiple challenges by Forbes and shoot past Keelan.

Docherty then brought on Young for Daly. Such a move when a team is ahead is usually a batten-down-the-hatches manoeuvre but, if anything, United attacked more (and Norwich got more defensive). Just as it seemed the match was sewn up, a United howler gave the visitors a big psychological advantage for the return bout at Carrow Road. Houston hit a weak back-pass to Stepney. Before the United goalie knew what was happening, a yellow shirt nipped in and whacked the ball into the net. The identity of that scorer? Ted MacDougall. One is tempted to add, 'Of course.'

***

Pearson's latest breakdown caused Docherty to make a peculiar decision. Instead of opting to utilise the strikers he had at his disposal – with Ron Davies, perennial substitute this season, the obvious candidate and young marksman David McCreery also someone one would have thought would be considered – he instead decided to take a player on loan. The player concerned was an even more curious choice. Born June 10 1945 in Gateshead, Tommy Baldwin was a Chelsea veteran of eight seasons and not exactly one of the country's foremost strikers, even if his League scoring tally of 74 during his time at the London club gave him a respectable ratio of one in approximately 2.5. Chelsea had already loaned Baldwin out to Millwall this season for six games. Docherty had known him during his own managerial term at Chelsea, Baldwin coming to Stamford Bridge as part of the deal that sent George Graham to Highbury. It's for perhaps this reason that Docherty opted to use the now 29-year-old as temporary cover. Baldwin made his first United appearance on January 18 against Sunderland and his second and last on February 1 against Bristol City and scored in neither. When Pearson got back in the side in February, his prolific scoring helped buy Baldwin a one-way ticket back to southwest London.

Baldwin playing in place of Daly was the only change Docherty made for the January 18 Sunderland match, a Saturday game at Roker Park with 45,976 present. Sunderland were clearly desperate to narrow the gap between themselves and their opponents at the top of the table. They had played Southampton the previous Tuesday but only collected a point in a match that wiped out their game in hand over the leaders. With both teams having played 26 matches, United were on 39 points and Sunderland 34. Third-placed Norwich were on 31 points, with 25 games played. The methods Sunderland used were to attack in numbers and to stifle United's attacks. They managed the latter by the remarkable strategy of marking the full-backs. With Stepney unable to throw the ball out to Forsyth and Houston and enable the Reds to build up an attack from the rear, he had to go the long-ball route. When he did, it was only to see Sunderland's Robson beat Baldwin to the ball just about every time.

Sunderland slipped up a little in the second-half, being less vigilant in their marking of Forsyth and Houston. Sunderland might still have won had it not been for a substitution on 66 minutes so strange – forward Finney was withdrawn in favour of defender Ashurst – that their skipper Bobby Moncur was literally seen to shake his head. All the press plaudits afterwards were for United, who had absorbed incredible pressure to keep the game goalless and cement their five-point security at the top of the table.

There were some worrying occurrences during the following week preceding the second leg of the League Cup semi-final on Wednesday January 22nd. Twice in 36 hours, the brakes and clutch on the United team coach were tampered with. The first incident occurred on the Tuesday, when two holes that looked like they had been made by a nail were found in the clutch pipe. On the Wednesday, there was more sinister vandalism. The club's driver Howard Wilson told the press, "It was a real professional job. The tap on the air pressure tank had been opened, draining everything off so the brakes didn't work. A nipple had also been removed and then replaced on the clutch pipe, so that was useless as well. Luckily whoever was responsible didn't realise there was an emergency alarm bell. When we tested the coach this morning, it rang and I knew immediately there had been another sabotage attempt."

The club reported the matter to the police but were dismayed by their response. Explained a police spokesman, "Because there has been no real damage, I can only report it as an incident and not a crime, unless you start pressing attempted murder charges. Maybe the CID will step in later." Docherty was scathing. "If this had happened to the prime minister's car, police would have been swarming all over the place," he said. "Does someone have to get killed before action is taken? The police reaction amazes me. These two attempts have left a nasty, uneasy feeling around and we will be all on edge until we reach Manchester safely. Fortunately the lads have taken it well, but I can't think what their wives and families must be feeling. It's clearly a premeditated campaign by some nut." The club decided to place the coach in a depot overnight. "But it still must be guarded," Docherty said. "My staff and I are prepared to share the watches." He revealed that he, Cavanagh, physiotherapist Laurie Brown and Wilson would be standing watch.

It's of course impossible to know whether all of this had an effect on the United players – subliminal or otherwise – and hence the result of the second leg of the semi. Suffice it to say that United were not in this game (for which Daly replaced Baldwin) as much as they had been in the first leg. Any adverse effects from the week's events were not helped by Macari's rough treatment by his compatriot Duncan Forbes, the Norwich captain.

Had the score remained 0-0 to the end, Norwich would have gone through: they had scored two in the draw at Old Trafford and United none at Carrow Road. However, the away goals rule did not need to be invoked because on 54 minutes a Norwich corner led to a headed Colin Suggett goal. United were now really up against it, requiring at least two strikes. They tried their hardest and Forsyth, McIlroy and Daly might all have scored had it not been for Keelan, who made some great saves. Ultimately, the 31,621 crowd saw the Canaries walk off the victors.

There was more humiliation for Morgan following the 1-0 loss. "The team had played great despite our defeat," Morgan later recalled. "The Doc stood at the dressing room door shaking hands with all the players as they came in – except me. When it came to my turn he just turned his back on me."

In the other second-leg semi-final that day, Aston Villa came out 5-4 aggregate winners against Chester, so the all-Second Division League Cup final predicted by many for this season did take place, even if it was unexpectedly not one that involved United. Villa at this juncture sat only one place below third-placed Norwich in the League table. Though it was a bitter disappointment for the Reds to be out of both domestic cup competitions, perhaps in the end it was good for their title hopes that these two particular teams were thus distracted.

\*\*\*

The final few days of January saw Docherty involved in controversy. The newspapers for January 28 carried Docherty's condemnations of Scotland manager Willie Ormond for not picking Lou Macari for the national team for their imminent European Championship match against Spain in Valencia. In a dispute that will bewilder these who are used to seeing managers protest about their men picking up injuries on international duty that rule them out of club fixtures (even taking into account Docherty's propriety feelings as the previous Scotland boss), Docherty complained, "It's like something out of Monty Python. Lou's not in but Charlie Cooke at 32 is selected. On top of that, they name Gordon McQueen and Graeme Souness when both are suspended, and fail to cover the centre-half position." The Doc said of Macari, "He's entitled to be sick. He's playing out of his skin, better than at any time in his life, and he's good for years. I'm only surprised Scotland haven't gone for Celtic's Billy McNeil, who's pushing 40 ... " Docherty added, bizarrely, though possibly jocularly "And how about my assistant manager Paddy Crerand, who's older than I am?" In fact, The Doc is Crerand's senior by more than a decade.

As if to make sure that Macari didn't feel left out of the verbal broadsides, Docherty had something critical to say about the little Scotsman's off-field activities. Macari had revealed plans to team up with a Lancashire businessman named Jack Trickett as a boxing promoter. They were planning to stage a four-fight bill at Salford Rugby League Club in just over a week's time. "He's told me nothing about it and he can't go ahead without the permission of my directors," said Docherty. "I want to see him in the morning to find out what it is all about." When contacted about this, Macari said, "I've not been able to keep the boss informed because we've had a five-day break from training." Macari added, "Let's face it – this hasn't been my day. You know when you've been doing well enough to play for your country, and I'm ready."

Greenhoff was absent for United's home match against Bristol City on Saturday February 1, replaced by Baldwin. An injured Daly gave way to Young on 18 minutes. The gate was 47,118, a figure that took the total number of visitors to Old Trafford in this campaign over the million mark. The reward the Red fans got for their loyalty this season – and their bravery in ignoring a bomb scare in the 35th minute – was the end of the Reds' unbeaten home run. That said, the only goal of the game was a sickener, for United – despite being well below par – were easily the dominant team. Steve James hit the crossbar and in the closing minutes had two shots blocked on the line, one after the other. With the referee now playing time added-on for injury, Bristol's Keith Fear broke away, went to the byline and crossed for Don Gillies to side-foot home. It was the last kick of the game. Despite the loss, the Reds were still top.

Earlier in the season, Docherty had been caustic about Bristol City's defensive approach in front of their own supporters, but now he was contemplating the fact that they were the only team so far this season who had defeated the Reds both home and away. Perhaps unsurprisingly then, this time around he was more critical about his own men. "Even sitting on the bench, I could smell that goal coming," he lamented. "They should have got the scent of it. too. They should have decided among themselves on the field in those last 10 minutes that they had worked hard to earn a point. They should have chosen to hold onto that instead of going forward to try and get a winner. That's what Leeds and Liverpool, the really top professional sides, would have done. The trouble is that there is not enough talking among our players out on the field. They do all their talking in the bath afterwards, when it's too late." He did admit, "One problem of course is that the Old Trafford crowd keep urging them on to attack and the players tend to respond without making sure it's safe." The Doc concluded, "Well, they've paid for it … I suppose it's all part of a team growing up."

Another part of a team growing up is knowing that no one is guaranteed a first-team place. Docherty seems to have been trying to make that point in his selection for the match at the Manor Ground on Saturday February 8. McCalliog, Baldwin and Daly were out, and Young, Pearson and Greenhoff in. One could plausibly claim that this was mainly a matter of first preference players returning after injury, but in his choice of goalkeeper Docherty seemed to be making a point about the loss of recent form that had seen United win only one of their last eight matches, get knocked out of two cups and notch up just six goals in the process: Paddy Roche made his debut senior appearance.

The Doc's team changes did not bring about a change in luck, nor did the augmentation of the 15,815 crowd by the *Match Of The Day* cameras. That's luck, not form, because United dominated the match, sweeping the ball up the pitch in pretty, tidy patterns. Oxford responded simply by defending grimly. It's not known who would have taken a penalty demanded by Pearson in the 10th minute, what with Daly, McCalliog and (ahem) Stepney all absent, but the referee adjudged that Pancho had merely fallen over Oxford's Light, so it was all moot. Oxford scored the game's only goal. Derek Clarke unleashed a left-foot shot on 35 minutes that went in off the far post. Though United's play improved when Morgan was taken off in favour of Davies, there was no improvement in the scoreline.

It was the fourth successive match in which United had failed to score and their second consecutive League loss. Making this loss more humiliating was the fact of United's 4-0 thrashing of Oxford the previous November. Though the Reds were still top, Sunderland had closed the gap to three points. It wasn't just a bad day football-wise. Hundreds of United supporters were unable to get in and milled outside menacingly. (Some clambered onto roofs adjoining the stadium to get a look at the proceedings.) In an ugly scene, Oxford director David Meeson was punched in the stomach. There was also fighting on the terraces.

Mick Martin made a comeback for the home match against Hull City on Saturday February 15, Morgan the man displaced. There were no other changes. Martin says his recall was part of a mini-trial Docherty had arranged for him: "He said, 'I can't make up my mind about you. One day you look as if you're going to be a great player for us and then you seem to lose interest.' Which I found very strange, 'cos I was never like that. But nonetheless, he did say to me eventually, 'Right, I'm going to play you five games on the trot and after them five games I'm going to make my mind up whether you're going to stay here'."

In the second minute Houston scrambled in a Forsyth free-kick. However, Hull's roughhouse tactics saw James stretchered off, Davies taking his place. Not surprisingly, United's players became disinclined to engage in their normal trickery. McIlroy, at least, was effervescent, taking men on regardless. He also helped make the second goal, his cross finding Davies, who headed back into the goalmouth where a lurking Pearson was ready to blast the ball into his old club's net.

The 2-0 win wasn't an overwhelming victory but a victory of any kind must have been a relief to Docherty, his men and the red part of the 44,712 gate. United's lead was now four points again, and none of the clubs in the top four had a game in hand over them. Aston Villa, in fifth place, had two games in hand but could boast just 33 points compared to United's 42.

It was Villa whom the Reds played next, meeting them at Villa Park on Saturday February 22 before 39,156 supporters. Villa were playing Norwich in the League Cup final the following Saturday and Docherty himself said beforehand, "Villa will be playing for their Cup places." However, few could have predicted that United (unchanged since the Hull match apart from the fact that Stepney was back and that Sidebottom replaced James) would be, in the words of one reporter, "unbelievably bad". In a 2-0 defeat, United sometimes gave the impression of being unwilling rather than unable to fight back. Docherty was not amused when one player came over to the bench for treatment to a cut lip and another to request a tie-up for a sock.

Afterwards, Docherty held court in the office of Ron Saunders. He described his team as "lethargic", and joked of their incompetence today, "When we got to the dressing room, one of our players tried to jump in the bath, missed and fell out of the window." A less humorous Docherty quote about the Villa result was, "Our display was a disgrace. We played like schoolboys." He said he fancied Villa for the League Cup but warned Saunders – looking bemusedly on as The Doc kept the journalists laughing – "Norwich won't make it as easy for you as we did today. They won't care how long it takes – they'll be prepared to go to five replays." When Saunders asserted that Norwich had never played defensively during his time at Carrow Road, Docherty retorted, "Norwich never *played* when you were there", a somewhat dangerous comment for a man whose team had just been completely outclassed.

Back in October after the 3-0 victory over Blackpool, when United had lost only once, Docherty had been asked by a reporter about the possibility of the Reds' run of great form coming to an end. "Every team has an indifferent period and it could come up for us before long," he conceded. "The important thing is we don't go to pieces but struggle through with a few draws. You might go eight games with only the odd win, but if you can hold on to a few draws you can finish a poor spell with eight points – and that could be enough to keep you in the running. People say, 'Look at that team, they have not won for ages but they are still up there.' That is what I hope they will be saying about us if we go off the boil at some stage. That way we will still be able to finish with 60 points, which is the figure I believe will win the Second Division this year." With United after the Villa capitulation on 42 points and still four points clear of Sunderland and Norwich and five points clear of the only team in the vicinity with a game in hand, who were in fact Villa, it could be argued they were still "up there". However, it was another loss, just when the Hull victory had indicated they had turned the corner and some were now beginning to write the Reds' obituaries. Reporter Clive White predicted that Villa would do well in the top flight if they got promoted but that if the Reds also ascended to the First Division, " ... they could be sent straight back down again." He went on, " ... on Saturday's evidence, they looked not unlike the team who were relegated last season, and with much the same problems: a dithering, sluggish defence, no 'brains' in midfield, and no height in attack. What was particularly disturbing was the lack of effort or urgency about their play, especially after the eager way they had worked earlier in the season." White dismissed the suggestions by Docherty that they had suffered from Pearson's absences. He also didn't seem to concur with the suggestion that heavier winter grounds had made United's short-ball playing and occasionally physically fragile team members struggle. Instead, he pinpointed the problem as central defence: "Before they lost the daunting centre-half Holton … United were romping away with the Second Division."

For his part, Docherty's patience over the recent bad form was at a loss. Comfortably top of the table they may have been but the manager clearly felt that that initial collective confidence had ossified into personal complacency and took steps above and beyond a dressing room bollocking to rectify it. The players *en masse* were forbidden to make derogatory comments about their fellow professionals – colleagues or opponents – to the press on the grounds that the ill-feeling generated was distracting. Some players were taken aside individually and told to rein in their night-life. In order to make players aware that they had no guarantee of an automatic first-team selection, he also did something he had not lately much felt the need to: buy.

The Doc's remedy worked wonders and United immediately re-captured the exhilarating form they had shown in those heady first two months of the campaign. It started the following Saturday when the hapless Cardiff City paid the penalty of Docherty's launching of rockets up United players' backsides by being the victims of a 4-0 March 1 hiding at Old Trafford. Changes were inevitable for the match. Sidebottom was replaced by James and Martin by Daly. Morgan also returned to the side, replacing Young. No doubt Docherty pinched his nostrils as he put the winger's name on the teamsheet for a match that needed a good result. Meanwhile, sitting on the bench that day was an unfamiliar figure. The name of this short, serious-looking young man was rendered in the programme as "Kopel", probably a United old-timer's assumption that he was related to 60s Red Frank Kopel. Presumably, that old-timer hadn't seen or paid close attention to some eye-catching press coverage 19-year-old Steve Coppell had just received. One paper carried a quote from Docherty in its report of Coppell's £40,000 purchase from Third Division Tranmere Rovers wherein the Reds manager said, "Bill Shankly told me a couple of months ago that if he had still been manager at Liverpool, Steve would have been in the team."

Though Cardiff were a bottom three club, the first half was goalless. Approaching the hour mark, Coppell was given his blooding. He was sent on in place of Willie Morgan – to a big chorus of complaint from the 43,601 crowd. It's not known whether Morgan feels he was recalled for the purpose of being deliberately humiliated by being withdrawn for a kid, but it can probably be guessed at. This substitution was somewhat symbolic, for that exchange of players would ultimately become permanent. No doubt it helped Coppell's nerves that Houston scored (a fine header) from the corner whose award gave the opportunity for the substitution in the first place, but it must have been an even greater boon when, with his first touch of the ball two minutes later, Coppell crossed for Pearson to get a second with a tap-in. McIlroy scored in the 87th minute, powering toward the opposition goal from his own half and thumping a low shot into the netting to the left of Cardiff keeper Irwin. Coppell's second significant touch of the ball came with a minute of normal time left. It was by his own admission a complete mis-kick, yet it found its way to Macari who was powering into the Cardiff penalty area and who promptly put United 4-0 up. Though the opposition was hardly wonderful, a comprehensive victory is a comprehensive victory, and United could point to the fact that putting four goals past a team who had resorted to placing eight men in front of their goalie was quite an achievement.

"Stuart Pearson lent me a pair of his boots because I didn't have any with me," Coppell revealed after the match. "It was fantastic playing here. The boss told me to play wide on the right and enjoy myself and that's just what I did. The atmosphere, the crowd and the lads in the side were marvellous. They talked me through the match. I didn't get time to feel nervous. This is definitely the place to be." Opined Docherty, "He's a great prospect. Just wait until he gets stronger and training full-time." Docherty's comments about Morgan were somewhat less glowing. "When we came off the park, he'd gone," said the manager. "It's never nice for a player to be substituted. They don't like it, but Willie Morgan must realise this is a 12-man game. Anyway, I was right. The result proved it." Asked if there was now a question mark over Morgan's future at Old Trafford, Docherty said, "I'm not prepared to discuss the Morgan situation, but if he played well enough, he would keep Coppell out – and vice versa. That's the way it has to be."

A Sale resident named Elizabeth Wynne was so incensed by Morgan's substitution in the Cardiff match and subsequent disappearance from the first team that she started a petition demanding his reinstatement and a clarification of his future at the club. Though her comment that Morgan seemed to be being victimised seems in retrospect insightful and prescient, Docherty did actually provide a plausible defence: that the 4-0 victory justified his actions and that replacing a right-sided winger with another in the match was logical and ensured he didn't have to engage in a reshuffling of the team. Morgan's subsequent sidelining was down, he said, to that old football wisdom that you don't change a winning team. To his credit, Morgan – Coppell has stated – showed no antagonism to him.

The day of the Cardiff match also saw the occasion of the League Cup final. It was won by Aston Villa by a single goal in a match that lives in people's memories because it proved the rule in soccer – much debated in pub arguments – that a player can score off the woodwork after failing to convert a penalty if an opponent has touched it first: Graydon put the ball away after Keelan had initially saved his spot-kick onto a post.

\*\*\*

Mick Martin was a casualty of the shake-up Docherty engineered, and of course in dropping him for the match The Doc was reneging on his alleged deal with the Irishman to give him five games on the trot for evaluation purposes. Martin clearly feels he had played well enough in the last two games to be immune to Docherty's attempt to stiffen up the team's backbone, although his memory of the Hull match's scoreline is inaccurate: "We beat them four or five," he says, "I think I'd made two of the goals and I'd hit the post and I'd hit the bar." The Villa match was to be Martin's last start for the club. "I never played in the five games he promised me," he says. "So that was hugely disappointing. I got disillusioned with Tom over that ... I knew there was nothing there for me once I only played one game when I was promised five."

Another casualty of the Cardiff result turned out to be Arnold Sidebottom, who would never play for United again and departed to Fourth Division Huddersfield Town in January 1976 on a free. Such a move ostensibly only increased the height problems of The Doc's Devils: never again in Docherty's reign would the club field on a regular basis a man of Sidebottom's height (6'1") or over it, with only Stepney and Houston – both six-foot-even – coming close. Yet the side's relentlessly attacking style somehow made their veritable midget constitution irrelevant.

Meanwhile, Jim McCalliog had been transferred to Southampton. Unusually, the departing player's issue was not with Docherty but with his assistant. "I had a wee problem with Tommy Cavanagh and that was it," says McCalliog vaguely. Was the problem Cav's disciplinarian approach? McCalliog: "No, not really because I'd never been one for getting in any bother. It was a wee thing that blew up between me and the Cav. I wouldn't back down." Asked if there is anything he can divulge about the disagreement, he responds, "No, not really. It was just one of them things. Dressing rooms are dressing rooms." He does add, "I wasnae treated badly." McCalliog went to speak to Southampton about a move. "I could have gone back to Old Trafford," he says. "It was the hardest thing in my life not to, but I wanted to enjoy my football. I didn't really want the hassle of it all, so I went down and spoke to [manager] Lawrie

McMenemy, and Micky Channon was there and Peter Osgood and they were telling me to go there. I said I would have three or four days down there and then I would see what was happening. It hurt me terribly to leave United. I think for United and I think for me it was the best decision. I've seen Tommy Docherty, I've seen Tommy Cav afterwards, I've always spoke to them. Life's too short to keep vendettas and what have you ... I didn't regret leaving. It was the right decision so if you make the right decision it's not a regret." McCalliog was transferred to the Saints in February for £40,000.

Coppell would transpire to be not merely a gee-up for over-comfortable players but one of Docherty's most important long-term signings. Coppell loved to take defenders on. A compact, business-like figure, he was not graceful in the manner of Daly or, later, Gordon Hill, but what he did, he did very well. Once at the byline, he would fire in a cross and had an impressive knack of doing so without having to slacken his pace, thereby catching defenders on the wrong foot or even facing in the wrong direction. If dispossessed, he would chase back and try to retrieve – another contrast to Daly and Hill, who had neither the inclination nor ability to tackle. His work ethic was also manifested in the way he would take the ball to his opponent over and over again: whereas Daly's and Hill's dribbling was characterised by spur-of-the-moment inspiration, Coppell's was a percentage type. In addition to all of this was an utterly professional temperament: Coppell didn't get involved in arguments or petty feuds, even when, as all skilful players do, he got violently treated by defenders.

Coppell's performance was good enough to ensure that a kid signed as a prospect for the future immediately became a first-team regular. That neither Coppell's present nor previous employers had envisaged his gaining a consistent first-team place so quickly seems to be indicated by the fact that built into the £40,000 transfer deal was an additional £20,000 for Tranmere when Coppell had played 20 League games. United's board may have had misgivings about needing to make that payment as soon as September of the following season, but Rovers were left with their own qualms about the deal. Tranmere chairman Bill Bothwell went on record as saying that the fee agreed on by manager Ron Yates should have been one of not less than £100,000. When one considers that before the season was out, Coppell had been watched by England manager Don Revie, Bothwell's seems to be the valuation closer to Coppell's true worth. Coppell would miss only one of the season's remaining fixtures, a run that coincided with a recovery of form for United. Of course it would be absurd to suggest that the winning streak was solely down to Coppell, but it is indisputable that United had been having a bad patch before his arrival and regained form when he made the team. "He is the kind of player who buzzes and is infectious," observed Docherty. "A new player, if he is good enough, shakes other people up and this is what Steve did for us."

Coppell's best friends at his new club were McIlroy and Greenhoff. Coppell explained that this was because the three of them used the reserve-team dressing room before training, only earning a place in the first-team dressing room the following season. His comment revealed a peculiar situation: though Greenhoff may have made his debut relatively recently, he had been at United since 1968, while, young though he was, McIlroy was very much a veteran.

Coppell's arrival meant that Martin Buchan would now have a companion at the table he commandeered on the team coach for his language studies. The winger was combining football with an attempt to get a degree in economic history. Now in his second year of the course, Coppell had not found the twin tasks of footballer and student difficult to combine hitherto, partly because the Liverpool native, born on July 9 1955, had been studying at his city's university and was therefore within easy reach of Birkenhead-situated Tranmere. The first year of his course coincided with him staking a first team place for himself at Tranmere, where his 12 goals made him the season's top scorer. Playing for a club located in Manchester, however, was a very different proposition and Coppell considered putting aside his third year of studies, at least temporarily, as he prepared to take on the responsibility of turning out for United. Docherty, though, told him to carry on studying, and here we see the good side of a man whose faults have been frequently and vengefully highlighted. Coppell was just one of several United players to whom he showed not merely good man-management (which, however apparently caring, can be manipulative and ultimately about the good of the club) but something genuinely pastoral. One can just imagine the type of intellectually challenged characters English football management was then full of (and still is to some extent, despite the influx of more cerebrally-oriented foreigners) telling Coppell that he had to make up his mind whether he was serious about his football and informing him in no uncertain terms that burying his nose in a book would not get him in the first team. Despite the fact that his own academic career had not progressed beyond the age of 14 and it had not done him any apparent harm in terms of personal fulfilment and financial security, Docherty gave every imaginable assistance to Coppell's studies. With The Doc's blessing, the winger's training regime at Manchester United was spotty rather than vigorous, usually consisting of a visit on Tuesdays for one session of group work. Coppell was trusted to take up the slack as best he could at home. Cavanagh gave him a stopwatch and a schedule to adhere to. While his colleagues were doing exercises and holding practice matches at The Cliff, Coppell attended lectures four mornings per week, only missing one when it occurred on a Friday and United were travelling.

Considering the way the newcomer instantly slotted into the team and began turning defences inside out, few could have any cause for complaint about preferential treatment. Certainly not Buchan, who pays Coppell an amazing compliment when he says, "Although I played with Law, Best and Charlton, they were of a previous era really, and I always say that of my time at Old Trafford, Stevie Coppell was our most valuable player. I would say that without a shadow of a doubt."

***

When United played Bolton Wanderers on Saturday March 8, there were 34 arrests outside and inside Burnden Park. 73 people were thrown out of the ground and nearby windows were smashed. The depressingly familiar bad news about the behaviour of United's fans was at least not mirrored by what went on on the pitch, where United notched up their first victory in six away matches.

The team was unchanged from the last match, with the exception that Coppell took Morgan's place. The latter didn't even make the sub's bench, where Young resided. Coppell's second match for the club was a much less happy affair than his debut. Not only did he fluff a golden scoring opportunity but he got booked when, lining up in a wall, he didn't hear the referee's command to retreat the requisite 10 yards. One might think that, though this was an irritating injustice, it was also not that big a deal. However, one of Coppell's ambitions up to this point was to go through the whole of his career without incurring a caution. Still, it was Coppell who took the corner that led to the Reds' 29th-minute goal, the only strike of the match. Houston went up for it and his header cannoned off the bar. Pearson found the back of the net by getting his head to the rebound.

Houston had to depart on a stretcher 10 minutes into the second-half as a consequence of landing awkwardly in the back of the net when heading a ball off the line. A star of the match, he received a round of applause from the 38,152 crowd. "It was worth it to get the ball away," Houston declared afterwards. United, of course, were still top of the table after the 1-0 win. Bolton manager Ian Greaves said, "I've no complaints about the result. United will go up and we are still in with a mathematical chance of promotion."

A team with somewhat more than a mathematical chance of promotion were fourth-placed Norwich, whom United entertained on Saturday March 15 with an unchanged line-up, including Houston, who lived up to his bionic man reputation in taking his place in the side: he had barely been able to hobble after the awkward fall the previous Saturday. Maybe he willed himself to get fit for a confrontation with a team who would be good candidates for United's nemesis this season: they had been the first team to beat them in 1974/75 and had shattered their Wembley dreams in the League Cup.

Coppell was making his full Old Trafford debut. Meanwhile, Ted MacDougall was playing at Old Trafford for the first time since joining Norwich. He was made Canaries captain for the day. England manager Don Revie was one of the 56,202 crowd and saw a lively first-half in which both teams tried to attack and United – performing with pleasing style – probably had slightly more of the play. Six minutes into the second half Coppell – who had been playing with confidence and centering well from the byline – delivered a low cross. McIlroy must have heard a call from Pearson for he left the ball and watched as Pancho eased it over the line from point-blank range for his fourth goal in five games and his 16th of the season. United gained in confidence from there and it was against the run of play that Norwich obtained an equaliser. With grim predictability for Docherty, it was the man who supposedly couldn't play who got the ball in the back of the United net on 68 minutes, MacDougall scoring his fourth goal against the Reds this season.

Perhaps fearful of seeing victory turn to ashes, Docherty took off winger Coppell and replaced him with midfielder Young. Not that United ground out a draw, a policy Docherty had declared a few weeks back was alien to his men in a comment that contradicted his "They should have chosen to hold onto a point" observation after the Bristol City home match. However, the score remained level and the honours shared. United were still five points clear of Villa at the top of the table, even if Villa had (like, Norwich, who were fourth behind Sunderland) a game in hand.

United's next port of call was the City Ground on Saturday March 22. Official attendance was the implausibly round figure of 22,000. Brian Clough was in the early stages of doing with Nottingham Forest what he had already done with Derby in taking a lowly club up the divisions to unlikely top-flight championship glory. There was to be no glory for him in the immediate future though and today he had to be content with the fact that his side's loss to the visitors was not worse. The Reds – unchanged – were classy and controlled, if never completely over-powering. The one goal of the game came nine minutes before the interval when an unmarked Daly knocked in Coppell's pass. Villa's game in hand now looked less important: United were seven points clear. Cloughie adjudged United, "the best side in the Second Division." Though a man who had shown he knew a thing or two about football both as a player and a manager, he certainly had a viewpoint on the potential of the Reds different to that of Clive White. "Good luck to them in the First Division, because they've done it with skill," said Clough. "I have seen enough of the other promotion-chasing clubs to know United are playing at least 30 per cent more football."

United's visit to Eastville on Good Friday, March 28, saw Docherty indulging in the unique luxury this season of fielding an identical side for the fourth match in a row. However, just as he must have been thanking the gods for not presenting him with injuries for once, James had to be taken off in the 19th minute with a recurrence of an ankle problem. Morgan came on, with Greenhoff dropping back into defence. It didn't make too much difference as United proceeded to control another game against a relegation-threatened side. As with Forest, though, United's domination of Bristol Rovers was not converted into many goals. The only one the Reds managed came on 35 minutes when Houston whipped in a low cross that left a row of Rovers defenders watching it. Rovers keeper Jimmy Eadie wasn't as quick as Macari to the ball, the Scotsman unleashing a right-foot shot that hit the roof of the net. The United defence seemed to have gotten over their recent wobbles and regained the composure of the season's opening months and a serviceable victory seemed assured. However, in the dying moments, David Staniforth proceeded toward United's box. When Stepney advanced to narrow the angle, he found Staniforth playing the ball square to substitute Bruce Bannister, who left a couple of defenders standing as he darted in and – to the horror of the United fans in the 19,000 gate – executed a left-foot drive into the empty net. There were 32 seconds remaining on the clock. "I'm disappointed at having victory snatched from us right at the end and I feel sorry for the lads because of the way they worked," Docherty rued afterwards. "It was really ironic because Alex Stepney had had nothing to do. At one stage he appeared so frozen standing on his line that I was thinking of going round and giving him my overcoat. Nevertheless we have got a valuable point, so it's not too bad a start to the Easter programme."

Though he had Arnold Sidebottom available to him to fill in for James, Docherty elected to keep Morgan in the side and leave the line-up as it was at the end of the Bristol Rovers match for the next day's home fixture against York City. Though Docherty might have preferred to keep Morgan out, there may have been a reason for his retention of Morgan that had nothing to do with his immediate tactical plans but were part of a long-term strategy.

York's manager Wilf McGuinness was making his return to Old Trafford in front of 46,802. York defender Barry Swallow later said, "Wilf was more nervous than the players. It was a big thing for him coming back here." There was some amusement when a linesman was unable to continue after 28 minutes due to a pulled muscle. Docherty jokingly offered to take his place. Eventually a Tannoy announcement procured somebody from the crowd prepared to run the line. The opening strike came in the 76th minute. Possibly Docherty bowed to the gods in acknowledgment of their sense of irony when he realised it was Morgan who had headed in Forsyth's free-kick from close range. Within a minute, United were in York's penalty area again. Macari threw his arms up in appeal when he was sent to the deck but when he saw the referee wasn't interested, he quickly sprang up and drove the ball home.

Afterwards, Macari said, "I was going for a penalty, but I'm glad we didn't get one because it was far more satisfying to end up scoring myself." Irritatingly for United, once again they fell victim to a late goal, Seal pulling one back two minutes from time.

Though the 2-1 victory may have confirmed the fact of, as one reporter put it, "the hard work … United are making of the final run-in to the Second Division title," United were left seven points clear at the top of the table again. Third-placed Villa had two games in hand but were eight points adrift. Moreover, though no one could apprehend it at the time, the day marked the beginning of something special in the shape of the long-term strategy mentioned above, something that would become the defining characteristic of Docherty's tenure at United, as well as the most exciting sight in English football for the next two seasons. Though Docherty had started the 1974/75 season with a determination never to return to negativity on the pitch, this was the first match in which he utilised a formation that was capable of generating more excitement amongst the spectators than any other: 4-2-4. To that purpose, with Greenhoff picking up the defensive slack, The Doc instructed Willie Morgan and Steve Coppell to occupy the flanks, with McIlroy and Pearson inhabiting the space in the middle as the strike force that would hopefully be the recipient of the chances created by their jinking and centering. The fact that it was midfielder Macari and Morgan himself who scored that day doesn't disprove the wisdom of the plan. Rather, that it was a sound idea was illustrated by the fact that United created half-a-dozen other scoring opportunities, even if all happened to be wasted. At this moment, Docherty's plans for 4-2-4 were in their raw stages, compromised by the breakdown of his relationship with Morgan and a little lop-sided due to the fact that both Morgan and Coppell were right-sided players. However, the winged approach would triumphantly reach fulfilment starting from the following November.

\*\*\*

Oldham Athletic visited Old Trafford on Easter Monday, March 31, to take on an unchanged United. The crowd was swollen to 56,618 by the opposition club's proximity. Reporter Ian Gibb opined, "It was United's finest showing at home for many weeks – and that had a lot to do with the revitalised comeback of Willy [sic] Morgan, whose first-half showing should have helped to put United well clear by half-time." It was Morgan who laid on the opening goal, McIlroy finding the net in the 22nd minute from his cross. Three minutes after the interval, Oldham grabbed an equaliser. Four minutes later, a Morgan corner was back-headed by McIlroy further into the Oldham box and, following some confused activity, the ball somehow ended up in the back of the net, with Macari raising his arm in triumph.

On 74 minutes. Coppell got his first goal in a United shirt when he fired in a shot from an acute angle. Young headed Oldham back into the game with 15 minutes left, but the score remained 3-2. Macari was now getting into the habit of perhaps unwise candour in post-match interviews. Today, he admitted that the goal that deprived Oldham of a badly needed point was illegal. "When the ball came over from McIlroy's back-header, the goalkeeper was shaping to save it," he revealed. "I knocked it in with my elbow."

Young was back for the visit to the Dell on Saturday April 5. Morgan kept his place while Coppell was dropped. Martin had gotten a run-out as sub in the last match, but this fixture saw 19-year-old defender Jimmy Nicholl serving as 12th man. With Southampton lodged right in the middle of the table, the game meant nothing to them in these closing weeks of the season. However, a victory for United would confirm their promotion to the top flight. The crowd was – we are told – 21,000, another suspiciously round figure that highlights how unscientific counting of gates sometimes was in those times. United – playing in blue today so as not to clash with Southampton's red-and-white stripes – almost went behind with the second half 11 minutes old. When Stepney brought down Steele, Channon stepped up to take the penalty. It's not known whether the sight of thousands of United supporters screaming abuse and discouragement at him from the away, Archers Road end caused Channon – after his usual fast run-up – to strike the ball so wildly that it hit the outside of a post, despite sending Stepney the wrong way. However, if he had scored, everybody would have been observing how remarkable it was for him to do so in the face of such distraction. Perhaps the United fans were not inclined to display sportsmanship because of the behaviour today of Peter Osgood. 'Ossie' was booked in the 26th minute for a challenge on Morgan. Before long, he had committed an offence against Macari so severe that Docherty was still fuming about it after the match. "Osgood does nobody any favours when he acts like this," he said. "He could have broken Macari's leg with a tackle that was so diabolical and I told him so at the time." Actually, that was the version the papers saw fit to report – one journalist said the real version was "unprintable". Buchan, who had adroitly organised the soaking-up of Southampton pressure, had to miss the last five minutes through injury, giving Nicholl his debut. Even in his short time on the pitch, the debutant was the target of the malice that afflicted Osgood today. Recalls Nicholl, "I remember the first thing I did was take an elbow right in the face from Peter Osgood." The only goal of the game was scored by Macari in the 76th minute, running 20 yards onto a pass to fire low into the net. The Scotsman later said, "I was so angry after that tackle that it was a case of me getting sent off or scoring a goal. I was desperate to score and when the goal came, I ran all over the pitch to try to find Osgood. But he seemed to disappear." Appended Docherty, "Ossie had crawled into a hole. You should have seen his head drop. Who wants players like that?" Well, The Doc had last season, in actual fact.

Macari's goal was his fourth in four games and a nice bonus to add to the fact that he had recently been recalled to the Scotland squad. It was somehow fitting that this reborn player – for many the club's man of the season – should score in this particular match. There were still fixtures remaining and a championship to settle, but Macari's winner had sealed the club's promotion. His transformation from club exile to saviour (or one of them) was complete.

Reporter John Samuel was put in mind by United's unfamiliar blue shirts of another club who played in blue more regularly whom Docherty had taken up into the First Division at the first time of asking. Docherty's Chelsea team had been of tender years. According to Samuel's calculations, the United line-up today had an average age of 22 years and three months, and that was including the been-round-the-block Stepney. Samuel's maths were wrong – the Reds' average age for the Southampton match was 23¾, while removing Stepney made it about 22¾ – but he had a point about youth. "Chelsea went straight back then and with some maturing eventually won the FA Cup," recalled Samuel (who could have made it clearer that Chelsea took the aforementioned trophy under Docherty's successor). "United, under Docherty, could prove the same sort of team – hyperthyroid [sic] and urgent, provocative, a United, as ever, to love or hate."

Buchan and Young were absent for the home match against Fulham on Saturday April 12, with James and Coppell coming into the side. Though in the season's early weeks they had been a fixture in the top three, and had even led the table in the beginning, Fulham's promotion hopes were now a matter of the most improbable mathematical formulae. However, they had something almost as good to look forward to: the FA Cup final, in which they were due to meet West Ham on May 3. The Cottagers now had nothing to lose except a place in the Wembley line-up caused by injury. The competing theory that they would be playing for the places at Wembley seemed disproven by a noticeable lack of motivation. Even so, despite 20 shots at goal and 18 corners, United had scant reward for their efforts. Gerry Daly scored the only goal, lashing in a shot after the Fulham defence had been torn open, not for the first time today, by a McIlroy run.

Though some of the United fans in the 52,971 gate would have taken note of another example of a worrying trend lately whereby United won by an inexplicably narrow margin, most were probably not inclined to agonise over a victory that left the club eight points clear. The Stretford End roared "Champions, champions" at close of play. Not quite. Second-placed Villa had two games in hand and could technically overtake them. Afterwards, Docherty spoke of his hopes and plans for the future. He talked of wanting to improve his current lop-sided winger situation. He also said regarding progress in the top flight, "To do something like Jack Charlton has done at Middlesbrough – that would be great."

Buchan was back for the visit to Notts County on Saturday April 19. Morgan was absent from the team, never to return. There were no other changes. United took the lead on seven minutes when Houston rose above everybody else to thump a free-kick into the far corner with his forehead. Celebration turned to dismay when violence erupted on the terraces. Part of the approximately 7,000-strong United element of the 17,320 crowd spilled onto the pitch in an attempt to get into Meadow Lane's County Road stand. "That was quite scary," Buchan recalls. "It was so distracting. We were trying to finish off the game and they were all getting stuck into each other." Five minutes before half-time Daly crossed for an unmarked Greenhoff to score the second United headed goal of the day.

Docherty later said that the hooliganism had taken the gloss off the day for him, but he should have been at least as concerned at the way that in the second-half United – though laziness, arrogance, confidence or all three – allowed what should have been a 2-0 triumph to turn into a draw. In fact, the match almost ended in a disastrous away loss. A County corner in the 49th minute was headed in. On 65 minutes, Kevin Randall secured the match's only goal scored with a boot when he got on the end of a cross. With 10 minutes to go, Stepney had to make a great save to keep another headed attempt on goal out of the net.

Depending on your point of view, United had either earned a point or squandered one but the result was enough to secure something very important. Though their seven-point advantage at match-end over second placed Villa would be reduced to three when the last ball of every fixture had been kicked this season, this was the match that won the Reds the Second Division championship. They had assured it with 59 points, one fewer than the number Docherty had predicted back in October as a requisite for taking the division title.

United's final match of the season on Saturday April 26 was preceded by a victory lap, a deafening ovation greeting the players and especially Docherty as they paraded the Second Division championship trophy around Old Trafford, followed by a crocodile of kids toward whose presence the police displayed a benign tolerance. After that, there was the small matter of a match to play. For United's farewell to the Second Division, it was only fitting that they should take on – and thrash – Blackpool, the team against whom their masterful performance in October had convinced many that they had demonstrated they were simply too good for Division Two. That the return engagement was a home fixture was even better, enabling an exhibition in front of the fans – 58,769 of them – who had shown such tremendous loyalty in their reduced circumstances.

Blackpool had been bubbling under the top three but promotion was now impossible so they had little to care about today except the professional pride of putting up a good fight. However, an unchanged United – convincing today in a way they had rarely been lately even in victory – were too strong. The first goal came on 20 minutes, a lurking Pearson knocking in a loose ball. Ten minutes into the second-half, Pancho again took advantage of a loose ball, this time the result of a fierce shot from McIlroy. Macari grabbed an opportunist's goal in the 79th minute. Greenhoff added a fourth in the 83rd. There were several narrow misses for the Reds, especially a McIlroy effort following a typically impudent dribble which ended in the Irishman hitting a post.

The end-of-season crowd invasion went ahead as usual, this time the kids at least waiting for the final whistle before covering the turf in a sea of red and white, although there was some unpleasantness when a section broke through the police cordon around the players' tunnel and a few fists started flying. The crowd was still on the pitch when Docherty addressed the stadium from the directors' box. "I feel this is just the beginning of great things for this club again," he said. Maybe so, but some present were somewhat ambivalent about their achievement. Though it would have been unthinkable to not run a victory lap that day, more than one participant was mortified by the celebrations. If truth be told, some of the United supporters who applauded their team as they jogged around the ground holding the Second Division championship trophy aloft were surprised to discover that there *was* a trophy involved with coming top of Division Two. And nothing could persuade Buchan and Macari that winning this bauble was any more cause for celebration than finishing 23rd in Division One, of which, of course, it was kind of the equivalent. Finishing the season with the prize of promotion to the top flight is understandably not exactly a matter for untrammelled joy for those who have previously known far headier heights. Both Buchan and Macari have said that the celebrations were an embarrassment for a club of United's stature. Macari later revealed, "I … couldn't get to the dressing room quickly enough." For his part, Forsyth says, "I'm just glad of any medal. Doesn't matter what it is. I was just delighted and honoured I was representing that club."

\*\*\*

In amassing their final tally of 61 points, United had won 26 of their League games, drawn nine and lost seven. "We went through the Second Division like a knife through butter," Docherty later said. Brian Greenhoff offered similar sentiments: "We hit that division so hard we had it sewn up almost before anyone realised we were there."

"Dead easy," McCalliog says of the Second Division. "It was a stroll in the park … We just felt we were a step above them." McIlroy, asked at what point in the season he had thought it inevitable that the club were going straight back up to Division One, says, "Oh I would say after 10 games, even that early. The way we were playing, the confidence right throughout the side. I thought, 'We're going to do it', and, without being over-confident, all the side thought we were going to do it as well. No matter home or away, we always felt we were going to win the game." Mick Martin says, "Well, I knew it virtually after two or three games. You knew that what you had was better than what was around ... There wasn't an awful lot of defeats because I remember saying, 'God, I'm never going to get into this team because they're winning all the time'." Greenhoff says "I must admit I expected us to come straight back and once he made a few signings then I think all we had to do was keep playing the way we knew, how we finished the [previous] season."

Buchan, though, insists that the campaign wasn't as effortless as some have assumed or suggested. "Lou Macari always says it was easy," he says, "but I qualify that statement because, as a forward, if Lou Macari didn't fancy chasing the ball he could let it go, but as a defender you always needed to be on your toes. You couldn't say, 'Well, I'll not bother with that one, the keeper might get it.' I think you had to concentrate harder playing in the back four. I don't recall it being as easy a ride as Lou seems to remember, although knowing him, he probably just says that to wind me up. I changed next to Lou for ten years in the dressing room at The Cliff and he did take great delight in winding me up." Buchan's mischievous Scots colleague did whatever the opposite of winding up is for the Old Trafford faithful: the Manchester United Supporters Club gave their Player of the Year award for this season to him.

Meek: "I thought they might have a good season in the Second Division because it was the Second Division and there were players still who had something to offer, albeit not in the First Division. And it was the players that he started to sign really when United took off again ... I enjoyed that season and I enjoyed it because of the swashbuckling football that he played. I enjoyed going to all the different grounds and the challenge of trying for promotion I found very exciting and as a journalist it was something a little bit different to write about." Would he subscribe to the view that relegation had turned out to be a good thing? Meek: "No, I think that's a silly attitude. It's never good to go down." Houston: "We came up a better team but in terms of saying it was the best thing that could have happened, I'm not quite too sure about that. I think this team would still have developed its way in the First Division at that time in its own way, but maybe it gave us the confidence and the momentum. That's maybe one of the plusses, so when we went back into [Division] One, we were still very, very buoyant as against staying in the First Division that year and maybe just finishing sixth from the bottom. We definitely hit the ground running when we went back into [Division] One." Forsyth, says, of relegation, "That was maybe a good thing. Learned us all different things." Buchan offers,

"The year in the Second Division didn't do them any harm at all because it might have given a lot of players confidence back in winning more games than not." This is a point of view that Docherty never agreed with. He felt that Division Two benefited from United's presence but, "I could have done without that club having had that experience."

As manager and the man who, rightly or wrongly, is publicly viewed as responsible for the relegation, it's an understandable perspective. However, a man of far greater experience and achievement than The Doc did agree with the idea. Matt Busby had been patently distraught at the climax of the previous season. Now, the relief and joy were evident as he talked of what the Second Division championship augured, so much so that he was throwing around phrases like "A blessing in disguise" and "A spell out of the First Division can act as a breather" in regards to the relegation, although did at least acknowledge that it was easy to be wise after the event. Busby pointed out that Liverpool and Leeds United, at that point two clubs indelibly associated with both the top flight and with long-standing success within it, had as recently as the 1960s been Division Two sides. In what was a motif in comments by United players, staff and sympathetic journalists, he said, "No club has a divine right to be in Division One, but I think that most people would accept that our return there is putting a club with the stature of Manchester United back in its rightful place."

When the dust had settled, United chairman Louis Edwards and the board were able to look with satisfaction at some remarkable statistics. United had not only attracted more supporters to their home ground than the season before, but had obtained the highest attendances of any club in the Football League, regardless of division. The Reds were the only club in England to attract a million spectators to their ground during the course of the campaign. Accordingly, they made a record profit. This will have been of some relief to Edwards and the board, who had, despite the drop, decided to go ahead with a £425,000 executive suite development. Additionally, there was hope for the future inherent in the fact that though the team had gone down with a dismal goals-for record of 38, they had gone back up having netted 66 League strikes.

From the point of United's ascension to the top of the table at the end of August 1974, they had never been knocked off the summit. Whilst it's true that mid-January to the end of February 1975 saw mediocre form from the Reds – encompassing four losses in a season in which they suffered only nine defeats in total – they ended up with an impressively low goals-against total of 30. They had also topped and tailed the season with unbeaten streaks, going 10 games before experiencing their first loss and, from the Cardiff home match onwards, embarking on an unbeaten closing run one better than that initial display of unassailability.

While Buchan, Stepney and (though Docherty might disagree) Morgan had confirmed the talents everybody already knew they possessed, several players had come into their own in this campaign. As previously noted, Macari was a transformed man. Pearson himself had proven a great buy, even despite his injury problems. Daly had blossomed impressively, something that wasn't only indicated by the fact that he hadn't missed a single one of the 10 penalties he'd taken. Houston, too, had proven himself a good purchase. Despite his initial uncertainty, Greenhoff had been impressive wherever he was played. Coppell, meanwhile, was clearly a star in the making.

Sammy McIlroy would later admit that the Division Two season was the making of him. He had exploited his time in the second tier to finally assert himself and prove the worth he had hinted at with that goal on his debut three seasons ago. Having seen all the kids his age who had been at the club when he signed disappear from Old Trafford, McIlroy had felt some anxiety at the start of the 1974/75 campaign, and wasn't about to let the fact that he was the top League scorer the previous season fool him into thinking he was doing well: finishing best marksman with a tally of six merely meant that the team was doing even worse than him. "Tommy Docherty had given me a fair crack of the whip and I knew I would be on my way out if I didn't do something soon," he later said. "One day I suddenly woke up and realised I had to try and show people what I could do, even if I did make mistakes." This going-for-broke approach worked wonders – and no doubt playing against a slightly lower grade of player in the second flight assisted his confidence. McIlroy attributed some of his improved form to Docherty. "He is urging me to take people on and go at them, especially in the penalty box," he said. His next words in a way summarise Docherty's new footballing philosophy at United: "He has told me not to worry if I lose the ball trying to do something and has got me to understand that I can't beat everybody all the time, so not to lose heart when things don't come off." Enjoying his partnership with Pearson, McIlroy's form was such that for the first time in the three years he had been making the first team at Old Trafford, he became something other than a man drafted in when somebody more important got injured. "For the first time in the Second Division season I felt like a first-team player," he later said. "Then I knew that the team was looking to me to do something and I liked the responsibility." He now says, "That was the season I really kicked on. All the car crash, everything had gone behind me, I was fit again, I'd no injuries whatsoever. I enjoyed it. We kicked off well, continued, confidence grew right throughout the side. We were filling grounds, record receipts away from home, we had a fantastic support who stuck with us and it was a fantastic experience really."

One of the silky skills for which the Stretford End loved McIlroy was his nutmegging. This is the term for a footballer sticking the ball between the legs of an opponent and running around him to retrieve it. The tactic is guaranteed to raise a cheer from the crowd, partly because it's so difficult to do – keeping their calves together is instilled in defenders – and partly because, as a consequence of that difficultly, it's humiliating for the opponent. Jimmy Greenhoff has described McIlroy as the best nutmegger he has ever seen. Skills like that were rewarded with the ultimate accolade from the Stretford End. It must be one of the sweetest things a footballer can experience to find that he is the subject of his own chant. This was the season that McIlroy first heard "Super Sam!" thundering from the terraces. Explains McIlroy, "It just came out of the blue. I think it actually came from a paper headline after a game I'd scored." In fact, the "Super Sam!" headline appeared in a Sunday newspaper after his brilliant point-salvaging goal against Notts Forest in September.

Tommy Docherty had written in a newspaper article the previous season after United's traumatic relegation, "Don't weep for Manchester United. Out of the ashes of last season will rise a team good enough to take on the world." Seeing as those words were printed only a few months after Docherty had felt compelled to drop George Graham, the man he had once posited as a new Gunter Netzer, many could be forgiven for viewing this as what is described in polite company as hyperbole and on the terraces as bollocks. However, though he was indeed sometimes given to leaving hostages to fortune and to silly bravado, in this case (and not for the last time) an apparently wildly optimistic prediction by the United boss came true. After the final match of the 1974/75 season, a jubilant Docherty said, "This is only the beginning. Give us two years and we will be back in business, competing for the major honours again." Again, it's a comment that sounds like hyperbole, but in fact it transpired to be a pessimistic statement. Excluding the close season, it would be more like two months before Manchester United were tussling with the biggest clubs in the domestic game in serious pursuit of its greatest prizes.

# PART FOUR

# 1975/76: Revitalisation

During the close season before their return to the First Division, Manchester United embarked on a five-week world tour. Their trip to Europe, Tehran, Jakarta, Hong Kong, Australia, New Zealand and America was a far more primitive affair than the type of tour seen in modern close seasons, where it has been known for United to take advantage of their valuable brand-name by fielding three different teams in three different countries more or less simultaneously. Nonetheless, it was a cold-eyed affair – as it needed to be to fulfil its remit of generating additional revenue to enable the club to finance the players' escalating wages. Such jaunts invariably involved exhibition matches against usually inferior local opposition in front of starstruck spectators to whom, in an age before global television football coverage, top European clubs were still semi-mythical.

In the press it was announced that Morgan had refused to go on the tour. It was also stated that Mick Martin would not be travelling on the grounds that he was looking for another club. Both men dispute these stories. Morgan's précis of events is dealt with in depth later. Martin says he was given no explanation for not being taken on the trip despite initially being informed he was. "I was looking forward to it because it's a place you don't get the opportunity to see on a regular basis," he says of the Australian leg. "We were all measured up and the bib and tucker for our jackets and trousers and suits and bags and all the stuff that you required to travel to Australia for three weeks in them days and, for some reason or other, I just got a message to say that I wasn't being included in the travelling 16 or 18 to Australia, which was very disappointing. I thought that I should have done. It wasn't Tommy Docherty who said it to me. I can't remember who it was. It might have been Paddy [Crerand]. They were the sort of things that would upset you. Whether it was too difficult just to take a young lad away to Australia, rather than not take him, I don't know. He maybe just wanted to bring someone else and make them happy. I remember talking to big Jim: 'I'm looking forward to this', I said, 'I'd like to see a bit of Australia.' Football gives you this opportunity, and funnily enough I've never been since."

Martin was not to be at the club much longer. He moved to West Brom in September 1975 for £20,000. "I'd done pre-season training with them and then we got going," he says, "but I had two or three clubs very interested in signing me at the time and I knew that and I knew that I wasn't going to start off in the Manchester United side and I knew that Tommy Docherty wasn't going to keep me any longer so I was preparing for life elsewhere … I was even contemplating going back to Ireland, I was so fed up at not playing football, because I came over to play football. A former Manchester United player Johnny Giles, who was a good friend of mine, international colleague, was appointed manager of West Bromwich Albion and he was keen to bring me down. It meant that I had to go back down to the Second Division, and when I went they were fourth from the bottom of the Second Division. We finished up getting promoted at the end of that season. The following year, I was playing against Manchester United."

Martin's omission from the travelling squad was curious considering that five youth-team players were named as part of the 19 who would make the trip: Jimmy Nicholl, David McCreery, Arthur Albiston, Peter Loughnane and Tony Grimshaw. There was good news for those who felt United's relatively poor second half of the season had coincided with the loss of Jim Holton. The centre-half had passed a fitness test on the eve of the tour. "I am delighted to have made it," Holton said. "I hope to get in a few games before the tour is over. My leg feels fine. It has been my heel holding things up. What I desperately want now is to play some matches and that is why I am so pleased to be going with the lads."

There was some light relief in the States, where the Reds got a glimpse of the way the Americans had altered soccer to meet the requirements of the more razzamatazz-oriented US public. In a match against Dallas Tornado, the United players watched in astonishment as their opponents made an entrance on horses, dressed in cowboy outfits. A stagecoach executed a dramatic appearance just before kick-off. The Reds noticed that several of the players looked a bit ill-at-ease in their Wild West personas – hardly surprising considering that many of them were players from the English leagues. However, that was one of the few happy moments of a tour that saw unsavoury incidents which, whatever the triumph of United's bounce-back to the First Division and their rediscovered footballing values, underlined for many that Tommy Docherty was simply not in the same class as a human being as his fellow Scottish United manager Busby.

There was ill-feeling in Switzerland when Buchan temporarily resigned the captaincy. Having gone out with the team with Docherty's permission and honoured the midnight curfew imposed by the manager, Buchan was offended when he found out that Docherty had sent Cavanagh to check up on the team. Entreaties from his colleagues persuaded Buchan to readopt the captaincy. However, things had been far worse in Australia. The Scottish players who had been on international duty for a match against Romania on June 1 joined the party at this point, namely Buchan, Macari, Forsyth and Houston. Lou Macari had a suitcase full of dirty laundry which he naturally sent to be cleaned. He was amazed to be told by Docherty that the laundry bill would have to be paid by him out of his £2 per day spending money. Macari refused and was threatening to fly back home. He was only prevented from doing so when United secretary Les Olive wouldn't give him back his passport. Nonetheless, he still declined to pay the laundry bill. Houston's recollection is, "I got to Brisbane and I had a contact from Scotland and four or five of us went up there after the game. By that time we'd been on the road quite a long time and our friends in Australia welcomed us in, some Scottish friends, and did all the washing for us." Though Steve Coppell, who had joined the tour late due to an appendix operation, had only been at United a few weeks at this point, he was amazed that the smooth-running club he had known thus far should be stricken with conflict over such a small problem. The mini-crisis was averted by Busby, who mysteriously materialised from the other side of the world. (He was on the same plane as Coppell.) Busby soothed things over, and the spending money was bumped up to £6. Discontent had only been quelled temporarily, however.

Unbeknownst to the squad, Docherty had arranged a head-tennis tournament in Perth featuring himself, McIlroy, Greenhoff and Coppell. Explains Greenhoff, "It was an old football and you just had to play it on a tennis court ... You both two-touch or three-touch. It was a bit of fun, and if you'd have watched The Doc's game, you'd have been falling about laughing." This may sound the type of sporting event that nobody would go to see even if it was being staged in their back garden, but at the time head-tennis was considered in some quarters to be the coming thing and, indeed, a crowd of 100,000 packed into the relevant stadium to watch it. But in arranging this bizarre event, Docherty had broken the sacrosanct tradition of the players' pool: the unwritten but long-standing rule that all money for off-field activities generated in the name of the club should go into a pot for equal distribution.

The deal came to light when Stepney casually asked McIlroy one day where he was going and the Irishman told his colleague about the competition. Stepney enquired if his remuneration was going into the players' pool. McIlroy later revealed, "When I said that as far as I was concerned, the fee being paid was to me, and that it would be my own money, Alex got a bit upset." Docherty had arranged a fee of 150 Australian dollars for the trio but, said Coppell, "When the other boys heard about the deal, it was decided that all the money should go into the general pool, and though the fees were not much it would at least have paid the cleaning bills." McIlroy now declines to criticise Docherty over the issue. "This head-tennis was arranged against four Australians," he says. "It was a packed audience in the arena and Tommy Docherty picked the players and everything else went into the players' pool [pause] in the end." However, in his 1980 autobiography, he said that, " ... I was in a thoroughly bad mood when the tournament ended [about] losing what I considered to be cash I had earned ... " Greenhoff also recalls the situation as being less than amicable. "The players said, 'You're on tour, you split the money'" he recollects. "They said they wanted the money, otherwise they wouldn't have us in the players' pool and all that ... We finished up we threw the money on the floor and said, 'Right, split it, if that's what you wanna do'."

Perhaps it was the fact that the issue was a culmination of the bad vibes of the tour that made the players demand a meeting with Docherty. Said meeting took place in a room at the team hotel. Stepney has recalled Docherty sitting at a table with a bottle of brandy and a glass. The Doc knocked back the liquor as he listened to the grievances of the assembled players. He continued doing so as he made his responses, although his comments weren't quite the explanations or appeasements the players had no doubt been seeking but, according to those present who have spoken of the meeting, thoughtfully targeted insults. Stepney says he was told "You will never play for Manchester United again" and that Houston was informed that he had never even played in the First Division. The quote if true (and Stepney's autobiography indicates that his memory is not completely reliable) is strange, as Houston, on top of his turn-outs for Chelsea, had played 20 Division One games – for Docherty's United. Coppell has confirmed he was called simply "a cunt". (Perhaps knowing the kind of thing he was going to say in advance, Docherty had prohibited Arthur Albiston and his tender ears from attending the meeting.) With those and other epithets and threats uttered, Docherty stormed out, leaving an empty bottle behind him.

Of course, some of this unseemliness is the consequence of the type of remuneration 'enjoyed' by footballers, especially Manchester United players, in that era. In *My Story*, Docherty published a list of the weekly wages of the club's 1974 playing staff. While three of the players were receiving £160 per week gross, the majority of the squad were earning around half that, and a significant number considerably less than half (even if around 50% were on a £20 appearance bonus.) We now know that the value placed on soccer in the 60s and 70s by the television industry was a complete underestimate: a succession of contract renegotiations raised the money paid by broadcasters to clubs by a massive amount even before the invention of satellite television and pay-per-view took such revenue into the stratosphere. This makes the wage levels detailed above obscenely low. That players at the most glamorous and well-supported club in Britain should be reduced to squabbling over a few dozen pounds is pathetic, but it is not their fault. There is a difference, however, between an employer with tight purse strings and a manager deceiving his charges and issuing threats when his machinations are exposed. It's perhaps unfair to continually make comparisons between Docherty and the supposedly sainted Busby, but one simply cannot imagine Sir Matt engaging in such behaviour. This would not be the last example of Docherty's eye for a buck leading him to act in a way that might be said to sully the reputation of the club and explains a deep disquiet about him among some people – both players and staff – who had been at United longer than he.

Considering all of the above, Willie Morgan might have cause for thanking his lucky stars that he hadn't gone on the trip. However, at the time the circumstances of his non-participation were a source of some grievance to the winger. Morgan later told journalist Jim White that Docherty had approached him at the season's end and informed him he wanted to be friends. Telling him not to bother to come on the tour, Morgan asserts that Docherty said, "Take the wife and kids and the club will pay for a holiday and I'll see you when I get back." Morgan continued, "The next thing I see is the front page of the *Manchester Evening News*, 'Morgan refuses to go on tour'."

June 1975 saw Morgan transferred to his old club Burnley for either £30,000 or £35,000. Whatever the true sum, some were surprised at its modesty. Initially, the newspapers were talking of £70,000. The original outlay in the other direction had been £117,000, a club record at the time. During a period in which there was a dearth of high-quality wingers in English football, it seems unlikely that clubs would not have been prepared to part with £70,000 for a still relatively young (30) player like Morgan. It also seems strange that a manager like Docherty – who always publicly took pride in his ability to balance the managerial books – should have agreed to make Morgan, as one paper put it, a "cut-price bargain". It may be that this derisory sum was what Docherty now felt to be the true worth of the man of whom he had said as recently as 1974, "I cannot think of a better player in his position in English football, nor in the world." However, Docherty had a responsibility to obtain the highest price possible for his outgoing players and a corresponding obligation not to engage in a high-profile gesture of contempt.

Morgan's journey from best right-sided winger in the world to cut-price cast-off within a season may reflect more the idiosyncrasies of Docherty than his own footballing worth, but just how good was the winger who was born in Sauchie, Stirlingshire on October 2 1944?

When it comes to posterity, Willie Morgan had the misfortune to play alongside a man to whom he seemed the 'Lite' version. George Best and Morgan were both wingers with dark hair worn fashionably long who excited the fans by weaving past strings of defenders. There, though, the similarity ended. Morgan was a very good player but he would have had to step up several levels to have even some of the other attributes possessed by Best, which included the ability to make superb tackles (rare for a winger), to execute powerful headers (remarkable for a man of Best's relatively diminutive stature), one of the most extraordinary capacities for acceleration ever seen on a football field and what can only be described as ball-sense, a sort of symbiotic relationship with a football that created moments of breathtaking improvisation and inspiration that no degree of coaching could ever confer.

That Morgan was considered to be Best's Mini-Me rankled with the Scotsman. The *Manchester United Football Book No.7*, published after the 1971/72 season, featured a chapter on Morgan punningly entitled "I'm Not Second Best" in which he grumbled about the unflattering comparisons. Morgan was at it again in the *Manchester United Football Book No.9*, complaining, "In many ways I was too similar in style and appearance to George Best. From the point of view of publicity there was only room for one of us at the club ... and George was the one." Yet Morgan's resentment went further than his words indicated, for observers at the time noted that Morgan actually thought he was Best's equal. The late John Doherty, a United player in the 1950s and someone who so closely observed the goings-on at Old Trafford afterwards that he published books in which he profiled every person who ever pulled on a first-team shirt there since his era, said, "The saddest thing about Willie Morgan was that he appeared to believe, in all honesty, that he was as good, if not better, than George Best ... To labour under such a colossal delusion must be very damaging to anyone's health." Indulgent amusement is the response of Sammy McIlroy and Mick Martin, who both played alongside Best and Morgan, when the subject is brought up. McIlroy: "Willie was very, very confident in his own ability. Willie and George obviously with the long hair looked very, very similar when they were playing. But you're talking to the wrong person because I'm George Best's biggest fan and I thought nobody was better than George." Martin: "To try and compare yourself with George Best in itself would be a privilege but no, George was the top man. Willie was a good player, but not a George Best." Alex Forsyth (completely unprompted, it should be pointed out) says, "Willie Morgan was trying to be a superstar. Willie done well but he always thought he was better than George and he'll never be as good as George. He thinks, 'If he can do it, I can do this. I'll train harder, I'll train better, I'll look after myself'." Meanwhile, Colin Waldron – who was a colleague of Morgan's at Burnley both before and after Morgan's tenure at Manchester United – says of his obsession with Best, "I always felt that was his problem. I just felt it was a lost cause from day one, because, one,

Willie couldn't head a ball; two, he couldn't tackle; three, he was frightened to death; four, he'd no left foot. Now that's just from quick memory, and you're trying to compare yourself to George Best who had all of them."

Best himself told Michael Parkinson that when he made his return to Old Trafford under Docherty, all of the players were very welcoming and encouraging to him with the exception of Morgan ("Willie always fancied himself as taking over from me and I think he was a bit choked to see me back"). Though Morgan insisted that there had never been any bad feeling between him and Best, ("The only thing that did annoy me was that even if I had a good game I seemed to get overlooked") this seems to be contradicted both by Best's observation and by Morgan's own, previously mentioned caustic assessment of Best when the Irishman had announced his retirement in 1974 ("George thought he was the James Bond of soccer"). Possibly Morgan's conviction of his parity with the Irishman partly stems from a match in March 1969 during Morgan's first season at United. The Reds slaughtered QPR 8-1 at Old Trafford. As might be expected, Best got a brace. However, Morgan did even better. Not only did he get a hat-trick, but one of these goals was worthy of Georgie himself, involving a dribble that started in his own half and saw him leave several QPR defenders eating his dust. Then there was the fact that – however inconceivable it seems – the United supporters' Player of the Year award for both the 1971/72 and 1972/73 seasons did not go to one of the Holy Trinity but to Morgan.

That Morgan's belief in being in the same quality bracket as Best was a deluded one is instantly proven by the fact that while football history books speak of Best in the same breath as they do Di Stefano, Pele, Cruyff and Maradona, not a single one has ever done the same with Morgan. That Morgan is doing himself a disservice by his delusion is illustrated perhaps by the fact that this writer has been discussing him here almost as if only to refer to this delusion. Morgan, in fact, was a fine player, the kind who looked good in a Manchester United kit: purpose-built to have that red shirt flapping outside his shorts as he tore down the wing, his stylish mane flying in the breeze. United could have done with more of his type of skill and box office attraction during Docherty's first two grim seasons at the club.

Few though would argue that Morgan's ego merited the treatment dished out to him by Docherty, whether it be the conflict created between him and Graham over the captaincy, Docherty's later libel suit or the storm surrounding Morgan not accompanying United on their tour at the end of the 1974/75 season. The latter marked the end for Morgan's tenure at United. At a subsequent showdown, at which Morgan was accompanied by a friend who was also a solicitor, Docherty demanded the winger leave the club. Morgan, not only furious at his treatment but mindful of the testimonial he was due, refused. He said Docherty offered him a payment of £5,000 and implied that he would never play for any United team at any level again. "He said there wasn't room for me in the Central League or 'A' teams because he wanted to give the youngsters a chance ... " Morgan claimed. "He went on to tell us how he'd chopped Wyn Davies' legs off because he wouldn't go to West Brom and how he'd done the same thing to other players. My friend was surprised by his attitude."

It's difficult to assess Morgan's insistence that Docherty's claim that he was a depleted player after his eye injury was a pretext for getting rid of someone he didn't like. After all, a player's form is a subjective matter. Long-term United watcher David Meek was also of the opinion that Morgan's form in the Second Division wasn't as impressive as it had been against the sharper defenders of Division One, though gave equal weight to the reason for this being fatigue caused by his participation in the 1974 World Cup. Blunstone, however, disagrees. "I didn't even know he'd got an eye injury," he says. "I hadn't seen a great deal of him before then but I think probably Tommy might have been covering himself a little bit there. Here's a good one for you: they didn't see eye to eye!" Morgan could point to the fact that his Division Two ratio of four goals in 42 games was a higher one than in his previous two seasons under Docherty and that one of those four goals was spectacular. Additionally, he continued playing for another seven years.

"When Doc joined the club Willie Morgan and he were inseparable," says one source who prefers not to be named. Brian Greenhoff is happy to go on the record with his comment, "Tommy Docherty and Willie Morgan were best mates. When it all turned pear-shaped, I think everybody was surprised." Morgan's Burnley colleague Colin Waldron offers, "I've never had any problems with Willie but I've known Tommy Doc and it's just chalk and cheese, because you cross Willie and you're dead and you cross Tommy and you're dead."

There was, by the way, another tour refusenik story from the close season expedition. Tony Young failed to turn up at Old Trafford to join the party leaving for the airport. Docherty told the press that he had rung Young's home and spoken to his mother. Docherty said, "She told me Tony was not available and he had told her not to pack his bags for the trip. We assume he had made up his mind not to go with us and when we got to the airport, the directors and myself decided to fine the player. Tony Young is fined two weeks' wages and placed on the transfer list." Yet again, the player's story differs from the manager's. "I'm already on the list," Young averred. "I asked for a move last Tuesday and it was granted on Wednesday." He went on, "I realised then there would be no point going on the tour. People will say I am giving up a great holiday but I would not have enjoyed it. It would be better for me to stay here and see if anyone comes in for me. I rang the manager on Friday to tell him

I wouldn't be going, but he had gone to London for the England-Scotland game and I wasn't able to get hold of him. This is not going to look good for me, I know, but I just could not see any point in going on the trip."

As to why he had asked for a transfer, Young explained, "This was not a sudden decision. I have been unhappy at United for some time. I played only seven League games last season and came on eight times as substitute and this is not good enough. I need regular first-team football, so a change of club will help me a lot." Young was a victim of United's transformation. When he became a first-team regular, the club were in dire straits and it wasn't too difficult to stake a claim for a place. At the end of the 1974/75 season, Young's type of player was in short supply at Manchester United. Young was competent but anonymous. He made little impression in his years at United, his name now merely a fading memory for Old Trafford old-timers and a bell-ringer for former boyhood collectors of bubblegum cards. Such players proliferated back in December 1972 when Docherty took the helm, but looking at the team line-ups of the final games of the season that had just ended, the only other player of that workmanlike type appearing in a red shirt was Steve James; the rest of the names are ones that no United fan of the era has trouble recollecting. United – and this is a measure of how much Docherty had already changed things – were now a team of stars and stars-in-the-making.

That transfer Young was hoping for in the close season didn't come and it wasn't until January 1976 – before which he made one last appearance for the Reds when he came on as substitute – that he moved to Charlton Athletic on a free, dropping down a division in the process. Steve James, by coincidence, also left that month, also on a free, moving to York City.

At the same time as it was announced Young wanted to leave, it was also revealed that United had made a new signing in the shape of Nottingham Forest's 28-year-old midfielder and Northern Ireland international Tommy Jackson. Born in Belfast on November 3 1946, he was obtained on a free. Docherty said of him, "This will be a good investment for us. I have been impressed with his performances in the home internationals and he'll go straight into the first-team squad."

*\*\**

With Morgan having been dispensed with, it would seem that Docherty now had his gun-sights set on the other senior squad member and the last surviving reminder of the European Cup-winning team. Shortly before United were to play the first of a series of friendlies in Copenhagen on a pre-season jaunt, Docherty took Stepney to one side and informed him he was no longer first-choice keeper. Because he was going for youth, Paddy Roche would now be between the sticks. Stepney had sometimes felt that his presence reminded Docherty uncomfortably of the Class of 1968, but – even if it was consistent with what Docherty had said in Australia – he was amazed at the turn of events, protesting that he had let in only 29 goals in his 40 League matches the previous season. Docherty was unmoved and told Stepney – according to the goalie – there was no use arguing. The manager proceeded to inform the reporters covering the trip of the news he had relayed to Stepney. Morgan wasn't surprised. Speaking publicly of the matter, he said, "Apart from Pat Crerand and Alex Stepney, he's just about got rid of all Matt Busby's players. And Alex is next. That's obvious after recent events. I've just picked up the cash from bets with supporters who wouldn't accept that Alex wouldn't be first choice after two brilliant seasons."

The Danish tour saw some more controversy. Holton got sent off in the opening match against Halskof. In the 57th minute of the Reds' match against Hosterbro, Macari received his marching orders when he got involved in an incident with John Bastrup only seven minutes after being booked along with the Dane for behaviour more suited to a wrestling match. Afterwards, Macari said, "This boy Bastrup had been up to all sorts of tricks. When we first clashed, he grabbed me. The second time all I know of [was] that somebody had gone down with me and that was that. Nothing sinister happened." Macari somewhat undermined his victimhood by acknowledging he had advanced toward Bastrup to punch him after the red card had appeared: "When I realised I was being sent off for such a trifling offence I thought I might as well earn it with a proper punch. I thought better of it at the last minute." Referring to a then-successful British boxer, he added, "Perhaps I'm due a crack at John Conteh soon." Though the referee stuck by his decision, he said he would not be reporting the matter to UEFA on the grounds that it was a friendly match, thus sparing Macari any ban back in England. Pearson was also booked that day for retaliation. Afterwards, Tommy Cavanagh – who oversaw the match in Docherty's absence – said, " … there could well be a lesson for us to learn here. There will undoubtedly be First Division players who will get us going and we must obviously learn not to retaliate." Contacted by Meek, Docherty echoed his coach's words, commenting, "Once the season starts, that kind of thing could cost players wages in fines."

After the Scandinavian matches, there was a pre-season home friendly against the legendary Eastern Europeans Red Star Belgrade. It occasioned a bit of a set-back for Holton during a pre-match kick-about. Forsyth: "I had a terrible habit of whacking a ball from maybe 20, 30 yards out and making a shot at goal. Big Jim was stretching up across the 18-yard line. He was just jogging across it. I thumped it off from 30 yards and it hit him right on the side of the head." Holton was unable to play through concussion. Forsyth: "He got carried off on a stretcher. I said to him, 'I'm really, really sorry Jim.' And Big Jim had a look at me – nae teeth in – and said, 'You effing dirty so-and-so, how the eff are you doing this in my first game back?'" The match finished 4-4, despite the visitors being 2-0 up within 25 minutes. Daly, McIlroy, Jackson and Coppell were United's marksmen.

An indication of what very different times the 1970s were is the fact that there was then in existence a government pay-rise deadline which even private companies had to observe. With said deadline approaching on August 1, Manchester United's board decided to extend Tommy Docherty's contract. The Doc's original three-year deal was set to expire in November. The new document would theoretically keep Docherty at Old Trafford through to 1979. Docherty signed it just before departing on the Danish tour and the deal was revealed to the press when the team arrived there. Louis Edwards commented, "The new [contract] was drawn up last May and we felt we had to make some move towards recognising what the manager has achieved so far." One newspaper talked of a salary of over £25,000 per year and of Docherty therefore becoming the highest-paid manager in the domestic game, although that figure would seem dependent on fulfilment of certain targets. Another said the deal was "believed to be £70,000 over a three-year period" and that there had been a "substantial increase of basic salary". Docherty commented, "The financial part of it is very satisfying but the main thing is the gesture of confidence which the board has shown. This gives me the time necessary to complete the team rebuilding job and make United into a force everybody will respect. I believe we will see big things from this team within the period of my new contract." Ironically, Docherty's new contract and pay increase were agreed just before he was locked in hard negotiations with four unnamed players, negotiations that had only just ended. The figures aren't known but in those days, players were paid substantially less than managers, a situation that has – in the top flight at least – been completely reversed today, so we should assume a certain relativism to be implicit in Docherty's comments on the settlement with the 'pay rebels': "This club is generous almost to a fault."

The Reds' return to top-flight football saw them turned out slightly differently. On the collars and cuffs of their shirts could now be discerned four red stripes. Additionally, United's white away-strip now featured four lines, these ones vertical and black, running down the left-hand side of the torso, and the deployment of black shorts, although white shorts would be used if they clashed with the opposition's. (Though most associate United with the colour red, the away kit was actually a development of United's normal away-strip, which had been predominately white since 1961 and had originally been a 'negative' of the home kit – that is, white shirts and red collars – and had then become all-white in 1969.) This change to the strip, minor though it may be, was the first since the 1971/72 season, at the start of which

United's manufacturer Umbro exchanged United's neck hoops with squared collars and swapped their old plain red socks for black socks with tops of three stripes consisting of a white band sandwiched by two red ones (the latter a return to a design from the late 50s). The only alteration between then and 1975 was the fact that the following season the now iconic Red Devil Manchester United crest made its first appearance, on the left breast of the shirt.

That Umbro kit change had made some sense. The 70s was an era of clean lines and clever (or at least high-falutin') concept. Those hooped collars seemed very old-fashioned compared to the much more modernistic-looking pointy type, while the all-red socks looked a little generic and were identical to those of other teams such as Liverpool. Less logic and more commerce was involved in the 1975 tweak. Said alteration alluded to the design of the corporate logo of Admiral, who had taken over from Umbro the task of manufacturing United's kit: four thick horizontal lines beneath a loop (which logo appeared on the right-hand side of shirts and shorts of the new United strips). The deal with Umbro had for the first time seen the strip available to buy at United's official souvenir shop at Old Trafford. Purchases of replicas of the strip netted United a guaranteed 10% royalty. The switch to Admiral (actually then still called Hurst and Cooke) saw United guaranteed £15,000 per year, plus 5% royalties on sales over that figure. There were also bonuses on offer to United from Admiral of £10,000 should United reach the FA Cup final and another £6,000 should they win it. These figures seem peculiarly small from today's perspective, even taking inflation into account, but the phenomenon of the replica shirt had not yet taken off. In those days, most of the people seen on the streets in their team's kit were children. It took a decade or more for shirts to replace scarves as an expression of allegiance at football matches. Today, the sight of scarves in club colours being held above heads or worn on wrists has become largely a thing of history and football stands are full of identikit rows of fans all dressed in the latest version of the kit shirt, which changes every season.

Though for some the phenomenon of the ever-changing replica kit is one of the most pernicious things in the modern game – indicative of the cynicism and greed of increasingly corporate clubs – and the engagement by United of Admiral's services marked in some senses the beginning of that trend, it should be noted that Admiral's white-black United away-strip was a thing of genuine beauty, those black shirt lines seeming less a company's corporate marque than something organic and art deco-like. Gordon Hill is not alone in thinking he and his colleagues looked elegant. "Beautiful," he says. "Admiral done us very proud."

\*\*\*

When Manchester United stood at the starting line with the rest of the First Division at the beginning of the 1975/76 season, they were not accompanied by either Luton Town or Carlisle United. Both clubs had been promoted to Division One in the same season that United had been ejected from it. Though Middlesbrough, the Second Division champions that year, had thrived in the top flight, Luton and Carlisle had basically lived up to the adage that being second and third in the Second Division only amounted to being 24th and 25th in Division One and had returned whence they came the following year. It should also be noted that though United had given the impression of dominance during their season outside the top flight, in fact their record in Division Two was far less impressive than that of Middlesbrough, who had won the division by a massive 15 points. Not only that, but the fact that United's closest rivals in the Second Division – Aston Villa and Norwich – took each other on in the final of the League Cup may have served to flatter them. Though it's unlikely that any circumstances could have prevented United from being promoted that season, without Norwich players being mindful of the danger of picking up an injury in a League match which might rule them out of their big day at Wembley, they might have amassed more points than United. It's more difficult to cite the possibility of Villa's results indicating a fatigue or lack of commitment due to their League Cup endeavours. However, they finished the season in greater style than did United, winning all of their last eight games and knocking in 26 goals in the process.

In short, though United had defied many expectations by bouncing straight back into Division One, the odds weren't necessarily in their favour when it came to staying there, let alone doing well in it. David Meek went as far as to say that though he felt the promotion side would hold their own in the top flight, challenging for top honours was out of the question until two signings – one in midfield, one upfront – were made. Docherty's response was that he intended to give the team that had won the Second Division championship a chance to prove their worth before taking such a measure. (He added, in a comment that is retrospectively hilarious but at the time must have seemed reasonable, that the imminent introduction of freedom of contract in football – players being able to leave for the club of their choice once their contract was completed in contrast to the way their clubs previously could deny a move unless they secured a transfer fee to their satisfaction – meant that the days of big-money signings were over.)

Speaking just before the Denmark trip, Docherty was cautious about the club's chances in the top flight. "I'll be well satisfied if we finish halfway in the First Division this season," he said. "I see us having a fair season. But I don't want to put too heavy a burden on the players, the club or myself. I'll be happy if we go through the season without too much pressure on us, never looking like winning anything and never being in danger. If we get near to a place in Europe, I'll be delighted. And if we win anything it would be an achievement beyond my wildest dreams. But I figure we might be too young a team for something like that to happen." Reflecting on what he had achieved so far at the club, he said, "We have completed six years' work in 30 months. 40 players have gone since I arrived as boss. There had to be a lot of weeding out … the players who retired, players past their best and the players who cheated. When I arrived there was a lot of whispering and too many cliques inside the club. Some unpopular decisions had to be made, but now we have a foundation for the future."

According to newspaper reports (and contrary to his stated aim of giving the Second Division champions a chance), Docherty tried to build on that foundation a few days before the start of the season with a major new signing. On Saturday August 9, it was said, he and Cavanagh travelled up to Scotland to watch the Scottish League Cup match between Celtic and Aberdeen at Parkhead. Playing for Celtic was the colossally gifted striker Kenny Dalglish, who was reputed to be unhappy about his pay at the club. Perhaps the combination of the revelation by Louis Edwards just one day previously that the club had made a £170,000 profit the previous season and the fact that Docherty knew of Dalglish's abilities very well (the 24-year-old was yet another player he had given his international start in his tenure as Scotland boss) had changed Docherty's mind. Then again, perhaps there was no substance to the story. Either way, in the end, although Dalglish did move south of the border, it was Liverpool who took him into the English First Division, and not until the 1977/78 season.

With Roche preparing to make his debut in the season's opening fixture against Wolves, tragedy struck for the Irishman when his father died. Stepney found himself the beneficiary of the bereavement as Roche flew back to Dublin. Nonetheless, Stepney claims that Docherty was telling everyone that the arrangement was only temporary and that Roche would be back in goal for the season's second fixture the following Tuesday at Birmingham. Stepney's frustration seems to have boiled over when he turned up for the subsequent first-team training session. His hurried recall meant that his gear had not been laid out for him as it would usually have been and he had to cobble together a kit from what was available. His unkempt appearance did not go down well with Cavanagh, who prided himself on being a stickler for neatness. In his autobiography, Stepney said that he explained to Cavanagh that his numbered kit was at The Cliff and that Cavanagh affected not to hear him and continued to bawl him out. The third time the coach did this, Stepney ran over to him, grabbed him by the throat and told him, "Don't you ever talk to me like that again." In his own memoirs, Macari remembered the incident slightly differently: "It took a lot to rattle Alex's cage but the next thing Tommy was picking himself up off the floor. Alex had whacked him. Cav had basically taken it on the chin for The Doc, whose treatment of Alex had ultimately fuelled the violent response." Macari said that Cavanagh was not a man inclined to hold a grudge and never mentioned it again. Meanwhile Stepney reported with some amusement that the fracas had caused his fellow colleagues, preparing their first sprints, to speed to the other end of the training pitch as though cued by a starting pistol. He also claimed, with some disgust, that Docherty pretended not to see the incident.

\*\*\*

United took to the field at Molineux on Saturday August 16 with a line-up of Stepney, Forsyth, Houston, Jackson, Greenhoff, Buchan, Coppell, McIlroy, Pearson, Macari and Daly, with Nicholl on the sub's bench. Holton's comeback was going to have to wait a few weeks longer: it transpired that in the accident before the kick-off against Red Star Belgrade, he had twisted ligaments in his knee as he fell.

It could be argued that having put three top-flight sides out of the League Cup last season, United had proven that their skills had not atrophied outside the First Division. However, the psychology of a cup tie – in which footballers can play above their normal game via the adrenalin that comes from knowledge of its status as a knock-out competition – is distinct from that of the week-by-week grind of the League. Asked if he was worried about United's prospects back in the top flight, Daly says, "No. The confidence then was sky-high and it didn't matter to us who we played. Everybody was that year older, bit more maturity was coming into the team. We knew one another's game inside out. I think we all were of the opinion that we were going to do well." Steve Coppell, though, has admitted that he was "extremely apprehensive" before the season started about whether he would be able to hack it in the unfamiliar and elevated environs of Division One. Pearson had also never had his skills tested in the top flight and, even though he might not share Coppell's uncertainty about being able to cope, many observers did. However, the new United, who now had an unmistakable Docherty brand, were about to find out that though there might be a gap between First and Second divisions, there wasn't one between the First Division clubs and Manchester United. What followed in front of the 32,348 gate was the most heart-lifting return to the top flight the club could have hoped for.

Forsyth recalls a slight change of strategy for the club's return to the top flight: "We needed to tighten up a wee bit ... Obviously you couldnae just go and attack the A-teams. They would destroy you." Perhaps the defender is talking only about the division's top sides, for there didn't seem to be anything defensive about the Reds' play this day. "It was like a bad dream," said a shaken Wolves manager Bill McGarry afterwards. United were brilliant, their play, as one reporter put it, "colourful, ambitious football". Both goals were second-half Macari efforts, one a side-footer, the other a loft over Wolves keeper Phil Parkes. United also had two goals disallowed. Afterwards, Docherty made a comment that constituted what would be a motif in his quotes during the rest of his time at the club: "We shall always play like that. We might win some 3-2, lose others 4-3, but whatever happens, whether we are top or bottom, we shall continue to play like that. We can't play any other way. We don't want to play any other way."

In the meaningless table after the season's opening day, United were sixth. Though it was a fine start to the season and though it is in the nature of managers to not want to change a winning team (and Docherty in particular would display a penchant for sticking to a regular crew), Stepney was still amazed that Docherty came into the dressing room afterwards and – contrary to what he says he had told him and everyone else about the goalkeeping situation – announced, "Same team Tuesday". Despite Stepney maintaining his first-choice position for the next two months, neither that nor the fact that United began achieving quite unexpected success imbued him with confidence about his long-term position at the club. Recent events had made him convinced he was "playing on borrowed time".

Tuesday August 19 saw United play their second away game in the Midlands in succession as they visited Birmingham. Docherty, in fact, wasn't able to field the same team because Pearson had picked up a knock in the opening match. He was replaced by McCreery in the only change. The yob element of the United supporters among the 33,177 crowd did the club's declining off-field reputation no favours as they chanted and sang their way through what was supposed to be a one-minute silence for recently deceased City chairman Clifford Coombs.

It's slightly amazing that United kept a clean sheet in this game, for the man between the sticks for almost all of the second half was not Stepney but Brian Greenhoff. Stepney had to be taken off injured on 47 minutes. (Nicholl was brought on to fill Greenhoff's outfield place.) Stepney's ailment was lockjaw, the result of damage done in a nasty early collision with Bob Hatton that left the Reds' goalie in the back of the net. "It's ridiculous," Stepney said after the game as he was taken to hospital for X-rays. "I just shouted for the ball and my jaw cracked and locked. It left me in agony." "'Cos I was the best," Greenhoff laughs when asked why he was chosen to deputise for Big Alex. "Simple as that. We were short of keepers once and I played at Preston [in] the 'B' team in goal. And then we were short again so I played in the 'A' team. I used to do all right." Of his performance today, he says, "I was quite fortunate really: the United fans were all behind me. The first save I had to make was off Jimmy Nicholl. I had to dive and I caught it. It was going in. I felt okay then. After that, I had another few saves to make, both off Howard Kendall. Just one nervy moment where I flapped a little bit but after that I was okay." Before long the United fans were sarcastically chanting, "Greenhoff for England!"

Two minutes after Stepney's departure, McIlroy at the Blues' far post sent a thumping header past Birmingham keeper Dave Latchford. It was McIlroy's name on the scoresheet again as the second and final goal of the game went in six minutes from time. Docherty was ecstatic about the character United displayed in losing a goalkeeper while the game was goalless and going on to secure a 2-0 victory. "I've had few prouder moments in football than tonight," he said. "Brian Greenhoff was great, but so was everybody." Their second successive 2-0 victory left United sitting at the top of the table, a point clear of Arsenal. Many refused to take that position seriously, which was perfectly understandable this early in the season when all sorts of strange League positions are thrown up by the few number of games played. The first game of the campaign had left Coventry City at the top (naturally by goal average, eight teams having collected the maximum two points that Saturday), hardly title contenders that season. Similarly, Arsenal and Newcastle were in second place after United's second and third games, and neither had scintillating seasons. However, when United remained perched atop Division One when the number of games had mounted up to the point where the cream was rising, many still declined to acknowledge that this signified anything other than a fluke. Many would soon be eating their words.

Saturday August 23 saw United's first home fixture of the season. Their opponents were Sheffield United. United provided the gate of 55,948 something special. To quote reporter Frank Green, "[Sheffield were] 'sandbagged' by the power, pace and devastating blend of a Manchester United determined to open their home account in a style to match their first two away performances." He added, "Undoubtedly, Sheffield escaped lightly, despite the scoreline." A pretty remarkable statement. That scoreline was 5-1, the joint-highest United match goal tally of Docherty's reign so far. A recovered Pearson was back in for McCreery in an otherwise unchanged team and it was he who opened the scoring on 11 minutes. The other goals came from Macari, Pearson again, Daly and McIlroy. Throughout Coppell, Daly, Forsyth and Houston fired in low crosses, something that would prove to be a new and often very effective Red tactic. After the match, United led Newcastle by a point at the top of the table.

Recalls Jimmy Nicholl of the low-cross strategy: "I remember practising that on a Thursday. If we were doing our crossing and finishing, if you were overlapping once a ball came to you, you just had to fire the ball in. You'd to fire it as hard and low as you could. I remember them vividly shouting, just when you were about to overlap, 'Violence!'" Blunstone adds in explanation of the strategy, "We didn't have big centre-forwards. Stuart Pearson was five nine, five ten." McCreery: "We always knew if we got to the byline or whatever, someone would be in the six-yard box. It could be a defender, it could go in-off. We got a lot of goals that way."

The team were unchanged for the home match against Coventry City the following Wednesday, August 27. The crowd was, impressively, 52,169, only 4,000 fewer than for Saturday's match. Coventry, like United, were unbeaten and showed it in the toughest match the Reds had had thus far. In the 23rd minute, Pearson launched a low, rasping shot from 20 yards that keeper King could only vainly grasp for. Coventry came away with a point – the first United had dropped in the campaign – by virtue of a blunder, Alan Green the ultimate beneficiary of an intercepted Greenhoff back-pass.

The Sheffield United match had been significant because it coincided with the newspapers printing their first League tables of the season. With that table showing United at the top, waves of excitement were no doubt beginning to ripple though the Stretford End. Possibly in response to this, Docherty's programme notes for the Coventry game saw the manager warn, "I do not intend to go overboard about our prospects this season and I hope you fans won't either. There is an awful long way to go yet and we shall most certainly have setbacks." Docherty's disinclination to publicly exult in his success might have been a sign of maturity, but his imploring the Old Trafford faithful to show similar caution was doomed to failure. It had been a long time since United fans had had the opportunity to chant the terrace favourites "United, United, top of the League" and "Now you're gonna believe us, we're gonna win the League" – outside of the Second Division, anyway – and they were hardly going to forebear now. Even with the unnecessary conceding of that late equaliser, the Coventry match still left United at the top, albeit on goal average over West Ham.

In any case, Docherty was sending out mixed signals about how to respond to United's good form. In the early weeks of the season, Docherty and Busby were naturally sought out for their opinions about United's spectacular First Division comeback by pressmen hoping for some good-copy-making superlatives. Busby was cautious, stating (somewhat presciently as it turns out) that he would rather speak in September about how good the team were. Though Docherty again spoke of being satisfied with a mid-table position at season's end, he couldn't resist a piece of hyperbole that utterly undermined such caution. He said that United were playing a little like the Dutch national team had at the 1974 World Cup finals. "Our full-backs are coming forward like the Holland defenders did," he said. "Our central defenders even attack and our midfield men get into the opposition box as often as possible, again like the Dutch." While nobody could dispute that Manchester United were a team who liked – loved, even – to take the game to the opposition and that their defenders were versatile, to invoke the glorious Total Football of Holland in West Germany in which the likes of Krol, Neeskens, Rensenbrink and especially Johan Cruyff mesmerised the football-loving world was not only unwise but absurd when he was trying to dampen over-expectation regarding his young team.

\*\*\*

Saturday August 30, saw United visit Stoke City. The gate was 33,092. Though the Reds' players were unchanged, Docherty made Greenhoff captain for the day, just as he had for the last fixture of the 1973/74 season and clearly for the same reason: Brian's big brother Jimmy was Stoke's captain.

United began to show how they had made the top of the table by going on the attack, knocking in those low, dangerous crosses again. The connection that Daly made with the ball on the volley in the 16th minute was sweet, but he could count on a bit of luck that it hit the back of the net, for it went in off a Stoke player. United did not really trouble Stoke's goalie Shilton further after that goal.

Their willingness to attack notwithstanding, scraping a one-nil victory via an own goal is hardly 'Roy of the Rovers' stuff. Few, though, could begrudge the usually adventurous United their continued status at the top of the table once the match was over, now leading West Ham by a point. However, reporter Edward Giles was in the Sceptical Admirer camp. "For how long can United continue to flourish by taxing the stamina of so many of their players?" he asked. "At the moment, confidence born of prosperity is lending wings to United's scurrying feet but the warning lights are already beginning to flash. It will be interesting to see how they react in adversity, and there must surely be some modification of tactics when the heavy grounds come along." (Incidentally, Giles demonstrated that, however injudicious and over-the-top Docherty's Dutch comparison, the thoughts were not unique to him: Giles said the Reds'"fluid style" was "excitingly reminiscent of Holland's in the last World Cup.") Says McIlroy, "A lot of people say that we were gung-ho, we attacked just for the sake of attacking and there was no plan. Now I disagree with that. We always played with pace, we always played with tempo, we always got people in the box. We [were] told to go up and down, defend from the front, everyone defend, everyone attack. That was the way we were. We were full of energy and Tommy Docherty knew that and he didn't want to hold us back." Greenhoff: "I think that did surprise us how well we did but we were just a young side with no fear. By this time the only experienced player we had was Alex. Even Martin wasn't old. I think we took a lot of teams by surprise." "Everybody kept expecting the bubble to burst, but we just kept on surprising people," says Buchan. Including themselves? "Maybe to a certain extent, yeah. But the season in the Second Division had given us a breathing space and helped Tommy Doc's signings to settle in and play together ... That season in the Second Division just revitalised the club. It eased the pain of relegation, the fact that we came back up right away and then acquitted ourselves so well ... So it was a pleasant surprise, but it wasn't a major surprise. I knew we were a decent team." Asked how much harder it was to play First Division players who are inevitably sharper than Second Division competition, Buchan says, "Physically it probably wasn't any harder, but concentration-wise, because of the higher quality of the finishing in the First Division, you had to be on your toes, particularly at the back." Docherty's eldest son Mick – a footballer with Burnley since 1968 – says "No, not at all" when asked if he recalls his father being surprised at United's form at this juncture. He goes on, "I think he knew what he had at his disposal. He knew he had a good side, a young side. He had a good dressing room, which is vital. When you've got a group of lads who are all pulling the same way, it can out-do and outshine an awful lot of other clubs very easily simply by the belief they have in themselves, in the manager, and once you've got something rolling it's a difficult thing to stop."

In 1962, Alf Ramsey had sensationally landed the First Division championship for Ipswich Town after bringing them out of the Second Division the season before. Asked if United were daring to think now that replicating this achievement might be possible, McIlroy says, "It was still difficult because we were young. People were saying we were on a crest of a wave and we were just flying through and it was still a very, very hard league to win. But we were on top and there was that belief about it. No matter who we played, we knew we had a chance." Blunstone: "I did think we could win it. I certainly did. 'Cos the players they had there were as good as anywhere else and they'd got a wonderful crowd behind them." Though his view might be one through the prism of sober maturity, Houston sort of disagrees: "At the time we probably thought we'll give it our best shot and we'll be there or thereabouts, but possibly we knew people like Liverpool were seasoned campaigners, etc. We knew ourselves we'd do well to win it."

\*\*\*

Nicholl replaced Forsyth in an otherwise unchanged United team for the home match against Spurs on Saturday September 6. Attendance was 51,641. It would soon become clear that Docherty wanted to ease Forsyth out and that Nicholl was the right-back heir-apparent. Few would understand why from today's match, in which Nicholl had a torrid time.

Nicholl fouled Tottenham's Jimmy Neighbour early on. When Jones caressed the ball into the far corner of the United net from Neighbour's resultant fourth-minute free-kick, United found themselves a goal down for the first time in the season. "I thought, 'Jeez, what a start this is'," recalls Nicholl. "A stupid clumsy challenge and they scored from it. The enthusiasm of youth and being clumsy." To those reasons for the mistake could possibly be added the inexperience of Nicholl playing at full-back when he had long been a centre-half. "Martin Buchan was doing that well, I was never going to get in the first team at that position so they changed me then." he explains. To some extent, Nicholl would never get over his feeling of disorientation in the full-back role: "I've done it so many times," he says of his instinct to challenge. "I was told to stop doing it and just jockey. And then whenever I started jockeying my opponent, I felt I wasn't doing my job. I always found it a bit strange at right-back and yet I ended up playing the bulk of games [there] right through my career."

As usual these days, United responded to adversity like a red-swathed army, with Coppell, McIlroy and Macari amongst the busiest of busy bees. With the Reds seeking an equaliser, a flashing light suddenly appeared on the roof of one of the dug-outs. Shortly thereafter, a loudspeaker message asked the crowd to look around to see if they could spot any suspicious packages, as a telephone warning had said half a dozen bombs were due to go off in the stadium at 3:30pm. Macari has said that Spurs and United were too busy concentrating on a fast and furious match to register much of this. The crowd themselves clearly thought it was a hoax, which bomb scares at that time tended to be more often than not, as they continued to cheer their teams on. However, some have reported that there was a certain dimming of the noise as the seconds ticked by to half-past.

An explosion did come adjacent to that time, but from the United fans in response to the results of a high-paced, medium-height Macari cross that caused confusion in the Tottenham defence. Smith and Pratt both failed to clear, and Pat Jennings was sent the wrong way by a rebound off the latter. More United pressure yielded a penalty just before the interval. Daly sent Jennings the wrong way with his spot-kick. Daly nabbed his second in the second half. When Nicholl fouled Neighbour again, the sanction was a penalty. Though Neighbour hit the bar from his spot-kick, Spurs suddenly seemed re-motivated and on 83 minutes substitute Chivers left Stepney helpless with a fine, fierce shot.

Docherty wasn't too worried afterwards by the visitors' late goal. "We will always concede goals, especially at home, because we don't have the men to close a game up," he said. "That's the way we play." Perhaps Docherty was mindful of the pleasing fact that the 3-2 victory could have been a win by a significantly greater margin were it not for the quality of the man between the Tottenham sticks. "He's still the best in the game," The Doc said of Jennings. "Without him it would have been a massacre."

The match meant United had taken an impressive 11 of the 12 points that had been available from their opening six games. Needless to say, they were still top of the League, one point clear of West Ham. Their continued dominance of the division naturally engendered more analysis of their qualities in the press. Reporter Mike Ellis said of the Reds' style, "Imagine 90 minutes in the front seat of a fairground rollercoaster and you get some idea of what it is like watching Manchester United these days. It's breathless, heady excitement with a hint of danger thrown in – a non-stop slam-bang which is going wonderfully well right now but could go spectacularly wrong at any time." Another journalist, Tom German, invoked, as many were now beginning to, the Holy-Trinity-era United in his match analysis. Naturally, he said there was no comparison ("The old United could suddenly pluck a magic spell from nowhere. The new version keeps working for 90 minutes with a spirit … ") but the very fact that he conjured the names of Law, Best and Charlton to point out that the red revival was not yet up to those standards rather than to launch into a "How did it come to this?" broadside – as he probably would have done only two seasons ago – indicated how far United had come under The Doc.

***

Nicholl's foul-ups in the Spurs match had evidently not troubled Docherty overly: United were unchanged for the visit by Brentford for the League Cup second-round tie on Wednesday September 10.

Forsyth says of his displacement by Nicholl, "I felt as though I was still playing well when I got dropped. Everybody does. Obviously he wanted to change it around a bit, so there's nothing really you can do. When you play in the reserves you're back into the first-team squad on the Monday, so it wasn't as if you were left away out. You train [with] 18, 20, 22 players in the full squad. You weren't just cast aside. I wasn't anyway." Indeed, Forsyth is unusual – almost unique – in not finding his out-of-Docherty's-favour status the harbinger of exile or transfer. "He never says to me, 'Well, I want to move you on' or anything like that," he reveals "I got on well with Doc." Did he feel The Doc valued him as a player? "Obviously he did or he'd say to me, 'Well, it's time you were moving on, I want rid of you'." Forsyth suspects that his versatility is what saved him: "He must have thought I'd be alright there for cover. I could play either full-back, right or left." Forsyth's bookend Houston, asked if he understood Docherty's preference for Nicholl, says, "I could and I couldn't. I suppose he felt that Jimmy was going to push Alex. I think every club needs somebody to push the other guy on. That's the way I looked at it at the time: 'He's brought him in to push Alex.' But that's the case at most clubs. They've got to have competition for places. Both were similar in many ways. I think Jimmy was a little bit sharper, a little bit quicker feet than Alex. I wouldn't say he was much, much better offensively than Alex." He adds, "He was a bubbly character, Jimmy, and showed a lot of enthusiasm."

Before the Brentford match, Docherty accepted a cheque for £100 and a gallon of Bell's whisky, his reward for being named Manager of the Month by the corporate sponsor. He had won a divisional award twice the previous season, but few at the time would have predicted at that time his club's progress in Division One warranting him such a prize this season.

As Stewart Houston's old club were a Fourth Division team while United sat astride the domestic game's pinnacle, some might have expected the massacre Docherty had said the result on Saturday could have been. Yet when four minutes after the interval, the rather paltry Old Trafford crowd of 25,286 saw the first goal of the evening, it came from a rather shocking source as Brentford defender Lawrence propelled a good header past Stepney from a free-kick. Docherty responded by pulling off Jackson and giving 17-year-old Tony Grimshaw his first senior appearance. Perhaps he agreed with the conclusion aired by some afterwards that United had shown a complacency. Either way, it seemed to work as United began mounting attacks with more sense of purpose. Shortly afterwards, Coppell was felled. Macari executed a curling 20-yard shot from the free-kick. Glazier got to it but it popped from his hands and crawled inside the near post for a 53rd-minute equaliser. United won the match when Houston floated in a free-kick and McIlroy got to the ball in a crowded penalty area, stooping to guide in a header.

***

In the run-up to United's visit to Loftus Road on Saturday September 13, Docherty admitted, "Frankly, we've been amazed how well we've started. If we'd got six points from the first six games, we would have been well pleased. I've got a young side without too much experience of the First Division. If you take away Alex Stepney, the average age isn't quite 22. We know we'll have our bad spell. I also know the character is there among these lads to pull through." Cavanagh was more effusive, though not inaccurately so. "The greatest club in football have got back their self-respect," he said. "And it's down to Doc."

In some ways, the QPR match was United's biggest test since their return to the top flight. Dave Sexton's team were formidable opponents – like them, unbeaten so far – and would, along with Liverpool, transpire to be United's main competitors for the championship this season. They boasted wonderful talent like Gerry Francis, whose dark, sideburned figure struck terror in defences as he tore for goal, wayward winger Stanley Bowles and rock-solid goalkeeper Phil Parkes (not the identically named Wolves goalie).

Greenhoff was injured, so Houston moved up the field and Albiston came in to fill Houston's normal position, making for two teenage full-backs. As if to emphasise that United would have to be even sharper against teams like QPR, the Londoners scored before United had even got a touch, a movement from a free-kick won straight after kick-off eventually seeing the ball propelled over the line by David Webb. Not even the psychological fillip of Stepney saving a Bowles penalty could help United overcome the deficit. They were lucky in fact that it wasn't substantially greater. That an important player was missing, that their defence was reshuffled and that they lost Jackson to injury before the first-half was up (Tony Young, still unpurchased, coming on for him) were all mitigating factors that didn't quite make up for the fact that conceding the free-kick that led to the QPR goal was unnecessary, that the marking at that free-kick was terrible and that throughout the match Stepney was repeatedly left exposed. In fact, the Reds had Stepney to thank for the fact that the score wasn't something adjacent to 4-0. He gave a masterclass in goalkeeping to the assembled 29,237, both with his hands and – on one occasion – his knees.

Docherty's attacking mantra after the match was different to previous versions only in the fact that its defiance followed a defeat, not a victory. "We'll continue to play the way we do," he pledged. "We'll lose some games, give away goals, but attacking football is the only way to attract supporters in large numbers into grounds." Docherty was wrong on the latter score: Liverpool and, especially, Leeds had been playing football that was not based on all-out attack and been packing them in over recent years. It would have been more honest to say that he was sticking with attacking football simply because that was his taste and his wont, and if he had nobody would have thought any the worse of him. He could also have plausibly posited that attacking teams are likely to prosper. Despite their first defeat since their return to the top flight, United still sat ahead of West Ham at the top of the table, courtesy of the superior goal average engendered by their relentlessly laying siege to opposition goalmouths.

That day, United's reserves had been playing Bury. The match caused heartbreak for Jim Holton, who had already suffered the nuisance of a delayed comeback after the freakish incident against Red Star Belgrade. He had to be carried off after 35 minutes of the Bury game. Following nearly a year of recuperation from his broken leg, fate had sadistically flicked him back just as he was climbing to the lip of his personal pit. Almost unbelievably, the diagnosis was a broken right leg again. To add insult to injury, Holton wasn't even involved in a challenge at the time but had merely been standing watching his colleague Lindsay McKeown tackle Bury winger Peter Farrell. Explained Holton afterwards, "I was holding back waiting to see what would happen when the Bury player fell over my leg. As soon as it happened, I knew it was broken. It was a pure accident." Though he was reported to be close to tears as he was carried off, Holton was in a more philosophical mood as he spoke from his hospital bed. "The break is about three inches above the ankle, in exactly the same spot as the first break," he said. "But it is a clean break and I don't think I will be out for too long." Big Jim also said, "Don't worry. I'm going to battle back again ... Funnily enough, it wasn't as bad mentally as the first break. I could adjust to it a bit better." Alex Forsyth, playing in the same match, said, "It could be hell for him on his own, so we will all make sure he has plenty of visits."

\*\*\*

Greenhoff was fit again for the home match against Ipswich Town on Saturday September 20, so Houston went back to his usual position, displacing Albiston. McCreery – making his home debut – stepped in for the injured Jackson.

Both sides were curiously subdued at times in a match that failed to live up to its billing. Ipswich were a high-flying team: the previous Saturday had seen them beat Liverpool, and in midweek they had defeated Feyenoord in Rotterdam in the UEFA Cup. Docherty expressed his puzzlement afterwards that Ipswich weren't more motivated for a clash against the League leaders at Old Trafford. The red part of the 50,513 gate seemed to feel there was a lack of motivation on the part of their team. Boos from the Stretford End greeted United's at times slow play – and the Reds didn't even have the excuse of a recent sea-trip of 10 hours each way to the Netherlands. The ultimate difference between the two sides was that United converted one of their hardly plentiful chances. On 28 minutes, a Coppell corner found the elevated head of Houston. The full-back's effort was not one of his best but Ipswich keeper Cooper – distracted by a colleague's legs around his body – let the ball go through his hands.

Reporter Ronald O'Connor wrote that United's success, " ... was not the conclusive one needed to convince pundits that they are rightful League leaders and can sustain their magnificent start to the season." Another journo, Tony Stevens, concluded simply that they were, "Leaders without conviction, except in their own eyes ... " Nonetheless, they *were* still leaders, although they continued to be above West Ham only by virtue of goal average.

The Reds were unchanged for their visit to the Baseball Ground the following Wednesday, September 24. The gate was 33,187. United were not overawed to be encountering the reigning champions. One reporter said, "Derby rarely looked at ease against this slick, quick-touch football from a young side bursting at the seams with ambition." But luck was running Derby's way, Charlie George scoring from play generated by an apparently unjustly awarded free-kick. The Rams were bossing United for some of the second-half, but in the 83rd minute, United seemed to have snatched a point when from a corner Gerry Daly found the back of the Derby net with an exquisite volley. In the 85th minute, though, Stepney couldn't hold onto the ball after an impressive save and George was quick to nip in and poke it past him for a hardly deserved winner.

The dreadfully unlucky defeat knocked United off the top of the table, even if QPR only led through goal average. Losing to the title holders at their own ground was not too much of a shock, but the fact that the Reds' first two losses of the season had come against the tougher competitors gave ammunition to those who felt that the superiority implied by United's position had been an illusion created by them not having yet faced the quality sides. Some may even have been put in mind of the 'false position' allegations made when United had been top of the League under O'Farrell's regime in 1971. In the end, United's collapse in form that season would seem to have proven those allegations correct, something that may have put a chill into the heart of United fans who recalled it now.

*\*\**

In contrast to the frequent, sometimes bewildering changes Tommy Docherty made to Manchester United teams in his first two seasons, he was now beginning to rely on a consistent nucleus of players. United's line-ups for this season and the next can be recited effortlessly by fans of the era. The current selection of Stepney, Nicholl, Houston, Jackson, Greenhoff, Buchan, Coppell, McIlroy, Pearson, Macari and Daly would rarely be changed through to November, when a new signing and tinkering with the goalkeeper's position would introduce unfamiliar names.

Following the difficulties involved in taking on three top teams in succession, the Reds now faced the prospect of a local derby at Maine Road. Docherty kept the side unchanged for the occasion on Saturday September 27. What followed was a wonderful advertisement for both football and Manchester. What a spoilt individual was the Mancunian faced with a choice of pledging his allegiance to Docherty's reborn, attack-minded United and a no less positive-minded if somewhat more sophisticated City presided over by Tony Book which included the classy likes of Joe Corrigan, Asa Hartford, Colin Bell, Joe Royle, Rodney Marsh and Dennis Tueart.

As well as an entertaining game, it was also a clean one, with no bookings. The match's four goals all came in a breathless period of under a quarter of an hour in the first-half. In the 20th minute, Corrigan executed a long clearance that Royle made a beeline for. Though Nicholl had an otherwise good game, he was panicked into putting the ball into his own net. Nine minutes later, a shot from Pearson was blocked but the rebound found McCreery – like fellow Belfast boy Nicholl, appearing in his first derby – who performed a low shot to equalise. A corner by McIlroy just after the half-hour mark found Macari's forehead and from there the back of the City net. Just one minute later, though, a Doyle ball reached an unmarked Royle on the United far-post and the latter poked the ball home. The second half couldn't help but be an anti-climax for the 46,931 spectators but honours-even felt like the right outcome for this game.

United were now down to third in the table, a point behind leaders QPR and second-placed West Ham. Jimmy Nicholl also felt his fortunes were tumbling. Nicholl was aware of the fact that he had displaced a man who was very popular with the Old Trafford faithful and his hesitancy in his unfamiliar position and attendant blunders were now attracting derision. "I found it really difficult," he recalls. "I was just a totally different type of player [to Forsyth] and I just had to keep my head down and get on with it, but I do remember getting serious stick from the crowd. I made mistakes alright because I was that keen to impress that I used to fly into tackles. I just lost my way a wee bit." He also found no assistance from the manager or his staff: "I was never once pulled aside by anybody and told try this and do this, or you're not doing this, you should be doing that. You were left to sort it yourself. I was getting more help from the senior players than what I did from management. But that's not a slant on the management. It was the fact that he kept you in the team and away you go." One thing about his role with which he did feel comfortable was Docherty's insistence on his full-backs overlapping. Nicholl: "You go up there and you're still young and enthusiastic and you want to go to impress, you want to do a job. If I ran down the wing, Stevie Coppell would come inside. Sometimes it was a decoy run, you never got the ball." Was it awkward between him and Alex Forsyth? Nicholl: "No, not at all. We used to travel [together] in the mornings."

\*\*\*

That on Saturday October 4, the Reds made heavy weather of gaining a goalless draw at home against Leicester City – a side without a win so far this season – gave further ammunition to those sceptics (more of whose voices were raised today) who claimed that United's elevated position was some kind of fluke. The visitors played a brisk, two-touch game in the pouring rain and went into the dressing room at the interval looking like the dominant side. Docherty must have been as dismayed as the 47,878 crowd at what he was seeing. Though he made no alterations for the second-half to the line-up of a team that was changed from the last fixture only by the reintroduction of Jackson at the expense of McCreery, judging by the fact that the Reds came out and dominated the final 45 minutes, he had clearly stated that dismay in no uncertain terms. However, though they had most of the play, United couldn't finish.

Such are the vagaries of football – and the truth of the adage that other people's results can be as important as your own – that after this thoroughly unconvincing performance, United found themselves back at the top of the table, albeit on equal points with QPR and West Ham.

The teamsheet remained the same for the League Cup third-round match on Wednesday October 8, atttendance at which was 41,447. As it was an away fixture, as opponents Aston Villa were the holders of the trophy and as United's form had dropped off somewhat of late, the average Red fan had no great grounds for optimism. The pessimists were vindicated to a degree by the way Villa overran United in the first half. At the heart of their attack was Andy Gray, who came close to scoring in that first-half more than once, as United tried to fend off wave after wave of claret-and-blue attack. Stepney (brilliant saves) and Jackson (line clearances) could take the credit for keeping the first-half goalless.

Once again, United came out refreshed for the second half. Villa managed to contain the resurgent Reds until the 63rd minute, when Macari headed home a Houston free-kick. On 73 minutes, another headed goal – this one by Coppell – put United two-up. Two minutes before the end, Gray got the goal he had looked like scoring all night – yet another headed strike – but there was no time for his team's lost ground to be regained.

***

It was off to Elland Road for an unchanged United on Saturday October 11. Leeds United had been in the European Cup final only five months earlier and they had beaten division high-flyers QPR in their previous League fixture. However, they were also lacking a trio of injured Scots internationals. On the half-hour mark, Coppell put a stinging shot past reserve Leeds keeper Stewart. Leeds came out for the resumption with evident new purpose but were unable to make headway. On 50 minutes, as United were setting about replacing an injured Houston with Grimshaw, McIlroy decided to take a flyer from a distance of 20 yards. Stewart, perhaps taken by surprise, ended up helping the ball into his net. When Leeds favourite Duncan McKenzie was substituted with 15 minutes to go – to the vocal disgust of the Leeds part of the 40,264 crowd – it seemed obvious that the home side's manager Jimmy Armfield was feeling a little desperate. Hope flared for Leeds in the 80th minute when Madeley crossed for Clarke to slide forward and get the ball over Stepney's goal-line, but the Reds managed to keep the score to 2-1 to the final whistle. As if to prove again the fact of the vagaries of football tables, despite the win the Reds were now standing second in the table, QPR leading by goal average.

United were unchanged again when they entertained Arsenal on Saturday October 18. Coppell, in a game in which he once again bewitched the opposition defence, put United ahead in the 35th minute with a left-footed shot that was deflected past Gunners goalkeeper Jimmy Rimmer. The latter, like team-mate Brian Kidd, was making his first-return to Old Trafford. Kiddo had a quiet game, provided little support by a team more concerned with containing United's attacks, and contained himself by Greenhoff.

Arsenal equalised in the 39th minute. Three minutes after half-time, Nicholl embarked on a 30-yard run at the end of which he centered. Pearson chested the ball down, span to evade his markers and unleashed a shot from 15 yards that sailed over Rimmer's head. As the net ballooned, the stands rose to their feet. In the 67th minute, Coppell got his second, with his right foot this time. Coppell almost got a hat-trick, but just when he was celebrating a goal he found Rimmer reaching behind his own right shoulder to miraculously tip the ball round the post. Coppell vividly remembered the quality save in his 1985 autobiography – but misidentified the keeper as Pat Jennings. The 3-1 victory put United back at the top of the table, two points clear of QPR. In third place were West Ham, who like QPR were on 17 points but had a game in hand over both the top clubs. The Reds were due to travel to Upton Park the following Saturday.

Before that match took place, something of an epiphany occurred for the man who had been the provider for Pearson's goal. On the following Monday, Docherty approached Nicholl. Recalls the latter, "He said to me – a simple, simple thing – 'Are you alright now?' I said, 'What do you mean?' He says, 'Are you happy now?' I says, 'I thought I was going to be left out, six, seven, eight games in a row.' He says, 'Aye, you would have been if you'd stopped trying to get the ball. Once you'd walked into a position you couldn't receive a ball from your team-mate, I'd have dropped you. But because you kept trying to get the ball and you kept trying to do things, I don't care. Even if you get a thousand touches and make 999 mistakes, I'm not worried. But the minute you turn your back on your team-mate and put yourself in a position you can't receive a ball from your team-mate, you'd have come off.' Them weeks and weeks and weeks of not talking about your position and how you're doing, and that's the reason I stayed in the team. And at the same time I was getting loads of abuse from the crowd. It didn't matter. Well, that meant more to me than anything. All the nervousness and all the anxiety of getting booed by the crowd, it never bothered me after that. I turned around and I've said, 'That's good enough for the manager, that'll do me lovely.' I just had a different slant on the game altogether."

United were unchanged for the West Ham match on October 25. The 38,601 crowd saw a wonderful game. United were in fine fettle, with Coppell, Jackson and Macari building attacks that a dangerously lurking Pearson was keen to get on the end of. Reporter John Moynihan said of Pancho, "Manchester United have had two great centre-forwards since the war, Jack Rowley and Tommy Taylor, and Pearson is showing these days that he could well join their league with his finesse, skill and dangerous shooting."

It was the home side who went ahead, however, even if the goal was a bit of a fluke. In the sixth minute, West Ham's teenage *wunderkind* goalkeeper Mervyn Day launched a huge clearance and Hammer's striker Alan Taylor chased it as Buchan stood frozen in hesitation. The exposed Stepney was beaten by Taylor's header. In the second-half, the game had to be stopped for nearly 20 minutes as fans battled on the terraces and spilled onto the pitch. Two minutes after the referee brought the players back on, Macari scored with a header from close range. Though it took a while for West Ham to get back into the swing of things, they went ahead late in the game. Docherty brought on McCreery for Daly but United failed to reply.

The 2-1 loss meant that the top three clubs – now, in descending order, QPR, United and West Ham – were all on 19 points. Despite the result, West Ham's Trevor Brooking, an elegant midfielder and striker and England international who would go on to provide analysis for the BBC upon his retirement, was mightily impressed by his club's opponents that day. He later said, "They came at West Ham more than any other side that has been to Upton Park. Their strength is their emphasis and belief in attack. At Old Trafford, the crowd lifts them, but they still go forward away from home." Despite the waves of attack he had seen his defensive colleagues endure, however, and perhaps partly due to the fact that the Hammers had just become only the third side to beat the Reds this season, Brooking mocked the idea that United could be championship contenders, predicting that they would blow up in late November or early December. When mid-season arrived and United were still tussling for pole position, Brooking had the grace to publicly eat his words.

Stepney has stated that one of the Hammers' goals resulted from a Buchan mistake, and it's obvious which one he was thinking of. For Docherty, however, it was the keeper who was at fault. Stepney felt it was the excuse that Docherty had been waiting for to drop him. Stepney was informed in Docherty's office the following Friday that Roche was going to be first-choice keeper. He later said, "He just called me in and told me it was over ... 'What was I to do?', I asked. 'Finish your time in the reserves', he said. I respected his reasons – I was no chicken and he wanted to give Paddy Roche a run – but I didn't agree with him." With his team top of the table and having contributed to that position by letting in only 13 goals in 14 League games, Stepney had justification for his dissension. Docherty proceeded to tell Stepney – the goalkeeper has claimed – he had been out of order in not sticking with Roche from the beginning. When an irritated Stepney replied that he was out of order now, Docherty responded that he would never play for United again. This induced *déjà vu* in the keeper, who recalled him saying it in Australia a few months back. Docherty then told journalists of Roche's promotion and that Stepney had had a good run but the time had come for change. Stepney has recalled that Docherty then proceeded to behave towards him in the way that several other out-of-favour players have complained of, what George Graham called the "leper treatment," not even speaking to him to say good morning.

\*\*\*

Roche was the only change to the United side for their home match against Norwich City on Saturday November 1. Though Norwich had come up with the Reds from the Second Division, they weren't thriving and were currently mid-table. United were the dominant team but for much of the match were frustrated both by tenacious Norwich defending and bad luck. Just as some of the 50,587 were streaming away, Macari powered past two defenders and pushed the ball forward to Pearson, who had moved intelligently into space. Pancho had gone in a diagonal line from left to right and now sent the ball back the other way, angling it to go inside the far post. This 80th-minute winner put United back on top of the League, sitting there by goal difference over not QPR now but West Ham – who still had a game in hand over them and QPR, as well as fourth-placed Derby.

Roche had not really been tested during the match. The closest he came was when a careless piece of play by Houston gave the ball to Norwich forward Boyer when Roche was well off his line. Boyer did the right thing and tried a lob. Roche was helpless but Boyer's touch was slightly off and the ball bounced on top of the crossbar. With a clean sheet and one reporter noting Roche's excellent distribution of the ball with throws, Docherty could have been forgiven for thinking that he had made the right decision in dropping Stepney. United, however, were about to embark on a disastrous stretch during which Roche's goalkeeping was the central issue.

\*\*\*

"United will die on November 8" read a piece of graffiti on a concrete slab on the motorway between Manchester and Liverpool. The United team – unchanged from the Norwich match – didn't quite expire at Anfield in the clash with their local, mutually red, rivals, although during and after the match one of their number – Paddy Roche – might have wished he had.

It was a rumbustious affair in front of a 49,137 crowd in which both teams looked like the championship contenders they were (even if Liverpool were slower off the mark than expected with their challenge this season). The first goal came on 12 minutes. Ian Callaghan crossed from the right flank. Roche and Greenhoff, conscious of the presence of John Toshack, both rose for the ball at the penalty-spot and collided. The ball fell from Roche's hands and Heighway – with almost sarcastic care – guided it over the line. Greenhoff says, "I went to head it and Paddy shouts, 'My ball.' Next thing, he comes over my shoulders. I'm thinking, 'What you *doing*?' It was easy header away. He should have just let me do it. Paddy wanted to impress, I think." Perhaps Greenhoff was puzzled by the call, for it was the type that rarely came from the keeper he had been playing in front of throughout his career thus far. For the record, one reporter, Tom German, noted what a good match Roche had otherwise: "If Roche blushed at such a blunder beneath the noses of The Kop, he concealed it admirably behind some subsequent safe catching and several fine saves."

The remainder of the first-half picked up to an unlikely greater pace but there were no further goals. A fence erected to keep apart the supporters at the Anfield Road end didn't prevent fighting on the terraces during half-time. All eyes were on the fine action on the pitch, however, when play resumed. On 47 minutes, Kevin Keegan received the ball from Kennedy out on the left. Roche was let down by his defenders as they all looked for an offside decision, leaving Keegan free to advance, draw Roche out and then pass square to Toshack, who thumped the ball into the roof of the net. United didn't let their heads drop at the deficit or the derision from The Kop. Clemence was to blame for the goal United pulled back in the 52nd minute. Houston unleashed one of his cannonball specials. Clemence threw himself on it at the near post, but just when it seemed he had dealt with it, it slipped away from him. Coppell nipped in and put the loose ball away.

The match could have gone either way. In the 78th minute, though, when a Hall corner was flicked on by John Toshack, Keegan, whether by the telepathy he and Toshack were renowned for seeming to have or by simple anticipation, surged forward to get his forehead on it and score the final goal of the game.

The 3-1 loss saw United take something of a tumble, from pole position to fifth, even if such was the cluster at the top of the table that they were still only one point behind leaders

The young Doc at home,
July 4th 1961

# IT'S DOC'S JOB!

## United will name him as boss soon

TOMMY DOCHERTY, manager of Scotland, will have full control of trouble-shattered Manchester United within the next fortnight.

Paddy Crerand, temporarily in charge of United's first team following the sackings of manager Frank O'Farrell and assistant Malcolm Musgrove, will become the Doc's deputy.

The press announce
The Doc's imminent arrival,
December 1972

# HAVE A NICE ONE BOBBY!

## The Mirror message to Britain's greatest sports ambassador as he plays his last League match

IF the Soccer fans will forgive the expression, it doesn't matter a damn who wins today's clash between Chelsea and Manchester United.

They should save their cheers for the man of the match. That's Bobby Charlton—even if he plays a stinker.

### Favourite

Because today is the day that Soccer's favourite son hangs up his boots. Bobby is pictured on the right arriving in London yesterday for his 751st game for United—and his last.

Farewell to a legend,
April 1973

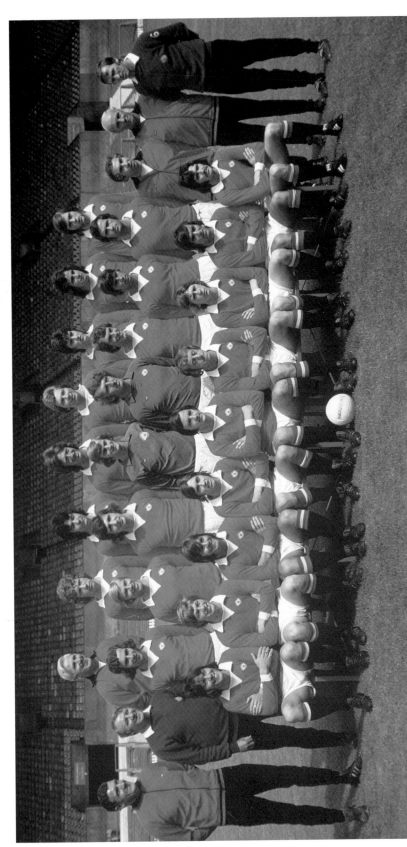

Manchester United 1974-75: Back row, left-right: Tommy Cavanagh (Trainer), Jimmy Nicholl, Alan Kirkup, Arnold Sidebottom, Paul Bielby, Jimmy Kelly, Arthur Albiston, Tony Young, Middle row, left-right: Bill Foulkes (Coach), Tommy Docherty (Manager), Lindsay McEwan, George Buchan, Steve James, Paddy Roche, Alex Stepney, Stewart Houston, Martin Buchan, George Graham, Laurie Brown (Physio), Jack Crompton (Trainer), Pat Crerand (Assistant manager), Front row, left-right: Stuart Pearson, Brian Greenhoff, McCalliog, Sammy McIlroy, Alex Forsyth, Mick Martin, Gerry Daly, Lou Macari, Trevor Anderson. Note: neither Kirkup nor McEwan ever played a game for the Reds, and George Buchan was shortly gone.

The Doc, July 31st 1975

The 1976 Cup Final Squad, April 1976: Back row, left-right: Jimmy Nicholl, Paddy Roche, Alex Stepney, Stewart Houston, Middle row, left-right: Tommy Cavanagh (Trainer), Arthur Albiston, Gerry Daly, Steve Coppell, Tommy Jackson, David McCreery, Brian Greenhoff, Alex Forsyth, Laurie Brown (Physio), Tommy Docherty (Manager), Front row. left-right: Stuart Pearson, Lou Macari, Martin Buchan, Gordon Hill, Sammy McIlroy

# FA CUP FINAL AT WEMBLEY

Manchester United ..........0     Southampton ..........1

# The latter-day Saints

## Doc did not order this

IT WAS a final that never really caught fire, but it left Manchester United with the taste of ashes. Two or three weeks ago the double of the League championship and the FA Cup was a feasible target. Now they have nothing tangible to show for all those months of inspired and adventurous football, for a long string of performances that represented the most exhilarating flourish of the English season. What had seemed an irresistible surge has stuttered, and died like a racing car that runs out of fuel a few yards short of the chequered flag.

To say all this is not to belittle the positive achievement of Southampton, whose victory owed as much to the soundness of their technique as to the firmness of their will. The entire team played with an honesty and boldness of purpose that reflected the values of their Geordie manager, Lawrie McMenemy, one of the most appealing and forthright spirits in the game. They deserved to win and it will be right and natural if their memories of yesterday afternoon at Wembley glow in a way that no neutral's ever could.

Yet for those of us who are obliged to be objective, this final and its result had more to do with jobs well done than with grand gestures accomplished; more to do with conscientiousness than inspiration, with efficiency than with glory. Thus the defensive covering of Steele and Blyth, and the ceaseless harrying by Gilchrist, did at least as much for the winners as the long, telling passes of McCalliog and the forward probings of Channon and Osgood; and the stifling of Manchester United's vaunted threat along the wings (which led to the substitution of McCreery for Hill) could be

considered as decisive as that late, beautifully executed and unmistakably fatal blow by Stokes.

Southampton won the Cup because they did a first-class job of work on the day. Manchester United lost because their capacity to do much more deserted them when they needed it most. Even in my hospital ward 40 miles from Wembley the intensity of their misery, mercilessly revealed by television cameras, was physically painful.

So Tommy Docherty, who has still to scale a major peak in his extraordinary career as a manager, finds himself back at base camp yet again. If there is any justice, Manchester United will surely dominate one or other of football's high places next season.

Press reaction to the 1976 Cup Final defeat

The Doc flanked by Steve Coppell and Gordon Hill

# JUST 5 MINUTES OF PURE MAGIC

THE STEALTHY goal burglars of Manchester United brought their guile to Wembley's Jubilee Final and went away with the most famous piece of silver of them all, the F.A. Cup,

I hope the Soccer chroniclers record more than the statistics. These are briefly concerned with a magical five-minute spell in the second half when Stuart Pearson and Jimmy Greenhoff always lurking with the intention of ransacking Liverpool's treble dream, scored goals either side of one by Jimmy Case.

## *British boost*

Here was a game of such grandeur, so memorable for its sportsmanship and grace, that British football can proudly reflect that the occasion was stage-managed to perfection.

Most of all I cherish the sportsmanship. The teams applauded each other at the end. Liverpool cruelly disappointed, buried their unhappiness and sought out the United man who severly damaged his ankle two weeks ago, Stewart Houston, to shake his hand.

And curly-haired, baby-faced Arthur Albiston, the 19-year-old Scot who took his place, had to be prised out of Houston's arms before he could collect his medal from the Duchess of Kent. Afterwards, in the noisy dressing-room party, Albiston tried to press his winners' medal upon Houston but the man on crutches would not

The 1977 Cup Final victory over Liverpool is heralded in the press

Bringing the Cup back to Manchester

Punished for love affair, says
Soccer boss as 'moral code'
United tell him: You're sacked

Mary Brown

Mrs Docherty

# CLUB WIVES OUST DOC

Who will
take over
at Old
Trafford?
Back Page

**TOMMY DOCHERTY** hit out bitterly last night after being sacked as manager of Manchester United, one of the top jobs in football.

Directors' wives at the club, which is proud of its family image, helped force him out. They acted from shock and embarrassment over his love affair.

The United women put pressure on the board following Docherty's announcement two weeks ago that he is setting up home with Mary Brown, wife of the club's physiotherapist.

Docherty, 49, who recently shook hands on a new four-year contract worth £100,000, after United won the F.A. Cup in May said: "I've been punished for falling in love. This is the most shattering experience of my football life.

## In just 30 seconds, Old Trafford gets its new boss

# Sexton: I'll be a winner

It's all over – The Doc is ousted in the press and his replacement announced, July 1977

West Ham. Liverpool – fourth-placed – were now ahead of United for the first time in the campaign. Despite being losers, the Reds impressed Liverpool's great striker Kevin Keegan (who would soon be voted Footballer of the Year) for their willingness to attack away from home, a willingness that was in stark contrast to his own club's cautiousness on opposition grounds. One United player in particular would impress Keegan this season. "Martin Buchan is the most extreme example of the ball-playing defender," he said of a trend that he thought was making the stopper centre-half a thing of history. "He sometimes takes breathtaking risks to retain possession rather than hit an optimistic pass." Buchan says of this habit now, "What you may see as a risk from your seat in the stand is maybe not so apparent when you're actually on the pitch in the situation with the ball. It could be little things: you can sense that your opponent is committed to going one way, you can see that his weight's on one foot ... A lot of things you do instinctively. I remember one thing I did in a game at Blackpool. A through-ball was coming at me on the deck at the same time and at the same speed as one of their forwards and without thinking I let the ball go through my legs and I flicked it with my right heel to Stewart Houston who was standing at left-back position. Afterwards he said, 'Jesus Christ, how did you manage that?' I said, 'Stewart, I haven't a clue.' I just did it instinctively, without thinking." The result of his unexcitable temperament? Buchan: "Well, maybe that's a good thing if you're playing in central defence. Or maybe the ideal combination is one of each: whatever Jim Holton was and a calm head beside him. Up-and-at-'em centre-half, and a calm sweeper-up."

\*\*\*

If playing at Anfield had been something of a baptism of fire for Roche in his prospective new life as United's first-choice goalkeeper, the following fixture was little easier. The Reds had been drawn against Manchester City in the League Cup for the second year in succession and the fourth-round tie took place on Wednesday November 12 at Maine Road. Docherty left the side unchanged. The gate was 50,182.

"We were the type of side that played to win. We didn't worry about how our opponents played or what they did. It was how we played." Those words have a familiar ring to them. Many will assume they emanate from Tommy Docherty and that he is speaking about United in this period. In fact, it is a quote from City manager Tony Book, speaking in January 2008 about *his* team in that period. Explaining that he was merely continuing the tradition of City's positive approach to football (one that had been far more consistently and successfully upheld than United's in recent years, it should be pointed out), he added, "We had always been an attack-minded side when I was a player so I didn't change that as manager." City certainly attacked United that day. United were a goal down after 38 seconds, and it didn't get any better from there. In the 13th minute, the home side were two up via Asa Hartford. A few minutes before the half-hour mark, Tueart sent in a shot that Roche dived for but which went in under his body. Docherty was no doubt in a filthy mood at half-time, which may explain the incident that occurred in the interval in which Crerand was asked by Docherty to leave the dressing room. "I felt humiliated ... " Crerand later wrote. "I wanted to hit him. But what could I do? I went to sit on the bench by myself. He came out for the second-half as if nothing had happened." Docherty withdrew Jackson in favour of McCreery on 56 minutes. The switch didn't seem to work – although of course you could make the unprovable assertion that United would have lost by an even more miserable margin without it. City fans had already begun chanting "Easy, easy ... " when Royle got their team's fourth, and last, in the 77th minute. Ironically, triumphant City manager Book would in many people's eyes soon be imitating United's style quite blatantly.

Roche couldn't be blamed for all the goals his team conceded, but the one that went under his body was an obvious howler, and coupled with the comedy of error between him and Greenhoff last time out, he was beginning to get a reputation as a blunderer. Mick Martin: "Paddy was a decent goalkeeper but to be asked to go in and play in a situation where there's 50,000 supporters and you're coming from a level of football that's well below the standard of football that you're used to playing is very hard and it's pressurising. I've seen him have some very good games for Manchester United, but when his mistakes were made they were highlighted and he was coming after the great Alex Stepney and that put pressure on him also."

\* \* \*

"In my mind, that was the end," Crerand later said of his dressing room humiliation that day. In fact, though it may have been a turning point, his tenure at Old Trafford would last a while longer and would leave him with some of the bitterest feelings of anybody who ever worked with Docherty – which is saying something.

In his book *My Story*, Docherty states that after a few months of the 1975/76 season, he went to United's board and told them his decision to appoint Crerand his assistant was a mistake. He claims that the two were incompatible in their working practices, vaguely talking of "time keeping, how to present yourself in a managerial capacity, that sort of thing" as their points of difference. Crerand had a much darker tale to tell. He had one day been astonished to be confronted by Busby who had somehow acquired the idea that he was drinking on the job and was not punctual, allegations he strongly denies. Crerand suspected that Docherty was behind Busby's suspicions. Again, we have two conflicting stories here, but this suggestion of Docherty whispering into ears before moving in for the kill is highly reminiscent of the train of events that Willie Morgan says led to his departure. Crerand also came to the conclusion that Docherty had deliberately made him look unpunctual or foolish or both by giving him the wrong time for the departure of a coach taking the United team to watch a match. Crerand also found Docherty deceitful over his testimonial match, which was played on November 26 1975, although Docherty's alleged lies were this time farcical rather than malicious. Busby arranged for Crerand to have his testimonial, but a few weeks afterwards Crerand claims that Docherty came rushing up to him telling him that he had sorted out a testimonial for him as though it was a generous act of his own.

More serious than any of those things are the circumstances surrounding a prestigious job failing to come Crerand's way when Docherty was sounded out by a Celtic director about Crerand's suitability to cover the absence of Jock Stein, who had been injured in a car crash. By Docherty's admission, he told Celtic that Crerand wasn't up to the job. However, Crerand claimed that when he approached a director of Celtic, he was told by him that Docherty had not just questioned his ability as a potential manager – his prerogative because a matter of opinion – but had falsely claimed that he was a member of the IRA, a very serious allegation at a time when people in Britain were losing their lives as a consequence of the activities of the Northern Irish paramilitary organisation.

Crerand began to hate coming into work, an experience unfamiliar to him since way back when he had worked on the Glasgow shipyards. "Long before the end, my position had become a sham," he said. "I didn't know anything that was going on. I stayed for two-and-a-half years only because I didn't have another job." Crerand theorised that Docherty didn't like the fact that he and Denis Law were still heroes in the United faithful's eyes and that this might explain the callous treatment of Law and himself.

*\*\**

While Crerand's long career at Manchester United was entering its final act, another was beginning. Sitting in the stands at Maine Road was Docherty's latest signing. Blunstone: "Bill Foulkes said he had a winger on loan to him when he was out in America, a lad named Gordon Hill, played for Millwall. So we had a look at him and we said, 'Right, it'll do it' and then we switched to 4-2-4." Hill had put pen to paper that very day.

Not long before the Hill signing, Docherty had been fulminating in the press about the price that had been demanded for a player in whom he had initially been interested before switching his attentions to Hill. He had made enquiries to Fourth Division Huddersfield Town about their 18-year-old reserve Martin Fowler. The Doc claimed that Huddersfield manager Tom Johnston told him he would have to part with a sum he found "ridiculous". Said The Doc, "I made a simple enquiry about Fowler and was told they wanted £100,000. Thank God I wasn't asking about a lad in their first team." Johnston countered, "It was up to Tommy to make an offer but it was a waste of time when he wouldn't even talk in terms of £25,000." Docherty was also not impressed by the sum – £125,000 – he claimed Millwall initially demanded for what would seem to be his second choice of signing, Hill. "He played well against us in the Second Division last season but I am not interested at that price," said The Doc. The sum eventually settled on was between £70,000 and £85,000. "This is the last big signing I'm going to make as United manager," said Docherty of Hill. "With this one in the bag, I believe I have now arrived at my perfect team."

"They got Gordon Hill to try and help me more because I was being so tightly marked," McIlroy later said. No doubt he's right, but that objective was dwarfed by a longer-term Docherty ambition. Steve Coppell was initially apprehensive when Hill joined, assuming that he had been brought in to replace him (the drubbing against Manchester City not helping his confidence). However, though Coppell had an admitted inferiority complex that was partly the result of him still being very much a part-timer because of his studies, he had no cause to worry, for Docherty saw Hill not as a rival for his place in the team but a perfect complement to him. With Coppell established as a right-sided wide player who could take men on and with the rest of a very good team in place, all Docherty now needed was somebody who could go past people on the left touchline to spray balls goalwards and his dream formation was realised.

Docherty had harboured many ambitions when he had taken over the manager's job at Manchester United, turning around their League fortunes, getting back into Europe and playing 4-2-4 football high among them. The last objective had been repeatedly hampered, and not just by the loss of wide players either involuntarily (Storey-Moore) or voluntarily (Morgan). To give an example of how long it took Docherty to achieve it, Blunstone recalls the winger ambition as being given new impetus as far back as the aftermath of relegation from Division One. He says, "We had a meeting the following week and Tommy said, 'What we gonna do about it? It's a tragedy going down.' So I said to him, out of the blue, 'What was the best team you had?' He said, 'Chelsea.' I said, 'What system did they play?' He said, '4-2-4.' So I said to him, 'Why don't we play 4-2-4 at United?' Tommy said, 'Because there's no effing wingers, that's why'. So we said in the whole of bloody Scotland, Ireland, England, they must be able to find two wingers, surely. And so we set out and that's what we did, actually, and the rest is history." Perhaps, but the fact that it took 19 months from that conversation to complete the process of obtaining the two wide players does underline Docherty's point about the scarcity of wingers.

"The signing means I can go ahead and play to a 4-2-4 formation that must make us even more effective," Docherty said of Hill's arrival. "This boy is sharp and confident and he goes past defenders. He will give our attack the extra width I am looking for." Said Hill, "I know I have just joined the greatest club in the world but it still hasn't really sunk in." The personal confidence to which Docherty referred was evident in Hill's next remarks: "I am not exactly overawed because fortunately I have got a belief in my ability that I hope will help me to settle down quickly. Mr Docherty tells me he is looking for a 4-2-4 formation which I fancy will cause sorts of havoc with defences, and I think I can deliver some of the goods for him. I've yet to meet a defender who can stop me without bringing me down. I don't look on myself as an arrogant player but I think you have to have confidence, otherwise you get nowhere." Hill was Millwall's top scorer so far this season with nine goals. "In this set-up there's got to be a few more for me," Hill predicted.

Docherty was taking what seemed a bit of a gamble with 4-2-4. The 4-4-2 formation, and the less defensive 4-3-3, had not become the norm over the last decade for no reason. Placing two of the outfield players who would normally operate in the middle permanently on the flanks was a wasteful use of manpower for many. Meanwhile, the type of player required to fulfil the role of winger was one of not only skill, but increasingly rare skill. The sight of a wide player booting the ball past a defender and relying on his pace to reach it before his opponent can turn and claim it himself, or dropping a shoulder or shimmying his legs to give the impression he is going one way before actually going the other (the opponent's move in the feigned direction gaining him a vital second or two to scoot from his orbit) had once been familiar on football pitches. Now that the byline was being reached via different methods, a declining number of players were versed in the art of dribbling.

Liverpool manager Bill Shankly had been the prime mover at club level in making wingers outmoded by securing success with possession football, wherein the individualism of dribbling was discouraged in favour of neat, short passing that diminished the chances for the opposition to obtain the ball. England manager Alf Ramsey had popularised it at international level by dint of winning the 1966 World Cup competition with a team dubbed the Wingless Wonders. Though it can't be denied that sometimes the sight of a well-drilled Liverpool team sweeping the ball from one end of the pitch to the other via a seamless and rapid succession of accurate passes could achieve the elegance and symmetry of a well-synchronised ballet, it also can't be denied that only the most jingoistic of Scousers or Englishmen weren't left with some doubt in their mind of the entertainment value of soccer players blandly, endlessly laying off the ball to each other. As McIlroy recalls, "Liverpool were the masters of keeping the ball, especially if they got in the lead. They could keep the ball for fun, and Liverpool were the best side in the world at giving the ball back to the goalkeeper, which you could do in them days. When they scored, they could pass it about and pass it about and edge it back to the back four and then back to the goalkeeper. They were one of the best sides at killing the game off and it used to frustrate you but they did it well." Not for nothing have the acknowledged outfield geniuses in soccer history – Di Stefano, Pele, Best, Cruyff and Maradona – all been wizards of the dribble.

Of course, a football manager's first duty is to win. Entertaining the crowds quite reasonably is of secondary importance to him. It was precisely because since the mid-60s the managerial assumption had been that winning was more likely with a formation that dispensed with wingers that wide players had begun to disappear from the game. Which is not to say that players who could run with the ball were extinct: every team had a wizard of the dribble (as labelled by their admirers) or a fancy dancer (the term used by their detractors), and usually they were the darling of their team's supporters. However, these players were generally not consigned to the flanks as it meant two players effectively being out of the game for large chunks of the playing time. Docherty had clearly decided that such logic was wrong.

Though they had the same role on the field, Hill and his counterpart Steve Coppell were chalk and cheese as both characters and players. Whereas Coppell was modest and studious, Hill was prone to vainglory and certainly not inclined to intellectual pursuits. This dissimilarity carried over into their wingwork. Blunstone says, "Steve was a strong dribbler. He'd knock it past them and run past them. He wasn't a dip the shoulder and get the defender off balance. He wasn't a great dribbler, Steve, but he was strong and he was quick. But Gordon was more get the defender off balance, go on the outside, get to the byline, pull [it] back." Even so, the names of Hill and Coppell would become so synonymous that several of the players interviewed for this book erroneously recall Hill playing for the Reds in Division Two, so unimaginable do they seem to find it that Hill could ever have turned out for United without Coppell bookending him on the opposite wing.

Meek approved of the new formation: "I thought it was very sensible and very shrewd of The Doc, because Matt Busby had always played with wingers. He believed in attacking football with individuals of individual talent able to express themselves, so for me The Doc was just fulfilling the Old Trafford tradition." Says Nicholl: "This is an argument I have with the coaches or managers and people I work with now. If you play 4-2-4, you've still got two sitting midfielders and the back four. You've still got six potential defenders. So the opposition's going to have to attack with either six or seven, and if they want to overload it and go for seven, that means there's only three at the back against our four. It's just being brave enough to do it. But you need pace at the back." He adds, though, "I don't think in them days you had to do anything dramatic tactically. There was no 3-5-2s and 3-1-4-2s and 3-4-3s. There was none of that … You didn't have to be a tactical genius in them days. It was man-management, personality and getting the best out of your players."

It should be noted, however, that whatever his penchant for attack, Docherty wasn't irresponsible defensively. Almost everybody questioned for this book about the 4-2-4 system he now adopted points out that The Doc's version of that formation was always flexible. Blunstone: "You've got to realise that you adapt. 4-2-4 can also go 4-4-2. Although we played 4-2-4, when we lost the ball it was 4-4-2." Buchan: "It was 4-4-2 when we didn't have the ball, because the wingers dropped back and helped out. You attack as a team and defend as a team."

Nonetheless, the format only intensified United's already existing attacking style. It also inevitably enabled opponents to catch United on the break, with the consequence of an even higher goals-against ratio. Blunstone: "What happened in quite a few of them games, we'd let three goals in. The press were always onto Tommy: 'But you let three goals in.' He said, 'I couldn't care less whether I let five goals in as long as we score six.' That was his attitude and that was brilliant. If you win every game, don't matter whether it's 6-5 or 1-0, you've won it and that's the important thing. What do people want to watch? United are brought up on Georgie Best, Bobby Charlton, Denis Law. Great players, great football. They don't want to see one-nil, one-nil, one-nil. Bloody boring." Additionally, for Blunstone this relentless attacking philosophy may also have ensured that the Reds' problems with lack of height were never really exposed: "We tried to go forward so much and put the pressure on the other team so they couldn't get at us. We didn't sit back and let them come at us." Buchan agrees: "Although Brian and I lacked height – we were both 5'10" – we managed by trying to keep the opposition out of the box for as long as possible. We didn't get exposed that often by big centre-forwards jumping against us." Greenhoff: "If you look over the records over the years, we didn't lose a lot of headed goals. We used to say, 'Right, come on, they're going to be bigger than you' – in them days everybody had a big centre-forward – and they said, 'Go challenge', and that's what we used to do. A good challenge and pick up the pieces … I'm playing centre-half which [is] a difficult position for me being so small – you're on a hiding to nothing when balls are knocked in the air – but in saying that my main thing once we got the ball was to set things going from the back." Greenhoff, incidentally, feels that Hill's purchase also helped to further the objective that the signing of Houston – a *bona fide* left-back – had begun. "On the left wing, we didn't have a left-sided player," he says. "The side needed balancing out, and I think that's what he did ... That's the thing that we always wanted. We were always struggling for somebody down there."

Asked how difficult it is for a defender to play against the new United 4-2-4 formation, Mick Docherty says, "It posed huge problems because ... his sides were very, very fit. They were capable of getting up and down. They had this work ethic whereby when we lost the ball we got behind the ball, when we got the ball we went forward, and it was a very difficult formation to play against when played with players of the application of Coppell and Hill and the others obviously around them. That's why they used to break sides down and consequently were very successful." How might the opposition manager combat this? Mick Docherty: "The manager would suggest we play 4-2-4, like-for-like, and you try and do that but, believe me, saying and doing are two different things and when you're playing against the likes of Gordon Hill who's willing to work hard up and down, it becomes a battle of wills and sometimes somebody's not stronger than another, one department lets you down, and you end up losing the game."

Gordon Hill was born in Sunbury-on-Thames, Middlesex in 1954. That his birthday is April Fool's Day would be considered significant by many who worked alongside him. Hill's family was large: he had five brothers (all older than him) and three sisters. "Because I come from London, I would obviously go to the local club, whichever one on the west side of London, Chelsea or Fulham or Brentford, was playing," he recalls. "Chelsea got a visit from me more than anything else but my big brother supported United." Hill was always a dribbler. "I just done what come naturally to me and it happened to be that I was quite good with a ball," he says. However, there was one art he never did master. "I never developed tackling because I didn't want to kick someone to get the ball," he explains.

Hill made his debut for Millwall in the 1973/74 season. "It's one of my fondest," he says of his memory of the three years he played at The Den. "You got groomed, you got kicked, you got pushed, you stood up and you played and it was a very, very, tough club, but that's what Millwall is all about. You have got to be a Millwall person to understand it."

The CVs of many of The Doc's Devils end with a series of clubs in the North American Soccer League, which entity tended in the late 70s and early 80s to secure the services of established players in the twilight of their careers simply because such players would not have countenanced spending their peak playing days in what was considered – despite the fees on offer – a Toytown league. (Of course, part of the reason it was considered such was the Catch-22 reason that so many of its players at that point were past their peak.) Hill was unusual in that he first made the journey across the Atlantic before he had become anything more than a cult hero in his home country. Also unusual was his timing: the NASL's raiding of foreign countries had yet to get into full swing. "I came over to the States for three months to help them out with a new franchise," says Hill. "I had a season at Millwall and then Barry [Fenton, manager] got the sack. Gordon Jago who was the manager at Millwall after Barry Fenton asked me to get a little bit more experience. He said, 'We will loan you out there just to get more games underneath your belt.' I said, 'Well, that's fantastic, because I'll be able to play out there, I'll be able to enjoy myself and I'll be able to keep fit.' When I come back, I still done the pre-season, but not as severe. I came back absolutely flying because I had such a good time."

As he was everywhere in his career up to and including his time at Manchester United, Hill was a sensation in the States during his three-month stay. His club was Chicago Sting, where Bill Foulkes was now head coach after taking his leave of Old Trafford. (It's not known whether his departure was due to the mysterious suspension-that-wasn't in January 1974, but, if it was, he doesn't seem to have borne a grudge about it judging by the close contact he maintained with United.) Hill's 16 goals in his single term there made him the club's top marksman and the second-highest scorer in the league, a remarkable tally considering that the NASL teams played just 22 games a season at the time. He was also responsible for seven "assists", NASL parlance for what British soccer fans then called setting up or providing goals. The Sting's second-highest scorer was Eddie May, with a mere seven strikes. Hill's form led to him being chosen for an incongruously named All-American team featuring the season's outstanding NASL players. It also led Foulkes – who, lest we forget, had played alongside some superb footballers from the other Busby Babes through to the Holy Trinity – to state, "In his season with us, Gordon Hill was the most exciting player in the American League – and that includes Pele."

At Millwall, so beloved had his trickery made Hill on the terraces that the fans had given him the nickname Merlin. Though Hill played against the Reds in their Second Division season, Millwall had been one of the three clubs relegated in that campaign. The move for him by Docherty, therefore, came as something of a salvation. However, Hill seems to feel that being rescued from the backwaters of Division Three was fairly inevitable. Hill: "I went back home [from America] and all of a sudden the lads would say to me, 'We won't be able to keep you, it will only be a matter of time before you're gone.' It wasn't a case of saying, 'I'm too big for this club.' I wouldn't have done that in a million years. I'd have quite happily played there for 10, 15 years. But obviously because of what I was doing, I'd attracted other clubs and obviously the lure of the money for the club was survival. I thought I was staying in London when I was playing for Millwall and I thought a London club was coming in to buy me because I'd not been outside London, so to speak. I was only a young pup. And then all of a sudden I find I'm going 200 miles up the motorway. Halfway through a game, I think I was playing on a slope at Wickham or something like that, they pulled me off and they said, 'Right okay, get your bags and bush, you're going up to United and see if you like it.' What a statement, eh? 'See if you like it'."

Hill has said he wasn't given much choice about the move (common in those days, when player power was still in its infancy), nor did he bring up remuneration. Not that it sounds like it would have mattered. "I got £60 per week at Millwall, I got £125 at United," he says. "You didn't become a millionaire out of that ... In them days you played for Man United not because you got paid the most money. You played for Man United because that was the best club in the world. They certainly weren't top payers."

Though he may only have signed Hill because his first preference was priced too high, when Docherty told the press, "That's it, I've completed the jigsaw," he wasn't engaging in hyperbole. Or if he was, in doing so, he had stumbled upon a truth. Though at 5'7", Hill might be viewed as adding to United's 'problem' of a lack of height, the new arrival was not just the left-sided wide player required for the fulfilment of the 4-2-4 dream, but massively gifted in other areas too. As well as his bewitching dribbling skills, he was possessed of electrifying pace and a propensity to score an uncommonly high number of goals for a winger. Macari would describe him as "one of the best strikers of a ball I have seen, especially on the volley". McCreery says, "For me, Gordon and Jimmy Greenhoff were the best volleyers of the ball I've ever seen." McCreery adds, "Gordon could shoot from any angle and score." Blunstone points out Hill's other main talent: "He was one of the greatest goalscorers I saw. If Gordon Hill got through on goal, he'd hit the target. I'm not saying he'd score – the goalie might save it – but nine out of 10 times he would hit the target. You get other players get through shoot wide, over the bar, anywhere. He wasn't a great header, but he was a lovely striker of the ball." Those traits naturally endeared him to his new manager. That Hill was also possessed of good looks, an endearingly chirpy personality and a propensity to make a disproportionate number of his goals spectacular were traits probably of less interest to Docherty, but they certainly sealed the affection for the player on the terraces. Hill would shortly become the recipient of the type of fan worship Old Trafford hadn't seen since the heydey of Jim Holton, even of George Best. When BBC commentator Barry Davies found himself working on a televised United match that season, his statement of Hill's name when the ball was sprayed out to the left side of the park was as often as not almost drowned out by the cheers from the Reds' fans as Hill took possession. "This crowd really have taken him to their hearts!" Davies marvelled.

At the same time as United obtained Hill's services, they took 17-year-old Port Vale striker Ken Beech on loan. "Tommy has offered to take him to give him a taste of life at United," explained Port's Vale's assistant manager Reg Berks. "It is simply a gesture to help the lad improve and nothing has been agreed yet." In fact, Beech was still at Port Vale in 1981, when he moved on to Walsall. He also played for Peterborough United, Stafford Rangers and the NASL's Cleveland Cobras. As for Huddersfield Town's Martin Fowler – the kid who could theoretically have torn up the wing for Manchester United in Gordon Hill's stead – though he had a perfectly respectable career, the fact that he plied his trade with lower-division clubs Blackburn Rovers, Hartlepool United, Stockport County and Scunthorpe United indicates that he was probably overvalued, whichever of the conflicting stories told by the respective club managers about Docherty's overture was true.

\*\*\*

United's home match against Aston Villa on Saturday November 15 saw Jackson relinquishing his place, which was filled by Daly. Daly's usual number 11 shirt meanwhile was taken by the latest addition to Docherty's squad. Used to crowds of around 12,000 at The Den, Gordon Hill found himself trotting out to appear before a gate of 51,682, and this despite a bus strike and unceasing rain. "A bit different," observes Hill. "In them days they stood up and they crammed them in and they chanted. You couldn't hear yourself speak to the next player. If you shouted for a ball, you had to shout at the top of your lungs."

Paddy Roche, having conceded eight goals in three games, would have been aware that many of those 51,000-plus pairs of eyes were on him, and not benignly. Rather ruthlessly, Villa had taken note of his recent troubles. Their defender Charlie Aitken admitted afterwards that they tried to quickly put Roche under a lot of pressure, thinking "He might crack." He conceded, "It didn't quite work out. He survived an uneasy time and then settled down to do well." Much the same could be said for the United team, who initially found tricky Villa right-winger Ray Graydon a nuisance. But United had a pair of tricksters of their own now, and Coppell and Hill used the flanks exactly as Docherty had promised they would to make United even more of an attacking side, if such a thing were possible. In the 15th minute, Coppell got his fifth goal in eight appearances (though also, strangely, his last of the season). On 68 minutes, United got their second courtesy of McIlroy, who span to thump in a Coppell corner. The Reds were very unlucky not to get a couple more. The 2-0 victory meant that United moved up to third in the table, on the same points as Liverpool and one point behind top-of-the-table Derby County. Perhaps more importantly, they seemed to have turned the corner on their mini-slump and Roche to have put his nightmares behind him.

Says Hill of his debut, "I was tired. It was a completely different level. It was the First Division as opposed to the Second [sic] Division and it was just a fitness factor and the occasion for me. I got cramp afterwards. I remember getting on the train back to London and I'd got a first-class ticket – we never travelled first class. I got on the train, I sat down, I put me feet up, I had a sandwich or something and lo and behold who comes down the platform playing Bury that weekend was Millwall, my boys. So all of a sudden they get in and they walk past and 'Hilly!', 'Come on, you ain't sitting here.' We're all sitting there and having a beer and the supporters came up from the beer wagon. I had a new suit on and I think it was Frankie Sewell turns round and says to me, 'I can see where the signing money has gone.' It was great, it was brilliant it really was and I travelled back with the boys, but they understood. They would never stand in my way."

United were unchanged for their visit to Highbury the following Saturday, November 22 attended by 40,102. Alan Ball scored for the Gunners – after 12 seconds. United lost McIlroy within the first quarter of an hour, stretchered off with a facial injury. McCreery took his place. In the 25th minute United were two down. Roche's response to a Nelson free-kick was inept: he came boldly out for it but missed it. Armstrong was lurking and Greenhoff, in his anxiety to prevent his weak connection with the ball crossing the line, helped it over. 17 minutes into the second half, Pearson reduced the deficit.

Late in the game, Roche got into a terrible flap, this one over an Armstrong corner, whose swing he misread. In attempting to compensate for that misreading, he ended up pulling the ball over his own goal-line. It wouldn't have made any difference to the result – it was in the last minute – but the fact that he was at fault for the second goal too meant the morning's newspapers were full of headlines about his continuing nightmare. The 3-1 defeat saw United tumble down to fifth place in a table of which Derby were still top. United were two points behind Derby and a point behind the clubs between them, two of whom had a game in hand over them.

Roche was by now in a vicious circle from which there was no immediate way out. On one occasion recently, the United fans had let out a comedic sigh of relief when he safely gathered a ball. This is the type of sarcasm which can crush a player already dispirited over his alleged failures. Getting stick from your own side's supporters as well as having to endure the contemptuous analysis of the media pundits and press reporters makes for an excruciating spotlight. As the keeper becomes ever more self-conscious, he is flustered in situations that would previously have presented no problem to him. In many people's eyes such a process had only recently destroyed the first-class career of Leeds United goalkeeper Gary Sprake, who made some high profile mistakes that meant he, in the words of one of his colleagues, "lost his nerve".

Greenhoff – whose collision with Roche at Anfield could be posited as what started the keeper's whole loss-of-confidence snowball rolling – says, "He wasn't a big lad, Paddy. As a goalkeeper, to weigh in at about 11½ stone, he's not heavy. Probably Alex would be about 13, 14 stone and if he came for the ball, people would know he was there. Whereas Paddy, slightest touch, unfortunately for him, he got knocked off the ball quite easy. He was a talented goalkeeper. His agility was fantastic, he'd got good hands, but to me he was always a bit lightweight and that's what I think stopped him becoming a very good goalkeeper." For his part, Buchan defends the keeper: "Paddy got a bit of a raw deal in my book, in that he came in at Arsenal where we never won, he was thrown in at Liverpool where we didn't have a great record and also at Maine Road. He played in all those matches and he got stick because we lost them all. Maybe Paddy was thrown in at the deep end when he might have got a bit more protection. Dare I say it, he got blamed for those three losses at three places we never really went looking for a win." Meek: "All goalkeepers let in goals and I don't think he particularly let the team down. They're all equally to blame – blame's the wrong word to use but they all [have] responsibility and it's totally unfair to point the finger at Paddy Roche and say that but for his mistakes United would have won ... I think his mistakes have been overplayed. He didn't have much luck. Some players come into a team and things go for them and others don't hit it off and they lose the confidence and make more mistakes. We've seen that in recent years with goalkeepers with Manchester United when they were trying to find the successor to Peter Schmeichel. Goalkeepers came and went much worse than Paddy Roche. It's a very difficult position to [fill]." McIlroy says, "It was a really tough baptism for Paddy and I don't think he ever really recovered from that again." Blunstone: "You've got to realise the standard is a lot lower in the reserves than it is in the first team. You're two standards below. You're playing Bury and some of them reserve teams, they're really struggling, so there was no crowd there to upset him. You're playing in front of 2,000, 1,500. And then he comes in the first team: 48,000, 50,000, big game. They can't live up to it, some of them, and that's what happened to Paddy. He got off to a bad start and the crowd got on his back a bit, and that made it even worse. Poor lad. I felt sorry for him, 'cos he's a nice lad. Tommy tried to be fair to him. He give him a good run. He didn't just have one bad game and throw him out. He thought, 'Right, if I keep with him and persevere, he might get through it', but he didn't. As a matter of fact, he went worse. You can never tell whether a player's gonna do it until he moves up into the first team." Forsyth: "Paddy was the most unlucky player I would say at United. Every game he put him in he made a blunder. Yet in training Paddy was smashing, great, doing well. The nerves got to him when he played. Eventually he had to keep him out of the side."

"I felt for him because we were on *Match Of The Day* three weeks in a row," says Nicholl of the exposure Roche's blunders had received in an era when television coverage of clubs tended to be fairly evenly distributed across the season on the grounds that the nation was only exposed to highlights (never live coverage) of five Saturday League matches – two on the BBC's Saturday night *Match Of The Day*, three on ITV's Sunday afternoon *The Big Match*. "Paddy was so laid-back, it was going to be one or the other. He was either going to be so laid-back he could handle the pressure or he's so laid-back that he can't handle it because he wasn't the type that was able to handle it. Until you're put in that position, you don't actually know what it's like." For Nicholl, part of the harsh nature of the methods of Tommy Cavanagh was precisely about making a player ready for the scorn of the Old Trafford crowds in adverse circumstances: Nicholl: "If you were in the reserves [or] in the youth team and somebody got injured in the first team and your name was shouted out to go and join them, you were nervous going over because you knew he was just going to blast you for mistakes and losing the ball. It got to the stage where they didn't want to go and join the first team because of Cav. This was at 16, 17, 18. And then when they become 20, 21, he'd turn round and say, 'Right, that's you now.' It actually was a test. It takes more than ability to make it as a player. You need something in your temperament and your make-up to convince people that you can do it, that you can handle being booed by 50-odd thousand people. We all love getting cheered by 50-odd thousand people but can you handle the other side? I found out later on when he was assistant manager with Northern Ireland and I spoke to him about this, that's what it was. If you're getting a bit of stick and you can't handle it at the training ground … They wouldn't take you aside and show you how to do your job but they were actually doing it without you knowing."

\*\*\*

On the Monday following the Arsenal defeat, Stepney was called into Old Trafford to see Docherty. A month after telling him he would never play for the club again, the manager informed Stepney that he was back in the first team for the home fixture against Newcastle the following Saturday. "When he called me back, I suppose I could have told him to get stuffed, but I didn't," said Stepney. "I enjoy playing for Manchester United and nothing and no one can take that away from me. But I couldn't look him in the eyes because I couldn't respect him." Stepney admitted that refusing to meet Docherty's eyes during this meeting and giving him the same silent treatment he had lately received caused an argument. Nevertheless, Stepney remained in the team, and would do so for the rest of the season. With one exception, two days after the meeting with Docherty, when a meeting between the current United side and the 1968 European Cup-winners for Pat Crerand's testimonial took place at Old Trafford. Though he was the only player in the world who qualified for both teams, Stepney couldn't play in two goals at once, so he pulled on a jersey for the veterans.

Matt Busby was manager of "Manchester United 1968", who even took to the field in the blue strip the club had unusually adopted for the European Cup final. Not that the team was exactly the same. Bill Foulkes and John Aston were missing, but nobody in the 36,646 crowd was going to complain about lack of purity when one of those vacant slots was filled by Denis Law, the man who if there was any justice would have played in that historic victory. Francis Burns took the other slot, with David Herd on the sub's bench. George Best – who walked out of Old Trafford in 1972 rather than engage in what he termed the hypocrisy of appearing in the testimonial of his nemesis Bobby Charlton – turned up to renew his partnership with the other two members of the Holy Trinity in support of their mutual friend. "Manchester United 1975" also featured a couple of anomalies. Pearson was nowhere to be seen, his shirt occupied by John Lowey, a man who would never appear in a United shirt in a competitive match. The absence of the injured McIlroy (his place taken by McCreery) was more understandable. Greenhoff was another absentee, Nicholl filling his usual position and Forsyth drafted back as left-back.

Best scored a good goal. Put through by Charlton, he bamboozled Roche before sliding the ball home. This time, Roche was not going to be blamed by anyone: even 22 months after Best's last competitive match, a one-on-one situation with him and a goalkeeper was only going to have one result. That was the second goal of what sounds like a highly entertaining game. The first had seen Crerand unfortunately gift Hill an easy goal after only two minutes. In fairness, the past masters were hardly going to be able to compete with the energy of the new generation of Reds, especially when Docherty decided to use five substitutes in the second half, even if they were obscure. Grimshaw, Albiston and Paterson were three of them, and they are superstar names compared to the others: Mountford and Storey. The modern

271

side ran out 7-2 winners. McCreery got an impressive four – a couple of them very good goals – and Coppell one, with Nobby Stiles putting though his own net. Law got the other goal for the vets, Stiles the provider. McCreery: "I scored one like a karate. A volley. For me to score four was incredible."

Back in the real world, the reinstatement of Stepney for the Newcastle game on Saturday November 29 was the only change from the line-up that had played Arsenal. Attendance was 52,624. United were in control throughout but there was only one goal, if a special one. Macari received the ball from Houston with his back to the opposition goal, flicked it over his own head and with awe-inspiring finesse turned and gave it to Daly, who virtually had only to let it hit his advancing body to send it past Toon keeper Mahoney.

Afterwards, reporter Gerald Sinstadt was slightly bemused by the proceedings. "As a game it was like a conversation with Tommy Docherty," he wrote. "One-sided, ceaseless, stimulating, wayward and utterly dismissive of any counter argument. Exhilarating while it lasts, this kind of experience tends to raise questions on reflection … If Manchester United's pace was less frenzied, would they make cleaner chances? And then would they take them more efficiently? Or is it their relentless onslaught which softens the opposition for the kill?" Had they a mind to, United and Docherty could ponder those musings in Majorca, where they were taking a four-day break in the coming week. They left behind a First Division in which they stood in fourth place, with Derby still at the summit.

*** 

Not too long ago, Docherty had spoken admiringly of the way that Jack Charlton's Middlesbrough had thrived upon their ascension to the top flight the previous season. As United prepared to meet 'Boro at Ayresome Park on Saturday December 6, Docherty could take pride from the fact that the Reds were currently doing better in the First Division than Charlton's mob, who after the previous Saturday's results had been in ninth place. With United having lost their last four away games, they could do with that psychological fillip.

United were unchanged except for Forsyth replacing Nicholl, who in turn displaced McCreery on the sub's bench. Docherty had told the young full-back that this was a long-term replacement beforehand. Recalls Nicholl, "He said, 'You're alright son – you've played 17, 18 games and it's coming up to winter. I'm going to bring Alex Forsyth back.' Which is fair enough. The process I'd been through. The Doc said, 'You're still young and the pitches are getting heavy'." The match – watched by 32,454 – was entertaining but goalless, even if

Pearson and Macari getting in the way, Keystone Kops style, is what prevented McIlroy and Houston scoring. Middlesbrough were also on the attack, but in a different way. In the 12th minute their John Hickton was involved in a collision with Stepney that knocked the United goalkeeper out. Seven minutes from the end, Forsyth was stretchered off after a tackle on Cooper. In both cases, no long-term damage was done. The result may have stopped the rot of United's away form but still left them fourth in the table. The League leaders were now, in descending order, QPR, Derby and Leeds.

There was a sign of troubles to come with respect to one player in one reporter's analysis. Though Ronald O'Connor was impressed by Hill ("He is full of confidence … He gave Craggs a torrid time, showing him the ball, then racing past him"), he had misgivings. One of those caveats would in the coming months and years – which saw many unforgettable goals by Merlin – prove to be ill-founded ("His finishing is wild at the moment and ruins his good work"), the other would come to be echoed by more than a few, not perhaps among the generally adoring spectators but among Hill's colleagues: "When he dropped back to help out his defence, he twice put them in serious trouble with injudicious back-passes, which once required Houston to clear off the line." Gordon Hill would never make a defender.

\*\*\*

Saturday December 13 saw a United with an unchanged starting line-up play bottom-placed Sheffield United at Bramwell Lane. The Blades of course had been thrashed 5-1 at Old Trafford and by the third minute the foundations for another rout were in place when Pearson thumped a shot home. "We could have had five or six by half-time," Docherty opined afterwards. Hill put the visitors two-nil up before the first-half was over, getting his inaugural goal for United with a superb strike.

Six minutes into the second half, the home side were awarded a penalty when Forsyth nudged Woodward. Keith Eddy was not the first opposition player to have to try to concentrate as he prepared to take a spot-kick against the madly distracting backdrop of a sea of United supporters' hostile faces and not the first to miss. However, Dearden was on hand to send the ball home after it rebounded off the crossbar.

Coppell set up United's remaining two goals, feeding Pearson in the 75th minute and then four minutes before full-time nodding down a corner for Macari – who had a masterful game – to make the score 4-1, a demolition watched by 31,741. Though the victory left the Reds in fourth place again, it was taking fairly complicated mathematics to sort out the succession in the congested upper echelons of the First Division. In descending order, QPR, Liverpool, Manchester United and Derby were each on 28 points, all having played 21 matches.

\*\*\*

The line-up for that second massacre of Sheffield United – Stepney, Forsyth, Houston, Daly, Greenhoff, Buchan, Coppell, McIlroy, Pearson, Macari and Hill – would enjoy a sustained run without change right through to the second week in March, a total of 18 consecutive matches. Houston feels this personnel consistency was important to the team's performance: "The continuity of the team week-in, week-out seems to give that strength and depth and understanding. And if it's doing well, if it don't need fixing, why change it?" This team – average age at this point with Stepney 24 years and 230 days and without Stepney 23 years and 272 days – cemented United's unique style of the period, one that was patently Docherty's.

Commenting on this new Manchester United for a new era at season's end, Matt Busby said, "This side puts the emphasis on the simple thing. They are all busy bees, working, playing and challenging for one another ... No one in the other side gets time to settle." Explains Buchan, "We had a very quick, mobile midfield. We didn't have any crunchers in there, but they could all get their foot in: Steve Coppell, Lou Macari, Gerry Daly, Gordon Hill, Sammy McIlroy – they were quick and they could all put people under pressure and get a foot in and jab the ball away, or make them part with the ball in a hurry, not giving people time on the ball. And we were a very sharp team. We were the best team in the country for spontaneously recovering possession. If we gave the ball away it wasn't long before we got it back, because we harried the opposition, just didn't give them a chance to settle." McCreery: "Everybody worked together as a team, as a unit. One closed down, the next one was there, the next one was there." What effect did that have on the opposition? McCreery: "I think it frightened them into mistakes, and I think we did capitalise on a lot of mistakes. It is like a high-tempo thing where you have to pressure for 90 minutes, but the team was so fit we could do that." Recalls Forsyth: "You done your training attacking-minded and he played his game attacking-minded. Unless you went through maybe a wee bad spell when you'd maybe do three or four days the defences back and working on it a wee bit. Mostly all your training was geared up for attacking all the time."

Hill says, "The football that the boss was producing was some absolutely sizzilating stuff. Even some us were absolutely mesmerised at the way we would play 100 mile an hour – but it was controlled." Hill recalls the crowd loving this "sizzilating" stuff as much as the players and this in turn feeding back: "That stage would make any player play better. It lifted you up. The fans are worth a goal ... The supporters at Old Trafford were very patient, they knew what we were all about, they loved the style that we were playing, they knew that was the Man United style." Integral to the style was Stepney's continued policy of not risking possession with hoofs upfield. Hill: "He'd get it out to either left or right and we'd try and work it up that way. We never punted it too long because we never had big enough people upfront, but put it on the floor, by gum it was like sticking glue ... "

Forsyth points out that the hustling style was something honed by much training: "You worked at that every single day, sometimes in the afternoon till you got it spot on." Additionally, he reveals for all the talk of Docherty being a motivator and not a tactician, much work was done assimilating those unfamiliar with the style: "If you brought in a new player, you were back in the afternoon going through all your different routines and all that." Yet Buchan also says, "It was a very sharp midfield and a lot of the training was based on short, sharp routines. Some mornings we would only be at it an hour and Tommy Cavanagh would send us in. I remember one chap coming over and he said to Cav, 'How long do you train – one hour, one-and-a-half hours, two hours?' And Cav said, 'My eye is my judge. When I'm happy with what I see, I'll send them in. We don't go out with any preconceived ideas'."

Because of their hyperactive style, United had to be fitter than most teams, but honing their physiques did not come at the expense of working with the ball. Despite the claims made by many for Matt Busby as a pure footballing man, George Best would later lament of the Busby era, " ... the training was a joke. Jack Crompton, the trainer, used to come out carrying these two balls under his arm and occasionally he'd let us have a kick but only after we'd knackered ourselves running up and down and round the pitch." "We always had plenty of the ball," says Buchan of The Doc's methods. Though Hill says, "When we had a hard session, it was a hard session. It was sick time," he also observes, "We always played with the ball. We did very little running." McCreery explains this apparent dichotomy: "We had a pre-season that was hard but very enjoyable. We went away and played a lot of games. We did a lot with the ball at The Cliff but we'd done all our pre-season work for the fitness side of it." Greenhoff also points out, "We trained hard but we rested. Sometimes in the week we'd get two days off. We'd play on a Saturday and we went in Tuesday, and then he'd give us Wednesday off. So we'd have a hard training day Tuesday and then he'd give us a day off, then we'd come in Thursday, we'd do all our bits and bobs what we had to do and sometimes we didn't even train on a Friday. Once you'd got your pre-season under your belt, you just need topping up. 'Cos games keep you fit and if you're playing two games a week, which most of the time you were then, you'd no need to really train. You just keep ticking over. They were very good at that."

The Manchester United playing style in the Docherty era was certainly not the consequence of lectures. The 1970s was a time when coaches and managers began analysing soccer to death and many were the hours that footballers found themselves sitting in front of blackboards. Macari has said, "Under The Doc we were never big on tactics. We'd just go out and play. We were a rampaging, instinctive side. We were organised in the sense that every player understood the responsibilities of his position, but beyond that we didn't plan much." Coppell has said, "There were few team talks and the training was often limited to lively games of five-a-side." Even those five-a-side games don't seem to have been taken that seriously: Alex Stepney was allowed to play in an outfield role, as was his wont. Apparently Stepney would score so prolifically during these matches that he was always picked first.

Jimmy Nicholl says he was never even told to mark anybody in a match: "You had to sort it out yourself. If you've seen you're up against Peter Barnes, all these boys, after you've played them once and you realise their strengths and weaknesses, you can either handle it or you can't." Says Daly, "I can't honestly say that we had a rigid formula that we stuck to. A lot of the play was off the cuff ... From a midfield point of view, neither myself or Lou Macari would have any inhibitions about trying to get forward and score goals because we were both in the same vein. You have to have a little bit of organisation at the back to know what other people are going to be doing but [for] the rest of us it was just get out and play." "As for strategy," Coppell has said, "our only speciality was to come rushing out of defence to ensnare opposing forwards offside." He also said, "We were encouraged to go forward and go for goal, there was never negative thought and no one told you off if you made a mistake."

Though people like Law, MacDougall, Wyn Davies, Graham, Morgan, Stepney, Crerand and others have deep and apparently justified grievances about their treatment by Docherty at Old Trafford, it cannot be denied that Manchester United at this time was a happy berth for most. The players interviewed speak of an atmosphere that was almost blissful. Remembers Buchan, "By and large, it was a sort of all-for-one and one-for-all feeling in the squad. We'd done all the heavy physical work at the start of the week and, much to the groundsman's chagrin, we used to train at OT on a Friday morning. We'd do a few 100-yard runs and then 50-yarders and some short sprints. A good warm-up, then some stretching and then we'd run through some set-pieces for the following day. We'd finish with an eight-a-side or whatever in a quarter of the pitch and then we'd go upstairs into the old directors' room after training and have a team talk and a cup of tea. We'd all sit around after the team talk had finished. Nobody rushed off. And you could sense the atmosphere in the air for the next day. It really was a great time to be at Old Trafford. Just because of the group of people that we were, and there was a feeling you could give anybody two goals of a start at Old Trafford and still beat them, because the crowd were behind you. That's why I say that spell was the happiest two years of my playing career." McCreery is in complete agreement: "You used to go in and think to yourself, 'We're never going to get beat here.' It was such a lovely, lovely atmosphere of people involved. Man-management was good. He was a joy to work with." Steve Coppell wrote in his autobiography, "United was, in every sense, a very happy club and, at the same time, very down-to-earth." Pearson later said, "It was a wonderful time. There were no bad apples in the dressing room and most of us lived in the same area. So we used to go out for a few pints together early in the week or meet up at Sunday lunchtime." Says McIlroy, "Tommy Docherty wanted to get on with the players. He was like a comedian at times. He was very, very quick-witted. He had the players in stitches with some of the quick one-liners that he used to do. He took his football serious, he was a winner, but when the time was for a laugh, he had a laugh with the best of them." Nicholl: "The Doc would come in and make light on a Monday morning. Used to love going in – win, lose or draw – on a Monday. He'd create the atmosphere." Houston: "It was a great place to be, it really was. There was wonderful moments and the momentum was going. The stadium, especially on European nights, was unbelievable. They really were outstanding, the way Old Trafford support got behind the team ... We had a banter going at the club at that particular time just because things were going well, the team was doing well. We felt good about ourselves and we were enjoying ourselves. It really is a joy to be at a club and playing good football." Hill says of United under Docherty, "I loved it. I think it was just the camaraderie. You didn't have to be the best of friends in that team, didn't have to mix with them after the game, but on the field it gelled." McCreery, incidentally, cites the practical jokers (of which all teams have some) in this disparate but happy cast as Macari, Houston and – perhaps surprisingly – Buchan. He adds of the latter, "But Martin wouldn't like it back!"

Matt Busby, it seems safe to assume, was a happier person than he had been for a long time. It also seems safe to assume that the club's grand old man now felt a little more comfortable about his back seat role and that as the 4-2-4 system began to reap dividends he was no longer having to bite his tongue. Hill: "Sir Matt was always around. I talked to him quite a lot, but only because I was very intrigued and very interested in what he was doing and [to] talk about a game or something. I thought that I could always get advice and go to Sir Matt because he'd sit down and wouldn't talk to you as a manager, he'd talk to you as a person, as a player and a friend. The boss would do exactly the same. When you've got two expert voices coming at you it was just nice. Most people nowadays can't even get one." Blunstone says of Busby's role at the club during his time there, "He was brilliant. He was a figurehead. He came every day, but he never interfered. He'd come and say, 'Hello Frank', 'Hello Tommy' and shake hands and have a cup of coffee with us and say, 'How's things?', blah blah, but he never got involved in the football side at all."

*\*\**

Wolverhampton Wanderers, who had just suffered three successive defeats, can't have been relishing their visit to Old Trafford on Saturday December 20 to face a United who were still unbeaten at home. There was some consolation for them: the gate was the lowest one for a League match at Old Trafford so far this season – a 'mere' 44,269.

The visitors were in actual fact plucky and in the opinion of some unlucky to lose, even if they concerned themselves more with defence than attack. As United sent in the usual waves of red shirts, Wolves resisted impressively. When the occasion did arise to attack on the break, they did so skilfully. Wolves were playing with ten men in the last half-hour following the dismissal of McAlle, who paid the penalty for his multiple offences against Pearson. Departing the field at the same time as McAlle was Greenhoff, who had received a blow on the head after colliding with Stepney. He was replaced by Jimmy Kelly, an 18-year-old defender. It was partly as a result of the Pearson incident that the referee played an inordinate amount of time added on. The only goal of this match arrived in the third minute of it, scored by Gordon Hill. It was the type with which United fans would become ecstatically familiar over the next two-and-a-half seasons. A corner was deflected away from goal. Receiving the ball well outside the penalty area, Hill controlled it and then let rip with a fizzing, head-high shot. The football purist might complain that the ball was aimed at the middle of the goal, a tactic the coaching manuals don't advise on the grounds that it makes it much more likely that the goalkeeper will stop it. However, that doesn't take into account the fact that on some occasions – such as this one – the shot is so hard that the goalkeeper barely has time to be conscious of it before it balloons his net. His first goal at Old Trafford was a moment for Merlin of appropriately mystical significance. "I felt the ground accepted me," he later said. "By the ground I don't mean the stands or the terraces. I mean the actual ground, the turf, where all them greats had trod. I felt it saying, 'You'll do for us, son.' That was great, beyond words, really." The match left United second in the League, behind Liverpool only on goal average.

Though Hill was loving his new club and clearly settling in well, there would be one adverse factor about life at Old Trafford that he and his then-wife would have to get used to: he permanently ponged. Hill: "We used a special oil which was called Five Oils which was just manufactured for us, and it was a smell that went through the uniforms and through the hamper baskets where the boots were and through the kit. You could smell it in the skips because it had been used time after time after time. And it was so hot that you wouldn't go into the toilet after somebody had been there, because you sit down on the toilet and you burnt your balls. It was quite funny, but it was a smell that you could only smell when you went in. Peter Shilton said [sniffs], 'We know we're at Old Trafford'."

One reporter said Jimmy Kelly replaced Greenhoff "most adequately" and that he was "a collected young man". Kelly was born on May 2 1957 in Carlisle, though is a naturalised Scot. Docherty, as ever, was effusive over his new prospect, stating that he was one of the club's most skilful players and adding, "He is as good a ball player as people much senior to him." Which makes it all the more mysterious that Kelly was never seen by the Stretford End again. Signed in April 1972, he left for American soccer precisely five years later with that one substitute appearance to his name.

Of course, it's perfectly natural that Docherty should encourage his players with this kind of praise, and he would have been a strange human being indeed, let alone manager, if he did not talk up their attributes to the media. But it was one of several predictions about the products of the youth set-up that Docherty would make that would prove to be spectacularly wrong and which calls into question the quality of the youth stream which Docherty, Cavanagh, journalist David Meek and others at the time were praising to the skies. The man in charge of the youth policy, however, was making no great claims for it. Though Frank Blunstone could point proudly to the fact that he had nurtured Arthur Albiston, Jimmy Nicholl and David McCreery into first-team footballers, he also said, "If I can get two players worth £200,000 from this programme, I will be more than satisfied." Certainly that price tag would not prove to be applicable to players whose names were at the time bandied about as prospects but who quickly faded (Jonathan Clark, Peter Coyne, Jim Kelly and Steve Paterson) or who never made the grade at all (David Jackson, Kevan Poppett and Peter Sutcliffe).

***

United visited Goodison Park on Tuesday December 23. Everton were a fairly useful side, lying in ninth place after Saturday's results. The 41,732 crowd was healthy for a midweek match.

In the 27th minute, a headed Everton clearance found Macari on the edge of the penalty area. Macari was standing with his back to goal, but his recent displays had proven that that was no impediment to him. He controlled the ball, juggled, then flicked it up as he fell backwards and sent an overhead kick into the back of the net. Five minutes before half-time, the home side equalised via Latchford. The score remained at 1-1 until the final whistle. The draw had ensured United had given themselves and their fans a nice Christmas present: they were now back at the top of the League, and furthermore not on goal average but by a clear point. That second-placed Liverpool had a game in hand over them – and, indeed, that United had played one, sometimes two games more than any other club in the division aside from today's opponents – was something that no doubt they would postpone worrying about until the turkey was digested.

United's next fixture took place on Saturday December 27, a home match against Burnley. It was a big-ish day for both Stepney (making his 350th League appearance for the Reds) and Willie Morgan, facing the Reds for the first time since his departure in unhappy circumstances. Despite the fact that he was greeted warmly by the United fans in the massive 59,726 crowd (largest in the League this season so far), Morgan no doubt had a hankering to stick it to Docherty. This presumed latter ambition was on the surface a difficult task: the two clubs were at opposite ends of the table. In actual fact, though, Burnley were United's equals for large parts of the match.

For the second time in as many games, Gordon Hill made an opponent feel compelled to try to prevent his progress with a foul that earned him a place in the referee's book. United were noticeably feeding Hill as much as possible, but his crosses for Pearson and Macari were being dealt with comfortably for the most part by Burnley's full-backs, one of whom was Tommy Docherty's son Mick. It was Burnley who opened the scoring. In the 33rd minute, Morgan left Forsyth and Greenhoff for dead and unleashed a shot. Stepney blocked but did not hold and Hankin was there to put the ball over the line. Six minutes into the second-half, a rebound led to the scores being levelled, McIlroy striking after a Forsyth effort hit the post. The teams still seemed evenly matched and it was only when Burnley's Collins had to limp off injured, that Macari found the space on the pitch that he had wanted all afternoon. (Pearson also had to go off, complaining of stomach trouble.) With ten minutes to go, United were awarded a free-kick. Houston came up to take it and the uncleared rebounded ball was put in the back of the net by Macari with a good shot. The 2-1 victory left United second on goal average, Liverpool having taken advantage of their game in hand to go top.

\*\*\*

The third day of 1976, a Saturday, saw the beginning of United's FA Cup campaign in the shape of a third-round home tie against Oxford United. The 41,082 present witnessed a not altogether convincing victory against Second Division opposition whose leading scorer, Mick Tait, was ruled out with flu before the kick-off.

It was Oxford who in the dying seconds of the first half went ahead when Derek Clarke flicked up the ball and executed a perfect overhead kick that bounced in off a post before Stepney was aware what was happening. Docherty made an interesting tactical substitution for the second half, replacing Forsyth with Nicholl. The Doc could claim that his decision reaped immediate dividends, at least in the sense that his side promptly equalised. United's attack direct from the re-start saw McIlroy sent to the deck. Daly stepped up for his first penalty since September. That he converted may sound predictable, but it should be noted that Burton got both hands to the ball. There seemed little dispute over that decision, but when five minutes later a tackle on Pearson in the penalty area saw the whistle shrill again some were surprised. Daly's second spot-kick of the day had the feel of a double-bluff: Burton went in the wrong direction as Daly placed the ball in the same corner as the previous one. Oxford pluckily continued fighting but despite a few near-misses United kept the scoreline at 2-1 to the final whistle.

Forsyth kept his place in the starting XI for the home League fixture against QPR on Saturday January 10 and remained on the pitch for the full 90 minutes. Rangers were, like United, one of five clubs separated by only three points at the top, so the match was also the archetypal 'four-pointer'. Though Rangers were outclassed, few would agree with any suggestion that this was partly due to losing glamour player Stanley Bowles with a groin strain on 35 minutes: his only notable contribution up to then had been a horrendous back-pass in the 15th minute which allowed Hill to drive a left-footed shot into the back of the net from the edge of the box after an attempt from Pearson had rebounded his way. Hill's goal was an equaliser, for the visitors had dismayed the majority of the 58,312 crowd by going ahead in the ninth minute via Givens. In the second half, Rangers seemed to flag a little, while United were showing ultra-enthusiasm in chasing every loose ball, with Coppell and Hill rampaging bookends. McIlroy got the Reds' winner on the hour.

The 2-1 victory put United back on top by a point. Second place was now occupied not by any of the other teams to whom United had been adjacent when they had previously occupied the table's top spot but by Leeds United, who were demonstrating that even after the departure of Don Revie they were still a team to be reckoned with, something underlined by the fact that Leeds had a game in hand. "United are the best team we have played," said QPR manager Dave Sexton after the match. The bamboozled and booked McLintock (Hill inevitably his victim) said, "They have a lot of quick boys, very snappy." David Meek joined in the effusions.

The reporter who had been watching United for longer than some of their fans had been alive wrote, "I can't remember a Manchester United team that has strung passes together with such a devastating red flow … They have a team that doesn't possess any real superstars. But they don't need them, because every man is a very good player whose sum total is baffling the rest of football." He spoke of the "sheer zest of their players allied to quick, accurate passing with a tactical dedication to attack" and "total team-work with wave after wave of assault." The Manchester United of 1976, he said, was "the best combined footballing team that they have perhaps ever produced".

Despite the sceptical tone of many of Meek's journalistic colleagues throughout the season, the campaign saw United pick up praise within the profession left, right and centre. Some examples: Roy McFarland (Derby County and England): "United have brought back so much good into the game and given the public a taste for football once more." Alan Ball (Arsenal and England): "[United] have taken the First Division by the scruff of its neck." Martin Dobson (Everton): " … a credit to the game and wonderful to watch." Emlyn Hughes (Liverpool and England): " … fantastic in the way they have come back into the First Division and played such good football." Tony Currie (Sheffield United and England): "They have given football a new lease of life, and other teams have followed them." Billy Bonds (West Ham United): "The most exciting team I've seen this season … their style is refreshing and good for football." Jimmy Greenhoff (Stoke City): "Manchester United have swept teams aside by sheer energy, but their pace also tends to overshadow the tremendous skill in the side." And back to a QPR player for a final testimonial. Gerry Francis who, as well as being Rangers' stylish midfielder was also then England captain: "We thought we could play them off the park. But they proved me wrong with their unique brand of attacking football."

One journalist who was not sceptical was David Miller of the *Daily Express*. After the QPR game, Miller asked Docherty what benefits had accrued to United from employing wingers. "It stops the opposing full-backs from attacking us," he said. Miller noted that the width Hill and Coppell's runs down the flanks had given their team was pulling defences apart, QPR being a case in point: for much of the match, Rangers defenders Frank McLintock and David Webb had had to man-mark Stuart Pearson and Sammy McIlroy, lest the United marksmen get on one of the endless balls being sent their way from the sides. Many years later, Buchan would also reveal another benefit to having wingers: "If we were under the cosh, we could feed the ball out to them, they would embark on long runs and the pressure would be lifted." Miller, never a fan of the football that had resulted from the way that Ramsey's Wingless Wonders had made wide men unfashionable, was for his part delighted. "After 10 years of the counter-productive, post-Ramsey theory of attacking full-backs and defensive wingers, this bogus philosophy is at last exposed – and wingers are once more respectable," he rejoiced.

*\*\*\**

Some of the 49,189 crowd who attended White Hart Lane for United's match against Tottenham Hotspur on Saturday January 17 were still queuing at the turnstiles when a roar greeting a goal emanated from inside. Gordon Hill had taken a fourth-minute corner which probably made contact with colleague Daly and opponent Chivers, but the strike ended up being credited to him when the ball crossed the goal-line.

A highly enjoyable game ensued, helped in no small measure by the fact that Spurs, like United, employed wingers. Spurs got the equaliser they deserved after an hour. It was the last goal of the match, putting paid to the feeling the Reds must have had after that early goal that they were about to achieve their first victory in London this season. However, they were actually lucky to come away with a point. Both Tottenham's manager Terry Neill and Docherty were of the opinion that the home side should have had a penalty five minutes after their goal when Duncan went down after being challenged by Buchan. United were still a point clear of Leeds, who still had a game in hand.

Alex Stepney was an uncertainty to make the starting line-up for the fourth round of the FA Cup on Saturday January 24 due to having ricked his back the day before. He was receiving treatment right up to a couple of hours before kick-off. United kept the fact as quiet as possible but had Roche standing by in case the physiotherapy didn't work. In the end, Docherty took a gamble and decided Stepney was fit. The man whom he had tried to ease out of the picture only a couple of months before was now deemed so vital that The Doc was prepared to run a risk of playing him that could blow up in his face.

Ex-Manchester United legend Noel Cantwell was the manager of Peterborough United, the Reds' Third Division opposition. The gate was 56,352. The visitors were two down after just 11 minutes of play. Forsyth got the first goal on eight minutes, unleashing a 25-yarder. "I think it [got] maybe a wee deflection," admits Forsyth. On 11 minutes, a possibly offside Pearson put through Hill, who delivered a perfect cross to the head of McIlroy, who made it 2-0. Perhaps sensing a rout, United continued to press. However, the drawback of taking a two-goal lead at such an early stage is that with more than a hour's play yawning ahead, the opposition are just as likely to realise there is everything to play for as become disheartened. Peterborough – perhaps mindful of the fact that United had been less than completely convincing against non-First Division opposition in cup competitions this season – took the former attitude. On 35 minutes, Cozens, following a chase for a long ball that Greenhoff lost when he slipped, sent a low shot past Stepney. If anything, Peterborough were the dominant side for the remainder of the half and came out for the second-half full of the proverbial beans. 20 minutes from time however, Gordon Hill put the match beyond the plucky underdogs. The winger would make a habit of scoring crucial and/or spectacular goals in cup competitions for United. Its arguable that this one was crucial but it was indisputably spectacular. A cross from the right flank reached Hill 25 yards from goal. Most players would have laid it off. Hill was not most players. He turned to the side, drew back his leg and caught the object cleanly on the volley, throwing the kind of shape familiar less from real life than from 'Roy of the Rovers'. Peterborough's Eric Steele, like so many goalies to come, could only watch as the ball whistled past his immobile form. Not for nothing had Hill's former manager at Millwall Gordon Jago already described him as, "The best volleyer I have ever seen."

Afterwards, Cantwell endeared himself to many by describing the 3-1 defeat as "a wonderful experience". Meanwhile, Hill had endeared himself further to the United fans, if indeed such a thing were possible, with his fifth goal in eight games, a strike rate that was extraordinary for a winger but which – unlike fellow winger Coppell's flurry earlier in the season – would be in no way unrepresentative of his time at Old Trafford. "He employed me for that, that's what he said," says Hill of Docherty. "He and Tommy Cavanagh used to say, 'Just get us one today.' And when I got two they said, 'Right okay, but you should have got three.' So they kept you going with their confidence ... " He points out that those familiar with his exploits at The Den wouldn't have been too surprised at his high scoring rate: "I was the top scorer at Millwall. I'm very, very fortunate to have been able to score goals and still been able to produce it down the lines. I'd score, say, 20 and I'd create 30." As for the adoration that was currently seeing the Stretford End erupt into a cheer every time the ball found its way to him, Hill says, "They knew something was gonna happen."

Beloved by the fans Hill might have been but one person at United (at least) never could stand him. "I have lost count of the number of times Hill left me feeling thoroughly disgusted with him as a fellow professional and a human being," Alex Stepney later said. Little glimmers of the perception of some in the United dressing room of Hill as an over-cocky, work-shy London buffoon did occasionally leak out in the media but only in a fairly bland fashion that could be mistaken for football club banter. Most Stretford Enders would have been shocked at the very idea that anybody wouldn't love the man the thought of whose presence on the pitch would make them quicken their step on the way to the ground. What wasn't to adore about someone who tore defences to shreds, laid on endless goals from the byline and who, though he seemed to insist only on scoring when a thunderbolt straight out of 'Roy of the Rovers' was in the offing, still managed to out-strike the 'real' front-men? Most United fans would have assumed that Stepney and Hill especially would have been pally, being 'Cockneys' (what Northerners erroneously tend to call all working-class Londoners). "Just because we come from the same part of the country it doesn't mean to say that you're the best of friends," says Hill. "I mean, Alex was way older than myself." Fair point, but what makes more surprising the fact that Hill and Stepney were like opposing magnets is that they both had the same grounding at Millwall FC.

But Stepney was oblivious to Hill's charms, both personal and professional, viewing him as a selfish player interested only in his own performance, a criticism that would be fairly common in the United dressing room during Hill's time at the club. It was a perspective that Docherty never seemed to share. Though he did acknowledge the grievances of some of Hill's colleagues, stating in 1976, "He can frustrate you and I think he is still slightly re-adjusting his game after playing in the Third Division," Docherty otherwise seemed indulgent of Hill's foibles. In his autobiography, he simply said of Hill, "His attitude and character were first class", something so contrary to what some of Hill's colleagues thought of him as to be quite eyebrow raising. The fact Hill mentions that he was separated in age from Stepney by a full decade is also significant. Not only were Stepney's generation – both in football and in society generally – possessed of a somewhat different attitude than the influx of whom Hill was a member, but as previously noted Stepney seems to have been a bit of a dry old stick even by the standards of war babies.

Though his contempt for Hill was at the extreme end of the scale, the goalkeeper was by no means the only one of his United colleagues whose goat Hill got. Says McIlroy, "Gordon was a character. He was like a one-off compared to us because we'd never seen anything like it, this bubbly Cockney … He was easily wound up in a nice way if you know what I mean. He was a little bit strange at times, but we got on with him." His words seem to constitute the attempt of a diplomat to acknowledge fault without criticising. Others are less polite. Recalls Daly: "I remember when Docherty introduced him to us up at Old Trafford when we were having a pre-match meal. Docherty says, 'This is the new signing here, he's Gordon Hill.' And everybody went, 'Oh, hullo.' I can remember him turning around and saying, 'If you like, you can call me Merlin.' Everybody sort of looked at each other and took a bit of an instant disliking to him. Talk about the rest of us – the inhibitions of youth, the cockiness – but he was an exception altogether."

Hill defends his apparent egotism by saying, "I knew I had to be confident. I think it was just my shyness underneath, because when I left the club, I would go home after a game and I'd be on my own." However, vainglory was by no means the extent of the problem some felt existed with the winger. Buchan agrees Hill was "a wonderfully talented player" but had two misgivings about his play. One was his lack of defensive awareness. The other was his finishing: "He would score maybe 20 goals in a season, but you couldn't help feel, with the amount of chances he had, that he should maybe have been scoring more. That's what I felt. He was never one to do the simple thing when the flamboyant would suffice."

In this ambivalence about Hill's on-pitch behaviour, Buchan is representative of his colleagues. Forsyth: "Stewart Houston used to pull his hair out with Gordon Hill. You would overlap with Gordon Hill, he'd never give you the ball. When you're caught out he wouldnae get back and help you defend. Stevie Coppell was absolutely magnificent. He's the best player I've ever played beside. If you were overlapping he'd get back and defend for you, great attitude for the game. He was absolutely brilliant, Stevie, so he was. Gordon skill-wise, absolutely brilliant but *ohhhh*. He could throw away the game for you. Absolutely brilliant player but oh dear, oh dear, at times he could really let you down and no' play at all and it just wouldnae go for him." Houston, the last line of defence on the wing up which Hill rampaged, also has ambivalent feelings about Merlin. "I would go on the overlap and Hilly at times would end up losing [the ball], so in the end I could be doing twice as much bleeding running," he says. "But not all the time, because he was a fit lad, Hilly, and he could get back. But he was more offensive-minded. So I had to be careful how I timed my runs. That's what I quickly learned. He had the ability to get back but he just had a wee bit of a lazy mentality. When he got to the halfway line he didn't really want to cross it. You used to have to keep reminding him to come back but at the end of the day I had to make my own decisions. The problem would arise if the opposite full-back came and he didn't track – I'm playing two v. one. That's when possibly words were said." Houston denies that Hill received unconditional love from the terraces. "Supporters are not daft," he says. "Don't kid yourself. They know when players are trying and they know when players are not trying. If somebody's trying all the time and they make mistakes, supporters don't have a problem with it. When supporters see somebody and they might not try, they have a problem with it. I think that's how the supporters looked at Gordon at times." Greenhoff: "Stevie Coppell [would] be up and down all day helping the full-back out and suddenly you've got Gordon who'd be strolling back. It was difficult to take."

Daly agrees with this analysis and adds a further complaint: "When Gordon had the ball out on the left wing, you were making your way into the box on the right-hand side waiting for the cross to come in and invariably it didn't come in because he tried to do too much on it. I do remember Stewart Houston having more problems with him. The amount of times where Hill would take the ball up and Stewart would go on one of his overlapping runs and then for some God-given reason the ball wouldn't be delivered to him and it'd break down and Gordon would just stand there and Stewart would have to run by him and get back again … "

Blunstone was a little more indulgent, possibly through the paternalism developed as youth coach: "He's a cocky little lad. I liked him, he's alright Gordon." However, even he acknowledges a couple of deficiencies. Blunstone: "Gordon was a pure outside-left, nothing else. Couldn't play him anywhere else. Pure winger. Very left-sided. I bend down and let him kick my arse, he wouldn't hurt me with his right foot." Then there was his laziness: "If you asked him to do it and said, 'Look, get back and work', he'd do it. But he'd get away with what he could." "Supporters even said it in them days: 'If Gordon's not scoring he's doing nothing'," says McIlroy. "A lot of people said that … " However, he adds, "I think it's a bit harsh in a way because if you're going to judge him with Stevie Coppell, you can't. Stevie Coppell worked up and down. That wasn't Gordon's strengths. He was more of a liability in our defensive area."

1976 saw the publication of *Only a Game?*, a diary by Millwall player Eamon Dunphy of his club's 1973/74 season. Irishman Dunphy had been a kid at United in the mid-60s but hadn't made the first team. He'd subsequently had a solid career in the lower divisions. That season covered in *Only a Game?* was Gordon Hill's first in professional soccer and Hill in a sense is the star of the book, although not always in a good way. Refracted through the prism of Dunphy's sometimes glacial disapproval, Hill comes across as alternately a twerp and a naïf, but Dunphy – who would go on to have a journalistic career that included a myth-busting book on his old manager Matt Busby and a somewhat less well-received tome on compatriot rock band U2, on which he was clearly on less familiar ground – knew what made good copy and Hill anecdotes pepper the text. Discussing 17-year-old Hill after he had played his first home game following a couple of away appearances, Dunphy said, "It is amazing to think that he has only been at the club a few months and is already in the first team. He is not ready yet. He needs to spend a lot longer in the reserves learning the game." Dunphy felt the youngster's unpredictability and habit of giving the ball away made him impossible to play with, but had to acknowledge that the crowd "have taken to him in a big way. There is nothing like a few tricks on the ball to get a crowd going, even if the tricks don't get you anywhere and just put the rest of the team in trouble." Footballers, certainly English ones, aren't the greatest of readers, but those United players who bought or borrowed a copy of *Only A Game?* will no doubt have been amused at sentiments that mirrored those of many at Old Trafford who considered Hill a fancy dancer. Others, like ex-Millwall boss Barry Fenton, Hill fans and Hill himself might have detected just a hint of jealousy in Dunphy's resentment that Hill had made lightning-fast progress up the career ladder. Interestingly Dunphy also said of Hill, "We are probably wrong in our judgment of him." He also made an admission that, if Docherty agreed with it, might explain the indulgence The Doc always showed to Hill: "If you try and instil too much common-sense in him, you will destroy his capacity for the spontaneous, the unusual. Which is a considerable asset in this game."

\*\*\*

United's home match against Birmingham City on Saturday January 31 in front of a 50,726 crowd ended in ugly scenes that were not representative of the match as a whole, but the result of a certain sense of both injustice and frustration on the part of relegation-threatened Birmingham.

"That was a frosty winter day and we played with an orange ball," Forsyth recalls. Gordon Hill, though, seemed immune to the conditions as he danced around Birmingham players, probably aware – as any self-respecting wizard of the dribble would be – that the conditions made it hard for defenders to turn. Also having a good game was Forsyth, who got his second goal in as many games on 37 minutes when a corner-kick came to him. "I hit it straight on the volley and it went in like a rocket," he says.

Just before the interval, McIlroy made it 2-0. The visitors protested that the Irishman had been offside during the build-up but the referee decided there was no interference with play. Birmingham got over their anger sufficiently to pull one back, but when Macari took advantage of a subsequent terrible Blues pass to score the Reds' third, it was all over bar the shouting and the fouling. United had retained their place at the top, clear by a point. Liverpool were now the second-placed team. Leeds still had their game in hand but they had slipped to fourth and, on 35 points, were three points adrift of United.

Forsyth must have been hoping that Docherty was watching the media reaction to his goal. Granada TV's *Kick Off* programme may have been a provincial affair – broadcast in the Manchester region – but who would not feel proud of getting, as Forsyth did, the programme's Man of the Match award? Additionally, Forsyth recalls the praise of Crystal Palace manager and football pundit Malcolm Allison: "Malcolm Allison says, 'He's the best two-footed player about in the country'." Which begs the question of whether Forsyth ever agitated for a regular role as free-kick taker? Forsyth: "Not really. Free-kicks we left to Gerry Daly, Willie Morgan. Gordon Hill liked to bend them in. So we had three or four players all wanting to take them. I liked to take penalties. Later on [after] I left United I took all penalties for Rangers, Accies and all that. So I'd have liked to have took penalties at United." However, he does concede, "Gerry was a good penalty taker."

Saturday February 7th saw the Reds visit Highfield Road to take on a Coventry City currently hovering only a few places above the relegation zone. The 33,922 spectators saw thrilling, end-to-end football throughout. Coventry had clearly been told by manager Gordon Milne to shoot whenever they saw the whites of Stepney's eyes, and on 31 minutes it was just such a long-range effort that Stepney was powerless to stop. Hill was United's man of the match. Coop was the hapless opponent this time out who picked up a booking for taking umbrage at his repeated weaving past multiples of defenders. The equalising and final goal of the match came a minute after McCreery replaced Pearson, Macari – completely unmarked – nodding in yet another cross from Hill in the 77th minute.

United dropped a position as a consequence of the result, now behind Liverpool on goal average. Though Coventry climbed a place, Milne was much less relaxed then Docherty after the match. "It was a good match for the public, but not so good for the connoisseurs," Milne – somewhat bafflingly – noted. A twinkle-eyed Docherty proudly fielded questions about Hill. "He lacks confidence at the moment – he only thinks he's the best left-winger in Europe," was one of his wry observations about Merlin. "He doesn't just make the ball talk – he makes it answer him back," was another.

United's FA Cup campaign continued the following Saturday. The St Valentine's day fifth-round fixture at Filbert Street saw them take on Division One opposition for the first time in this year's competiton. Furthermore, Leicester City boasted class players like powerful striker (and all-round smoothie) Frank Worthington and midfielder Keith Weller.

United were incredibly lucky to survive the tie. They made the early running, going ahead in the eighth minute through Macari. Worthington replied on the half-hour mark only to be adjudged offside. Three minutes later, Gerry Daly (described by one journalist after today's match as "like a British Rivera", in reference to the sublimely gifted Italian playmaker nicknamed the Golden Boy) executed a shot on the turn past Leicester keeper Wallington. Though he didn't score, Pearson had a good game, displaying an energy and form that had been lacking recently, though the lately sublime Hill was noticeably recovering from flu and replaced by McCreery on 83 minutes. For Coppell, the rampant, hyperactive Macari was one of the men of the match in the 2-1 victory and a recurring memory he had of the Scotsman's role was him shouting the bewildering war-cry "Timpsons!" It actually meant "Boot it!", Timpsons being a chain of shoe shops.

Leicester were not keen to suffer the humiliation of being beaten by a bunch of kids on their home turf. Hardly slouches in the first-half, they mounted a ferocious second-half fightback. Bad luck on Leicester's part kept the ball out of the United net – that and the brilliance of Stepney. When Bob Lee pulled one back in the 60th minute, few were surprised. A draw at least seemed likely, and the fact that the replay would be at Old Trafford would not have overly daunted a team who had held United to 0-0 at the Reds' home ground in October. But United's defence was impregnable, especially the 33-year-old element of it. Stepney has recalled that Docherty tried to use this match to do his equivalent of kissing and making up. Noticing Docherty running towards him after the final whistle sounded, Stepney realised with some horror that the manager intended to throw his arms around him. Stepney pretended not to see him and searched for the opposition goalkeeper to shake hands. But Docherty caught him and Stepney then had to endure having pictures taken with the ostentatiously grateful manager in the dressing room. "It was his way of saying the difference was over," Stepney later recalled. "After that you couldn't say we were friends, but at least there were exchanges of views!" While the photographers were allowed access, Alex 'Hurricane' Higgins wasn't. The stylish but wayward snooker player (his sport's version of George Best, right down to the Irish roots) was, like many of his countrymen, a huge United fan. This cut no ice with Cavanagh, who prevented him offering his congratulations to the players by stating, "I couldn't care who you are, you're not coming in here", and slamming the door in his face.

Leicester manager Jimmy Bloomfield declared with magnanimity afterwards that the display that had been put on before the 34,000 crowd was "a victory for football". Reporter Robert Oxby was so impressed by what he had seen that he opined of the "effervescent young United team" that they would "bring a new dimension to the club's history" and were "worthy successors of the young men lost so tragically at Munich".

\*\*\*

Despite the fact that United's next match took place on a Wednesday, a massive crowd of 59,709 clicked through the turnstiles to see it, for the fixture on February 18 saw them play host to Liverpool in a match that would put United on top of the League should they win, as well make up for that beating they had taken at Anfield in November.

With their supporters roaring them on, United made most of the early play. Liverpool weathered the storm and then began displaying their own particular brand of football, which was stately where the home team's was rip-roaring. However, no matter how many times Coppell beat Neal or Hill ghosted by Tommy Smith, no matter how many times Macari – impressive tonight – showed his skills in midfield, and no matter on how many occasions Kevin Keegan and John Toshack tussled with Buchan and Greenhoff, a state of deadlock prevailed. A below-par McIlroy was replaced by McCreery on 70 minutes, but that made no difference and the ultimate 0-0 scoreline seemed to prove that there was as little between the quality of the two teams as the goal average that separated them in the table.

It was obviously disappointing to the United players that they didn't obtain the extra point that would quite possibly have installed them as favourites for the title. To their credit, though, none of their frustration manifested itself in on-field nastiness. Docherty later recalled the Liverpool manager Bob Paisley coming into United's dressing room and complimenting them on the low number of fouls they committed.

United visited Villa Park on Saturday February 21. The Reds were playing some delightful football in the opening half-hour for the 50,094 assembled but Villa dealt with it coolly. In the 39th minute, Villa went ahead. United equalised five minutes later. Hill had now been discovered to have yet another weapon in his armoury: long throw-ins. Accordingly, he switched wings to take one and sure enough propelled the ball a remarkable distance, especially considering his diminutive stature and correspondingly short arms. From it, Pearson sent a backward header into the penalty area, where Macari was waiting to hook in his 14th goal of the season.

Villa had the better of the play in an exciting second-half. On 61 minutes, Macari had to withdraw with a groin strain. He was replaced by 17-year-old Peter Coyne, who had already scored 38 goals for the youth team this season and was being hailed as a superstar-in-the-making by some at Old Trafford. The substitution occurred just before Villa scored again, Gray's volleyed strike effectively the last word in a clash that ended United's 14-match unbeaten run. The result left the Reds in third place, two points adrift of table leaders Liverpool. While United had the same number of points as second-placed QPR, the Londoners had a game in hand.

With United due to meet title contenders Derby on Wednesday, Macari's injury couldn't have come at a worse time. In comments that seemed to admit a lack of strength in depth, The Doc said after the Villa match, "Our biggest danger is injuries. There is nothing you can do when they happen. You can make excuses but they upset the balance and blend of any side." He added a comment that suggested his purse-strings had been tightened by the board: "It's not a question of buying players to plug the gaps. That's something I won't do."

\*\*\*

Local lad Peter Coyne – born in Longsight, Manchester (not Hartlepool as many sources claim) on November 13 1958 – was signed by United in October 1973. Coyne says Docherty was "very instrumental" in signing him. "United had followed my career, if I can call it that, from Manchester Boys when I played under-11s," he recalls. "Today. I don't think anybody ever hears of them, but it was a massive achievement to play for Manchester Boys when I played, and of course you either went to United or City. I was about 13, 14 when United and a couple of teams started to take notice." United would invite Coyne over for training. "I never, ever went but they kept watching me and they got to know me dad and they were always asking me to sign ..." Docherty even invited Coyne to travel on the first-team coach to a Southampton away fixture. "Me being such a shy lad at that age, I didn't take up the opportunity." Coyne did train with Manchester City a few times – but only because his older brother Ged was a centre-half there. To some extent, Coyne did the rounds, having trials at several clubs like the junior England players he associated with. "England boys [would] say, I'm going Chelsea next week for a trial', 'I'm going Arsenal ... ' I suppose it's the England boys saying they were here, there and everywhere. I thought, 'Well I'll just keep me options open' but I don't know why. Me brother used to say, 'Why don't you just sign for United? You know you're going to.' I was a massive United [fan] ... My whole family are Blues so I don't know why I ended up a Red. I was one of them used to go to bed in a United kit." Ged – two years his senior – joined Peter at United when released by City.

Coyne became famous among his Manchester contemporaries when he scored hat-tricks for England Schoolboys against France and West Germany. In fact, his fame spread beyond the city, because England Schoolboys matches were now being televised. Coyne: "The next day everybody knew you. Of course being linked to United as well ... You got to be well-known in Manchester. It was a massive thing." Though he wasn't as powerfully built as many centre-forwards nor possessed of huge skill, Coyne's quick instincts and unashamed goal-hanging habits meant he – to employ the phrase used to describe players with a high strike rate – scored for fun. "I think it's a goalscorer's instinct," he explains of his gift. "You can't coach where to be. Your legs just take you to somewhere where you think the ball's going to end up and lo and behold it does. It's taking a chance, gambling that the goalie's gonna drop it or a defender's going to make a mistake. Always think they're going to make a mistake and take a chance 'cos when the opportunity [comes], you're there."

After Coyne finally signed on the dotted line with United, Docherty continued to nurture – even spoil – him. Coyne: "I went on an England Schoolboys trip to Australia and The Doc said come down to Old Trafford the week before and he kitted me out with three pairs of football boots. Every Friday, even while I was at school, I had to ring up Old Trafford to find out if I was in the 'B' team the next day, and he'd sometimes be on the phone and have a little word, which for a kid of that age to get to chat to a manager, it was a massive thing. You can't help but be impressed that he's took the time to have a chat with you. I couldn't speak highly of him enough when I was 15." Tommy Cavanagh, of course, was a less benign figure: "When I signed full-time I found out it was like good-cop, bad-cop. Although The Doc could be a bad cop as well. But the results proved at United that it worked well, what they had going ... The Doc used to say to me ... 'You've got a lovely habit of scoring goals. While you're doing well, I'm your best mate. When you step out of line, I'm your worst mate'."

Having previously broken the Manchester Schools scoring record set by United's Tony Young, Coyne found himself bet by Docherty in 1975/76 that he couldn't reach a figure of 40 goals for a United youth team for whom he was scoring prolifically. Coyne: "The Doc used to go up to these strikers – reserves, 'A' team, I think it was mostly young ones – at the start of the season and just say, 'If you score 40 goals this season, I'll give you a fiver.' By Christmas I was on 38 and I got a message to go and see Tommy Docherty at Old Trafford. I thought I was in trouble. Walked into his room. They were all there: him, the chief scout, Tommy Cav. I was scared to death. He said, 'Do you know what you're here for?' I said, 'I can't think.' He said, 'Do you remember the bet I said at the start of the season if you scored 40 goals? Well you've got 38 now. Did you [know]?' I went, 'No.' and he just got his fiver out and said, 'There's your fiver.' It were fantastic. As a kid then five quid was quite a lot, so I was chuffed to bits."

Of his first-team debut, Coyne recalls, "I had no idea I was even being thought of because I was playing for the 'A' team. The odd game for the reserves, then back in the 'A' team. They used to put the teamsheet up at The Cliff every Friday morning for the 'B' team, the 'A' team and the reserves, and you'd do your training then look who you're playing for the next day. My first thoughts are to look at the 'A' team. Nothing there. There was a 'G. Coyne', number nine, obviously my brother. I looked at the reserves. Nothing there. I thought, 'I wonder if they've made a mistake with the 'A' team with the "G"?' I went to make enquiries and they said, 'No, you're with the first-team tomorrow.' No one give me any [indication] or anything during the week."

On the day of the Villa match, it was uncertain until 12:30 whether Coyne or fellow junior Ray Storey would be substitute. "The other lad was older than me, he'd had more experience, and I think he thought it was gonna be him," says Coyne. "But no, The Doc said, 'In case you're wondering what you're doing here, I've phoned your dad, your dad's on his way, you're sub'." So swift was Coyne's elevation, that it led to a surreal scene before the match: "I remember doing the warm-up before the game. Some of me mates actually shouted at me in the crowd: 'What are you doing here?' I said, 'I'm sub!'" Coyne says he was not nervous: "I wanted to get on." He got his chance when Macari got injured. "I was warming up. Next minute, he's coming off. The game stopped while I went on for Lou. The free-kick was taken and they scored, Andy Gray, made it 2-1. That was my start to professional football." As for his memories of the rest of the game, he says, "It's like a blur. I was so excited. It's your [dream] as a kid to play for United."

By a remarkable coincidence, the very day of Peter Coyne's debut saw the youngster gain a splash of publicity. Coyne was the subject of the 'Sports Star of the Future' feature in the boys' weekly comic *Action* cover-dated February 28 1976 (the publication appeared a week before its cover-date). Under the headline 'United's Goal Getter!', Coyne gave a précis of his career thus far: "If there's one thing I really like it's scoring goals! And playing for Manchester United, I've got to make sure I do – or Mr. Docherty will have something to say! I've always got a real thrill out of slamming 'em into the net – ever since my primary school days. They put me on the wing because I was small – but it wasn't long before I moved into the middle where I could use my shooting skills. Reckon I got about 300 goals altogether. I went on to play schoolboy games for Manchester, for Lancashire and for England. I'll always remember those games I played for England. I managed to score two hat-tricks against West Germany and France, at Wembley. The goals were not blistering Bobby Charlton-type rockets – but reflex shots inside the box. I'm 17 now and signed professional for United last November. Mr. Docherty is really keen on discipline. He told me to get my hair cut – pointing out that with a great big mop over my eyes I wouldn't be able to see the ball. But he's got bags of confidence in me – and that's great. He took me to one side early in the season and said I should set myself a target of 40 goals in 1975/76 – or better still … 50!" All pretty anodyne, of course, but this gushing prose would ultimately become poignant because of the tragic ending to this story.

\*\*\*

Ironically considering Docherty's morose injury-related ruminations, come Wednesday – February 25 – United were able to field an unchanged team yet again. And Macari, in fact, proved to be the man of the match, thrilling the 59,632 at Old Trafford by providing the impetus from midfield for most of United's attacks.

United were the dominant side and took a deserved lead on 27 minutes. The Reds gained a free-kick when Coppell was fouled. Hill's powerful long-range effort – free-kicks yet another of his talents – almost earned him a spectacular goal, but the ball hit the bar. Pearson, though, was hovering. Pancho must have been relieved to see his header go in – it was his first goal in 12 matches. Derby played more like the reigning champions they were in the second-half, having had one serious attempt on the United goal in the preceding 45 minutes, and they equalised in the 56th minute. The 1-1 draw left United third, one point behind both Liverpool and QPR. Rangers had played a game more than the clubs either side of them. United were ahead of fourth-placed Derby only on goal difference.

The crowd of 57,220 for the match against West Ham United on Saturday February 28 marked the point at which the Old Trafford turnstiles had clicked only 21,000 shy of a million times this season, thus virtually guaranteeing that the next fixture would take them over the million mark. As if to celebrate the occasion, the Reds shrugged off the relative torpor that had seen them acquire just two points from three matches and gave their loyal fans a goals bonanza.

The Reds were lacklustre for much of the first-half but four minutes into the second they began a demolition job. Coppell had a shot cleared off the line, but Forsyth was hovering. "That was a 20-yard volley through other players," Forsyth recalls. Seven minutes later, Daly executed a brilliant volley to make it 2-0. At that point, an injured McIlroy was pulled off and replaced by McCreery. The sub got his name on the scoresheet on 76 minutes when Pearson set him up by sliding the ball through after bursting free of two West Ham players. West Ham were now hanging on for grim life, not least because the wingers had found their stride and were knocking in centres repeatedly. One might think that the way Hill set up United's fourth and final goal two minutes from time – juggling the ball on a toe before flipping it up for Pearson to head home – was showing off, but frankly the dividing line between run-of-the-mill play and showboating for Hill was so blurred as to be meaningless. Though United were still third in the table after the 4-0 triumph, it marked an improvement: not only was it just goal average that divided the top three – Liverpool, QPR and United all had 43 points – but United had a game in hand over QPR. The title race was still wide open. McCreery recalls feeling confident about United's prospects that season: "I think definitely when we went up so high in the League and Old Trafford was a fortress at the time." Asked if he personally was surprised that the club were doing so well in their first season back in the top flight he says no, citing the number of internationals in the team's ranks.

Certainly, the Reds had far more of a chance than West Ham. After the Hammers had beaten United at Upton Park in October, West Ham were in third place, one position behind United, but on goal average only and with a game in hand. Today, the London club were languishing in ninth place. Almost as if predicting his side's humiliation, Trevor Brooking – a perennially nice man even if his judgments are not always 100% accurate – had publicly marvelled at United's form shortly beforehand. Interestingly, his praise was shot through with observations on factors that would normally prevent a side achieving the form and results United had been, factors which may have influenced his pouring scorn on their title chances earlier in the season: United had neither a traditional stopper-half like Jack Charlton nor a midfield destroyer like their own former hero Nobby Stiles; they lacked height in the centre of defence; their all-out attack exposed them to the risk of counter-attack. None of these things seemed to matter because, Brooking pointed out, Greenhoff and Buchan may only have been 5ft 10in, but they handled danger by holding a line at the edge of the penalty area, only going into the penalty-box to pick up an opponent if a wide player had got down a flank and was preparing to cross. Additionally, he said, Stewart Houston covered well for his central colleagues, presumably a reference to the fact that at six feet the left-back was a veritable giant compared to the other defenders.

By now, it was obvious that however peculiar the combination of Greenhoff and Buchan as centre-halves, it was working. As well as constituting a diminutive but robust line of defence, it saw the two complement each other. Buchan sacrificed the goalscoring he had occasionally provided for Aberdeen (he netted nine times in 136 League matches at Pittordrie, which may not sound much but he notched up only four strikes in his 456 matches in all competitions for the Reds), because he knew that in Greenhoff he had a defensive colleague who was unusually comfortable going forward. Says Greenhoff, "It was the only way I could do it. I couldn't just go and be an out-and-out defender because I wasn't good enough to do that. My thing was defend the best I could to help the team, knowing I had a great player alongside me, Martin Buchan, and then once we got the ball set things going, and if I could join in a bit more I would do. I think Martin was always happy to sit back and let me go forward and I was always happy to go and challenge for balls and then pick the pieces up. It was a good marriage."

On the same day as the West Ham match, the League Cup final took place, fought between Newcastle United and Manchester City. Ordinarily, City's 2-1 victory would have been of only passing interest to Red fans but it rankled with some that City were playing a type of football that had come to seem to them Docherty's trademark. Docherty of course didn't invent 4-2-4, but it was hardly the fashion when City manager Tony Book had recently started using it in what some saw as a particularly audacious (considering that imitating your arch-rivals is not usually something that goes down well with football fans) example of monkey-see, monkey-do. Book, though, could plausibly claim that his winged wonders were more than just copycats: he had at his disposal players of the class of keeper Joe Corrigan, veteran midfield workhorse Colin Bell, Asa Hartford – only famous to many as the footballer who hit the headlines when a transfer was scuppered after a medical revealed he had a hole in his heart but actually a classy midfielder – and Joe Royle, the long-serving Everton striker who had moved to the club in 1974. Book's wingmen were, for some, even better than Coppell and Hill. Dennis Tueart, like Hill, combined skill at running with the ball with virtuosity: whereas Hill scored with thunderous volleys. Tueart netted with dramatic overhead kicks. Tueart's wing partner was *wunderkind* Peter Barnes, a teenager who would be named the PFA's Young Player of the Year that season. Nonetheless, the reaction of some United fans to City's current style is best expressed by Richard Kurt and Chris Nickeas, authors of *The Red Army Years: Manchester United in the 1970s*, who wrote, "The thieving bastards had copied our 4-2-4 style and won a trophy with it, pinning our own fourth-round scalp to the ribbons. However much Reds' dads chirped that this was 'good for Manchester', it grated."

\*\*\*

Saturday March 6 saw at Old Trafford before a 59,433 gate the beginning of what would transpire to be an epic struggle between Manchester United and Wolverhampton Wanderers for a place in the FA Cup semi-finals. Wolves were one from bottom of the First Division table, but they proved United's toughest opponents thus far.

The story of the match is revealed in the statistics for corners: 19 for the home side, two for the visitors. United mercilessly overworked the Wolves defence, using the unusual strategy today of lobbing high, long balls over the midfield in order to counter Wolves' ultra-defensive approach. If it was something of a miracle that the game was goalless come half-time, a certain Phil Parkes (the other one) was God's representative on earth. On the hour mark, Wolves shocked Old Trafford by going into the lead ridiculously against the run of play. Equilibrium was restored 10 minutes later when Daly drove an angled shot inside the Wolves far post. The Irishman can recall almost none of his strikes for United (including even his first) but says of this one, "I remember scoring that goal and running toward the Stretford End. That one always sticks out for me." In the dying moments, McIlroy volleyed goalwards but Parkes capped his magnificent performance by tipping it over.

The Molineux replay took place the following Tuesday, March 9. Wolves, encouraged by a crowd of 44,373 – the biggest at this stadium since May 1972 – were attacking from the start. In the 19th minute, forward Steve Kindon rose well to head home a cross. Before United even had time to gather themselves, they were behind by two when John Richards adroitly brought down the ball with his chest and smashed it beyond the reach of Stepney. Just 21 minutes had passed. Worse, United had the distraction of having to fend off more attacks from a Wolves team as adventurous as they had been unambitious on Saturday.

10 minutes later, Docherty took drastic action. Lou Macari, whose participation had always been risky due to both groin and toe injuries, was taken off and Jimmy Nicholl sent on in his stead. "I don't think Lou should have played that game," says Greenhoff. "He played because that's what you did in them days. Not like now. If you've got a little kick, you're out for three weeks. Because you've got such a squad you can play who you want. In them days, how many times you played with an injury, it's scary." It was Greenhoff in fact who – Nicholl being a defender – had to move into midfield. What followed was possibly the greatest Manchester United performance of the Docherty era. It didn't take too long for this make-or-break measure of Docherty (who later said of it, "I thought we might as well lose 4-0 as 2-0") to start working. In the 36th minute, Pearson's relentless hustling paid dividends as he headed home a Hill corner. United continued applying the pressure in the second-half. Wolves, though, were refusing to be dominated, as indicated by a powerful shot from Steve Kindon. Some Wolves fans were already celebrating a goal before it thumped against a post and rebounded fully 20 yards. Finally, in the 75th minute, the pressure – especially from the two wingers – that saw United win a total of 15 corners in the match as opposed to Wolves' three yielded an equaliser. Greenhoff was the man responsible.

As the whistle blew for the end of normal time, it was back to square one for everybody. Even Wolves' home advantage could be said to be negated by the psychological fillip given the United players by clawing their way back to even-stevens. Six minutes into extra-time, McIlroy raced in to put United ahead for the first time over the two ties. Wolves never recovered.

For the Doc, the man of the match seemed to be one of those who didn't get on the scoresheet: Steve Coppell. Marvelling at the way the young winger ran at Wolves' Derek Parkin over and over again, he said, "He just never gives in … Repeatedly, Parkin stopped him but Steve persisted and in the end he destroyed him to win the match for us."

The Reds' fightback was not only a superb victory, but the kind of recovery that creates that football virtue no amount of skill can equate to: strength of character. For Buchan, it was a defining moment of Docherty's era at Old Trafford. "I think that epitomised the fighting spirit that The Doc had instilled in us," he says. "There was a great sense of togetherness." Does he look back on that Wolves match as the greatest match in which he ever played, in terms of a footballing spectacle? "It must come very close. It's got to be up there with the greatest performances of my time at [Old Trafford]."

United knew by now that their semi-final opponents would be no pushovers: reigning League Champions Derby County. Even so, Coppell has recalled Docherty calling a meeting to tell the players not to engage in media debate about the club's prospects, pointing out that they had enough pressure on them already without discussion of what trophies they might secure. Almost unbelievably, considering the situation they had been in two seasons ago, people were now talking about the possibility that United could pull off the FA Cup and League double.

***

Macari's injury necessitated the first change to United's starting line-up since December for the home match against Leeds United on Saturday March 13. McCreery was given the chance to recast himself from eternal super-sub to striker, a situation that would persist for six matches. To facilitate this, McIlroy was moved back to midfield. Gerry Daly meanwhile helped to take up the slack engendered by such a hyperactive player's absence by taking on more on-field responsibilities. Ironically, though McCreery's role upfront could not really be termed a success in terms of goals scored, the other two players shone in their changed roles. Docherty would later coo over Daly's happy-go-lucky temperament (which assisted his nervelessness in spot-kicks) and noted his improved stamina. Nice though it is for a player to be commended in public, Docherty simply went too far in his praise for McIlroy. Though few would dispute his judgment that the Irishman was a "revelation after he switched into the middle after the injury to Lou Macari," it was typical absurd Docherty bombast for him to declare, "He could become another Johan Cruyff." It's doubtful that any player – least of all one as level-headed and modest as McIlroy – would have been thanked to be compared to the man pretty unanimously considered the greatest footballer in the world at the time, with all the potential for ridicule that created.

Leeds' title challenge had somewhat fallen away of late, not coincidentally because Billy Bremner had been out injured for seven matches. His return made something of a difference today. Leeds seemed to have been instructed to stop United by foul means and fouler and the Reds' free-kick on three minutes was not their first. Forsyth took it, Pearson hooked it on and Houston charged in to head it past David Harvey. The hapless Harvey then found himself the victim of an avalanche of attempts on his goal, with the bulk of the 59,429 spectators roaring the Reds on. Forsyth made his way to the byline, whereupon he sent in the now archetypically Manchester United hard, low cross. The objective of these crosses was demonstrated almost textbook style by Pearson as he coolly sidefooted home. 15 minutes into the second-half, United looked to have it wrapped up when McIlroy executed one of his impudent nutmegs and, as the Stretford End jeered at his victim Yorath's embarrassment, centered for Daly, whose header flashed past Harvey. United's players were now virtually lining up to have a shot at the Leeds goal.

United might have learned valuable lessons in the Wolves replay but they were still young and inexperienced. In contrast to the way that this Leeds team – at least up until a couple of seasons ago – had an ability and a penchant to guard even a one-goal lead like their lives depended on it, United proceeded to become careless. The old, medal-bedecked warhorse Bremner could smell weakness and in the 87th minute put Cherry through on goal with a wonderful pass to which his colleague did full justice by beating Stepney from a narrow angle. Even then, United didn't tighten up for the remaining three minutes and within one minute of the Cherry goal it was Bremner scoring for Leeds.

The 3-2 scoreline was an illusion, of course, and Leeds returned to Yorkshire knowing they had been outclassed. Reporter Tom Gorman, while noting the liveliness and mobility of Coppell, McCreery, Pearson and McIlroy, was particularly impressed by the class of Daly: "Lean and pallid, he is the stylish fulcrum of much of his side's fine work. One moment he was piercing Leeds with short, sharply-angled passes, the next giving width to the play and always looking for space." United were still in third place after the match and leaders QPR had now opened up a two-point gap over both them and second-placed Liverpool. However, United had played only 33 games, in contrast to Liverpool's 34 and Rangers' 35. That double that no one in the United side was allowed to discuss with the press was still very much a possibility.

An unchanged United visited Carrow Road the following Wednesday, March 17. Hill put the Reds ahead within nine minutes. Forsyth had fed Pearson with a cross and Pancho in turn flicked it to Hill who executed a low, curling shot into the net from 14 yards. In the 69th minute, Norwich got a goal they well deserved for the way they had fought back. At the end of a thrilling match, the 27,782 present gave the teams a standing ovation.

United climbed to second in the table, one point behind QPR and one above Liverpool, with the pleasing knowledge that QPR had played an extra game. Docherty said afterwards, "I was happy with a point. It was that kind of game." He also said, "Whatever happens, I'll promise you this. There's one thing we're sure of winning this season and that's public respect – everywhere." Norwich manager John Bond said, "That was something special – just what football is all about." As if proving The Doc's point about respect, he added, "That's why I want United to win the title."

United, unchanged again, played Newcastle United away on Saturday March 20. A wind-swept St James's Park played host to an all-ticket crowd of 41,427 who saw surely the Reds' most bizarre match of the season.

On the 12-minute mark, a lobbed back-pass that was weakened by the blustery conditions was pounced on by Pearson to put the visitors ahead. Three minutes later, Bird executed a highly creditable volley which seared across the goal-line. Unfortunately, it was the Newcastle man's own. Burns took full advantage of a back pass blunder of United's (accounts differ as to whether Buchan or Hill was the culprit) to pull one back on 17 minutes. Malcolm Macdonald scored one of the only goals not dependent on horrendous play or horrendous bad luck when on 27 minutes he thumped in a fine header. Just before the interval, Macdonald executed a shot that would probably have been dealt with by Stepney but hit Stepney's ex-United team-mate Alan Gowling on the leg and left him bamboozled as it changed direction.

The ridiculous mood of Lady Happenstance was on display again four minutes into the second-half when the Reds pulled level via a McIlroy corner that was headed into his own net by Howard. 11 minutes later, Pearson glanced the ball in off his forehead to put United 4-3 ahead. At this point, the Reds finally began showing their trademark attacking finesse, although Houston stopped the ball on the line on two occasions. The Reds held out for a remarkable 4-3 victory. Afterwards, Docherty said, " ... they were bombarding our goal in the last five minutes. I have to admit we were lucky but full credit to Houston, who covered the goal-line as if his life depended on it." One reporter described the affair as "one of the most exciting, entertaining, comical, mistake-bespattered First Division matches ever to miss the eyes of the television cameras".

However they had been obtained, the two points had almost certainly brought about a milestone: a return to the European stage on which the club had been pioneers and had achieved such glory. "With 48 points we must be certainties for Europe ... " said Docherty. He described this as a "bonus" and added, "I want to win that championship. With four games at home and three away still to come, we must have a chance." This was a rare example of understatement from Docherty. United were placed second again after the match, their 48 points putting them one point behind QPR and one above Liverpool. They still had a game in hand over Rangers. Liverpool had today achieved an impressive away victory against Norwich. The 1-0 scoreline, however, gives an indication of the fact that – as Macari later put it – "There are times when they put discipline before entertainment." Indeed, Norwich manager John Bond said after the match that it would be better for football if United or

QPR won the championship rather than Liverpool. That couldn't be put down completely to sour grapes: Norwich had engineered a stunning 3-1 victory at Fortress Anfield only the previous November.

The following Saturday, March 27, saw United, unchanged again, playing host to Middlesbrough. 'Boro managed to keep the first-half goalless even though United showed a panache beyond the wildest dreams of Jack Charlton's men. In the second-half, United were finally able to translate their footballing superiority into goals, and not because the visitors had come out to the chorus of derision now traditional from the Stretford End. A handball saw a penalty awarded and Daly did his usual efficient job – this time a low, casual effort – from the spot. McCreery got the second not long afterwards when the ball came to him following a scramble in the Middlesbrough goalmouth. Hill (magnificent today) provided the third, and something of a *coup de grace*, not long after that when he was put through on goal with a well-weighted pass. He chipped beautifully over Platt. With United now rampant, Middlesbrough did well to keep the scoreline to 3-0.

A crowd of 58,527 had seen the rout. United were second in the table. A point behind QPR and level-pegging with Derby, they had a game in hand over both. (Liverpool were now fourth.) One journalist detected Docherty fighting a losing battle with an instinct to be cautious after the match, and few could blame the manager: with League form like this and the FA Cup semi-final the following Saturday, who would not be intoxicated by the whiff of glory in the air?

*** 

The Derby County versus Manchester United FA Cup semi-final was to be played at neutral Hillsborough on Saturday April 3. The United party had been booked into a Buxton hotel for the match. However, Docherty recalled later that he was worried when United got there by how insalubrious the establishment seemed. He asked to see his room before the checking-in took place, only to find a dirty room with an unmade bed. When another room he was shown transpired to have suitcases in it, Docherty ordered everyone back onto the team coach. The United party booked into Mottram Hall, a Cheshire hotel with which they were familiar from using it before home games.

On paper, Derby were far and away the superior side. Not only was their winning of the League championship the season before a symmetrically superior achievement to United having been champions of Division Two, but they had won the championship twice in the previous five seasons. Their team was stuffed to the gills with household names: Archie Gemmill,

Leighton James, Colin Todd, Bruce Rioch and substitute Francis Lee among them. Luckily for United, another household name normally to be found on the Derby team-sheet – Charlie George – was absent through injury. However, United themselves were significantly depleted by the continued absence of Macari. Though the Reds were unchanged, it would appear from McCreery's recollection that Docherty had hoped that the little Scotsman would recover fitness in time for the match only to have those hopes dashed. McCreery: "I remember in the hotel Tommy says, 'You're playing'."

United's unexpected dominance of Derby was demonstrated by the responses of two of the County team, even if they were greatly contrasting reactions. Forsyth had been given the job of marking winger Leighton James, whose touchline prowess had recently seen him purchased by Derby for the then staggering sum of £330,000. Forsyth was conscious of the necessity to stop James centering for Derby's tall forward Roger Davies. Asked how he dealt with the threat of James, he says, "Just like I dealt with the other players that had a bit of pace and all that. You just marked him tight and gave him a couple of wee good hard tackles early to make sure he knew that we were there and that." Forsyth was left bemused by the result of his grimly tight marking. "In the second-half he just didn't want to know," he claimed of James not long after the match. "He was chatting about the crowd and what a nice day it was." Asked about this now, Forsyth explains, "Sometimes if you're on top of your game, the player says, 'Oh, how can I try and put the opponent off?' and he starts chatting to you or doing this and that and thinks you'll maybe back off a bit. Just a tactical thing, 'Oh, start talking, maybe he'll not come in so hard the next tackle and maybe lay off a wee bit and give me a yard'." Derby's fiery midfielder Rioch, meanwhile, expressed his frustration in a more spiteful way. "Bruce Rioch was kicking me all over the place," recalls McIlroy. Is it difficult not to react to that kind of provocation? "Well, he was a lot bigger than me so … I was a little bit flattered to be fair because he was giving me special attention and my thought was to get through it and hopefully get to Wembley." Though McIlroy walked away from the trouble, Pearson remonstrated with Rioch, who responded with a punch that referee Jack Taylor missed. Pearson's brawling days may have been largely behind him, but a man who had acquired a nickname that was a bastardisation of 'Puncho' was hardly going to take this lying down. Later, he went looking for Rioch and caught him with a boot, which earned him a booking. McIlroy: "He was a class referee. There are not many like Jack Taylor these days, but in that game it was helter skelter. It was going a hundred mile an hour, there was a lot of tackles flying about. Derby could put it about with the players they had in the side, and it was a tough game to manage."

Tommy Cavanagh and The Doc had used a Matt Busby line before the start, telling the players "go out and enjoy yourselves". On a lovely Spring day in front of a 55,000-strong and for once peaceful crowd, the players did so. Their relaxed state may partly have been to do with the fact that the other semi-final today at Stamford Bridge was between Southampton and Crystal Palace, Second and Third Division sides respectively. If they got through this, United were facing a final whose likely difficulty factor did not even approach the previous Wolves encounter and their current tussle with the champions.

As ever, the Reds were on the attack from the kick-off, and seemed in no way inhibited by the absence of Macari. There was not a bad performance by the United players across the park. Journalist Donald Saunders said of the defence, "Greenhoff, refusing to be upset by a series of early errors, combined with the calm, authoritative Buchan to ridicule suggestions that United's defence has a soft centre." Meanwhile, Macari later said of Hill today, "He was almost impudent at times as he took men on and beat them."

In the 12th minute, Hill received the ball with his back to the Derby goal. He flicked it up to Daly, and seamlessly turned and ran onto the return, whereupon he controlled it with one touch and proceeded to curl it beautifully around Derby keeper Graham Moseley from 20 yards. United continued to hold the advantage, with Pearson surprisingly often going wide, and McIlroy and Daly pouring into the gaps he left. Eventually though, Derby gave cause for the Red Army's hearts to catch in their throats. Hector and Rioch performed a neat little exchange that released Davies. Greenhoff and Forsyth were stranded. Davies teed up and shot. But that archetypal line-keeper showed that he also knew when to abandon the goal-line: having seen the danger, Stepney tore forward to block the shot. Had Davies laid it off for his team-mate Hector, he would have found a man in front of an open goal. Hector was later taken off in favour of ex-Manchester City star Francis Lee. 'Franny', as he was referred to, was a formidable if unsubtle opponent and had one of the hardest shots in football. Coppell remembered Lee's entrée as the only time Derby gave United problems that day, but they weren't problems big enough to change Derby's luck. At one point, David Nish apparently beat the United offside trap by cleverly hooking the ball over the line of red shirts and running around to collect it, leaving him with only Stepney to beat. The ball made its way into the back of the net but the referee's whistle had shrilled at an offside signal from the relevant linesman. Many thought it an utter injustice. Though it was true that there were several Derby players in an offside position, Nish's original touch of the ball that took it past the last United player could only have activated the offside law if he had intended it as a pass to one of his colleagues. Jack Taylor clearly decided that this was indeed the case.

In the 82nd minute, the frustration Derby were feeling as the seconds ticked away without them managing a reply – or an officially acknowledged one anyway – manifested itself once again in overly physical behaviour. Coppell tore off on one of his characteristic calm but speedy runs. Finally, just outside the right-hand side of the Derby penalty area he was brought down by a Derby man who was no doubt mindful of the proven scoring prowess of the lurking Pearson. He didn't seem to have taken into account the well-established dead-ball prowess of Gordon Hill, who moved across to take the free-kick. By this point, Hill had no right to still be playing well: he, Docherty and Coppell had accompanied Docherty and their hotel's head waiter on a (fruitless) rabbit hunt the previous day that left the wingers with stiff legs. However, though Coppell by his own admission had an average game, Hill was indefatigable.

It's perhaps the distance from which Hill had to shoot that stopped Derby assembling a wall that was anything more than perfunctory, which makes it somewhat ironic that part of that badly constructed wall was possibly what caused Hill's shot to go in. Debate will rage forever – at least among Derby fans – as to whether Hill's powerful, curling effort would have found its way to the back of the County net had it not been for the deflection it took off the Rams' Powell. Says McIlroy, "It's easy to say if it wasn't deflected it wouldn't have went in, but I seen the ball move and there was plenty of power in it and the goalkeeper had no chance really."

Spurred on by the madly fluttering red-and-white scarves on the terraces, United didn't stop there. A low shot by Greenhoff could have made the debate about the disallowed goal irrelevant, but it went just wide. Bruce Rioch was more accurate with his vicious punishment of Sammy McIlroy for playing for time a minute or two later, leaving a trail of stud marks down his leg before taking him by the throat. Taylor would have done well to send him off, even if his bath would only have taken place a few seconds before those of his team-mates. Instead, Taylor blew for full-time and took issue with the Derby man in the manner of a particularly ineffective schoolteacher in front of a riotous class. A somewhat more strenuous protest came from a teenaged United fan, who invaded the pitch and let Rioch know what he thought of him while aiming a boot in his direction.

"He won us the semi-final himself," says Forsyth of Hill. "Give Gordon a bit of space, he would destroy you. Running at you, he'd tear you to ribbons." Some might suggest that Forsyth had been no slouch today in his suppression of Hill's counterpart. Meek now says, "Big things in the build up were expected of Leighton James, but in fact compared with Gordon Hill he was a damp squib." Hill has a pre-match recollection that gives an interesting extra layer of insight into the stinker that James had today: "Leighton James was coming down the hallway as we were going into our changing room and he said, 'It's not worth turning up today boys.' Well, I'll tell you what, that's a red rag to a bull for us. Charlie George has just grabbed hold of him by the throat: 'You stupid idiot, what the fuck you saying that for? You're winding them up.' And at the end of the game Charlie wouldn't talk to Jamesie."

Brian Glanville was one of the reporters impressed by the way the team of tender years had overwhelmed the reigning champions and even partially withdrew earlier caveats he had expressed about the Reds. "It has been said of Manchester United ... that their success has been a matter of momentum ... they are a team which swings the bucket so fast that the water does not spill. Perhaps as we saw for much of this game, this is something of an over-simplification." In support of this, Glanville pointed out that Coppell and Hill did a tremendous amount of running back to help not only their midfield but the defence, too: this was why when Greenhoff found himself in possession early on, he was able to feed Hill in a move that led to the first goal. Cavanagh simply said afterwards, "They played like the innocents they are and their enjoyment brought victory."

With their Wembley place booked and with their opponents now known to be Southampton, United could knuckle down to trying to win a championship they had just as good a chance as anyone of taking. And of course they were now the only team capable of winning the double this season.

Says Hill, "I think what the boss instilled upon us is that the League is your bread and butter and the FA Cup is your jam and we'd concentrate on the League because that was a tough one to win. We were still going for both. We didn't know if it was feasible, but all of [us] were told to take a game at a time." Buchan offers, "I never tempt fate, me. It's an old cliché: you just take one game at a time. If you look too far ahead, you can sometimes end up very disappointed. I never really gave it a thought that we might be in position to win the double."

There was something working against the possibility of achieving that dream, however much or little they were allowing themselves to think about it. United had five League matches in April over the course of 15 days from Saturday 10 through to Saturday 24, an especially onerous workload for such a young and inexperienced side. Accordingly, Docherty tried to reduce wear and tear by keeping training between matches to a bare minimum. However, there were other activities occupying the players over the course of that month, ones that some feel were disastrous.

\*\*\*

Saturday April 10 saw United take on mid-table Ipswich Town, away, in front of 34,889. United were unchanged from the team that outclassed the champions but seemed to have been replaced by impostors identical in every way except in the area of application, of which there was very little. Just when United were gaining a dominance, Ipswich went ahead, Mick Lambert executing a superb chip that sailed over Stepney and went in off the far post. From there it never looked like the Reds were going to make headway. In the 78th minute, Ipswich went two up. The rout was complete with eight minutes left when Johnson placed the ball past the advancing Stepney.

Before the match, Stepney had said, "We have a new philosophy at United. Laugh like hell when you win, and don't moan when you get beat." Still ebullient after booking a place in a Cup Final in which they were the firm favourites, he probably wasn't expecting to have his bluff called so quickly by fate. However, he kept a smile on his face today as he spoke to journalists after what was his team's biggest League defeat of the season. "It's going to be difficult to land both now but we'll still keep trying," he said of the League and Cup competitions. "Ipswich lifted their game to new heights today, and good luck to them. That has been happening all season, because United are once again the team everyone wants to beat." Maybe so, but did the Reds have to surrender so limply? Docherty later said that only Stepney, Buchan and Coppell were steadfast throughout.

Asked if he could say with his hand on his heart that at this point in the season he was as committed in League matches as he would normally be, Hill fesses up: "No. I would say with my hand on my heart that you was wary of the situation, you wanted the result but you didn't want to work as hard as you normally do for it." Forsyth semi-agrees: "You're never really terrified but it's in the back of your mind you've got a Cup Final coming up and you want to play and you don't want to get an injury and you don't want to pull any muscle or anything like that. It's your first chance of going to Wembley and you just don't want to miss it."

Considering the way United's results continued to be dire after this match, many will nod their heads in understanding at these comments. However the comments are not representative. Blunstone says, "I don't agree with that. Players go out and play. Once you get on that park, you don't think about injuries, you just get on with it and try and win and give 100% and play well. I don't care whether you're in a Cup Final or not. I don't think that's anything to do with it. Not at all. The press jump on that. So easy to jump on it and say players aren't trying. They just lost form and didn't play well. Simple as that." McCreery too finds the idea of lack of commitment implausible: "You had to go out and prove that you were going to play in the final. I don't think at Old Trafford at the time there was a player that was guaranteed a position or a starting. Obviously you get the likes of Martin Buchan, whatever, but you knew you had to give it your all. You couldn't sit back and be expected to be picked because Tommy would be the one to come down on you if you didn't give 100%." Houston concurs: "Alright, you're obvious[ly] not [wanting] to get injured but he could leave you out in the final, so you've actually beaten yourself." McIlroy, for his part, says his playing was not affected: "It was great getting to Wembley but obviously we wanted to win the Championship because it hadn't been won since 1967. We wanted to win everything. Things just sort of came off the rails a little bit. Not meaningly, not that we're thinking, 'Oh, ease off'." Buchan also says his own playing was unaffected: "I always felt you were more likely to get injured if you were half-hearted. I liked to win every tackle in training, never mind in a match." However, he does not make the same claim for all of his colleagues, and nor does he restrict his claim merely to the matches after the semi-final: "Some of the lads were distracted by the Cup run ... There's no doubt that some of them soft-pedalled a bit. Maybe unwittingly ... There were ... matches we could have won and we didn't because some of them were saving themselves for the next Cup tie."

Did Docherty lose his temper in the dressing room after the Ipswich match? "If he had to say something, if he had to make a point, he made it," says McIlroy. "I never seen him threw cups or anything like that, but he got his point across. Him and Tommy Cavanagh, they let you know they were always on their toes. They were always quick to point out mistakes and encouragement, so they were lively characters the two of them and they let you know if they thought you weren't going 100% or whatever. But you got to realise as well, we were a young side and to go for the Cup and the League, it was a big ask and I think Tommy Cav and Tommy Doc knew this. It was a great achievement to get to the Cup Final and we were still doing well in the League, but they didn't really slaughter us when we lost a few games and stuff like that because they thought it was part and parcel of growing up and getting to know what this was all about."

For Buchan, as he watched his team's terrible form from the Ipswich match spill over into the subsequent fixtures, there was a cancer infecting United's team much worse than the fear of injury. As was traditional at this point in football history, the FA Cup final occasioned a chance for players – who were still very far from being hugely remunerated workers – to make a few bob. It was decided that newspapers that wanted interviews and photographs should pay £250 each towards the players' pool. Parts of Fleet Street were furious. Some of the Sundays were not inclined to take the attitude that as the features generated by such access helped them sell papers, the players were entitled to stop making money for others and look after themselves. "Scroungers" was the verdict of the *News of the World*. "Go to hell" was the response of the *Sunday Express*. It was a lot of ill-will over what was, when divided up among 17 squad players, a paltry amount of money. The TV companies – in those days just ITV and the BBC – were more realistic and would give the players £1,500 for the privilege of setting up camp at the hotel in rustic St Albans that the team and staff holed up in from the evening of the Thursday before the final.

In addition to the conflict with outside parties, there was discord within the United camp. Some players were getting involved in their own publicity work, the remuneration for which they thought should be exclusively theirs, whereas other players felt everything should be divvied up equally according to the players' pool principle mentioned previously. The activities were, for some, something of a distraction from football. United players found themselves spending a whole day at a shoe factory and an entire afternoon having suits fitted. They also took time out to cut a record, 'Manchester United' (with a B-side, 'Old Trafford Blues', written by guitar aficionado Martin Buchan), which reached number 50 in the charts.

The team had decided not to employ an agent, which might have occasioned losing 10 or 20 per cent of their earnings in commissions but would also have lessened their burden of work at a time when minds might have been better concentrated on the League campaign. Martin Buchan was disgusted by what was happening. Daly was puzzled. "Everything seemed to change leading up to that Cup Final," says Daly. "Little things like bringing in a masseur the night previously and people having rubdowns in their room and all that jazz. We never had any of that when we were going up to play at Old Trafford, for God sake, when we used to stay at Mottram Hall. Little things like that. I'm not saying it was an absolute distraction, I'm not saying that wasn't the right thing to do, but it was certainly different." McCreery: "We had to do a lot. It was a busy time doing other things. Get measured for your suits, going opening places, going to schools and this and that."

Nonetheless, things weren't so bad as a first glance at the League table positions after the Ipswich match had suggested. Though the third-placed Reds were now five points adrift of QPR and four behind Liverpool, they had two games in hand over both. The championship was still achievable if they wanted it. The scoreline against Everton on Saturday April 17 suggested they did. Perhaps it was Old Trafford's crowd of 61,879 – the biggest in the Football League that season – that made United buck up their ideas enough to secure a win, even if the 2-1 scoreline flattered the Reds. Docherty was able once more to field that familiar roll call of Stepney, Forsyth, Houston, Daly, Greenhoff, Buchan, Coppell, McIlroy,

Pearson, Macari and Hill. However, though Macari was fit again, the good luck Docherty had had in avoiding injuries over the three months before his absence started did not make a reappearance. The Reds lost Coppell after 32 minutes when the winger was hurt going for a 50-50 ball with Mick Lyons. With the exception of one notable match, that familiar roll call would not take to the field again.

Even before this misfortune, though, United had had their wings clipped. Or perhaps that should be wingers. Everton manager Billy Bingham decided upon a strategy in which he virtually exulted after the match. "We stifled their wingers, kept United's full-backs occupied and frustrated their normal pattern," he said. "Everything was dictated by us for long spells … We made United change and play long balls out of defence." Fair enough, but it didn't earn his team a point, even if the visitors scored first.

Nevertheless, it was only luck that saved United's long-running unbeaten home record. In the 55th minute, a United free-kick pinged back and forth between three Everton defenders before a deflection from Kenyon beat his own keeper. United now finally began playing with some conviction. In the 80th minute, McCreery, who had come off the substitute's bench to replace Coppell, executed a brilliant 20-yard shot to give the home team the vital two points that to some extent made their unconvincing display irrelevant.

Bingham actually went so far as to say, "In this match possibly lay the crux to who walks off with the Cup. We offered Southampton a few sound hints. If they adopt them, United could have problems at Wembley." A member of the crowd who may have taken note of Bingham's words was Southampton's assistant manager Ted Bates.

Following the match, the radio broadcasts that United doubtlessly cranked up in the dressing room told them that though Liverpool had won, Derby had drawn and QPR had actually lost. Liverpool were now back on top. Third-placed United were now only four points adrift of Liverpool and three behind QPR and had two games in hand over both. The championship was most definitely still a possibility. However, there was a major problem: Coppell's injury. He would miss all the League games before the Cup Final. And as fate would have it, who would United be playing in their next fixture but Burnley, who until just the previous month had been home to a player who would have been the absolutely ideal replacement for the injured Coppell: Willie Morgan. (Morgan had been given a free transfer to Bolton Wanderers in March after falling out with the Burnley regime.)

*\*\**

McCreery may have felt slightly resentful at automatically resuming his position of bench-warmer now that Macari was fit again, especially after having tasted the glory of an FA Cup semi-final and particularly because he was left contemplating the implication that though he had helped United make the final he would not be competing in it. However, the fact that he scored against Everton sort of affirms the wisdom of Docherty allowing Macari back into the side: McCreery had only managed one in a striker's position in six starts but back in his substitute's role, he found his goal-scoring touch.

David McCreery's match statistics sum up his tenure at Manchester United. He made 57 starts for the Reds. He also made 52 substitute appearances. Few players come off the bench for part of the match on almost the same number of occasions as they are on the pitch from kick-off. Interestingly, McCreery is an exact contemporary of David Fairclough (both born in 1957, in McCreery's case on September 16), a Liverpool player who like McCreery seemed perennially doomed to having his football restricted to short periods at the end of matches. Fairclough's tendency to hit the back of the net after coming on for tactical reasons or to replace tired legs (he averaged a goal in every three games for Liverpool despite starting 92 times as opposed to his 61 substitute appearances) led to a nickname being coined for him, one that has now come to be used for just about any footballer who consistently makes an impact after coming off the bench: "Super-sub". Some cruelly characterise such players as the kind of player who would be the best in the world if football matches lasted 20 minutes.

Belfast native McCreery was signed by Docherty after being discovered by (that man again) Bob Bishop. "I went straight from school," he recalls. "I used to travel over since I was about 13, 14. I'd never gone away to teams on trial. It was only Manchester United. I'd go over in the summer for two to three weeks at a time. While I was a schoolboy, I used to fly over and play in one of the youth games and then fly back to school again. I was playing for the Northern Ireland schoolboy internationals in midfield, and that's where I thought I was. Then when I joined the older set of lads [at United], I went from the 'A' team and I think I bypassed the reserves and straight into the first team when I was 16. So I was playing midfield when I went over there and then with Tommy Doc I changed to playing upfront. No problem. I felt comfortable because I was quite quick in closing people down."

Breaking into the first team, though, is different to breaking into the starting XI, something McCreery was never quite able to do on merit (as opposed to through another player's injury) in his time at Old Trafford, regardless of manager. Perhaps McCreery's inability to force his way into a line-up that always had players a bit more talented than him in it would have been made more bearable if he possessed Fairclough's extraordinary ability to

311

make a huge impact in a limited amount of time. McCreery concedes, "David come on and scored spectacular goals and I think I was just more workmanlike." In fact, time seemed to prove that McCreery was initially miscast by Docherty as a striker – something that had been apparent to some early on due to his diminutive (5'7") stature. Given that chance in the attack during March and April 1976, he failed to make much headway and there was certainly no likelihood of him being retained in the starting line-up when Macari was fit and the team could revert to its normal shape. McCreery was then remoulded into more of a midfielder, although that didn't increase his chances of making it onto the teamsheet with a number other than 12 beside his name. Says Hill, "David could play, come on and give us a little bit of a buzz, but couldn't give you 90 minutes. He was great when you was tired. The Boss would say, 'David, just go on and be busy', and that's what David did. David could play in several positions to accommodate the players. He'd play in midfield if one of the players was not feeling too clever or had a bit of a dummy time, he could play defender. David was one of those players." Says McIlroy, "He was a tremendous little competitor. I played with him in Northern Ireland. Brave as a lion, only small, fantastic engine. When he started in games he did really well, but he just couldn't command a regular place. But The Doc had great faith in him because he could play various positions." McCreery: "I went in for Lou Macari, I went in for Stuart Pearson, I went in for Jimmy Greenhoff, I went in for Sammy. I played right-back once in a quarter final."

Docherty continued to value McCreery's willingness to work and his lightning pace (for which some sources state McCreery was given his nickname of "Roadrunner", although others cite his habit of racing up and down the touchline when preparing to come on as the source. Additionally, Colin Waldron recalls his nickname as being "Chick", for some reason). The Doc also – perhaps somewhat callously – deployed him for psychological reasons. McCreery: "If a game was going not our way, Tommy would just say to me, 'Just go and get warmed up on the touchline, you'll see them all looking around' and it would give them a gee-on." Wasn't that cruel to him? McCreery: "It was, but I never felt that way. I was really young." He is too modest to also point out that he is exceedingly good-natured, which probably played a large part in his endless patience over his perennial 12th-man role. "You're just glad to be involved," he says. "Just to play and for me to be sub for Manchester United was people's dreams." Did he ever complain that he felt he should be in the starting line-up? McCreery: "Not really, because I was appreciative of him and Tommy Cavanagh, what they'd done for me and whatever. When you're at United, it's such a club and such a team ... " No doubt, the *esprit d'corps* at a club that was a happy breed of men at the time also militated against any inclination to harbour resentment.

That McCreery was a character who was slow to take offence was just as well for Docherty, because he might have faced an assault claim from a less temperate individual after an incident that occurred when United were travelling back from a fixture in the Midlands. Some wag on the team decided to lock Docherty in the coach toilet. (McCreery: "I think it was probably Louie.") When the manager managed to batter his way out, it was to find a sea of amused faces. According to McIlroy, a furious Docherty picked on the first person he happened to see to exact retribution: Docherty grabbed McCreery's head and banged it against a window before marching back to his seat. "I was only young and I got the blame for it," recalls McCreery of the incident now, laughing as he does.

Though he was never an automatic first choice, neither was McCreery on the fringes of the team. As Gordon Hill says, "Davey was as much part of the squad as Louie Macari or myself." The fans didn't see him as semi-detached either: he was one of those players who embedded themselves in the Stretford End's affections. Meanwhile, being substitute didn't prevent McCreery making his international breakthrough, which came in the 1975/76 season when he was included in the Northern Ireland squad that played in Israel. The Belfast boy would rack up a tidy 67 caps for his country.

\*\*\*

When Manchester United and Burnley met at Turf Moor on Monday April 19, Burnley were fighting for their very First Division survival. However, it may not have been this that caused United – unchanged except for McCreery replacing the injured Coppell – to struggle but the fact that the absence of Coppell was compounded in the first-half by Pearson having to limp off with an ankle injury. (Tommy Jackson replaced him.) Then there was the state of the pitch. "It was like playing in a dust bowl," recalls Buchan. "The pitch had hardly any grass on it. It was unbelievably hard. Look how it's changed now. They don't play on bad pitches now, do they?" Furthermore, United were having to play in a 4-3-3 formation to which they were now very unaccustomed. United's usual carefree "push-around" football (to use a phrase that was fashionable to apply to their game at the moment) was little in evidence.

In the 57th minute, Macari sent home a saved McIlroy shot for the game's only goal. When the match was over, the home side's supporters in the 27,418 gate were glumly cognizant of the fact that their team would be playing in Division Two the following season. The United contingent, meanwhile, while no doubt pleased at the maximum points, must also have been uncomfortably conscious of the fact that like Saturday's win, it was a somewhat unconvincing victory. Both Liverpool and QPR had won as well, so the situation remained

313

that the Reds were four points adrift of Liverpool and three of QPR, though with two games in hand on both. They could still overhaul both clubs, but as well as having injury problems, they were running out of matches. They had three League games left, two of them before the Cup Final.

The first of those matches took place just two days later. Pearson was going to be out for at least this fixture. Having to cope with the loss of the man who would be their top League scorer that season was a blow, especially in conjunction with the continued absence of Coppell. McCreery and Jackson were on in their places. Docherty moved McCreery into the centre of the attack, with McIlroy on the right. United at least had the consolation of this being a match at Old Trafford – that fortress whose impregnability now stretched back 15 months – and their opponents being Stoke City, who were only 12th in the table. They had of course beaten Stoke way back in August when people were still scoffing at the idea of a team fresh back in the First Division vying for title honours. United were watched again by Ted Bates, this time accompanied by Southampton manager Lawrie McMenemy.

Knowing what they had to do and what was at stake, the Reds attacked relentlessly. It was the misfortune of those replacements for two of United's key forwards to not only have big shoes to fill but also to be up this night against a man who was by consensus either the best keeper in the country or on his way to becoming it. Peter Shilton was simply impassable.

On the half-hour mark, Nicholl was instructed to replace Jackson. The 53,879 crowd then witnessed the extraordinary sight of Jackson – who hadn't played a full game since the end of the previous year and hadn't been having a stinker or anything like it today – refusing to leave the field. Eventually, the distraught player gave in to the inevitable, and received an ovation from a sympathetic Stretford End. Nicholl went into his normal place in defence, with Brian Greenhoff switched to midfield as the Reds tried to work out the puzzle of how to keep alive their championship hopes in the face of what must have been stiffer opposition than they had expected from a team who had nothing particularly to gain. Docherty had of course won apparently lost matches before with audacious substitutions and switcharounds, so the Stretford End could end up cheering him yet should this one work. United may well have gone ahead before the interval but for a bizarre moment when McIlroy was in a position to shoot but found an over-eager Hill nipping in to take the ball off him and have a go himself. The winger's shot was wild – which is what could also be said for McIlroy's visible feelings about the incident. Hill almost made up for it, but his 44th-minute angled effort only muddied the paintwork on the far post.

In the second-half, as though conscious of time ticking away on their title hopes, United seemed confused. Greenhoff was upfront for a while, but then seemed to switch with Macari. As if to underline an increasing desperation, Buchan, well out of his usual orbit, unleashed a good effort that forced Shilton to make a diving save. The impasse continued. With the minutes mounting up, United attempted to break the deadlock by pushing everyone up. It was a necessary tactic at a juncture in the season where one point simply would not do, but it proved disastrous, both for this match and for the campaign. Stoke City broke and defender Alan Bloor took advantage of the space left him in United's penalty area to head a Kevin Sheldon cross beyond the reach of Stepney and into the corner of the net. It happened at a point where there was no way back: the 87th minute.

It was a hell of a time for United to suffer their first home defeat for a year-and-a-quarter. The headlines said it all: "LAST HOPE GOES FOR UNITED", "LATE STOKE GOAL ENDS UNITED HOPES OF THE DOUBLE." The game in hand United continued to possess over both Liverpool and QPR was virtually worthless: the maximum number of points they could now obtain this season was 58 – precisely the number Liverpool had already achieved. The Reds needed the not-in-this-world eventuality of both those clubs slipping up in their respective one remaining fixture and to themselves win both their remaining games to stand a chance of even taking the title on goal average.

"I'll go to my grave believing we could have won the League championship in 1975/76," Buchan said in the book *Match of My Life – Manchester United*, where he pointed out that just five of the six points available from the final three matches would have secured United the title. Whereas Buchan's opinion is, "It was the Cup run that cost us the championship," McIlroy, in his 1980 autobiography, blamed the results during the Roche run, asserting, " ... if we hadn't conceded the goals during this patchy spell, we would probably have wound up by taking the championship of the First Division." Either way, the dream was over. Unlike other clubs who had seen their championship hopes evaporate, though, United were still pursuing another honour.

*** 

The Burnley match was notable for the absence in the opposition line-up of Colin Waldron, the central defender who had become something of a star for the Clarets since Chelsea had sold him to the club for £30,000 two days after Docherty had ceased being their manager in 1967. Born in Bristol on June 22 1949, Waldron played 356 games for Burnley over nine seasons. Naturally, he didn't get up the field to score many goals for them – 18 in all – but one of them was pretty decisive: the winning strike in a 1973 match against Preston that won his club the Second Division championship. Another goal from him won his club the Charity Shield the at the beginning of the following season in a match against Manchester City. (FA Cup winners Sunderland and League champions Liverpool had both declined to participate, making for an ersatz event contested by City, the previous year's Charity Shield winners, and the Second Division champions.) Waldron – and other players – had become *personas non grata* at Turf Moor since the club had dispensed with the services of manager Jimmy Adamson in January 1976. Says Waldron, "They were just culling the Adamson players and I think they took the captaincy off me for no reason, and they just pulled us out the side." Within weeks, Docherty had swooped to make Waldron yet another player with whom he was familiar from his Chelsea days who he'd signed for a second time.

Despite what some might describe as his tantrum in the Stoke match, Jackson got a place in the starting line-up for the Reds' away fixture against Leicester City on Saturday April 24. He even got to play the entire game. Not that he could read much into that. Throughout the course of this match, the United contingent in the 31,053 crowd chanted noisily about the fixture their team were playing the following Saturday on neutral territory. It was obvious that Docherty also had his mind more on that game than the present one. Coppell, McIlroy, Pearson and Daly all sat in the Filbert Street stand. Docherty gave Daly's shirt to Nicholl and moved McCreery to the right again. The other striker's position was occupied by 17-year-old Peter Coyne, making his full debut. Coyne recalls such a relaxed atmosphere in the dressing room before the game that TV cameras were allowed in to bear witness to Gordon Hill doing his impersonation of comedian Norman Wisdom. Meanwhile, the only reason Houston, suffering a slight cold, started the match was because the man Docherty wanted to play in his stead, Albiston, had a headache. Once the headache had cleared, Docherty made a 39th minute substitution.

Says Coyne, "I think I knew the night before that I was going to be playing. He'd already told me he was resting Stuart Pearson. I knew I'd be at least sub, but when you look round the people, you think, 'Well, they've got no striker, it must be me'." As with the Villa match, he wasn't nervous: "That's all I ever wanted to do, was score goals and play for United. It was more excited than nerves." Though the absence of four of the most exciting players in the First Division, as well as a lack of commitment on the part of some Red players who could clearly see Wembley's twin towers even from Leicester, meant that the match was never destined to be a classic, it was a reasonably attractive affair. "They were a fantastic team," Coyne says of the opposition. "They absolutely battered us that game. Alex Stepney played out of his skin. He was absolutely fantastic. They had chance after chance after chance."

However, Coyne insists that he didn't get the impression that the performance of his own team was half-hearted. "It was a fairly youngish team and when you've got people like Martin Buchan and Brian Greenhoff playing for you, they're the type of players who'd go through a brick wall for United." Nonetheless, his opinion on the latter point seems to be a minority one. The Reds' goal deficit at half-time could have been greater than the one goal it was, so patently half-hearted were some of the United players' efforts.

A minute after the interval, the home side went two up. However, United showed a bit more life in the second half, although the goal they pulled back came from a most unexpected source, for who should get the ball in the back of the net but Coyne. Put through by Greenhoff in the 59th minute, the youngster span and struck a fierce 20-yard shot. Remembers Greenhoff, "Turned Jeff Blockley and he tucked it in the corner. Cracking goal." Coyne: "It was a bobbly pitch and the ball just broke free on the edge of the box. A challenge ... went on for a few seconds. Brian Greenhoff was trying to head the ball. I'm stood more or less on the penalty-spot and he just toe-poked it. I was quite quick to react and I just turned, looked up and smashed it. At the end where all the United fans were as well. I didn't know what to do but luckily all the first-team players came and mobbed me and some fantastic comments that I'll never, ever forget from them. Martin Buchan, I'll never, ever forget what he said. Obviously he was playing at the back and he was one of the last ones and he shook me hand, put his arm round me and said, 'Well done son, first of many.' I actually say it to people meself now. I coach young kids and when they score their first goal, first thing I say to them [is] 'First of many'."

Coyne's strike was captured for posterity by the television cameras. The footage shows a young man who, when he turns away from goal, grinning broadly, looks like a gauche version of Rod Stewart. Nonetheless, he took his opportunity in his first match in the starting line-up for United, and only his second-ever taste of both first-team and top-flight football, with the assuredness of a veteran. Docherty would seem to have a real prospect on his hands. However, it wasn't enough to stop United going down to their third defeat in a fortnight, even if this loss was profoundly less bitter than the other two. The 2-1 result left United third, five points behind QPR, four behind Liverpool. QPR had played a game more than Liverpool. Few United staff or fans cared, of course, as thoughts now turned to Wembley, where their opponents were happily not the sort of high-class outfit with whom they had been tussling in the League all season. Journalist Clive White summed up the feelings of many after the Leicester match when he wrote, "Manchester United go into the FA Cup final next Saturday as such overwhelming favourites that there seems little point in Southampton, their opponents, turning up."

\*\*\*

Before the Wembley date, Docherty completed the signing of Waldron. Though his former charge was only 27, The Doc obtained him on a free, something that Waldron acknowledges was a gesture of contempt by Burnley chairman Bob Lord. "Bob Lord were getting rid of three players," recalls Waldron. "Tommy Doc's son was one, I was another and Doug Collins was another. In essence we were three Jimmy Adamson men and he wanted us off the books and Mick Docherty obviously told his dad. Mick Docherty consequently signed for Man City and his dad came onto the phone to me. I'd had two offers." Of Mick Docherty, Waldron says, "I don't think Tommy would have employed his son," though does concede, "If you're the best player in the world, he'd have signed him." Bizarrely, though, Waldron actually believes that Docherty signing him may have been bound up in the fact of the club for whom his son signed terms. Though Waldron knew his own worth ("I was a First Division player with over 400 league games at centre-half. I was just reaching me peak and I was on a free transfer"), he also theorises another reason Docherty would find his presence on United's books attractive: " Mick lived near me and he had a lengthy driving ban. If Tommy Doc signed me for United, I could give Mick Doc a lift to work every morning and bring him home at night. I've always felt that might have been the case."

"I don't think there was ever any chance of me playing at Old Trafford under dad," says Mick Docherty. "That was one of the reasons as a young man I left Chelsea. I served my apprenticeship at Chelsea and then I moved to Burnley because I was getting to professional age – 17 at the time – and dad felt that the nepotism type of thing might creep in. Because I'm his son, if he picked me they might think it was favouritism … I don't think after the Chelsea situation where he felt like father and son wouldn't work that he would instigate that at Old Trafford … It was never even talked about. It was something that I certainly felt would never happen. He had some great players there as it was." Nonetheless, defender Mick Docherty had a very respectable career: "I played at a good level. I played a lot of football in the old First Division, against great sides, United being one of them. I played against Denis, I played against George and Bobby, Brian Kidd and all them. Every week you were up against perfect players. I was happy at Burnley, I was married and settled and I spent nearly 10 years as a player there." He was, of course, following in the footsteps of a decent footballer but says, "I never really modelled myself on anybody. I saw dad play but I was only five, six and seven. I didn't really have any recollections of how good a player he was but by all accounts he was a good, good player. You had to be to play at the level he did. He was a hard act to follow if you like but I didn't set myself targets. I thought, 'Well, if I can do half as well as dad then I'll get a good career out of it'."

Mick seems to have adopted the regional accent of Burnley, after a childhood spent in first Preston, then London. He says, "I think it's quite odd actually. I moved down south with dad when he was at Chelsea and obviously as a young man [grew] up with a lot of houses in different places, 'cos dad had, as the old saying goes, more clubs then Jack Nicklaus. My base every three years could change so I never really had a settled childhood, but I don't think it's done me any harm." Referring to the management career he has intermittently pursued since 1981, he says, "I've had a few clubs on this side of the fence as well. I've had my fair share of moving around." Mick found that being the son of a well-known manager had long-term advantages as both player and manager: "I always leant on his experience, his advice, although he never proffered it. He said, 'I'm here if you want me' and I used to pick his brains occasionally and I was fortunate to meet the likes of Shankly and Matt Busby and Malcolm Allison. So I was very privileged to go into the coaching and managerial side having the knowledge of [having] actually listened and sat and talked with these people. It was a bonus rather than a negative side of things. It never fazed me. I always knew I was never going to surpass dad but it was a lovely target to aim for."

To a certain extent, Waldron was almost family himself. "[When] I went to Burnley, his son was at Burnley by pure coincidence, so over the years, I would bump into Doc," says Waldron. "I'd retained all my friendships, if you like, with Tommy Docherty. I knew him well … I had a friendship with him that I'd built up through his son and I had socialised with him. To this day I'm still close to his son." However, once he signed on the dotted line at Old Trafford, Waldron realised it would be unprofessional to flaunt that friendship in front of his colleagues: "When he signed me I thought, 'Well, I've got to be careful here.' So I tried to stay away from it. I wasn't a first-team player so for a reserve team player to be close to [the manager], it would have been a joke."

He did get in sufficiently close proximity to Docherty to form an opinion about how much he had changed since he was his boss at Chelsea, and the verdict was: not at all. "Always been the same," says Waldron. "A great motivator. Always got a joke or a one-liner, a funny man … He wasn't a coach. He had Cavanagh as a coach. He just motivated players." Not that, for Waldron, the United team he was joining needed much in the way of formal tactics: "Because the side was so gifted, it was a case of saying, 'Look, you're good enough, if you all play the way you can play, you shouldn't fear anybody' and little talks to individual players. He could come up to you and just make you feel 10-foot tall." As for himself, Waldron considered he had matured in a professional capacity since his disastrous spell as centre-half under Docherty at Chelsea: "In 10 years I'd grown, I'd learnt about the position, felt I'd become a decent player that could hold me own." Nonetheless, he knew that he was not going to be an automatic first-team choice. "Just a squad member," he says. Docherty was hedging his bets over the recovering Jim Holton: "He'd had a long-standing bad injury and they didn't know how he was going to come out of it." Waldron observed that Docherty needed cover because United's squad was threadbare even for the era: "He basically had the team that he put out, which picked itself every week, and after that you'd got young kids. Kids everywhere and I mean not just 20, 21, I mean 17, 18-year-old kids in every position. Even with me, I don't think the squad was particularly large, apart from kids. You took an injury and you'd be down to the bare bones."

For his own part, Docherty explained of the signing that getting Waldron on a free transfer was an opportunity too good to miss. With United destined for European competition next season – the UEFA Cup was already assured, but the club would elect to participate in the more prestigious Cup Winners' Cup instead should things go the right way at Wembley – Docherty saw Waldron as cover for Brian Greenhoff in matches with continental sides. A recuperating Jim Holton could only watch proceedings with dismay but Docherty insisted, "I must have an experienced reserve straight away ... Broken legs take time."

Though unhappy with events at Burnley, to some extent Waldron had fallen on his feet. Firstly, "When you were transferred in the First Division from one club to another, you could not have your wages diminished. You had to be paid the same or more. When I got on a free transfer from Burnley my basic wage was as good if not better than anybody at Man United." Secondly and thirdly, "We'd been relegated so we were in Division Two. To go back to stay in the division was fantastic, but to go to Man United was just unbelievable." Waldron was making his way to Manchester about a year after Willie Morgan had travelled in the exact opposite direction with a £35,000 price tag that had seemed a gesture of contempt similar to Bob Lord's zero valuation of Waldron. However, Waldron says Morgan did not try to contact him to warn him of the trouble he had had with The Doc, although this sounds like this would be less to do with lack of concern about what his colleague might be getting himself into than the fact that Morgan might not have felt he had the right to: "I got on well with Willie without being close to him. I don't think many people got close to Willie. Willie wouldn't ring me about that."

Docherty's comments about the signing, incidentally, did not make the papers immediately upon Waldron agreeing to become a United player. Though the transfer occurred before the FA Cup final, it didn't become public knowledge immediately, deliberately so on United's part. Explains Waldron, "He didn't want anybody upsetting the apple cart with the knowledge of extra players being signed. You've got a Cup Final team away and the last thing you need is the news that they're signing players, so it was kept quiet and it only broke a week or so after the Cup Final."

***

Over the course of the previous few seasons, the United hooligan element had been busily proving that just about nothing was sacrosanct, including the voice of Matt Busby, whose PA system-broadcast entreaties to stop the violence they had ignored on more than one occasion. There was no reason to believe, therefore, that the yobs wouldn't do the previously unthinkable and ruin football's showcase match. Louis Edwards went to the trouble of appealing for good behaviour from the Red Army in the run-up to the Cup Final. "Some of those who follow the club have let us down so often in the past that it is something which cannot be ignored," he said. "All we can do is hope everyone attending the game will go in a spirit of good sportsmanship … and if the day goes against us, then to give due credit to our opponents."

Before the final, snooker player Alex Higgins – he of the thwarted dressing room entry after the tie against Leicester – sent each United player a poem, individualised with their names, a somewhat expensive measure considering he used the method of telegram and an unusually tender gesture for a man with a reputation for tempestuousness.

The day before the Cup Final, both teams made a trip to Wembley. Ostensibly something to acclimatise themselves to the ground, Southampton's Jim McCalliog says of the tradition, "You're a bit bored really. I think it passes the time and for managers it keeps the players together and they're not wandering off anywhere." McCalliog enjoyed the opportunity to catch up with some of his old friends from his days at Old Trafford. "We were out on the pitch and then the United boys come out," he recalls. "Stuart Pearson, who was one of my pals at the club, and Stewart Houston come over and we were just talking and chatting. The Cav come up. They said, 'Well, you should be playing for us tomorrow.' And I said, 'No, I don't want to do that Cav, 'cos we're gonna beat you tomorrow'."

***

McIlroy remembers Docherty's pre-match address to the troops on Saturday May 1 1976 as being, "'Come on, you have done brilliant, it's been a fantastic season – go and win it'." He adds, "I'm not saying Tommy Doc was over-confident, Tommy Cavanagh or anyone like that, or us, we were just told to go out there and win the game." Hill

321

says, "He just said 'Guys, listen, you got to respect them, you got to go out there and play, they're no dummies, you got to go out there and just play the way you can play." Blunstone: "I think he just said go out there and enjoy yourselves. He didn't say that you're going to win."

As Docherty and Southampton manager Lawrie McMenemy led their players out onto the Wembley turf, both would have been happily conscious of the contrast their respective situations today constituted compared to two years previously. At this stage in the 1973/74 season, both Docherty and McMenemy had suffered the agony of the drop into Division Two. Though McMenemy had yet to effect the escape back to the top flight for Southampton that Docherty had managed last season (he would do that at the end of the 1977/78 season), it was a huge achievement for him to be now taking his team out onto the Wembley pitch, an achievement not diminished in any way by the fact that the appearances in the Cup final of Sunderland in 1973 and Fulham in 1975 had lately made Wembley no stranger to Second Division clubs.

The playing careers of Lawrie McMenemy and Tommy Docherty did not reveal many similarities. Whereas Docherty played professional soccer to a very high standard, McMenemy never played in the Football League, although admittedly that may have been something to do with the fact that his career was ended by injury when he was still in his mid-20s. McMenemy had started his managerial career in a much lower strata of football than had The Doc, inching his way up the greasy pole after obtaining a position as player-coach at Gateshead. At non-League Bishop Auckland, he turned the side into Northern League champions. A couple of years biding his time as coach at Sheffield Wednesday landed him the job of manager of Doncaster Rovers. Grimsby Town was his next port of call. His work in obtaining them the Fourth Division championship piqued the interest of Southampton, whom he joined as assistant manager in the summer of 1973, becoming manager at the end of that year.

Southampton's journey to the 1976 Cup Final had started shakily indeed. In their third-round home match against Aston Villa, they had been trailing 1-0 until the last minute, when Fisher provided an equaliser that neither he nor his colleagues nor his manager could have predicted would pave the way for a journey that would four months later see them contesting the second-biggest prize in British football. After defeating Villa 2-1 in the replay, the Saints claimed the scalp of Blackpool in a 3-1 home win. It took two matches to dispense with West Bromwich Albion in the next round, even if their one-all draw away was followed by a comprehensive 4-0 triumph at The Dell. A 1-0 away victory against Bradford City took them into the semi-final, in which, remarkably considering it was this stage of the competition, they took on a club even lowlier than they in the global scheme of things, Third Division Crystal Palace, whom they defeated 2-0 at Stamford Bridge.

Though the United players walking in file behind the brown-suited Docherty were dressed in white tracksuits with black stripes redolent of their second kit, beneath they wore their normal red first kit. Having lost the strip toss-up, Southampton were wearing their away yellow-and-blue colours. Recovery from injury for all key players meant that Docherty was able to pick what he obviously felt was his optimum team, that roll call that had become so familiar over the course of the season: Stepney, Forsyth, Houston, Daly, Greenhoff, Buchan, Coppell, McIlroy, Pearson, Macari, Hill, sub. McCreery. More than half of those players – Stepney, Forsyth, Houston, Greenhoff, Buchan, McIlroy and Macari – had shared, as first-team regulars, in Docherty's relegation agony in the 1973/74 campaign. Although some of the team had played on this pitch in international matches, none of them apart from Stepney had experience of any sort of final here. Despite his long career, Stepney himself had not played in an FA Cup final before: a winner's medal for that trophy was the only major honour this League Championship and European Cup winner did not possess. Meanwhile, Gordon Hill, who had started the season in the Third Division, now found himself playing in a theatre of dreams he had only previously visited to watch Speedway racing.

Though Docherty had most certainly been to Wembley before, both as player and manager, it had never been a happy experience for him. He had played for Scotland at England's premier stadium four times and never emerged on the winning team. In 1954, he had played on the losing side as Preston North End were defeated by West Brom in the FA Cup final. In 1967, as manager of Chelsea, he had seen his side beaten by Spurs in the FA Cup final. (Of course, had the two legs of the League Cup final in 1965 not been played at the respective grounds of the competing clubs, Docherty's Wembley jinx would theoretically have ended then.) Docherty, naturally, was never the kind of person who would show any sort of vulnerability in public, but privately he must have had ominous feelings about the stadium. Even when they're not superstitious, football folk are simply human, and any human being must begin to submit at some point to the feeling of being cursed at a ground at which they have never been victorious, however illogical they know the conviction to be.

Today, that seemed destined to change, and United's status of favourites was only enhanced by the size of the pitch. Cathedral of football though it might be, many players don't like the physical fact of playing at Wembley (whether it be the old version or the new one opened in 2007), which has such a large playing area that their calves can start groaning after only a few minutes of play. Yet Old Trafford's 116 x76-yard dimensions made it one of the biggest pitches in the Football League and the expanse of Wembley accordingly less of a shock to Red systems.

Unusually, the national anthem was played by the marching band before the players were introduced to the visiting dignitary, on this occasion the Duke of Edinburgh. The referee was Clive Thomas, the man who had ordered off the entire teams in the Maine Road Manchester derby in 1974 in order to assert his authority. By his own admission, Thomas had deliberately stopped warranting the nickname 'The Book' about a year previously when he had decided that he shouldn't follow the letter of the law as rigidly as he had previously. True to his new philosophy, he would keep this game moving, playing the advantage when the offended-against team had the ball and having a quiet word with players when tempers frayed or dissent was aired rather than reaching for his pocket. In fact, he even seemed to err on the side of caution today – certainly from the probable point of view of a sometimes grimacing and hobbling Stuart Pearson.

Southampton may have been the underdogs because of their Second Division status but they were also a team of seasoned players with much familiarity with big games. Peter Osgood had been part of the Chelsea FA Cup winning team of 1970. Jim McCalliog had been on the losing side when Sheffield Wednesday lost the 1966 FA Cup final to Everton. Club captain Peter Rodrigues was also blooded in an FA Cup final – he picked up a loser's medal with Leicester City in their 1969 clash with Manchester City. Not only that, he was something of a warhorse. In fact, the man who had played for three other cubs since his professional debut in 1963 looked almost impossibly old for a footballer: moustachioed, thin, grey and balding. "They had a wealth of experience," Buchan says. "If you added up all the first-team appearances of our team and theirs, I think they would have been miles ahead of us." But experience can also be a synonym for slightly past one's best. Buchan: "Yeah, but every now and then they can reach the heights. If they're all on top of their game on a certain day, they can still produce the goods."

Not only were the Saints well-versed in the arts of football but – for Macari – they also knew a thing or two about the craft of 'kidology'. "Southampton didn't do anything to destroy the illusion that they were indeed the underdogs," he later said of the run-up to the final. "In fact … I feel that Southampton made the most of a confidence trick … They knew that if anyone was going to be under pressure because of this favourites tag, it was us."

Martin Buchan once famously remarked that some United players thought that they only had to turn up at Wembley this day to collect their winner's medals. Stepney was another who later alleged that some players felt the result was a formality. "I detected that the attitude of many of the younger players was wrong," he opined. "All that was required of them was an appearance at Wembley on the day and the Cup would be theirs." A further player who was more than a little concerned about the over-confidence of some of his colleagues was Macari, who later recalled that the memory of a Scottish League Cup final defeat against the unfancied Partick Thistle in 1971 when he wore the green and white hoops of Celtic had given him an early lesson about the surprises football can throw up – Celtic lost 4-1 to a side boasting Alex Forsyth – and that he had admitted his fears about the 1976 final to some of his close friends beforehand. "It was fact," says Hill. "There's no ifs and buts about it. Over-confident. We'd gone in there and it was a formality: turn up, pick the trophy up." Blunstone says he got the feeling that Docherty too was taking the match for granted: "I think we all did. And I think the supporters felt that way too. The club felt it, we all felt that: we thought, 'Oh, we can beat Southampton.'"

It must have been easy for Docherty and his charges to be swept up in a general sentiment in the air, perhaps best summed up by a column Brian Clough wrote for a tabloid on the eve of the final. Though undeniably pompous, as a man who had only recently won the First Division championship for Derby County Clough's words carried some weight. In his article, Clough said of Docherty's United, "I'm glad to be in football when I see them. They've helped me out of bed on a Monday morning … Youngsters Gordon Hill and Steve Coppell are the most exciting combination since Tom Finney and Stanley Matthews … I can see England boss Don Revie and his counterparts ripping the heart out of Manchester United. They'll be planning international fixtures around Old Trafford commitments, won't they? … They are not using their brains yet. They are playing with legs, hearts and lungs. I want their game to go on flowing naturally, without them having to think … England leads the world in nothing at the moment … But can anybody deny that United are carrying the torch for our football?" As for the Cup Final itself, Clough boomed, "I can't see Southampton touching them … I can't remember another Wembley where one team could look at the other and say truthfully that they wouldn't swap a single player." One bookmaker was making Southampton 5/1 to take the Cup, astonishingly long odds in a two-horse race. Not only had newspapers been asserting that United's name was on the Cup this year as far back as that fifth-round defeat of Leicester – the intellectual *Observer* no less than the tabloid *People* – but giant-killing in the final was almost unprecedented, so much so that Sunderland's shock defeat of the mighty Leeds in 1973 could be dismissed as a fluke, never to be repeated.

If United were arrogant, this might be assumed by some to partly stem from a remark Docherty had made before their semi-final tie. In reference to the fact that whoever won the Derby-United semi-final would have either Second or Third Division opponents in the final, he said that the semi in which his team were involved was, "The first time the Cup Final has been decided at Hillsborough." It seems an astonishingly unwise comment from The Doc, not just because of the way it might undermine any advice he might want to give to his players before the Cup Final to not take a victory for granted, but also because it displayed a presumption bound to infuriate the Southampton players and get them playing above and beyond their normal capabilities. Blunstone says, "That's Tommy. We didn't take any notice of it. All Scotsmen are like that." Surprisingly, though, McCalliog says the Southampton players didn't take any notice of the remark either: "We didn't feel anything about that at all because that was what Tommy Docherty was about. There's nobody had more up and downs with The Doc than myself but if you know The Doc, The Doc has got a fantastic sense of humour. He not only takes the piss out of people, he gets the piss taken out of him and as far as I was concerned I just thought that was a typical Tommy Docherty thing to say. I just think he felt so confident with his team that what's wrong with that? Jose Mourinho's done it, like 'I'm a special one'. I think I'm speaking for the whole Southampton [team] because me and Ossie knew The Doc because we'd grown up with The Doc and obviously Micky Channon had been with the England squad, so he knew the story. I don't think there was a problem with that at all and I think it was probably rightly so, because at the end of the day it was a Second Division side and a Third Division side in the other semi."

McCalliog recalls his team was pretty confident of their own chances too. Asked if the Southampton players felt intimidated by the prospect of meeting United in the final, he says, "Not at all, not at all. Man U were an up-and-coming side but we had players there were terrific value. You look at Peter Rodrigues. He had I think it was 31 caps for Wales. You look at Peter Osgood. You look at Micky Channon, who was the most wanted forward in the country. And then there was myself. And we also had Jim Steele in the back. And we had quite a good little lot of young players around us." Indeed, so experienced were the Southampton men that McCalliog says McMenemy's address beforehand would have been perfunctory: "Lawrie never really told us anything. How can you tell Mick Channon, how can you tell Peter Osgood, Peter Rodrigues, myself? We've all played the game, we know the game. The only one who hadn't been in a Cup Final before I think was Micky. So there's no point. The good thing about our team was before that we were really not particularly a good dressing room, but the wee Cup run kind of bonded the team a bit more together. Before that we had a bad atmosphere at Southampton." Saints captain Peter Rodrigues later recalled, "I recall shaking hands with the United skipper Martin Buchan and he seemed very nervous – so I turned round and told our lads."

Though the match would be relatively open despite the bittiness engendered by offside traps, it was fairly predetermined that this final was going to be no classic, mainly because of the heat. FA Cup finals are often soporific affairs in the best of circumstances, courtesy of being played in the late Spring, recipe for sluggish play, legs tiring quickly and players squinting uncomfortably in the glare. This, though, was 1976, when heat records were broken left, right and centre and the inhabitants of Britain got used to seeing photographs in newspapers of recently flowing rivers reduced to bare, cracked mud. It was not really a day for that 'busy bees' style of play. Hill: "You can check the records, it was the hottest day there has ever been at Wembley. I think Southampton handled it better than we did." Buchan: "At that time in the month of May when they play, it always has the potential for being a very warm day and the hot air is trapped in the bowl as well, so it did have a bit of a reputation for being stamina sapping." He adds, "I would have thought that was generally felt more by the team that was losing."

In the first few minutes, Coppell cut inside and launched an impressive effort with his weaker, left foot. Southampton's goalie Ian Turner saved and when Macari dashed in for the loose ball, the whistle blew, though no one seemed sure whether it was for feet-up or for something the whistle would blow for many times during the match, offside. On the latter score, United were usually the team caught out, something that was almost an inevitable consequence of their throwing so many men forward, but was also a deliberate McMenemy stratagem. Five times in the first seven minutes the whistle of Clive Thomas shrilled as United players hared toward goal only to be adjudged to be level with or past the second-to-last opposition player when the ball reached them. Docherty would later make caustic comments about the Southampton offside trap, but of course United were playing their own well-drilled one too.

Stepney may have been the veteran in the United team and the only man in their otherwise young ranks who had tasted glory at Wembley, albeit not in this competition, but that didn't stop him getting a rollicking from his captain in the first few minutes when Buchan felt he should have come for a ball which Buchan ended up having to hoist into the stands.

On 13 minutes, the ball was poked into the path of Hill. As he raced for it, it was realised by the suddenly excited crowd that – clear through on goal – he was not offside. Turner raced off his goal-line as Hill approached the penalty-area at a rapid pace. Having come as far as he could to handle the ball legally, Turner went down at Hill's feet at the margins of his area just as Merlin tried to flick the ball over him. The ball hit Turner's arm and the threat was averted. McCalliog: "I thought the first 15 minutes was tough. It looked like they were going to get a few goals, but I think the longer the game went on, the more I came into the game, then the more we controlled the game."

327

Toward the half-hour mark, Hill executed a beautiful backheel on the run that left his marker going the wrong way and sent the ball travelling diagonally into the penalty-area, momentarily causing chaos among a bamboozled Southampton defence. It was, though, one of the few moments of Merlin magic today. However, Hill wasn't the only one having a subdued game. McIlroy was also noticeably failing to make the play one would expect of a player of his calibre. "I was very surprised with the way they played," admits Daly of the Saints. "They had a chap by the name of Holmes. He practically marked me and made sure that I wasn't going to do much. The same happened with a lot of the lads."

Coming up to half-time, a lovely long ball from McCalliog found Mick Channon tearing toward the United goal. Stepney knew the danger of the man with the fancy sideburns and the Wiltshire accent and raced off his line to narrow the angle. He stuck a foot out and the swelling noise of the crowed turned into an "Ooh!" as the ball bounced off his boot to safety. Channon's provider, McCalliog, says, "There was a bit of spin on it and Micky didn't judge the spin and he hit Stepney with it. Micky should have put that in." McCalliog, incidentally, would be one of the men of the match and Gerry Daly observes of the player with whom he had been close at Old Trafford, "I don't think he got on too well with The Doc and if ever there was a player revved up for one particular game it was Jim McCalliog."

In the 42nd minute, Pearson went down on the right edge of the Southampton penalty-area, but there was – mystifyingly for many – no whistle for an incident that left the striker hobbling for what was the second time in the match.

15 minutes into the second-half, Hill took a corner. Pearson at the near post executed a backward header to send the ball into the six-yard box. McIlroy was standing at the far post. "All of a sudden it came through a crowd of players," recalls McIlroy. "I stuck my head out and it hit the underneath of the bar." When the ball bounced down and off the turf, it was hooked to safety by a Southampton man. McMenemy later stated that he turned to one of his colleagues on the bench at that point and said he couldn't see United winning this match.

On 65 minutes, McCreery was standing at the touchline with Tommy Cavanagh. In Cavanagh's right hand was the substitute card, bearing the number of the man about to come off. Alert TV viewers and those close enough in the stadium to read it were shocked to see that the number it bore was 11. Today, a substitution does not carry the significance it did in 1976. With teams now allowed to throw on up to five extra men, some managers exploit the opportunity to make changes almost casually, while some are forced to introduce fresh legs simply because they know that the opposition manager is going to do so. In 1976, teams were only allowed a single substitution, so managers had to exchange players carefully. Frequently they chose to make no change at all. A decision by a manager to pull off a player, therefore, was a significant statement, almost a rebuke to that substituted man. Gordon Hill had been many United fans' player of the season, even though he had only joined three months in. His Cup performances, especially against Derby in the semi, had been to a large part responsible for United getting to Wembley in the first place. He had been expected by many pundits to be the FA Cup final's man of the match. But now he was jogging grimly toward the touchline to cede his placing. Hill would later state that he had had his final against Derby.

Though Blunstone wasn't surprised Hill was substituted ("The way he was playing was bloody awful") he also says, "I don't think I'd have taken him off because he's the type of player who could play bloody awful and all of a sudden he'd break through and let fly and score. When you're losing, you don't want to take goalscorers off. Take 'em off when you're winning 5-0." Blunstone's essential humanity shines though in another argument he makes for not substituting Hill: "The danger with doing that, especially Gordon Hill, a very cocky player, it'd knock him down a bit. 'Cos he was that type of boy." Buchan, though, observes, "It's not like today [where] you can say, 'I know he's not having the best of times but we'll leave him on, we'll take somebody else off.' I think he felt that he had to do something to change it." Did he remember feeling during the match that Gordon wasn't having the best of days? Buchan: "I remember feeling the team as a whole wasn't having the best of days." McIlroy himself admits, "I think he could have took anyone off that day. We just didn't perform." Nonetheless, it can't be denied that Merlin had not been tearing down the left flank and bewitching defenders in his normal fashion and that Rodrigues – though he looked old enough to be his father – had been a big part of the reason for that. "Oh, my gosh I had a nightmare," says Hill, "I had an absolute horror in the final and I was tired. It was the heat and that's no excuses, but I felt as though my energy had just gone. I felt very, very dead. And I tried and I tried." Hill admits of the substitution, "I was upset." However, his upset was tempered by the sort of caustic wit that was part of The Doc's make-up. Hill later recalled, "As I walked to the bench, I turned to Tommy Docherty and said, 'What? Fucking me?' and he said, 'No, the whole fucking team'. Even though I was so disappointed I had to chuckle."

Whatever the wisdom of the choice of the withdrawn player, it certainly seemed to be a sign of concern on Docherty's part about the way this match was developing. As the game wore on, Southampton seemed to be becoming less and less afraid of their opponents. McMenemy's tactics were working. Like many managers, he had known that 'clipping the wingers' was desirable but unlike many he had succeeded in this objective. Though Coppell had had more success on his flank in taking the ball to the byline, too often he had found himself overwhelmed. He had also often found himself unsupported, for also considered important by the Southampton boss had been preventing those ever-energetic midfielders Daly and Macari slipping the attentions of Southampton men and getting behind the defence. This too had largely been achieved. To make matters worse, on 76 minutes Pearson was visibly struggling again. Having already made their permitted substitution, there was nothing the United bench could do about it. Though Southampton would no doubt consider it churlish to give significance to this, it seems fair to say that Pearson was not playing to his full capacity and that this would seem to be the consequence of the unpunished knock(s) he had taken.

Macari's misgivings about the complacent attitude of some of his teammates had been eased by the match's opening minutes when they had pushed the ball around well and had two early chances. However, as the match wore on without the Reds scoring, the alarm bells had started distantly ringing. "I began to sense that it was going to be the Stoke match all over again," he later said in reference to the recent League defeat that had seen United's title hopes destroyed by a late goal on the break. "The same sort of pattern was beginning to emerge." His worst nightmare came true in the 83rd minute, at the same time as Jim McCalliog's biggest dream was realised. "Old players, by and large, come back to haunt you," Docherty admitted one day far into the future. The propensity of fate to send Docherty discards back to bite him on the posterior did indeed occur yet again today. McCalliog: "Don't forget it was only about 16 months since I'd left Man U and what The Doc had always said was that a good clearance, everybody pushed up." This time round, United's use of the offside trap found McCalliog in possession. Referring to team-mate Bobby Stokes, McCalliog says, "I could hear little Bobby shouting and if you watch the video you can see me lift it over the top right into that inside-left position 'cos I knew that's where Bobby was going. I put it in his path."

Throughout the match, the linesmen's flags had shot up again and again as United headed for the Southampton goal. But as the ball made its way to an isolated Stokes 30 yards from the United goal, this time the linesman saw nothing wrong. As the United fans in the 100,000 crowd howled in protest and a ragged line comprised of Forsyth, Greenhoff and Buchan furiously chased him, Stokes – by now just outside the penalty-arc – angled a low, first-time, left-footed shot toward the far post without looking up. Forsyth: "I was the last man who tried to get near him ... I thought he might have been slightly offside but I came across. If he'd took it on I'd probably have caught him but he hit it just outside the 18-yard box ... He's hit it well out and I thought, 'Well, big Alex will get that' and, before you know it, it's creeped into the bottom left-hand side. I couldnae believe it ... It seemed to take forever. It wasnae a rocket shot." McCalliog: "I think it must have bounced the most times I've ever seen in my life." In Greenhoff's eyes, the right-back let him down. "He just ran across Alex and ran behind me," says Greenhoff of Stokes. "All Alex [Forsyth] had to do was shout to me but I didn't get a call and next thing he's gone, 'cos you haven't got eyes in back of your head … I wasn't far away … Once he's run across Alex, then he should have shouted 'Brian!' I might have reacted and it might have just changed the game. I didn't get it and the next thing I know he's behind me and I'm thinking, 'How the hell's he got there?'"

Because of the few cameras and therefore angles involved in television football coverage then, for many there remains a question about the goal that put Southampton 1-0 up. McCalliog: "For people to say it was offside – which The Doc said as well – just wasnae true". Says Buchan, "I can remember seeing clips of Bobby Stokes scoring the goal and every time I see it, he seems to get further and further offside. Or maybe that's just an illusion." Coppell has said, "I thought at the time that goal was offside and, having seen the replays on television, I still do." Greenhoff: "Yeah. Half a yard's offside in them days." Hill says, "The guy took the goal, he got away with it, good luck to him … Defenders will be the first person to say he was offside by at least a yard. This is always a difficult one and what we see was marginal. We look at the replay again and say, 'Yes, he was offside.' But he got away with it." Houston: "It's very difficult. I'm 10, 15 yards in front of Martin, so there's no way I'm even involved in looking along the line. When we looked at it again, it did look offside." Forsyth: "I've looked at it umpteen times on the telly and obviously in them days you only had the one camera whereas now you've got a camera everywhere. I think he's just slightly offside." In his 1980 book, McIlroy disagreed, stating, "The referee and linesman were proved to have been right in allowing play to go on and the goal to stand." Nowadays, perhaps feeling less encumbered by the obligation to be seen as a good loser, he sings a different tune: "Bobby Stokes was two yards offside when he scored." Docherty has said, "To this day, it was offside." Blunstone: "The goal was offside. Definitely. Don't forget in them days, it wasn't when the ball was played, it was when you received it. They've changed the rules since then." McCreery: "I think it was controversial. The referee was Clive Thomas who we'd had a few run-ins with before." Daly is one of the few who don't have an opinion either way on the matter. "I don't know," he shrugs. "But that doesn't matter. It was given and that was it."

When the question is put to David Meek, he gives a laugh that suggests he has been asked this many times before. "There was the tendency from the United point of view to feel that it was offside but I don't really know," he says. "I wasn't in as good a position as the linesman and I accept that it was not offside. It was one of the 50-50 calls and the linesman was being honest and I don't think anybody can swear that it was offside." If Stokes *was* onside, it would seem Buchan was the culprit: his form trotting back to his own goal in the centre of the pitch would have been the one making the Southampton man level with play. The fact that the United captain was just out of the television camera's frame when Stokes received the ball would seem to be the cause of the lingering uncertainty over whether the decision was correct.

Some, though, state that whether Stokes was onside or not is irrelevant and that no top-flight goalkeeper should be beaten from the distance Stepney was. Muttering among those who felt that Alex had been a good servant to the club but that he was past his best must surely have intensified that evening. Docherty, of course, had already made his feelings known about Stepney via his abortive attempt to ease Paddy Roche into his job earlier in the season, so it should come as no surprise that *My Story* saw Docherty opining that Stepney was too slow off his line and that he should have narrowed the angle for the Southampton man. Says McIlroy, "I'm sure Alex would have saved that nine out of 10 times, but it went in and that just sort of summed up the day." "I think Alex was disappointed", Greenhoff says, using the euphemism beloved of football commentators too polite to say that the relevant player bungled. "I don't think I'm talking out of school when I [say I] think he thought he should have had it."

Some defend Stepney. Forsyth: "You couldnae blame the goalkeeper. You couldnae blame anybody." Stepney's future United colleague Waldron, watching on television, didn't fault him either. He adds, with the benefit of subsequently getting to know the keeper, "I would think that Alex has saved far, far more goals, one on one, than most goalkeepers and he had a system about how he did it and obviously it's not going to work every time, and it didn't work on that particular occasion." Even Gordon Hill – who baldly states of Stepney, "I think he had his best days with the 1968 side" and who was far from being best mates with the goalie – defends him. "I don't think any goalkeeper in the world could have saved that because it bobbled," he says. "It went right into the corner. I think he caught everybody by hitting so early. I don't think Ray Clemence or Shiltsie would have got that." Stepney himself said, "It was a mis-hit across me and it bounced just in front of me and accelerated fiendishly off the turf. It was the bounce that defeated me … "

For Daly, the goal was a reality check:. "It was just unbelievable in the fact that they could actually go and score a goal," he says. "And it wasn't the best of goals either. It was only after that goal did we start thinking to ourselves we might end up losing this game." McCreery: "We had all the play. It was just a bolt out of the blue … I think once the goal went in, it just drains you." A minute after Southampton had scored, Daly was through on the Southampton goal, but Turner bravely dashed out and smothered the ball. It was the last good chance United would get.

\*\*\*

After the final whistle, all was devastation for United. This time last year, Docherty and his men had been holding aloft a decidedly ersatz prize in the shape of the Second Division championship trophy. In a sign of just how much their expectations of themselves had skyrocketed in 12 months, the United team and their manager were today bereft in a way that the footballing cliché sick as a parrot just cannot convey. It's easy to ridicule soccer players for taking the sport so seriously that they are sometimes as stricken over a loss in a big game as by a bereavement but, examining it objectively, it is perfectly understandable. Football is not just a job but a vocation, furthermore one that is inextricably bound up with the emotions and dreams of the supporters whose vociferous figures they play in front of every week. The media build-up to finals of knock-out competitions and other big matches serves to ratchet up the intensity of emotion and hope even further. Add to this a fragile emotional state created by the fact that United were a very young side – much closer to the age when every mishap seems a crisis than to the position on life's timeline where one realises the world goes on and devastation will be soothed by passing years – and one can began to understand how distraught United's players were. Of course, the case can be made that the relegation of a couple of years ago was far more traumatic – in terms of its symbolism and implications for the future – but by the nature of a relegation fight, it was a gradual thing. Sickening as its final confirmation was, it didn't quite have the sudden, devastating impact involved in the result of this match.

It should be pointed out that there is not a consensus on the idea that the Reds were over-confident. Forsyth: "It doesn't matter who you're playing, you're never over-confident with anybody. We always thought we had a right good chance obviously, but we were never over-confident because you just don't know how you're going to perform on the day." "I don't think we underestimated them", says McIlroy. "I really don't. We just didn't play on the day, I think the occasion got to us, They had an absolute experience all over the park and we just got caught up as certain winners. We didn't mean to go out there and play the way we played. The game passed in a flash. I couldn't believe it that we got beat. It was our first experience of a day at Wembley in a Cup Final and it just passed us by." Buchan comes out with similar comments, at least in one respect: "I can't remember too much about the game. That was my first final and they do say the first time you play it goes in a flash."

Meek, however, recalls, "I think there was a confidence in the team. They felt they were better, although they'd come from a rather chequered background. I think they felt that they just had to play their normal game and they would win ... I remember after the game going into the dressing room. Tommy Docherty was sitting alongside Tommy Cavanagh and they were more shocked than me because I think they really thought they had it in the bag. Their first reaction was, 'Don't worry, we'll be back next year and we'll win it.' It's easy to dismiss it as bravado and there was an element of bravado, but at the same time I think they really meant it." Was the reporter surprised what difficult opponents Southampton were? "I was actually. I thought Southampton played out of their skins."

Docherty later said that he felt Coppell was consistent in his effort this day but that Hill, Macari and McIlroy were under par. Hill, in reference to Docherty's pre-match instruction to the team to play the way they could, says, "And we didn't." He adds, "But I still think the over-confidence factor was evident ... We were such a flamboyant team in the way that we were playing and everybody said, 'Oh, I love watching United and this is a new era, this is great', and I think that got to a lot of us. There's a few players that played well and a few players that just went through the motions." Daly: "Maybe a bit of complacency came in, maybe the occasion got to some people, I don't know. All I can tell you is I can't remember one of us on that particular day actually performing to anywhere near the ability that we possessed. Maybe what won the day for them was the experience that they had on the pitch. Osgood and Channon and so on: it was once in a lifetime for them. Maybe we looked upon the situation, 'We've got years to come after that' and for them people it was probably the last throw of the dice ... There's a lot of things you can put forward. I'm not going to blame the heat, because it should have been easier for us. We could run all day and they had older legs. Maybe it was just the occasion got to everybody." Forsyth: "On the day, we just played terrible. We didnae do nothing. We were nothing like ourselves, the way that we could play. Fair dues to Southampton. They got a softish goal. It wasnae an all-time classic goal ... But we never played nothing like we could do. I thought maybe the nerves got to us because Wembley can drain you: it takes a lot out of you. It's a big stadium, the atmosphere ... We had a few chances here and there, had a lot of possession. I feel we were the better team on the day but we didnae destroy them. They played well, you've got to hand it to them. They [won] the Cup and their name's in the history book so fair dues to Southampton." Houston: "We didn't play anywhere near the potential of the team, and I don't know if it was a bit of stage fright. We never really played. We seemed to freeze on the day. We just didn't get going." Blunstone: "We just didn't turn out. Whether the occasion got to us or not, we didn't play as well as could play, but sometimes you've got to realise the bounce of the ball goes against you. They got the offside goal and that was one of them days. That's what happens." Brian Greenhoff: "We bombarded them for the first 15, 20 minutes and didn't score and I think if we'd have scored early, we'd have gone on and won comfortably. In the end they hit us with a sucker punch." Greenhoff remembers an eagerness rather than a nervousness amongst his colleagues and says, "I don't think we were over-confident because The Doc would never let us get that way. I just think it was their day. Your name's on the Cup ... "

"I didn't think they were in the game," McCalliog demurs. "They had Macari in midfield, Gerry Daly – I don't remember then touching the ball. [Coppell and Hill] never got a kick either." Does it irritate McCalliog that so many still insist the goal he laid on was illegal? "No, I just think that's their opinion and I think that's what happens in the game. It doesn't irritate me at all. It's down in the history books and no matter what they think, I know what's happened. It's all over and I enjoyed a lovely day out at Wembley and I got quite a lot of the ball and that's it." McCalliog's bantering prediction to Cavanagh, Pearson and Houston the previous day had come true, and he had played a major part in it by laying on the goal. Echoing Docherty, he says, "An ex-player is always dangerous, because he can come back and bite you." It wasn't even the first time McCalliog had done this to The Doc: "I remember leaving Chelsea and going to Sheffield Wednesday. I left in the November and in the March we beat them in the semi-final of the Cup at Sheffield Wednesday and I scored one of the goals. I've done it everywhere I've left. I've always come back and had something to say." McCalliog declines to couch it in terms of revenge: "It's a pride thing, it's not a get-at-you or anything like that."

After the game, McMenemy made the point that most journalists writing off the Saints' chances beforehand hadn't actually seen much of his team this season, as writers for national newspapers predominately covered First Division games; those in the know would not have been as quick to assume that the advantage was with the Reds.

Docherty may have been considerably older than his charges but had his own awful mixture of emotions to deal with, no doubt prominent in which was the fact that he'd been through this more than once before. When the final whistle blew, he sportingly went over to congratulate McMenemy and his colleagues on their victory but his inner feelings were closer to those of Brian Greenhoff, who he was shortly having to console as the defender failed to prevent tears springing. (Greenhoff: "I am quite emotional anyway.") Docherty has subsequently said that sitting in the dressing room afterwards – crowded but silent, as only the dressing rooms of shell-shocked losers can be – he thought to himself that what he was feeling must be worse than dying, on the grounds that at least if you were dead you didn't have to read about it in the papers the next day. He has also said, "I was more disappointed after that game than [I was] when we got relegated, because I was so sure we were gonna beat Southampton." Forsyth: "We were all sick after it. Just hardly talked. Had our bath. We had a great chance there and we blew it. Everybody knew it. It was very, very quiet. A team like us against Southampton … No disrespect to them, that should have been our Cup and we just let it go." McCreery recalls of the team, "Distraught. Disbelief. Everybody moping around and no one would speak. Just so devastated." Buchan, ever contrary, was more stoical. "I just felt it was a great opportunity missed," he says. "Running about stomping your feet's not going to change things is it? You've just got to resolve to do better next time you're in that position."

A red-eyed Brian Greenhoff was shortly to be seen outside the dressing room door clutching the dead weight of good-luck telegrams. "The one thing that's holding us together is that we are young enough to come back here one day," he said. It was a sentiment echoed by Sammy McIlroy, who commented, "We're sick about it but at least we are young enough to come back. We're good enough, too." Young was not a description that applied to his colleague Alex Stepney. For the keeper, the fact that repeated viewings of the goal would convince him that it was offside provided a truly sickening quality to the aftermath of what he was assuming was his last big occasion in football. "I looked upon the match as ... my chance to go out of the game with a memorable flourish," he said. He also admitted that he openly wept on the way back to Manchester. Blunstone: "It was a blow. We had a dinner at night and it weren't very pleasant. Everybody was down."

"They have given much pleasure and entertainment all season and their day will surely come," opined football correspondent Geoffrey Green of the Reds. Maybe so, but not this configuration. The match was the last time Stepney, Forsyth, Houston, Daly, Greenhoff, Buchan, Coppell, McIlroy, Pearson, Macari and Hill would play together. Due to a combination of Docherty's preferences changing, injury, a significant new signing and a surprising sale, the roll call was soon no more.

One good thing came of the day. When it most mattered – at domestic soccer's showpiece match – the United fans behaved impeccably. Many of course clung to the belief and recited the mantra that the hooligans weren't really football fans. This is of course a nonsense that refuses to acknowledge the obvious overlap between the two, demonstrated by such things as programme-sellers outside grounds being attacked and deprived of their wares so as to enable the robbers to cut out the tokens the accumulation of which gains access to a Wembley ticket should their team reach the Cup Final. Today, the hooligans were subdued. Perhaps even they were in a mellow mood: possibly a combination of the jubilation of being at Wembley two years after the ultimate humiliation for a club of United's stature and being drained by the shock of defeat to the underdogs. According to the hooligan memoir industry that has bewilderingly grown up in recent years, violence at 70s football matches usually involved hooligan attacking hooligan, with the non-violent fans sportingly left alone. Maybe, in that case, the boot-boys usually to be found seeking out opposition supporters to give a kicking to were among those United fans giving a thumbs up to the Southampton coach as it left the ground. Police, railway officials and coach operators were unanimous in their praise of the Red Army, with Robert Ryan, the police commander on duty that day, going so far as to say, "They were easily one of the best crowds we have had to handle in recent years."

Jimmy Nicholl might or might not have had a better time of it if he had played. "I thought I had a good chance of being sub," he recalls. "I was disappointed in a sense because you wanted to be part of it. We ended up with our wives and our girlfriends sitting in the stands obviously getting beat, so it wasn't a great weekend to be honest with you. Southampton weren't bad but I didn't think they were going to lose it, United. When they scored the goal, you always had this feeling that, 'Alright, they'll come back and they'll win it.' I was a wee bit flat anyway because of not being involved … You don't know whether that particular moment is going to be your last opportunity or not." There was a humorous post-script to his day: "I remember getting back on Sunday night and supporters turned round and said, 'Well unlucky lads – but we backed Southampton at 13-1. It paid for our weekend'."

\*\*\*

There were more tears for the beaten finalists the next day as United returned to Manchester where 20,000 attended the city's Albert Square to greet their open-topped bus. Stuart Pearson unashamedly bawled like a baby as the crowd sang, "We don't mind, we don't mind." They also sang, "Next year, next year." In his speech from the bus top deck, Docherty did a peculiar thing. Though he was wont to engage in hyperbole, it was not usually the kind of stuff that left him wide open. The previous season when most people were already declaring United Second Division champions by the last week of September, he had made sure to forebear from predicting even promotion until the cusp of the second week of December. His comments about the FA Cup final being decided at Hillsborough could be (and apparently were) dismissed as banter, Meanwhile, comparing George Graham to Gunter Netzer and declaring Willie Morgan the best right-sided winger in the world were merely matters of opinion, however outlandish, not predictions that could be disproven by the passage of time. But Docherty brazenly declared this day, "We'll be back next year, and we'll win it." Meek, who was present, says, "That was just really repeating what he'd told me in the dressing room immediately after the match and I think he really meant it." A defiant remark in the confines of a dressing room is one thing, but surely repeated in public it potentially becomes a hostage to fortune? Meek: "Yes it does, but that was Docherty. He never really avoided issues. He wore his heart on his sleeve and what he felt, he said. I think he genuinely felt a little bit aggrieved, let down or whatever, that they'd not won it and that they would make up for it the next year. I don't think he blamed himself and I don't think he blamed the players. I think he just blamed the referee. He felt it was offside. He just felt they'd not had the rub of the green and that they were capable of playing a lot better."

Perhaps even more extraordinary than making this remark to a journalist who might print it in an article or uttering it in public from the top of a bus is the fact that Docherty also made it in private to someone whom he was neither using as a potential conduit to the supporters nor trying to console, namely his son Mick. Says Docherty *fils*, "He walked a very lonely figure into the Russell Square hotel and he says, 'Michael, I'm going to win this next year, son.' He was always very, very positive. I felt, 'Well, he's maybe just saying that out of anger or frustration or disappointment.' It's an easy thing to say but it's much, much harder thing to do." However, Mick is adamant on one thing: "I'm sure he believed it."

To some extent, it was also what the players, not just the fans, wanted to hear. Buchan points out that at that age, players aren't inclined to contemplate the statistical implausibility of ever getting another chance to contest a Cup Final. However, he also says of the comment, "I'm quite sure there's not too many of them would remember it by the time the third round of the Cup came round the following January."

***

Three days after the devastation of the Wembley defeat, United had to pick themselves up and dust themselves down as best they could to play their final League match of the season. Though the championship had yet to be decided, for United their fixture on Tuesday May 4 was the archetypal dead rubber. QPR had played their last game on April 24 and were going to finish either first or second, depending on Liverpool's result today against Wolves. (Liverpool, in fact, would win 3-1.) With United trailing QPR by five points as they went into this match, they had no chance of finishing even second, but were also too far ahead of Derby to relinquish third place. Such meaningless matches after a devastating loss are one of the worst aspects of a footballer's profession.

However, this obligation wasn't quite so bad as the team's requirement following their 1974 relegation to drag their bodies over to Stoke for a fag-end fixture. In the first place, it was a home game. Secondly, the fixture was a local derby. Not only would the game give them the energy boost of playing in a packed stadium in front of a noisy, partisan crowd, it would enable them to try to give their fans a treat by compensating in some way for the Wembley loss with a victory over their arch-rivals. Said notional victory would be all the sweeter for the point it would enable them to prove to Book's allegedly 4-2-4 clothes-stealing Manchester City, whose own cup victory – albeit the less prestigious League Cup – added salt to the wounds of any United player or supporter inclined to brood about the copyism. In this season of near misses in League and Cup, this was one thing at least the United players were able to do. In front of a crowd of 59,528, the Reds gave an example of why so many neutral observers had felt their return to the First Division this season had been good for football.

Greenhoff and Macari were absent today – presumably injured, as there was nothing for Docherty to save them for – and replaced by Albiston and Jackson respectively. United made most of the play in the first half, even if their finishing was off. Despite the fact that nothing was at stake except pride, there was a little bit of nastiness. Tueart went in heavily on Hill, who was visibly shaken. The red element of the crowd roared in outrage. The blue element responded, "Show us your cup." The opening goal was scored, appropriately, by Gordon Hill, the man who had done so much to make United such an exciting proposition this season. As if to assert his worth after the bitter disappointment of his substitution on Saturday, Hill was man of the match, bossing proceedings on his touchline and surging into the City half at will. Four minutes into the second-half, he embarked on a 40-yard run that left two City men in his wake before unleashing a ball that Joe Corrigan had no chance of stopping. Super Sam was another man who might have been determined to make amends for being below-par on Saturday and his 53rd-minute goal certainly went some way toward achieving that. Stepney put his own nightmare of the Cup Final behind him to keep a clean sheet.

In an example of the genuinely clever chants that English soccer fans are apt to come up with, the Stretford End were to be heard declaiming to the tune of 'If You're Happy And You Know It', "We'd rather win the derby than the Cup." Not true of course, but closer to the truth this day than almost any other, for United's 2-0 victory was, unbelievably, their first home win against City for a decade.

"We didn't really want to play," says McIlroy of the fixture. "Obviously we were still gutted about losing the Cup, but I suppose if you're going to have a game, play it against Manchester City at Old Trafford and that was at least a decent end to the season." Forsyth sounds somewhat bewildered by the switcharound in form in four days that saw United beat significantly superior opposition to Southampton. "We absolutely destroyed them yet in the Cup Final we were terrible," he says. "I just don't believe it."

\*\*\*

When the dust settled after the last fixtures, Liverpool emerged as champions by one point. United's third place was achieved with 56 points, three fewer than QPR and three more than fourth-placed Derby. The Reds had won 23 of their League matches, drawn 10 and lost nine. Macari was magnanimous about the Merseysiders' victory in a season in which they also won the UEFA Cup, disagreeing with John Bond's assertion that their championship was bad for the English game. "They emerged as champions worthy of the name," he said. However, he added, "We have a certain quality called elegance about us. During the first 18 months of my career at Old Trafford, I think we were all searching for that formula which provided entertainment, yet also produced the right results. Finally, we got it." Houston: "It was a highlight in many ways but was a big disappointment not to pick up anything from our efforts during the season. It left us a little bit hollow, but there was still a lot of positive things from that season."

That United's third-place finish was achieved with 56 points raises an interesting point. The previous season had seen Derby take the title with just 53 points. Nonetheless, however valid talk of the high standard of competition in the League that year may be, for some – including Martin Buchan – the title was United's to give away, and that is what they did. McIlroy had said after the FA Cup victory against Wolves that it would be a tragedy for the game if Manchester United didn't win anything this season. That tragedy had come to pass.

After the 3-0 loss to Ipswich in the season's closing stages, Docherty had, almost defiantly, said, "But even if we wind up with nothing, it will still have been a marvellous season. We have been the saviours of English football." His point was partly proved by the one honour United did win that season. They topped the *Daily Mail*'s Fair Play League, finishing in front of Liverpool by a comfortable margin. In a League whose points worked on a reverse principle – the more you picked up, the worse you did – United amassed only 648 points. The Fair Play League saw a team given a point for each free-kick conceded: the Reds had conceded only 433 free-kicks during the season, as opposed to Liverpool's 504. Bookings attracted 20 points and United had only seen a player cautioned on 10 occasions. As for the offence that attracted the greatest Fair Play League sanction – a sending-off, worth 50 points – United had completely clean hands. "We have been too busy playing football to worry about kicking people," said Buchan at the time. However, he added, "I still think we concede too many needless fouls. We can get better." Docherty was awarded a cheque of £1,000 for the achievement. He said, "It augers well for British football that successful teams like Liverpool and ourselves are doing things the right way. The players have worked hard in setting an example and I'm pleased for them that we have won the trophy." The award was made by ex-Liverpool manager Bill Shankly, whose old club had scored 724 points in coming second in the Fair Play League. "My gospel was always to play the ball and never bother with the man," said Shanks. "And not to argue with the referees because the only one you upset is yourself. Manchester United have been refreshing from the very beginning, they have been brilliant for a bunch of boys. I remember when Lou Macari wanted to referee every match himself. If Lou sees the light, there's a chance for everybody in the game."

The Fair Play Award wouldn't have been a huge consolation to a team who had come so close in two competitions and emerged empty-handed. But for that dwindling band of players who had been in the first team in Docherty's first two seasons as manager when United had a reputation for play that was anything but fair it must have at least aroused a scintilla of pleasure. And as Brian Glanville might have pointed out (even if to the accompaniment of smoke appearing from the ears of fans of a certain soccer knight), it would also have been an award that Matt Busby's teams would have had some difficulty winning had it existed in his day.

Meanwhile, United's board of directors were probably at least partly consoled by some rather pleasing statistics staring back at them as they took the opportunity provided by the close season to reflect on their club's situation. Once again, Manchester United were the only League club to pack a million people into their ground over the course of the campaign, the April 17 match against Everton securing that figure with two home matches left to play. (Although, of course, they had secured that figure by March 6 if one takes into account cup fixtures.) In playing host to an average attendance of 54,750 – an increase of 6,000 per match on the previous season – United had achieved their best crowds since 1968, when they notched up a post-War record average of 57,696. All rather symbolic, because they were currently playing their best football since that year of glory.

What all this meant in practical terms was not that the club were rolling in it but that they were now climbing steadily out of financial dire straits. Club accounts for the year 1975 revealed, despite a record profit of £164,826, an overdraft secured by a mortgage of more than £500,000. Those straits had been entered into in 1971/72 when O'Farrell had started spending heavily in the transfer market. Although he was right to do so – the fact that United had bought a mere two players in the five years preceding his appointment is simply absurd – O'Farrell failed to balance the books in a day and age where television money was not high enough to compensate for transfer-market profligacy. The club's loss that season of £245,000 was their first in eight years. Not that Docherty was any better: he ensured a loss of £390,000. The climbing gates and the fact that Docherty had all but abandoned big-money signings, as well as the fact that he was practising a book-balancing policy of one-out, one-in, were all combining to ensure that the bleak days in Old Trafford's accounts department were becoming as distant as their once wretched form on the pitch.

Pearson was the top League scorer for the club with 13, but Macari was top scorer overall, having added three Cup (League and FA) goals to his 12 First Division strikes. McIlroy had also done well, his tally of 13 only one behind Pearson's strike rate from all competitions. Macari won the United Supporters' Association Player of the Year Award, equalling Willie

Morgan's previous two consecutive victories. Some might have been surprised at the choice, given the voluble appreciation of Hill from the terraces during the campaign, but the Supporters' Association could possibly be argued to be connoisseurs, appreciative of more nuanced skills than dazzling wingwork.

Matt Busby had of course been pleased at United's First Division bounce-back the previous year, but this time round he could reflect on a season whose accomplishments had been more gratifying than merely regaining a place it was felt they should never have lost in the first instance. The Reds might have won neither of the big prizes for which they were major contenders in 1975/76, but that they were contenders at all was significant. Furthermore, they had challenged for the honours in style. The resurrection of the wingmen was something that particularly warmed Busby's cockles, his memories of United wide players going back not just to George Best and John Aston but to the likes of Charlie Mitten, Johnny Berry, David Pegg and Albert Scanlon. Of Hill and Coppell, Busby observed, "They are giving the rest of the side room to play. There is creation, movement and excitement." Busby didn't just credit Docherty, Coppell and Hill: he extended his gratitude for more positive football to Manchester City's manager Tony Book and Derby bossman Dave Mackay for placing similar faith in wingers.

One of Busby's great teams, of course, had been known as the Busby Babes because of their unusually young average age. The Doc had his own team of babes and for Tommy Cavanagh that might explain why the side had had such unexpected success. "The innocence of the players has taken us into the unknown," said the coach. "They sometimes do things that more experienced players would not attempt ... When they have lost their innocence, they might not be as good."

# PART FIVE

# 1976/77: Retribution

Shortly before the end of the 1975/76 season, it was announced that Pat Crerand would be leaving his post as Docherty's assistant to seek work as a manager elsewhere. Said Crerand in the press, "The reason for my parting is ambition … I'm going with no hard feelings and there is no question of me being pushed out. This decision is mine … Tommy Docherty and the chairman have promised me all their help. I can stay here until I land a new job, but I'm hoping to get fixed before the end of the season." Docherty was quoted as saying, "Pat is a great bloke and has been a tremendous servant. He wants a manager's job and the best way is to let everyone know he's available."

Those who weren't on the inside at Old Trafford would have accepted the statements at face value, especially as shortly thereafter Crerand obtained a managerial post at Third Division Northampton Town. Docherty has subsequently admitted that he had told Northampton Town – as with the previous overture from Celtic – that he didn't think Crerand would be up to the job. On this occasion, his failure to give a reference was ignored in favour of more positive comments from Matt Busby and ex-Manchester City and England caretaker manager Joe Mercer.

The miserable time that had caused Crerand to lately hate going into Old Trafford reached a crescendo in a *contretemps* between him and Docherty at a civic reception in Manchester following the FA Cup final defeat. Crerand later said of the incident, "I almost had a fist fight with The Doc. I had a go at him about everything I thought was wrong and it became heated."

Docherty's version of events was that Crerand had followed him to the toilet, " ... threatening me". It has to be acknowledged that Crerand had by his own admission a penchant for violence. Barely a chapter of his autobiography *Never Turn the Other Cheek* goes by without Crerand talking of an incident in which he responded to provocation real or imagined by using his fists or threatening to. On one occasion, he remonstrated with a passing football journalist who had written something he didn't like, which perhaps might not have seemed so intemperate had he not at the time been working for Piccadilly Radio and been live on air. Though many attest to the warmth and humanity of Crerand, he clearly has a darker side and it cannot always have been comfortable to work alongside such a hothead, even for someone hardly angelic like Docherty himself.

Crerand has spoken of the incident that led him to depart the club permanently. "I turned up at the training ground and found that no kit had been laid out for me," he recalled. "I asked why and was told, 'Mr Docherty's orders'." Crerand did not return to The Cliff or Old Trafford after that. Docherty later claimed, " ... it was his decision to leave the club. The board didn't say to him, 'You're no longer assistant manager' and neither did I. I knew it would get back to him that I'd said I'd made a mistake in appointing him. So he decided to go his own way."

Frank Blunstone to some extent seems to possess a quality of innocence. Just as the youth coach managed to get through his time at Old Trafford without even becoming aware that Docherty and Morgan were at loggerheads over an alleged eye injury, so he says of the Crerand departure, "I didn't see it coming at all. I don't know what happened there." He doesn't appear to be being disingenuous and nothing sinister can safely be read into the fact that he was a beneficiary of Crerand's resignation. Before the start of the 1976/77 season, Blunstone stepped up to fill the assistant manager role Crerand had vacated. He retained his responsibility for the youth team and reserves. Blunstone: "Tommy Cavanagh got a bit upset about it, but Tommy [Docherty] said he wanted somebody to be at the club when he was away. 'Cos I was with the second team or youth team, when they were playing away I'd be at Old Trafford. I could do the job at Old Trafford, whatever come up, where Cavanagh was with him all the time."

Blunstone asked Docherty permission to spend a week during the summer break in Germany watching the methods of celebrated former Borussia Mönchengladbach coach Hennes Weisweiler, now working at FC Cologne, with the object of improving the training of United's kids. "I brought back quite a few of them methods, what they were using," Blunstone says. "[United] used to warm up just lapping and that sort of thing, running, but they warmed up with ball work all the time. And they had grids 16-yards square, a grid with cones or little things they'd put on the floor. In the middle they had two players trying to win the ball from the people on the outside. If the people in the inside won it off one of the outside players, whoever gave it away on the outside had to go inside and the inside player went outside. It was encouraging them to keep the ball under pressure. It was brilliant. And it was a good warm-up: you could have two-touch, one-touch. You could do all sorts of things with it. It's complicated but it's very good … I brought all that in. Forwards versus the defenders, a lot of shadow football, that type of thing." What had been intended as training methods for United's youth players became first-team practices: "He watched a few of them and he liked it and he introduced it to the first team."

The close season saw Docherty make a new signing, obtaining forward Alan Foggon for £25,000–£27,000 from Middlesbrough. Born in Chester-le-Street, County Durham on February 23 1950, Foggon had been in the same 1969 Fairs Cup-winning Newcastle United team as Wyn Davies and his approximately one in 2.5 scoring ratio for 'Boro suggested a useful striker, despite an unusually chunky build for a footballer that had led to the terrace nickname "Fatty Foggon". Docherty had so desired his services that he travelled thousands of miles to secure them. Foggon had been spending the close season playing in the North American Soccer League for Hartford Centennials when he received a call from 'Boro manager Jack Charlton to tell him of United's overture. "Then as now, if Manchester United were interested, you listened," explained Foggon many years later. "Unfortunately Tommy couldn't get a US visa so they got me on a little six-seater plane to Montreal … I had dinner with The Doc and then we went to bed." Those who might imagine the last sentence is unintentionally comical bad wording would be wrong. A crowded Montreal was at that point hosting the Olympic Games. Foggon: "Unfortunately it was the only hotel room in the whole of Montreal."

\*\*\*

The foreign tour on which United embarked in the close season caused Colin Waldron to be "astounded" by the size of his new club. He recalls, "My first game was in a friendly. It was for Jimmy Johnson and Bobby Lennox's testimonial match at Celtic, so I go up there for a testimonial match thinking this is a joke. 72,000 inside and 20,000 outside in a testimonial game, and from there we went to Ireland where the entire population of Ireland comes to a standstill while the bus goes through. And from there to Canada, America, Bermuda, Belgium, Holland, Germany, Yugoslavia, all within a matter of months, and wherever you go it's like the bloody Pope arriving. It was just absolutely incredible."

In Yugoslavia, United played a friendly against Red Star Belgrade (the attendance at which Waldron estimates as 72,000). In a 2-1 loss, Macari was substituted and wasn't happy about the decision. He let journalists know about it afterwards, and before long yet another war of words between him and Docherty was taking place in the press. Macari said he had been "singled out" and had been "no better nor worse than a few of the other players." Docherty countered with, "Lou had not been playing as well as he can on our tour and when I took him off it was because I felt I had to do something about it." Credence was given to The Doc's decision by another comment Macari made: "As soon as the prizes are there to be won I'll really be playing. I am only at my best when there's something important in front of me." However, that both men had learned lessons from their previous confrontations was indicated by the fact that both held back from outright condemnation of the other. Though Macari said, "All I'm asking is for a fair deal … It was not clear to me if I was really wanted," he was anxious to point out that, "I would not want to leave Manchester United. I have no intention of making a major issue out of this." And though Docherty caustically said, "This is not the Lou Macari Football Club but Manchester United FC," he also stated, "I now regard it as a storm in a teacup. It is now over and he will be playing … against Birmingham in our opening game of the season."

Someone who wouldn't be playing against Birmingham was Alex Forsyth. Not too long before the season started, Forsyth got a nasty shock. Docherty told him that Nicholl was now his first choice right-back. Naturally, Forsyth was frustrated and a little bewildered. After all, a player usually expects to be dropped after a loss of form or due to age, not at the start of a campaign and aged just 24. "Alex was quite naturally disappointed," admitted Docherty, "but he took it very sensibly. He has been out of the side before and has fought his way back. He knows he has the chance to do this again." Forsyth told the press, "I am terribly disappointed, but the boss picks the team and I can't argue about his decision. I don't want to leave Manchester United and I'll fight hard to get back into the side." Forsyth says that Nicholl was as puzzled by the decision as he was: "Even Jimmy said to me, 'Look, I don't know why he's put me in the team. You're playing well and that.' I said, 'Och, no it's nothing to do with you Jimmy. If you get your chance you've got to take it. If you're in front of me, good luck to you. If I get back in, that's just the way it goes.' I don't know why he did it. Obviously he saw something in Jimmy that he thought was better than me."

Reasons McIlroy, "Alec was good, he had a fantastic shot on him, he had good feet, but Tommy was always one to improve the side, especially after that year." Buchan, as was his nature, didn't bother concerning himself with the situation: "I don't know what was behind The Doc's thinking, and I never challenged it. It wasn't my job to do that. You see, a football captain is not like a cricket captain. In cricket the captain has a lot more say in things, he's involved in the selection of the team. I was never asked what I thought, who should be playing, and more important, I would never presume to offer an opinion unless asked."

Though born in Hamilton, Canada, on February 28 1956, Nicholl was raised in Northern Ireland. "When I was growing up in Belfast, it was Man United and Liverpool," he says of the footballing loyalties of the kids in that city. "I would say it was half-and-half on the estate where I grew up." Nicholl himself was a Manchester United fan: "That was from the very start with the Geordie Best connection and then once they won the European Cup, that was it: straight out in the streets and everybody had their own player. I remember it vividly, everybody in our house in Belfast just watching the game, and straight onto the grass up the park and just re-living the dream. Of course then Sammy Mac went." Nicholl followed in the footsteps of Best and McIlroy when spotted by the same man who had recognised their talents, Bob Bishop. Nicholl: "I was playing for the 7th Newtownabbey Boys' Brigade and I was only 14. I was playing for my boys club on Saturday morning and then I was supposed to play for the juniors on Saturday afternoon but one of the senior players got injured and I was told I would go and have to report for seniors. We were playing away and Bob Bishop was at the game and it was very fortunate I was playing that day because at half-time our BB captain says, 'There's a fella here who wants to speak to you and he's a Manchester United scout.' First of all [Bishop] said, 'Are you with anybody, have you signed any papers?' I said, 'No.' He says would you like to go to Man United on trial?' He took my details, name and address. We had no phones in them days – we hadn't anyway. And then he came to the house and spoke to my mum and dad and that was it. I signed the form that night. That would have been 1970. I went for a few trials with Abbey. It was just a process of elimination. I finally got chosen to be an apprentice. Frank O'Farrell was the manager then." When he signed terms, Nicholl wasn't playing in the full-back role for which he would become known: "I was midfield for some of the time at my school and I was centre-half as well. I was centre-half-come-sweeper in the youth team at Man United and then, even in the reserves when I was breaking through, a few times I played in the middle of the park." He remembers those reserve-team games fondly: "I remember playing with George Graham and Jim McCalliog and all these. It was a great education. Tommy Docherty, he'd brought all these older players to try and avoid relegation but when they got relegated they were still at the club with the reserves 'cos he was bringing in all the younger ones."

With the centre-half position in United's team well and truly taken, Nicholl was groomed for a new role: "Three or four weeks I played in the reserves and Frankie Blunstone would do a wee bit of work with me after training. I didn't realise what they were doing until he says, 'That's it, you've got to start thinking as a full-back now because you won't get in before Martin Buchan.' In order to get in the first team I had to go and change positions. If I had been at any other club, I think my career would have been in that Martin Buchan sort of role. Not heading balls like big Jim Holton and McQueen but just playing at centre-half and reading the game and tidying up and sweeping and passing."

Nicholl credits Docherty for being prepared to give youth a chance. "One of the joys of growing up at The Cliff was going to the notice board on the Friday and then looking to see what squad you were in," he says. "You could be in the 'A' team or the reserves but you could be in the first-team squad. You just didn't know until that Friday. It was great. If a fella in the first team wasn't doing it, you were in. You can't say that too often about a manager." Not that Nicholl was blind to a fault in Docherty that many who admired him failed to pick up on. Nicholl: "Tommy Doc liked conflict with senior players. I knew it was happening ... I always find it difficult if I'm raving and enthusing over The Doc. I'm probably being selfish because he's been good for me, but he probably liked nothing more than a fight with the senior players." Having said that, he points out, "I never, ever felt going out on Saturday that players weren't playing for him."

Many managers would be very happy to have the dilemma of having to choose between two such quality full-backs as Forsyth and Nicholl and many managers would have inclined toward Forsyth on the grounds of the Scotsman's versatility but Docherty was less impressed by his two-footedness, dead-ball prowess and dribbling abilities than Nicholl's talents, which also included two-footedness as well as good aerial abilities, good passing and – once those early hiccups were over with – a general unflappability. Nicholl's combination of red hair and footballing wiliness would earn him the nickname 'the Fox'. That wiliness quickly got him noticed. His precocious gifts led to the Canadian footballing authorities sounding him out about whether he wanted to play international football for them but Nicholl unsurprisingly opted for an international career in a green shirt. His first full cap came in October 1976 in a match in which in a perfectly symmetrical example of fantasy-turned-reality, he found himself lining up alongside his former idol George Best, who was making his return to international football.

\*\*\*

In the week before the start of the season, Docherty told the press that he wanted to hear less chatter about brighter football and see more of it. "Talk is cheap and there has been a lot of it," he said. "It's what happens on the field that's important. And the time comes around on Saturday for the talking to stop and for clubs to practise what they preach." Of the promises he had heard from fellow managers to deploy attacking football and from the football authorities about clamping down on foul play, he said, "I just can't shake off that feeling that I've heard it all before." Asked if his own team's attacking style would be quite so effective in this campaign now that the opposing teams knew what to expect, he said, "They know what to expect from us but they themselves have got to do something about it. They have got to attack as well or run the risk of emptying their stadiums. Despite all the talk about entertainment and adventure, I have the feeling it will be the same as last year, with just a few clubs really going out and doing something positive to achieve those things."

Asked if there was there any thought about tempering the attacking style in this season so as to concede fewer goals, McIlroy says, "No, no, no. We went out and played. We went to play the entertaining [football] and score more goals than the opposition. That's the way we were. That's the way we wanted to do it as players. We didn't want to be held back ... The boss just said, 'Listen, do what you're doing, that's what's got you where you've got. Don't change. This time you'll learn to wrap things up with a little bit more experience'." For Blunstone, the question – because of the fact of Docherty being in his eyes a great motivator, not a great coach – is sort of irrelevant. "I don't think he'd go and say 'We're going to defend more', because I don't think he'd know how to do that," he says.

***

Waldron was not surprised to start the season in the reserves. He was, though, surprised by what he saw on the day of the first game: "I get to Old Trafford at 10 o'clock in the morning to travel with the reserves. There's 10,000 people outside and you see your Rome supporters club, Belfast, Oslo, from all over the bleeding world. I'm thinking, 'This is unbelievable.' A huge club. None bigger, I don't think." While a gobsmacked Waldron travelled to Derby on that Saturday August 21, the first team had a home match against Birmingham City. United's line-up was Alex Stepney, Jimmy Nicholl, Stewart Houston, Gerry Daly Brian Greenhoff, Martin Buchan, Steve Coppell, Sammy McIlroy, Stuart Pearson, Lou Macari and Gordon Hill. Alex Forsyth was the only starting-XI absentee from the roll call that had become so familiar to the Stretford End the previous season. Tongues would also have tripped when reaching the 12th man, for where the roll call rhythm would usually culminate in the name of David McCreery, instead there was a name alien by its unfamiliarity, that of Alan Foggon, who came on in the 78th minute. Though the right-back position was occupied by a relatively unfamiliar face, the face in the goalkeeper's position couldn't be more recognizable. Over the blistering summer of the close season, Alex Stepney, who had thought during the previous campaign that he was living on borrowed time, felt his relationship with Docherty had stabilised and he started 1976/77 as first-choice goalkeeper.

The match was watched by what was predictably the day's biggest attendance, 58,898. A more than lively first-half contained all four of the fixture's goals. It was Birmingham who opened the scoring with a free-kick on 16 minutes. However, the run of the play was always with United. Four minutes after that opener, a McIlroy corner found Coppell who executed a powerful, close-range shot into the back of the opposition net. On 29 minutes, a thumping Pearson header put United into the lead. Just before the interval, though, the visitors secured the psychological fillip of going in for their oranges on level terms: a shot by Burns was deflected into the net by a hapless Nicholl, who seemed to be continuing the habit of failing to justify Docherty's preference of him over Forsyth.

It was amazing to those watching that United didn't win. Docherty admitted afterwards that his team wasted several chances. Pearson meanwhile was aggrieved that what he and many in the crowd felt was a winner was disallowed: he was insistent that his 75th-minute header was a foot over the line before being scrambled to safety. On a bad-luck day for the striker, another of his efforts hit the bar. Following the day's results, the meaningless and imaginary start-of-season table (made more meaningless by the fact that neither Leeds nor Liverpool played today) saw United occupy 12th position.

On the Monday after the season opener, Docherty went to see United's reserves play against Coventry. Though he was a frequent presence at reserve matches, he had a specific job to perform this evening, namely to watch Jim Holton embark on his second comeback from a broken leg. Holton had spent the close season in America. The 16 games he had played for Miami Torus had convinced him that he was on the brink of a return to the first team. He told a reporter just before the season began, "I feel better than at any time since my bad luck began when I first broke a leg. I am enjoying my football again and I want to fight my way back." Holton, though, was due for heartbreak when Docherty told him after the match that he was no longer part of his plans. Blunstone: "He was still determined and still a good tackler, but you lose a bit of pace. I broke my leg twice playing, and when you come back, I don't care what you say, you lose a bit of pace." "I think this sort of parallels the Jaap Stam situation," Buchan says, referring to the Manchester United defender whom Alex Ferguson peremptorily sold in 2001, ostensibly for making allegations about misconduct by Ferguson in his autobiography. "I think the Jaap Stam book business was a smokescreen. I think the club genuinely felt that he was never going to be the player he was after his injury. That's my take on it, and I think it was probably the same with Jim." Meek concurs about The Doc's rationale with Holton: "I think Docherty felt he'd lost something with the injury and he wasn't the player he was." Did he agree? Meek: "Yes, I probably did."

Docherty himself has said that he was mindful of the fact that Greenhoff and Buchan had built up a good understanding in central defence during Holton's absence and, with the recent signing of Waldron, he felt he had in him and the so-far untested but promising Steve Paterson adequate cover should either Greenhoff or Buchan be injured. "Whilst he had been out injured, we had developed a different way of playing at the back, which was more mobile a game than he was suited to," Docherty said of Holton. One wonders whether there was an additional issue in Docherty's mind. He has admitted that he was "proud" to have been in charge of players with such a good disciplinary record that they were clear winners of the Fair Play League. Would it have crossed his mind that he didn't really want to go back to the type of match report in which it was asserted that United were "a very difficult team to love these days"?

Whatever the reason for Docherty's decision to inform Holton he was superfluous to his requirements, David Meek found his attitude toward the situation so objectionable that he actually remonstrated with the manager. "He told me he was going to 'get rid' of Jim Holton," says Meek. "I said, 'You're talking about one of the most popular players at this club among the fans. Just because he's had a broken leg and you're ready to pass him on, you can't talk about getting rid of him in terms like that. It's insensitive and it'll upset the fans, never mind Jim Holton.' But that was his style. Not to put too fine a point on it, he was a bit ignorant when it came to that side of things. Docherty is ... not a very sensitive soul and when a player's usefulness to him is over, he's downright ruthless and cruel. If he's decided the player's no more use to him, despite what he might have done, his loyalty and achievements, he boots him out." And Docherty's response to his remonstration? "His reaction was to say, 'Oh, you can't get soft with players. They'd steal the milk out of your tea and then come back for the sugar'."

\*\*\*

On Tuesday August 24, the Reds' first team played Coventry at Highfield Road. The team that took to the pitch was unchanged, though McCreery replaced Foggon as sub. The gate was 26,775. The game was one of contrasting footballing philosophies, the positivity of United juxtaposed by the ugly tactics of the home side. Coventry proved dangerous on the break but played five at the back and scythed down players who ran with the ball.

On 19 minutes, Macari smacked home from four yards. Perhaps an equaliser would have afforded the home side a sense of comfort that would have made them quit with the rough stuff, but seven minutes into the second-half their continued nastiness saw them reduced to ten men. On 65 minutes, United got the second goal their silky play deserved. Hill jinked his way down the wing and sent in an angled shot that Blyth got his hand to but couldn't prevent rifling into the back of the net. In a peculiar move, well before the days when substitution was employed to eat up time, Hill was replaced two minutes before the end. The 2-0 victory left United in third position. Notional though such a table was no doubt some who had mocked their title pretensions when early results had seen them flying high the previous season now hesitated before doing the same this time around.

The following Saturday, August 28, an unchanged Reds visited the Baseball Ground, which contained 34,054 for the occasion. Derby paid the Reds the compliment of playing five at the back to counter their four-man strike-force. Their own star striker Kevin Hector was out. Nonetheless, a good game ensued, even if Stepney only had to strain three times. Afterwards, Derby manager Dave Mackay had to concede that the offside decision that disallowed a goal from a Daly 20-yard free-kick was wrong. Fate gave Derby their own grievance to nurture on 70 minutes when a Rioch effort seemed to be blocked by McIlroy more with his arm than shoulder. The Irishman probably wasn't inclined to agonise about the legality of his clearance considering the brutality he'd suffered at the hands and feet of Rioch the last time they had shared a park. The match ended goalless, with a solid performance from Jimmy Nicholl cited by at least one reporter as a reason for the Reds keeping a clean sheet. United dropped a place in the table following the final whistle, although, emphasising the lack of import to be read into tables at this stage of the campaign, the top nine teams (of which Aston Villa were first) were all on four points.

United's second-round League Cup match on Wednesday September 1 saw the first team make their debut appearance under Old Trafford's new floodlight system. (The reserves had already enjoyed the privilege of playing under the new lights – installed at a cost of £50,000 in the close season – in their recent Central League fixture against Coventry.) After the Derby County match, reporter Bob Russell had opined of United, "With so many outlets, it's inevitable that the goal-flow will resume shortly – possibly with a League Cup flood against Tranmere at Old Trafford on Wednesday." A cigar for Mr. Russell. The demolition job by a United whose starting XI was once again unchanged was made all the more remarkable by the fact that Tranmere were inordinately determined to keep the scoreline as low as possible. As his ex-employers, the club were cognizant of just what a danger the United right-winger was. Consequently, Coppell was marked suffocatingly tightly. This in combination with some surprisingly nimble football from the Third Division side meant that when the whistle blew for the interval, the minnows had ensured that they were goallessly level-pegging with the giants.

Though much has been made of Docherty's off-the-cuff football, as proven again today when the occasion demanded it The Doc was able to do more than tell his players to go out and enjoy themselves. At half-time, he moved decisively and quickly: he told McIlroy and Coppell to swap places for the second-half. Tranmere were completely bamboozled. United triumphantly exploited the opposition's confusion, banging home five goals in the space of 30 minutes. Daly started the spree on 54 minutes with a crafty lob from 20 yards and provided the *coup de grace* in the 85th minute by sending substitute McCreery's flick-on of Hill's cross into the net. Between those Gerry-built bookends came strikes from Macari (a low shot from outside the area on 55 minutes), Pearson (stabbing home a block of a Coppell effort in the 63rd minute) and Hill (converting a Macari pass on 80 minutes). When the visitors retreated to lick their wounds after the final whistle, the only thing with which they could console themselves was a nice pay-day: in an age where away sides took a cut of the home gate receipts, there was a considerable amount to divvy up from the admission fees of the 37,586 crowd.

It goes without saying that United were unchanged for their visit to White Hart Lane the following Saturday, September 4. The day before, Docherty – clearly still ebullient after the League Cup match – told a reporter of the imminent League fixture, "Unless we do something really stupid, nobody can beat us." From the opening whistle, United took up where they had left off against the hapless Tranmere. Spurs manager Keith Burkinshaw said after the game that his team were merely "making up the numbers" in the first-half. Not only was Coppell's wingwork superb today, but he opened the scoring with 17 minutes gone. Seven minutes later, Coppell sent in one of United's trademark low crosses. Pearson had to shoot twice but the outcome was a two-goal lead.

One match report that day implied that Docherty had instructed his young, rampant lions not to be complacent at half-time. If he did, his players did not appear to have taken note, for come the second-half they proceeded to do the "something really stupid" Docherty had plainly felt was not plausible the previous day. The massive crowd of 60,723 possibly proved United's undoing. The Red Army (which, considering Spurs' average home-gate was then 30,000, may have outnumbered the home supporters) kept urging their team on and, Docherty later opined, made his players feel obliged to be concerned less with possession than attack. There were other theories flying around after the match for United's second-half collapse – among them the fact that five of the Reds might have had international call-ups for midweek on their minds – but whatever the reason, United proceeded to amaze everybody present by throwing the match away. On 56 minutes, Ralph Coates swung in a corner which some observers claimed had gone directly in, George Best-style, but which others insisted had brushed the head of Martin Buchan. On the hour mark, Spurs equalised. In the 78th minute, John Pratt decided to unleash a speculative long-range effort. His 25-yard shot sailed past Stepney. The home team could even have made it four but Buchan – having a grisly day – brought down Neighbour when he was in a clear scoring position, though sanction there was none.

It was early enough in the season for Docherty to be able to exhibit a relatively relaxed attitude. "Spurs are away feeling better than the Great Train Robbers," he quipped. "That lot ended up with 30 years … Spurs got two points." However, it's perhaps the case that his true, probably shell-shocked, feelings about the 3-2 defeat were revealed in another comment that day: "I do not know what went wrong." United tumbled to eighth place after this bizarre result. Villa maintained their pole position on goal difference, a new system that had been introduced this season in place of goal average and which was not only less complicated to calculate than the old system but would in theory benefit teams like Docherty's United for the way its formula rewarded high-scoring teams.

On the other side of London on this day, incidentally, George Best made a return to English football. It wasn't in the top flight – he was turning out for Second Division Fulham – but few long-term Best fans could fail to be pleased by the performance put in at Craven Cottage by the man whom they had thought was lost to soccer forever (unless you counted his recent appearances in the gentler, some would say Toytown, environs of the North American Soccer League). Not only did Best prove he could still play, but he scored his side's only goal in a win against Bristol Rovers with a mind-boggling curling, low shot virtually from the touchline.

\*\*\*

The following Saturday, September 11, took United to St James's Park. Newcastle had sold 39,000 tickets but conditions were so miserable – high winds and approaching rain – that only 29,642 attended. United were unchanged except for their substitute. (Foggon – here instead of McCreery – got a cheer from the fans of his former team when he replaced Hill in the 73rd minute.)

On 13 minutes, the Reds' offside trap led to them conceding the first goal. United players froze in hesitation when a linesman flagged, but the referee concluded that the relevant player was not interfering with play, allowing Cannell to execute a diving header. United equalised four minutes later through Pearson. Nicholl – despite that own goal, recipient of good notices since the season's start – was involved in his team's second goal, which arrived on 32 minutes, although the main credit goes to Greenhoff, who on receiving the right-back's pass stepped forward and unleashed a 30-yard rising shot that hit the underside of the Newcastle crossbar before crossing the line. Burns equalised for Newcastle not long after half-time. The score remained at 2-2 until the final whistle, which saw the players dart almost comically quickly for the warmth and dry of the dressing rooms. United remained in eighth place in a table whose summit Liverpool had mounted, albeit only on goal difference.

\*\*\*

Those who ventured into Tommy Docherty's office at Old Trafford would often notice the pennants from foreign countries pinned up on his walls. The number had proliferated in the past couple of years as Manchester United had increasingly played matches against top continental sides. Not competitive matches, of course, as entry to European competition was dependent on trophies – and, in the case of the UEFA Cup, high final-table placings – that had lately been lacking at Manchester United. The friendlies that Docherty had ensured had regularly taken place with clubs from across the Channel was all part of a design by the manager. As the club who had pioneered English participation in European club competition, United – for Docherty, as well as many others – belonged in Europe. With their top-three placing in the League the previous season, United had finally earned the right to participate in that particular theatre of dreams again following an absence of eight years, their last European campaign being the 1968/69 attempt to retain the European Cup. Poetically, their return to European football with their participation in the UEFA Cup marked the 20th anniversary of their first European campaign.

For Docherty, though, merely being in Europe wasn't enough. The two-leg format of the rounds often engendered negative football, with clubs sometimes happy to accept low-scoring defeats away if they had done well, or felt they were going to, in front of their home crowd. The Doc insisted that United were not going to play that game. "I know you've heard it all before ... he said. "All the stuff about, 'We'll attack over there, not defend ...' Talk has proved cheap. But for us this is the big pay-off."

Players at English clubs of the era loved the European matches. It gave them the opportunity to take on opposition that was more challenging than they were used to, not just because by definition such tournaments feature the *crème de la crème* of the participating nations but because English football could in those days be characterised by a pedestrian quality that sophisticated continental sides often disdained. Another reason was the glamour associated with participation, whether it be because of the fact that all such matches took place at night and created the atmospheric thrill of floodlit football or because of the legendary names – names made more legendary by the exoticness conferred by foreignness – with whom they found themselves sharing a pitch. The fans clearly felt the same way about such matches. United's home games in the UEFA Cup this season – all midweek matches – attracted crowds of 59,000, several thousand above the attendance of a lot of Saturday domestic fixtures.

There were few club names more glamorous than the one with whom United's was paired for the first round of the UEFA Cup on Wednesday September 15: Ajax. Since the late 60s, the Amsterdam club had become synonymous with a revolutionary type of football, one which had been co-opted by the Dutch national team in recent years and with which that national side had come tantalisingly close to winning the World Cup in 1974: Total Football. Ajax's star had waned a little lately, particularly since the departure of their genius Johan Cruyff and other luminaries like Rep and Neeskens who had been at the epicentre of the swirling, all-hands-to-the-tiller nature of their play, but the aura they carried from having won the European Cup three years in succession from 1971 through 1973 was considerable to say the least. Docherty, who didn't normally have teams watched on the grounds that "I believe in imposing our style on them", took the precaution of making sure the Dutchmen were observed in action twice by Frank Blunstone in preparation for this match, explaining, "Ajax are new to us."

So precious was European football to Docherty that he was to be heard expressing his concerns before the match that the hooligan element might ruin it all for the club. UEFA had recently imposed sanctions on Leeds, Real Madrid and the Welsh national side over crowd disorder and The Doc was painfully aware that the consequences for United could be disastrous if even a few troublemakers got out of hand. "I therefore ask our fans to cheer and support us to the full, but to behave themselves," he said. "If we are beaten, they must accept defeat sportingly, as they did when Southampton pipped us in the Cup Final last May … The club have taken all possible precautions but if there is hooliganism, that could put us out of Europe. We could even get the situation where we might not have a second game at Old Trafford at all." Docherty also warned his own players to keep out of trouble on the pitch. "If they do get involved in anything serious, I will pull them off and put on a substitute. I am confident though that they will not get involved. They have been told to accept decisions and walk away from trouble."

The club precautions Docherty spoke of included only allowing sales of their 6,000 ticket allocation through the Supporters' Club and arranging transportation to Holland through approved travel agents. The warning went out that chartered coach and boat trips would be cancelled if there was any trouble on the journey over, while arrangements for the fans' speediest possible departure from Amsterdam had been put in place. These arrangements had been somewhat undermined, though, by Ajax themselves who had put the remaining 30,000 tickets on open sale. (Confusingly, the conflicting statistics for official attendance go no higher than 30,000.) The travelling United fans were isolated from the rest of the crowd, surrounded by 100 police.

The fact that United came away 1-0 losers after the first leg match in the Olympisch Stadium might indicate that Docherty was indeed talking cheap, such a scoreline being common for clubs playing away in Europe. However, the scoreline belied a brilliant performance by the visitors. United (playing in an all-blue strip redolent of their kit in the 1968 European Cup final) repeatedly swarmed around the Ajax goal: Macari hit a post, a Pearson effort was blocked on the line and the home side's goalie Piet Schrijvers had to pull off a series of impressive saves. One shot he didn't contain according to both Pearson (standing very close) and *Manchester Evening News* photographer Clive Cooksey was a powerful effort by Houston two minutes into the second-half: both claimed it crossed the line before he flipped it out. With the away-goals rule that dictated that strikes in foreign territory counted double in the event of an aggregate draw, it would have been invaluable. At the other end, a sweeping quintessentially Total Football move saw Ajax captain Rudi Krol score in the 42nd minute.

Though United were desperately unlucky not to come away with a draw, an ebullient Docherty was telling the Ajax president after the match that the Dutch side hadn't done enough. His tone was less gloating with the press: "I'm happy with the performance and satisfied with the result. I was surprised that Ajax played so defensively and if we had been a bit quicker we could have done so much more."

It was after this match that Sammy McIlroy took the extraordinary step of asking Docherty to drop him. The Irishman had had a below-average season thus far, certainly as far as his non-existent scoring was concerned. McIlroy said he felt he didn't deserve to be in the team, partly because he was conscious of the fact that front-line players Alan Foggon and David McCreery were unable to claim first-team places at the moment and might actually do better in that role. Mixed in with McIlroy's unhappiness was a feeling that he wasn't playing in his best position. The injury to Macari in the 1975/76 campaign which saw McIlroy dropping back in the formation had confirmed in the Irishman's mind a feeling he'd had ever since he had admiringly watched his team-mate Bobby Charlton spraying long passes across the field, namely that he wanted to be a midfielder. He had even begun to regret the spectacular start he had made to his career when he had scored three goals in his first five starts, because it has resulted in him being miscast as a striker. Though McIlroy reported that Docherty gave him a fair hearing, the manager seems to have been fairly unsympathetic otherwise. Docherty told McIlroy that though he agreed that midfield was his best place, the team was doing well and he was happy with McIlroy's own form and that he wasn't prepared to drop a player simply so he could feel happier about his own game. Accordingly, McIlroy was in the team for the next fixture against Middlesbrough. He was also still in the team, and fulfilling a striker's role, at the end of the month when he finally got on the scoresheet. Nonetheless, before long, as the fact that McIlroy was not one of life's natural goalscorers was increasingly exposed and as this contributed to a run of bad form for his club, McIlroy would get his wish granted for a switch in position.

*\*\**

United entertained Middlesbrough on Saturday September 18. The starting XI was the same for the 11th match in a row. However, though McCreery had come on against Ajax on Wednesday, Foggon was back as sub against what was another of his old clubs. Last Saturday's results had seen Jack Charlton's team, currently unbeaten, sitting in second position in the table.

Before the match, both Charlton and Docherty had been mouthing off to the press, as might be expected of two of the game's larger-than-life characters. This may have been the reason for both the rugged nature of the play and the vitriol aimed Charlton's way by parts of the 56,712 crowd (Old Trafford's lowest so far this season but still the biggest in English football that day). The home side proceeded to respond to their crowd's lust for all-out attack and the pressure brought a goal on 21 minutes, albeit an own goal: Houston thumped in a low cross that was so powerful that McAndrew, running back to cover, ended up helping it into his own net. On 76 minutes, Houston lofted a pass that seemed to leave 'Boro's defence frozen in indecision, a condition that could never be said to afflict Pearson, who sped through the middle and placed the ball beyond the advancing Platt. The 2-0 victory was a nice way for Stepney to celebrate his 34th birthday.

Afterwards, Charlton was unusually taciturn, simply stating in reference to the stick from the crowd, "I've had enough intimidation for one day." Some of his players were more forthcoming, defenders complaining to reporters of theatrical responses to challenges, especially from Hill. Docherty was also taciturn, though was clearly a far happier man than Charlton. "My players did the talking for me this time," he said. United's first home League victory of the season saw them climb to fifth in a table in which Middlesbrough had dropped to fourth. Liverpool were top, leading Manchester City by a point.

Just before United's third-round League Cup home match on Wednesday September 22, a story appeared in the papers stating that Jim Holton was in talks with their opponents in the tie, Sunderland, about moving there. Docherty said, "Jim is desperate for First Division football." He would need to be, for Sunderland were currently bottom of the table. Holton did indeed move across to Roker Park but, in what some might consider a semi-insult, Sunderland, apparently fearful of a recurrence of his injury problems, would initially only take Holton on loan. (The following month, Sunderland made the deal permanent with a £40,000 transfer fee.) Sunderland manager Bob Stokoe was honest enough to observe of the move, "It's no use kidding Jim that he's coming to the greatest club in the world, because he's probably just leaving it. But he is the type of ready-made top-flight player that I'm seeking." Perhaps it's poetic justice that Docherty's callous offloading of Holton would come back to haunt him, for there would be a point in the season when United desperately needed to both fill a hole in central defence and raise sagging morale. Notwithstanding the reservations expressed about Holton earlier in the text, Big Jim would have been just the ticket on both those counts.

Though Sunderland were propping up the division and United possessed home advantage, the Reds were unconvincing to say the least. United's starting XI was changed for the first time this season, with McCreery taking the place of an injured Coppell. On six minutes, the United fans in the 46,170 crowd who idolised Gordon Hill got an idea of why their hero could drive his colleagues to distraction. Inhabiting his own penalty-area, he revealed himself as completely out of his element, firstly by ignoring a shout from Stepney and then by engaging in play with Buchan that resulted in United losing possession. Sunderland's Ray Train was on hand to grab an early and unexpectedly gifted lead for his team. Accusing faces and disgusted voices lambasted Hill from both the field and the dugout. Merlin, used to more adulatory noises, seemed shaken and was a subdued presence on the pitch for the remainder of the match. United obtained an equaliser after 10 minutes via Pearson, lurking at the far post for a corner. An upset seemed on the cards when Sunderland went ahead in the 79th minute and United began to panic. Their equaliser came in the nick of time and by farcical good fortune. McCreery's 87th-minute cross was put in his own net by Jeff Clarke as he stretched to block it.

Maine Road was United's destination the following Saturday, September 25. A recovered Coppell reclaimed his place in the starting line-up and McCreery returned to the bench. However, the sub wasn't there long: Pearson had to hobble off with a damaged thigh muscle after 13 minutes. McCreery was one of the Reds' outstanding players, as was Hill who – apparently determined to make up for the fiasco in midweek – dazzled, refusing to rein in his dribbling despite the rough treatment by City defenders, including Tommy Docherty's son Mick. (The Doc opined afterwards that the "boy" was lucky not to get sent off – or, as it would come to be known from October when a new system for demonstrating sanction was introduced in the Football League, 'red-carded').

City struck first when Brian Kidd – now back playing football in his home town – crossed in the seventh minute and saw Tueart stoop to nod it over the line. Coppell equalised on the quarter-hour mark. 10 minutes later, McCreery poked the ball home. On 68 minutes, City were convinced they had scored an equaliser but the relevant linesman insisted that Buchan – lying on the ground – had hooked the ball away before it crossed the line. Not even the *Match of the Day* cameras were able to resolve the dispute. On 70 minutes, United delighted their supporters in the 48,861 crowd when they flicked the ball around beautifully to set up their third, the sphere making its way from Hill to Macari back to Hill to Daly, and the latter slicing it past Joe Corrigan. Only a block by Doyle on the line from McIlroy stopped the visitors scoring a fourth. Not only had City been unbeaten in the League thus far, but the 3-1 victory was United's first win at Maine Road in five years. The result sent United up to third place, a point behind Liverpool and Middlesbrough.

*\*\*\**

It turned out that the knock Pearson picked up against City was serious enough to rule him out of Ajax's visit for the second-leg UEFA Cup match on Wednesday September 29. Discounting the loss of Coppell for the Sunderland League Cup tie, this was the first of several injuries to key players that would plague Manchester United up to Christmas. Macari meanwhile was only playing at his own insistence: after the derby he had had a double X-ray. Coppell was also on the pitch despite not being 100% fit. Docherty put the ever dependable McCreery on in Pancho's place.

Shrugging off his discomfort, Macari got the opening goal of the game with a poacher's effort. However, the fact that that goal didn't come until the 43rd minute was a worrying development for the Reds. Even if Ajax lost 2-1 on the night, the away goals rule would put them into the second round. On 60 minutes, Docherty made another of the canny tactical decisions that seem to give the lie to the idea that he had little or no organisational ability. He took off Daly and replaced him with Arthur Albiston, ordering the young defender to take over from Houston at left-back, with the latter moving into Brian Greenhoff's central-defensive role. Greenhoff in turn was told to play upfront. The reorganisation seemed to work and five minutes after it was instigated Greenhoff was at the heart of the second United goal. Working with Coppell, he found McIlroy who eased the ball into the Ajax net.

Hill took a knock and Docherty took advantage of the extra substitute allowed in European competition to replace him with Paterson with 20 minutes to go. Buchan later admitted that the second-half was "very tense" for a United *au fait* with the fact that one mistake could lead to Ajax grabbing that vital deciding away-goal but – with the aid of some excellent goalkeeping from Stepney – they kept the score at 2-0 for the rest of the match.

Afterwards, Docherty described Greenhoff as the best player on the park. He said, "Of course, he came to us as a midfield player and it does him good to have a run there once in a while." Greenhoff exhibited no particular desire to stay in midfield after the match. "I have won my England caps so far as a defender and I think that is where I play best," he said. "I didn't know until I saw Gerry Daly being called off that I was going to be moved upfront. Nothing was said at half-time. All I know is that I finished the game completely whacked." Buchan's nomination for man of the match was Macari. Either way, it was an impressive victory over a top foreign side and set up a second-round clash with another legendary club, Juventus of Italy, who had just put out Manchester City. Docherty seemed to be implying that there were reasons to be extremely optimistic about United's future progress in the tournament when he said, "I don't think we will meet a better team than Ajax in the UEFA Cup this season."

The massive crowd of 58,918 guaranteed United a bonanza of £80,000, something that went nicely with the announcement at the club's annual shareholders' meeting that week that they had made a record profit the previous year of £301,438.

***

Saturday October 2 saw United visit Elland Road. The Reds' line-up was Stepney, Nicholl, Houston, Daly, Greenhoff, Buchan, Coppell, McIlroy, Pearson, Macari, Hill. Leeds were currently at the bottom of the table and with Billy Bremner and Johnny Giles no longer part of the set-up, the Revie era was clearly passing into history. Even so, every one of their players today was a full international.

Things started happily for the visitors, so happily that after only nine minutes the away terraces were resounding to the sarcastic chant of "There's only one United." Some people in the 44,512 crowd were still finding their seats when Daly put the Reds ahead with a spectacular 18-yard volley with five minutes gone. Within four minutes, the Reds were two-up courtesy of Coppell. Two minutes later, McIlroy almost got one himself but after breaking clear he was no doubt confirmed in his own mind of his goal jinx by missing. The rout that all this seemed to presage didn't quite happen, but the 2-0 victory left United on top of the table for the first time this season, albeit only on goal difference over Manchester City, Liverpool and Middlesbrough, who also had 11 points.

Afterwards, Docherty claimed that thanks to the attentions of the Leeds men Pearson and Macari were doubtful for the next match and that Coppell, Greenhoff and Houston also needed medical attention. He fulminated, "I fear for the image of the game. Unless we do something we will drive people away. There had been a lot of talk about a clean-up but nothing has happened. I'm making a plea to the authorities to issue a new directive to referees. This season only two have given us any protection. But this concerns everybody, not just Manchester United."

Leeds manager Jimmy Armfield was dismissive of Docherty's complaints, but the following Monday, October 4, did indeed see a severely weakened United team take to the pitch at Roker Park for the replay of the third-round League Cup tie against Sunderland. The Reds – playing their third match in six days – were without Pearson and Macari. They were also up against a team that included the newly signed Jim Holton, who no doubt felt he had a point to prove to The Doc. Docherty was warning fans not to expect much. This might have been kidology but when United went a goal down in the second minute from a penalty and then Greenhoff had to be taken off with an injury 15 minutes into the second-half, even the manager must have been inclined to write off the League Cup for this season.

At the start, Brian Greenhoff was played as a striker, with Colin Waldron given his United debut in Greenhoff's normal position. McCreery also got a place in the starting line-up and in the front line. Greenhoff worked well enough in his makeshift position to score the equaliser before he departed, even if his long-range effort on 50 minutes was actually a cross that the Sunderland goalie and a defender each thought the other was going to deal with. But Sunderland seemed to have settled the match in the 87th minute when Ray Train fired home. Needing only to hold it steady for three minutes, however, a Sunderland player dismayed the home support in the 30,831 crowd with a moment of madness when he dealt with a shot from Daly with his hand. That player was Alan Foggon, who only two months after he had joined

United following that trans-Atlantic dash for his services and following just three substitute appearances, had been sold by Docherty for £30,000 (admittedly, a profit of £3,000–£5,000). Daly stepped up for his first penalty-kick of the season and did his usual clinical job. Extra-time was now required. Things were still deadlocked after the additional 30 minutes. To compound a tiring schedule for the Reds, the second replay was set for two days' time.

The occasion of Waldron's first match for United is probably a good time to discuss Waldron's impressions of a club he had previously analysed from the outside. "The team that I joined in '76 was a bloody good side," he says. "Man United were balanced. They had the two wingers Coppell and Hill, one left-footed, one right-footed, both had good skill, both had engines and both would run their socks off for you. When they were going forward there were four forwards, it was 4-2-4. As soon as they lost it, back into midfield, 4-4-2. Difficult to beat. They had Lou Macari upfront with Stuart Pearson: Little and Large. They'd good defenders. I was a defender and I'm not being biased, I think if you look at any great team that wins championships they win it on the back four. The left-back was Stewart Houston, who was all left peg, the right back was all right peg, Forsyth. He wasn't a great defender Alex, but he could put the boot in. Your two central defenders complemented each other very, very well. Brian Greenhoff could play a little bit and liked to go on runs. Martin Buchan was extremely quick and could leave a boot in if he wanted to. Christ, they were a cohesive unit."

Waldron had been used to being captain of the clubs he played for but of course now found himself taking directions from a skipper himself. He was both bemused and impressed by Martin Buchan. "He wasn't what I'd call a popular captain," he says. "If players had thought of me what they thought of Martin I'd have been a bit concerned. He was a complete loner, an intellectual, a clever lad. I had no problems with him. I found him a nice lad, and I found I could talk to the lad, but that wasn't the case with a lot of the other players … I had a lot of time for this lad. And he was a man of high morals and decency." However much he was bemused by the concept of a skipper who was not one of the boys, Waldron was impressed by his footballing skills: "You put a ball at Martin's feet and he wasn't a great passer of the ball or a user of the ball, but he was an excellent defender, great pace, which got him out of an awful lot of trouble and covered other people. He was a lad with an immense amount of confidence in whatever he did. I think he was so confident in his ability that he felt he could take chances. If he did get caught, his pace would pull him out again." Of Stepney, with whom he roomed, Waldron opines, "One thing I've always wanted from a goalkeeper is a mouth, shouting whatever, and Alex could shout with the best of 'em. He was fabulous to play in front of."

Waldron found the training methods at United different to what he was used to: "I've been at nine clubs and the training at Burnley was beyond belief, ahead of its time. But when I went to United it was more or less play with the ball, lots of skill or whatever." He adds, "They had us doing time and time again getting to the byline, like Coppell and Hill did, but when you get there, you weren't allowed to look up, you had to smash the ball across and it couldn't go above four feet from the ground, because if you did you had to do it again. You'd have Tommy Cavanagh there shouting, and the word he used was 'Violence'. You had to kick this ball with *violence* and smash it across." He says this was, " ... quite an effective training system for the formation that you'd got. As a defender, as a six-foot defender, I would want the ball lobbed up in the air because I were going to kill it. I didn't want the ball coming at 50-mile-an-hour a foot from the deck, when it could have gone anywhere." Isn't the approach of randomly hitting in a low ball as opposed to a flight toward a specific head something of a crapshoot? Waldron: "Well, it is and it isn't. It depends on how much room you've got. Let me tell you, if it becomes a crapshoot, I don't want a crapshoot in my box, I want it lifted safely up in the air so I know where it's going. I can see it. When it comes in like a ping-pong it can go anywhere."

\*\*\*

Docherty had Macari – who passed a late fitness test – back for the second replay of the Sunderland League Cup tie at Old Trafford on Wednesday October 6. Greenhoff dropped back into his usual position, displacing Waldron. At least initially.

A healthy crowd of 47,689 indicated that the Reds' fans were not losing interest in this marathon tie, but things remained at an impasse until seven minutes into the second-half, Docherty decided a fresh player was needed to spark something. Hill was taken off. Substitute Arthur Albiston occupied Hill's outside-left position for a few minutes before being instructed to fill the left-back role with which he was familiar. Stewart Houston moved into central defence, allowing Brian Greenhoff in turn to occupy the midfield. Ajax had been similarly confused by such switching. Docherty must have felt more than the usual happiness at his side scoring when the scorer of the only goal of the game turned out to be none other than Greenhoff. It was in truth against the run of play but United could perhaps claim that they deserved the 1-0 victory purely on perseverance over a series of matches in which Sunderland had led four times and United just once.

After an exhausting six matches in 15 days, international fixtures saw United get a 10-day break from competition, although of course some of their men were playing for their countries in this period. United's next match was on Saturday October 16 when they visited the Hawthorns for a League fixture against West Bromwich Albion. Pearson was able to reclaim his place from McCreery but just as United got back their star striker, they lost a player further back in the formation who may not have had a striker's glamour but whom events would prove to be far more crucial to the success of the side. Martin Buchan had torn a thigh muscle playing for Scotland in Prague in midweek and would miss both this match and the next ten fixtures. Waldron took his place today.

The opposition's manager had also been on international duty in midweek, which is not the sort of sentence that crops up very often. The boss of West Brom was Johnny Giles, who had departed Leeds United to take up a player-manager's role for the Baggies. Also playing for West Brom today was Mick Martin, who had thrived at the Hawthorns after leaving Old Trafford. "John would get more out of me because he showed an interest in me," says Martin. He also admits that he was motivated to prove his worth to his ex-boss in his performance. As if understanding this, Giles made Martin captain today.

Giles set the perfect example for his team on six minutes with a 25-yard shot that gave him his first home goal for his club. His team of ageing pros and journeymen then began to tear the visitors apart. Symptomatic of United's disastrous day was the fact that when they seemed to have been offered a way back into the match in the 25th minute, Gerry Daly proceeded to miss a penalty for the first and only time in his career at the club. Ray Treacy had signalled to West Brom goalie John Osborne to dive to his left, his insight possibly due to the fact that he and Daly were fellow Eire internationals.

The substitution of Macari for McCreery made no difference and parts of the Red Army in the 38,037 crowd – already reduced to a very low decibel level – began streaming away before West Brom scored their fourth and final goal. United's players must have wished that departing the scene of their misery was as easy. Recalls Waldron, "It was just one of those days where everything went wrong and we were out-battled in every department. I don't think we ever looked like scoring. 'Four-nil drubbing' about summed it up." Afterwards, Docherty revealed, "With 10 minutes left, Tommy Cavanagh said he wished we could get a goal. I simply said I wished we could get a shot." Docherty baldly stated that it was the worst performance since he had become United manager. It wasn't the worst scoreline; it shared that 'honour' with the League Cup defeat by Manchester City last season. Curiously, though, both those 4-0 losses took place well after Docherty's United had turned the corner: even in their relegation season United had not experienced such a whitewash. The result saw the Reds plummet to eighth place. Liverpool were back on top on goal difference.

That United should be beaten so comprehensively in the first match of the season in which Buchan did not participate was symbolic. His eleven-match absence was a run that coincided with a collapse in United's League form (although, curiously, not their cup form, at least initially). It was a situation United had not known since Buchan's arrival: incredibly, he had previously missed just one match in the four-and-a-half years since his move to Old Trafford. Blunstone: "A lot of people didn't realise how good he was. He was so decisive. He read the game well. When he tackled, he won the ball nine times out of 10, and that is a class player. When they get injured, you miss them. You just don't get another Martin Buchan." However, he adds, "To lose a player of his ability is a blow, but one man doesn't make a team so there's no excuse. We just went down. They just didn't play."

It being the case, as Blunstone points out, that no team should fall to pieces because, an individual player, no matter how talented, isn't match-fit, this disastrous spell would seem to prove the assertion of some that Docherty's United were only a great team on the surface, that they were guilty of an essential flimsiness as a consequence of a severe weakness in squad depth. Further evidence of this is provided by the fact that Docherty tried a variety of different players in Buchan's position over the following couple of months – Waldron, Houston, Paterson and Greenhoff – and none of them was able to stop the goals flooding into the United net and the defeats piling up.

One wonders whether this was all due to Docherty's propensity to move players on once they weren't making the team and investing his faith in players coming through a youth system whose qualities – of which he was publicly known to boast – he was mistaken about. The season might have turned out very differently for United if, for instance, they were able to plug the gap left by Buchan with Jim Holton. One also wonders whether Docherty's faith in the youth system stemmed from a desire to prove himself in the same class as Matt Busby, whose reputation was to a large part founded on the way he had nurtured players from promising kids into superstars. Though Frank Blunstone's boys won the Blue Star International Youth Tournament in 1976, in terms of talented players making the graduation from junior and reserve teams to first team, history has shown that Docherty's youth system was largely mediocre. Docherty's placing so much stock in it may have fatally undermined United at this juncture.

Frank Blunstone seemed to admit the manpower-related fragility of United's capacity for success when he was interviewed at the end of the season. He said, "There's a thin line between success and failure and if injury took away Martin Buchan or Lou Macari, it would be hard to bear ... " He now says, "There wasn't the players coming through. There's nobody in the reserves could have come through and played. I agree he sold 'em too quick. Tommy, if something happens, [is] very quick to make his mind up and do things. A bit too hasty at times." Waldron is in no doubt about the threadbare nature of United's squad at the time. "We hadn't got strength in depth," he states. "We had a bunch of kids. Very few of them actually made it. Chick McCreery had a reasonably good career. Arthur Albiston had a really good career. They were the two squad players that you could probably count on. Dave McCreery a bit lightweight, Arthur would have been fine. After that, Paterson was never going to make it ever, and I can't remember any other names. Nichols [sic] had a decent career ... The reserves had a lot of young players clearly destined for the lower divisions and I think that reflected in the League form. Every time you had got a hiccup with an injury, you're going to struggle a little bit."

***

The following Wednesday, October 20, saw United entertain Juventus at Old Trafford for the first leg of their second-round UEFA Cup tie. This time out, Docherty tried plugging the Buchan-sized hole with Houston, Albiston coming in to take Houston's normal place. United were otherwise unchanged.

For Blunstone, Docherty's pronouncement that United were unlikely to meet a team superior to Ajax after the previous round was incorrect. "Juventus were a better side," he says. "Juventus had bloody six internationals in their team." Of course, United had more internationals in their team, but the point Blunstone is making is that those Juventus internationals were all in the top-rated Italian national side, not spread across the teams of the four countries of the United Kingdom, some of whom could not afford to be too fussy about who they picked. In any case, a prediction by The Doc of relatively easy progress by his team based on not meeting a side equal to Ajax seems naïve, for superior skill is not always what football is about. When United met the Italians, they quickly found out that some teams weren't interested in Total Football, or even, on occasion, football at all. Blunstone: "The Italians were up to their tricks, spit at you and all sorts." Juventus were at times brutal. Having already dispensed with Manchester City in the tournament, they weren't going to be intimidated by a tie with City's neighbours, nor were they about to feel obliged to abandon their win-at-all-costs *modus operandi* in the face of United's celebrated positive footballing values. Even a crowd of 59,000 didn't faze the visitors.

Coppell later recalled that when Docherty warned his charges before the match that every trick in the book would be used against them, he had been slightly dismissive. Though not unaware of the reputation for gamesmanship of Italian sides, Coppell felt as a player who enjoyed running at full-backs that there couldn't be much he didn't know about defenders' tactics. He discovered how wrong he was in the opening minutes when United got their first corner. He took up his usual position at the near post and was hardly surprised that his marker, Marco Tardelli, followed him. However, he *was* surprised when Tardelli proceeded to stand on his foot and grind his studs into his instep. Instinctively, Coppell pushed the defender away – and was astonished when Tardelli collapsed to the ground in paroxysms of fake agony. The referee came over and Tardelli protested to him, whereupon the astounded Coppell found himself being sternly admonished. Throughout the rest of the match, whenever Coppell backed into Tardelli, the Italian spitefully pinched Coppell's flanks.

Juventus' grim, take-no-prisoners approach, though, belied genuine talent, individual and collective, which could have given them one or even two potentially devastating away goals when the match was still less than 20 minutes old. The sole goal of the game, though, came from Gordon Hill. It was only fitting. Juventus coach Giovanni Trappattoni conceded of Merlin after the match, "Sometimes there were three or four of my men on him but still he got through. A very clever player indeed." With 31 minutes gone, Merlin performed a shot that was special even for his brand of magic. Says Hill, "A player called Cuccureddu was marking me. I went into the middle of the box because I knew the corner was coming over and at the last moment he was still in the box. I'd pulled out about three yards and the ball dropped and I hit it smack on the volley, and it was straight into the left-hand side of the goal and it was like – *whoo*." An Exocet of a strike, clean and powerful, even the great keeper Dino Zoff was helpless to keep it out.

The visitors were more restrained in the second-half, not wanting to incur a sending off. They settled into defensive mode, allowing United to attack them but absorbing everything they threw at them. Though Coppell hit a post and a free-kick from Houston sizzled tantalisingly wide, and though Docherty pulled off Daly in favour of McCreery on 58 minutes, the Reds were unable to improve on their one goal and Greenhoff later admitted, "We had tried everything and were running out of ideas."

Juventus might have lost the game but it could not necessarily be inferred that they were unhappy with the 1-0 defeat. As the final whistle blew, unused substitute Colin Waldron followed the match players into the tunnel. He was surprised by the sight he beheld there. "They were going down the tunnel jumping up and down and throwing their arms in the air," he says of the Juventus team, "and I couldn't understand. They'd got beat one-nil and they were treating it like a massive victory."

\*\*\*

That week, Docherty delved into the transfer market, signing 21-year-old winger Chris McGrath from Spurs for £30,000. Born in Belfast on November 29 1954, McGrath had impressed a few seasons back by gaining a first-team place at Tottenham when just 18 and helping the club to a place in the UEFA Cup final via five goals in eight games. Though lately struggling to get in the Spurs first team, McGrath was already a Northern Ireland international and his propensity to take players on was in the best United tradition. Tommy Cavanagh, who had been working part-time with the Northern Ireland squad, had the previous week seen McGrath score a goal for his country in a World Cup qualifier against Holland. (That 2-2 draw, incidentally, was the match that marked the return of George Best to international soccer, and Bestie played a blinder against a Dutch team that included Johan Cruyff.) "We have watched McGrath for six months … We just waited to judge Chris' character and he came through that test very well," said Docherty.

The Doc also sounded a word of warning about big-money football transfers. "Clubs spending heavily are heading for financial ruin," he said. "The days of six-figure signings at United are gone forever. It's a policy of madness." Docherty also let it be known at this juncture that he had his eye on a replacement for Alex Stepney, namely Jimmy Allan, 21-year-old keeper at Third Division Swindon. The Doc had had the Scot, who was valued at £80,000, watched recently and was now set to make his move. However, the future Docherty envisaged for Allan as a replacement for Stepney (and apparently Roche) proved as inaccurate as his predictions for the end of spiralling transfer fees. Though Derby also expressed their interest in Allan, he remained at Swindon.

Docherty named McGrath as substitute for United's home game against Norwich on Saturday October 23. Attendance was 54,356. In the only starting XI change, Waldron occupied Buchan's usual place, with Houston full-back once more. The Canaries' Suggett brought the perky Hill down in the box, providing Daly the earliest opportunity – at least in the League – to put his recent penalty miss behind him. Three minutes before the interval, Kevin Keelan was beaten again, this time by a curling Hill free-kick. The fact that the 2-0 lead did not reflect the play so far seemed to spur on the visitors in the second-half. It's possible that John Ryan meant the diagonal ball he sent into Stepney's penalty area on 71 minutes as a cross, but the goal still counted when the swirling wind tricked Stepney and bent inside the far post. With six minutes to go, Boyer nodded a cross home.

At this point, Docherty, perhaps fearful of a repeat of Spurs' recent 3-2 victory after the Reds had led by two goals, pulled off McIlroy and gave McGrath his first appearance in a red shirt. The role that Docherty envisaged for McGrath – and the future role that he at this juncture was considering for Coppell – was indicated in the fact that McGrath went wide and Coppell moved inside. The fantasy debut for the ex-Tottenham man, of course, would have seen him score the goal that gave his side victory. It almost happened. He unleashed an effort that one reporter described as the best shot of the match, only to see it hit a post. The score remained 2-2 until the final whistle. United were left ninth in the table, which Middlesbrough led by a point.

Waldron had his own problems. "I remember standing in the players' room afterwards and, Christ, my temperature must have been through the roof," he says. "I remember looking at one of the waitresses behind the bar and her nudging the other waitress and I thought, 'What are they looking at me for?', and I realised I were absolutely pouring sweat." It became obvious that there was something wrong, which fact Waldron had suspected for the past week: "After the West Brom match, I was really struggling with me breathing." Yet more bad luck was about to afflict United, the loss of Buchan now being compounded by his obvious replacement being put out of commission. Says Waldron, "Me first match of the season, I've developed a blood infection ... which took a good while to diagnose. Even then United's medical facility was just fantastic but they couldn't get to the bottom of it. If I'd have had an injury like a ligament or ankle or whatever I could have handled it far better. I started questioning, 'Do Man United believe me or not?'"

Docherty dropped Waldron for their home League Cup fourth-round match on Wednesday October 27 against Newcastle United. Houston filled the role in the centre once more, with Albiston deputising at left-back. There were 52,002 spectators.

By the sixth minute, the Reds were ahead, and if there was a large element of fortune about the 25-yard Houston bender that bounced under the Newcastle keeper, what followed could hardly be put down to a fluke. In the 11th minute, Hill scored with another non-textbook (too close to the keeper) but unstoppable long-range effort. Newcastle pulled one back within five minutes and maybe would have equalised had they not had to replace an injured Gowling on 20 minutes, but it's doubtful. Thanks to Pearson, the Magpies were soon 3-1 down. "It was probably the best goal I ever scored in my life," says Jimmy Nicholl of his first-ever strike for the club, which made it 4-1 two minutes into the second-half. Nicholl recalls, "I played a couple of one-twos, picked the ball up again and just hit this thing from about 30 yards." It was a spectacular strike, but Nicholl modestly says, "To be perfectly honest with you, it was a wet night and the Newcastle goalkeeper actually should have held it but he didn't." Does a goal mean more to a defender than an attacker? Nicholl: "Oh aye. Providing it's not a consolation goal. It's no good if you haven't done your job." Nicholl was to be disappointed when he sat down to watch the TV highlights: "They only showed the first two goals or something. Something happened to the camera and they never got the rest of the game, so I've never seen it."

In the 52nd minute, Hill scored goal number five. Coppell scored four minutes later. 10 minutes after that, Daly found Hill, who proceeded to obtain the first hat-trick of his career. Newcastle managed to wrest a shred of dignity from the evening with an 80th-minute strike from Burns.

Though, as was the tradition with hat-trick achievers, Hill took the ball home ("I gave the ball to [some] kids and they were kicking it around in the streets out the front"), to this day he insists that the triumvirate that inspired headlines like "HAT-TRICK HILL LEADS SEVEN-GOAL SLAUGHTER" should actually be recorded by history as a foursome: "People say I scored three. I scored four. To this very day, I say check it again, if you've got footage, check 'em." Not altogether convincingly – considering his penchant for having a pop at goal on the half-chance when other players were better positioned – he adds, "I mean I didn't care who scored. I didn't care as long as it was in the back of the net." "I can't remember him scoring four," says McIlroy. "Unless he hit one and it was deflected three times and he's claiming it. That's more like Gordon."

Docherty must have been left bemused by the seesaw life of a football manager. A fortnight before, he had been reeling at the joint worst defeat in his time as United manager but today the 4-0 drubbing by West Brom must have seemed a million years ago as he exulted in a 7-2 victory that was the best in his Old Trafford tenure so far and, he surmised, "probably in my whole career". He must have been even more bemused by football's seesaw nature in the following fixtures, though not in a good way.

Understandably, Docherty kept the team the same for the home match against Ipswich Town on Saturday October 30. However, if he was assuming that the League Cup triumph meant that the problems associated with the absence of Buchan were over, he was to be proved completely wrong. The tone was set when the Reds gave away a soft goal in the second minute. It's not known to what the barrackers in the 57,416-strong crowd attributed their team's below-par performance, but there was a contingent in the United support that made their displeasure with the team audible throughout. The crowd also contained home secretary Merlyn Rees, making himself visible in order to express his government's concern over football hooliganism.

United overall were so poor that at the interval Docherty took the unusual step of sending out the team for the second-half with a change. Macari was the player who failed to reappear, McCreery taking his place. United heaped on pressure in the opening stage of the second-half, but there were no further goals. The 1-0 loss left United 11th. (Liverpool were top by three points.) "I don't want to make excuses, because Ipswich worked hard for each other and for their victory," Docherty said afterwards. He did have reasons, though for the defeat. " ... we had four players right off form ... " he said, as well as, " ... the attitude of that small but noisy group of barrackers didn't help. Perhaps some of our spectators have had too much success too quickly." One takes Docherty's point about fans throwing their rattles out of their prams at the first sign of a dip in form (a situation which has today escalated to absurd levels where anything less than endless success is posited as a crisis by self-important supporters groups), but a mathematical indication of how badly things were going compared to last season was the fact that United had now already dropped as many points at home as they did over the entire course of the previous campaign.

\*\*\*

In the days preceding the Reds' UEFA Cup away match against Juventus, some pundits were predicting that their 1-0 victory at Old Trafford would not be enough to see them through to the next round. Manchester City had gone to Turin with the same slender one-goal cushion in the first round and had soon found themselves going back to Manchester 2-0 losers and with their European dream in tatters for another year. Docherty said that United had been more cautious than they should have been against Ajax in their home city because it had been their first game back in serious European competition. "Our natural game is to attack," he now said. "This is when we are at our best. We shall certainly attack in Turin, because basically we cannot play any other way." Despite his defiance, even The Doc wasn't speaking in terms of a victory at Juventus' home ground, instead hoping for "a draw or even a 2-1 defeat." He added, "Away goals count double in the event of an aggregate draw, so if we manage a goal in Italy then we can lose the match but win the tie." He did admit though that the Reds would have to play a "lot better" than they had during the West Brom drubbing and "concentrate a little harder" than they had at Norwich, where they had let a two-goal lead slide into a draw. "We have lacked consistency this last couple of weeks," he said. "We are playing in fits and starts. Basically I believe we are a better team than last season, but we haven't achieved the same high level of consistency. But then footballers are not machines. You cannot expect them to go on turning out high-class performances indefinitely. There must be patience at some stage of the season and I believe we have just been going through one of those unfortunate phases that come sooner or later to the best of teams. I am now looking forward to the challenge of Europe to snap us out of it and we shall travel to Turin with every confidence, I assure you."

The reference to patience was probably partly inspired by the stick United had begun to receive from a section of their fans (although not the Stretford End). "Barracking by a section of the crowd has caused as much embarrassment for the players as the hooligans have for the club," claimed Docherty. "These demos are destroying the confidence of some of the youngest players and it is against that background that I have to try to lift them for the Juventus game. This is a very young side but I will not be swayed away from a youth policy just because some of the crowd are becoming a problem. If anything, it will make me more determined than ever." Docherty's words were nonsense on more than one level. The idea that the dispirited feeling that some of his squad many have been experiencing because they were getting stick from a minority of supporters bore any comparison to the pariah status in English football to which hooliganism was in danger of reducing Manchester United was absurd. Meanwhile his talk of not being swayed from a youth policy was baffling. None of the fans had ever given any indication of having a problem with his emphasis on youth, only with poor results. In any case, the only way his team was appreciably younger compared to last season was in the shape of Jimmy Nicholl. Perhaps Docherty had a guilty conscience about inexplicably dropping Alex Forsyth to make way for Nicholl and was feeling the heat insofar as United's results with Nicholl could be argued not to bear comparison to what they had been when he was in the reserves. He certainly seemed a little chastened by events at the moment. The man who was famous for predicting all manner of success for his teams also said, "We may have to settle this season for a comfortable League position and success in one or other of the three cup competitions."

For the Wednesday November 3 match against Juventus in Turin, the United starting line-up was unchanged from Saturday, with Docherty also sending on subs McCreery and Paterson at stages. The familiar rainy conditions was just about the only thing in the Reds' favour. They were playing in front of a crowd whose size – 66,632 – even Old Trafford at the time could not match. They were also subjected to treatment even more brutal than in the first match. Waldron, once again an unused substitute, found the penny dropping as to the strange jubilation he had witnessed on the part of the opposition players after their loss in Manchester: "After 30 seconds in Juventus, I knew why, because the gangster element had come in. They'd thumped Sammy McIlroy, nearly knocked him out off the ball, they'd whacked Dave McCreery and it was just unbelievable what they got away with." Juventus coach Trappattoni made sure that his team's tormentor from the first match, Hill, was shadowed, and quite viciously, throughout the match. However, it couldn't be

373

denied that Juventus were impressive when they did try to play football. Notwithstanding their rough treatment, United were less so. They had a single serious attempt on goal. Despite what the ultimate scoreline might suggest, Stepney had a good game, making a fine save as early as the second minute. However, he was unable to stop Tardelli scoring on 30 minutes. Half-time saw ugly scenes. Hill: "We go into the extended tunnel and they start kicking us from behind. It was like a full-scale fight. Tommy Cavanagh's closing the changing room doors as we're trying to swing at them. Oh. it was like fucking handbags at ten paces but Sammy's got an eye that's swollen, I've got blood coming down the back of my head … "

When Juventus went three up in the 85th minute, even the prospect of scraping through on the away-goals rule moved like a mirage into the distance for the tired, battered and outplayed United team. Blunstone: "We found it hard in Europe. Being a young side, it was a big step up." It was the first time United had failed to reach the quarter-final of a European competition.

*\*\*\**

With Docherty's European dream – which had looked halfway plausible after the Ajax matches – over for the season, he had to turn his attention back to the already faltering League campaign. In that competition, Aston Villa were their next opponents, the clash on Saturday November 6 taking place at Villa Park. Villa had been placed seventh after the previous weekend's matches. The crowd, strictly segregated in a day when that was still unusual, were treated to an exciting, seesawing match. Macari was dropped, with Coppell playing in his position, and McGrath – getting his first start in a red shirt – occupying the latter's normal role on the right flank. The winger who shone, though, was Hill, whose effervescence was praised by reporters, whereas the lack of either plaudits or brickbats for McGrath indicates he was anonymous.

Pearson headed in the first goal on 24 minutes. United's neat play following that – as well as Stepney smartly saving a 6th-minute penalty – promised good things for the doldrums-inhabiting Reds, but six minutes before half-time a powerful shot from 25 yards defeated Stepney. The second-half was only 14 minutes old when Villa got their second. Almost immediately afterwards, Hill equalised, even if his goal – the ball hit both posts before trickling over the line – was hardly his usual blockbuster. Andy Gray scored a third for the home side in the 54th minute. The neutral observer would have suggested a draw would have been a more just result than Villa's 3-2 victory.

"The First Division needs clubs like Villa who can produce 50,000 crowds," said Docherty afterwards. (In fact, the gate was 44,789.) He wasn't just being generous: the former Villa manager still had shares in the club. However, even a man who was later strongly alleged to be financially dubious is above suspicion as to his grim feelings about the result. The Reds' second-successive League loss left them in a mildly shocking 14th position. (Villa were now third; Liverpool were still top by three points.) "It's disappointing to lose," The Doc said, "but at least there was some consolation in our display." Unlike the Ipswich game, there was no complaint from The Doc about anyone being out of form: "I was pleased with my own players."

Wednesday November 10 saw United taking on Sunderland at Old Trafford before 42,685. Perhaps indicating a manager beginning to panic, the United line-up was much changed for this fixture. Roche replaced Stepney in goal, Nicholl was absent (Albiston occupying a full-back position), Paterson and Waldron formed the central defence, Coppell was back in his winger's role (with McGrath dropped) and Macari also returned. Greenhoff was moved upfield to replace an absent McIlroy. On 34 minutes, Paterson, playing his full debut, showed uncommon control and delicacy of touch for both a defender and a man of his hulking physique when he sprayed a beautiful ball to Hill on the left flank. Merlin cut inside, mesmerised the defence with a wriggle of his hips and sent in a low shot from 15 yards that beat Siddall. United gave their lately disaffected supporters even more reason for good cheer seven minutes later when Pearson made it two.

Nine minutes into the second-half, the visitors clawed one back. Two minutes later, Greenhoff scored with a header. Even 3-1 down, though, the Wearsiders refused to yield and replied within two minutes. Docherty chose this moment to do yet more team reshuffling: Waldron made way for 17-year-old Jonathan Clark, making his debut, while the defence was rearranged so that Houston could move into midfield. A heartfelt groan must have made its way across the Stretford End as Lee's header ballooned the United net on 75 minutes. Surely their team wasn't going to squander yet another commanding situation? Lo and behold, as visibility got progressively worse with advancing fog, United failed to obtain the goal needed for maximum points. 15th was the uninspiring, even worrying, position the 3-3 draw left them occupying in the table, one that Liverpool now led by five points.

Waldron's appearance today would mark his farewell to United. The club he was destined for were today's opponents – who, in a remarkable act of symmetry, had also been the opponents in his first appearance for the Reds. November saw Sunderland appoint Jimmy Adamson as their manager. Waldron's boss at Burnley for 10 years had no hesitation in seeking the services of the defender. Waldron had worked his way back into consideration for the United first team after taking matters into his own hands over his mysterious malaise. "Unknown to Man United, I had a friend of a friend who was a top cancer surgeon who I went to, I was that bothered by everything," he says. "They gave me some tests and he came back to me and said, 'Listen, how have you been feeling?' and I said, 'Well, to be fair I've been feeling better.' When I was training I couldn't run the length of the pitch without absolutely being on my knees. He said, 'Well, it looks like you've got some kind of infection, but from the tests it looks like the infection is on the wane.' I've wasted two or three months and I just started picking up again and Sunderland came in. Tommy Docherty was absolutely brilliant. I didn't see a lot of him because I didn't want to mess him about in any way. He had his own problems with being a manager. He's got a squad of like 20 or 30 players. I'm only one and obviously I wasn't being any form of asset to the club in the condition I was in. But when the time came to go he helped me all he could. I went to Sunderland on loan for six months or whatever it was. He was brilliant with me, kept me informed." Waldron was eventually transferred to Sunderland on a free.

The Sunderland match would also mark the last senior United appearance for Jonathan Clark, despite it also constituting his entrée. Clark was born in Swansea on November 12 1958. Docherty later said of him, " ... at 15 you would have staked your mortgage on his future as a top class player ... he didn't make the grade and his career fizzled out." Docherty also admitted, "There was a host of players just like him," although he appeared to feel this was more because of the fact that a football youth system was "like planting a batch of seeds knowing that only a few will bear fruit" than any shortcomings in United's particular youth set-up at the time.

***

"If I'd realised what a good player I was, I would have gone for more money," quips Martin Buchan about the disastrous run of results during his absence. He adds, "I think a lot of it was coincidence." Whatever the reason for the recent form, previous claims by Docherty to be the best manager in the land were now being used to ridicule him. One joke making the rounds was that Tommy Docherty now had initials after his name, but the OBE being referred to was not Order of the British Empire but 'Out By Easter'. The provenance of this crack is unknown, but few would be surprised if it had originated with notorious Manchester comedian Bernard Manning. Docherty would often take in the act of Manning at the latter's trendy club in Manchester and was quite able to endure the ridicule to which Manning would proceed to subject him if he spotted him in the audience as simply what was to be expected from a Manchester City fan. But the joke was beginning to turn sour. The sale of

Jim Holton was looking an exceedingly unwise move now that a huge injury-caused gap existed in the United defence that he would have plugged perfectly, while for some at least he could have injected a bit of backbone in a team who were too good-natured for their own good. Meanwhile, the fact that, unless you count the League Cup, Docherty had never won anything as a manager was beginning to nag at some people's minds again as the trajectory that had taken Docherty's United from Second Division champions to FA Cup runners-up and third place in the League now looked like it might actually have passed its apex. Naturally, many opposition supporters were currently expressing their delight at the way the high-and-mighty had fallen with some ribald terrace chants.

Docherty had in his office a framed copy of *If*, the Kipling poem that is now a cast-iron cliché of pseudo-philosophy but was probably viewed as less hackneyed then. The Doc's stance, however, didn't quite seem to chime with that piece of verse's advice that triumph and disaster are both impostors to be treated in an identical manner when he defiantly told the *Sunday Express*, "I say I'm the best manager because I want my players to believe they are the best in the world. They wouldn't if I was going around saying I was rubbish." Nonetheless, Docherty knew he had to strengthen his squad. United's current goal drought, which had translated into a run of losses, concerned him. Curiously, he evinced no concern about the gap in defence Buchan's absence seemed to expose but instead seemed to feel it was down to the goalkeeper. While Stepney was undeniably getting on a bit, one wonders whether old enmities – either with Alex or with the very concept of any overhang from the Busby days – were influencing his thoughts. Either way, the opportunity to obtain both a striker and a keeper came in the second week of November 1976 when Stoke City had the misfortune to lose the roof of their Butler Street stand during a storm. The only way the club could afford to repair it was by offloading one or more of their prize assets.

Docherty has recalled Stoke manager Tony Waddington phoning him and offering him their veteran striker Jimmy Greenhoff. Docherty recalls he said "Yes" immediately and then added, "I'll take Peter Shilton off your hands as well." Blunstone recalls it differently: "I said to him, 'Go and get Jimmy Greenhoff and get Peter Shilton'." Whether or not one agrees with Docherty's apparent analysis of what currently ailed his side, not many would dispute that Shilton would be a huge benefit to it. Then 27, he was entering the stage where he would be at the peak of his powers, and those powers were considerable. Blunstone: "We were struggling for a goalkeeper at that time. They weren't quite good enough. Paddy wasn't really up to it. He was very consistent, Alec, but it was only a matter of time. As you get older it gets a bit harder. Tommy was building for the future and Peter Shilton would have been a good replacement and a good name, which United would have appreciated, because they're always looking for top-class players." Docherty himself felt that Shilton ranked alongside Liverpool's Ray Clemence and Juventus' Dino Zoff as the world's best goalkeeper. Docherty's estimate of how many fewer goals per season United would concede with Shilton's presence between their sticks has varied down the years between 20 and 30, but not his judgment of what those saved goals would constitute: the difference between winning the championship and being also-rans.

At one point, everything seemed set for Shilton to become a Red. Stoke indicated they were prepared to let him go, Shilton indicated that he was enthusiastic about coming to Manchester, and the United board – after some humming and hawing over the £275,000 being asked for Shilton at a time when goalkeepers didn't often go for high sums – agreed to the transfer fee. It's a measure of how much Docherty thought of Shilton that he was prepared to break the low-spending, no-stars transfer philosophy he articulated to a journalist this season: "As a general rule, my policy is to find and produce our own players. It makes more financial sense; it's good business and you can create a better team spirit and harmony. If I buy a big name for a lot of money, he has to go straight into the team and it's disheartening for players working at promotion. But if I buy a 20-year-old … then he is happy to go into the reserves, improve and wait for his chance. It makes much more sense."

In his books *Call The Doc* and *The Quest for Glory*, Docherty claimed that the deal he had arranged with Stoke City was for a cash sum and an exchange of either Roche or Stepney. In *The Quest for Glory*, he also cited his negotiations as being with caretaker manager George Eastham, which would place the events after March 1977, and said that Shilton was anxious to leave the club because they had just been relegated, which would place them at the end of the 1976/77 season. It could be that Docherty's memory is confused. It could also be that negotiations with Stoke were quite protracted and that they might have started in November 1976 but continued throughout the season. Extraordinarily, Shilton was so interested in playing for United that, according to Gordon Hill's recollection, he was virtually soliciting a move. "When I was with the England squad, Shiltsie used to say to me, 'I know that you're looking for a goalkeeper and I'd love to come to United'," says Hill. "I said, 'Shilts I'd love you to come to United.' He said, 'Could you put a word in?' and I went, 'I'll speak to the boss for you, sure I will.' I said to the boss, 'I've been speaking to Shiltsie and he'd love to come, boss'. So he says, 'I know Gordon, we're trying to get him, but it's just the cost. The board are humming and hawing about it.' So then he came to play us and he was walking down the tunnel and he said, 'Hey Hilly, any news on it?' I always remember he was wearing his rain mac. I said, 'Well listen, I tell you what I'll do, I'll mention it to the boss again for you and see what it is.' Well the boss happened to come past and I said, 'Hey boss, he's as keen as mustard'."

Whatever the timeframe involved, the mischievous cosmic forces that had seemed to conspire so often against Docherty when trying to get rid of Stepney now set to work again. According to Docherty, Shilton's move to United foundered for the most absurd and petty reason. Shilton's agent cited a desired wage, presumably one adjacent to the £400 per week Docherty has said Stoke were then paying Shilton. Whatever the sum was, it was apparently one that would make the goalkeeper United's highest-paid player by a margin of £50 per week. Docherty felt Shilton was worth this kind of money. He claims the board said they didn't. "United were a club at the time that didn't pay massively," says McIlroy. "There was a lot of clubs [where] people were on more money. A lot of people didn't really realise that, but that was the truth. United were decent payers but they weren't the highest. I think it started with the Ron Atkinson era. I think that was when the change came, where money began to change." As might be expected, Buchan has a philosophical view on the situation: "We were relatively well paid by the standards of the time," he says, and adds, "We weren't the best-paid team in England, but then again we weren't the best team in England in the 70s, so that makes sense to me." Docherty later said it was the only time the board refused him permission to buy a player. Hill: "If we'd have got Peter Shilton in, that would have been it. I think Alex would have retired or done something else or gone to another club ... Alex has been a great servant and it was no disrespect to him. We're a younger side and Shilts is number one. What a collection, if we'd had Shilts then. I think that would have been the crowning ..." Pearson, speaking in 2004, agreed with this assessment: "With Peter in goal, I'm sure we would have won the title."

Docherty did at least get his striker, Brian Greenhoff's big brother Jimmy joined United for either £100,000 or £120,000 in the second week of November. Jimmy Greenhoff later said that Waddington had tears in his eyes when he informed him of the need to sell him. Waddington told the press, "It's a sad day for me to lose such a player. I did not want him to leave – but we need the money." "It was a shock to learn that Stoke were prepared to sell me and a surprise when I found that I still do not qualify for a testimonial," Greenhoff said after signing. "But now it is done it is not a wrench. Money isn't everything. I've lost a testimonial payout but I've got a great move. This is the most exciting day of my career, and I can't wait to play in a home game here. One of the biggest disappointments of my career has been my lack of international honours, but this move more than makes up for it." Greenhoff could have insisted on Stoke honouring his contract by keeping him on their books and staging his testimonial. Docherty paid tribute to him for not doing so: "I think that Jimmy is giving up a hell of a lot because of this situation. It's a big financial sacrifice to make even when joining a club like United. It's a tremendous decision, particularly when players are being slagged all over the place for being greedy and selfish. I hope this player gets every medal in the game over the next five or six seasons. He deserves every one of them. Jimmy has come here obviously because he believes we have great potential and he wants to be with us when we start winning things."

Some eyebrows might have been raised by the number of years Docherty was projecting 30-year-old Greenhoff as playing with United. Greenhoff's snaggle-teeth and receding hairline certainly didn't give him the appearance of a man in the first flush of youth, or with his best days as a footballer anything other than behind him. Some eyebrows might also have been raised at another comment by The Doc wherein he described the newcomer as the last piece in his jigsaw. Though Greenhoff himself understandably found the comment "gratifying", many would have recalled that Docherty had said the same thing about Gordon Hill.

"We thought [he] had two or three good seasons [left]," says Blunstone. "Also we thought the balance would be right. We thought him and Stuart Pearson up the front would work well together. Stuart was aggressive, determined, and Jimmy had the bit of class. His reading of the game, his coming off, his control. He was a class player." Nicholl offers another possible reason: "The Doc probably felt at that time we were going through a bad time and it was a big test for us and we needed more experienced players. You had young ones like the Coppells and Hills and all these boys and it probably did need an old head there upfront just to settle things down, slow things down, clam everybody down, and he certainly did." McCreery: "I think for Manchester United at the time he was the best buy they've ever had. Stylish. He could hold the ball up, bring players into the game. He could pick a pass. Score goals. Shoot from both feet. He was just a fantastic all-round player."

Brian Greenhoff was in Italy for a World Cup qualifier when he got the news that the man to whom he refers as "our kid" was coming to join him at Old Trafford. "I just got a phone call from Kath, the receptionist at the time," he recalls. Kath put him on to The Doc. "He just says, 'I've got someone who wants to speak to you'. [Jimmy] was in the office. He says, 'I've done a deal and I'm going to be signing and I'm coming'. When I came back, the next day he came to our house and I took him to The Cliff." Asked if the purchase of a 30-something by a manager who had spent the last few seasons building for the future surprised him, Brian offers, "Well, it wasn't a daft price. A proven player. We were desperate for another striker to play alongside Stuart. Smashing player Sammy was, he wasn't a striker for me. He was always better playing in midfield or out wide 'cos of the ability that he had. Who else did we have? Pete Fletcher had gone the other way. He fetched in Ron Davies, then he fetched in Tommy Baldwin, but they were all sort of [stop]-gaps." Greenhoff concedes that The Doc may have also viewed his brother at this stage as a stop-gap, bridging the time it took for youth-team goalscorers like Andy Ritchie and Peter Coyne to mature. In the end, though, Jimmy Greenhoff would have a true Indian summer with his new employers. In his four-year career at the club, he would be a darling of the terraces and play a vital part in Docherty's finest hour.

Jimmy Greenhoff was born in Barnsley on June 19 1946. When he was young, plenty of scouts tried to obtain his precocious skills for their club. Greenhoff took the advice of his father and signed for Don Revie's Leeds. Jimmy worked his way through the Leeds junior teams and the reserves as a midfielder but came to realise the dubious wisdom of joining a club that boasted such quality that men like Giles, Bremner and Hunter formed a queue before him for selection for the first team. Used as sweeper in one match, he may have been put in mind of the old joke of the player finding himself increasingly to the rear of the formation: "Any further back I'll be behind the goal-line." At one point Jimmy asked for a transfer but ultimately stayed at Elland Road to battle for a place. His break came by accident. In 1966, during a reserve match, Jimmy was switched to striker because of an injury and his good performance was reported back to Revie. Leeds striker Alan Peacock was injured at the time and Revie – mindful of the big money he would have to part with if he were to replace Peacock from outside – gave the 20-year-old his chance as centre-forward. His game in that position was against Preston in the League Cup. In Leeds' 4-1 victory, Jimmy scored one of the goals. He proceeded to nab seven goals in his first 11 games in that position. "It's great," he enthused to a newspaper reporter. "I love it. I've found my true position at last." The media speculated that this was the kind of form that merited England selection, and this proved not to be hot air when Alf Ramsey took the trouble to watch him. At the end of the 1966/67 season, he was picked for a Middle Eastern England Under-23 tour. However, in what turned out to be a portentous event for his international career, he didn't play, on this occasion having to pull out through injury.

Jimmy picked up League Cup and Fairs Cup winners medals the following season, but almost as quickly as his ascent at Leeds had come, a combination of bad form and injury saw him increasingly fail to get picked and ultimately unable to even get on the sub's bench. Revie agreed to his transfer request and Jimmy joined Second Division Birmingham City in the opening weeks of the 1968/69 season for £75,000. He scored 12 goals in nine games and quickly became a fan favourite. He was therefore astounded when Birmingham manager Stan Cullis decided that he wasn't scoring enough. His dismay began to be reflected in his form for the club and he was relieved when Stoke City took him back to the First Division in August 1969 for £100,000.

To this day, many Potters fans will tell you that Jimmy Greenhoff was a Stoke City player and that his time with Manchester United was merely the fag-end of his real career. Certainly,

Jimmy has the long association and success with Stoke that links a player indelibly with a club in the minds of both that club's supporters and the wider public. He played 260 League games for Stoke, netting 74 goals. Stoke were the type of club who were never really destined to win championships but were widely admired and able to attract quality players (the much-loved Alan Hudson also passed through the club's ranks in the 70s). Honours were not beyond them either, as Greenhoff's 1972 League Cup winner's medal attests. Though the club and Jimmy only parted company because of that spell of bad weather in the Potteries, in 1976 he had lately been unsettled at Stoke after being pressed into a midfield role when both he and all the statistics (including the fact that he was top scorer the previous season) insisted he was best upfront. Knowledge of his availability led Everton and West Ham to express interest but Greenhoff resisted the overtures of both. After his move to Old Trafford, he said, "It was always a boyhood ambition to play for Manchester United. It has taken me some time to achieve it ..."

***

The starting line-up for United's match against Leicester City on Saturday November 20 in front of a crowd of 27,071 at Filbert Street read: Stepney, Nicholl, Albiston, Daly, Greenhoff (B), Paterson, Coppell, McIlroy, Pearson, Greenhoff (J), Hill. Macari's absence was through injury.

United conceded a soft goal in the eighth minute. Though the match was entertaining, the Reds were so far from the swashbuckling side they had been until a few weeks previously that Hill and Coppell – outplayed by their markers – eventually dropped back. On 84 minutes, United obtained a penalty for alleged handball. Though the consensus was that the penalty award was unjust, United could point out that an upending of Jimmy Greenhoff (who did well on his debut) late in the first-half had not brought the spot-kick it seemed it should have. Daly did his usual sterling work in the situation. United were pleased no doubt to take a point back to Manchester with them and to climb two places in the table, but the circumstances of the 1-1 draw were hardly convincing and it was now the fifth successive game in which the Reds had failed to chalk up a victory. Docherty said afterwards, "People say something has gone wrong with us, but the talent is all there and the results will come in time."

It seemed conceivable that that turnaround in fortunes might begin with the next fixture, a home match against bottom-of-the-table West Ham on Saturday November 27. Nicholl and Paterson were missing from the previous game's line-up, replaced by Forsyth and Houston. The gate was 55,366. Those barrackers whose presence Docherty had lamented recently had good reason to make their displeasure known as they saw United succumb to a team who hadn't won away in a League match in over a year. In Macari's continued absence, the United midfield was particularly below-par, something that posed a serious problem for a team whose 4-2-4 formation made the midfield more vulnerable than other clubs'.

After a 2-0 defeat that sent them back down to 15th, Docherty told the press, "We are basically the same side who did so well last season." This produced a scathing response from columnist Frank McGhee, who opined that though Manchester United had broadly the same players, they were not the same team and were not producing the same exciting standards as before. He said that, " … the whole Manchester United team have lost their momentum, enthusiasm and confidence." He detected an absence of the ceaseless running that he estimated had been 60% of their game and a newfound inability or unwillingness to win 50-50 challenges. "Heads are no longer held high," he asserted. "Too many chins go down onto chests. They have lost the zest they brought back to English football last season … Against West Ham, too many of them were hiding, pretending, shirking … That doesn't call for patience, Tommy Docherty. That calls for a real, old-fashioned Glasgow Gorbals rollicking."

Perhaps The Doc did deliver that rollicking McGhee recommended, but it would have been like flogging a horse with a broken leg, for between then and the next fixture – the fifth-round League Cup match against Everton at Old Trafford on Wednesday December 1 – United's injury woes got worse. Not only were Buchan and Macari still out, but new boy Jimmy Greenhoff was also ruled unfit and Houston was absent with stomach trouble. Docherty did what he could to patch up the side by recalling the rookie Paterson and giving Tommy Jackson his first game of the season. Attendance was 57,738.

The euphoria of United's League Cup fourth-round demolition of Newcastle was followed by their own humiliation in the fifth round of the competition. Remarkably, the 3-0 loss could have been considerably worse, with Stepney pulling off several excellent saves. Substituting Daly for McCreery made no appreciable difference to a team that failed to gel.

The statistics about their form after the match were depressing reading for the Reds. It was their fifth defeat in seven matches. Even more worrying, the team that until April the previous season had not lost at Old Trafford in more than a year were now contemplating their third defeat in four home matches. Says Hill, "It was really the inexperience of the side coming to the forefront. Older squads or more experienced squads would have wrapped up and said, 'Right, okay, close the doors, that's it.' The boss used to say, 'All we need is one good result and we're off again'."

\*\*\*

Perhaps mercifully for the Reds, there were no official matches between their ejection from the League Cup and their visit to Highbury on December 18. During that two-and-a-half week hiatus, however, United did keep their hand in. On December 8, they played a friendly match at Ninian Park in Cardiff against a South Wales XI made up of players from Cardiff City, Swansea City and Newport County. This peculiar fixture was a result of Docherty's more pleasant side. Reading the papers in his Old Trafford office one morning, he noted a story about the dire financial straits that Newport County were in. Docherty has said, "Irrespective of which club you support, play for or manage, I have always believed, collectively, we are all a part of the great family of football." Accordingly, he decided to arrange a fixture that could fill the ailing Fourth Division club's coffers and hopefully help them avert bankruptcy. United were able to use the match to give Martin Buchan a chance to see if his injury had healed. The starting line-up was: Stepney, Forsyth, Houston, McIlroy, Greenhoff (B), Buchan, Coppell, Greenhoff (J), Pearson, Macari and Hill. Roche, McGrath, Daly and Albiston came on in the second-half. The match attracted a surprisingly healthy crowd of 13,003 considering the fact of the Rugby Union match between Cardiff and Newport taking place at nearby Cardiff Arms Park the same evening. United waived their normal fee, which meant Newport had a cheque, after expenses, of £6,000 to put toward their £100,000 debts. The only goal of the game came not long before half-time when Cardiff defender Sawyer headed home a Dwyer centre. However, the score hardly mattered on such an occasion. Newport chairman Cyril Rogers said, "United are one of the biggest crowd-pullers in the country and to have them appearing at Ninian Park for us is a magnificent touch of sportsmanship. We shall never forget United's splendid effort."

On Saturday December 18, Martin Buchan finally made his League return, lining up to take on Arsenal. Macari and Houston were back, too, Jackson and Albiston making way for them. However, with Coppell ruled unfit with a hamstring injury, McCreery started the match, although it was actually McIlroy who played on the right wing. There wasn't even room for Daly on the sub's bench, where sat McGrath. (The latter came on for Brian Greenhoff.)

This was the first match in which McIlroy was played in midfield since Jimmy Greenhoff's arrival. He would remain there for the rest of the season, something that Buchan found appropriate: "Sammy wasn't a centre-forward. Sammy was somebody who played off the front players." McIlroy's redeployment may have been in Docherty's mind when he decided to buy the elder Greenhoff. Speaking before the season of McIlroy's sterling work in midfield in the 1975/76 season he said, "I don't know which is his best position … Perhaps 15 goals is his limit as a striker but he will still get 10 as a midfield player. His change of position added a new dimension to his game." When McIlroy began struggling in his striker's position this season and told The Doc so, Docherty's own words may have echoed through his mind.

Ironically, McIlroy found his scoring touch again in the Arsenal match. The 39,572 crowd at Highbury saw a rip-roaring start, with each side scoring in the opening seven minutes. On five minutes, Malcolm Macdonald – now tending his famous sideburns down south after being transferred by Newcastle – crashed in a cross. United were level within two minutes courtesy of a solo goal by Super Sam, who weaved past three defenders before putting the ball past ex-United colleague Rimmer, a brilliant way to end his scoring duck.

With that reply and the fact that Buchan was back, the Reds' fans must have thought/ hoped/prayed that this was going to be the match that would see a turnaround in their fortunes. A minute before half-time, though, the Gunners scored again, and on 53 minutes 'Supermac' got his second. The 3-1 defeat meant that United had suffered another hat-trick of losses, one that now left them 17th. In a League of 22 clubs, that placing was ominously reminiscent of the positions in which the club had found themselves during the relegation season. Meanwhile, in the upper echelons of the table – which had become somewhat distant to United recently and its goings-on therefore of abstract rather than immediate interest – Liverpool, who had been top, were now second, although with two games in hand over goal-difference leaders Ipswich.

After the humiliating December 1 League Cup home loss against Everton, Docherty had told the press, "We face a psychological problem. We need a few good results to give the lads their confidence back. We have just got to bat along. It may take a week or a month but I know in the end it's going to come right." His comments may have struck some as the desperation of a bewildered man, and rendered no less so by comments elsewhere that there was nothing wrong with the quality of his players. Though the latter was undoubtedly true, the same could largely be said of the players who had not been able to prevent United being relegated. In the end though, Docherty was proved right. United's turnaround in fortunes began on December 27 – just within the month's outer limit for recovery he had mentioned – and, suitably enough, came against Everton. A crowd of 56,786 attended Old Trafford. The prosaic explanation for this unusually high attendance for a Monday-night fixture was that Christmas had fallen this year on a Saturday, so the Monday was a Bank Holiday. However, the more poetically inclined might suggest that the turnout was down to the fact that the recently glum United faithful were somehow expecting what transpired. The rain might have fallen ceaselessly but everything seemed sunny at Old Trafford as the visitors were thrashed 4-0. It was no flash-in-the-pan victory either, but instead marked the beginning of a remarkable run of results for the Reds. Significantly, the match saw the first goal for the club by Jimmy Greenhoff, somebody who would proceed to be one of the stars of the remainder of the season. Even more significantly, it marked the debut of the second major fixed line-up of Docherty's reign. As with the previous roll call, any United fan of the era can recite it to you as easily as a times table: "Stepney, Nicholl, Houston, Greenhoff (B), Buchan, McIlroy, Macari, Coppell, Greenhoff (J), Pearson, Hill. Sub: McCreery." Docherty himself said the United team ran off the tongue like a well-known nursery rhyme. "Irrespective of how many games we played, I was reluctant to change the team," he stated, "and only did so when forced to through injuries."

The observant will have noticed that that roll call does not include the name of Gerry Daly. Though the Irishman had played such an important part in the process of turning Manchester United from a joke into a class act again, the fact of McIlroy being pushed back in the formation by Jimmy Greenhoff's arrival had created a competition for a midfield place which The Doc had adjudged him to have lost. Meanwhile, the fact that Nicholl had returned to left-back after Forsyth's longest run in the first team this season was final confirmation that the Belfast boy was now Docherty's first choice in that position. Though Forsyth and Daly would be fondly remembered, Docherty's instincts were proven right. The new fixed line-up – what we might call the 'Roll Call Mark II' – clicked instantly. The new regular cast had a significantly higher average age than the "innocents" Cavanagh had spoken of (although of course this was partly because it was now over a year since the first roll call had played together): with Stepney, it was 26 years and 11 days, without Stepney 25 years and 249 days.

All four goals came in the second-half, the first a nod-in from a Pearson loitering on the far post. On 61 minutes, Jimmy Greenhoff was finally able to silence those inclined to question the wisdom of signing a player of his vintage. Hill got on the scoresheet in his inimitable style, impudently lobbing the Everton keeper from 30 yards. McCreery, who had come on for Coppell in the 77th minute, laid on the fourth goal, scored by Macari from close range.

Amazingly, the margin of the victory could have been significantly greater, with Everton scrambling off the line on three occasions and United having what seemed a legitimate penalty claim turned down. Brian Greenhoff had to be stretchered off in the closing minutes. However, as if to underline the fact that fortune was now smiling on his team at last, the numbed right leg that he thought was broken turned out to be nothing worse than bruised. United's biggest League victory of the season and their first win in nine matches left them in 15th position.

\*\*\*

With no new injuries, Docherty, needless to say, left the team unchanged for the New Year's Day home fixture against Aston Villa the following Saturday. Villa, fourth in the table, were very much championship contenders. The gate was 55,446.

On 17 minutes Pearson and Burridge went for the ball, but Pearson got there first (or, in one reporter's estimation, headed the ball out of the keeper's hands). Six minutes later, Pancho volleyed another goal from eight yards. United could have made it a 3-0 victory when McCreery – sent on in the 85th minute for Pearson – was brought down. McIlroy opted to take the spot-kick. However, though he may have won the battle for a midfield role with Daly, apparently McIlroy did not have his penalty-taking talents and missed. United's victory left them 13th in the table. Liverpool led by four points, although second-placed Ipswich had four games in hand over them.

It was Ipswich, in fact, who were United's next opponents, an away fixture on Monday January 3 1977. The knee injury that had led to Pearson's late substitution against Villa proved sufficiently non-serious to allow him to play. Houston and Coppell were not fit. Though it would be implausible to blame the fact that United proceeded to lose the game on their replacements, Albiston and McCreery, it seems significant that one of the few occasions during the rest of his tenure at the club that Docherty was not able to field the Roll Call Mark II marked one of the few occasions that United were unable to secure at least a point.

Within the first minute, it looked ominously for the home fans in the 30,105 crowd – already suffering through bitterly cold weather – as though it was going to be the visitors' day. Pearson thumped the ball into the roof of the Ipswich net after only 23 seconds. Just before half-time, Hill scored in his favoured spectacular fashion, volleying the ball from the edge of the penalty area into the far corner. It was disallowed, because either he or Jimmy Greenhoff (no one seemed sure) was offside. "If that had happened to us, I would have been sick," admitted Ipswich manager Bobby Robson. "Hill struck the ball perfectly, it went in like a rocket, and even if another player was in [an] offside position, there is no way he could have been interfering with the play."

With 10 minutes to go, Ipswich's Clive Woods sent a cross in the direction of colleague Bertschin. Brian Greenhoff saw the danger, but in his attempt to deal with it he lost his footing and ended up heading into his own net. In the final minutes, Woods executed a half-volley for an 84th-minute winner. At this point, Hill must have considered kicking himself (and his colleagues contemplated joining in) for an earlier miss when he had successfully managed to round Ipswich goalie Paul Cooper only to shoot wide of an open goal.

Ipswich, now unbeaten in 14 games, were left only two points behind League leaders Liverpool with three games in hand. In contrast United slipped a place to 14th and their 18 points looked decidedly paltry compared to Liverpool's 32.

*\*\**

This season would give United two opportunities to avenge FA Cup defeats of recent seasons, both of which had seen underdogs achieve shock victories over them. The first occasion was at the start of their campaign on Saturday January 8. In the competition's third round, United were drawn against Walsall, the team who had knocked them out of the competition in the same round two years previously. Walsall, though, were in no mood to roll over and play dead, nor be overwhelmed by either an Old Trafford crowd of 48,870 or the fact that United had since put another division between the clubs. As Docherty observed after the match, "If Walsall played like this every week, they would be in a higher grade than the Third Division." The Doc later said that it was United's hardest match in the competition that season. Docherty was able to field the Roll Call Mark II, although Daly, as opposed to McCreery, was the substitute. The fact that The Doc was able to employ such a gifted player as the Irishman as bench-warmer was a very pleasing indication (for Docherty anyway, maybe not for Daly) of both how strong were United's available midfield players and how the injury crisis now seemed well and truly over.

The Reds went ahead just before the break, Hill unleashing a low drive into the net. Despite Hill sending over balls from the left like he was on a quantity bonus, United failed to build on the lead or even to give the impression of being cognizant of the two-division gulf between the clubs. Approaching the hour mark, Docherty felt compelled to pull off Coppell and replace him with Daly to shore up the midfield. It worked sufficiently well to see United maintain their one-goal lead through to the final whistle. It was hardly an auspicious start to the objective of making good Docherty's promise the previous year to bring the FA Cup to Manchester.

Docherty came down with a virus before United's next fixture, so Frank Blunstone took over for the home match against Coventry City on Saturday January 15. United were unchanged, apart from McCreery taking Daly's place on the sub's bench. "I enjoyed it," says Blunstone of his single match in charge in his tenure at Old Trafford. The same might not be said of Gordon Hill.

United were pretty much in control throughout, playing nice flowing football in the first-half that left Coventry clueless. Though the visitors came back a little in the second-half – a familiar process in football that is a testament to the power of the half-time manager's bollocking – they couldn't find a way past a rock-solid Buchan. Lou Macari was scintillating, even if the Scotsman's first goal was a fluke. Coventry's Dugdale later said, "I was heading the ball clear and it struck Macari on the back of the head and went into the net." The powerful and accurate low shot that got Macari his second goal was no accident though.

The only real danger for the Reds came from themselves. In this game, Buchan's discontent with Hill's deficiencies came boiling to the surface. The United captain found himself confronted near the halfway line by Coventry's diminutive bearded frontman Alan Green. Buchan: "He tried to take me on down the line, our left-hand side of defence. He went to the byline and he still couldn't get his cross in and I shepherded him back down the field, almost back to the halfway line. At this point Mick Coop, the Coventry right-back, is standing on the halfway line and he thinks to himself, 'If I go up the touchline, Alan'll be able to play me in.' And Hilly looks at Mick Coop, sees him start to run, does a half-hearted couple of paces and says to himself, 'Fuck it, I'm not going to bother' … The [players] we had weren't built to make crunching tackles but there was nothing stopping them putting opponents under pressure, sometimes by merely standing close enough to them to make someone else think twice about passing a ball to them … So of course Alan Green slips the ball to Mick Coop and he's off up down the touchline. I'm running past Hilly and I slapped him on the back of the head and said, 'Why don't you waken up?' or words to that effect."

If the 46,567 spectators were astonished by Buchan's assault, they were no less so than Hill, especially when he realised that – contrary to his initial impressions – it was not a Coventry player who had laid hands on him. The memories of the two players differ when it comes to precisely what words were exchanged when Hill caught up with the defender. Hill said to Jim White, "I told him if he did it again I'd kill him." Buchan says, "I get back just in time to launch myself into a diving header and put Mick's cross for a corner. I'm sucking air through my backside, leaning on the post trying to get my breath back. Hilly comes up to me, he says, [Cockney accent], 'You do that again, I'll kick you in the bollocks.' And I just said, 'Gordon, get on with the fucking game'." That the dispute was more heated than Buchan seems to be suggesting is indicated by the fact that the referee waded into it, ordering the pair to calm down lest he have to make personal history by sending off two colleagues for arguing.

The 2-0 victory left United 11th in the title, but inevitably some of the papers were less concerned with the Reds' incremental revival than with the flare-up. Buchan: "I can assure you that if The

Doc had been there, after the match when we came up the tunnel he'd have said, 'Right you two, zip it, say nothing to the press.' Of course Gordon had a say, Frank Blunstone had a say, and it was a big story." Opined one journo, "Leadership, we are told, should be inspirational, coming from example and firmness. Buchan is a great player. But a great captain will keep his temper. Diplomacy remains an essential part of his job. Fists never settled anything except a world championship fight." Blunstone: "The press tried to make a lot of it. I noticed it but I told them I didn't. It happens. Christ, I've been on many [pitches] where somebody's had a go at somebody. Gordon's a cocky lad and Martin was very decisive and he didn't like it if Gordon was fiddling about. It was all over in the dressing room, good as gold after, no trouble. He had justification [for] being angry but you can't just hit people 'cos you're angry, can you?"

Hill agrees the matter would have been less sensational had Docherty been around to deal with the press on the day. In the week following the incident, Docherty did his belated best to quell the controversy in the papers, "Martin Buchan is the gaffer on the field and he has to play it the way he sees it," he said. "He sets such a high standard for himself that he sometimes gets frustrated if other people don't match him. But even so it was all a storm in a teacup and I shall be having a quiet word with both of them." And yet there was something of an ambivalence in Docherty's comments, for he then said, "Some of our defenders should have a bit more consideration for Gordon. He tries to help out in defence but he is not as strong as Steve Coppell. But then again Coppell doesn't score the goals that Gordon does. We know how difficult it is for a winger to have to keep chasing back. All we are trying to do with Gordon is to strike a happy medium."

Waldron offers an explanation for Docherty's confused message: "Whatever was happening, they were winning, so things were looking good and even if there is that flaw in the system and you keep trying to address it, you're not going to take it out, because whatever you're doing it's working." Buchan: "He probably weighed up the pros and cons and he thought he [was] worth a place in the team. For all his (in inverted commas) 'faults' or for all his 'foibles', he was worth keeping in the side because he had some wonderful gifts." Offers McIlroy, "Tommy I think felt we had enough people that could go about defending and we had a solid defence line. Maybe some of the lads thought Gordon wasn't pulling his weight, but as a manager if you've got a player who can get you 20 goals what do you say to him? Where do you want him to work? I just think The Doc wanted Gordon to do his business in the final third and leave the defensive sort of things to the rest of the boys. Now whether that is fair or not, it didn't really bother me. I knew what Gordon was all about." Daly offers, "I think it's something to do with the Manchester United bit. You couldn't just play for Manchester United and be ordinary. You had to do something. They were brought up on

Georgie Best and that business, Denis and all that, and all the great players previous to that. You couldn't just go out there and pick the ball up and pass it two yards and then get on your way. You had to be seen to do something with the ball and I think that was Docherty's attitude as well. You couldn't just go out at Old Trafford and win. You had to entertain." However, McIlroy does say, "I'm definitely sure The Doc wouldn't have said to Gordon Hill, 'Don't you worry about tracking back', because he wasn't that type of manager. Everyone had to pull their shift in." Asked if Docherty was indulgent of Hill in terms of failing to deliver bollockings, Greenhoff responds, "That's all about man-management. Some need patting on the back when they've had a bad game, and some need bollocking when they've had a bad game. No two players are the same. You treat them all the same when it comes to the rules but when it comes to getting the best out of them you've got to have your own ways of doing it. I think he did need a cuddle, Gordon. He used to do it different with me. He used to get Tommy Cav to have a go at me and liven me up, but that's fine. If it gets the best out of me then I'm okay." Blunstone acknowledges that Docherty was indulgent of the winger: "Oh, he liked Gordon. Tommy likes a laugh and *he* liked a laugh. Both of them were very similar, that's why they got on so well. He accepted it, Tommy, because he was such a good goalscorer. The trouble is, if you start making them come back and work harder for the team, they don't score the goals. Steve had to come back and work harder than Gordon because he didn't score the goals that Gordon scored. Once you start getting them to come back and defend, you've taken away their assets. You can't do that with them type of players. You've got to accept they won't run back and track back now and again." When the suggestion is put to him that Hill couldn't do two jobs – tracking back and scoring prolifically – Buchan says, "I don't know. That's your opinion. We can both see the same situation and form different opinions about it." He also says, "Some of the games that we played, when he didn't make much of a contribution and he got a winning bonus, he wasn't going to say, 'Oh, you lads have my bonus because I never did the business today.' It's a team game. Look at Kenny Dalglish, one of the most talented players ever to play in the English First Division. He wasn't above doing his share of the work."

Nicholl actually recalls the Alan Green incident as effecting a change in the general attitude toward Hill: "If he did come back, he would try and dribble out of defence or he'd try and do a wee trick. He was actually more of a hindrance … It was after that, we turned round and said, 'Right okay, we'll defend without Hilly coming back'." However, either Nicholl's memory is failing him here or he is mistaking the indulgence of himself, Docherty and others for a general acceptance that Hill was above the rules. Dressing room resentment towards Hill for his lack of effort seems to have become something of a cancer within United. The resentment wasn't restricted to the criticism that the winger left gaps by not chasing back. Stepney would later say that Hill "hid" during matches, footballer's parlance for not making himself an obvious target for a pass from his team-mates, an accusation usually only made about a player when a match isn't going well for his team. "I wasn't one of those players that you can say it's all-round," concedes Hill. "I was an out-and-out striker, crosser and a scorer. I would agree that I left gaps, I'd agree that I'd lapse in maybe my defending qualities." He adds in a somewhat confused, even cavalier remark that perhaps gives a flavour of the attitude that infuriated some colleagues, "But it wasn't because I didn't want to do it, it was a case of well, I just didn't do it."

Hill does say, "I never got permission to not defend. I got my fair crack of bollocking if I didn't do something." Yet he adds something that almost suggests a feeling of scapegoating: "If a ball goes in the back of the net, Alex [Stepney] could have said it about a lot of people, but I was there and I think I was maybe the one that they looked at. I was an outlet. Which is fine. Which is no skin off my nose, because I'd get, shall we say, a whack on the back and then the next minute I'd put the ball in the net and I'd get a pat on the back." However, he does contend that he was not complacent about the shortcomings others asserted existed in his game: "I accepted the bollocking and then I would try harder next time. If I got a bollocking I was aware of the situation that I got a bollocking in." Does he feel he developed as a player? "Yes. Not only experience-wise, I think I got a bit of an understanding of other people as well."

*\*\**

On Wednesday January 19, an unchanged United met Bristol City at Old Trafford in front of a 43,051 crowd. Though City started the match third from bottom of the table, United wouldn't have forgotten that back when both teams were in the Second Division, City were the only team to beat United home and away throughout the campaign. However, if today City looked like repeating those victories over the Reds, it was not through the quality of their football. Afterwards, the visitors' roughneck approach had Docherty fuming.

City got a goal in the fifth minute through Keith Fear after Houston hesitated when he thought the ball had crossed the touchline. Perhaps unsettled by that rookie-like mistake, Houston didn't have a particularly good game. Neither did Nicholl on the other defensive wing. Meanwhile, United's attacking play was stymied by both a defensive blanket and City's less than subtle challenges. The Reds finally broke through the thicket of bodies just after the interval when Pearson headed in a chipped Coppell free-kick. It was his 14th goal of the season, a significant number, because it meant that he had already equalled his final tally for last season. With 10 minutes to go, Hill had a crack at goal. His shot seemed destined for the area wide of the post when suddenly Brian Greenhoff stuck out a boot and did what his brother had been striving to all match in vain: projected the ball into the back of the City net.

The 2-1 victory – United's fourth successive home League win – saw the Reds climb to ninth in the table. Of greater immediate concern to The Doc though was the fact that Coppell looked doubtful for Saturday's fixture as he was receiving treatment for a damaged ankle. Docherty once more publicly appealed for a clampdown on foul play. "We will never have a great international team in England until referees start giving more protection to the skilful players …" he said. He went on, "We are the cleanest team in the Football League. That is a fact, otherwise we would not be top of the Fair Play League. The referee never had control of the game. Bristol tried to provoke us. It was … too much for the young ones." However, Docherty was able to wrap up his state-of-the-union address with a certain degree of satisfaction: "Victory went to the team trying to play football. Bristol City got what they deserved – nothing."

\*\*\*

The Bristol game had seen Gerry Daly yet again go unpicked. He had made just one appearance, and that as a substitute, since the Arsenal match a month before. Accordingly, not many will have been completely surprised to have seen stories in the papers following the Bristol match that stated Daly wanted a transfer. "I have spoken to the manager and made my feelings plain," he was quoted as saying. "I've told him I want a move and there is no going back on it. The reason must be obvious and I'm determined to go through with this." The same story relayed the information that Docherty was insisting that the Irishman would not get his wish fulfilled. "I've told Gerry to put his request in writing," said The Doc. "I've also told him he's wasting his money on the stamp because there's no way he will be leaving. There are one-and-a-half years of his contract remaining. He'll see that through and he'll be here while I'm manager. I've already spoken to my chairman and directors and they are of the same opinion. Gerry is a great player and a great lad but this reaction is a bit misguided to say the least. He should know that if he's playing well he will be back in the first team, and that if he isn't doing it in the reserves there's always the 'A' team. I have Daly, Macari and McIlroy, three first-class players, for two midfield places, and I wouldn't trade any of them. But while I've decided to leave Daly out for the moment, the ball is still very much in his court. Provided he adopts the right attitude, there's a tremendous future for him here."

Daly, though, says something about this story that calls into question many other quotes reproduced in this book from contemporary newspaper reports about bust-ups between The Doc and his players: "I didn't put in a transfer request." So how does he explain this quite detailed published quote supposedly from himself saying precisely the opposite? Daly: "Maybe Docherty put it in ... That was probably the done thing in them particular days. Get the crowd, the supporters, to think, 'Oh, he wants to go so what's the difference, let him go' and make him look the good guy."

\*\*\*

Thankfully, Coppell's ankle recovered sufficiently for Docherty to be able to field the Roll Call Mark II for the away match against Birmingham City on Saturday January 22. Intriguingly, Daly, not McCreery, was sub. He would come on for Hill in the 85th minute.

Before the Birmingham match, Docherty was publicly reflecting on the change in his side's fortunes. "We are playing as a team again," he said. "We had an excellent away record early this season before our lean spell and I am sure we are on our way back towards playing well away from home again as well as on our own ground." In terms of grander ambitions, he said, "We have set our sights on qualifying for Europe again and I am quite confident we can finish in fifth or sixth place."

Birmingham's skilful international Trevor Francis opened the scoring in the 22nd minute. United recovered within a minute via a Houston header. On 27 minutes, Jimmy Greenhoff tapped a low cross over the line. Pearson got the Reds' third. A dangerous challenge from Jones saw Brian Greenhoff hobble off the field but he quickly returned to the fray at the insistence of Docherty. One could understand why when, late on, Emmanuel scored for Birmingham.

For Trevor Francis, the Greenhoff goal should never have stood. He said of a linesman, "First of all he flagged for a foul throw by Lou Macari in the build-up to the goal. But he dropped it when the ball finished up in our net. At one apiece the goal came at a very critical time for us." The 3-2 victory in front of 35,316 people left United eighth in the table. Liverpool led by a point, but second-placed Ipswich had three games in hand over them.

Saturday January 29 saw the Reds take on Queens Park Rangers at home in the fourth round of the FA Cup. The starting XI trotted out unchanged again in front of a gate of 57,422. Perversely, the wingers seemed to thrive in treacherous conditions that had left one side of the pitch soft-going, the other hard and dry. The two wide players were both involved in the goal that came in the 16th minute, but then so were a lot of people in a movement that summed up United's hyperactive and intermeshed style. It was Macari who ultimately headed the ball into the Rangers net. QPR were as determined as Walsall had been in the previous round and actually hit the woodwork twice in the second-half, as well as creating a scramble in the United goalmouth that saw McIlroy hit the underside of his own bar. The final whistle went with neither side having added to the scoring tally.

The combination of good luck and good team-work that had seen them through another close FA Cup victory made some of the United team – notably Alex Stepney and Steve Coppell – begin to feel that this year the FA Cup had their team's name on it. The Docherty pledge from the bus in Albert Square the previous season was, for Coppell, typical Docherty bravado and what the crowd wanted to hear. The players, he felt, were glad that this "pie-in-the-sky" stuff was going down so well. But he also felt that Docherty honestly meant what he was saying. By Coppell's account, it was not a pledge restricted to the emotional aftermath of the final. "He was to repeat it so often throughout the next season that we eventually became convinced as well," Coppell said. Says Meek, "I think sometimes a team does play as if they believe their name is on the Cup, which is the key thing, and it does work out it's a particular team's year."

With seven victories in eight matches going into the Reds' League fixture against fast-sinking Derby County at Old Trafford on Saturday February 5, it was little wonder that Docherty was named Bell's Whiskey's Manager of the Month. The injured Hill was replaced by Daly in the only line-up change.

"We failed to cope with the steamroller start United make so often at home and got caught by a goal early in each half," reflected Rams manager Colin Murphy afterwards. That steamroller start – delighting the United fans in the 54,044 crowd – culminated in Macari putting the ball in the net in the ninth minute. Nine minutes into the second-half, Houston nodded in from close range. On the hour mark, an attempt by Derby's Powell to clear a McIlroy cross saw him getting on the scoresheet against his own team. Derby got a consolation goal with 10 minutes left, but, said The Doc, "Derby only played as well as we let them – it's as simple as that." Liverpool and Ipswich were still top of a table in which United had now climbed to seventh.

The Wednesday after the Derby match saw Old Trafford play host to Alex Stepney's testimonial. A healthy crowd of 37,988 turned out to pay their respects to the man who had racked up nearly 500 appearances in all competitions for the Reds. Logically, United were playing Benfica, the team who had been the opposition during the greatest victory of Stepney's footballing career, and whose Eusebio had given the goalie the opportunity to immortalise himself in United lore with that crucial save in the dying moments of normal time. Some might have felt that this match was a distraction, particularly at this stage of the season, but Docherty was employing the same philosophy that had seen him arrange friendly matches with top European sides at a time when United weren't fit to be on the same pitch as them: this was no nostalgia-fest involving the aged, mostly retired teams from the 1968 clash but the current sides of the respective clubs. The manager knew the experience would do his team good in any European competition to which they might obtain entry the following season.

Little can be read into the happenings of a testimonial match but observers thought it was played fairly seriously for such an affair and that Stepney made some genuinely good saves. United won 2-1, Coppell scoring on seven minutes, Macari on 12, and Chalana replying for the opposition in the 75th minute. England were playing Holland that night at Wembley. At one point, the Old Trafford scoreboard flashed up some dismaying latest news: "England 0 Holland 2." "Stepney for England!" chanted the Stretford Enders in response.

Stepney's match tally for United put him – at the time –behind only Bobby Charlton and Bill Foulkes, but after the game he stressed that the fact of the testimonial should not be taken to imply that he was thinking of retirement. "I want to keep going," insisted the man who was nearly halfway through his biblical three-score-and-ten.

*\*\**

The following Saturday, February 12, United visited White Hart Lane. Hill had recovered from his injury, so it was back to the Roll Call Mark II. That Tottenham had lately tumbled toward the relegation zone made no less impressive the way the Reds took them apart. Certainly reporter Norman Fox was enthused. "Their fast interchanging of positions was far from typical of the League game," he wrote. The visitors were ahead by the third minute via Macari. McIlroy got the second on 32 minutes. Three minutes after that, Tottenham gave the impression of having at least half a chance when Jones scored. However, they failed to build on that goal and on the hour mark, Hill underlined the reality of United's dominance by beating Pat Jennings from an acute angle.

Docherty admitted after the 3-1 victory that his team's marking was slack and could have cost them the lead. "But we'll carry on our way even if occasionally we come unstuck," he said. United were up to sixth in the League and this climb of 11 places in the space of seven weeks now had Docherty seriously thinking about not finishing in fifth or sixth place, as he had recently been publicly contemplating, but rather his club's prospects of catching up with leaders Liverpool and Ipswich. He cited the forthcoming March 5 derby at Old Trafford as the fixture that would decide whether the Reds had a real chance of recovering that ground they had lost during their poor spell. "They are the best side I've seen," he said of United's neighbours, currently lying third in the division. "If we can win that one, I think you can start talking seriously of us in terms of being dark horses for the title."

Macari scoring was sweet for the Scotsman for more than one reason. Macari had become almost convinced that he was jinxed in the capital. Remarkably, this fixture marked the first occasion in which a team containing Macari had won in London. What with the fact that the FA Cup final was of course a London event, might this not be another little sign that a certain Manchester team had their name on a certain trophy this season?

Though the Tottenham fans in the 45,946 crowd might not have been disposed after this humiliation to agree with Lou Macari's post-match boast that United were "the top entertainers in the country" they would be in a minority. More than one journalist made a caustic comparison between United's skilful, sophisticated play and the clod-hopping performance England had given in midweek against the Dutch. Though Scots and Irishmen made up half of their team, the Reds also had plenty of players eligible for England. Brian Greenhoff and Stuart Pearson had been on England duty on Wednesday and Hill was currently on the fringes of the national team. However, Don Revie never took full advantage of the opportunities the Manchester United side of that era offered him. Reporting on the match, journalist Harry Miller said, "If England boss Don Revie, of the ever changing mind, means it when he suggests it will be back to wingers and a target man, then United have got something for him: Gordon Hill and Stuart Pearson." He could have added that United had something else for him: Steve Coppell and Jimmy Greenhoff. Though Hill, Coppell and Pearson all played for Revie at various points, the England boss never capped the elder Greenhoff. Neither did any other England manager.

His uncapped status made Jimmy Greenhoff a real rarity at Old Trafford at this point. As Hill points out, "All our squad was away when we had internationals. During the week, there was nobody at the training ground. Alex Stepney used to get a breather." By the time of Greenhoff Major's arrival, there were just two first-team regulars who had not been capped at senior level for their countries. Those players were Coppell, who made his full England debut a few days after Jimmy Greenhoff signed for United, and Jimmy Nicholl, who made his Northern Ireland debut the month thereafter. This statistic is made all the more lamentable by how bewildering it is. Though the elder Greenhoff was unfortunate enough to play in an era in which he was in competition for an England place with the likes of Kevin Keegan, Mick Channon and Joe Royle, many who saw him in action shake their head in utter mystification

397

that he didn't get at least a smattering of international appearances. Hill speaks for many when he describes Jimmy Greenhoff as "the best uncapped player around". "I was like most people – I was very surprised that he hadn't been capped," says Brian Greenhoff, but he also points out that his brother's uncapped status was partly down to misfortune: "There's a few instances when he did get picked and things happened so he couldn't play. He was actually picked when he was at Stoke but I think the club had a game. When it was only a friendly, it was club before country, so he had to pull out of the squad. Another time, he was going to be picked in the squad but got injured."

Though Revie had plenty of good strikers to call on, it would have been interesting to say the least if he had done what some were urging him to do and picked the entire Manchester United front-line for the national side. If Coppell, Pearson, Jimmy Greenhoff and Hill were tearing defences apart for their club, the chances were they could have achieved the same for England. While some might suggest that Hill especially always underperformed for England, that misgiving is easily countered by the fact that the familiarity of working with his club colleagues at national level would surely have raised his game. Brian Greenhoff: "Course it could have worked. They all knew what each other was doing. We did it in the Under-23s against Hungary: we had Stevie Coppell on the right, Stuart Pearson at centre-forward and Gordon Hill on the left. I played at the back and it worked. England tried it once with Liverpool in the 70s when they put about six or seven of them in the team." It was not to be. History records a prosaic and underachieving England team at this juncture rather than a swashbuckling, Red-led side that rolled back the legacy of the Wingless Wonders.

\*\*\*

Though a home fixture, United's next match – on Wednesday February 16 – was a more difficult game than their recent run-outs against relegation battlers. Though Liverpool had had an indifferent spell lately, especially away from home where they had lost four times in recent fixtures, they were without question championship contenders.

The match was the usual contrast of styles between the collectivism of the possession football of Liverpool and the individualism United – unchanged from the last match – favoured. Liverpool's machine-like offside trap – which halted play time and time again – did not go down well with the United fans in the large gate of 57,487. Having said that, there wasn't much negative about the way Liverpool went on the attack, heedless of the intimidating atmosphere of a packed Old Trafford. The first-half was Liverpool's by a small margin. The second-half saw United get more into the match, but the impasse continued. The game ended

0-0. Though the Merseysiders had brought a halt to United's seven-match winning streak, the home side had prevented the visitors from obtaining their first away victory for more than two months. United were still placed sixth in the table, seven points behind leaders Ipswich, who led Liverpool on goal difference.

Newcastle United were the Reds' next competition on Saturday February 19, a home fixture watched by 51,828. Newcastle were one of the division's more attractive sides, so the game was one of enjoyable, open football. However, the Magpies were simply overwhelmed by a team whose ground almost always brought them slim pickings. Even so, while the Reds (unchanged from the Liverpool match) had many chances, only one man made the most of his: Jimmy Greenhoff. In the ninth minute, Greenhoff senior sent Mahoney the wrong way when he scored a typically classy goal by allowing the ball to glance off his boot from a Pearson shot. His second, on 35 minutes, had a whiff of offside about it – he seemed to be past the last man as he executed a simple tap-in – but in any case, in the 73rd minute he got a legitimate third when Coppell's corner found Houston's head, then his. Newcastle's consolation goal came in the 31st minute. The occasional wobbliness of United's defence was mentioned in despatches today and it was a common theme in match reports of the period. But then so was the dependability of Buchan. His ability to deal with threats from forwards – today Gowling and Mitchell – seemed to compensate for the frequent inconsistency of the United backline, which can probably be put down to youth.

After the match, Liverpool were top of the table, leading Ipswich by two points, Manchester City by three and United by seven. However, the result left United in fourth place, and – with a game in hand over Liverpool – they were now serious title contenders for the first time this season, unless you counted their brief occupancy of the pole position on goal difference in October. As Brian Greenhoff said after the match, "It's amazing when you remember that terrible run when we could not do a thing right. We scraped three points out of 16 and now we have lost only the same in ten matches. We are right in the groove. There is a long way to go and a lot of good teams in the hunt but if folk are looking for the dark horses then I suppose we are not a bad bet."

Jimmy Greenhoff's hat-trick was only the fourth of his career. It couldn't have come at a better time for the veteran, for although few were doubting his delicate touch and footballing intelligence, his two goals in 14 appearances in a United shirt before today was not exactly a prolific rate for a man in his position, even if you could state the (reasonable) defence that a team with as many forwards as Manchester United didn't actually expect strikers to be as productive as did other teams. It was a point Greenhoff made afterwards. "I was happy to get those goals," he said, "but unlike Stoke, where I was often a lone ranger up front, there is no pressure on me here to score. At Manchester, we play four up and get men into the box all the time. Someone is bound to score a few in that situation and while it was my turn I benefited from the hard work of others like Stuart Pearson." Brian Greenhoff now says of that initial goal drought on the part of his brother, "It was obvious what he was adding to the team. You've got runners like Stevie on right, you'd Gordon on left, you'd Lou and Sammy in middle – all good athletes and they could make a run knowing that he'll just knock the ball into their path. It was just a matter of most strikers, once they get a goal, they're up and running."

The partnership the elder Greenhoff had formed with Pancho was impressive, for many had initially felt that the two were too similar in their playing styles and might cancel one another out rather than complement each other. The English footballing tradition was for a pairing of strength and skill: a big, powerful centre-forward working in combination with somebody less capable of physical prowess but with tidier feet. But just as Pearson displayed delicate touch while being nobody's pushover, so Greenhoff's lovely control didn't mean he wasn't capable of giving as good as he got from defenders. Meanwhile, at 5'10", Greenhoff was little more imposing than Pearson. Buchan says, "He developed very quickly a great understanding with Stuart Pearson and it was a treat to play with him. You felt you could stand with the ball in the middle of the back four and close your eyes and punt it upfield and one of the two of them would be on the end of it. It was almost uncanny." Says Nicholl, "Sometimes your defence is under pressure for not holding a ball up upfront but Jimmy, it would stick to him." All the more remarkable is the fact that there had actually been a rumour at the time of Greenhoff senior's signing that this partnership was something not even envisaged by Docherty and that he was contemplating Greenhoff as a replacement for an arguably out-of-form Pearson. "We meshed perfectly," Jimmy later said. "It seemed that we knew each others' intentions instinctively, so that if one of us received the ball, the other was running instantly into the right place for a pass." Stating that their understanding at times seemed almost telepathic, Jimmy said, "We both liked the ball to feet, we both tried to keep the game flowing, but we were capable of shielding it if heavily marked." "They would always make themselves available," says Brian Greenhoff of the combination of his brother and Pancho. "They were very easy to play with." Steve Coppell simply said of the elder Greenhoff, "He was the best player I ever played with."

Apart from their temperaments – Jimmy Greenhoff was endlessly benevolent, while Pearson could have his prickly moments – one way the members of the strike force weren't similar was experience. Jimmy Greenhoff had only three years on Pearson, but unlike Pancho he had vast knowledge of life at the very top of the game. Consequently, the younger man could see, and learn from, the extra tricks and layers of ability that came from that greater experience. Greenhoff's extra years also made him a target for defenders: because he was a known commodity as a goalscorer, opposition teams wound up marking him, which took significant pressure off Pearson.

Jimmy Greenhoff immediately loved United, and not just for the no doubt great pleasure of playing in a team with his brother. "Everything about United is big, every game a Cup Final" said the veteran, who also marvelled, "I feel like a young lad starting all over again."

***

"The Cup's got our name on it" is a line dismissed by many as footballers' crackerbarrel philosophy, but it was remarkable how fate this season seemed to be lining up opportunities for United to exact revenge for previous FA Cup humiliations, with the implication of it being a laying-of-the-ground for a grander ultimate prize. Just as the third round had enabled them to put Walsall in what might be termed their proper place, on Saturday February 26 they had the opportunity to obtain payback for what had happened at Wembley last year. Since the Southampton defeat, the wound of that notable day had had salt rubbed into it by the opportunity to see the winning goal on television replays. The consensus was that the goal was offside and a sense of injustice lingered in the air in the run-up to the fifth-round fixture between the Red Devils and the Saints that took place at The Dell. Asked if footballers really do think of such an occasion as a – to use a tabloid phrase – grudge match, Brian Greenhoff says, "Oh, aye. You do like that: 'Ooh, God, got them. Good. We owe 'em one'." Asked if he was seeking revenge for last year, Docherty said, "No, we are not looking for that. The lads just want to get to Wembley again to make up for last season."

To some extent, this was a different Southampton team to the one that had, fairly or unfairly, beaten United last year, with only five of the Cup-winning side remaining. Jim McCalliog had now fallen from favour, Alan Ball having usurped him in the first team. Interestingly, though, another of Docherty's discards was now playing for Southampton and scoring prolifically: our old friend from this narrative, Ted MacDougall. When Docherty was asked about MacDougall, he admitted, "I have had more letters about him than any other player I have sold or released." Defiantly, he appended, "But I have always done what I thought was right for Manchester United." In another defiant interview before the Southampton tie, Docherty attacked those who had criticised him during United's lean spell at the end of the previous year. "There were plenty of pony soldiers waiting in the bushes with the long knives," he said. Asked about whether he had thought of making wholesale changes to the United team following the Cup Final defeat the way he had with Chelsea, he made a comment that indicated he regretted letting valuable players leave Stamford Bridge. "People won't accept that I've changed since the days when I turned Chelsea inside out," he said. "They can't see that I've got no intention of throwing away the best job in the world ... It was certain we'd go through a bad patch. When that followed the defeat at Wembley, I looked hard at the team we'd got and considered whether I ought to try to strengthen it. But the more I considered, the more certain I became that there were very few players better than those we already had. Jimmy Greenhoff brought a little maturity ... because that's one commodity with which you cannot endow players. I couldn't tell them how be to be mature. They had to learn. In its way, losing the Cup Final was a very sobering experience for some of the lads. We brought in Greenhoff and a couple of good characters to ginger up the competition for places, but by and large the composition of the team hasn't changed. But they are a bit more aware of what it's all about. That bit more grown-up. So I believe we've come out of it all as a better side."

A real seesaw of a match followed and a thrilling spectacle for the 29,137 crowd, whatever their loyalties. United – unchanged – seemed a little nervous at the start. The sight of Buchan tripping MacDougall from behind and Brian Greenhoff virtually wrestling Alan Ball to the ground was somewhat disconcerting for the many who viewed The Doc's Devils as English football's nice guys. Macari got the opening goal in the 13th minute by heading in an excellent Jimmy Greenhoff cross. Approaching the half-hour mark, Houston showed yet another sign of what seemed a desperation not to be humiliated again by this club by bringing down Channon. The resultant penalty was scored by David Peach. Hill silenced the faithful at The Dell temporarily in the 39th minute by scoring – not for the first time this season – from an acute angle. But a side who had beaten the Reds against all the odds the previous summer were not going to surrender easily. Just before the interval, Mick Holmes drove the ball home with his left foot.

In the second-half, Southampton seemed to be turning things their way and matters weren't helped when Jimmy Greenhoff had to go off injured in the 63rd minute, McCreery replacing him. Some Reds – players, as well as supporters – must have been relieved when the referee blew for time, and a replay with home advantage beckoned.

"But for Alex Stepney we would be out of the Cup," gushed Docherty afterwards. Stepney resisted the opportunity to retort that if the manager had shown such faith in him the previous season they might have been reigning champions at this point. An even more intriguing comment from Docherty after the match came regarding the penalty. Docherty readily conceded that Houston had committed a professional foul on Channon – deliberately denied him a goalscoring opportunity – and apologised to Channon and the Southampton fans for the incident.

\*\*\*

On March 3 1977, one of the signings that Docherty had said he'd made to "ginger up the competition for places" created a major casualty in United's ranks when Gerry Daly got his wish for a transfer. At least, that's what people would have believed at the time because of the story that had appeared in the newspapers six weeks previously.

Daly's destination was Derby County, ironically the club against whom he had made what turned out to be his final appearance for Manchester United in February. It was reported that Derby County manager Colin Murphy had twice had offers to buy the unsettled Irishman rejected by Docherty in the space of a fortnight, but that The Doc finally buckled when he was offered £175,000, a United club record for a departing player. (Some sources say it was £170,000, which would make it an equal club record with the fee MacDougall's sale fetched.) Said Docherty, "Gerry is a good player but this was an offer I couldn't refuse." Daly was said to have signed with Derby after six hours of talks and, according to the press, said, "There was no major problem over my signing for Derby. It was just a big decision and took me some time to make up my mind. I am going to help stave off relegation but they are also eyeing me in the long term." Another contemporary quote from Daly about the move was, "I am leaving United without any hard feelings." Today, Daly says this was nothing like the truth.

"We used to go to Blackpool for day outs, for saunas and things," he recalls. "We were on the coach and Cavanagh walked up to me on the coach and he said, 'The manager wants to see you in the office ... ' Not even having the balls to tell me why the manager wanted to speak to me ... As soon as I got off the coach, the coach left. And I thought, 'Well, that's strange. Something's going up here' ... And all the players are looking out the window at me as I'm walking in the door and they're all sort of going, 'What's up?'" When Daly entered Docherty's office, what turned out to be 'up' was a bit of a shock: "He just said to me that Derby County had come in and made a bid for me and the club has accepted it. I said, 'I don't want to go.' And he said, 'Well look Gerry, the way I see things is I want you to go and as far as I'm concerned you'll never, ever play for the first team again.' I said, 'Well, I don't care – I'm not leaving'." While that meeting was a jolt for Daly, following it he had another one that was rather peculiar. Daly found himself approached by the pair who had been his mentors at the club. "Sir Matt Busby and Jimmy Murphy told me that they didn't want me to leave Old Trafford," says Daly. "They said to me, 'There's something going on. We can't tell you what it's about but all we can say to you is we want you here at Old Trafford, so don't go.' Then I told them that Docherty had said to me, 'Well, you'll never going to play for the first team again so you may as well be on your way.' They said, 'Well, we can't comment on what he said to you but all we're saying to you is don't leave Old Trafford'."

However, a crestfallen Daly became resigned to the idea of leaving: "I decided then that after what the manager had told me that that was it. But when I agreed to go and meet the Derby people down in The Belfry in Sutton Coldfield, we went upstairs and had a meeting with Colin Murphy and I said, 'No, I'm not happy about the situation, I'm not going.' So then next thing I know is Murphy is on the phone up in the room and he's obviously speaking to Tommy Docherty and then Tommy Docherty comes up to the room and we had a bit of an argument when I said I didn't want to go. Actually my wife was there and I remember her standing up and saying, 'Don't you ever speak to him like that.' That was it. The both of us left. There was a chap by the name of Norman, he was the coach driver at one time and then eventually he used to sit on the bench. He was there 'cos he'd obviously driven up with Docherty. Docherty decided I think to stay over at The Belfry that particular night and I said I wanted to go back to Manchester with my wife and Norman had to drive us back. But then we had a discussion about it all night and then decided, 'Okay, 'I'll sign for Derby'." However, he adds, "I never wanted to leave Manchester United and since then I've been proved correct in the amount of phone calls that I got from players that played there [saying] how disappointed they were that I'd gone. 'Cos I think they were all of the opinion that this is what I wanted. I also know from the letters that I received and from the years gone by since that the supporters didn't want me to go either." Of the suggestion implicit in press coverage of the transfer that he was not prepared to fight for his place in the team, he says simply, "That's a load of crap. It's a load of bullshit, that."

The turn of events was distressing and bewildering for Daly. "In the early years, when he brought me over, I liked Tommy," he says. "I thought he was great. I thought he had a great sense of humour. You're playing, you're happy, you're delighted to be at Old Trafford, everybody is treating you well, you're doing the best you can out on the pitch, everything is going swimmingly. And then for some God-given reason, things change. I can't give you an explanation as to why it changed. I just don't know." An indication of how quickly things had turned around for Daly is his fond memories of the close season after 1975/76 when he travelled over to Malta to accept the Player of the Year award from that country's Manchester

United Supporters Club (the oldest United supporters association in the world). Daly recalls, "He arrived over there when they were making the presentation to me. We had a great time."

What must have made it particularly galling for Daly to find himself exiled was the fact that he had previously rebuffed an approach by Ajax for his services in, he estimates, 1975. Daly: "When I was at Old Trafford I opened up a shop in Manchester. It was like a newsagent and then there was a greengrocers. It was my wife actually that done it all ... I used to go in after training and things like that, just stand behind the counter to try and get some customers in because they all knew, because my name was over the bloody door basically ... While I was there this bloke walked in and he was a foreign sort of chap ... He said he was an agent for Ajax in Amsterdam. I remember him saying 'Would I fancy coming out?' I said, 'Why would I want to go out and sign for Ajax when I'm at Manchester United?'"

Asked if he thought The Doc rated him as a player, Daly says, "Oh, I think he did." So why sell him? Daly: "I was always of the opinion that he needed to sell somebody to finance the [Jimmy] Greenhoff deal ... I think a lot of it had to do with Tommy Cavanagh. I didn't get on particularly well with Cavanagh. I wouldn't say me more than most. It could have been anyone as far as Cavanagh was concerned, because I can't remember him actually getting on with anybody." In light of Daly's conviction that The Doc was selling him for financial as opposed to football reasons, it's interesting to note a purse-strings-conscious comment Docherty made in the press at the time of the sale: "There won't be any more big-money players being signed by me this season – unless we are hit by a calamity. I believe I have got the necessary resources to cover most situations with the players now in my first-team squad. There won't be any big-money recruits just because we have let Gerry go." It should also be pointed out that it was in Docherty's interests to falsely claim – as Daly is effectively saying he did – that the player wanted a move: a club transferring a player without the player's consent is breaking his contract, which costs the club money that the player forfeits if he formally submits a transfer request.

The sale of a high-quality player like Daly seems exceedingly unwise. Whether the decision to part so readily with Daly was a consequence of that over-eagerness to get rid of players who were not currently in favour noted before, Docherty's impulsiveness (also noted before) or the consequence of Docherty's one-in, one-out transfer policy (again, previously mentioned) is unknown. McIlroy (who remained good friends with Daly even when they were competing for a place) revealed where he stood on the issue in his autobiography in which he said, "Tommy Docherty will make decisions on the spot, whereas most other managers will stop and think – and think again ... I reckoned the decision to sell Gerry Daly was made in haste and possibly repented at leisure … I believe … he should never have been allowed to leave Manchester United." Hill says, "I thought Gerry was a great player and I was surprised. I never delved into it but I think you always ask the question why." McIlroy also said of Docherty's regime, "There was never a day when you went down to the ground for training without wondering who was coming and who was on his way, for players came and players went in quick succession." Speaking today, McIlroy, though he admits Daly's sale was "a bit of [a] shock", suggests the move was part of the pattern of Docherty's endless tinkering with and refining of the team/squad: "He would bring people in and let people go. That's the way that The Doc did [it]. He was always trying to add to the squad and change the squad."

Blunstone recalls, "Tommy didn't fancy Gerry Daly. He liked a drink, he liked a smoke, he was a bit airy-fairy and a bit of a airy-fairy character. He weren't a bad footballer, don't get me wrong, but even when he went to Derby he didn't pull any trees up there. Tommy would have accepted his lifestyle if he'd have done it on the field all the time. He was in and out, Gerry." Meek agrees with Blunstone's and (allegedly) Docherty's assessment of the Irishman: "Gerry Daly did extremely well, but I think he played above himself basically. He wasn't a top-drawer player. He would have been found out if he'd continued much longer. I think he felt that Gerry Daly had given him as much as he was capable of giving."

The logic involved in the unanimous feelings of Blunstone, Meek and (allegedly) The Doc seems peculiar. Either a player does well on the pitch or he doesn't. Daly had been considered by most observers to be thriving. Meek's comment about Daly playing above himself seems almost to suggest that the reporter thinks Daly was hypnotising people into believing he was a better player than he was, a smoke-and-mirrors feat surely impossible in what was even back then the toughest and most closely observed League in the world. Only the previous season, a reporter had made a flattering comparison between Daly and Rivera, widely considered one of the world's greatest players during the 70s. Daly chuckles at Meek's comments. "I think it's a load of rubbish," he says. "It's water off a duck's back to me now. (It wouldn't have been at that particular time.) My response to that is there's an awful lot of clubs that wanted to sign me that I didn't end up playing for."

In matches later this season, it would have been handy, to say the least, to have a player of Daly's class around, even if only to bring him on as a substitute when the occasion demanded. With no disrespect to the useful McCreery, replacing the tired legs of McIlroy, Macari, Coppell or Hill – to cite the most obvious names whose positions Daly could slot into – with a player of Daly's calibre would have been an option that might have made all the difference in some matches in this campaign between the Reds winning and losing.

And that is not even mentioning matches where injury required Docherty to field relative novices and/or mediocrities from kick-off.

*\*\*\**

The names of Derby County and Tommy Docherty were publicly linked again the following month. In early March, stories began appearing in newspapers claiming that the club to whom Docherty had sold Daly were interested in making Docherty their manager. Lately the Rams had seen their fortunes tumble to such an extent that they were currently bottom of the First Division. One of said stories alleged that things were not as happy as they might appear at Old Trafford and that this might prompt Docherty to jump ship. The source of that unhappiness was supposedly Matt Busby's continuing influence at the club, particularly over Louis Edwards. 'One of Docherty's friends' was quoted by the paper as saying, "He has not been able to resolve what he regards as a problem and is likely to do something more about it." It was presumably this 'friend' who cited as another reason for the manager's restlessness "little troubles" between himself and unnamed United players.

'A friend' is often cited as a source by newspapers in the event of the information contained in the story coming from the story's subject when that person wants to be quoted without attribution. Though it's perfectly plausible that Derby had made overtures to Docherty, some suspected that the story had been planted by Docherty in a bid to get United to extend his contract despite the fact that his contract had been extended and its terms improved at the beginning of the previous season. The story would rumble on throughout the season.

At around the same time, it became publicly known that Martin Buchan was considering his options. The skipper's contract expired at the end of the season and at 28 he was looking for security. Though Buchan was hardly a prima donna, he can't have been unaware of his importance to the team, as underlined by their disastrous form when he had been absent earlier in the campaign. However, Louis Edwards claimed that the club was caught between Buchan's desire for a significant wage rise and the Government's pay freeze. "I know 100 footballers in the same plight," the chairman was quoted as saying. "I don't know if there is any way round this ... He'll have to ask [prime minister] Mr Callaghan."

*\*\*\**

Saturday March 5 saw the match Docherty had recently spoken of as a litmus test for his team's championship chances: the fixture against Manchester City at Old Trafford. United were unchanged again for a game watched by 58,595 people. The team The Doc had recently described as the best he'd seen this season were going through a poor spell, having lost considerable ground via four consecutive defeats in their most recent encounters. The crackling atmosphere of a local derby – albeit one afflicted by strong winds – did not serve to perk up the Blues, who seemed less committed than their red counterparts throughout and uninterested in going forward. The star of the match was Macari, who – as he always seemed to in these derbies – raised his game and commitment above even his usual high levels. The opening goal saw Pearson calmly side-footing home. The next goal was a low drive from Hill who – as per – evaded a defender before striking and – as per – scored from an implausible angle. The home side's third came eight minutes into the second-half when Coppell volleyed superbly from the edge of the area. City replied through Royle.

Whether or not this 3-1 victory was indeed the litmus test Docherty had suggested, the prognosis afterwards was certainly good. The Reds, who had defeated their arch enemies by the same scoreline that they had managed at Maine Road in September and who were now the only team to have beaten City both home and away this season, had chalked up their ninth win in 11 League matches. United were still only placed fourth but they had beaten a team higher in the table than them (City had started the match third and finished it third). Liverpool, meanwhile, were top by two points but had played two more games than the next seven teams. The title race was wide open and Manchester United, a – perhaps *the* – form team, had as good a chance as any of the clubs at the top of finishing it in first place.

Before continuing that race for the title, however, United still had the not inconsiderable matter of their FA Cup campaign to attend to. The home replay against Southampton took place on March 8. Though a Tuesday, a massive crowd of 58,103 packed into the stadium.

An unchanged United asserted their authority on their home turf in the fifth minute when Jimmy Greenhoff stooped to head the ball in. From there, United were the dominant force in the first-half, but four minutes before half-time they were back to square one when a race for a loose ball by Buchan and Southampton's Steve Williams saw the latter tumble groundwards. Buchan mimed a dive and many referees would have waved play on but, unfortunately for United, the referee that day was Clive Thomas. 'The Book' may have been too officious and self-important for some but to his credit was also hardly the kind of person who was going to allow a partisan crowd to dictate his decision. Southampton defender David Peach put the penalty past Stepney's right hand.

Naturally, Southampton were re-energised and were a somewhat more vital force in the second-half. However, the Reds had a deafening wall of support at their backs and pressed forward themselves. United broke the deadlock on 69 minutes when Jimmy Greenhoff's hooked shot found the net, albeit after a deflection off the Saints' Jim Steele. Barely had play re-started when Steele brought the elder Greenhoff down from behind, his second bookable offence. With his dismissal necessitating Peter Osgood being switched to the back-four for the rest of the match, the Saints' Cup campaign for the season stalled there.

United were still on the road to Wembley but once again it was hardly via an overwhelming victory, one which again turned to some degree on fortune (and in this case the opposition's self-sabotage). As suggested before, paradoxically, many people feel winning with such unconvincing form is not an indicator that a Cup campaign is doomed but a sign that it is a team's destiny to lift the trophy, Lady Luck smiling on you supposedly being more important than scintillating performances. United were certainly hoping so. Some of the team had allowed themselves to be convinced the League Cup this season was virtually theirs for the taking because their 17 goals in five matches had been complemented by the fact that many of the top teams got knocked out unusually early, but we know the heartbreak that had ended in.

*\*\**

In their next League match – Saturday March 12 – the Reds met fellow FA Cup quarter-finalists Leeds United at Old Trafford. For parts of it, the red element of the crowd, apparently still drunk on euphoria after the Southampton match, sang the refrain, "Wem-ber-ley, Wem-ber-ley ... " Docherty was able to field an unchanged side yet again. That the ground played host to its second-biggest crowd of the season so far – 60,612 – suggests a certain specialness about the affair but the action on the pitch failed to live up to this implied status. The only goal was symptomatic of a bitty match. After a 12th-minute corner, Coppell prodded the ball toward the Leeds net. The deflection it took off Cherry's chest sent it past the Leeds keeper. It was a win nonetheless and though the positions of the top four teams were unchanged, United were inch-by-inch closing the gap on the three clubs above them, all of whom they now had one to three games in hand on.

The march to "Wem-ber-ley" resumed on Saturday March 19 against Aston Villa in front of 57,089 people. Though it was a plus factor that United – unchanged once more – had a home fixture in this sixth-round match, it's a matter of debate whether the situation their opponents currently found themselves in worked in the Reds' favour. That situation was an epic or interminable (delete according to taste) League Cup final against Everton which (in an era before penalty shoot-outs) had already resulted in two draws, with another match due in April. Villa's legs and minds were probably a little tired as they prepared to meet United.

Additionally, they were without key players, including Andy Gray. At the same time, though, they were getting very used to big occasions.

It was Villa who opened their account first when Brian Little unleashed a magnificent 30-yard shot. Around the 25-minute mark, Houston executed one of his own long-range specials following a pass from a free-kick. It found a gap in the opposition wall and flew past Villa keeper Burridge just inside the post. A groin strain saw Brian Greenhoff depart the field, replaced by McCreery. The latter actually filled a full-back position, with Nicholl moving up to the centre of the defence. It was a curious reshuffling, but both players coped well with their unfamiliar roles as Villa came out for the second-half with an apparent all-or-nothing attitude. Somewhat less impressive were Hill and Coppell, who were not having their best games, credit for which went to Villa defenders Robson and Gidman. Just when another replay seemed on the cards, in the 76th minute Macari settled matters empathically when he unleashed a shot from the edge of the penalty-area as impressive as Little's opener, with the same net-ballooning result.

Afterwards, Villa manager Ron Saunders claimed, "Apart from five minutes in each half, we matched United everywhere." Some observers agreed with the analysis, but the 2-1 victory meant that Manchester United were now due to play their 12th post war FA Cup semi-final, while Villa were left hoping they could salvage something from slender-ish championship contention and an increasingly diminished League Cup competition. (For the record, Villa won that third League Cup final match, which as it happened took place at Old Trafford, 3-2.)

\*\*\*

West Bromwich Albion visited Old Trafford on Wednesday March 23. The knock Brian Greenhoff had picked up against Villa necessitated one line-up change for this League match: the drafting in of Albiston, who played at full-back while Houston occupied the younger Greenhoff's normal position. The astute Johnny Giles seemed to have instructed his men to make the most of Greenhoff Minor's absence. Attendance was 51,053.

In the 18th minute, David Cross scored for the visitors. West Brom did not sit back on their lead but kept pressing, spraying the ball around with some panache, with United old boy Mick Martin often at the centre of the action. On 35 minutes, young Bryan Robson increased the lead with a header. (The rookie, would of course, go on to have a magnificent career at Manchester United himself from 1981 to 1994.) As Stepney came under additional pressure, people's memories were rushing back to that four-nil demolition of United at the Hawthorns back in October. However, three minutes before the interval Jimmy Greenhoff was felled in the penalty area – the body-barge by Robertson actually knocking him briefly unconscious – and United had a spot-kick. Following McIlroy's failure in the Villa match to convert their first penalty since their ace spot-kicker Gerry Daly had lost his place, the Irishman's appetite for the job appeared to have deserted him. Perhaps inevitably it was Gordon Hill – that man of irrepressible confidence – who stepped up to take it. Merlin (otherwise unmagical today) put the ball to the left of Godden. Hill would become United's regular penalty taker from hereon, and do well in the role. Only his inability to defend to save his life prevented him being the player who had everything.

Still trailing 2-1, United were hampered further when a limping McIlroy had to go off, McCreery replacing him. The Reds' unbeaten run – standing at 14 League and cup games going into this match – was almost becoming a curse insofar as people – including, by dint of human nature, the United players themselves – were increasingly wondering how long it could possibly last. With the minutes ticking away, the reporters at the match were no doubt preparing to write the Reds' obituaries, while Docherty and his men were becoming increasingly desperate to avert that mini-disaster. With just two minutes to go, Coppell finally broke through the tight West Brom defence. His first shot hit Godden but when it rebounded back to him, he put the ball in from close range.

Ipswich were top of the table, leading Liverpool on goal difference. United were now fifth, Newcastle having sneaked ahead of them. The Reds had two games in hand over the Magpies. However, nine of the Reds' remaining 13 fixtures were away matches. Impressive though their 15-match unbeaten run was, 12 of those matches had been at home, and there were few more pronounced examples of home advantage in English football than the supportive roar of the Old Trafford faithful.

*** 

When Peter Coyne had been profiled in *Action* comic on the day of his debut last season, the youngster had said, "I guess if things work out I'll probably get into the big money one day – but I'm not that interested in having a flash car and things. I'm quite happy to hop aboard the No. 53 corporation bus which passes our house *en route* to Old Trafford – and think about those goals I'm going to score!" If the level-headedness communicated by the quote was genuine, it was just as well, for in March 1977, Manchester United terminated Coyne's contract. Those who remembered Coyne scoring on his full debut for the club in the previous season's away fixture against Leicester would have been surprised by the news. Many of those who were *au fait* with the status of star-in-the-making Coyne had enjoyed at Old Trafford the last few years would have been flabbergasted. The next club Coyne turned out for was Ashton United, a non-League outfit. From the most glamorous name in football to a club residing in the Cheshire County League was a drop so massive as to be barely comprehensible.

In the *Manchester United Football Book No. 11*, published at the end of the 1975/76 season, David Meek waxed lyrical about United's youth system and one prospect in particular. The veteran United observer said, "I have no doubt we shall be soon ... be hearing a lot more from teenager Peter Coyne." This appeared alongside effusive quotes from Docherty in which the manager spoke of Coyne replacing McCreery as the regular first-team reserve. "I think he will get 25 to 30 goals a season when he is in the first team," asserted The Doc. That Coyne had scored on his first game in United's starting line-up only seemed to confirm the youngster's potential and his imminent permanent elevation to the first team. Yet following the Leicester match, Coyne never got another game for Manchester United. Nor did he go on to find glory elsewhere. After the spectacular splash he had made as an England schoolboy and a United debutant, his career trajectory after his departure was bewildering in its lack of achievement.

Like every United player of the era asked about him, Buchan readily remembers Coyne. Of his fading away, he says, "He didn't have outstanding pace and physically I don't think he was strong enough." Colin Waldron wasn't surprised at Coyne's fate. "From my recollection of Pete Coyne, he wasn't a dedicated draw," he says. "It's just that if you're going to be a pro you've got to be dedicated and as a young kid, particularly in Manchester or a big city, you're going to be tempted. I don't know if he was tempted or not, but I questioned whether he would have made it in the big area. I always thought it was questionable." McCreery, who recalls Coyne as a "very confident lad", says, "When you saw Peter and he trained with the first team, everybody thought, 'There's only one way he's going to go and that's up.' It just tapered away for Peter." Was there a question mark over his application? McCreery: "There was. A lot of people were saying he didn't have the heart for it." Brian Greenhoff: "He was a cracking finisher. One of the best finishers I've seen for a young lad. But he couldn't pass a bookies. He was a bit of a gambler I think. Nowadays they'd offer him help."

When this writer brings up Coyne with the man who guided him through United's youth system by referring to a "football tragedy", Frank Blunstone says with a weary tone to his voice, "I know who you're going to tell me: Peter Coyne." He goes on, "He was a classic, he was. He came to us with a great reputation. He scored a hat-trick at Wembley for England Schoolboys, the first one to ever do it, I think. But you've got to be dedicated, determined, to be a footballer. Peter Coyne wasn't. He wasn't dedicated whatsoever. He turned up for training late. I sent him home. He was that late, he'd get a taxi and try and get in on time. I warned him two or three times. I said to Tommy, 'I'm gonna suspend him and try and shake him up a bit.' I suspended him for a fortnight. After a week he came back and said he wanted to come back. I said to him, 'No, you can't, you stay till your fortnight's up and then you can come back and we'll see how you go from there.' But he had a girlfriend, he was [at] Bellevue." Of Coyne's frequenting of Bellevue dog track in Manchester, Blunstone says, "On the grapevine that's what came back to me. There was nothing to say that he couldn't go to the dog track, but it's just unusual for a 15-, 16-year-old to go." He summarises, "He just wasn't dedicated and it's shame, because he had ability." Blunstone also says, "We sent him out on loan. Bolton Wanderers came in for him. We said okay. It was arranged for him to go. Next thing we get a phone call from Bolton: 'Where's Peter Coyne?' He just didn't turn up, and that's the boy he was. Them people don't make it. He had all the ability, he had everything, but he didn't have the determination and professionalism to be a footballer. If Peter had had Ged's determination and professionalism, he'd have made a brilliant player. They're completely different. I spoke to his dad many times. He said, 'It's a pity he's not like Ged'."

"I don't blame anybody else," says Coyne. "Looking back now, it was purely and simply my fault. It was an attitude thing. Whether I got in too soon, I don't know. If I had to do it all over again, I would aim ... to get physically stronger. Get faster and get fitter ... They never, ever told me I wasn't good enough. I was quite behind the rest of the lads in training. I found that very, very hard. Can only think I wasn't putting enough effort in. All I wanted to do was score. I didn't want to do all the nitty-gritty, all the up-and-down stuff, and sweat, I just wanted to score. But obviously that wasn't enough. [Docherty] saw that wasn't enough."

He admits he did visit Bellevue and bet quite frequently: "We had White City Dogs as well, which was right next to Old Trafford. I'd be paid on a Friday, an hour later I'd be at the White City Dogs. We had a Ladbrokes right outside Old Trafford as well. It was only pounds and two pounds. I was only on £40 a week at Old Trafford. Used to come out with £28, I used to pay me mam's keep a tenner, so left with 18 quid. But I was brought up with gambling. Me dad was dogs-mad, so it was in me blood like football, But they obviously didn't like it. With United, wherever you are, someone sees ya and I found out people would be on the phone and me youth team manager would [say], 'What were you doing at dogs last night when you've a game the next day?'"

Lateness, too, he concedes was a fault – and it was partly down to the fact that, contrary to what he told *Action*, he wasn't happy to take the No. 53 bus: "I used to get a lift off Tony Young. He used to pass our house and pick me and my brother up on the last minute. It was either that or about an hour's journey on the bus. We'd screech into the car park about 25 past 10 and all the lads would be coming out to train and we'd be running in. That didn't go down too well. The gambling, not training hard enough, attitude – I think it was an accumulation of things ... And it's not as if I didn't have enough warnings. But while The Doc was warning me every week, saying your attitude blah blah blah, I was still scoring left, right and centre for any team that I played for. He said, 'Look, if you don't sort yourself out, you'll be going, you'll be going ... ' Lo and behold I got the old dreaded, 'Go and see The Doc at Old Trafford' and you knew what was going to happen then."

Coyne arrived at Docherty's office to find the manager, Cavanagh and Gordon Clayton, the scout who signed him, inside. "It was a real bad experience," he says. "Exactly the opposite of when they called me in to give me my fiver. I more or less knew what was happening because the day before someone had had the same message to see Tommy Doc and he'd been given a free transfer, so I was prepared for it a little bit." What Coyne wasn't so prepared for was an atmosphere that was not exactly appropriately sombre. "Getting bad news is bad at that age but when you're treated as though they couldn't care less, it made it all the worse," he says. "It was like a laugh to them. I thought they could have been a bit more feeling about it, 'cos they could see I was upset." He adds, "The worst thing was going home and telling me parents the bad news." Coyne rejects any suggestion that being a spoilt younger brother explains his lack of the professionalism and dedication his less skilled older sibling possessed: "Gosh, no, I had a very strict father. I had to be in on time. Me dad used to preach to me about dedication. I wasn't a spoilt brat." If anything, the psychology would seem to be the reverse. Asked if he chafed at the restrictions of his upbringing, he says, "I did a little bit. I think if me dad was here now he would say maybe he was a little bit ... "

Of course, many is the footballer with a far worse attitude than Coyne's whose skills made his club prepared to overlook his faults. Coyne offers a couple of reasons why Docherty's patience may have snapped unduly early with him. First, "I may have been an influence on the rest of them 'cos I played for England Schoolboys and all that and I think he saw me as a bad example to the rest of the lads." Additionally, "I think I was a bit unlucky 'cos a year below me was a young lad called Andy Ritchie ready to take my place. I think it made it easier for him, knowing Andy [was there]. Andy was a fantastic prospect and looking back it was a fantastic decision that he made 'cos I might have kept Andy back another year, but with me out of the way Andy was promoted a little bit … If Andy Ritchie hadn't have been there, I might have got another season to sort me attitude out."

However, the Bolton Wanderers loan fiasco to which Blunstone refers above seems a more complicated story than the one Blunstone proffers as another example of Coyne's sloppiness. Recalls Coyne, "They gave me a free transfer. They had to tell you early doors in them days. They sent a letter to you and then they circulate your name to all the clubs to see if they're interested. Your contract runs out the end of June, so it gives you a few months to try and sort another club out. You just have to wait for a phone call. The very next day Bolton Wanderers rang Old Trafford and asked to take me on loan. Tommy Docherty rang my house, spoke to my father – I wasn't in – and The Doc said to me dad, 'Tell your Peter [that] Bolton want him on a month's loan.' So when I came at night, me dad told me and I thought, 'Oh, I'll just hang on and see if City come in.' Went training the next day, did me morning sessions. We was up in the canteen at The Cliff having a drink, absolutely packed out, and The Doc comes in. Of course when he shows his face everyone goes a little bit quiet. Came over to me in front of everyone and says, 'What are you doing here?' I was so embarrassed. 'I've been training, boss.' He said, 'You're supposed to be at Bolton.' And I just says, 'Oh right, I thought I had a choice.' And he went, 'Get in my office *now.*' He phoned Ian Greaves, the Bolton manager. Before he did he said, 'You tell Bolton now you want to come on a month's loan.' That's the way it was put to me – like I had no choice." At this point, Coyne agreed to the move to Second Division Bolton – but then changed his mind. "I played the next day at Everton in the reserves, went back to Bolton the next day on my day off and asked Ian Greaves to release me month's contract. I wanted to go somewhere else. That was Ashton United. The owner of Ashton was an old schoolteacher of mine who I respected very well. He always used to say to me – he kept in touch – 'If anything ever goes wrong in football there's always a job here. You can come and play football for me.' And sure enough when me brother was given a free transfer, he give Ged a job. So when I got a free from United, he was straight on the phone, Mr. Donnelly. Looking back, what a bad decision. I had a fantastic opportunity at Bolton." As well as sentimentality swaying his decision, Coyne was impressed by the remuneration on offer at Ashton. "It was more or less five times what I was getting at United. It was a massive amount of money for me. With hardly having to [do] any work as well. It got a lot of publicity for [them]: a United player going straight to Ashton United. So I think he got his money back."

Coyne's tenure at Ashton was only a few months in length. Coyne: "I was doing okay there and scoring plenty of goals. In the papers, 'Clubs are watching Peter Coyne again, blah blah blah.' Next minute, they told me Harry Gregg's interested at Crewe." As a former United man and Munich air-disaster survivor, the retired goalkeeper Gregg had many contacts at Old Trafford, although he had also gone to Ashton to watch Coyne a few times. Recalls Coyne, "I met Harry with me dad and I remember being very impressed by what he had to say. I knew a couple of lads that were already there, couple of Manchester lads, and that helped influence my decision a little bit, but Harry was so impressive. He's a larger-than-life figure." One of the ex-Reds at the club was fellow Docherty-discard Wyn Davies. Coyne established a good striking partnership with Davies – who was literally old enough to be his father – and, despite an uncertain start, by the end of his first season at Crewe was once again scoring goals for fun: in the closing stages he knocked in eight in 11 games, making a total for the season of 16.

In the close season following his first Crewe campaign, Coyne played in America for Los Angeles Aztecs alongside the great George Best. "I just got a phone call [from someone] who said he was George Best's agent asking me if I was interested to go and play in America. As soon as he mentioned George Best, I couldn't get over there quick enough ... It was just an unbelievable experience just being in the same dressing room as him. I did find out that [Best] was the one who'd asked Harry if he would let me come over, 'cos I think he had a big influence in the team and all that. That's what Harry Gregg told me. [Best] made me feel so welcome, 'cos I was a Manchester lad first time in America. I'll never forget that as long as I live. I was there three months but after a week being there George got transferred. What a bummer. But I can always say I played in the same team as George Best. How many people can say that?"

This is all very well, but a player who had made such a name for himself at such as young age as Coyne could surely do better than a Fourth Division club and an NASL outfit. It seems to be the case here that the man who coupled a refusal to give a job reference to Pat Crerand with a scurrilous claim that he was a member of the IRA was up to his dirty tracks again. Coyne: "I did hear – whether it's true or not – the expression was, 'You're going to be buried.' I don't want to make excuses, but I thought I might have got a little bit higher, but it seems that my name was pretty much, 'Attitude's terrible, don't touch him.' Ian Greaves at Bolton, he was willing to take a chance on me – it was only a month, he had nothing to lose – but I have been told that my name was really, really bad. Whether that was The Doc or not, I don't know ... I suppose if I'd have left United and signed to City the next day and gone on to have a really good career, it would look stupid on United." Coyne would never appear in the top tier of English football again.

Coyne netted 16 goals again for Crewe in his second season. Injury blighted the season after that for him, but he did get the chance to prove he could play in midfield in that term. A new manager saw Coyne drifting out of the first team, despite maintaining his status as leading club scorer (in a team incidentally which now included another former Docherty-era United player, Jimmy Greenhoff). It was back to non-League football for Coyne the following season as he was given a free transfer to Hyde United. He was still just 23. "It was the old Stoke manager, Tony Waddington," he says. "He just didn't fancy me as a player." Lining up alongside Coyne at Hyde for some of his time there was his brother Ged, who despite Blunstone's singing of his praises in comparison to Peter, never – unlike Peter – got a first team game for Manchester United before being given a free.

For Hyde, Coyne scored 63 goals in 117 games, but after four years there he had begun to feel that his chance had passed. "I was applying for full-time jobs, nothing to do with football," he says. "I had a young son, mortgage to pay. You just think you've missed the boat." But then the Old Trafford magic circle provided an escape route again, poetically partly via the man whose substitution had given Coyne his first chance in professional football: "Lou Macari got his first job at Swindon, and then next minute he took Harry Gregg as his assistant. Harry had always said, when he left Crewe, 'Wherever I go there'll be a place for you.' I thought that's a nice thing for him to say. You don't ever think it'll come true. Sure enough when he got assistant manager, he was the first person that phoned. He said, 'Lou wants you to come down and train with us, I've told him about ya.' 'Course, Lou remembered me from United. He probably remembered the lazy little teenager who could score. I don't think he was that bothered at first, but Harry is very convincing and persuaded him to let me go for a little sort of a trial for a couple of weeks and then he asked me to sign."

Macari played Coyne as both striker and midfielder. Coyne feels his attitude was now much improved. "When I went with Lou and Harry at Swindon, that's when I found out what football was all about. If you were lazy with Lou Macari, you were out the door. You had to be fit or there was no place for you." Coyne scored 14 in his first season with Swindon and 11 the season thereafter, one in which the club took the Fourth Division championship. Coyne scored the club's only and winning goal in their last game of the latter season against his old club Crewe. The 1986/87 season saw Swindon gain promotion for the second time in as many seasons, although the early months of that campaign saw Coyne struggling to hold his place in the first team. Coyne scored goals in both the semi-final and final of the play-offs, which system of deciding promotion hadn't existed when he'd first signed terms as a professional footballer. Ironically, assisting said promotion helped bring the curtain down on his own Swindon career: "As we got higher in the league, Lou was signing better players and there was more competition for places. I picked up a few injuries. I was out for three months with one injury and that put me really on the back foot. I never really regained me form after that injury. When I did get back I was never the same. Lou left Swindon. Ossie Ardilles took over and again he either fancies you or he doesn't fancy you. He didn't fancy me. I wasn't a regular when he joined. I was injured and all that. He didn't know much about me."

With non-reserve appearances becoming few and far between, Coyne accepted a loan to Aldershot and it was there – not yet 30 – that he made his final appearances in the Football League. However, he continued to play for non-League sides like Colne Dynamoes, Radcliffe Borough, Glossop North End and Wilmslow Albion until he was nearly 40. "I started to play for teams like that rather than do nothing on a Saturday … The slower I got, I used to drop down a little level. Wherever I went, I was a regular scorer. You can't beat that feeling, hitting the back of the net."

Coyne began a security job at Manchester Airport in 1990. It is a role that has meant he has had several meetings with a visiting Tommy Docherty. Was the first encounter a bit awkward? Coyne: "I think it might have been more for him than me. It's all forgotten now. He did what he thought was right at the time. He probably was right at the time. It's nice to see him now … He always comes over and says, 'Hello, how are you doing, how's your brother?'" Echoing those elsewhere in this text who testify to Docherty being prepared to play someone regardless of his youth, he says, "One thing about The Doc, he gave me a chance. If it had been another manager, I might not have got a chance."

Asked if he thinks he would have coped in top-flight football if he had not been sold, Coyne admits, "Not the way I was. I wouldn't have survived. I didn't have the strength … You watch them on telly, think 'I could do this, I could do that.' Until you've actually played against these guys and you realise how strong they are and how fast they are. Unless you actually are right next to them and feeling the strength and the pace of them and how fit they are, that's when you realise what football's all about … I would have worked a whole lot harder to survive at that level on my physique. Just looking after your body a lot more, resting when you should be resting, sleeping at nights. Just thinking and living and eating football. You have to, and I didn't." Perhaps the fact that Coyne is a bit more understanding of The Doc's fateful decision now is down to the fact that he is these days on the same side of the fence as Docherty was then: "I've done a few of me badges. I mostly coach primary school age now."

Does he understand why some people use his name as a byword for footballing tragedy? Coyne: "Well, yeah. 'Cos it's like you had the world at your feet." Is he embittered? "No, not at all. Me dream was to play for United. I scored for United. That'll do for me. It was on telly as well, and I've got the goal on video ... All the great players that I've played with and all the places in the world that I've been to ... Played at Wembley. I've got memories that only other kids can dream of, so I don't look back with any regrets. If I had me time again, I'd train a lot harder. But playing with the people that I've played with – no one can take that away."

Though no one would deny Coyne his right to be proud of his achievements, they are paltry compared to what they surely would have been had he fulfilled the potential he was universally perceived to possess as a teenager. Coyne's face beaming out of another *Manchester United Football Book* (in this case *No.10*) and the superlatives in the accompanying picture caption are a salutary reminder that football may provide glory but can also produce disappointment no matter how elevated one's starting point.

Having said that, the idea that Coyne's story is a tragedy seems laughable in the context of the destinies of two components of the United youth system of around his time. Full-back Martyn Rogers – another England Schoolboys player – signed for the club in either August 1975 or May 1976 (sources differ). Born in Nottingham on January 26 1960, he hadn't been picked for a first-team game before The Doc's departure and racked up a solitary appearance under the reign of his successor. In July 1979, Docherty, now at QPR, took him to Loftus Road for a paltry £7,500, where he got a couple of games in the 1979/80 season, the last two fixtures of the campaign, both of them victories. From there, Rogers disappears off the Football League radar: Docherty's successor Terry Venables let him go on a free in May 1981 and The Doc demonstrated once more that he hadn't forgotten him by taking him Down Under to Sydney Olympic, which he was currently managing. Rogers played six seasons in Australia. He then returned to Britain and played non-League football in Nottingham. Following the end of his career, he worked as a lorry driver.

It is of course inevitably disappointing for any player groomed at the biggest football club in the world to realise he is not going to make the grade, and even more disappointing if he tumbles down to the very backwaters of the game. Some – like Steve Paterson and Paul Bielby – manage to rise above their disappointments to achieve other sorts of triumph in their lives. Others may or may not get over their disappointment but survive somehow, at some level. In the case of Martyn Rogers, he was evidently sadly unable to find solace in either his professional or personal life over the way being one of the apparently chosen few turned into being one of the anonymous many. On Saturday February 29 1992, he made two phone calls, one to his mother, whom he told he was in Singapore, another to a girlfriend, whom he told he was in Australia. He then drove his car to the New Forest, where he attached a hose to the exhaust pipe and fed it into the car. His lifeless body was found in the vehicle's passenger seat. He was just 32. Tommy Docherty attended Rogers' funeral. When contacted by the press about the suicide, he had said, "This is shocking. I just can't believe it." His shock may not have been unrelated to the fact that Rogers' death was possibly a copycat suicide. Less than a month previously, his ex-colleague at United, Alan Davies, had gassed himself in Wales. Davies had obtained a professional contract at Old Trafford in the year after Docherty's departure and then had a reasonably successful career that encompassed an FA Cup winner's medal with the Reds and stints with Newcastle United, Charlton Athletic, Carlisle United, Swansea City and Bradford City. Davies left behind a young daughter and a wife who was eight months pregnant.

"I remember Martyn Rogers," says Blunstone. "Martyn was quite a useful player. Left-back. He had a chance, but the trouble is he had Arthur Albiston to compete with at the time, so it was difficult. Martyn was very quiet. The lads got on well with him. He was quite respected by the other lads. He was quite a sensible lad. I would never have thought he'd have done that. Never."

\*\*\*

Saturday April 2 saw the first of the Reds' piled-up away games, a visit to Carrow Road. Only the injured Pearson was absent from the roll call for this match, McCreery fielded instead. McGrath took McCreery's usual place on the sub's bench. The match was watched by 26,125.

Inconsistent United's defence may usually have been but today they were simply often slack. On seven minutes this was demonstrated when a soft clearance by Buchan only went as far the edge of the box and Norwich's Colin Suggett drove it home. Just after the half-hour mark, Kevin Reeves rounded Buchan and slid the ball past Stepney. Two minutes before the hour mark, United got one back, although only because Buchan's floated cross was headed by the Canaries' Tony Powell past his own keeper. At this point, United finally seemed to rally. However, the Reds then had to contend with the loss of Hill through a knock on the knee. Consequently, when the referee blew for time, he was also bringing down the curtain on United's three-month, 15-game unbeaten streak. "Get at them and they are definitely vulnerable," said Norwich manager John Bond of his side's 2-1 victory, "but they are still a team with the right blend whose heads never go down."

Bond's assessment was actually a lot kinder than that of Macari, who said, "Well, that's it. It looks like the championship's been flattened once and for all now. While that long unbeaten run was safe, every one of the lads felt the same way … the title was still up for grabs. But this defeat has put it well out of reach, and we can't complain, the way we played." Macari's gloomy prognosis seemed a little premature. True, the match had left United sixth in the table and they now no longer had games in hand over those clubs above them. However, there were still a dozen League fixtures remaining for the Reds, including potential four-pointers against Leicester, Leeds and (especially) Liverpool, who were now leading the table from Ipswich by two points.

Whether or not United's title hopes were receding was a subject of little interest to those who felt that other proceedings observed at Carrow Road constituted a crescendo of the Manchester United hooligan problem. Docherty had had to go onto the pitch before kick-off to appeal to his team's fans to cease their riotous behaviour, with limited success. Red supporters wrecked a stand, threw staves at police and opposition supporters, overturned cars and left hundreds of windows in the city with no glass. David Smith, chairman of the Manchester United Supporters' Club, advocated an away ban if the police could not guarantee public safety. He said of the hooligans' behaviour in Norwich, "It was the worst exhibition of wanton, all-out destruction I have seen. It was disgraceful. Some of the United followers – you can't possibly describe them as fans – behaved like a bunch of Vikings out to pillage everything. There was no question of a confrontation between rival fans. Norwich have their idiots but the crowd was not really involved. We sold 5,000 tickets to our own fans and between 600 and 1,000 got mixed up in this trouble. I saw them fighting, getting into trouble, smashing windows and wrecking cars. From the back of the stand, I watched them ripping down the boards and generally smashing things to pieces. The police were powerless."

Docherty was sceptical about the events. "It got blanket coverage on TV, and I was always suspicious of a set-up on this day," he later claimed. "It smelled of being staged for the benefit of the cameras." Meanwhile, the claims of some that a lot of the hooliganism was by people flying under a red flag of convenience seems to be borne out by a newspaper article published after the trouble at Carrow Road which said, "Court statistics show that as many as 90% of the people who fall into the hands of the police come from areas outside Manchester."

The behaviour of the hooligans brought about an emergency parliamentary session. The upshot was an effective ban on United supporters at opposition grounds. Bristol City independently announced that they would be making history by declining to sell tickets to anyone outside their own area for the fixture against United on May 7. On the same day, sports minister Denis Howell announced that the Sunderland match on April 11 would be the last time that the Reds' fans would be able to buy tickets for the terraces (or, if the home side decided, any at all) at away grounds. The logic was that hooligans couldn't operate in seats, and couldn't afford them either. That the effective away ban affected not just the hooligans but everyone was not really the concern of populist politicians.

\*\*\*

Pearson was back for United's away match against Everton on Tuesday April 5. However, Macari was injured, so McCreery played in his stead. Albiston was substitute, and – like McGrath had in the previous match – managed to get some time on the pitch before the final whistle blew: following an outstanding game, Hill was pulled off after suffering another knee-knock. Ironically, this fixture saw United up against opponents striving to preserve their own impressive unbeaten record. Going into the match, the Toffees hadn't lost in 11 games. Attendance was 38,216.

The visitors scored in the first minute, Hill putting the ball in the back of the net despite being surrounded by the enemy. The match proceeded at a frantic pace and a high temperature. When on 21 minutes, Lyons made a careless pass to no one in particular, a red-shirted figure pounced. The loss of possession might have meant no danger with most other players but this was Merlin, who had the vision to see Lawson six yards off his line and the sublime skill to do something about it: he executed a perfect chip over the Everton keeper into the back of the net.

There should have been several more goals for United, but nobody took advantage of their chances the way Hill had, although in fairness Coppell and Jimmy Greenhoff seemed to have good claims for penalties turned down. 17 minutes from time, Everton got a goal and thereafter stormed forward with greater impetus, no doubt feeling the same desperate emotions as United had when trying to preserve their winning streak recently. The Reds' sturdy defence was enough to maintain the 2-1 scoreline, to end Everton's winning streak and (though Macari might have disagreed) keep United in the title race. They were still sixth. Ipswich now had the lead at the top over Liverpool on goal difference, though the latter at this point were the ones with a game in hand.

It was back to a full-strength Roll Call Mark II for the home match against Stoke City on Saturday April 9. For a team facing relegation, as Stoke were, a visit to Old Trafford was not a nice prospect. Their desperation to maintain their First Division status and their nervousness at having to face a largely hostile crowd of 53,102 seemed to be manifested in rather nasty play in which there was no room for sentiment – or even humanity – for their old boy Jimmy Greenhoff, who hobbled off on 25 minutes after several collisions with their defence, replaced by McCreery.

After a first-half in which both sides played poorly, the second-half saw United awarded a free-kick from which the ball eventually came to Houston, who executed a looping header just beyond the straining Peter Shilton's fingers. 10 minutes later, Macari, half turned away from the Stoke goal when a clearance came in his direction, spun and hooked the ball past Shilton in one fluid motion. Hill had a couple of good attempts on goal but in the 82nd minute it was Pearson who got the third and final strike. Perhaps worryingly, the 3-0 victory over a relegation-haunted team did not seem at all overwhelming and there were few scintillating performers in red shirts today. (Two reporters independently cited Coppell and Buchan as United's men of the match.) Nonetheless, United rose to fifth place. Things in the top two places were unchanged.

Jimmy Greenhoff hadn't recovered in time for the match against Sunderland at Roker Park the following Monday, April 11, so McCreery got another start in the only change to the line-up that took the field. The crowd of 38,785 was surprisingly low, and some were suggesting that the fear of violence that now attended the visits of the Red Army may have been to blame. This was the last match before the away ban came into effect and the supposition was that the boot boys would go out in a crescendo of destruction. In the event, there was no trouble. Those who stayed away missed an excellent, exciting match, as Sunderland strived to stave off relegation while United attempted to maintain their place in the championship race.

Sunderland were ahead within three minutes. When McCreery was upended, Hill took the 15th-minute penalty to make the scores level. Within four minutes, though, Nicholl squandered United's lead by bringing down Holden. Buchan didn't even bother contesting the penalty decision, instead bawling out his colleague. Tony Towers drove a low spot-kick to the right of Stepney. Perhaps United could have taken away a point, or even two, had they not had more injury woe: Macari didn't reappear on the pitch for the second-half, replaced by Albiston. Their 2-1 victory took the home side out of the bottom three for the first time in months, leading manager Jimmy Adamson to joke, "We'll win this championship yet." The championship looked slightly less likely for the Reds today. Though they were still placed fifth, it was a loss of two vital points which might prove crucial in the final weeks. Ipswich still led Liverpool by a point, and Liverpool still had a game in hand. Though United had nine points fewer than Ipswich, they at least had played three fewer games than them. Similarly, though they trailed Liverpool by eight points, they had two games in hand over them.

On the teamsheet for Sunderland today was Docherty's son Mick, who had ceased requiring Colin Waldron's taxi service not long after his move to Manchester City, playing only eight League games for them before moving to Roker Park. He remembers the match well. "It was the quickest I've ever played in," he says. "I just remember sitting in the dressing room after the game and thought 'Where the hell did that go?'" Of the opposition, he says, "They were a wonderful, terrific, free-flowing side and the game went so quickly it was just scary. I remember thinking, 'By God, they're gonna be a force are this lot.' We were lucky to win that day." He adds, "We were fighting against relegation and United were riding high and yet we nicked it 2-1, so it didn't go down too well in the Docherty household that weekend!"

Also playing for Sunderland was Colin Waldron. "I played well," recalls Waldron of his performance against his recent colleagues. "I was pleased to show that I could be a good player because I thought that United and the fans would think I'm a very ordinary player, which I didn't think I was. I never got a chance to really prove it, but I would not want to switch my time at United for anything." Nonetheless, he had declined to return to Old Trafford despite the fact that the offer was open to him: "I was on a monthly contract and every month that went by I knew from talking to people what I could do and what I couldn't do and I knew I could have come back at any time, but by then I was hooked into Sunderland. I'd got my health back, I was starting to play okay and I was back to normal, which was a big thing for me, confidence-booster or whatever. Also Sunderland had stood by me." There was, though, an unfortunate aspect to Waldron signing full terms with Sunderland: his repeat displacement of Jim Holton: "I arrived [at Old Trafford] and they shifted him out to Sunderland, and six months later I went to Sunderland, and replaced him again. He was never the same after the injury wasn't Jim, but he was a big, lovely character." Not that Waldron subscribes to the party line of others fond of Holton that he was clumsy rather than malicious: "[He] would snap you in half if he got a chance ... The word malicious exists in every First Division defender when we played and to say anything different would be a blatant lie, because you were allowed to do it. We were allowed to get away with murder and referees hadn't got a clue. Referees hadn't got a clue."

***

Jimmy Greenhoff was back for the home game against Leicester City on Saturday April 16, but with Houston ruled unfit (replaced by Albiston) and Hill reduced to the sub's bench (McCreery deputised) because he decided an hour before the match that he didn't want to risk a suspect knee over a full 90 minutes, there were worrying signs of the injury curse that had afflicted United before Christmas. The match, watched by 49,161, was generally unremarkable and United's performance not exactly committed, with the exceptions of Macari and Buchan, both of whom were ironically not 100% fit. Leicester went ahead on 13 minutes. Jimmy Greenhoff managed to reply in the 62nd minute. Buchan picked up a groin strain in the match but – with Hill having already replaced McCreery – insisted on staying on. Pearson dropped back as cover, but Leicester seemed uninterested in pressing home their advantage and the score remained 1-1. The point United earned/dropped meant that they were still fifth in the table. Afterwards, Buchan explained of his staying on, "The way things were going, we were in danger of losing and with every single point vital for Europe next season I wasn't going off to leave us with only 10 men."

One newspaper interpreted the loyalty and stoicism Buchan had displayed in this match as an indication that the club did not have to worry about the possibility that he was preparing to leave at the end of the season over his pay demands. That rumbling story had just hit the papers again, this time in conjunction with the report of the similar desire of Lou Macari – another man approaching the end of his contract – to have pay parity with other major First Division footballers. What with Docherty's continued unsettled contract state – *The Sun* was claiming that Derby County had made a £28,000-a-year overture to The Doc, which was around £10,000 more than he was currently getting at United – Louis Edwards could have been forgiven for feeling that his problems were piling up on him somewhat: though Docherty had signed a new contract only the previous year, in those days managers could break their contracts and jump clubs with impunity. However, the profit of £750,000 United were projected to make this season may have alleviated the chairman's anxieties to a degree. Eventually, Buchan did sign, as did Macari. Buchan: "I remember Doc coming to Lou and me and saying, 'Swum the Channel for you two, got you what you wanted, didn't do so well for myself.' I thought, 'That'll be right!'"

\*\*\*

The valuable home point dropped against Leicester could be compensated for if United took all the points from their fixture at Loftus Road on Tuesday April 19.

London bus workers refused to supply transport on 10 routes that passed near QPR's ground for fear of trouble. The match had originally been scheduled for December and 8,000 tickets had been provided to United back then. (Attendees today bought a programme that was the magazine printed for the originally scheduled date with a few new pages wrapped around it as a puny way of disguising how out of date it was.) However, United supporters who didn't yet have tickets had no problem buying them, despite the supposed away ban. As one paper noted as the tickets were snapped up at the ground, "It was impossible to tell the difference between Rangers and United fans." The gate was 28,848.

QPR had had a thin time of it lately, and were hovering only four places above the relegation zone, in contrast to Leicester's mid-table position, so theoretically clawing back that squandered point was not a hugely difficult task for the visitors. However, United had a double-pronged injury problem that turned out to be disastrous. Hill was not available, his knee continuing to cause problems. He harrowingly describes his experience: "[An opponent] went across my right knee and he chipped a bone and I got back to Old Trafford late that night and the doctor said to me, 'What I suggest we do [is] give you an injection with cortisone.' They held me down as they put this needle in and it hit me bone. And I tell you what, that's the worst thing I've ever had in my life. They said, 'You should be alright now.' So I went home and I went out with my wife for dinner and my knee was getting stiffer all night long and then when I got up to get out of the car, I fell over. It didn't lock, it froze – it was glued together ... It got stiffer and stiffer during the night and then I phoned up Laurie the next morning and I said, 'My knee's not working, my knee's solid ... ' I had the next four days going in for manipulation because they'd stuck too much stuff in. I was in tears with manipulation ... That's why I've never had another injection in my knees." "He wasn't the bravest but he was a nice lad, there's nothing wrong with that," says Laurie Brown. "Some can put up with it better than others."

Also absent was Buchan, whose decision to remain on the pitch in the previous match would seem to have been unwise. Though both men would be absent for only one game, the loss of the skipper's authority and composure at the back and Merlin's dazzling wingwork upfront allowed the home side to simply walk all over the Reds. Additionally, there seemed a whiff of fear of being injured for Saturday's FA Cup semi-final in the lethargy of United's men. Docherty himself seemed to have already made up his mind that though the championship was mathematically possible, it wasn't worth thinking about: with the Reds behind at half-time, he took off Brian Greenhoff and gave Alex Forsyth a rare outing. Albiston and McCreery had kept their places in the starting line-up, with Houston playing in Buchan's usual place.

QPR, meanwhile, seemed like a team reborn rather than a club struggling to stay in the top flight. This may have been something to do with the fact that their star player, England captain Gerry Francis, was back after a long-term injury. Rangers' first goal came on 30 seconds, and by the 20th minute they were two-up. United continued to be under the cosh in the Brian Greenhoff-less second-half. By the hour mark, Eastoe had added a further brace for the hosts. Coppell shot over the bar toward the end and Forsyth actually rattled the woodwork, but even had either, or both, scored, it would have leavened the misery of United's evening by a negligible degree. The catastrophic 4-0 loss was, it felt, by no coincidence whatsoever the same scoreline as occurred on the occasion of the beginning of Buchan's last absence. It was the final nail in the coffin for any hope the Reds – marooned in the same fifth place afterwards, nine points adrift of table leaders Liverpool – might have still nurtured that they could take the championship.

With all hope in that direction having been extinguished, the club could perhaps step back and acknowledge that it had never really been on the cards. Significantly, United had led the table only once during the entire season, and even that had been on goal difference. Macari later opined that the team had experienced "second season syndrome". For the Scotsman, it wasn't that the Reds were trying any less hard or going backwards but that "other teams were on to us. Coppell and Hill were squeezed by opposition defences. They worked out how to break up our play." Houston offers, "What you tend to find, the first season up, everybody's a bit fresh. The new League don't quite know you. After the first season up, the teams begin to know you, so they start doing different things. We were okay but we weren't flying as much as we were the year before."

Docherty could only thank his lucky stars that early in the second-half a wonderful Francis goal was adjudged offside. A 5-0 scoreline would have brought uncomfortable comparisons with where Docherty came in: the humiliation at Crystal Palace's ground back in 1972. Realistically, though, any such comparisons would have been mildly fatuous. United's next match was their second FA Cup semi-final in as many years.

*\*\**

In the run-up to the semi, Docherty gave an interview to journalist Alan Hubbard that read like a gambit to get that improved contract that had not been forthcoming despite the story linking him with Derby County more than a month previously. "It just doesn't make sense to me," said Docherty of the failure of United to grant him the terms he desired, now allowing himself to be quoted directly instead of insisting on the 'friend' attribution. Hubbard also claimed (although without any quotes) that Docherty had admitted another club ("almost certainly Derby County") had approached him but that he strongly denied that he was using this as a lever to get what he wanted from the board. Docherty, it was claimed, wanted security for himself and Cavanagh, which Hubbard interpreted as meaning "A job for life".

Hibbard quoted Docherty as saying of his existing contract, which still had 15 months remaining, "I'll honour that contract and see it through." With regards to the terms of that contract, The Doc said, "[If the] board want to do something about it, marvellous. If not, well, I'll just have to get on with it … Oh, I know there are a few people around who would like to see me leave Manchester United, but they've got another think coming. I'm not going to give them that satisfaction." He went on, "This is a great club and if I couldn't be happy here, I couldn't be happy anywhere. It is just one or two things that niggle and upset you. But I want to make one thing clear. I'm not after more money. The government would take it all anyway." The latter was a reference to taxation rates in an era when some high-earners had to yield up 98% to the exchequer. Docherty went on, "I have been described as a pay rebel, but that's nonsense. All I want is the chance of security … This is going to be a great side and I want to be here in charge of it when it starts really producing the goods. I want to finish the job off. I don't want someone else cashing in on it, as happened at Chelsea, and to some degree Aston Villa. I don't want anyone else to step in and get the credit for what myself and my staff have done … What does upset me a little is that the board could have stopped all this speculation by doing something about it … It's the sort of thing I feel you shouldn't have to push for and it would have made us feel that we're wanted."

Also in the run-up to the semi-final, Docherty was publicly reflecting on the progress of his team and declaring himself satisfied. "It's true that I considered we were at a crossroads when we launched into the present season, but I have seen enough now to know that our playing staff have temperament as well as talent," he said. "This was proved to me by the way they recovered from the disappointment of losing the Cup Final at Wembley to open their present campaign with great heart and relish. Their healthy attitude was underlined by the setback we received for a two-month spell just before Christmas. We had injuries and nothing seemed to go right. But the lads stuck at it and we came through to move into a challenging position for Europe in the League again, and they fought through to the semi-finals of the FA Cup. They showed character to pull out of a terrible spell. They are going to be tested again now as we tackle our remaining programme which is loaded with away fixtures. But I am confident they will pick up enough points to qualify for the UEFA Cup again and of course we have high hopes of winning at Hillsborough to reach Wembley again, which would be no mean achievement … "

\*\*\*

Docherty received good news for the match at neutral Hillsborough on Saturday April 23. All of his preferred players were fit for the semi. It was the Roll Call Mark II, therefore, that trotted out to face Leeds United.

Docherty said beforehand, "Although Leeds are the team I wanted to play, rather than Liverpool or Everton – we've beaten them the last four times we've played – I have a lot of respect for them. They're going through a transitional period, rather like we did. Jimmy Armfield has had to bring in one or two youngsters and discard some old stagers, as I have had to do here. People don't like to see old favourites go, but sometimes they have to, and the quicker the better." In the same interview, The Doc said, "We can't win the League this season – in fact, we're a team that until we get a little more experience will always finish third or fourth – but I believe that if we can get past Leeds we can win at Wembley."

The transitional period for Leeds was not quite as drastic as the one United had gone through. Their propensity for trophy winning had seemed to depart with legendary manager Don Revie, who had given them a second League championship in his final season to go with the other honours he had secured them: the FA Cup, League Cup, two Fairs Cups and the Second Division championship, along with a host of runners-up positions. However, this paucity of honours since Revie took up the England manager's job in the summer of 1974 hardly compared to relegation. Moreover, in terms of reputation, their stock if anything was actually higher since Armfield had arrived. The presence of Tony Currie in the present line-up proved this: a fabulously gifted footballer and irrepressible character, he was simply too good-natured to adopt the bullying tactics that for just about everyone outside the city of Leeds had blighted the undeniably talented side throughout Revie's reign. However, though the infamous form of defender Norman 'Bites Yer Legs' Hunter was gone, several of the old cast of Leeds villains were still around. As was, clearly, a penchant for gamesmanship. When the buzzer that signalled the teams should leave the dressing room sounded, the Reds dutifully lined up in the tunnel. However, after four or five minutes, their opponents still hadn't appeared and they had to ask the referee to go and get them. When Leeds did deign to materialize, the contrast of the average heights of the two sides became comically apparent as towering players like Paul Madeley, Joe Jordan and Gordon McQueen trooped past a team compised save for Stepney and Houston of shorties. So much so that Leeds defender Gordon McQueen yelled that Leeds were going to crush the United midgets.

However, as the teams made their way onto the pitch, it became apparent that Leeds were themselves dwarfed by the support for their opposition in the crowd of 55,000. McIlroy: "I went out that day and I was surrounded by Manchester United supporters all around the park. It was unbelievable. It even affected the Leeds United players, because they couldn't believe it. They're in Sheffield, they're in Yorkshire, and Manchester United have got three-quarters of the stadium. It gave us a proper lift. Hillsborough was jammed to the rafters and all I can remember seeing is red and white everywhere."

As if worried about Leeds' lingering nastiness, or the fact that their opponents' progress in the competition had been more convincing than their own (Leeds had disposed of four First Division sides on their way to the semis), United attacked the Yorkshiremen right from the kick-off. Observers were left startled by the way the Reds combined aggression with their usual positive football values. Leeds meanwhile were left stunned by an opening quarter of an hour that left them two goals down. In the eighth minute, United won a corner. As usual, Houston trotted up to lend his (relative) height. His back-header from Hill's corner befuddled Leeds' Frank Gray and Jimmy Greenhoff was on hand to pounce and hit the ball into the roof of the net. It was another slice of satisfaction for Greenhoff Major, who had spoken of his happiness at his brace in the fifth-round match against Southampton: he had seen the devastation of his little brother after the Cup Final against the same team the previous season. In the 14th minute, Hill played a neat little one-two off Pearson's head. Merlin, as was his wont, unleashed a fearsome shot at goal. It bounced off Paul Madeley in front of Coppell, who put his recent mediocre form behind him by volleying it into the right corner of the net. Coppell wasn't sure it had gone in until the ecstatic reaction of the United supporters hit his ears. Said Docherty afterwards, "The lads all know the importance of a quick breakthrough, but two goals in 14 minutes were more than I ever dared to expect."

With a two-goal deficit to make up, Leeds now had to do all the running. They were naturally up for it, but United managed to hold them off until just before 20 minutes before full-time, when Joe Jordan was brought down by Nicholl. With Jordan out wide in the Reds' penalty area and nobody in support, it was a completely unnecessary offence and showed that for all the good work Nicholl had put in during this Cup campaign, there were still faults in his play which only experience could iron out. Allan Clarke converted the penalty – Stepney did get a hand to it – but the fresh hope instilled in Leeds turned to heartbreak as the minutes ticked away without them managing a follow-up. When the referee blew for full-time, United were no doubt less preoccupied with the fact that they and their opponents had provided a fine footballing spectacle than that they were at Wembley for the second year in succession.

Speaking at the end of the season, Docherty said of the semi-final, "We had gone off the boil a little in our previous League games. So much so, in fact, that most of the critics were tipping Leeds to win." He did concede, "We are not lethal finishers, otherwise we would have had four or five goals." Brian Greenhoff avers, "The semi-final was our best performance. The score says 2-1 but we won it quite a lot more comfortably than 2-1."

Nicholl offers an interesting memory of this season: "I can't remember thinking about the League. I don't know when we lost the opportunity. I only remember just everything being the Cup, the Cup, the Cup, the Cup and I can't remember ever being conscious of, 'Come on, we'll keep this going and we might be able to do the double'." Brian Greenhoff concurs about the League: "It never entered our minds that year. You're trying to get a strong finish to try and get in Europe."

\*\*\*

Following the Hillsborough match, a curious story appeared in the *Sunday People*. A feature by John Maddock claimed that had United lost, Docherty would have been sacked. Maddock alleged that the "controversy" surrounding the departures of Willie Morgan and Pat Crerand had turned several figures at the club against the manager. He further asserted that Matt Busby was "disturbed" by Docherty's image, particularly the way he would make public outbursts against opposition sides and individuals. Additionally, Busby's reaction was "annoyance" when Docherty was "forced to bring the issue [of his new contract] into the open". Maddock quoted what he described as "an influential member of the United fringe" as saying before the semi-final, "I hope we're beaten, then we can get rid of Docherty." We have no way of knowing the reliability of Maddock's quotes, although it should be noted that subsequent events make all of this ring true.

Maddock's story isn't even particularly undermined by the quotes from a 'friend' of Docherty he included. In a syntax strangely reminiscent of that of The Doc himself, the friend said, "Every club has its share of outside influences. People who think they control the directors, players, managers and training staffs. United are unique. There are more political figures trying to exert their influence than any other club in the land. There are people who would be delighted to see Tommy Docherty get the sack and he knows it. He won't go along with what they want." The friend's comments on "outside influences" and "political figures" would be echoed in later quotes bearing Docherty's name about what he and Cavanagh called the club's "junior board". Maddock's entire story would ultimately be given massive credence by events at the end of the season.

\*\*\*

Theoretically, Manchester United's remaining seven League fixtures retained some importance. Should they finish in the top four, they would be playing European football next year, specifically in the UEFA Cup. However, in reality it was a lot more complicated than that, even leaving aside the possibility that some of the United players were not going to give their all in League matches when one knock could rule them out of the FA Cup final. The way the season was going had thrown United a curveball, to use a term from another sport. United didn't yet know who their Cup Final opponents were going to be. The other semi-final between Liverpool and Everton had ended 2-2. An Everton victory in the forthcoming replay would suit United in terms of apparently increasing their chances of winning the Cup, what with their 4-0 victory over the club in December. However, should Liverpool be United's opponents at Wembley, it was likely that United wouldn't have to finish at any particular place in the table or even win the FA Cup Final to be guaranteed European football next season. Should Liverpool maintain their present position at the top of the League through to the end of the campaign, they would be eligible for the European Cup once more. They would not therefore be participating in the European Cup Winners' Cup even if they became eligible by winning the FA Cup final – it being impossible to play two European competitions – so their place in the European Cup Winners' Cup tournament would automatically be taken by Manchester United as FA Cup finalists. Even should Liverpool not finish as champions this year but win the European Cup – whose final they were already through to – they would automatically gain entry to next season's European Cup competition as holders, with the same beneficial by-product for Docherty's team.

These permutations of possibility were no doubt dizzying many heads at Old Trafford. Some may have been able and willing to cleave to the footballing maxim of "One game at a time", but most mortals – even supposedly simple-minded footballers – don't have that capacity for deliberately blinkered vision. One thing seems indisputable, though: the protestations of the majority of those questioned that players did not play below-par in the final League fixtures last season because they had their eyes set on the FA Cup final seem to be undermined by the fact that an identical collapse in the team's League form occurred in this campaign once they had booked their place at Wembley – even if this year the United players could at least point out that they weren't sacrificing the championship via their poor play.

On Tuesday April 26, United played Middlesbrough away. A crowd of 22,000 saw a full strength Mark II Roll Call crumble to a team who hadn't won at home for 10 weeks, even if they had beaten title chasers Ipswich at the weekend. Manager Jack Charlton had already decided to quit the club, so he had little left to lose, but his team played as though his reputation, if not his job, was on the line. Meanwhile, United were playing football involving many back-passes and a strange disinclination to tackle. The opening 'Boro goal came on 22 minutes. The United keeper blundered the ball into his own net in the 32nd minute from a corner, although he was being harassed at the time. The home side got a third and final goal in the 64th minute and only awful finishing prevented them getting more. The defeat left United in sixth place.

The following day, Liverpool ran out 3-0 winners in the replay of the FA Cup semi-final at Maine Road, meaning that though United had been unequivocally the favourites in the final the previous year, this time round they were going to be very much the underdogs, arguably even more than Southampton had been in 1976. Not only had Manchester United beaten Liverpool just once since 1969, but Liverpool were a club sweeping all before them: they were now on for a treble of League, FA Cup and European Cup. An indication of just what favourites Liverpool were is given by David Meek's response to the question of whether he had believed this season that United's name was on the FA Cup: "I did until they reached Liverpool in the final."

*\*\**

As fate would have it, on Saturday April 30, less than two weeks after United's demolition by QPR at the Londoners' home ground, came the return engagement at Old Trafford. With United – unchanged – able to field their preferred team this time, they played to a somewhat higher standard than they had at Loftus Road, even if they weren't exactly convincing. Still, the red element of the 50,788 crowd were at least treated to a victory, albeit one very late in coming. United dominated the first-half, Rangers the second. With the match still goalless on 67 minutes, Docherty decided to send McCreery on. The man he pulled off was Hill, who was neither injured nor having a bad game. Though this was the 10th time he had been substituted this season, it marked the first occasion where match reporters noted Merlin expressing annoyance at the decision. He wasn't alone, however: the crowd in the main-stand barracked Docherty. McCreery went into midfield and the Reds adopted a 4-3-3 formation. In Docherty's defence, things livened up in his team's attack at this point. With three minutes to go, Macari thrillingly dribbled his way through the Rangers defence before putting the ball past Parkes. Almost immediately afterwards, QPR seemed to equalise through Eastoe, but the ref disallowed it for pushing.

The 1-0 win was – in terms of avenging that 4-0 drubbing – something of a Pyrrhic victory. United – still sixth – had seen their championship hopes evaporate that grim night at Loftus Road. An indication of how empathically the title had slipped away from them was the fact that though the Reds had played an identical number of games to leaders Liverpool (37), they had a mere 43 points to Liverpool's 52.

Hot off that irony-dripping QPR fixture, Tuesday May 3 saw fate having a little fun again regarding United's opponents. The Reds visited Anfield for a League match that was inevitably billed by the media as a dress rehearsal for the FA Cup final.

In the QPR match, sighs of relief had occurred when Buchan waved away treatment after gingerly feeling his thigh, but the injury turned out to be serious enough to make him sit out this match. Brian Greenhoff, too, was unfit. With the duo who had proven to be the heart of the United defence absent, with United's players possibly determined not to risk injury, with United aware that Liverpool led the table by two points and had at least one game in hand over all their closest rivals and were therefore favourites to win a championship that would make their own participation in the Cup Winners' Cup next season a certainty and with the opposition needing to get as many points and goals as possible in the race for the title, one would have expected a massacre. That United kept the defeat down to a single goal was fairly impressive, though God alone knows what kind of conflicting impulses and emotions they were experiencing during the proceedings, which were watched by 53,046. Forsyth and Albiston were drafted in to replace Buchan and Brian Greenhoff (the only changes), although they played as full-backs, with Nicholl and Houston comprising the central defence.

Liverpool applied pressure early and on the quarter-hour mark it yielded the match's goal when Kevin Keegan defied his diminutive stature to climb for the ball and send a thumping header into the angle of post and bar. It was Keegan's 20th goal of the season, and a reminder – as if United needed one – that he would almost certainly be the danger man in the final. Docherty decided to send on McCreery at almost exactly the same juncture as in the QPR match, Jimmy Greenhoff this time the man who gave way.

Their 1-0 victory may have sealed the title for Liverpool – they were now four points clear of second-placed Manchester City with both clubs having played the same number of games; United were sixth – but little or nothing about the Cup Final could be extrapolated from this match. As Nicholl points out, a United away loss to Liverpool was not exactly unusual: "I can't remember being in a winning team at Anfield in my days there." Hill observes, "We used to get nothing from Liverpool. We used to get a cup of tea and a shower." In fact, the only thing that the game decided that was relevant to the Wembley fixture was the kit in which the sides would play at the aforesaid stadium. With both teams possessing a first strip of red, it was decided that the coin toss at the beginning of this match would dictate not just the right to choose in which half of the pitch to start play today but which club would have first choice of colours for the big day. Lou Macari, acting captain, won the toss and the club decided – naturally – that they would play in red come May 21st.

Meanwhile, the long-running saga over Docherty's contract was reaching its conclusion. Docherty's wife Agnes subsequently recalled that it was the day following the Liverpool match that her husband came home in an ecstatic mood, wanting to celebrate his new deal.

Presumably he had received the news that day, although of course The Doc could conceivably have been told it over the course of the previous two days, during which time Agnes may not have spoken to her Liverpool-bound spouse. Some might have felt the saga would never end. Gossip about Docherty in Manchester, especially among his detractors, was rife and the fact that Easter had come and gone, as had the FA Cup semi-final, without the issue being resolved was making some nod their heads sagely. After all, why would a club in danger of losing the manager who had turned them from a laughing stock into championship and FA Cup contenders not fall over themselves to ensure that he wouldn't be lured away by a better offer? Yes, Docherty had given public assurances that he would honour his current contract, but it would be an unusual club that placed much stock in such a pledge. Louis Edwards had made sure to publicly state his desire to retain Docherty's services, saying, "Tommy has done a wonderful job for this club. If I have my way, he will be with us for the next 40 years." Yet despite this effusiveness, the notable absence of a new 10-year contract for Docherty that some of the papers were speculating about, or a contract for Cavanagh, who had no written agreement with the club, made many postulate that despite the success Docherty was bringing to United, some on the board had severe doubts about him, not so much as a manager but as a man.

Matt Busby was forced to publicly deny that there was a rift amongst the directors. Louis Edwards claimed that the Easter holidays and so many midweek fixtures had prevented the board being able to meet to settle the matter. David Meek, close to the centre of the action at Old Trafford, later said that the board resented the pressure they felt had been applied to them by media coverage of the topic. It was a pressure, according to Meek, for which Docherty was responsible. Meek claimed that for his part Docherty was "hurt and dismayed" at the way the matter hadn't been resolved and that it was a situation that was "made public in the press at his own instigation". Docherty has recalled that Derby County approached the United board for permission to speak to him before the FA Cup semi-final and offered him a £10,000 salary rise to £28,000, exactly the figures that had previously been reported in *The Sun*. The aforementioned impunity with which managers could then break their contracts meant that this formal approach was a cause for alarm, even if Docherty told the United board (he says) that he had no interest in joining Derby.

Finally, after two board meetings and – significantly for some – after the Cup semi-final, the board agreed to give Docherty a new four-year contract. It was far from the "job for life" previously spoken of by journo Alan Hubbard, but it was widely reported that its basic payment terms and incentives were a substantial improvement over his previous one. Cavanagh got his own three-year written agreement..

*** 

Even less than from the Liverpool match could be extrapolated from United's away fixture against Bristol City on Saturday May 7. Despite the home club's supposed banning of anyone without a Bristol accent, there was a significant Red Army presence, albeit reduced from its usual 10,000 to about 2,000. City blamed alarmist newspaper stories suggesting there would be more United fans for the fact that the gate of 32,166 indicated that 5,000 City fans had stayed at home. Though Buchan was mercifully recovered, the United line-up was suspiciously unfamiliar. Docherty went as far as he dared in resting players at a time when fielding weakened teams was something that attracted sanctions by the football authorities. (Liverpool were fined for fielding a team of reserves in their final match of the season, which happened to be against Bristol City.) Hill and Pearson sat the match out, while McIlroy only came on as substitute. Jackson, McCreery and Albiston got places in the starting line-up instead.

After having just taken on the treble-chasing table leaders, United were now up against a team smack bang at the bottom of Division One. Bristol City were clinging to the belief that their games in hand over some of the clubs above them might prevent their relegation. Perhaps this explains some of the unseemly incidents during the proceedings. Those stigmatised Reds who managed to get into the ground by hook or by crook must have been left wondering whether those looking for hooliganism today would have been better advised to observe the happenings on the pitch. Sammy McIlroy, for instance, took several clatterings, and he only appeared – replacing the injured Houston – on 25 minutes. That there was no action from the referee drove the Irishman to distraction and a punch-up ensued that saw both him and Gow dismissed. As Docherty shepherded McIlroy off, words were exchanged and Gow had to be prevented from reaching the United manager. The home side scored after six minutes. Shortly after half-time, McCreery was brought down in the City penalty-area. With Hill in the stands, it was Jimmy Greenhoff who stepped up to take and convert the spot-kick. The match stayed at 1-1.

Afterwards, Bristol manager Alan Dicks complained that Docherty's comments as McIlroy and Gow came off were provocative. "A player would not react like that without good cause," he said of Gow's touchline flare-up. "Docherty got involved with our players during the match. That is bad for football and should not be allowed." Docherty claimed his angry words had been directed at McIlroy: "I was telling him how stupid he had been."

Considering both the roughhouse nature of the game and the United players' apparent terror of injury, it was an irony of the bitterest kind that though the heartbreak of an

FA Cup final-depriving injury did occur in this match, the incident that caused it was a wholly innocent one. Jumping for a ball with Chris Garland in the 25th minute, Houston fell awkwardly. "When I landed I thought I'd got cramp," he recalls. "When I turned over, my left ankle was at 90 degrees to my shin." The ankle injury was so serious that it was instantaneously clear that the left-back was not going to make it to Wembley. "It was nobody's fault," admitted Docherty.

"I wasn't too far away from him and I heard it go," recalls Buchan. "I knew he was in trouble right away." Even Hill heard the injury from the stands. "It's shitty at Ashton Gate and right in the middle of the field was sand," Hill says. "Stewart tried to turn with the ball and you heard a crack." Houston: "I don't remember a snap. It didn't feel in the ankle. It felt more in the calf. But when I looked, I thought, 'Oh my God, I'm just looking at something horrific here.' A lot of the players reacted as well and came over and quite normally just had to turn their head away because it was quite horrific ... I dislocated the ankle and was stretchered off and taken to the hospital. I was in very good hands: one of the Queen's surgeons operated at Bristol Hospital. But that was it. My ankle was shattered and so was my season." The most disappointing moment of his career? Houston: "Absolutely. No question about it. You just feel as if the world's opened up and swallowed you. You just felt hollow." Possibly even worse than missing out on the FA Cup final was losing what transpired to be his only real chance of playing on soccer's biggest stage. "I was picked to go to Argentina the year before the World Cup," he points out. "But then that went completely out of the window as well." Houston would never add to his solitary international cap, obtained against Denmark in October 1975.

A disconsolate-looking Houston later posed for the papers propped up in his hospital bed. "Even losing in the Cup Final a year ago was not as bad as this," he said. He revealed that he did have some cause for relief: "You always fear the worst when this sort of thing happens but the injury is not as bad as many people suspected. The bone has just been chipped slightly and I'm expecting to be in plaster for six weeks. Now I'm looking forward to the start of the next season."

Docherty had actually announced his Cup Final team after the semi-final. Naturally, it had been the Roll Call Mark II. Alex Forsyth – usually a right-back but a two-footed player able to play on either flank – was not given a chance to harbour even a fleeting hope that he might plug the new gap. Docherty told Arthur Albiston on the coach home from the Bristol City game that he would be playing at Wembley in Houston's absence. Considering that Albiston was merely a Scotland Under-21 and Under-23 player, whereas Forsyth had 10 full Scotland caps, Forsyth could be forgiven for imagining Docherty had a grudge against him. When asked about his decision to play Albiston, Docherty – who appears to have told journalists of it before Albiston – explained with a metaphorical shrug, "He is a good player." Says Buchan, "Not only did I have a lot of respect for Stewart as a player, he was one of my closest friends at the club. The good thing was that Arthur was a Scot, so we were halfway there. That's half the battle." Nicholl says of his stricken full-back bookend, "He was a great pro, a great lad, looked after us young lads. He was brilliant. Wee Arthur got his opportunity, but for that to happen to big Stewart, it was a disappointment to everybody." It would be nearly a year before Houston was back in United's first team.

\*\*\*

The 1-1 draw against Bristol City left United sixth in the table. The rest that had been intended for McIlroy but which had been scuppered by Houston's injury was now going to be an enforced one. He had accumulated enough disciplinary points to warrant a one-match suspension, which would coincide with the away match against Stoke City the following Wednesday, May 11.

In the Stoke game, for which Albiston took his place at full-back, Hill was present but the strike force of Pearson and Jimmy Greenhoff was absent, replaced by McCreery and McGrath. (United claimed that this was through genuine injury.) Tommy Jackson stepped into McIlroy's place. One might imagine that such a depleted line-up would not put up much of a fight against their relegation-battling opponents, but what transpired turned out to be a fine game of football. In the 22nd minute. Hill jinked in front of Shilton and when the keeper had been persuaded to advance off his line lifted the ball over his head to open the scoring. As soon as play kicked off again, McGrath dispossessed Johnson and fed McCreery. Super Sam shot across Shilton to make the scoreline 2-0. Three minutes before half-time, Stoke pulled one back and added another six minutes after half-time. However, United took the lead again when Coppell skipped in to intercept a bad back-pass and slid it across to Hill. Merlin experienced the novelty of scoring from close range. Stoke could consider themselves lucky to get the goal which made the final score 3-3 and over which there was a referee-linesman consultation but considering their pluckiness few would begrudge them the draw. The match – which took place in front of 24,632 – left United sixth in the table again.

Midweek saw Docherty in off-field drama. According to at least one report, he narrowly escaped death when he was involved in a crash on the A74. He had been travelling back from the Scottish Football Writers' Association presentation of the Player of the Year Award (made to Celtic full-back Danny McGrain) where he had been a guest speaker. His Mercedes was totalled in a pile-up near Beattock Summit. "I'm very lucky to be alive," Docherty said. "A car towing a trailer overtook me and suddenly jack-knifed. As it swerved across the central reservation, the trailer bashed into my car and the next I remember I was climbing out of the wreckage." The Doc abandoned his car by the side of the road and hitched a lift back to Manchester from a United fan who no doubt couldn't believe his eyes when he realised who the man with his thumb stuck out was. (Docherty's wife Agnes later claimed that The Doc reneged on a promise he made to his rescuer of two tickets for the Cup Final as a reward.) That Docherty's story may not have been the gospel truth was suggested by the fact that, seven days after the crash, he was banned from driving for six months after pleading guilty to travelling at 50 to 55 miles per hour in a 30mph zone.

\*\*\*

Saturday May 14 saw the United team that people knew would be – barring late injuries – their Cup Final configuration trot out to take on Arsenal at Old Trafford, essentially the Roll Call Mark II with Albiston taking Houston's place. This drew the approval of journalist Tony Stevens, who said of the League matches United played between the previous year's FA Cup semi-final and final with a fluctuating team, "[Bookmakers'] punters who saw United during that flabby period [and] realised how difficult it is for a machine of 11 parts, after a month of messing about, to reconnect the threads and restore the rhythm at the blast of the Wembley whistle, were duly rewarded for their perception."

For the first match in half a dozen, Docherty's side were not taking on either championship contenders or relegation battlers. With not even a place in Europe plausibly on the cards, Arsenal had nothing to lose or gain. Combined with the home team's disinclination to jeopardise Wembley appearances, the result was a good-spirited and gentle affair that often resembled exhibition or charity football. Despite this having been a distinct possibility at the outset, 53,232 attended what was the last Manchester United home fixture of the season. Contradicting the gentle pace, three players got booked, including McIlroy and Buchan. The Reds – which it was still appropriate to call United today, as Arsenal were in their yellow away-strip – went ahead in the 11th minute, Jimmy Greenhoff driving home. On 36 minutes, Macari made it 2-0. Five minutes after the interval, Arsenal's Liam Brady scored the type of goal that deserves to win a match when he embarked on an epic run in which he left Buchan and Brian Greenhoff tackling his shadow before sliding the ball past Stepney. Not long afterwards, Hill scored. In the 78th minute, a Graham Rix shot was deflected by Frank Stapleton past Stepney.

The 3-2 scoreline was how it remained to the end, upon which Pat Rice delivered his opinion on United's Cup Final prospects to the press. "I have tipped United to take the Cup all along, but if they carry on like they did today, I am going to be way out," said the man who had been in the Arsenal double-winning side of 1971 that it so happened were the last team to beat Liverpool at Wembley. "They were wide open at the back. They must really tighten things up defensively." Rice's comments were considerably leavened with some genuine good wishes for United: "I would love to see them win it for all the pleasure they have given in the last couple of years."

For those who cared, United were fifth in table after this result on a day that confirmed Liverpool as League champions when they drew 0-0 at home against West Ham. The unlovely efficiency of the Liverpool machine was for some epitomised by that score and the fact of their previous two results, a 0-0 draw away against Coventry and a 1-1 away draw against QPR.

Should the Reds fail to win the Cup, this season there would be no opportunity for a consolatory post-final League win like the defeat of Manchester City last year. Their final League game occurred on Monday, May 16 at Upton Park, with the Cup Final the following Saturday. The day before the West Ham match, Docherty, Hill and Pearson went off to do some advertising work for Gillette. The relationship between the three and the shaving razor manufacturer had, according to Coppell, begun when he had received a letter from the company inviting him to appear in a TV commercial. A novice in these matters, he had sought permission and advice from Docherty and then had been somewhat bemused at the way Docherty proceeded to hijack the project so that it also featured his manager and his wing bookend. The resultant advertisement was shot on a freezing cold day on the television gantry at Old Trafford. Coppell had possibly originally been approached by Gillette because such a clean-cut player provided the right image for a product – the new G2 blade – that gave a close, neat shave. Leaving the presence of The Doc aside, the introduction of Hill into the equation also made conceptual sense: two wingers advertising a razor with two blades with the strapline "The Old One-Two." Until, that is, you started thinking about it: Hill and Coppell played on opposite flanks, so the occasions when they might exchange a one-two pass were rare indeed. Coppell, coincidentally, also observed that as well as getting in on the appearance fee, Docherty seemed to have engineered other benefits for himself. "Doc, inevitably, was the star of the show and it was his car boot which was full of razors and blades rather than mine," Coppell said.

\*\*\*

Those who swallowed the United line that Docherty had not been repeating the strategy of last season in resting key players in the run-up to the final would seem to be disproven by the fact that Roche played in goal against West Ham. (Unless we are to accept that The Doc was seriously thinking at this point of playing Roche in the final, an act of cruelty towards Stepney – who apart from the Sunderland match in November had been first-choice keeper all season – that would be unprecedented even for Docherty.) Additionally, three minutes into the second-half Docherty pulled off Jimmy Greenhoff for McCreery.

United's unexpected early enthusiasm was manifested in a goal scored within 22 seconds. Macari released Hill with an excellent pass and the winger put the ball past Mervyn Day – as he had so many goalies this season – from an angle that appeared impossible. In the 30th minute, Frank Lampard – father of the current England star of the same name – unleashed a 25-yard shot that went in off a United post. Just before half-time, referee Clive Thomas befuddled most of the people in the 29,232 crowd by adjudging Macari to have fouled Trevor Brooking in the penalty-box. For those who detected no contact in the challenge, it was only just that Pike sent the consequent penalty over the crossbar.

That substitution of Jimmy Greenhoff seemed to weaken the Reds. Certainly, it marked a change in the home team's fortunes. On 52 minutes, Pike rifled the ball in from 20 yards. Five minutes later, the Hammers were 3-1 up courtesy of 'Pop' Robson. Though Pearson got one back with a brilliant 66th-minute volley, on 75 minutes, Robson sealed a 4-2 West Ham victory and another season in the top flight for his hitherto relegation-threatened team.

The only real matter of import for the Reds in regard to this for them meaningless fixture was that it left them in danger of losing Martin Buchan for the Cup Final, something they well knew to be a truly nightmare scenario. Recalls Buchan, "Everybody was up for a corner except me. West Ham clear it and Trevor Brooking's coming towards me in the centre circle. I managed to get my leg out and get a foot on the ball and Trevor fell over my outstretched leg. You must have seen the way Trevor runs – that sort of gangling style. Anybody else would have safely vaulted my outstretched leg, but not him. He fell right on top of me and opened up my knee ligaments." Buchan only became aware of how serious matters were later that evening. "I went out with Tommy Jackson to see a dear friend of mine, a singer called Bill Fredericks, singing in cabaret at Quaglinos night club and I felt my knee stiffening up and I couldnae walk in the morning. I needed crutches. I said to Tommy Doc, 'You might as well give me my train ticket and I'll go back up to Manchester because there's no way I'm going to play on Saturday'."

\*\*\*

Buchan excepted, it was a relaxing week for Manchester United before the Cup Final. With them out of the running for the League title, they had been able to take it as easy as professional pride allows for the West Ham fixture. Meanwhile, on Docherty's orders there were no commercial activities this week. This lack of distraction leading up to the final complemented the way the players had ensured that the semi-chaos that had reigned over their attempts to financially exploit their finalists' status last season was avoided this time by them hiring agent Dennis Roach. McCreery: "He took over the players' pool. And I don't think we did as much as we did the year before, the appearances and stuff." As Docherty observed, "As they know only too well now, all the fringe activities add up to very little if it all goes wrong on the big day."

The team and staff moved out of the Royal Garden Hotel in central London that had been their base for the West Ham fixture and repaired to Selsdon Park Hotel, near Crystal Palace, in Croydon, south London. Buchan was surprised at the price of a pint down in London but probably more surprised at the choice of hotel: "It was the wrong side of London to be for a Cup Final." Hill offers an explanation: "We changed from our old hotel in North London and we stayed at the Selsdon Park where Southampton stayed the year before. All Cup-winning teams had stayed there."

Alex Stepney this time around felt the mood among the players was just right, the complacency displayed by some before last year's final replaced by a hunger and a determination. "Southampton had, at least, taught us something," he later said. (He also felt a new warmth toward Docherty, partly because the manager had been very helpful over his testimonial earlier in the season. The Doc, he felt, wanted to like him but their relationship had been complicated by his status as the survivor of the class of 1968.) Macari later said that the difference between this and United's last visit to Wembley was "incredible" and attributed it to the fact that 12 months before the Reds, as huge favourites, were under "enormous pressure" to beat Southampton. Macari: "This time there was no pressure on us whatsoever because Liverpool were on for the League, FA Cup and European Cup treble and everyone expected them to do it."

Docherty gave a team-talk on the Friday before the final that was, it goes without saying, stirring and heart-felt. But as he finished it, he amazed the United players with a flourish. He told them that if they won, he would give the team £5,000 out of his own pocket to share, the approximate equivalent of nearly £25,000 in today's money. It was the type of flamboyant gesture that Docherty had made throughout his entire career. Considering that it was unlikely to make a jot of difference to how the team played – footballers would actually pay for the privilege of appearing in a Cup Final were they required to, a fact that an ex-player like Docherty would have known full well – one suspects that it was the gesture of a man who was a servant to impulse, and one rather similar to that completely unnecessary promise he made to Millwall when in the act of signing Stepney to Chelsea way back when that if the keeper played for England they would get an extra £10,000 on top of the agreed transfer fee.

\*\*\*

Happy to be underdogs this year United might be, but at the backs of their minds there must have been a terrible fear. The tearful scenes after their Wembley defeat the previous year illustrated just how devastating it is for a team to lose in English football's premier knock-out competition. How unbearable, then, would it be to get to a Cup Final for the second year in succession and once again lose? For Docherty that fear would have been even worse. The previous year he had thought being a three-time FA Cup final loser was "Worse than dying."

Docherty spoke publicly of that record before the final. "I'm not being haunted by the thoughts of losing again," he insisted. "Wembley is not about me. It's about the players, the supporters and the club." But he did admit, "I want a major trophy for peace of mind." Elsewhere he said of his alleged Wembley hoodoo, "A jinx is there to be beaten." However, that Docherty was nervous seems to be suggested by the fact that he was very carefully not repeating that claim he had made in Manchester at the end of the previous season that he would bring back the FA Cup. "I cannot say we will win, of course, because only fools and gamblers can pretend to know what is going to happen in a football match," he said. Separately, he commented, "I'm not casting a vote either way because I'm a fatalist."

Of the previous year's Wembley match, Docherty said, "I'll not be travelling south again with the same inexperienced team. We were like a coach-load of excitable schoolboys. We weren't ready. We had found the glory road too quickly from the Second Division. We thought we were going to Wembley merely to pick up the Cup and come home. The size of the occasion, the meaning of the day, hit those young men when we lined up in the Wembley tunnel. I'm sure some of them were saying inwardly: 'Mum, dad, come and help me.' They are one year older now and some have international games under their belts. They are going there as underdogs too, and that is better still." He also said, " ... there will be no problem motivating the team. Pride was hurt at Wembley last May and I think we all learned a valuable lesson. Obviously, no one wanted to go to Wembley and play badly. On the day I think everyone tried to the limit of their capabilities. But in the light of defeat I think there may be more motivation in the preparation for the match."

All the motivation in the world was, of course, meaningless without fit players and on that score United had a couple of worries. The first was one they had known about for a fortnight, namely Stewart Houston's unavailability. The man who had been a tower of strength in 36 league matches and six FA Cup rounds – and who was the only tall man in a defence lacking height – was a serious loss. That 19-year-old Arthur Albiston (height, incidentally, 5'7") was considered by Docherty his most obvious replacement may have been for some an expression of The Doc's faith in youth. Others may have considered it proof of The Doc's Devils' lack of strength in depth. In the three games in which Albiston had taken Houston's vacant place, United had let in nine goals and won just three of the six available points. While few were going to be blaming Albiston for the poor form of a team with Wembley patently preoccupying their thoughts, neither can this run have done much to quell the nerves of those who realised what an asset Houston had been and how inexperienced was Albiston, the veteran of a mere 23 starts.

Meanwhile, Laurie Brown was working on Buchan's knee. "Tirelessly" is Buchan's adjective. "Desperately" some might feel inclined to suggest. Most players would have insisted to the manager that they believed they could recover before the big day. Buchan though – as befitting a man of admirable if sometimes pompous integrity – had swiftly pronounced himself unfit for the final. Recalls Brown, "Martin thought he had no hope. In fact he wanted his ticket to go home. He didn't want to stay with the squad." It must have put the fear of God into the manager. Already wrestling with the unhappy knowledge of the inexperience at the back of the Wembley team and his own history of failure in the competition, Docherty now had to deal with the probable loss of the player whose presence (as proven by results) United's success was to a large extent contingent upon. No wonder Docherty had ignored Buchan's advice to give him his train ticket home.

"He left it up to me," Buchan says of Docherty's position with regard to his ability to play. "I remember having a few beers with Stewart on the Wednesday night actually thinking I wasn't going to make it." Brown: "You keep trying... We trained together up until the Friday morning. He was strapped up and played in a little five-a-side on the Friday morning. It was a calculated risk. Martin said on the Wednesday or the Thursday, 'If I play in this match, you can have my medal.' He hadn't done that much damage to it but it was enough to cause him bother and pain and a bit of swelling." By lunchtime of the Thursday, Buchan noticed an improvement. "For my fitness test on the Friday morning I stood in the goals of a five-a-side just kicking balls off the line and I played with a strapping," he says. In the end, this, the fact that Buchan wanted to be there to help the rookie Albiston and the prospect of a duel with Liverpool marksman and footballer of the moment Kevin Keegan made Buchan decide to play: "I declared myself fit and I got away with it. Another day I might not." "We strapped him up and tried to hide the strapping as much as we could for the Saturday," says Brown. Docherty himself must have known that Buchan was playing on a wing and a prayer even as he proceeded to put his name on the teamsheet. Afterwards, Docherty – in a comment that suggests the fitness test to which Buchan refers was so perfunctory as to not be considered a formal one – said, "It was so close that he went to Wembley without even a fitness test. But Martin's presence was as important to us on a psychological score as his actual play."

Stepney recalled the atmosphere in the dressing room before the match as electric, as well as serious and determined. Blunstone says, "It was a different atmosphere because they thought they were going to beat Southampton but they thought, 'Liverpool – different kettle of fish'." He adds, "I wasn't confident. Especially after the year before. It puts a bit of a doubt in your mind." Says Nicholl, "The year before, the players that were involved were over-confident. They made the mistake of being over-confident because [they] were the big favourites. [This year we thought] 'We came unstuck – we're not going to let that happen again.' We knew we were underdogs against Liverpool. It's a different approach and a different attitude and the fear of losing – if you have that all the time, you're going to win more games than you lose." Brian Greenhoff admits that Liverpool's stature had him worried that the eventuality that had caused him to publicly weep the previous year could very well be repeated: "I'd never played on a winning side against Liverpool. I'd drawn once and every other game we'd lost against them." However, he also says, "The thing is, it's one game." Nicholl adds a comment that also suggests the possible terror of losing consecutive finals could be mitigated by a philosophical approach: "Well you're not losing to another club along the lines of Southampton. You're losing to Liverpool, who's going for the treble. Now providing it's a good game and you've given everything, as hard as it is to take losing another final, you can live with it." (Of course, Nicholl hadn't played in the previous year's match, but his point is still valid.)

McIlroy says of Docherty's pre-match troop address this year, "'We're here. We let ourselves down last year. Go and win it this time for the fans' and then we had that in our minds that we were going to go out and do a better job. Well, we knew we had to because it was Liverpool." Blunstone: "He said something like, 'Right, now we've got another chance. We lost it last time. Make sure we take it this time'."

The Liverpool side that Bob Paisley led out had a surprising omission: David Fairclough was not even on the bench. Instead, Ian Callaghan was sub. For Brian Greenhoff, this was a double dose of the unexpected. "We were surprised that Ian Callaghan didn't play," he says. "We thought he would have started." However, Liverpool's starting XI were hardly weak-looking even without their midfield veteran and their super-sub: Ray Clemence, Phil Neal, Joey Jones, Tommy Smith, Ray Kennedy, Emlyn Hughes, Kevin Keegan, Jimmy Case, Steve Heighway, David Johnson and Terry McDermott were all instantly recognisable and respected names. Though Liverpool had made heavy weather of defeating Third Division Crystal Palace in the competition's third round (Palace had impressively held them to a 0-0 draw at Anfield before losing 3-2 on their own ground), their road to Wembley had – up to the semi-final stage – been pretty straightforward. In fact, easy, with them blessed by draws that consistently gave them both home ties and, almost as frequently, lower division opposition. They had beaten Second Division Carlisle United 3-0 and Oldham Athletic, also of Division Two, 3-1. Middlesbrough, their first top-flight opponents, were subjected to a 2-0 defeat before that replayed semi against neighbours Everton.

For the superstitious, there was a good omen when Buchan won the toss to decide which way his team would kick in the first-half. This, of course, followed the previous good omen of Macari having won the toss that ensured they were playing in their red first strip. (For some reason, Stepney wore a blue, rather than the traditional goalkeeper's green, jersey today.) As in the previous FA Cup rounds, United's shirts commemorated the 25th anniversary of Queen Elizabeth's II's coronation via a silver silhouette of the FA Cup and the words 'Silver Jubilee 1977', both items placed below the crest.

Jimmy Greenhoff later said of their opponents, "Of course, Liverpool were a great side, but The Doc reckoned they were terrified by our pace." Docherty has recalled that his intended strategy had been to take the game to Liverpool from the kick-off. Clearly conscious of the fact that Liverpool were a fearsome proposition when in possession, he instructed his men to close their players down quickly, especially in midfield. However, Liverpool were not the pre-eminent British side of the era for no reason. Bob Paisley had clearly told his men to do the same and the first-half was dominated by the Merseysiders.

In the opening few minutes, Arthur Albiston neatly dispossessed Phil Neal. Immediately afterwards, he robbed Jimmy Case. Both tackles brought huge cheers from the United fans. If the young stand-in was nervous, he wasn't showing it. Albiston's fellow full-back also had a good day. "The only reason I was nervous is because I was playing against Stevie Heighway," says Nicholl. "He was quick and he could cross a ball fairly well with his left foot but he could come inside on his right foot and lay and move. He wasn't just one of these wingers that stood there. You're just hoping to get in a good tackle to start off. I felt alright. I'm sure Heighway went over to the other side to wee Arthur during a period of time and then Jimmy Case come over. He chopped and changed a few times."

Kevin Keegan's first threatening moment saw him being smartly dispossessed by Buchan after the ball was punted toward him in the penalty box. Keegan was naturally expected to be Liverpool's star today. However, the sights Liverpool fans were so used to when they fixed their eyes on him – the diminutive but muscular figure bustling around the field, his shoulders moving in an instantly recognisable rolling manner, his chunky legs flowing as though oiled – were simply not as vivid as normal. That early example of dispossession by Buchan would be representative of the day. Reveals Buchan, "You can't man-mark someone for 90 minutes unless you're playing the sweeper system and you've just got that one job, but the plan was for me to pick him up whenever possible." In contrast to the way Keegan had been rampant in the League match between the two sides just three weeks before, in the Cup Final he was anonymous. In Coppell's opinion, Buchan neutralised Keegan. Brian Greenhoff says, "Sometimes you're only allowed to play as well as you're allowed and I think Martin marked him very well when he was in his area and I think I did the same."

When Clemence received a long back-pass for the second time Liverpool were booed for the tactic. However, it should be pointed out that in what was one of the better Cup Finals, both teams spurned the Cup Final tradition of caginess and attacked as if it were a home match.

In the eighth minute, Liverpool defender Tommy Smith was dispossessed in his own half by McIlroy. He pursued the Irishman and got the ball back in a challenge that left McIlroy writhing in pain on the ground but the referee Robert Matthewson surprisingly waved play on. Dubious character and footballer though Smith might be, he provided a useful litmus test for Buchan and his fitness worries: "Quite early on in the game I had a 50-50 with Tommy Smith on the halfway line, centre circle, and I thought, 'Well, if I got through this, I'll get through the game'."

In the 14th minute, Macari proved what an incredibly hard worker he was by dispossessing Heighway – on United's goal-line. A minute-and-a-half later, Gordon Hill produced his first burst of magic of the day with a shot whose long, leisurely flight made it resemble a cross but forced Clemence to tip it over the bar. On 18 minutes, a Liverpool attack was abruptly halted by the referee's whistle because all the red shirts were in Liverpool's half. It was neither the first nor the last time the offside trap would work for United today, but it was living dangerously. One slow pair of United legs or one unheard command from Buchan to push up could leave Stepney defenceless and few needed reminding of the way that Bobby Stokes had (arguably) beaten the Reds' offside trap the previous season.

Three minutes before half-time, Case, on the right-hand side of the United penalty box, floated an excellent cross to Kennedy on the far post. Kennedy's head connected with it and as it travelled toward the goal from the six-yard line Stepney was caught going the wrong way. However, Stepney stuck out his right foot and prevented it sneaking inside the post.

When the whistle blew for the interval, Docherty had the task of motivating his men for the resumption of hostilities after a first 45 minutes that few doubted Liverpool had had the better of. However, though United had not taken the match by the scruff as he had wanted, at least it was even-stevens and so far United had been at worst spirited. Docherty has said that he told the team that they were doing well but that they would have to do better to win. He wanted them to be more positive, particularly the wingers, and put the opposition under pressure by attacking in numbers. He instructed Pearson and Jimmy Greenhoff to go roaming, therefore pulling their markers out of position and leaving gaps for Macari and McIlroy to exploit. United were playing with the mild advantage of the wind in the second-half.

Not many seemed to have noticed in the euphoria of the Reds' FA Cup run that Stuart Pearson – despite scoring prolifically in the League and League Cup – had yet to rack up a goal in the competition this season. In the 50th minute, Pancho finally broke that duck. Not only did Pearson's first goal of the Cup run come in the perfect match, but it was a truly archetypal Pearson effort. When he hared toward McIlroy's pass on the right-hand side of the Liverpool penalty area, it at first seemed as though the close attention of Liverpool's Joey Jones would thwart him. But the fact of Jones towering over him, the fact that he had to ride his challenge and the fact that he was being steered into an awkwardly narrow angle clearly mattered little to the terrier-like form that appeared on the far side of the Liverpool man, the ball surprisingly still in his possession. Ray Clemence, covering the near post, provided yet another obstacle. In the split second he had to execute his effort, Pearson defied the odds by both overcoming the drawback of moving at high speed and by finding the part of the goal that was protected by Clemence. Rapidly running out of pitch, Pearson rifled a low shot inside the near post. The combination of power and subtlety in his goal was as quintessential Pearson as the fist he proceeded to raise in the direction of the United supporters who erupted in approval. An elated Coppell leapt onto Pearson's back.

Just as some had blamed Stepney for Southampton's goal in last year's final, so some felt that Pearson's strike today was less down to his talents than to a mistake by a goalkeeper who should have known infinitely better. "Ray was a little slow going down," said Pearson. Coppell, though, has said that Clemence made the same mistaken assumption he did: that

Pearson was going for the option most strikers would have – aiming for the unprotected far corner. Buchan says, "He hit his shot quite early and caught the goalkeeper by surprise."

Nicholl: "When he scored, you turned round and thought, 'Oh Jesus – great, now we've actually got a chance of winning this.' And it become even more intense, because you've got something to hold onto." No sooner had United finished their celebrations, though, then Stepney was on the deck, his face buried in his arms in despair at the fact that he had failed to stop a Jimmy Case shot ballooning his net. It had been two minutes since the Reds had scored. "There's no way he could have saved that," says Hill of Case's strike. It was certainly a gloriously taken effort. Receiving the ball with his back to the United goal, Case controlled it with his thigh, flicked it to his left, turned and unleashed a half-volley from fully 18 yards. The ball flew into the far corner of the net. "A very cleverly executed goal," admits Buchan. "I didn't appreciate that at the time, but when you see it, he took it very well." It was an appropriate goal for one of the match's outstanding participants. Hill: "I said to Jim, 'I'd have been proud to score that one Jim.' He said, 'Yeah, I just turned and hit it, that's all. It could have gone anywhere'."

It was an abrupt crash-down for the recently jubilant Reds. Buchan: "You think, 'Oh no. Wembley. Liverpool. 1-1'." Hill: "It was, 'Oh my God, we're going to go to overtime, especially on this big field, especially with this heat'." Blunstone was more philosophical: "You expect that. You don't play teams like Liverpool without them coming back at you. They're not going to sit down and die. You've got to be on your mettle."

Within three minutes, United were ahead again, though there was nothing of the class of Case's strike about the goal. Firstly, there was some argy bargy between Jimmy Greenhoff and Tommy Smith leading up to it. The two were entwined, pushing at each other and locking arms as they struggled to gain possession. Some felt the United man had committed an offence. Others – including Docherty – that it was a six-of-one scenario frequently to be seen on a football field and impossible to adjudicate on. Others, mindful of all the times Smith had assaulted fellow human beings on the pretext of a tackle, simply couldn't give a toss. Either way, Greenhoff toed the ball to Macari. "Jimmy was almost in my way," Macari later recalled. "He was trying to get out of it because he was in my line of vision. His movement distracted me a bit. I mis-hit the shot slightly ... " Jimmy Greenhoff later confirmed, "Afterwards we had a joke that we'd worked it out on the training ground, but actually I was trying to get out of Lou's way when he hit it!" Luckily for the team, the striker failed in his objective of removing himself from Macari's line of vision. "Louie when he hit it, it was going into the fourth row at the back," says Hill, "but Jimmy's chest was there and it hit Jimmy's chest and spun into the goal. I saw it because I was in the penalty box, going in on it." Hill was one-up on Macari, who had no idea that the shot had come off his team-mate as he rejoiced. Macari later recalled that at the time he honestly believed he had hit the ball as cleanly as he could and that it had just sailed into the net. "It never occurred to me that it might have hit anyone else on the way in," he said. "In front of 100,000 people at Wembley you don't stop to think when the noise hits you and I was off celebrating as soon as it went in." Though Hill cites Greenhoff's chest area as the point of contact, it would probably be fairer to say that the ball hit Greenhoff's stomach, possibly by way of his forearm. This whiff of handball has been the subject of surprisingly little comment down the years, even if any contact with his arm would clearly have been accidental.

"No, didn't see it at all," says Blunstone. "Because we were low there, on the bench. I hadn't got a clue. *They* didn't, so I don't know about us." Had Blunstone thought to glance at the scoreboard, he would have solved the mystery of the scorer's identity like Brian Greenhoff did. "I thought Lou had scored, 'cos I run straight to Lou," says Brian. "And then next thing it come on the board. Just looked up." When he subsequently saw it on television, Blunstone " ... thought actually how lucky it was because I don't think it was going in till it got a deflection." "I don't agree that it was a fluke," says Meek. "I know it took a deflection but it was a well-hit shot and the deflection was not right in front of the goalkeeper, it was quite well out. I think it was a good goal."

"Once that went in, it was like – that's it," asserts Hill. "They will not come back at us. If you looked at it very carefully, they tried but they couldn't get through." Nicholl's memories about the remainder of the match are somewhat less relaxed: "Once you go 2-1 up, then you're back the way you were when you're one-nil up. Then every minute that goes on becomes more and more tense. I remember thinking, 'Jesus if we can just hold on here.' If you knock a ball down the line and it doesn't go to anybody, you're not too bothered. You're just holding on ... "

Within a minute, United could have gone further ahead when Hill hit a low cross in the direction of Jimmy Greenhoff, but it flew past the striker and Jones hit it over the bar to safety. On 67 minutes, there was a rare flash of 'fantasy' from Hill this day as – apparently pinioned at the corner by two Liverpool men, his back to goal – he executed a Cruyff turn and a flip-up that released McIlroy. Immediately afterwards, Callaghan came on for David Johnson. Says Brian Greenhoff: "When they take a striker off, you're pleased, 'cos that means he's not doing well." Some later surmised that Paisley must have wished at this moment that he had the hyperactive services of David Fairclough to call on.

On 80 minutes, a long cross floated into the United penalty area and bounced in front of Brian Greenhoff. Greenhoff executed a header that Stepney had to perform a salmon leap to keep out of his own net. It seemed a rare lapse for the younger Greenhoff, a man whose tenacity – especially in the air – would make him many people's man of the match but Greenhoff says in fact that it was all intended: "It was a perfect shout from Alex. If you watch it on the telly, when I run away, I just turn round and clap him. It was a funny ball in from Phil Neal. It sort of bounced up. Alex shouted and I just knocked it to him. Looking back, you think, 'Ooh, that's a little bit risky, that', but I think at that particular time, I was having a decent game, it just seemed the natural thing to do."

Though 2-1 up in a Cup Final, Docherty's team were continuing to play the high-risk offside trap, as had been illustrated in the 74th minute when Neal tore after a through-ball but found himself alone in acres of empty space with the whistle shrilling. Blunstone denies this was a living-with-danger approach ("If he hadn't played offside, [Liverpool] might have scored more goals") but whether it was or not, Docherty showed caution in the substitution he made in the 81st minute. Here, The Doc proved that whatever indulgence he might have shown Gordon Hill previously, he wasn't going to let his fondness for his eccentric winger jeopardise his Cup Final prospects. Merlin found himself being pulled off at Wembley in favour of McCreery for the second successive year. Hill was visibly angry, and the United fans audibly so. Once again, Hill had not been as involved as much as people had been expecting and though Albiston had been nerveless and rock solid in defence, his inexperience had shown in the lack of service he had provided Merlin. However, Docherty has said that this time around the substitution wasn't for playing a "horror", as Hill had termed his performance last year. Rather it was his response to Bob Paisley's reshuffle of Liverpool's formation that had seen Case move into the attack when Callaghan replaced Johnson. McCreery was instructed to take up a midfielder's position to temper the threat. Blunstone: "It was a tactical thing. Two-one up, wanted to shore it up a bit more." McCreery: "It was just to try to hold the lead. I came onto the centre of midfield and it was to harry people. Just go and stiffen the midfield up." Tactical though the substitution may have been, Buchan feels Merlin's play in both Cup Finals had a shared characteristic: "I think the word you would have used possibly for both his performances was 'subdued' by his standards, because normally he was full of beans: 'Give me the ball, let me show what I can do'."

With the match into injury time, Kennedy crossed into the United box toward Keegan but as Keegan and Jimmy Greenhoff jumped for it, Stepney was raising his arms in jubilation: the final whistle had blown. The tension finally ebbed out of Nicholl. "I remember sheer relief," he says. As United players and staff hugged each other, the Liverpool players collapsed in a remarkable picture of devastation in the centre circle. Case subsequently explained that the Merseysiders were gutted that their dream of winning the treble was in tatters. Docherty sportingly went over and shook hands with all of them.

When Buchan ascended the stairs to the Royal Box to do his captain's duty of lifting the Cup, those viewers who were watching the BBC's coverage of the event heard John Motson say in a remark that confirms the famous commentator's dogged research or anally-fixated dementedness, depending on your opinion, "How appropriate that a man named Buchan should climb the 39 steps to the Royal Box to lift the Cup." The Duchess of Kent presented the trophy to Buchan, who in his anxiety to show the trophy to the United fans, displayed such little interest in small talk that the member of royalty found herself congratulating his back. Remarkably, the United fans' cheers as the Cup was held aloft were almost drowned out by the Liverpool supporters chanting their team's name.

***

Had this been 'Roy of the Rovers', the match would have been won with a goal of the quality of Jimmy Case's. Though he concedes the winning goal was lucky, Buchan says, "I don't think we were unworthy winners. I think we'd stood up to Liverpool and did well to confine them to one goal ... They scored four goals in the European Cup final on the Wednesday, so all in all it was a good day's work." (Liverpool in fact scored three goals the following Wednesday.) "No, I wouldn't say we were worthy winners," disagrees Blunstone. "There was nothing between us. It could have gone either way. It was one of them games. We had the break of the ball, no doubt about it, that day. But we deserved it after the year before." The assistant manager would seem to be in a minority. McCreery: "I think we were worthy winners. We gave as good as we got, if not better." Brian Greenhoff: "I thought we thoroughly deserved to win in the end, 'cos, when you look, Liverpool hardly a chance." Meek also gravitates to the point of view that the scoreline accurately reflected the run of play on the day: "I felt that here was a team that believed in themselves and were out to make up for the disappointment the previous year. I was surprised, because they were playing above themselves."

The scorer of the winning Cup Final goal was traditionally awarded a Golden Boot, and according to Macari it was only when Jimmy Greenhoff walked into the dressing room carrying the said prize that he realised he hadn't scored. (Greenhoff's little brother sarcastically suggested a Golden Arm award would have been more appropriate.) "Jimmy and I could not have cared less," Macari said of the debate about who should be credited for the goal. "We had beaten Liverpool. That was the main thing."

Albiston had done brilliantly in the final, so much so that to some he was the man of the match. Houston says of the player who benefited from his misfortune, "It was really a huge step for Arthur to be thrown into the biggest game of his career, but he did terrific. On the day he was probably as good as anybody else on our team." Typical of Albiston's modesty and good nature, he tried to give Houston his own winner's medal in the dressing room. Houston's own modesty and good nature was demonstrated by his refusal to take it.

Naturally, the scene in the United dressing room was a stark contrast to the glum vista therein the previous year. Jimmy Greenhoff has recalled, "It was bedlam in the dressing room. Everyone was in the bath. Players, staff, kit men. And when we got back to Old Trafford my bloody strip wasn't there." A decade later, the elder Greenhoff was approached at an engagement in Cleethorpes by a man ("He was just a member of the public") who fessed up to the shirt-pinch. The man offered the shirt back to Greenhoff but the player was so impressed by his honesty that he told him he could keep it, though admitted he did later regret his generosity. Docherty, though, found himself with mixed feelings in his moment of triumph. "After the one in 1976 against Southampton, I was sick," he later said. "I was so sure we would win … that when we beat Liverpool the following year, it was almost an anticlimax. We had been such hot favourites against the Saints, and after that, I thought we'd no chance of beating Liverpool." No wonder he had been so reluctant to predict a United victory in pre-final interviews.

The players who took home medals for winning the Football Association Challenge Cup in 1977 would have found the idea of a future diminishment in the status of their triumph unthinkable. Though the competition may now be viewed as a lesser one, in 1977 being on the winning team in an FA Cup Final was a huge deal, the domestic club honour second in prestige only by a small margin to a League championship medal. With the exception of Stepney, it was the finest moment in the career of all of The Doc's Devils so far, and not at all down to the fact that the era in which they were playing marked an extended drought in United's winning of championships. Even for Stepney, it was special as the final missing accolade of a golden career in which he had won the League championship and the European Cup. After the previous season's Cup Final, with his biological clock ticking ever more loudly and serving a manager who had been equivocal about his faith in his abilities, Stepney had assumed that his chance to obtain the one medal not in his cabinet was gone.

It was also a particularly magic moment for both Greenhoffs. When Jimmy Greenhoff played for Leeds in the 1968 League Cup final, his younger brother – then 14 – had been one of the six ballboys supplied by Barnsley schools. Jimmy Greenhoff told a journalist at the time,

"My mum and dad have always said it would make their day if both their boys ever got to Wembley." It was a humorous comment that he had no way of knowing would come true properly, even if he had also said at the time, "Brian could be back as a player himself, for he's a good little half-back." Brian had helped make up for his tear-stricken devastation of 1976 in the best – in fact, the only – way possible. Jimmy had taken great pleasure in assisting in that aim via his three goals during the Wembley campaign (pre-final). Jimmy had also obtained for himself the domestic honour that had seemed destined to be forever beyond his reach. He had been on the losing Leeds team in the 1967 FA Cup semi-final. He had then been in the losing Stoke City team in two successive FA Cup semi-finals (1971 and 1972), both times against Arsenal, an experience of which he later observed, "I cried my heart out. It almost destroyed me." The Greenhoffs, incidentally, were the first brothers to play at Wembley since 1967, when Ron and Allan Harris had turned out for Tommy Docherty's Chelsea. Says Brian Greenhoff of the performance that brought about this familial joy, "Playing 12 months before helps you, because you're going back and you know what to expect and you know what it's like, and we had a go at them. We set off really well. I just think the team as a whole worked so hard. I passed it to Lou Macari and Sammy McIlroy, they seemed to run like a thousand miles in midfield. When they've got big players there it was a big ask for them but I thought they were fantastic ... It was one of them games where me and Martin, we really did defend well together."

Even the pain of his second successive Cup Final substitution couldn't take the gloss off the day for Hill. "I wasn't unhappy about it because we'd won the Cup and I knew that the boss had done something to secure that, so I wasn't going to argue 'cos the FA Cup's the FA Cup," he says. When asked if it was the happiest day of his professional life up to that point, even the usually unexcitable Buchan says, "Oh, it had to be, yeah – particularly when in the back of your mind is Tommy Doc in front of that huge crowd at the town hall, saying, 'Never mind, we'll come back and win it next year'. So it was like a fairytale come true."

For some players, part and parcel of the Wembley triumph was what it seemed it might herald. McIlroy: "We were a good young side with good players and we felt we could keep going from here on in." Blunstone opines that this victory meant more than beating their opponents the previous year would have done: "To beat Liverpool, it's fantastic. If they'd have beat Southampton, what would it have been? 'Oh, well so you should do – they're a Second Division team.' But if you beat Liverpool, you've beaten the best."

With Borussia Mönchengladbach, Liverpool's finalists in the European Cup final in Rome the following Wednesday, having that very day retained the West German championship, some were predicting that Liverpool's treble dreams would end up as the embarrassment of 'merely' winning the championship. "Once we got that trophy, we went up to them and we just said we wish you all the very best in Europe next week", says Hill of the Liverpool men. The United fans had been similarly sporting, applauding the Anfield crew on their lap of honour and chanting "Good Luck Liverpool." The latter was a particularly magnanimous gesture because some Red fans – possibly even the majority – did not want United's record of being the only English club ever to have won the European Cup sullied.

Football correspondent Donald Saunders spoke for many when he said that English soccer had cause to be pleased with Manchester United's success. "Failure at Wembley last season, followed by disappointment in Europe last autumn, might have persuaded United to abandon their policy of playing the bold football that entertains but offers little insurance against defeat," he wrote. "Instead they continued to set an enterprising example." No doubt mindful of the decline in football attendances in recent years, he also said, "Now, having achieved success, they may win badly needed converts over to their faith, which many believe alone offers English football salvation."

Waldron says of Docherty's Albert Square claim the year before that he would bring the Cup back in 1977, "I just think him coming out [with] that, it's an emotional thing. They've brought the open-top bus to parade through and they haven't got the Cup and it can lead you to saying things that could be hot air or whatever. The unbelievable thing is that he fulfilled it." McIlroy: "That was Tommy Doc. The media loved him, he made these statements. That was a fantastic statement to make after losing the Cup Final against Southampton when we were favourites, but he made that statement and he fulfilled it. He did it." Brian Greenhoff reveals he'd had a similar attitude in 1976: "We went to the hotel and I got my medal and I threw it to the wife and said, 'That's yours, I'm having the winner's next year'." He admits, though, that this was " ... bravado. You hope it'll happen." For Gordon Hill, though, the victory was preordained from the first moment of the season's competition, by which is meant not the smugness that had possibly afflicted the Reds' performance against Southampton but an almost mystical inevitability. His words suggest that some of his colleagues shared this belief. "We knew it the year before," he claims. "We talked on the train on the way back and we knew we would be back at Wembley. It's amazing. I can't tell you what and how, but all of us knew that we'd be back. It was funny. It was something that went through us as a team: we'll be back."

A banquet followed at the Royal Lancaster Hotel. While Cavanagh was understandably and expectedly ebullient, the other Tommy struck some as surprisingly subdued. Coppell certainly observed how quiet the manager was in the wake of the biggest triumph of his career. Docherty himself said later that people kept coming up to him to ask him why he looked so unhappy. The world would soon find out.

"I can now see a championship in front of us like never before," Docherty told the press afterwards. "I want it to be ours within [the] next two years. The win ... was the final confirmation that we are on a winner. Liverpool's system has been tested and proved over umpteen years as the hardest to break down, but our style beat them. All we require now is their kind of consistency. The ability is there – enough to make us champions." However, Docherty had grander ambitions than just improving the lot of his club: "What I want to do now is establish that the kind of progressive football we all believe in at Old Trafford is good not just for Manchester United, but the only way you can push home the message after winning the Cup is by winning the championship."

Hill's feelings about his second successive Cup Final substitution were discussed in the press. One tabloid reported that Merlin had asked The Doc if he had a future at the club. "No, nothing of the kind," says Hill now. "I went up to the boss and he just said, 'Gordie, I done it for the team.' I went, 'Fine no problem at all.' But the tabloids got hold of it and said, 'Gordon, was you unhappy?' I said, 'Yeah, very unhappy.' And that's what they put. They put their two and two and came out with five. If they'd have seen me afterwards, they wouldn't have said I was unhappy." Some though cite Hill's failure to rise to the occasions of his Cup Finals in conjunction with his mediocre form in his six England appearances as evidence that he did not have a big-match temperament. "You can't get no bigger than Juventus," he demurs. "You can't get no bigger than Ajax. I think it's just a case of settling down. It was the second year I'd been around in the team and as time would have gone on I'd have been more confident. Sometimes I wasn't confident, but I'd try not to let it show. With the England team, you didn't know if you was playing or not. I was on the bench for a couple of years with them. Every game they played – qualifying, because you never played a lot of internationals in them days – it was always, 'Well, he's going to play this formation' and the wingers weren't included."

On the train home, Stepney felt himself warming to Docherty again when the manager took hold of the FA Cup and placed it between the goalkeeper's two young sons. The hallowed trophy remained there all the way back to Manchester.

There was one last matter to attend to for the players: the £5,000 bonus to which they were eagerly looking forward. (Stepney, incidentally, does believe that the United team put in a bit of extra effort as a consequence of the cash inducement.) Their captain was deputised to collect it. Recalls Buchan, "Doc offered it to me to distribute among the lads not long after the end of the season, but some of the lads had already left on holiday so I told him to hang on to it until we were all back together for pre-season training."

\*\*\*

The Reds won 18 matches in this League campaign, drawing 11 and losing 13. Gordon Hill ended up United's top scorer of the season, with a total of 22 from all competitions. Pearson got 19 in total, Macari 14 and Jimmy Greenhoff 12. None of those players, though, got the Manchester United Supporters Association Player of the Year award, that prize instead going to redoubtable defender Brian Greenhoff. Says Brian, "When my brother came, that gave me a lift and I think me performances improved greatly. I think that's what it does to you. 'Cos you knew the standard that he played at, that you wanted to be up there." For the second campaign in succession, United won the Fair Play Award, something that must have pleased Buchan, who had said the previous year, "Our aim now must be to hold on to this trophy next season."

Liverpool went on to get a little bit of revenge on United the Wednesday following the Cup Final by winning the European Cup. No longer could the Reds claim their 1968 achievement of winning said trophy as unique for an English club. Part of the reason for Liverpool's 3-1 triumph over Borussia Mönchengladbach was that Keegan was marked by Bertie Vogts somewhat less well than he had been by Buchan. A measure of Buchan's achievement was that Vogts was a World Cup winner who had contained the great Johan Cruyff in the 1974 World Cup final. Another measure is the fact that Keegan, though he would finish runner-up in the poll to determine that season's European Footballer of the Year award, would go on to win that accolade back to back in the two seasons after that.

When it came to the League, Macari's glum assessment that his club's title hopes were dead after the defeat against Norwich back in April now seemed less unwarranted pessimism than a spot-on evaluation: United's ultimate position of sixth was exactly where they had been after that Carrow Road loss, and they had risen no higher than fifth in the interim. The teams between Liverpool and Manchester United in the final table were, in descending order, Manchester City, Ipswich Town, Aston Villa and Newcastle United. Liverpool actually lost their last game of the season, their away fixture against Bristol City, a 2-1 defeat that would ultimately save their opponents' First Division bacon, in which the Merseysiders' understrength team was clearly a gambit to save players for the approaching two cup finals. Though the swashbuckling nature of The Doc's Devils might have been proven by the fact that their strike tally of 71 meant that United had scored nine goals more than the Merseysiders this season, it was a rather shocking statistic that despite United finishing only five places in the table below Liverpool, they had conceded 62 goals to Liverpool's 33. Still, the fact that United had beaten the domestic and (shortly) European champions in the FA Cup final augured well for the side's future.

∗∗∗

Immediately following the FA Cup final victory, the United players had made themselves available for the television cameras. Sweat-drenched, swigging from 70s-style long-necked milk bottles and draped with the hats ands scarves traditionally pressed on players by jubilant fans on their way up to the Royal Box, they came out with the usual brief banalities to be expected of exhausted and happy athletes. Docherty was a little more articulate, but not much. There was, however, one moment in The Doc's exchange with ITV's Gerald Sinstadt that, in retrospect, is arresting indeed. The commentator was puzzled by the fact that Docherty's wife Agnes wasn't at the ground, assuming her to be back in Manchester. In fact, following the disappointment of last year's defeat, she had acquiesced to the insistence of Frank Blunstone's wife Doreen that, should the club get to Wembley again, the pair should watch the match on television in their hotel.

"You left your wife at home this year," said Sinstadt, "Is she going to be allowed to come next time?" "I thought you said I'd left my *wife* there," responded Docherty.

Sinstadt had unwittingly stumbled upon a truth. 26 days later, June 16, Tommy Docherty did indeed inform his wife Agnes, mother of their four children, that he was leaving her. He was setting up home with Mary Brown, a 31-year-old woman who had two children of her own. Mary was the wife of the club physiotherapist, Laurie Brown. Agnes would claim that before this date, Docherty had pretended to visit his sick mother for a week, during which time he moved in with Mary Brown. This theory tallies with the implicit admission in Docherty's account(s) that he moved in with Mary before telling his wife. Laurie Brown says he learnt of the relationship, "...the week after the Cup Final. Mary told me." Docherty had been involved in a relationship with Mary for some time. In *Call The Doc* (1981), the manager said it had been "a couple of years" after their first meeting in 1973 that they had formed an "attachment". According to Mary in a 1977 newspaper interview, the two had become lovers in approximately November 1976. In *My Story* Docherty claimed that about a fortnight after the Cup Final, he moved out of his family home in Hale Barns, Cheshire, and into the granny flat in the Browns' house with Mary. Because said flat was underneath the Browns' ex-marital home, this allowed Mary to give her two daughters a semblance of normality in terms of getting her children off to school, putting them to bed, etc. Nobody in the wider public knew about this state of affairs until June 18, when the story broke in the newspapers.

Meek: "It was complete surprise and shock. He'd conducted the affair in the utmost secrecy and I don't think anybody had any idea. I read it in the papers." So too did the players. "Me and Sammy were lying on a beach in Ibiza," recalls Hill. "Sammy had come back off an Irish tour, I'd just come back off an England tour to Australia, and we were trying to grab a week away before we went back pre-season. Sam said, 'Have you read the paper? The Doc, he's been knocking off Mary Brown for two years.' I went, 'Sam, don't be stupid'." McIlroy: "It was the summer holidays. All the players were at home or on holiday. We were only getting snippets from the press what was going on. No one ever contacted any of the players to say what was going on." Nicholl: "Absolutely no idea. I was sitting in Spain, me and the wife. It was big Alex Stepney. I met big Alec at the beach and he said, 'What about that?'" A penny, though, dropped for Nicholl: "You just looked back. I was sitting and thinking about the reception in the hotel afterwards: he was very subdued that night." Docherty has confirmed that his desire to be with Mary Brown was indeed the reason for his surprisingly downbeat mood that evening.

Coppell was probably one of the last to know. At the conclusion of the season, he was with the England squad on a South American tour. Because this was long before the age of the internet or 24-hour news media, he remained oblivious of the news reports of the affair until he was driving to his girlfriend's house from Gatwick Airport upon his return. The radio news report made him burst out laughing at the idea of a union between the loud, brash and relatively uncultured Docherty and a woman the winger had found on the few occasions he had met her to be quiet, well-spoken and even a little snobbish.

Docherty claims that he spoke to Louis Edwards' son Martin (a board member) about the new development in his life "about a week or so after the Cup Final" and was told by him not to worry as it was the sort of thing that had been going on since Adam and Eve. Docherty stated that he hadn't been completely reassured by this isolated opinion from one of the club's lesser figures but that he was unable to contact Matt Busby or the club's secretary Les Olive because both were on holiday. (Strangely, he has not mentioned feeling a need to contact Louis Edwards, whom one would imagine to be the most important figure at Manchester United.) Pat Crerand has claimed that it was he who informed Matt Busby of the breaking scandal, having received a phone message from a caller he doesn't identify the Saturday before the story appeared in the *News of the World* telling him of its contents (he possibly means the *Sunday People*, to which paper Docherty and Mary Brown had sold their story). Crerand was still close to Busby and rang him in County Mayo, Ireland, where Sir Matt was on a golfing holiday. He has recalled that his ex-manager's first words when he came to the phone were, "What's he done now?" That Crerand had not even needed to tell Busby who the subject of the call was seems to indicate that there was a high degree of dissatisfaction with Docherty, at least among some, behind the scenes at the club. When Busby was informed by Crerand of the nature of the story, he decided to travel straight back to Manchester.

What played out in the media over the following few weeks was akin to a soap opera. The *Sunday People* ran a story headlined "The Doc Runs Off With Team Wife", which looked at first glance (perhaps intentionally) as though it was a story about the manager taking up with one of his players' partners. From Docherty's account, the newspaper had somehow come upon the story and he and Mary had decided to cooperate with it. Agnes has said money was provided by the *People* for their tale (although that doesn't prove Docherty's version of events untrue). Laurie Brown says, "They found out very quickly. I think he broke it. He gave an exclusive I think and that was it – once one got it, they were all there. That wasnae very nice either. You had half the country's press parked outside the door and he was doing deals with papers, and if it was a rival paper, then he made sure that Mary did the deal." "We are in love," Docherty told the *People*. "We've got something special going for us and we've decided we would like to spend our future together. We haven't rushed into this. There's been a lot of soul-searching. The bond has grown between us over the last three years and we've decided to bring our relationship out in the open rather than live a lie." He went on, "This has nothing at all to do with football. It is a private matter and I've always believed in keeping my public and private lives separate. I shall continue to devote my time to keeping United a top team."

Laurie Brown, however, clearly didn't think anything could ever be the same again. Docherty said to the press, "We both have a job to do. Personally, I think we can still work together." Brown, however, told a reporter, "I have lost my job, my wife and two smashing kids. I have not been sacked – but could you work with a boss who has stolen your wife? I asked him in my home because I thought he was happy when he came here. I never dreamed he was seeing my wife. I had no inkling." Brown now says, "If my wife had run away with the milkman, I would have understood, because you'd have thought, 'You've been a bit selfish here and you havenae spent enough time at home' because it was seven days a week. But when she ran away with him – y'know: anybody but him." He says that at this point he was resigned to leaving the club. "When it came to it, I thought 'I'll leave here but I'll wait until I'm pushed. I'm not going to make it easy for anyone and jump'," he recalls. "I was losing my job, my life, my kids, my house, the lot… You think you cannae go into the ground, but I thought, 'Well why shouldn't I?' So I went in every day. It wasnae very nice. A lot of the staff, if I walked into a room, they all found a reason to leave. I think they thought, 'Wait a minute, Docherty's staying', I'll be going – they didn't want to rock the boat with the manager."

Docherty subsequently had a meeting with Louis Edwards about the issue. Afterwards, he told reporters, "There is no question of my leaving the club. I have seen the chairman, Mr Louis Edwards. He has spoken to the rest of the board and they want me to stay. The board have been absolutely marvellous. They feel like I do – it has not been a pleasant thing but it is a personal matter and has nothing to do with the football side of the club." The chairman. though. did not back up Docherty's story and his reaction to press enquiries was rather terse. "I am not prepared to comment," he said. "I will make a statement tomorrow but at this stage I am not prepared to say whether these remarks are true or otherwise." In light of Edwards' subsequent support for Docherty, his comments can be seen as flustered rather than ominous. Inevitably, Docherty was asked more questions about his working relationship with Laurie Brown. "I am staying here," he said. "Laurie must face up to that himself. I would like him to work here but it would obviously be very difficult for us both. It would depend on who is big enough to overcome it." Later that day, Brown told the press, "Obviously I have no future at Old Trafford if he stays."

Confusion then reigned. Docherty went off on a holiday to the Lake District with his son Mick and Mick's family. (Mick remains the only child Docherty had with Agnes who has maintained contact with him since the split.) On Wednesday June 29, Docherty was called back to Old Trafford for an evening meeting with Louis Edwards and Busby. He then returned to his holiday. Edwards and Busby had previously had a meeting with Laurie Brown. Rumours began circulating about what had transpired at the meeting between Busby, Docherty and Edwards. One report claimed that Docherty had been asked to resign but had refused to do so and that he had then been suspended on full pay. United put out a statement saying, "It is not true that Docherty has been suspended. The directors have had a normal meeting at which the situation regarding the manager and other members of staff was discussed. There is no change in their positions at the club." Docherty said, "I can't wait for training to start on July 21. I don't just want to win the Cup again. I want to win everything. I'll be back at my desk on Monday, and that's it."

Rumours continued to swell over the next few days that Docherty would be sacked, that he would receive a £100,000 golden handshake and that he had been offered a post at Derby County, the club whose overtures had caused United to extend Docherty's contract only weeks previously. Mick Docherty was caught up in all this drama. Asked if his father was worried at this point that he was going to be dismissed, he replies, "Seriously, it was never, ever discussed. I didn't even know the full implications. I knew about what was happening with dad and Mary and it was a very difficult position for me to be in, but in terms of his tenure at Old Trafford coming to an end, he never discussed that with me at all until it finally happened." Perhaps this was because Tommy Docherty had no particular reason to think his job wasn't safe. After all, on Sunday July 3, Edwards made his strongest suggestion yet that Docherty's position was not under threat. "The stories about us sacking Tommy are nonsense," he was reported as saying. "The rumours that he will be asked to leave get no encouragement from the club."

Brown now says he thinks the board's initial refusal to sack Docherty made the manager abruptly change an escape plan he had hatched. "He was going to Derby anyway and he was going to take Tommy Cavanagh with him," he says. "He told me." Brown dates this Derby revelation to prior to the Cup Final (and of course prior to him knowing about The Doc's affair with his wife). Brown says, "They were going to get more money and they werenae happy at Old Trafford... He was running away with Mary. I think he thought it would have been very hard for him to stay on at United... He had it all sorted out and it was only when Edwards said, 'Oh this has got nothing to do with football, he can stay' that he must have thought, 'Oh, well I can stay'." Though Brown's revelation about Docherty's interest in Derby being more than an exploitation of them as a bargaining chip to get higher pay at United is intriguing, his theory doesn't quite add up when one considers that Docherty had spoken in the *People* story– of which United seem to have had no prior knowledge – of intending to stay at Old Trafford.

The day following Edward's public support for the manager, Docherty was driven to the home of Louis Edwards in Alderley Edge, Cheshire, by United's kit man Norman Davies. (Docherty's driving ban had similarly meant that Mary had had to drive him to a previous meeting.) Before the meeting, Docherty declined to tell the press what it was about but did say that he expected the matter to be concluded, it being otherwise unfair "to the club, to the players and to myself". The meeting inside with the six directors of the club lasted no more than half-an-hour. When he emerged, Docherty was, according to one paper, "Grim-faced and badly shaken." Docherty later gave his version of what happened: "I went to the meeting of the directors today at 4:45. I had to stay outside, of course. They called me in and Mr Edwards read out a prepared statement saying that the board had dispensed with my services because of a breach of the terms of my contract. Nothing was said about what the breach was and even now I can't think of any way I could have breached the conditions. In a way the board has treated me worse than a shop steward or an industrial worker. Under the Industrial Relations Act they're supposed to warn people. I got no warning. There was nothing in my contract about my private life. I conducted my private life to the best of my ability but a lot of things can happen along the way. In all this I am sorry for the fantastic supporters and staff who have backed me all the way. They are the people who are in jeopardy now. I spoke to three or four players this morning. They said that what had happened in my private life didn't make the slightest difference to them. They hoped I would be staying. I have loved every minute of the job at Manchester United. But now I am looking for a job."

A statement by Manchester United was read out by club secretary Les Olive. It said: "A meeting of the directors has decided unanimously that Mr Docherty is in breach of the terms of his contract and his engagement is terminated forthwith. It is the board's intention to appoint a new manager as soon as possible and applications are invited from managers with experience and proven ability. They should be addressed to the chairman, Mr Louis C. Edwards, at the club." It was just 44 days since Docherty had done what no manager had since 1968: win Manchester United a trophy.

Gerry Daly was one of the few who did not find himself surprised by the sacking. "I obviously put two and two together," he says. "I thought to myself, 'This is the reason why Jimmy Murphy and Sir Matt Busby came along and spoke to me and told me that we can't tell you what's going on.' Because Sir Matt knew everything that went on at Old Trafford. I'm surmising that may be the reason." Laurie Brown was also not surprised. Having been resigned to leaving Old Trafford, a meeting with the United board persuaded him that his job was as safe there as Docherty's was unsafe. It's not known on what date this meeting occurred, though Brown says he had only one meeting with the United board about the matter and that he thinks it wasn't a Sunday because of the traffic he unexpectedly ran into on his way there – meaning it wasn't the day before the dismissal. Logic dictates that said board meeting can't have been on the day of Docherty's dismissal, both because the media reported a meeting with Brown prior to this and it is inconceivable that the club would have only consulted Brown at such a late stage in the proceedings. Brown recalls, "The meeting that I had with the board was at Louis' house very early in the morning. It was about eight o'clock. All the board were there. They wanted to know what I was going to do, and at that time I thought, 'I'm leaving, I've had it,' but then they asked me to stay on. I knew if they wanted me to stay on, he was going, because they wouldn't have asked me to stay on and say, 'Oh by the way, he's going to carry on as well.' That was an impossible situation." Matt Busby had been responsible for bringing Brown to the club as a part-timer in 1969, the year after which Brown became the club's first ever full-time qualified physiotherapist. Says Brown, "I think Sir Matt wouldnae have been too happy and I think he had a lot to do with me staying on." He adds, though, that the vibe he got off Louis Edwards was no different to that from Busby: "The board seemed quite united when I was there."

"This is the most shattering experience of my life in football and I am terribly disappointed in Manchester United," Docherty said. "During the past two weeks I have been treated like an animal ... hunted everywhere. Yet what I did belonged only to my private life ... I've been punished for falling in love – it's as simple as that ... If I had been sacked three years ago after we had been relegated I could have understood it but not over something which is private. But in a way I feel relieved that it is all over now. I know what I can do." Docherty alleged that he had more reason to feel aggrieved than might be imagined, claiming that two weeks previously, at the start of the controversy, a First Division club which he did not name rang Edwards to enquire about his availability. Docherty said he was in the room at the time that Edwards took the call: "The chairman replied that everything was okay, that the situation had created no embarrassment, that everything would blow over in 48 hours and that he wanted me to stay." Docherty then claimed that in fact the rumour that the club had strongly denied – that he had been asked to resign and that he had been suspended on full pay when he hadn't – was in fact true, which makes Louis Edwards' expression of strong support for him on the Sunday, several days after the logical date for this requested resignation, bizarre.

Docherty later claimed that at the meeting in which he was informed of his dismissal, Martin Edwards suggested he had been selling Cup Final tickets on the black market. Docherty doesn't deny this – and says he told the meeting he had also been doing it on behalf of Martin's father. The latter is a perfectly plausible scenario considering the subsequently exposed shady business dealings of Louis. In any case, of course, few doubt, including The Doc, that the Mary Brown situation was the real reason for the dismissal.

Docherty said he was particularly disappointed by Louis Edwards, who he thought was his "closest friend" on the United board. Edwards' *volte face* was double-fold, him having joined with Busby in asking for Docherty's resignation, then having insisted that talk of Docherty being sacked was "nonsense" and finally sacking him. Journalist Robert Oxby opined of Edwards's expression of support for The Doc on the weekend, "It is obvious that he was persuaded by his colleagues to take a different view." So what brought about he change of mind on the part of United and/or Edwards? Meek: "Because they'd not thought about it, but as soon as they sat down to think it through they came to the only correct decision which was it was impossible for the manager to work with the physiotherapist, two people who've got to work together very closely for the good functioning of the team. Obviously the relationship between them was extremely strained to say the least, so one of them had to go. You couldn't really sack Laurie Brown, so the only logical conclusion was that it was Tommy Docherty who had to be sacked. I think it was the right decision and they'd no alternative. Louis Edwards talked for a time about how it was a private matter but I think he was blinded by [the fact that] he liked Tommy Docherty, he wanted him to stay."

Docherty also felt that the club's Catholic influence had some bearing on the decision by Louis Edwards to go back on his refusal to sack him, although admitted that his belief that influential members of that religion had nudged Busby was based on hearsay. Meek says, "I think that was all tittle-tattle and supposition. They didn't need any influence from the Catholic Church or their wives or anything like that because it was so blindingly obvious that The Doc had to go."

Crerand has recalled that when told at an Old Trafford meeting that Louis Edwards wanted Docherty to say, Busby replied, "So does that mean that Laurie Brown will lose his job as well as his wife?" (Crerand doesn't reveal the source.) This sounds noble, but Docherty has claimed that Busby himself had what in Manchester is colloquially called a fancy woman whom he would visit when United played in the capital. Docherty has also said that at the meeting at which he was sacked he was told he had broken the club's "moral code", a phrase Docherty claims Martin Edwards, who succeeded his father as chairman from 1980 to 2002, reiterated to his face as the reason for his dismissal many years later. This phrase might raise some eyebrows among those who recall that the married Martin Edwards has been alleged to have hired prostitutes while on club business on more than one occasion. All of which goes to prove that life is far too complicated for people to assume positions on high horses too readily. But like it or not, the morality of the situation is in any case irrelevant. Legally, there is only one issue surrounding the relationship between Docherty and Mary Brown that might justify United's dismissal of The Doc. It was after his wife left him that Laurie Brown felt he understood why Docherty had repeatedly left him kicking his heels at Old Trafford. It has often been reported that Docherty forced Brown to work on Sundays so as to enable him to arrange trysts with his wife. Brown says the Sunday part is inaccurate – "I worked every Sunday with every manager. All the second team players and all the juniors who'd been injured on the Saturday matches came in for treatment on the Sunday" – but that the rest is true. Brown recalls, "He'd phone up and say, if I was at The Cliff, 'Go over to Old Trafford and I want to have a chat with you, I'll see you when I come back.' So I had to wait there until he came back. That's why it annoys me when [it's said] it had nothing to do with football, 'I was sacked for love' and all that crap. He knew there was no chance of me bursting in on him because he knew exactly where I was... Managers are supposed to be fairly busy but he seemed to find plenty time off to do what he had to do and make sure that I was well out of the road. So I just had to wait at Old Trafford for him coming back, which makes you feel a bit of a mug when you find out what's been happening." On this specific point, it could be argued that United had a clear case for sacking Docherty insofar as this constituted an abuse of his position.

\*\*\*

Laurie Brown said after the sacking, " … everybody seems to think that I've won because he's gone now, but it's not so. I'm not looking for that kind of satisfaction. Relatively speaking, jobs are ten a penny and what has happened today wasn't particularly what I wanted." He added, "Football is the least of my worries at the moment, though eventually I shall have to get myself back in the right frame of mind to do my job properly. What I want most of all is my wife and family back together with me." Brown's magnanimity didn't last long. When Docherty went back to Old Trafford to clear his desk, he was seen to be sporting a black eye. Asked about it by the press, he joked, "It's those razors I advertise on TV. I have been having trouble with them lately. This morning I shaved too high." In fact, as Docherty later revealed, the shiner had been given him by Brown. Docherty said that Brown had gestured to him as he was about to drive off in his car outside the house they effectively shared and that when he wound down the window to find out what he wanted, he received a fist in the face. The Doc claimed that – aware of the necessity to maintain good relations with Brown's children, who were in the car, along with Mary – he didn't retaliate. Brown says he was responding to a provocative comment by Docherty. Brown: "I think it was something like, 'Oh, you'll be alright for money now'. I think he thought that with me staying on, United would have had to pay me a lot more money – and that wasnae true. It was something stupid and I wasnae probably thinking straight at that time and I didnae feel very happy. He drove away, but he was going down a very narrow lane and I ran after the car and caught up with him. Then the car stopped." Brown admits that he half-expected Docherty to climb out of the car after he sent a punch his way, but Docherty hit only the accelerator. Brown: "I think Mary told him to."

Ultimately, Docherty would drive off with his wife and children in a broader sense. Brown: "They went to Derby. I thought, 'I'll keep the kids and live in the house and I'll get a nanny' and then you see a solicitor and they tell you, 'Unless you can convince everybody that Mary's a nymphomaniac or an alcoholic, fathers – especially in your job – you've got no chance of keeping the children and you'll have to sell the house and give her half the house'." Though Docherty was gone from Manchester United, Brown was less than happy with some of the remaining employees after his recent treatment: "Some of the staff would come up and put their arms round me but there were people there that I never felt the same about." Though his pain and humiliation at the time were acute, a third of a century has passed since the events in question and Brown has been able to reacquire a sense of happiness, though he says, "Took a long time." He explains, "I am married. It's my third time." He adds, however, "But I never intended to get married more than once."

A supreme irony is the fact that after all the skulduggery and negotiation involved in getting that extension to his contract, Docherty had never got around to signing it. He later claimed it was because he was so grateful to the board for the way they had stuck by him when he had made a bad start at United that he wanted to be open with them about the circumstances in his private life before putting pen to paper. It's a story that seems plausible, insofar as there appears no other logical motive to impute to a course of action that could potentially cost him a considerable amount of money. It's not known precisely how much he lost out on by this tardiness with his signature but if we can believe the papers' estimate of the worth of that new contract – £100,000 over the next four (some said five) years – and contrast that with the fact that Docherty's ex-wife Agnes claimed that he ultimately received a pay-off of £50,000 from the club (a sum which included £15,000 in bonuses he was already due for the achievements of the team in the 1976/77 season), then we can get a rough idea.

"I don't suppose I was top of his Christmas card list, and he wasn't top of mine," said Buchan in the aftermath of the sacking, "but I think we ended up with a grudging respect for each other. When I signed my new contract at the end of last season, we shook hands and I said, 'Well, here's to another three years of arguments … ' I have been shocked at the people who have kicked him when he is down. I'm only glad that when it happened the players were on holiday. I think if it had been during the season, we would have had intolerable pressures put on us." Macari has said that the last thing on the players' minds when the scandal broke was that The Doc would be sacked, but acknowledged that the situation of a high-profile employee playing around with another man's wife made it too awkward for the club to do anything else: "You could not have sacked Laurie Brown instead." Aside from Stepney, Macari was the present Manchester United player who had probably had the most bust-ups with Docherty but for Macari, "Though everybody had their ups and downs with The Doc, you could not dislike him." Though Macari was one of the witnesses Willie Morgan had lined up to give evidence against Docherty in his later libel trial, in *Red News* magazine in 2008 Macari spoke of his "fond memories" of the man with whom he had had so many *contretemps*. "He was that happy-go-lucky fella and he's very, very funny and very witty and I liked that," Macari said. " … there was a Jekyll and Hyde side to him but … you overcame that. You wanted to overcome that because you wanted to be in his company." He has said that the players were stunned by his abrupt departure: "One day he was wisecracking around Old Trafford, the next it was all over for him." Houston was also disoriented by the turn of events. "We'd put ourselves back on the map and won the Cup against the best team in Europe," he says. "From that point of view, everybody was on a high, then the next minute, it was like, 'What the heck's going on?' It was something to do with something completely outside of football. Nothing had happened on the field of play, nothing happened on the training ground, [in] the Final, whatever. So it was a hard one to swallow. On reflection I have to say Tommy was a very brave man by what he did in terms of bringing it out. I had to respect him a lot in one way."

At the time, Stepney said, "It was a strange business playing under him. We loved the matches and the training but in between there were times when you just had to put your head down, go home and put it all behind you ... In a way I feel sorry for The Doc. He seems to have a self-destructive thing in him. He built a brilliant team at Chelsea which nearly won the title, but then broke it up. I thought he'd never do the same again, but now he's blown it in a different way. It seemed he was a changed man when he managed Scotland. But perhaps that's the best sort of job for him. One where he hasn't got the players long enough to have upsets." By 1978, though, Stepney had come round to a form of compassion. In his autobiography, he wrote, " ... I feel they were wrong to sack him on a matter which was connected with his private life ..." Meek, though, is not inclined to be sympathetic. "I'm sure it did rankle with Docherty and I'm sure he felt badly done to," he says. "That doesn't mean that he's right. I've never asked him about it but I would think that if Tommy Docherty was honest he would say that the board reached the right decision. It was immaterial whether it was a waste or not. He had to go. Tommy Docherty had cut his own throat. It was a shame for Manchester United because he'd got something going there and then at the end of the day it counted for nothing. I'm not going to criticise Tommy Docherty. It was personal and these things happen in life and you live with the consequences, and that's what he had to do and that's what Manchester United fans had to do."

Asked if it was unjust that his father was sacked, Mick Docherty says, "It's a difficult one to answer because at that time – you're going back 30-odd years – Man United thought they may have to make a stand because of this situation and consequently did. In this day and age, who knows? They might stand by the individual, whoever it may be. They decided to do what they thought was the right thing. Consequently, dad lost his job. I'm sure he regrets it to this day but, having said that, you've got to move on and at the end of the day he's still with Mary after 30-odd years, so I wouldn't call it a fling." Mick Docherty in conversation is so plainly fond of his dad that it would appear to give the lie to the portrait painted by Agnes Docherty of The Doc as a distant and inadequate father. However, it should also be pointed out regarding his and other people's references to Docherty and Mary Brown's enduring love that Agnes Docherty claimed Tommy twice wanted to leave Mary Brown and come back to her. The first time, she said, was immediately after Docherty had left home and the second on July 26 1977 in a move she interpreted as an attempt to get back his job at Old Trafford, despite a new manager having been appointed by United less than a fortnight previously. (If the latter story is true, one wonders whether Agnes was underestimating Docherty's ability for Machiavellian scheming: would it be too implausible, considering his track record, that he was attempting to set up a phony reconciliation with his wife that would end as soon as the Old Trafford board had reinstated him?)

Hill is in the camp that feels that on balance Docherty should not have been sacked for the reasons he was. Referring to a subsequent United manager, he points out, "Ron Atkinson did the same thing. How can it be an affair when he's been in love with her and he's got a daughter from her and they're together now and they're as happy as pigs in muck? How can anybody turn round and say that's not right? The guy has just brought them a trophy. Nowadays if you get rid of a manager for that, there would be uproar. I personally don't understand it at all. Crumbs, nowadays, you'd have brought the manager and the physio into the office wouldn't you, you'd have sat them down and said, 'What's this crap?'" Asked if The Doc should have been given the boot, Nicholl says, "It wouldn't happen today. I'd have said 'No'. We all have private things in our life. It's difficult to talk about. I don't know the circumstances. Whatever happened happened, but I would say 'No'. It would have been up to Tommy to sort out his private life. If the private life was then affecting the football club the start of the following season for whatever reason, there's too much going on in his private life and it's affecting the club and if the players feel, 'Listen, he's not the same man, there's something not right … ' But just to do it the way it was done, I'd have said 'No'."

However, everybody questioned also concedes that it would have been impossible for Brown and Docherty to work together, thus bringing us back to the inequitable situation for Laurie Brown that – according to Crerand – caused concern to Busby. The excruciating nature of the dilemma is summed up by Brian Greenhoff's thoughts: "Something had to give. I know for a fact a lot of the players were really disappointed that it had happened. I was disappointed he went, I really was. I'm not saying Laurie should have gone." Meanwhile, Forsyth says, "It was just a shame what happened. Maybe let it go but what do you do? I think they done the right thing. I think they done the gentlemanly thing."

However, a twist in the tale was provided by the fact that before long it became apparent that it might be the case that the affair with Mary Brown was not the reason that Manchester United sacked Docherty, but rather a convenient excuse to get rid of a manager that some directors and quasi-directors considered an embarrassment. A conviction that Docherty was a character too unseemly to be manager of such a great club was something that may have taken root due to (or perhaps been confirmed by) the contents of a dossier that had been compiled on Docherty by a private investigation company. On the Sunday after the sacking, *The News of the World* claimed that a team of private detectives had been following Docherty for two years and had been building a report on his activities. The paper quoted Steve Hayes, a partner of Cheshire firm Contact Investigations Ltd. and a former Manchester CID officer, who said, "We have carried out an investigation concerning Mr Docherty's conduct. But it would be unethical for me to tell you the nature of our enquiries or who was employing us." The paper, however, cited their clients as "a group of wealthy and influential businessmen in Manchester". As well as Docherty's relationship with Mary Brown, the paper claimed the said group had, through the private investigators, looked into such matters as how tickets allocated to United for the club's two recent Cup Final appearances had ended up in the hands of touts, events at the football dinner which preceded Docherty's recent car crash, incidents at hotels during the close season tour and allegations that Docherty had slapped an 11-year-old boy's face outside a telephone booth (the parents were said to have brought a private summons which Docherty settled out of court). Wrote the paper's reporter, " ... I can reveal that extracts from the detectives' dossier, leaked by the businessmen to certain directors, may have played a part in Docherty's downfall." One wonders whether these unnamed businessmen broke the story of the Mary Brown affair to the press.

The story also stated that the businessmen behind the investigation were "not connected officially with the club. But they are all staunch United supporters. They are also long-standing friends of several players and certain directors." This description sounds rather like the previously mentioned "junior board". Docherty later wrote that the junior board was the kind of group that can be found at most football clubs: local businessmen in their 30s and 40s who are quite successful but only enough to have the sort of money that could buy them the vice-president status that the right type of season ticket confers rather than the sort of cash that could purchase places on the board proper. Such men are genuine fans and if they have a grievance about their beloved club being subjected to bad treatment might try to influence the real board, whose ear they generally have (if not as much as they imagine or want). The fact that some of the "junior board" at Old Trafford were also friends with United staff and players created, for Docherty, an additional problem, not least in their resentment of the fact that legendary players had been discarded by a man who had only been to Manchester for visits before taking up his post there. Of course, something not in Docherty's calculations (at least not publicly) about such men is that they would be more likely to resent the *way* players had been discarded as opposed to the mere fact of them being discarded.

Meek opines of all this, "I think that's all been quite exaggerated. [There were] people who probably thought they would like to influence the board and probably felt they were doing. Matt Busby had his friends and Louis Edwards had his friends and no doubt they would have an input, but I think it's insulting to suggest they weren't capable of reaching their own decisions. They might listen to other people but it's a conspiracy theory that I don't think really stands up." Docherty, though, claims that no less a figure than Shay Brennan – one of the legendary XI from 1968 – had warned him of the dangers of such people on a return visit to the club, his term for them being not the junior board but "the United clique". Such people, Docherty claims Brennan advised him, muttered about Docherty getting rid of players of the stature of Law and Best and replacing them with people like Lou Macari and Mick Martin.

Blunstone does believe that there was a conspiracy behind Docherty's dismissal. "Absolutely," he says. "He'd let certain players go and they were waiting for him to make a mistake and then moved in. It was nothing to do with the board. It wasn't Louis. Louis was a decent fella. I think sacking Paddy [Crerand] had a lot to do with it. I'll just say that. He was very popular. Not Paddy himself but certain people Paddy knew I think had something to do with it." He adds, "I don't think he deserved to be sacked, because as I say I don't think it was for that reason."

Whatever the reason, and however happy he was with Mary, life would never be the same, or as good, for The Doc again. Blunstone: "That was him finished, Tommy. It broke his heart." Mick Docherty says of his father, "He loved the club beyond reproach. He's down on record as saying, 'There's only way you go from Man United, and that's down'."

# PART SIX

# Requiem: Manchester United after Docherty

Frank Blunstone was appointed Manchester United's caretaker manager while the board – for the fourth time in eight years – pondered over who they would appoint next to guide the club's fortunes.

Docherty publicly gave the temporary appointment his blessing and said that the club should make it permanent. "Frank Blunstone is one of the family and he must be the one for the directors to appoint in keeping the line going," he said. "Frank has got the total respect of the players and at this moment I think it is important that the whole set-up should not be disrupted by a new arrival. It would be common sense to give him the job. It would be a marvellous appointment on a long-term basis. Continuity is one of the reasons why clubs such as Liverpool have been so formidable over the years. He has got the perfect temperament for his position and I also believe his image is just right." By the time of the publication of his 1991 book *The Quest For Glory*, The Doc had apparently changed his mind, stating, "Tommy Cavanagh should have been chosen to succeed me as manager," giving as his reasons, "He knew the club inside out, had played a vital part in the success of the previous three years and had a good rapport with the players."

Brian Clough, Lawrie McMenemy and Dave Sexton were all rumoured to be in the frame for the vacant managerial job. Blunstone, however, made no secret of the fact that he felt that he, not those larger-than-life figures, was the man the Old Trafford board should be considering. "Of course I want the job," he said. "I can't imagine a better one in football. But I've no intention of applying. If the directors don't know what I can do by now … I can handle it. I have the experience after 12 years in the managerial side. I learned under the best, Tommy Doc and Dave Sexton, and I was four years at Brentford doing everything – and that's the most invaluable experience of the lot. This is a worrying time for the club. There's a sense of not knowing what's going to happen, a fear of the unknown. I remember [the] feeling as a player at Chelsea between the managerships of Ted Drake and Doc. It's not pleasant until the position is resolved. Then we had a changeover from an office manager to a tracksuited boss. It worked out because Tommy was fortunate that he had basically a young side to work on." Echoing Docherty's words, he said, "The big thing is continuity. That's what Liverpool have proved with their attitude of keeping it in the family." He continued, "And I believe in what we have produced at United. We've had success over the last three years – the Second Division title, FA Cup winners, contenders for the double, and it took one of the best teams in Europe, Juventus, to put us out of the UEFA Cup. Doc must take the credit for that, but I'm proud of my share. I believe in what United believe – attacking, entertaining football. We've built on that premise. People in the game are inclined to disregard the public. But I don't believe they can be fooled. People know what they want – and that's to be entertained. Winning is important, but how you win is very important. I know the way United have been brought up and I've been bred the same way. I'm biased. I was a winger, and I like wingers. I don't care who's going down the flank, as long as someone is giving us width to the attack. And that way has been proved right by the crowds that United draw. No one matches our home average, and we outdraw even Liverpool away … I believe this club can do well in terms of honours. But the important thing is that an appointment be made before the players report back for training in a couple of weeks."

Though he concluded, "But if it's not to be me, there'll be no tears. I'll be happy to carry on as I am … ", all of the preceding sounds very much like the application Blunstone claimed at the time it wasn't. Now, though, Blunstone asserts that throwing his hat in the ring for Docherty's old job was the last thing on his mind. Says Blunstone, "He'd been a very good friend for me and he'd given me jobs and I thought, 'It's a bit much – if I apply for it he might think I've gone behind his back' and I wouldn't do that. So there's no way." When it's pointed out to him that The Doc was saying to the press he'd be the ideal replacement, he says, "I know, but I wasn't going to push myself forward for it. I was too friendly with Tommy to do that." Though he says, "Don't regret it at all," was he aggrieved that United didn't ask him but instead turned to an outside man? Blunstone: "I don't think so because I was friendly with Tommy and they'd just sacked him so they might [have thought] I would be upset as well."

Furthermore, he states that had he been given the job, he doesn't think he could have made a go of it: "I worry too much. That's why I packed in managing. I knew the game and everything but I took things to heart too much. When we lost, I couldn't sleep at night thinking about it: 'What could I have done, is it my fault?' and that sort of thing."

Of the three aforementioned candidates, either Clough or McMenemy would probably have gone down well with the United faithful. Clough had worked near miracles at Derby County, and of course McMenemy's capacity for success didn't need to be pointed out to United fans. But David Meek feels that United were not looking first and foremost at prospective managers' footballing *nous*. "If you study the managers that Manchester United have had, it's always the swing of the pendulum," he says. "Wilf McGuinness was the first: young, raw. When he failed they went for experience: Frank O'Farrell. And when he went, they went for somebody who was more extrovert than he was, which was Docherty. And then when he went, they went for somebody safe to restore the moral integrity, if you like, of the club and they went for Dave Sexton."

Dave Sexton was appointed Manchester United manager 11 days after Docherty's dismissal, quitting his post as QPR boss to accept the role. Sexton had something of a history of stepping into Docherty's shoes, having inherited his Chelsea team. Notwithstanding Meek's comments about the swing of the pendulum, United's board were no doubt mindful of the fact that Sexton had built a wonderful side at QPR who had squeezed United into third place in the title race two seasons before. "We are absolutely delighted that Mr Sexton has accepted our offer," said Louis Edwards. "The decision was a unanimous one by the board." He then added a comment that some might think confirms Meek's theory about the board seeking someone of moral integrity: "We wanted a gentleman as well as a good football manager." At least one person interpreted the comment as rather spiteful and pointed: Docherty subsequently issued a libel writ against Edwards over the supposed slur on his character. Whether one agrees with the implication that Docherty was not a gent, Sexton was certainly a very different breed to the average cocksure football boss. "If you go around talking all the time in this game, you are bound to hurt someone," Sexton said. "If you talk, you have to criticise and someone has to be the butt of that criticism ... I feel awkward saying 'We'll murder 'em!' and all those kind of things ... I prefer to win quietly."

At first, many were pleased with the appointment, and those who weren't were prepared to give it the benefit of the doubt. Meek: "He was a very good coach and the club needed to restore their dignity after Tommy had got them in the tabloid papers, and Dave Sexton was just the man to do that. I didn't quibble at all with that appointment." Though Coppell had been distraught at Docherty's dismissal and considered it "a terrible waste", upon hearing of Sexton's engagement, he thought it to the good and that Sexton might even add an extra dimension lacking in Docherty's management. Known for his strong sense of organisation, Sexton was the type of manager, Coppell felt, who could deal with the issue of Docherty's United being more enthusiastic than prepared. McIlroy felt that even had Docherty remained, his all-out attacking style would have had to be changed eventually anyway: " ... other teams would have twigged us, and worked out their counters." Says Buchan, "In fairness I felt 'Well, Doc's gone now, Dave Sexton's come from QPR, he had a good side there, quite an entertaining side in fact, so let's see how we get on'." This is consistent with what Buchan said to the press at the time: "The boss comes to us with a great reputation and I think he will give us a fresh approach. I admire the way Mr Sexton had studied the Continentals, especially the German leagues, so closely ... This is the best squad of players in my time at Old Trafford ... We suffered last season because some of our key men were heavily marked and our moves did not always come off. That's what I mean when I say a fresh approach will help us."

Sexton's ex-Chelsea colleague Blunstone says he wasn't surprised by his appointment, " ... because Dave was classy. He'd done a great job at QPR, he'd got a good name in the game, everybody knew him, he was a gentleman." But when the question is raised of whether such a quiet man was able to instil sufficient respect in his team, Blunstone admits, "That was his problem. Dave was a great coach and a great fella but I don't think he'd ever have made a top manager."

While the speculation had been raging about who would take over at Old Trafford, Colin Murphy was having to field questions about rumours that Docherty was about to be offered his job of manager of Derby County (almost certainly the club that had tried to make an overture to Docherty a fortnight back but been blocked by Edwards). Murphy sounded understandably rattled, commenting, "The Doc can't do anything for the club that I couldn't do." At one point the previous season it had looked likely that Derby would be relegated, but Murphy had hauled them up to finish in 15th position. However, such a lowly placing was something of a comedown for a club that had been League champions only two seasons before. That Docherty would supplant Murphy − a man whose appointment had been a surprise in the first place due to him never having played professional football and never managed before − was somewhat inevitable. Its inevitably was almost confirmed by other comments Murphy made at this juncture, ones that drip with tragi-comedy in their faith in the reassurances of club directors: "I'm not a bit worried about the latest rumours. I was given a vote of confidence by the board only two weeks ago and I know they will stand by it as men of integrity and honesty." Docherty's appointment as manager of Derby County was announced on September 17 1977, a month into the new football season and just under 11 weeks after his dismissal by Manchester United.

One of his new charges at Derby was Gerry Daly, whom he had despatched to the Baseball Ground in rather unsavoury circumstances. Asked if their first meeting at Derby was a rather awkward occasion, Daly says, "No, not really because that's the way Tommy was. He was brazen. He was as if nothing had happened." Before September was out, another component of Docherty's Old Trafford set-up came to the Baseball Ground. The Doc's first choice as his assistant had been Tommy Cavanagh, who was offered a three-year £12,000 contract by Derby. When the deal was matched by United, Cav declined Docherty's overture and publicly commented, "I just hope that TD understands the reason why I didn't join him. United made me an offer I didn't expect or ask for. They wanted me to stay and that means more than anything to me." Docherty was reported to be "disappointed". Cavanagh was now officially United assistant manager. Dave Sexton was quoted as saying, "Tommy is in charge of the senior squad with Frank Blunstone looking after the reserve and youth teams. There is no question of one being senior over the other." Yet Blunstone was so disgusted with the situation that he quit to become Docherty's assistant manager. He said of his departure from Old Trafford, "I think I have gone as far as I can here. I had four great years at Old Trafford, but I felt this was a good time for a change. United agreed to cancel my contract, which had a year to run. It's just that I now have the chance to work with a first-team pool. It will give me the stimulus I need and the atmosphere I've missed. It's a new challenge and of course it means I'm back with The Doc. You either love him or hate him – and I love him. There's something about him that's magic. He is the type of person who leaves you to get on with your job. But he can also be firm if necessary." Behind the diplomatic words was anger. Blunstone says now, "Tommy Cavanagh was never happy 'cos I was made assistant manager and when Dave come he wanted to be assistant manager. Dave said that he would make both of us assistant managers to try and get over it, and I said, 'No way'."

Sexton in fact also initially refused The Doc permission to speak to Blunstone. Docherty told the press, "As far as I know, Frank wants to come to the Baseball Ground and he will be trying to persuade United to release him." Though Blunstone would presumably have taken a pay cut to leave an unhappy situation, he seems to have benefited financially from the move, judging by the newspapers' estimates of his United salary (£12,000) and the value of his three-year deal at Derby ("nearly £40,000"). Blunstone adds, "Gordon Clayton came with us as well as chief scout."

*\*\*\**

Injuries plagued Sexton in his first season as United boss, with Jimmy Greenhoff picking a long-running one up in – of all worthless matches – the 1977/78 Charity Shield season curtain-raiser against Liverpool. Also afflicted by injury during what could comedically be called the campaign were Buchan, Brian Greenhoff, Macari and Pearson. Houston of course was still sidelined. Considering the way United's form under Docherty had collapsed with the absence of just one key player, it was inevitable that United's lack of strength in depth would be even more cruelly exposed this year. Rookie Andy Ritchie was drafted into the first team and proved to be a goalscoring *wunderkind*, but there weren't really any other potential stars waiting in the wings for their big chance. In any case, Sexton didn't appear to fancy Ritchie, only seeming to play him – judging by his paucity of appearances – grudgingly.

To some extent things remained the same at Old Trafford, as Tommy Cavanagh constituted a link to the old regime and many of the training routines were retained. Sexton also initially continued playing wingers. Said Sexton at the start of his tenure, "Whatever the system was here before I arrived, it will remain the same. I don't plan any drastic alterations." Like most other people in English football, Sexton was steeped in the lore of his new club, if from an unusually close perspective. "I saw Bobby Charlton's first game for the club," he said. "And I was there at Highbury when United played their last match in England before the Munich disaster ... I have always admired their style. And like United have always done, I believe in attacking football."

The second great Docherty roll call (Stepney, Nicholl, Houston, Brian Greenhoff, Buchan, McIlroy Macari, Coppell, Jimmy Greenhoff, Pearson, Hill, Sub: McCreery) never did take to the field again. The 1-0 home victory against – wait for it – QPR on April 30 1977 the month before the Cup Final marked the passing of that fondly remembered line-up. Even when lack of injury allowed Sexton to field a team vaguely resembling it, it still seemed very unfamiliar. The names were generally the same, the 4-2-4 system was evident but there was somehow something different. United didn't thrill the way they had under Docherty, didn't often exhibit flair anymore, were sometimes – inconceivably – dull. It was almost as if Sexton was only playing 4-2-4 under duress and that he really wanted to play a type of football characterised by far more caution. It was a paradox: Sexton's Chelsea and QPR teams had had no little flair, but if the United board had been expecting him to bring that flair up north, they were to be severely disappointed. Jimmy Greenhoff later remarked, "We all tried hard for Dave because we liked him so much, but it's fair to say we preferred The Doc's free-flowing game." Houston of course knew Sexton from Chelsea, so his more methodical approach was not a surprise to him. "I was quite aware of what he was about but the players at Old Trafford found it very different," he says. "They actually found it a bit strange and took a while to get into the groove of it."

None more so than Gordon Hill, who says, "The players knew what they were doing. It was a winning side. He didn't need to have changed the side. Sexton was from the FA. He was methodical and you found that out straight away. We'd be out trying to do things until the cows came home. We would be there until we got it right. Even if we walked through it. And he'd call you in and you'd look at pictures and 'This is what I want you to do, and this', and you'd look at films and he went home and he studied films. He was a very 'into-it' type of guy. He is a nice guy but in the game he was too deep. Everything had to be exact and prompt and this and that. The team he came into weren't like that. We weren't like that one little bit. We could play. He didn't have to tell us what to do. All he had to do was guide us." Hill feels that Cavanagh was as bewildered as he was by the regimen of tactical study: "You could see Cav was apart. You could see there was a gap." Even Brian Greenhoff – that player so dutiful he didn't care where he played as long as he played – objected to the new ways. He says, "With The Doc there, it was always fun. We worked hard, we always enjoyed ourselves and we always came off the pitch after training having a laugh. When Dave Sexton come, you never finished like that. You always had something else to do, so I didn't enjoy his training at all. You're training for nine, 10 months of the season – everything can't be serious. You've got to have a bit of a laugh and finish training having a giggle."

Sexton made clear to Hill that he had a slightly different role in mind for him. "He said to me he wanted me to defend and stop as many goals as I scored," Hill says. "It was unknown to me. He says, 'I want you to try and see if you can get back as much as you possibly can, but I still want you to get up front.' That was asking to do a double whammy, which I couldn't do. I needed all my energy and all my strength to attack." Coppell has reported that Hill struggled with the instructions he was given in Sexton's training sessions and that in matches he obeyed the orders to track back but then got himself into trouble when he started dribbling in his own half because he found that hoofing the ball clear was alien to him even when he was in front of his own penalty-area.

For the record, United actually led the First Division after the first two games of the 1977/78 season, albeit on goal difference, but this time round those early League positions really did turn out to be meaningless. At one point they tumbled as far down as 16th in the table. They also lost six home games in Sexton's first season – in contrast to the overall tally of six home losses in Docherty's last three seasons. But the real story of United's season – and of Sexton's four-year reign – is the fact that between March 15 and the closing fixture on April 29, the Reds bounced back and forth between 10th and 11th position, eventually winding up 10th. This was undiluted mid-table mediocrity, and while it's true that Docherty had had his ups and downs League-wise in 1976/77, there was no glimmer of solace in Cup competition for Sexton's

United. They were dumped out of the League Cup at the first stage by Arsenal in what was Sexton's first defeat with the club.

They had a more respectable Cup Winners' Cup campaign but in that competition Sexton's problems were compounded by the avarice of the Old Trafford board. When United played the Iran 'B' team in a friendly in Tehran on October 24 1977, it had disastrous consequences. Recalls McIlroy, "We got some injections. It made the lads' arms swell up a little bit. That knocked a few of the lads for six." Hill states that the side effects of these jabs for the visit to Tehran (for which he denounces the "greedy directors") were responsible for what happened in the club's Cup Winners' Cup second-round first-leg match against Porto five days earlier and their away League match against West Brom three days after that: both 4-0 losses. Hill recalls of the Porto fixture, "We are under the weather. We're sick. Jimmy, Brian, myself, have got colds and we go out there and Tommy Cavanagh said it's like somebody had taken a syringe and taken everything out of us. We couldn't run. There was nothing we could do. We got beaten 4-0 and we were so embarrassed, because of what we went through and then we came back after that and then we still had to like recoup, because we were dead. We were dead." Those who witnessed the Reds' second 4-0 drubbing by West Brom in as many seasons will attest to this lack of life. United battled bravely to reverse the Porto result in the second leg on November 2, but though they got five home goals, Porto went through 6-5 on aggregate.

Though Sexton had the excuse of inoculations and board greed beyond his control regarding the European competition, it was a full-strength side that got dumped out of the FA Cup after a replay in the fourth round by (that team again) West Brom. That defeat, coupled with an insurmountable mountain to climb in the League, meant that, with February just begun, United's 1977/78 season was over.

Paddy Roche was in goal in that fourth-round match, but that was not through injury to Stepney but because, Sexton explained to a bewildered Stepney in November, Roche might bring a "change of luck". Also playing in that match was a new striker. Sexton's £350,000 purchase of Joe Jordan in January 1978 heralded another departure from Docherty's strategies, for it signified that the days of the big-money purchases that The Doc had largely abandoned in 1974 were back. Jordan was to be joined by his equally towering ex-Leeds colleague Gordon McQueen, a centre-half, the following month for a then-staggering half-a-million pounds. Jimmy Greenhoff has recalled that the rationale of signing Jordan was Sexton's belief in a big man leading the attack (Jordan was 6'1", but his fearsomeness somehow made him seem even more imposing), with nippy people assisting him. Buchan, meanwhile, recalls the manager having qualms about the Reds' lack of height in central defence, hence the swoop for McQueen.

"Dave had his own ideas on football," McIlroy says. "You can't blame a manager for bringing in his own players." Hill is less understanding: "He wanted to take that team apart, because he didn't want The Doc's players." Houston actually approved of the two signings – a bolstering he considered The Doc's team, for all their qualities, needed – but he has to concede of Sexton's United, "There wasn't the same excitement around the place."

Few would dispute the talents of Messrs Jordan and McQueen but both men were unlovely arrivals from an unlovely team. The culture inculcated at Elland Road by Don Revie in his decade in charge there is, for Colin Waldron, summed up by an incident he recalls at a Leeds-Burnley fixture when he was going back to the dressing room with his Burnley colleague Doug Collins: "We have walked off at 0-0, six, seven yellows, two reds and the great Don Revie's rushed up to me and Doug and turned to face us as we walk up the tunnel and prodded him in the chest and said, 'When you come to Elland Road, we're going to break your fucking leg.' If the manager says that, what's the players going to be doing?" Though Hill found Jordan as "quiet as can be off the field", he wasn't impressed by his on-field behaviour. "I'll always remember Joe Jordan depressing John Wiles's cheek at West Brom," he says. "Sitting down on the edge of the box and Joe just got his elbow and went *bop* and it was a depressed cheek-bone which had to be pulled out. I was absolutely disgusted with it. I was playing in the game and I couldn't believe what I looked at." Already, Manchester United players were doing things that would have been inconceivable in the last two seasons of Docherty's reign.

Whether the gamesmanship and aggression endemic at their former berth had made McQueen and Jordan the players they were or whether they were born like that is not really relevant. The point is they were diametrically opposed to the clean-cut nature of the players who featured in Docherty's latter-day United sides, and it's surprising that Sexton – who actually had a better overall reputation than Docherty when it came to keeping it clean on the football field as both player and manager – should even want them in his teams. Additionally, the pair introduced an awkwardness United fans had not known for a few seasons and which those in the Stretford End young enough to have been blooded only recently had never known: having to cheer for somebody they had booed to the rafters only months or weeks before. Notwithstanding that Jordan won the United Supporters' Club Player of the Year award two years in succession, to this day some Red fans will tell you that Jordan and McQueen were not 'real' Manchester United players, that they were mere mercenaries flying under a flag of convenience, that they didn't really understand United's footballing principles or have the qualities it takes to be a Red. Some will also tell you the same applies to Sexton in his own way. Not that he was cut from the same snarling cloth as his two Leeds purchases, just that swashbuckling was not in his nature. As Docherty once said of his successor, "Dave's teams play dull, because Dave's dull." He was overlooking the excitement generated by Sexton's Chelsea and QPR teams, but you get The Doc's point.

Though Nicholl says of Sexton, "He was a lovely manager," he admits that Sexton's tenure was an uncertain time for him, with the new boss never showing the faith in his talents that Docherty had. Nicholl: "I was thankful I was in the team because Michael Duxbury played right-back, Dave McCreery played right-back, Brian Greenhoff played right-back. He tried a load of people at right-back and I was never 100% confident that Dave rated me as a player. I always felt I was playing for my place every week, so it took that wee bit of enjoyment away from me." He adds, "My game changed when big Joe Jordan came. All I had to do was knock it up to big Joe."

In a season marked by dreary underachievement, one of the Reds' more pleasing results interestingly came from the visit in January of Derby County. Though the United fans gave Docherty a rapturous reception on his return, the United players were merciless in their 4-0 demolition of the visitors. Hill scored two, including a penalty, Pearson another and even Martin Buchan made a rare appearance on the scoresheet. Though the result is not related to it, it was on this day that some of the sympathy his ex-charges felt for The Doc over his dismissal from Old Trafford started to dissipate as they realised that the unofficial £5,000 bonus they were due for helping him achieve the crowning glory of his career was not going to be forthcoming. After the match, Buchan approached Docherty about the money. The issue had been on the back-burner since the start of the season when the players had asked Tommy Cavanagh – with whom they suspected Docherty was still in touch – to approach their former boss about the debt. Stepney has recalled that Cavanagh brought back a message that they would be getting their money but it would be a few weeks yet as he had to sort out financial matters with the wife he had recently left. The players felt this was reasonable enough, and were conscious of the need for human compassion at a time of great trauma in Docherty's life. However, as the weeks dragged on without a resolution, it was felt that the visit by Derby would be the ideal opportunity to bring the matter up again, this time in person. As club captain and the man who had originally declined to look after the bonus over the close season, it was natural that it was Buchan who approached Docherty. Stepney having been dropped, he was not an eyewitness to the conversation but has related what he says Buchan told him: that Docherty said he wasn't going to pay the money because Macari and Stepney had told the press immediately after his dismissal that his sacking was a blessing in disguise. Stepney has said that he was staggered by this, as he was on holiday at the time so not only hadn't given his opinion to the media but hadn't even been asked it. Ditto, he says, Macari. Stepney was seething in his autobiography, published later that year, where he said, "We have not finished with him yet ... There will be no peace for The Doc until he honours the promise he made ... " Buchan was relaxed about Docherty's alleged treachery. "How can you lose what you never had?" he says. "I never fell out with him about it."

***

Having learned to live with McQueen, Jordan, lack of good results and sometimes dull football, in the last few weeks of the new manager's first season, United fans were given another bitter pill to swallow with the April 1978 sale of the beloved and talismanic Gordon Hill.

Sexton's ambivalence about Hill's qualities tipped over into apparent dismissiveness after a *contretemps* that followed Sexton dithering over whether to field him in a particular fixture. Hill: "The game that we were going to play was a QPR game, and he said, 'I'm going to play you', 'I'm not going to play you', 'I'm going to play you', 'I'm not going to play you.' And this was like the Thursday and Friday. Then in the end he phones me up and says, 'Yeah, I'm going to play you.' I said, 'I'd rather play for the reserves because I haven't got in that type of mind.' I went to Preston in the reserves. I was only on the field about 20 minutes and they said to me that Sexton has accepted a bid from Derby County. As soon as [Docherty] knew that I was in the reserves he knew straight away that Dave Sexton wasn't going to keep me." This wasn't the first approach that had been made for Hill's services but it was the first the winger had been prepared to countenance: "I'd been told that Wolves and Watford had been in for me, but it was 'No'. But the boss come in and Derby was always at the top of the tree and so I was staying at the top of the tree so to speak, and I was happy with it. I had no problem at all going over there. Really. It was £275,000, which was lots of money in those days." Indeed, it was the highest sum ever fetched for a departing Red by a margin of at least £100,000. "I went to Derby and started scoring goals." Hill adds of Sexton's decision to offload him, "I think he wanted to stamp his authority as well."

In selling Hill, Dave Sexton crossed a Rubicon. He wasn't merely offloading a player, he was making a statement about the kind of football his Devils would be playing. Sexton was declaring Hill's style a luxury that United could no longer afford. Docherty had tolerated Hill's maverick spirit and disinclination to cover areas like defence because of his high scoring rate and ability to produce moments of sublime, spontaneous skill that might turn a game. Such free-spiritedness and improvisation – no matter what the by-products – did not fit into Sexton's plans, in which every player had a pre-assigned role to which they must stick rigidly. Nicholl feels the addition of hard-men like Jordan and McQueen was necessary if the club wanted to win the championship. However, the loss of Hill surely cancelled out the benefits of that backbone of steel, as demonstrated by the fact that despite his departure with five games still to play, Hill ended up the Reds' top scorer of the season, even if his tally of 19 in all competitions (four more than second-placed Pearson) was boosted by seven penalty conversions.

Hill's departure left some parts of the dressing room dry-eyed. "Over the course of a season he was a liability," Alex Stepney later declared, asserting that Hill would shine when the team was doing well but that when his colleagues were trying to shake off poor form, he would hide out on the wing. "We were glad to see him go," he claimed. Stepney sounds like he thinks he is speaking for everybody at the club here, but it's clear that he isn't. Coppell said that the United players were sad that his skills could not be harnessed. Nor was Arthur Albiston in the good-riddance camp. Jim White wrote in *Always in the Running*, "Jimmy Nicholl … had the easiest job in the club playing behind Steve Coppell; Arthur Albiston, at left-back, must have come off after most games exhausted." Yet Albiston himself told Kurt & Nickeas, "Gordon Hill was a great loss to us. I know some people used to joke that replacing him with a 'hard worker' would save us left-sided players behind him from an early grave but you can't lose a 20-goal-a-season winger who can produce chances out of nothing and just brush it off. I certainly didn't notice my burden of work being eased anyway!"

Nonetheless, as we have seen from the Buchan clouting incident, Stepney was by no means the only player displeased by Hill's dilettantism. Recently, Gordon McQueen had been so disgusted with Hill that any newcomer's taciturnity had been overridden by his fury as he tore into him in a post-match inquest. Hill himself thought there was a conspiracy against him, claiming that he had been "driven out", a phrase that suggests he had in mind more than a tiny minority of players. Docherty publicly backed Hill's assertion of a vendetta, but Nicholl says, "I certainly can't remember that and I can't believe that for one minute. I don't see how that would work." David Meek, writing at the end of the season, said, "It was perhaps an exaggeration, but it contained an element of truth."

Hill's ex-boss at Millwall, Barry Fenton, had remarked a couple of seasons before that the free role he gave Hill at The Den – on the grounds that his sumptuous skills and sheer unpredictability could win apparently lost matches – did not go down well with team-mates. "It led to a lot of jealously from less talented players," he said. "I told the other players that frankly he was a genius and that I would never try to shackle him." Yet it must also be conceded that it wasn't only players in a non-glamorous role and therefore susceptible to the green-eyed monster who had a problem with Hill. In terms of occupancy of both glamour job and position of fan's favourite, Stuart Pearson was at least adjacent to Hill, yet Pancho was also known to deliver dressing room lectures to Merlin about his deficiencies. Sammy McIlroy – not a man comfortable with doling out criticism in the best of circumstances – admitted to often feeling Hill was "going it alone … and you felt an increasing sense of frustration because he wasn't getting anywhere." Macari – who won the United Supporters' Association Player of the Year Award twice to Hill's none – has wryly noted, "Gordon had to beat a man before he was interested in crossing to anybody."

Upon Hill's departure, Sexton said, "Gordon is a very selfish player and to accommodate him, other players have done extra work." "I think it's a bit harsh to say 'selfish'," says Buchan, "but maybe he just didn't think see it as such a big sin wasting possession. Maybe he felt that was worth the risk. Dave had had a very successful, skilful, hard-working team at QPR so maybe he was trying to make Gordon Hill fit the Dave Sexton mould … I was quite happy to see him get the ball on the halfway line and lose it trying to go past the full-back down the line. Now what I didn't like was when he tried to play a 70-yard cross-field diagonal ball to Steve Coppell and was always scratching his head because he couldn't understand why the full-back kept cutting it out. Even Pele didn't play 70-yard diagonal balls three times in a game if the first one was cut out. You think, 'Uh-oh, it's not on, this guy's reading this. I'd better try another ball.' But Gordon would persist trying to play that ball, like the golfer in the film *Tin Cup*, trying time and time again to play the difficult shot 'cos he knew he could. I think the phrase you use nowadays is he didn't always prioritise. Probably because he felt that he could play that ball every time. To have that level of confidence is a wonderful thing, but when it's not working, it's hell of a frustration because the rest of the team have to try and get the bloody ball back."

While one can perfectly understand the resentment of Hill's eccentricities by players whose work rate was higher than his, their allegations of him being a liability or a luxury player seem to be undermined by one thing: goals, both scored and (probably equally as numerous) laid on. David Meek observed after Hill's departure, "For some strange reason, the players had a blind spot about Gordon Hill's goals, and when they were pointed out, the best his team-mates could say was that he should have scored a lot more." Meek now adds, "He was a big, big plus for me and his lack of defensive awareness was in my view overplayed. His accent was on attack and that's what he did, and he did it better than most, so I was a Gordon Hill fan and don't criticise him at all." In the interests of balance, we should point out that Meek did in fact implicitly endorse Sexton's decision to sell Hill in the same *Manchester United*

*Football Book* from which the above quote about his colleagues' blind spot comes, wherein he said that although Hill's flair and goals would undoubtedly be missed, " ... if a system falters and the players are no longer making it work, then new tactics have to be tried."

"In anybody's career, there's always a time to come and a time to go," shrugs Houston of the Hill sale. "The team had changed round. Dave Sexton possibly wanted somebody different. That's a manager's decision. I wouldn't say he was forced out. I wouldn't have said it was as strong as that. His record was actually pretty good but every manager has to [consider], 'Is he a disappointing influence in the dressing room?' Maybe that's what Dave felt." Brian Greenhoff admits that some in the dressing room were happy to see the back of Hill: "There were [some], without mentioning names, because he was infuriating." However, Brian sounds like he wasn't one of those in the good-riddance camp: "Gordon could be infuriating but he could be exciting and win you games."

Interestingly, it is a defender who, as well as lamenting Hill's departure, seems to feel it was bound up in the disenchantment that escalated over the following few seasons among the Old Trafford crowds. Nicholl: "If you've got somebody like Gordon Hill pulling you out of trouble if you're not playing too well, if you've got somebody who's gonna get you 15 to 20 goals a year, it's going to be a big loss. I think that would have an adverse affect on the crowd as well if we're not playing entertaining football and we're getting rid of the likes of Gordon Hill. You end up you've really got to do something to turn the crowd in your favour. They'll take that for a certain period of time at Man U as long as you're winning, but there comes a time it's got to be done in a certain style and if we weren't doing it in a certain style I don't think it would have mattered even you'd finished runners-up. You'd still be looked upon as, 'Ach, alright, you've finished second but we didn't really enjoy that.' And I felt that. I felt that."

But then one suspects that there were issues at work other than Hill's on-pitch behaviour. Some at the club didn't like Hill as a person. Buchan sounds like he can plead 'not guilty' to this charge: "He was no shrinking violet, but I didn't have any problems with that. In the same way that he's labelled an extrovert, I was labelled a loner or whatever because I preferred to sit and read a book rather than join in the card schools and throw away my money. It's very convenient to pin labels on footballers". Others, though, seem to have been of the opinion that Hill's comedy turns weren't all as harmless as simple braggadocio and a propensity to adopt the hyperactive personas of game-show compere Bruce Forsyth and comedian Norman Wisdom. Hill appears to have come across to some of his workmates as a tiresome and not always benign jackass.

Some United fans made their feelings known about Hill's out-of-favour status. Recalls Hill, "The people were writing graffiti on the walls: 'Hill In, Sexton Out'." Hill himself feels that Sexton's buying Mickey Thomas in November 1978 for £300,000 was an appeasement gesture to the disgruntled members of his fan club on the terraces. Thomas – another left-sided man with an ability to pass defenders – was a decent player but it was striking how much he seemed an ersatz version of Hill. He could dribble but not as dazzlingly as Hill, he could score, but neither as prolifically nor as spectacularly as Hill. If he had fair pace it was nothing near Hill's blistering speed. The only quality Thomas possessed that Hill had not displayed to a superior level was work rate. Thomas was that contradiction in terms, a prosaic winger. His purchase sort of summed up Dave Sexton's reign at Old Trafford, and not just because Sexton agreed to pay £25,000 more for him than he got for the sale of Hill. Says Brian Greenhoff, "Mickey Thomas [would] go up and down the wing all day, defend, attack, defend, attack. A more defensive player, but he was never going to win you games like Gordon Hill."

Gordon Hill, like it or not, summed up the Tommy Docherty era at Manchester United. His *joie de vive* and chirpiness was a magnified version of the United team's zest and energy. His dribbling – the closest thing modern United fans had seen to the breathtaking mazy runs of George Best – triumphantly brought to life Docherty's dream of wingwork. His goals were frequently moulded from idealised versions of football, and deliberately so. He told Jim White, "I used to watch *Match of the Day* of a Saturday and if there was a spectacular goal, a goal of the month or whatever, I'd say to myself, 'Right Hilly, you're gonna do better than that.' And a lot of the time I would." Even his defensive deficiencies had the effect of underlining United's philosophy under The Doc. Though his near-heedlessness regarding defence can't be said to be what Docherty wanted, it does put one in mind of The Doc's regular post-match manta about not caring how many goals the opposition scored as long as his team scored more. In fact, on reflection, it might be more accurate to say that his joker's mien and his taking the all-out attack approach to the limit (and beyond) makes Hill not emblematic of The Doc's Devils but a cartoon embodiment of them.

The champions in the 1977/78 season, incidentally, were Nottingham Forest, who also won the League Cup. Their manager Brian Clough and his assistant Peter Taylor – the latter in many people's opinion essential to the success of the former – had achieved a remarkable feat that at one point in the 1975/76 campaign had seemed within United's grasp: a League and Cup double (if not *the* League and Cup double) the season after promotion to Division One. The following season, Forest would win the European Cup. The season thereafter, they won the European Cup again after qualifying as holders. Many were the United fans who at this point must have been wondering how things would have turned out if the Old Trafford board had opted for an unpredictable genius like Cloughie instead of a safe pair of hands. It also has to be admitted that this stunning litany of achievement puts Docherty's progress at United into perspective. While The Doc had impressively awakened a slumbering giant, Clough and Taylor took a club from nowhere to double European glory at a rate almost faster than the brain could assimilate – a double European glory that was making United's historical claim to be the first English team to take said trophy look increasingly less impressive.

***

The 1978/79 season marked 100 years since Manchester United had begun life as Newton Heath FC. They 'celebrated' their centenary by getting dumped out of the League Cup at the first stage at home to lowly Watford and via a string of uninspiring League results that culminated in a miserable performance on November 11 1978 at bottom-placed Birmingham, where they were beaten 5-1. Though United won their February 28 1979 home match against QPR 2-0, they were booed off the pitch by a crowd unimpressed by their pedestrianism. That crowd itself was a shockingly low one of 36,085. "It wasn't the type of football that they were used to," suggests Hill. "He might have been a nice man at Coventry or somewhere else but no way was he a Man United manager. The expectations was too great."

United finished ninth in 1978/79, though they come agonisingly close to winning the FA Cup. Arsenal were their opponents at Wembley on May 12 1979. The Reds' path to the final was speckled with some impressive scalps, them having dispensed with Chelsea, Fulham, Colchester United, Tottenham and Liverpool in the previous rounds. In the final, United were 2-0 down at half-time. There then followed probably the most memorable switchback in the history of the competition. Followed by another. When McQueen scored for United, only the most optimistic United fan thought it anything other than a consolation goal: there were just four minutes remaining. Sammy McIlroy, however, had other ideas. Weaving – perhaps stumbling – his way past Arsenal shirts, he slotted the ball past Pat Jennings and Wembley was suddenly heaving. Looking at the stunned faces of Arsenal players who had already been preparing to celebrate their victory, McIlroy was convinced this was now going to be his team's day. Enter Liam Brady, another silky-skilled Irishman. After jinking his way past defenders, he found Alan Sunderland on the far post, who in turn found the back of the net. And with 89 minutes on the clock, not even this unbelievable Cup Final was going to yield further surprises.

Laments McIlroy, "We didn't deal with Liam Brady to bring him down because we were still on a high. I'm not knocking anyone when you say it should have been discipline. We were on a high from getting back from 2-0 to 2-2. We were still celebrating really the goal and they just broke away again and got the winner." Having taken part in a thrilling spectacle and scored one of the best goals of his career, is it possible to come away from a match like that with any sense of enjoyment? "No, not really. Wembley is only a place for winners. You have lost the game and it's a horrible place to lose. To score a good goal at Wembley and not lift the Cup – it doesn't make up for it."

The close season saw Sexton sell Stuart Pearson to West Ham for £200,000 (or £220,000) after Pancho had the temerity to ask for a wage increase, something that suggests Sexton's 'nice guy' image may not be the full story. As do the comments of the perennially even-tempered Brian Greenhoff when he departed for Leeds United the same month for £350,000: "I couldn't work for that man – I just didn't like him." Greenhoff now says, "Some managers you get on with, some you don't and even though I could have stayed at the club – I'd no need to leave – I realised I had no working relationship with Dave Sexton. I thought as a person he was a lovely fella. I thought as a manager he was hopeless. His man-management skills were nil. The Doc was a great motivator, he knew how to get the best out of me. Dave Sexton was never going to get the best out of me." McCreery went to QPR at around the same time for £170,000–£200,000.

Chelsea's Ray Wilkins – then more commonly known as 'Butch' – was bought with some of the proceeds from those departures. Ostensibly the comings and goings were good business. The following season, the Reds were genuine championship contenders, finishing runners-up to Liverpool by just two points. Yet though it was their highest League finish since 1968, United never looked completely convincing, illustrated by the fact that they continued to suffer weird results, such as a shocking 6-0 defeat by Ipswich in March, which itself would have been 8-0 had keeper Gary Bailey not saved two penalties. The maximum number of goals any Docherty United team conceded in a competitive match was four. Nonetheless, come the end of the season, Sexton and Cavanagh were given new three-year contracts.

The 1980/81 season saw United finish a mediocre eighth and even that position was achieved only via a late run of form that saw them winning their last seven matches. During the campaign, United racked up a couple of unenviable club records: they went five consecutive League games without a goal and were involved in 18 draws (eight of them 0-0, 11 of them home fixtures). It's rumoured that only an informal banning of the poaching of managers during the season recently agreed between football clubs saved Sexton's job after a crisis board meeting in February. When that final winning flourish occurred, many were assuming that the manager would be deemed by the board to have turned the corner. Yet Sexton was dismissed in April 1981. The team sheet of his final game in charge read: Bailey, Duxbury,

Albiston, Moran, McQueen, Buchan, Coppell, Birtles, Jordan, Macari and Wilkins. The side contained only four survivors of the Docherty era, although McIlroy and Nicholl were also technically still part of the club set-up.

Slice it how you like, Sexton's reign at United was awful. Some United fans will never forgive Sexton for squandering the potential of the team he inherited. True, he didn't take the club down into Division Two, but then when Docherty did that he was dealing with a club in a state of decay, not assuming the job of managing the FA Cup holders. Sexton had dismantled a Cup-winning side with time on its side and was left with nothing to show for it. He'd also managed by the end of his run to shave more than 8,500 off what had been the average Old Trafford attendance during Docherty's last season in charge. Perhaps what sums up Sexton's reign as much as anything is that the one honour added to United's cabinet during it – the Charity Shield, a hardly much coveted trophy that is a two-horse race between the reigning League champions and the FA Cup holders – was actually not a full honour at all: in 1977, the match between United and Liverpool was a 0-0 draw, so the Charity Shield was shared. Docherty later observed of Sexton's appointment by the United board, "They got what they appointed and they deserved what they got." His words were those of an embittered man. But the vast majority of United fans could have done nothing but agree with them.

However, many of the players defend Sexton, and none of them think he was unsympathetic to the idea of attacking football. Macari has praised Sexton for his generosity and kindness to the players, something that must have come as a relief to the Scotsman after having seen the spiteful side of Docherty so many times. Though he found his reliance on analysis ("He knew everything about the opposition") to be very different to Docherty's approach and indeed antithetical to the approach of Manchester United *per se*, Macari did not find his methods overly regimented or defensive. Sexton's training was all about working out attacking strategies, so much so that defenders would complain that their roles were being neglected. Even Blunstone, despite his reservations about Sexton's potential as a manager, says, "I played under Dave as a coach. He was always an attacking coach. As a matter of fact, he was the first person to get full-backs to attack, 'cos at one time they never went above the halfway line. When we were at Chelsea he got Eddie McCreadie and Ken Shillitoe to go forward." McIlroy says, "He was under a lot of pressure. We went eight games unbeaten at the end of the season [in fact, it was nine] and he still lost his job, because it wasn't the flamboyant football that people wanted. He took a lot of stick from the press for being negative, but I don't think he was really negative. He wanted to play football. It was just the media side of things Dave couldn't handle as well as Tommy Doc. Tommy Docherty was fantastic in the media, they loved him. Every day United were in the papers. Dave didn't really like talking to the papers."

Of the booing that in the end would greet even a victorious Sexton side, McIlroy says, "It's up to the players as well to try to entertain and I think Dave was wrongly criticised at times because of that." "It wasn't through lack of trying," Buchan says of Sexton's failure to provide entertaining football. "I always found him a very positive guy." He also says, "Dave Sexton was the nicest man I ever met in football and he lived and breathed football ... "

Buchan – who points out that those seven straight wins at the end of Sexton's final season included a victory over Liverpool at Anfield, United's first there since 1969 – echoes McIlroy's comments when he says, "Dave was never comfortable with the press, and at the end of the day they destroyed him." He recalls, "I had the Burnley manager's job briefly for 1986/7. On the morning of my first League game, I was getting ready to drive to Burnley when Alex Ferguson rang me. 'Just to wish you all the best and give you some advice: never seek confrontations, they will find you. Don't engineer situations to prove you're the boss because situations will arise where you've got to stamp your authority. Always make yourself available to the press, and that way you can perhaps have some influence on what they write, otherwise they'll just write what they want'." The last piece of advice is something that Buchan feels Sexton could have used: "The way I best illustrate it, on a Friday at Old Trafford, Tommy Doc would get the press in after giving us a team talk. They rolled out of Old Trafford at 4 o'clock having consumed numerous glasses of wine and they'd get so much material from The Doc in those two or three hours, they wouldn't know what to leave out of their pieces at the weekend. With Dave they didn't know what to put *in* because he never gave them anything. That was the difference. In those days of the late 70s, football journalism had changed from being a reporter's considered opinion of the game as he saw it to mostly direct quotes from players and managers. Tommy Doc made their job easy and Dave didn't." Buchan might have a point, but what destroyed Sexton was surely not the press but both lack of trophies and lack of excitement.

\*\*\*

The man who in many people's opinion could, had he not been sacked, have won United the championship for which their fans were aching inherited a good side at Derby County but failed to win anything with them. One reason is that the team The Doc took over were, just like Manchester United had been in 1972, one with their best days behind them. Daly and Leighton James, plus Docherty's signing Hill, were three of the most gifted players in Division One but their youth put them in a minority. Blunstone: "Derby had a lot of good players. The trouble was they were all old players: McFarland Todd, Rioch, Nish, Tappy James. They were all 30-odd and they were all going over the top at the same time, so it was difficult. It was a hard job at Derby ... Tommy really struggled there," This time, there would be no dramatic rebuilding and re-energising of the club of the kind The Doc had engineered at Old Trafford. From Hill's recollection, this was partly to do with the lack of finances. "The situation was completely different at Derby. I think there wasn't the money," he says. "The club didn't allow the expenses. I think they just said, 'Okay. that's it, we've got it, let's see what we can do with it'." A certain Brian Clough, if he were alive, might have a wry smile at that considering what he managed to achieve at Derby (and Nottingham Forest) with fewer resources and far fewer quality players, but in any event there was another problem. "Tommy hit the drink there," reveals Blunstone. "He never came out training. His heart wasn't in it at Derby. It was very difficult there. I didn't enjoy it there at Derby." Additionally, Daly says that he wasn't surprised that Docherty wasn't successful at Derby because, "He fell out with an awful lot of the Derby County players then. He fell out with Colin Todd and Archie Gemmill. Leighton James. Kevin Hector. So things weren't working out." Docherty admitted to the *Daily Telegraph* in 2006, "I did a terrible job at Derby."

***

On Monday November 13 1978, Docherty's libel case against Willie Morgan and Granada TV started in the High Court in London. Docherty had instituted proceedings over an edition of the television programme *Kick Off*, broadcast in June 1977, in which Morgan described him as "about the worst manager there has ever been". Docherty claimed that Morgan's remarks had damaged his reputation in a highly competitive and precarious job. "I felt it was the remark of a bitter person," Docherty said of Morgan's "worst manager" remark, stating that it made him very upset. That Morgan was bitter was hardly in dispute, even if the cause of Morgan's bitterness was.

Morgan defended the case vigorously, not least because he stood to lose just about everything he had if he didn't, although the hatred that motivated him to make his comments in the first place must also have provided a certain impetus. No less hatred can be assumed on the part of two of the people Morgan called as witnesses: Pat Crerand and Denis Law. Morgan had made another remark in the *Kick Off* programme that was somewhat peculiar: "When he goes, I think the rejoicing in Manchester will be like winning the Cup again, and when that happens it will be a good club again." That Cup Final victory to which Morgan alluded made his predictions nonsense: whether he liked it or not, Docherty was a hero among United fans. However, the evidence that Crerand and Law were likely to give (in Law's case reluctantly) was liable to make the jury perceive just about all of Morgan's claims as fair comment. In the event, though, Crerand and Law did not have to give evidence, for while Docherty was in the witness box, just about all the dubious things he had done in the course of returning Manchester United to its former glories were brought up to ultimately devastating effect.

It was put to Docherty that he had been sacked by Manchester United for "bringing the club into disrepute". It was a factual error on the part of the defence counsel: United had publicly stated at the time that the reason for his dismissal was breach of contract, even if they'd not explained what the breach was. However, this was about the only mis-step by Morgan's legal team. Among the things that a surprisingly subdued Docherty was cross-examined over were his breaking up of the marriage of Laurie Brown; whether he had pocketed a £1,000 bribe to allow George Best to play a game for Southern League club Dunstable Town in 1974 (Best was still registered with United so professional appearances had to be approved by the club: Docherty said this fee had been agreed between him and Busby and that he had not personally benefited); that Fraud Squad officers had interviewed him over the Best fee shortly after his appointment by Derby County (no charges had been brought against Docherty); and whether he had performed an obscene and derogatory ditty about Willie Morgan in 1975 at the annual Catholic Sports dinner in Manchester attended by nuns, priests and a bishop (he was said to have sung: "Willie Morgan on the wing, He's a cunt, I'm going to sort him out"). He was also asked whether he had been abusive not only to Lou Macari but also his wife after Macari had refused to turn out for a junior side in a testimonial against a non-League club (presumably the Mossley match of October 1974); whether he had told Jim Holton that he should return to Third Division football following his injuries; whether he sold two Cup Final tickets to "a renowned supporter in the carpet trade"; whether he had asked Lou Macari to bring ticket tout Stan Flashman – a tabloid pantomime villain of the day – into the club's executive suite and then tried to put the blame on Macari when the tout was ejected; and whether he had asked Macari to hand over 200 tickets to Flashman before the 1977 Cup Final in return for £7,000, three times their face value.

He denied all the allegations, as well as others including that he put players on the transfer list without telling them; that he sold two 1974 Cup Final tickets for £100 as opposed to their face value of £10; asked Morgan and Stepney to complain about the behaviour of Tommy Cavanagh; sold Morgan for £90,000 less than his true market value as a gesture of contempt; and relieved George Graham of the United captaincy by grabbing the ball from his hands immediately prior to a match.

Docherty said of Graham in the witness box, "We had a good relationship. It all went wrong when I did my job and left him out of the team. In giving him the benefit of the doubt I gave him 27 games but in retrospect I think I allowed him to go on too long. That is when you become unpopular with the players." (Docherty in fact gave Graham 44 starts and two substitute appearances.) Docherty's response to Morgan's comments about his worth as a manager was that United were in a "terrible state" when he took them over. Not only had he bounced straight back up from the Second Division with "a very young, very attractive side" and finished third in the League, but he had transformed the financial state of the club from half a million pounds in the red to £850,000 in the black. (Louis Edwards would later dispute these figures but not the fact that Docherty had considerably enhanced United's profits.)

When it opened, the court case was projected to last until Christmas. However, it came to a juddering halt on the morning of Wednesday November 15, two-and-a-half days in. The court rose for a mid-morning break that turned into a two-and-a-half hour hiatus. When the court reconvened, Docherty's counsel Peter Bowsher informed the judge, Mr Justice O'Connor, that his client was not proceeding with the case. Docherty really could do little else: during the morning's cross-examination, he had seemed to confess to having perjured himself in his evidence. Docherty was questioned by defence counsel John Wilmers about the version of events he had given regarding the transfer of Denis Law. Law's free had been like a "golden handshake" and the player knew he was to be transferred, Docherty had told the court. But when Morgan's counsel put it to Docherty that, "You told a pack of lies to the jury about this, didn't you?", Docherty – amazingly – replied, "Yes, it turned out that way." This had been preceded by Docherty admitting that indeed he had transferred Law against his knowledge and furthermore that he had done so when Law was in Scotland to visit his ill mother. Docherty furthermore admitted he had known that Law's mother was ill.

Wilmers: "No decent competent manager would dream of treating a man like Mr Law that way?"

Docherty: "It was the wrong thing to do ... it was very wrong."

It was shortly after Docherty had answered in the affirmative when the "pack of lies" proposition was put to him that the court rose for the adjournment. When Docherty's counsel announced the abandonment of his case, Docherty was ordered to pay all costs, unofficially estimated at £30,000.

Though Morgan issued a statement saying he was "delighted that Docherty has by this withdrawal agreed that what I said was justified", he was surprisingly reluctant to talk about the case, preferring to concentrate on whether he would be selected for Bolton's next fixture on Saturday. Law was also not enthusiastic about public comment, though he did state, "I never wanted the problems I had with Docherty to cause difficulties for Manchester United."

Inevitably Laurie Brown was contacted. "Justice has been done," he said. Though those particular individuals had more of an interest in tearing into The Doc than most, newspapers and pundits were more vengeful still. This was all too much for columnist Frank Butler, who pointed out, "Not even Doc's best friends can defend his integrity after that High Court case, but I am sickened by all the soccer people now condemning him as a liar when some knew all about Tommy anyway and were happy to do business with him."

As befitting the author of *Never Turn the Other Cheek*, Pat Crerand had a few things to say. Though admitting that Docherty had a warm side and that "As a friend, he could be the greatest fellow on earth", he also said, " ... as an enemy he was vicious, vindictive, callous. And he often seemed to go for people for no reason whatsoever. For all his brashness, it seemed he never could tell anyone what he thought of them to their face. If he didn't want someone around he would demean their character." This, claimed Crerand, included alleging one discarded player had venereal disease. Continued Crerand: "But if you confronted him with his accusations he'd tell you, 'On my mother's life, I didn't say that.' That was one of his favourite expressions."

\*\*\*

It's difficult to overestimate the extent of the catastrophe the case constituted for Docherty. As well as being publicly humiliated, he was facing the prospect of losing his job at Derby County (who shortly suspended him), he was in all likelihood going to be charged by the football authorities with bringing the game into disrepute, and – most seriously – was inevitably going to be facing a criminal prosecution for perjury over his apparent confession of lying in the witness box. Meanwhile, newspapers were crawling all over other allegations that had been made in court – and denied by Docherty under oath – particularly the issue of whether he took a bribe to allow George Best to play for Dunstable. Docherty later described his decision to bring the libel case as the "biggest mistake of my life".

Martin Buchan subsequently suggested that Docherty should have simply publicly dismissed Morgan's assertion with the phrase "sour grapes". And surely Docherty – then ensconced in a £25,000 per-year job as manager of Derby County – couldn't truly believe his assertion in the witness box that Morgan's comments had meant he was "written off" as a manager? Perhaps one clue as to why he decided to press ahead with the case lies in an exchange he'd had with the *News of the World* the previous February. The Sunday paper had latched onto the story about the alleged bribe from Dunstable Town. Confronted by its reporters, Docherty said, "I'm not saying anything either way. I'm just saying that if I see anything published which I don't like I put it in the hands of my solicitors." He then added a phrase that some may find telling: "I am doing quite well out of that little legal sideline."

A deep mystery remains as to why Docherty should suddenly capitulate not only in the way he did but over the issue on which he did. After having sworn the falsehood of several accusations which were in fact provable, why did Docherty confess to having lied about the circumstances surrounding the transfer of Denis Law when they were a matter of his word against the player's and therefore impossible to prove either way? There is a school of thought that Docherty caused the case to be stopped because, had it gone any further, unsavoury material might have come out about senior figures at Manchester United. The theory seems implausible. If people who were worried about their reputations had persuaded Docherty not to proceed, why did The Doc not simply instruct his solicitors to inform the judge that he was giving up rather than jeopardise his own freedom by seeming to admit to committing the criminal offence of perjury? Yet the conspiracy theory seemed to be in the air at the time, too: one tabloid claimed, "Docherty was advised at the weekend by an influential source to drop the case ... " Perhaps this "influential source" was concerned about the fact that Docherty had admitted in his testimony to lying on United's behalf when AFC Bournemouth had brought a court case against the club over the £25,000 Bournemouth claimed was still outstanding from Ted MacDougall's transfer deal. (MacDougall had been lined up to give evidence.)

Those who believe the conspiracy theory might cite the fact that Docherty emerged if not unscathed from the case then at least not ruined financially, personally or professionally as had seemed reasonable to assume he would be on all counts. Though he was indeed tried for perjury in October 1981, he was acquitted on the grounds that he did not set out to lie. Yet Docherty appears to have seriously contemplated pleading guilty at some point, for he later told Terry Wogan on the latter's TV chat show that he had told an interviewing police officer he was going to do so and that the police officer had humorously replied, "I don't know whether to believe you, Tommy." Meanwhile, he was quickly reinstated as Derby manager after a one-week suspension following the libel case and carried on working for them until April 1979, only leaving of his own accord to reunite with Jim Gregory at Queens Park Rangers. Derby, though, would be his last top-flight berth.

\*\*\*

In October 1979, Docherty hit the headlines again when allegations of taking kickbacks – bungs – for transfers of Derby County players were raised once more. No charges were ever brought. Meanwhile, The Doc was trying to effect the reversal of fortunes with

Rangers that he had managed with Manchester United. Since they had finished runners-up to Liverpool in the championship race in 1975/76, QPR had experienced a shocking decline and were now in Division Two. (Docherty took up his post with one game of the season remaining but with the club already confirmed as relegated.) He had some great players – including Stan Bowles, Tony Currie, Gordon Hill, who he bought from Derby, and David McCreery, who he bought from Manchester United – and racked up some good results (including a 7-0 defeat of Burnley) and for a while QPR led the Division Two table. Unfortunately, they missed promotion by four points. Those crucial points might not have been dropped had it not been for a five-week period in which Docherty was unable to work after being attacked when leaving a train by a gang of youths whose obscene songs about him and Mary he took voluble exception to. (Bizarrely, Docherty claimed that he had met Denis Law on the train and that the two had exchanged pleasantries.) The club only won two points out of a possible 12 while Docherty was recuperating.

Docherty was sacked by QPR in May 1980 because Gregory was unhappy about his failure to move to London. Within nine days, the protests of supporters and players saw Docherty reinstated, although he did agree to relocate to the capital. With fewer than a dozen games of the following season played, Gregory again dismissed Docherty. The club were only halfway up the table, something Docherty attributed to key players being sold against his will, but the League position was not Gregory's concern, according to Docherty, but rather a press controversy over the club's failure to procure the services of Andy Ritchie from Manchester United. The Doc has claimed Sexton agreed terms with Gregory for Docherty's former protégé and Docherty even went to the airport to pick up his new signing, only to be informed that Sexton had changed his mind. Docherty publicly criticised Sexton – whom he suspected was nervous of the potential humiliation of Ritchie doing well under him – and insisted that QPR should be allowed to make a bid for a man now rumoured to be going to either Brighton or Chelsea. Docherty's statement that if he was Ritchie he would choose a First Division club – Brighton were then in the top flight, Chelsea in Division Two – resulted in headlines like "Docherty Tells Ritchie: Don't Go To Chelsea." Such press did not go down well with Gregory, who retained a lingering affection for Sexton, who of course he had employed as manager at QPR before Docherty's sacking at Old Trafford opened up a new job opportunity for him. This time Gregory did not back down over The Doc's dismissal.

Sexton's offloading of Ritchie amazed many. Though not picked often, he had scored 13 goals in his 32 starts and 10 substitute appearances. The move has been interpreted by some as Sexton's way of alleviating the financial burden imposed by his October 1980 £1.25m signing from Nottingham Forest of Garry Birtles, a man now chiefly famous for accompanying Peter Marinello and Alan Brazil at the top of English football's Expensive Failure League. Intriguingly, the late Manchester United historian John Doherty said of the sale of Ritchie, "It was Cavanagh who talked Dave into selling Andy, and he was proud of it! My language when he told me was not fit for family consumption." His quote puts one in mind of Daly's theorising as to why he was sold by Docherty.

Docherty then decamped to Australia to manage part-timers Sydney Olympic, whom he says asked him to stay once his initial contract period of eight months was over. But Docherty had been offered the manager's job at Preston North End, the first English club he had played for and the club at which he had spent the vast bulk of his playing career. Preston were currently a Second Division outfit attracting home gates of less than 7,000. During the middle of Docherty's brief spell there, his perjury case started. Despite the verdict, he is convinced that the stigma that continued to hang over him scared off other clubs who might have thought about employing him once Preston dispensed with his services near the end of 1981, with the club near the bottom of the table. South Melbourne FC, his next port of call, was hardly an illustrious name in football, and though he won a trophy for them in 1982, the Victorian Ampol Night Soccer Cup is hardly up there with the FA Cup. Docherty had another stint with Sydney Olympic before returning to England, where in June 1984 he took the helm at Wolverhampton Wanderers, a fallen giant then languishing in Division Two. A club whose ground bulged with crowds of 50,000 when Docherty was a young man now struggled to entice 10,000 to home fixtures. That the club were relegated to Division Three at the end of the season is something for which ultimately Docherty must take responsibility. However, his protests that his job was not exactly made easy by the club's parlous state – milkmen refusing to deliver over unpaid bills, electricity supplies cut off, players' wages having to be paid at one point by the PFA – deserve some credence. Docherty and Wolves parted company by mutual consent in July 1985 shortly after relegation was confirmed.

At this point Docherty decided he was "managed-out." After nearly a quarter-century of being a football boss, none of the offers on the table – and he says there were some – were attractive to him. Of course, he would probably have viewed things differently had one of the giants of the game offered him work, but time, fashion, court cases, police investigations and poor recent form had stripped his name of the allure it had once had for soccer's big clubs. There was one more sojourn into management when he took the helm of non-League Altrincham in 1987. He was there just over four months before resigning after a bust-up with a new chairman. After that, he did some scouting work for Burnley. Since then Docherty has earned an income from media punditry and after-dinner speaking. The latter is a role for which, many have observed, his ready gags and caustic sense of humour make him ideal: his quip "I've had more clubs than Jack Nicklaus" has long been established in football folklore.

Docherty's quarter-century of management produced only two major trophies: the League Cup with Chelsea and the FA Cup with Manchester United. This hardly constitutes failure but it is a miserable tally compared to the column inches he produced and the vainglorious boasts with which he was apt to come out. Many are the people who think he would have added to that tally had things not worked out for him as they did at Old Trafford, but his record post-Manchester United is mediocre. Jimmy Nicholl: "I think sometimes you're very lucky. You get a group of players and they respond to you. It depends what club you're at. If you were at Man United, you've got players there who want to do things, want to achieve things. They're delighted they're at a big club so they're going to do their best, so that's half the battle. And if you add your own personality to that, then you're going to have some reasonable success. You'd have thought he'd have gone and done something when he went to Derby, who were still a big club, but from then on it just didn't work out." Says David Meek, "I think there's always a peak in somebody's career and the peak for Tommy Docherty was managing Manchester United. He made a mess of it and he fouled up and was never the same again. It's just life. Everybody has their moment. Life doesn't keep offering moments."

\*\*\*

Post-Sexton, the vacant United manager's post was reputedly turned down by both Bobby Robson of Ipswich Town and Ron Saunders of Aston Villa. Southampton's Lawrie McMenemy would most certainly not have turned down the chance of taking the helm of the club but he claims that Southampton falsely told him that there had been no overture from Old Trafford. In June 1981, the job went to West Bromwich Albion boss Ron Atkinson, a man whose huge physical bulk didn't prevent him from being something of a peacock and whose twinkle-eyed gregariousness made him about the closest thing to Tommy Docherty there could be without his actually being The Doc. Was that a regression of sorts? Meek thinks it simply a matter of the Old Trafford pendulum swinging again: "When Dave Sexton went, they went for somebody who was extrovert and had a more colourful personality."

Atkinson raised some eyebrows by bringing in his own backroom team, which necessitated dismissal of the remnants of the old regime at a time when such wholesale clear-outs weren't common in football. "That was the end of me," says Laurie Brown. "I don't think I did anything to deserve to be sacked but when you get a new manager, as Martin Edwards said at the time, you have to back him up because if you ever want to sack him you can't have him turning round and saying, 'Well, you never backed me up to begin with.' That was said and after about ten minutes or so I realised was getting the sack. It took me a wee while before the penny dropped." As well as Brown and Tommy Cavanagh, other less well-known names lost their jobs. Meanwhile, the dwindling number of players remaining from the days of Docherty was reduced further with the departures of McIlroy, Nicholl and Buchan. Sammy McIlroy – who had already served five managers in his time at Old Trafford – could have been forgiven for experiencing a certain amount of weariness at the prospect of another new boss. He recalls, "I'd always think, 'This is the one that's going to change you, get you out the door'." However: "Ron was okay with me. I made a silly mistake in leaving when he bought Bryan Robson. He wanted me to play on the left side of Robbo. I should have done that. I spat my dummy out and said I wanted to play midfield and I was stupid. I could have done that job [on the] left-hand side. It was just my ego was a little bit hurt when Bryan came and Remi Moses came." Atkinson sold McIlroy to Stoke City in February 1982 and Jimmy Nicholl to Toronto Blizzard two months later. Though Ron Atkinson was an intelligent enough manager to know the qualities Martin Buchan possessed – he played 30 matches in Atkinson's first season – human nature dictated that Atkinson wanted to build for the future. Though Atkinson would no doubt have viewed Buchan favourably had he signed him himself, inheriting a player in his 30s was a psychologically different proposition and by the 1982/83 season Buchan found himself used only as cover. By August 1983, he had departed to Oldham Athletic on a free.

Atkinson spoke of a "dream team in my head" but though United seemed to give him a blank cheque, he failed to capture several players he had his eye on, at the same time as losing Joe Jordan to AC Milan. Though Frank Stapleton was a useful buy, the ageing Arsenal man was hardly in the same league as Glenn Hoddle, Mark Lawrenson and Michel Platini, men whom Atkinson was reported to be interested in, none of whom signed terms with the club. However the October 1981 purchase of Bryan Robson from West Brom was possibly the best signing Atkinson made in his time at the club, even if that rather demonstrates the declining quality of football in the 1980s: though his fierce tackling, awe-inspiring pitch coverage and 100% commitment made him such an inspiration that he became captain of England, Robson was hardly possessed of the silky skills associated with Old Trafford.

Atkinson was sufficiently different to his predecessor to consider re-signing Hill, a move that would have been hugely popular with the supporters. "He just said he wants somebody back that can play, Gordon's the man," claims Merlin, adding, "But then he went and got Peter Barnes." (The ex-City wide man joined United in July 1985 but only made 24 starts.) Gerry Daly also claims that Atkinson made noises about turning him into a prodigal son. "I remember playing against a United team at Dalymount Park," says Daly. "It must have been a testimonial or something. Ron Atkinson was the manager. I was in the corridor after the game and he said to me, 'How do you fancy coming back to Old Trafford?' Just out of the blue. And I said, 'That'd be nice.' And with that we parted our ways and I never heard about it again. I thought, 'Why say it?' Obviously if you think you have an opportunity to go back to Old Trafford, you take it, don't you? Not many people sign for United then get transferred and then go back."

There were several other comings and goings but United's League form remained mediocre. In May 1983, though, Atkinson gave United their first trophy since 1977 when the Reds beat Brighton in a replayed FA Cup final. Atkinson's contract was extended by two years. The following season saw the tragedy of Steve Coppell's career being terminated when he finally gave up on a knee injury that had been plaguing him since he had incurred it in a 1981 World Cup qualifier for England against Hungary. He was just 28. The club had strong runs in both the League and European Cup Winners' Cup. However, they finished fourth in the former and were beaten at the semi-final stage in the latter. Atkinson's private life hit the headlines this season but, unlike with Docherty, his extra-marital affair and the consequent break-up of his marriage were not matters considered by the board to have made him in breach of his contract, although admittedly his relationship was with someone not connected to the club.

The following season, League success continued to elude the club but Atkinson gave them a second FA Cup victory, the winning goal over Everton scored brilliantly by Norman Whiteside, a precociously gifted and fearsomely no-nonsense player who made his United debut aged just 16 and who shortly thereafter became the youngest player ever to appear in the World Cup finals. He was yet another discovery by Bob Bishop, the Northern Ireland scout to whom the debt owned by United cannot be calculated. Bulldozing striker Mark Hughes was another iconic United player of the Atkinson reign, and became one of the few players who was sold by the club and then bought back again. Both were products of the Old Trafford youth system and went at least some way toward making up for the fact that Atkinson had built a team comprised to a certain extent of expensive flops. This latter accusation stemmed from Atkinson failing, like all post-Busby managers, to obtain the First Division title. As McIlroy points out, "Manchester United from the Busby era through wanted championships. The FA Cup was great, don't get me wrong. It's a major honour, it's great for everyone to get a day out at Wembley, but a big club like Manchester United needed the League championship. Every manager tried and tried hard. Unfortunately it wasn't to be, so the crowd probably got frustrated with their neighbours down the road winning it season after season."1985/86 opened with a record-breaking 10 successive wins, and the Reds were unbeaten until their 16th game, but they again foundered.

The following season, they collapsed. In November 1986, the Reds were fourth from bottom of the table and had been ejected from the League Cup by Southampton in the third round. The board sacked Big Ron, although the poor form may have had only as much to do with the dismissal as rumours of a drinking culture amongst the players, dissatisfaction with Atkinson's transfer-market profligacy, alleged favouritism toward out-of-form players and declining attendances. Though Atkinson sidelined and then dispensed with him, Buchan offers this observation of his reign: "For a time both Tommy Doc and Ron Atkinson had their respective United teams playing a brand of football that was as attractive as any United team of any other era, whether it's the Busby Babes, or Fergie's best team. Ron Atkinson's team produced some enthralling stuff and we were quite exciting on our day, and I'd like to think that our best XI would have given Alex Ferguson's best team or the Busby Babes a good game."

The type of fantasy football match Buchan talks about sort of came to pass on November 23 1981 when Sammy McIlroy's testimonial at Old Trafford saw The Doc's Devils – or "Manchester United 1977 FA Cup XI", as they were billed – take on Atkinson's United. Though Docherty didn't manage to reassemble either his Mark I or Mark II roll calls in their entirety – the line-up was Stepney, Nicholl, Albiston, McIlroy, Holton (somewhat anachronistically), Brian Greenhoff, Macari, Jimmy Greenhoff, Pearson, McCreery and Hill, with Daly coming on as sub for McCreery and (completely anachronistically) current United man Alan Davies for Holton – it was as near as dammit. Though, bizarrely, Bobby Charlton played for Atkinson's men, the opposition was essentially Big Ron's current team. For Hill, the match was a vindication of the strength of The Doc's side and a measure of what the Old Trafford board had thrown away. "It was Ron's seven-million-dollar men," he recalls. "TD said to us when we were sitting in there, 'Listen, you should have been the next team, go out there and show them what you can do', and we went out there and we were 4-0 up at half-time against your Wilkins and all that and your Stapletons and all that. And they weren't taking it lightly because they knew we weren't. Kevin Moran and all that. They were saying, like, 'Wow.' We're still playing, although we're playing for different clubs, we're still the team that the boss put together." The Doc's team's scorers were Jimmy Greenhoff (3) and Gerry Daly. Hill: "Then we were asked to lighten up and let them score a couple of goals and it ended up 4-4."

*\*\**

One of the comments Docherty made after his sacking was, "United cannot take away my ability as a manager – and in the end will be the losers." It's the sort of they'll-be-sorry emotion to be expected in such circumstances. In a way, though, he was proven right, for it took nearly a quarter of a century for Manchester United to regain the momentum he had created for them. Only with the triumph of the Alex Ferguson era could it be said that the club looked as convincing as they had at the point when The Doc was fired.

United picked Ferguson to replace Atkinson before they'd even formally dismissed the latter. Though Ferguson had been boss at East Stirling and St Mirren, it was his achievements at Aberdeen from 1978 onwards which had caught Old Trafford's eye. That he had shattered the Celtic-Rangers hegemony in the Scottish top flight by obtaining Aberdeen three Premier Division championships, four Scottish Cups, the Scottish League Cup and the European Cup Winners' Cup clearly appealed to the United board, but no doubt so did his reputation as the sort of iron disciplinarian who would not show favouritism toward fading old pros in selection nor tolerate a drinking culture.

*\*\**

Ferguson actually got off to a very shaky start as United manager, his first half-decade marked by utter mediocrity and his scalp probably only saved by winning the FA Cup in 1990 and the European Cup Winners' Cup the following year. The coveted championship, though, remained elusive. With United's last League title receding ever further into the distance, one shrewd young fan was to be heard observing on television, "We've got a history, but that's all we've got." Such comments now themselves seem like ancient history. Technically, Ferguson never did win the First Division championship. By the time he first finished a season with Manchester United at the summit of English football's top flight – 1993 – it had been renamed the Premier League. However, by the summer of 2010 he had won for United what used to be called the First Division championship a staggering 11 times. He has also brought to Old Trafford the FA Cup five times, the trophy once known as the League Cup (now called after whoever is currently sponsoring it) four times and the UEFA European Champions League – previously known as the European Champion Clubs' Cup but informally referred to as the European Cup – twice. In addition, he has won the now defunct European Cup Winner's Cup and the FIFA Club World Cup, even if despite its grandiose title few view the latter competition as anything other than an international equivalent of the Community Shield (formerly known as the Charity Shield), which itself he has won outright with United seven times, sharing it once. He has made the FA Cup and League double – once so rare – seem almost laughably easy, having pulled it off three times. In 1999, he achieved with United the treble that the Reds had denied Liverpool in 1977: FA Cup, League championship/ Premiership and European Cup/Champions League. He is officially the most successful manager in the history of English football.

Going by bald statistics, and even factoring in the rebuilding necessitated by the 1958 Munich air disaster that wiped out most of the Busby Babes, this is a more impressive achievement than Busby's five League championships (and seven runners-up positions), two FA Cups and one European Cup over a slightly longer period. However, since the formation of the Premiership, the top flight in football has become – for whatever reason – a three-horse race between United, Chelsea and Arsenal (Blackburn's title in 1995 the only exception). Meek disputes that winning what is no longer colloquially referred to as 'the League' is now easier, saying, "It was difficult then and it's difficult now. Alright, there aren't as many teams competing with a reasonable expectation of winning the championship, but the ones who are your immediate rivals are stronger. It's like there're two divisions, but it doesn't make it any easier if you're one of the top four, so to speak." However, Busby – unlike Ferguson – achieved what he did without being able to buy players willy-nilly and without being able to entice footballers with top wages. Then there is the fact that Ferguson's achievements are essentially those of a big fish in a small pond: United's dominance of English football over his tenure has certainly not been matched by a commanding presence in Europe and his European Champions League victories were achieved by the skin of his teeth both times.

For those reasons, it's difficult to disagree with Frank Blunstone's assessment, "Matt Busby obviously is the top one." It's also difficult to dispute that Docherty ranks third behind Ferguson as a post-War United manager, not least because Ferguson put in place the kind of fruitful youth system that Docherty dreamed of but never realised. As Gordon Hill says of the home-grown crop of players who were blooded in the mid-1990s, "Never in football has it ever come. When Ferguson got Giggs, Beckham, [Gary] Neville, [Phil] Neville, Scholes and Nicky Butt, that's like winning the lottery. They got Giggsie from Man City, they got Nicky Butt from Man City, and yet they developed them and you've got now these young babes, these young players, you haven't spent a dime, and they were worth a fortune. They played together. Doc wasn't handed that, and Sir Matt wasn't handed that."

The "Giggsie" to whom Hill refers is Ryan Giggs. He made his League debut as a 17-year-old in March 1991 and at the time of writing (June 2010) is still a fixture at Old Trafford. It looks likely that his and Ferguson's careers will end at around the same time, testament to Ferguson's admiration for a man whom he considers the consummate professional, although to his credit he was always quick to dismiss the hyperbolic claims for the Welsh winger as the new George Best, pointing out that Best was "a miracle". Ferguson has had many great players under his wing at Old Trafford – and some genuinely iconic ones. Eric Cantona was an exquisitely gifted and thrillingly temperamental Frenchman who was crucial in that first Premiership. David Beckham was a man less gifted than he was handsome and fame-hungry but had one of the best free-kicks the game has seen. He also did what Pele famously tried to in the 1970 World Cup Finals (albeit with a heavier ball and boots) and failed: scored from the halfway line. Wayne Rooney is a fearsomely competitive forward with all-round abilities. Cristiano Ronaldo was also a special talent, but the Portuguese wing wizard was sometimes so over-elaborate in his dribbling that he seemed more like a computer game version of a footballer than the real thing.

The success Ferguson has brought United has come at a price. Affection for the club among neutrals has drained away somewhat as resentment has grown at Ferguson's distasteful and inappropriate martyr complex, at the way the club has been able to fund their success by piling up debt levels not made available by banks to their rivals and at the suspicion of increasingly preferential treatment from officialdom. "I never heard it when I was there that United would get a penalty because the referees were scared," says Hill. "Referees would more like give one against us." Additionally, Ferguson has sacrificed a certain degree of humanity in his quest for glory, perhaps exemplified by his humiliation of goalkeeper Jim Leighton, whom he dropped for the replay of the 1990 FA Cup final because he considered him to blame for the goals conceded in the first match. Additionally, Ferguson has turned Docherty's methods of quick despatch of out-of-favour players – regardless of their wishes and contract law – into an artform, as the likes of Paul Ince, David Beckham, Jaap Stam, Ruud Van Nistlerooy and others can testify. Even Docherty seems appalled, saying, "You fall out with him and you're finished." The knighthood conferred on Ferguson in 1999 raised many eyebrows: Matt Busby was considered the type of gentleman who merited such an accolade, but its award to a man seen by many as a ranting, red-faced bully was viewed as cheapening the honour.

*\*\**

Though Docherty may have been in Willie Morgan's opinion one of the worst human beings he ever met, even Morgan must surely on reflection admit that his assessment of Tommy Docherty as "about the worst manager there has ever been" is way off.

If we overlook the unfortunate matter of relegation – which most of reasonable mind are prepared to do because half the team then were not Docherty signings and there was a bigger malaise at the club which he had to sort out before he could start building for the future – the gradient of Docherty's career at Old Trafford was a steeply upward one: from Second Division champions to FA Cup runners-up to FA Cup winners in the space of three seasons is impressive. The trajectory of League form in isolation was less unequivocally upward, but to go from Second Division champions to finish third and sixth in the First Division in the following two seasons was no mean achievement. Of the 228 competitive matches Manchester United played when Docherty was manager, they won 107, drew 56 and lost 65. This may not immediately strike one as too remarkable, but nearly half of all his losses – 29 – were incurred in his first two seasons, the first of which wasn't even a complete season.

The $64,000 question is whether, had Docherty remained in charge at Old Trafford, the team's upward momentum would have given them each a First Division championship medal. Nicholl is among the doubters. "I don't think Man United would ever have won the League going about the job the way we used to go," he says. Talking of 70s hard-men like Norman Hunter and Tommy Smith, he laments, "We never really had players like that. It was an enjoyable time for me but in order to win things and keep on winning things, you need the Roy Keanes of this world, the Bryan Robsons, and we weren't like that. I'm only saying that now through experience. At that time, you'd have thought, 'Ah go on, we'll win it.' But then you realise that no, that style of football, and that type of player, probably mightn't have done. It's the same thing with [manager] Kevin Keegan in this day and age. His attitude's, 'Attack, attack, attack.' Well, you mightn't win. If you do win things like that, good luck, but the chances are you mightn't." Forsyth also has his doubts. He says of Liverpool's efficiency and QPR's technical *nous*, "I think that's what maybe we could have done with." He goes on, "You've got to have a bit of everything and The Doc was just really attacking and other managers played cagey. If you've got players that are just attacking all the time, you're just not going to do it ... You had your Leeds, Liverpools playing great stuff then and I just think you had to have a good defence as well as a good attacking team to go through and win championships and all that."

A third full-back is another of the nay-sayers. Offers Houston, "I think that team needed to be added to. In most of the positions. I've just got a little bit of doubt in the back of my mind." He concludes, not altogether convincingly, "I think they might have just been pushed to do it but I wouldn't have ruled it out." Brian Greenhoff says, "We needed more players. The squad wasn't big enough. I think really we seemed more of a cup team. I think at a club like United, I don't care who it is, you try and improve. If you see that there's a player who you think can make that position stronger, you make it stronger." Would The Doc have strengthened the side in the way he felt was needed? Brian Greenhoff: "I think he'd always look to strengthen the side. It's just about money, isn't it? He wanted to strengthen it with Peter Shilton. The club would pay the fee but they wouldn't pay his wages. That was always a problem at United." Though it may be easy to dismiss this latter caveat on the grounds that Docherty himself says the Shilton affair was the only occasion that he was refused the funds needed to secure a player, we should also note that many must have been the player who simply did not contemplate a move to Old Trafford precisely because they knew of the club's stinginess on the salary front. Blunstone is ambivalent for similar reasons. Although when asked about The Doc's title prospects with United, he says, "I think he might have done. Cup Final two years on the trot … ", he also says, "It all depends on the board, if they'll go with you and buy the players you want."

Some have no doubts that The Doc's Devils could have won the League. Steve Coppell has said that when he came back from England duty in the close season in the summer of 1977, he was convinced that in the coming season United would take the First Division title from Liverpool. For Coppell, Docherty's tenure at Old Trafford was an "unfinished symphony". Buchan says, "I always say we'll never know if that team could have gone to achieve greater things under The Doc," but his addendum indicates that he believes they could: "We'd won a major trophy in the FA Cup, which would have only increased the confidence of the squad." He does, though, acknowledge a weakness about The Doc's Devils: "The thing is we could raise our game against Liverpool and the other top teams. We could always do that in a one-off game, but we never mastered the art of going to Coventry on a wet Wednesday night and grinding out a 1-0 victory. Somehow we never developed the consistency to do things like that, as Liverpool did so well." McCreery offers, "The team that we had then were fantastic. You look at it and you think what would we have done if the team had stuck together, stayed with Tommy Doc? I think we had a very good chance at it." Hill: "I felt it was only a matter of time before we would have won the League and we'd have won a European Cup. We were gutted that the club didn't look to the future. They just said, 'This is a bad thing, this is a wrong thing, get rid of him … ' We were firing on all cylinders and it was disappointment because I knew for a fact in my heart of hearts, and a lot of other players did, that we'd have four or five years together." Meek: "I think he had every chance of building on that and maybe Manchester United would have reached the glory days again a little bit quicker than they did. It was like snakes and ladders: they landed on their head and they had to go back to the beginning again."

How many years would it have taken Docherty to win the League? Meek: "I wouldn't say the next season but within a couple of years. I think he was on the track to win the championship." McIlroy concurs. He says, "Lou Macari always seemed to think that we were a better cup bet than a League bet but once we won the Second Division and we got into the First Division and got to the Cup Final in '77 and won it, I just thought there was so many men of strength it evened the game. With the club on a high, the players on a high, who knows? Liverpool were still the team obviously to beat around them days but we *had* beat them in the Cup Final." Hill claims that ex-Liverpool boss Bill Shankly also thought a passing of the baton was on the cards. He recalls meeting Shankly after a United-Liverpool game: "I was coming up the stairs. The boss and Bill Shankly was walking down the steps and [Shankly] said to his boys, 'Guys, you're going to start losing your trophies. There's a team down the East Lancs Road there that is going to take it off of you'." Meek does state that though Docherty may have brought the championship to Old Trafford had he not been sacked, "I don't think he could have brought them the success that Ferguson had. Ferguson is a one-off. He's driven by football and in comparison Tommy Docherty was a dilettante, which gets you so far but it doesn't get you as far as Alex Ferguson."

And The Doc's view? In his memoirs, Docherty said, "I built a very attacking side, with a good defence, but we were more of a cup side than a League one. To win the FA Cup you have to win only six games, but the League is a different type of challenge." However, Docherty also said, "The team I felt would have won the League championship had I stayed on."

All of course is conjecture. We will never know if Docherty's FA Cup victory heralded the type of limited success achieved by Ron Atkinson, who won two FA Cups for United but never took the club above a final League placing of third, or whether he would have brought the club such success that he would have enjoyed the unassailable, unsackable position of Alex Ferguson, who has been United manager now for a quarter of a century.

What is not in dispute is that, financially, Docherty left United in a far better position than it was in when he arrived. The signings made by Frank O'Farrell were a long overdue recognition by United that they couldn't stand above the fray when it came to making big-money purchases and rely exclusively on the youth system to deliver them quality players. Unfortunately, that investment didn't result in the immediate dividends of honours, either under him or under Docherty, who proceeded to spend far more than O'Farrell had. By 1976, United's first ever overdraft of £234,000 had mushroomed into a walloping £495,188, even if part of the reason for it climbing to this figure was the club's investment in Old Trafford's Executive Suite and Grill Room in 1975. But Docherty ensured that the Reds maintained massive League attendances that at first were completely incongruous with their form and achievements. He also repeatedly and lucratively gave them lengthy runs in both domestic cup competitions and obtained them a place in the UEFA Cup (as well as the Cup Winners' Cup, even if he wasn't around to guide them through it). The Reds' two home fixtures in the 1976/77 UEFA Cup competition were watched cumulatively by more than 100,000 paying spectators. United's profit for the 1976/77 season was over £600,000. This may seem like peanuts today, even when factoring in inflation, but at the time it was a club record.

A note of caution should be sounded though, for one of the ways by which Docherty helped achieve that figure was his obsession with balancing the books in transfer dealings. Getting rid of dead wood for a tidy sum is one thing, but squandering valuable assets is another. The one-in, one-out (even sometimes one-in, two-out) policy that Docherty increasingly pursued at Old Trafford provided for an Achilles heel: lack of strength in depth. Eventually, Docherty seemed to completely spurn the philosophy he had espoused in his first few weeks at the club when he said, "We need at least 18 top-class players in our squad." Whether they are to one's personal taste or not, players like MacDougall, Rimmer, Morgan, Holton and Daly all had good service to give the club when he dispensed with them and their presence in the squad at various times would have provided him with options in team selection that may have made profound differences to progress in League and cups, progress that might have ultimately more than compensated for an immediate failure to balance the books.

The amateur psychologist might speculate that Docherty's habit of hastily clearing out players displays his discomfort at being around people he had deemed superfluous or with whom he had fallen out or that it may have been down to a guilt complex over the way he had presided over an unprecedented debt even as he plunged depths unknown in modern United history by taking them into Division Two. We don't know whether any of these theories are correct any more than we know whether The Doc would have won United the First Division championship. Perhaps he would have changed and learned to accept that such methods are unnecessary and counter-productive to long-term success. It's also difficult to extrapolate from his record with his subsequent clubs what he would have done at Old Trafford beyond 1977, because the budgets and legend surrounding Manchester United are exceptional and opportunities spring from them accordingly.

Docherty told Jim White, "Your biggest enemy as a manager is an old pro in the dressing room, poisoning the young minds, spreading the gospel – the wrong gospel, I might add. The best thing is to get them on their bikes as quickly as possible." Most of the players with whom Docherty fell out and therefore got rid of do indeed seem to have been in their mid-20s or older. Some have suggested that Docherty's tendency to treat older players dismissively is a sign that he felt more comfortable with the callow and the naïve because they were less likely to recognise his faults as man and manager. This may be so, but Docherty's caring attitude toward the players he nurtured was clearly genuine, as demonstrated by the support he showed Steve Coppell as he juggled his football commitments and his desire to continue his studies. (In the summer of 1976, Docherty even cut short a foreign holiday to fly back to attend Coppell's graduation ceremony at Liverpool University, although Agnes Docherty revealed that she suspected this was a pretext to pay a visit to Mary Brown.) When Coppell had been depressed about both his form and his studies. Docherty paid for Coppell and his girlfriend to stay at a hotel in the Lake District to help him refresh his batteries. The Doc did a similar thing for Brian Greenhoff when the latter's pregnant wife was feeling unwell, allowing the defender to take a break of several days in Anglesey, giving him a bag of kit to enable him to train on his own during his absence. Though McCreery admits of The Doc, "He could just fly off the handle," he also says the manager was a father figure to him: "Very much so. If there was any problems back home when the Troubles were on, he used to say to me, 'How's your family?' And if I said, 'Well, there's a bit of a problem', he'd say, 'Right, get yourself home for a couple of days'." Laurie Brown, though, points out the other side of this coin: "He did a few things with some of the young players, without telling older players: 'I'll give you this' or 'You can do this', and 'You don't have to put in', and when the older players found out they weren't too pleased about that."

Docherty was as caring about United fans as he was his favourite players. Coppell said, "He was smashing ... He would go around the country, visiting each supporters' club." There seems no more for Docherty to personally gain from doing this than from the charity work Coppell has also pointed out that The Doc engaged in, especially for sick and disabled children, whom he was able to put at their ease with humorous remarks while Coppell – a university student, so no dummy – was tongue-tied. Though Coppell was not unaware of Docherty's shortcomings as a human being – he found The Doc able and willing to direct reasonless abuse at players, unable to accept players answering back and inconsistent and impulsive both on and off the pitch – he has always been full of praise for the way his manager cared for him almost as though he were his own son. Docherty's concerned consoling of a tearful Brian Greenhoff as he walked off the Wembley pitch after the team had lost the 1976 Cup Final sums up his paternal approach and remains a truly touching image.

Meek though is unimpressed. "Brian Greenhoff still had a future, so he was taking care of him," he observes. "But Denis Law's career was as good as over, so no sentiment: out you go. Brian Greenhoff was a young player who was going to be useful for him so he went out of his way to help mend his sadness and upset. Very logical really."

It seems as much the case that Docherty didn't want to deal with older footballers as he didn't really know how to. The team he inherited at Old Trafford was stuffed to the gills with good players, from Stepney to Buchan to Morgan to Storey-Moore to Charlton to Law, and though some of those players were clearly not of the age to build the club's future on, they all had a season or two of service in them at the very least. Yet Docherty was unable to make a team with those fine footballers gel, even when they had been augmented by his also generally fine new signings, either that season or the next. Only when he started overhauling the team in the Second Division and filling almost all available places with youngsters who looked up to him and were grateful for the chance he had provided them did things click for Docherty's United.

The previously mentioned unimpressive youth set-up was of course another reason for lack of strength in depth in The Doc's Devils. Asked if he felt that there were a lot of good young players coming through the youth teams in his time at Old Trafford, Buchan says, "Not too many spring to mind." To be fair to Docherty, had he still been at the club when Andy Ritchie came through, the verdict on his youth system would have been at least slightly different. Probably not by much, though. Nicholl says, "I remember going to Toronto in '82 and Davey Fairclough came for six months on loan. I'm talking to Dave Fairclough about this. Liverpool had won the reserve League about 12, 13 years in a row." The contrast between the productivity of the clubs' respective youth streams makes Nicholl say of the suggestion that United's youth well was virtually dry, "Factually. it's right."

\*\*\*

Sir Matt Busby passed away in January 1994. The other giant of the United board in Docherty's era, Louis Edwards, had preceded him to the grave in February 1980, succumbing to a heart attack exactly four weeks after the *World in Action* exposé, which also alleged that he had obtained control of the club by corrupt means. When Edwards's son took over as chairman, he was accused by the fans of only being interested in money. Martin Edwards certainly did well for himself by floating the club on the stock market: he is reported to have subsequently made more than £100 million from the shares he sold. However, Edwards's enrichment went hand in hand with the enrichment of a club whose value climbed from £20 million in 1989 to more than £1 billion just over a decade later. While that off-field success may have been of negligible interest to most fans, the same cannot be said for the on-field triumph Edwards can also plausibly claim credit for by refusing to cave in to pressure from supporters to sack Alex Ferguson in his unsteady early years as manager..

In May 2005, United came back into private ownership when American Malcolm Glazer obtained sufficient shares to force a compulsory buyout. Glazer and his family have racked up debts at Old Trafford so large that the annual interest payments alone are £62 million. Meanwhile, members of the Glazer family on the board have taken tens of millions of pounds out of the club in loans and "management and administration fees." It can't be denied, though, that United have continued their winning ways under the Glazers thus far. However, in another outstanding season in 2008/09, only the £81m sale of Ronaldo prevented the biggest club in the world from making a loss. Many United fans had predicted such an eventuality when the Glazers had taken over. However, their response – setting up a football club pointedly called FC United of Manchester – seems a futile gesture. This lowly and homeless outfit are not likely to be causing the Glazers any sleepless nights, nor challenging for the Premiership.

Although the valuation of Manchester United had dropped to £800m by the point of the Glazer takeover, it was still an astronomical amount. It was also a testament to the way that the perceived value of football has shot through the roof since the 1980s. Wages have also skyrocketed, with weekly pay packets of £100,000 not uncommon. Such huge salaries have made footballers easy targets for posturing public figures who wish to curry favour with the public, possibly the most pathetic example being a television condemnation of players showing dissent to referees by an MP chiefly known to the public for being unfaithful to his wife in extremely colourful circumstances. Martin Buchan has strong views on this phenomenon: "It would be interesting to see how Tommy Doc would fare with today's press. Things were a lot simpler back then. For me, it changed in the mid-70s. In 1974 I went to the World Cup in Germany with Scotland and we were accompanied by a posse of football reporters. In 1978, in Argentina there were football reporters to cover the matches and news reporters looking for scandal or controversy and I think that's when coverage of the game changed. They seem to be more interested in what happens off the field now than what happens on it. And with camera phones these days, everyone's a potential paparazzo … When I was growing up, we used to say 'I want to be a fitba' player.' Nowadays these poor lads are expected to be role models for a society that has no leadership, appalling standards of behaviour and no discipline and a lot of them come from very ordinary backgrounds. They're probably cosseted too much when they get to a football club at the age of 16. They're expected to behave like paragons of virtue when actually the people who are writing about them are far from that. The politicians clamouring in the House of Commons about the behaviour of certain individuals are ten times worse and I think it's horrendous that these lads have been thrust into the public spotlight. But I suppose it goes with the territory. They get big money now, they get wall-to-wall coverage on TV and adverts. People feel they actually know these lads personally. When I played, I had a private life."

Though pandering to popular bigotry about footballers is one of the modern age's more tedious sports, Gordon Hill does have a point in his dismissive attitude toward present-day footballers who complain they are required to play too much. "We played nearly 50–60 games [per season] and never complained," he points out. "The fields were shit. You had players out there that could kick. Referees didn't protect players. Every defender wanted to take me out. Nowadays they'd be sent off."

Pitches on which there is not a blade of grass out of place and defenders required to play clean are just two things a 1970s soccer fan transported in time to today would be startled by. Football teams still only field 11 players at a time. The sport itself is still – to quote a football commentators' pearl of wisdom so hackneyed that it can no longer be uttered unselfconsciously – a game of two halves. In all other respects, though, soccer has changed profoundly since the days of Tommy Docherty's tenure as Manchester United manager.

Not only has the League Cup, which produced several exciting ties during Docherty's era, been completely devalued but even the FA Cup – the winning of which was Docherty's sole undiluted triumph in his tenure at United – is now looked at as an insubstantial bauble by many teams and managers, probably partly as a casualty of an influx of foreigners into the English game who don't appreciate that the tournament is not merely the equivalent of the knock-out competitions in their home countries but a contest steeped in a history that goes back to the very dawn of soccer. The FA Cup has been increasingly marginalized by the desire for a place in the European Champions' League, the competition that the European Cup has mutated into and which – logically – should itself have been seen as devalued when clubs finishing as low as fourth in their respective domestic leagues became eligible for entry. It must also be acknowledged that Manchester United themselves helped to devalue the FA Cup by electing not to enter it in 1999/2000 at a time when they were the holders of the trophy, opting instead to play in the Club World Championship (now known as the Club World Cup). Though United have demonstrated there was political pressure from the government of the time to participate in the Club World Championship, Ryan Giggs summed up the feelings of many when he publicly expressed puzzlement as to why United couldn't just field a weakened team in the early rounds of the FA Cup (as by now they routinely did in every round of the League Cup) rather than pull out of the tournament completely.

It is not just the League Cup and FA Cup that have been devalued, but the very language surrounding the game. Football followers are now obliged to refer to the third and fourth tiers of English league football – the old Divisions Three and Four – by their new titles of Leagues One and Two. Similarly, what was once the Second Division is now known by the quasi-Orwellian doublethink title of The Championship. The game as a whole has also arguably been devalued by the increasing use of penalty shoot-outs to decide matches. Though more sophisticated defences and hence a greater numbers of drawn matches may have made these necessary – the alternative being the kind of interest-sapping succession of replays that decided that 1977 League Cup final – the fact that penalty shoot-outs are more a matter of chance than skill makes many lose interest in the match outcome that they are utilised to decide. So much for the introduction of three points for a win in the English game in 1981 to encourage positive play.

\*\*\*

Even allowing for inflation, comments by Docherty such as "The days of six-figure signings at United are gone forever" have been proven laughably inaccurate. But then Docherty had no way of foreseeing the revenue that would pour into the game through advances in technology that were then in their infancy (pay-per-view) or the stuff largely of science fiction (domestic satellite television and the internet).

The Cliff, United's former training ground, is now used only for United Academy (kids) matches, having been superseded at the turn of the millennium by the sprawling, fortress-like Trafford Training Centre in Carrington. Old Trafford remains, but massively expanded and updated, a gleaming, high-tech edifice. The Stretford End, however, is no more. In 1993, it was replaced by the West Stand. Though Liverpool briefly overtook them in terms of home attendance in the late 1980s/early 1990s, United continue to achieve the highest gates in English football. Following reconstruction work (which affected United's gates for a while), the capacity at Old Trafford is now 76,000, about fourteen thousand higher than in Docherty's day, even despite the stadium's conversion to all-seater status. (Plans are afoot to upgrade to a 95,000 capacity.) Somehow, though, there is something missing. That increased capacity has not led to greater noise levels. Modern attendance figures are really ticket sales rather than the number of people present at the game: even to use the word 'attendance' nowadays is misleading. Additionally, the inhibiting fact of spectators being seated, the increasingly middle class nature of football fans and the growth of hermetically sealed executive boxes (peopled by the "prawn sandwiches" brigade that infamously aroused the scorn of United's Roy Keane) has gradually drained Old Trafford – like many football grounds – of much of its atmosphere. When he has visited the modern ground, Gordon Hill has been shocked by the low noise levels on match day. "I can hear people talk on the field," he says. "You can hear somebody from the far side shout out. You couldn't do that [in my day]. Sammy McIlroy and myself used to laugh sometimes because I couldn't get through to him and he couldn't get through to me." In their defence, the boxes have given rise to the modern football phenomenon of corporate hospitality, which enables ex-United legends to earn money as greeters. Brian Greenhoff has occasionally done such work. He explains, "When they're sat down, you just go walk round, have a chat with them. The earlier you get the team [sheet] the better usually, 'cos then you can talk about the team: 'What do you think? What do you think going's to happen today?' And they're given a sheet to write down the scorer and all this and they ask you what you think and they might ask you about your playing days, 'cos you do get some who are interested. A lot of the people who do it are from the 70s and the 80s, because they're all people who still need to work ... It's nice. I quite enjoyed it." He does add, though, "There's not many where you actually used to get outside to watch the match. We used to watch it on a telly inside. Sometimes there's just not the space for you."

Not everything is a deterioration. The hooliganism that blighted football in the 70s and besmirched the name of Manchester United more than that of any other British club has disappeared, squeezed out by the all-seeing eye of CCTV and then the practical restrictions of all-seater stadia brought about by the 1990 Taylor Report.

*** 

Though The Doc's Devils boasted no Holy Trinity-level players, the team ultimately were all luminaries. None of the regular players during Docherty's last two seasons at the club were anonymous. From the goalkeeper's position through the back-four, the midfield and the attack, all of the players were outstanding at their job. If they were greater than the sum of their parts, it was in one respect only: the fact that the goalscoring was spread across an extraordinary high number of players. United had no Ian Rush/Gary Lineker figure upfront, hanging around the penalty area for easy tap-ins. Strikers like McIlroy, Pearson and Jimmy Greenhoff had a much wider range than that and would use their layered skills to assist as many goals as they knocked in. While this meant that they didn't stack up goals in the numbers enjoyed by the Rush/Lineker mould of player, it didn't matter: almost everyone at the club seemed capable of hitting the back of the net, whether defender (Brian Greenhoff, Forsyth, Houston), midfielder (Daly, Macari, the redeployed McIlroy) or winger (Hill and Coppell). Perhaps in a way, it was indeed Docherty's version of the Total Football he vaingloriously claimed his team practised.

Blunstone says of The Doc, "Alec Ferguson is brilliant but Tommy'll go down in history with him, no doubt about that ... I think he'll go down as one of the greats." "What really ticks me off about United, they don't really play the Doc era up much," says Hill. "And what pisses me off, really pisses me off, is that from when we won the FA Cup right the way through, they haven't looked back. And yet no one recognises [that]. It's all Fergie, Fergie, Fergie, yet The Doc came back and he come storming out of the Second Division, he come storming up into the First Division. We were getting there." Though he acknowledges that, "Liverpool were the best team at the time," he also points out, "We were only puppies." He goes on, "I've got a lot of respect for the Busby Babes [but] coming out from the Second Division, back in the First Division, it was a new era for them. They'd said, 'Right, we've had our lull', and I still state this: from that day to this day, they haven't been out of the light. They just picked up more trophies."

Hill's assertion of an unbroken line of honours-winning post-Docherty is demonstrably untrue, and it would be easy to dismiss his comments as those of a man who has oft been accused of engaging his tongue before his brain and who is unashamedly biased in his fondness for Docherty. Yet the comments of David Meek – a far more thoughtful figure and someone with profound reservations about Docherty as man and manager – are not too dissimilar in content, although the journalist is better equipped linguistically to make the case that Hill is groping for. "Docherty, there's no denying, was the key to turning around Manchester United's fortunes after the retirement of Matt Busby," Meek says. "Because there's no doubt that the retirement of Matt Busby left them in some disarray. Docherty kick-started them again. He's very important in the history of Manchester United and I don't think – because he left under a bit of a cloud – he's been given enough credit for pulling the team round and providing a bridge to more successful days that we know and associate with them now."

Perhaps the last word should go to Hill, that player who embodied the spirit of The Doc's Devils, for good or ill. Hill: "I enjoyed it because he let me play, he let me be flamboyant. He let me do what I was born to do: play and enjoy and score. And believed in you … I always keep in touch … I phone him up for advice. He's still called 'the boss' to me … I've got a lot of respect. The guy give me a chance, and I respect him because he was the type of guy that would tell you upfront he's going to stab you in the back … You've got to be ruthless at times and you've got to be cold. I've learnt that now in the management world." The hurt and bewilderment of losing his mentor when the two were in a position to achieve great things together still apparently stings with Hill more than three decades later. "What they done to him was absolutely tragic," says the man they called Merlin. "Everybody at United now seems to forget the boss, The Doc. But I tell you what: he had some side."

# Résumés: the fate of The Doc's Devils

Note: In tallies of players' Manchester United games, starts are listed first, followed by separate substitute appearances in brackets.

**ARTHUR ALBISTON**
**Manchester United games: 467 (18)**
**Manchester United goals: 7**
**Full international caps: 14**

That unflappable performance in the FA Cup final of 1977 turned out to be representative of Arthur Albiston's abilities. Albiston proceeded to have a lengthy career at Old Trafford, becoming the club's longest-serving post-War left-back. Having survived the management regimes of Sexton and Atkinson, he found himself out of favour with Alex Ferguson, who let him go on a free to West Brom in August 1988, making him the last of The Doc's Devils to depart Old Trafford. Still only 31, he naturally wasn't yet prepared to hang up his boots and subsequently turned out for West Bromwich Albion, Dundee, Chesterfield, Chester City, Norway's Molde F.K. and Ayr United. Even when his League career was over, he could be found playing for various non-League sides, one of whom – Droylsden – he managed in 1996/97. Since then he has been a youth coach at United and has worked as a radio commentator. Albiston played a game in the 1986 World Cup finals.

**TREVOR ANDERSON**
**Manchester United games: 13 (6)**
**Manchester United goals: 2**
**Full international caps: 22**

Some were puzzled when Docherty let Trevor Anderson go to Swindon Town for £25,000 in November 1974. However, the Irishman averaged a respectable but not outstanding goal per four games or thereabouts for Swindon, so perhaps that lower tier of football was his true level. The other English team for whom Anderson turned out was Peterborough United, before he returned to his native Northern Ireland in 1979 while still only 28. There he enjoyed another decade in the game, playing more than 300 fixtures for Linfield and racking up nearly 100 goals for them. In 1986, he won the Northern Ireland Football Writers' Association Player of the Season Award, aged 35. Upon his retirement, he became Linfield's youth-team coach, before being appointed manager in October 1992. Though sacked in 1997, he had won several honours for the club by then. He later managed Newry Town, Ards and Dundalk.

## TOMMY BALDWIN
**Manchester United games: 2**
**Manchester United goals: 0**
**Full international caps: 0**

Following his brief loan period at United as cover for the injured Pearson during the Second Division season, Baldwin returned to Stamford Bridge. His two loan periods that season, however, indicated his Chelsea days were numbered. Though some felt injury had hampered him recently, it was still shocking that the next port of call for a man in only his early 30s should be non-League club Gravesend & Northfleet, where he ended up in the 1976/77 season, though he did at least get another taste of League football with Brentford before his retirement from the game in 1978. He is now a media pundit.

## GEORGE BEST
**Manchester United games: 470**
**Manchester United goals: 179**
**Full international caps: 37**

Following his storming out from Old Trafford in January 1974, George Best continued to be a celebrity. Still a young man and still extraordinarily handsome (he is reputed to have bedded three successive Miss Worlds), he engaged in various business ventures while occasionally turning out for football clubs who obtained his services for a handsome fee in the knowledge that his presence on the pitch would swell their attendances. Best played three matches apiece for Dunstable Town, Stockport County and Cork Celtic, as well as taking up a lucrative offer to appear in South Africa for, er, Jewish Guild. Matt Busby reportedly likened such activities to that of a performing flea. Though Docherty is the source for this comparison, and furthermore made it during his testimony in the witness box at his ill-fated libel trial, it rings true. The North American Soccer League (NASL) turned out to be Best's salvation. The boom in the sport in the States in the late 70s created a demand for the services of him, Pele, Cruyff, Eusebio, Beckenbauer and other legends somewhat past their peak but still blessed with such talent as to be able to fill stadiums. Turning out for Los Angeles Aztecs, Fort Lauderdale Strikers and San Jose Earthquakes as he did from 1976 to 1981, Best could enjoy his football and earn some money without needing to agonise about the thought of the crowds he was playing in front of making mental comparisons to his former abilities. However, it was perhaps that fear that meant his return to English football in 1976 was via a Second Division side. He joined Rodney Marsh and Bobby Moore at Fulham. His spectacular goal on his debut was the first of 10 in 47 appearances for the London club. His ratio of three in 22 for Scots Hibernian in 1979/80 was (just about) respectable, too. However, his scattered appearances for Bournemouth, Australia's Brisbane Lions and Northern Ireland's Tobermore United from 1983 to 1984 smack again of the performing-flea scenario, one made sadder by being at the fag-end of his career. As if underlining the latter fact, in Best's last appearance in a competitive match – for Tobermore in an Irish Cup fixture against Ballymena United – he was on a losing side that let in seven goals with no reply.

Best never found a vocation following his retirement. He once expressed interest in the then vacant Northern Ireland manager's role but stories of his occasionally failing to turn up for speaking engagements and an excruciating inebriated performance in 1990 on a live Terry Wogan TV chat show gave him an aura of unreliability that ensured neither that nor any other manager's post came his way. Nonetheless, he was always able to keep body and soul together by selling his views on the game he once dominated to newspapers and television. Occasionally he would find domestic bliss, even if all his long-term relationships eventually foundered.

Towards the end of his life, he seemed to finally be getting over the excruciating shyness that surprisingly few posited as a cause of his alcoholism. Yet the latter disease continued to hold him in its sway and nothing – including therapy, potentially fatal stomach implants and a liver transplant – could keep him away from the bottle for long. He died of multiple organ failure on November 25 2005.

Some felt that Best should have been called up by Northern Ireland when they finally reached the World Cup finals in 1982 on the grounds that even at 36 he was able to conjure magic, even if only used as a substitute. However, national manager Billy Bingham failed to select him. Jimmy Nicholl – who watched Best's dramatic Old Trafford comings and goings from the distance of the United youth team and would go on to play on the international stage with him – feels bringing him into the team at this point would have done Best "a disservice". Fellow NI international David McCreery disagrees, saying he would "definitely" have liked Best to be selected. And even Nicholl, recalling a late 70s Northern Ireland versus Holland match in which he played alongside Best, says of the man they called Georgie, "He nutmegged Cruyff and Neeskens in the one move and that was enough to prove to me that he was the best I've ever, ever seen."

## PAUL BIELBY
**Manchester United games: 2 (2)**
**Manchester United goals: 0**
**Full international caps: 0**

Winger Bielby was born on November 24 1956 in Darlington. Following his sprinkling of appearances for the Reds during that traumatic relegation season, Paul Bielby went on a free to Fourth Division Hartlepool United in December 1975, where he notched up nearly 100 games. His other League club was Huddersfield Town. Dropping down the divisions after having been scooped up as a boy by Manchester United must have been disappointing enough, but far worse was to come when a knee injury forced his retirement at just 23. Bielby turned his tragedy to triumph, firstly by working his way up to the position of director of Hazlewood Foods after starting as a sales rep, secondly by founding the Darlington Primary School Football Association and the Master Skills Football Academy, also located in Darlington. His determination to improve sports facilities for children earned him an MBE for services to young people in 2008. Speaking of his truncated football career after the award was announced, he said, "I watched television and saw lads I had played with at youth international level become household names. But I decided that I had to turn that competitive spirit into something else."

## GEORGE BUCHAN
**Manchester United games: 0 (4)**
**Manchester United goals: 0**
**Full international caps: 0**

George Buchan's transfer to Bury that Docherty stepped in to stop in the close season following the 1972/73 campaign ultimately did take place when Martin Buchan's little brother turned out in Docherty's opinion to not have quite what it took to play in the First Division. George played a couple of seasons for Bury before dropping out of the game. Explains Martin, "George's wife was a schoolteacher and he left Bury, joined non-League Lancaster and went to college to qualify as a teacher himself. For many years he worked [in a] secondary school in Oldham teaching PE and English."

## MARTIN BUCHAN
**Manchester United games: 456**
**Manchester United goals: 4**
**Full international caps: 34**

Martin Buchan had a testimonial match in August 1983 and then moved to Oldham Athletic, although not before turning down a somewhat more prestigious offer from Maine

Road. "I didn't think it was right to go across the city," he later explained of his decision not to join United's great rivals. Once again, the man of iron principles had done what he considered morally right, not financially convenient. He also turned down an offer to be professionally reunited with Docherty when the latter took over the Wolverhampton Wanderers management in 1984. Buchan: "He asked me to be player/coach at Wolves but didn't have the budget to allow me to stay near the club a couple of nights a week rather than travel up and down the M6 every day, so I signed for Joe Royle at Oldham for the same basic wage Doc had offered me and had a mostly enjoyable two years at Boundary Park." Buchan's principles saw him retire from the game through injury halfway through his second 'Latics season rather than sit out the rest of his contract.

Buchan's heightened intellect and no-nonsense attitude led some – including Buchan himself – to think he might have a managerial career ahead of him. Four months in charge of Burnley disabused him of that notion. Finding himself drowning in players' complaints that he didn't consider to be within a manager's remit was bad enough but informing young players that they weren't going to make it in the game broke his heart. Buchan spent 12 years working for boot manufacturer Puma before joining the Professional Footballers Association, where – judging by an overheard phone conversation with a lower league player who had not been paid recently – he handles members' problems caringly and conscientiously.

Buchan's son Jamie is a professional footballer, his exclusively Scottish career having started at Aberdeen. Martin Buchan remains the only man to have captained winning sides in both Scottish Cup and FA Cup finals.

**BOBBY CHARLTON**
**Manchester United games: 756 (2)**
**Manchester United goals: 249**
**Full international caps: 106**
George Best was sometimes ridiculed for whoring his talents around soccer's backwaters when he was well past his peak, but the same charge could, to a lesser extent, be levelled against his ex-team-mate Bobby Charlton. When his management of Preston North End resulted in the club's relegation from Division Two in 1974, Charlton decided to help the attempt to bounce back up by pulling on his boots again. As player-manager, he scored 10 goals in 48 matches but quit management that season. His taste for playing apparently having been restored, in the 1975/76 season he turned out for Waterford United – managed by his old colleague Shay Brennan – which surely must have been a surreal sight for fans of the League of Ireland club. He scored 18 goals in 31 games for Waterford. He also subsequently

played in apartheid-era South Africa, though the Teflon reputation conferred on him by his soccer saint status ensured this attracted little criticism.

Charlton served briefly as acting manager for Wigan Athletic in 1983, of which club he was also a director. Since 1984, he has been on the board at Manchester United. He is still revered by the public and media, although is apparently subjected to mickey-taking by less reverential modern-day United players who are amused by his taciturn nature. However, that he is neither a fool nor an establishment mannequin was illustrated by his 2007 autobiography *My Manchester United Years*, wherein he revealed his contempt for the people who had upheld the maximum wage for so long and highlighted the petty rules of the football authorities that led to the Munich air disaster. Additionally, the man who had always seemed to epitomise the old order in contrast to the 60s zeitgeist-encapsulating George Best – and thereby implicitly seemed conservative to his core – surprised many by engaging in work (pre-Blair) for the organisation Footballers for a Labour Victory.

Amusingly, in recent years Charlton has publicly renounced his 'comb-over', the disguise of his balding pate which he adopted in the 60s that would have been precarious at the best of times but with running around and windy conditions was always wrecked within minutes of kick-off and necessitated constant sweeps of his hand across his head.

Though the proliferation of international friendlies in recent years has seen the far less talented David Beckham overhaul his 106 caps, Charlton's goalscoring record (49) for England remains intact. In 2008, Ryan Giggs broke his record for most Manchester United appearances, but again Charlton remains the Reds' all-time top goalscorer. (Additionally, more than 100 of Giggs' appearances were as substitute, and in a similar number of matches Giggs was substituted.)

The inevitable knighthood for the soccer saint came in 1994. He had previously been awarded the CBE in 1974 to add to the OBE he was awarded in 1969.

## JONATHAN CLARK
**Manchester United games: 0 (1)**
**Manchester United goals: 0**
**Full international caps: 0**

Jonathan Clark was described by David Meek when he was on the verge of a first-team breakthrough as the best player to come out of Wales since John Charles. Blunstone says, "Jonathan never developed. He was a very complicated boy. He just stood still. He was only as good at 18 as he was when he was 15. You've got to progress and get better every year and Jonathan didn't." He was born in Swansea on November 12 1958 and signed full terms under the Docherty regime, for which he made one substitute appearance. In September 1978, he was taken by Docherty to Derby County for £50,000, thus apparently disproving Agnes Docherty's allegation of anti-Welsh bias on the part of her husband. Clark played more the 50 games for Derby before signing for Docherty again at Preston North End, for whom he turned out more than 100 times. Bury and Carlisle United were his other League clubs. Though this constitutes a fairly respectable career, Old Trafford insiders will tell you he never really fulfilled the promise he had shown as a youngster, when his elegant passing would produce coos of admiration from those watching him in practice matches at The Cliff. He is now a publican.

**STEVE COPPELL**
**Manchester United games: 393 (3)**
**Manchester United goals: 70**
**Full international caps: 42**
Steve Coppell was the Manchester United Supporters Club Player of the Year in 1978, despite a redrafting of his duties by Dave Sexton that for many made him too workmanlike. After his tragically early retirement, he started his management career with Crystal Palace, a club he has bizarrely returned to three further times. He reached the FA Cup final with the London club in 1990, though also famously suffered a 9-0 humiliation with them against Liverpool in 1989. He has also managed Manchester City, Brentford, Brighton and Hove Albion and Reading. With the last, in 2006, he won the Championship – or the Second Division as it was called when he played in it for United. In April 2010 he was made manager of Bristol City, but resigned after just four months, claiming he was retiring from management..

Many were disappointed with this usually dignified man's role on the inquiry team of a Football Association investigation into 'bungs' – managers and agents receiving under-the-counter payments during transfer deals – in the mid-1990s. The seemingly interminable inquiry (actually three-and-a-half years) smacked of dragging feet in order to gain time, which of course has a sporting metaphor: kicking the ball into touch.

**PETER COYNE**
**Manchester United games: 1 (1)**
**Manchester United goals: 1**
**Full international caps: 0**
Coyne's career is covered in part 5. An interesting footnote is provided by the fact that Peter Coyne's son Tony played for FC United of Manchester, the club set up in 2005 by United fans

disgruntled by the Glazer takeover. Coyne: "My son was a big City fan but everybody wanted to play for FC United when they started so he had a couple of seasons with them. I think they've gone as far as they can go now. The crowd's not getting any bigger or anything like that. I think the only way they can progress is getting their own ground and I think they're finding it difficult."

**GERRY DALY**
**Manchester United games: 137 (5)**
**Manchester United goals: 32**
**Full international caps: 48**

Though Daly emphatically did not want the transfer from Old Trafford to the Baseball Ground in early 1977, the Irishman says, "I went to Derby County and I probably played some of the best football I'd ever played in my life." He also reveals, "Leeds United tried to sign me. It was when I was at Derby County. Probably one of the best managers that ever lived was the manager there then and his name was Jock Stein." However, the interest from Elland Road dissipated over Daly's commitments in the North American Soccer League. "I went out to America in the summers – the Boston Teamen." The Teamen's manager and assistant manager were former Manchester United legends Noel Cantwell and Dennis Viollet.

Daly recalls of his time with The Doc at Derby: "I remember us having a meeting once. We were joking and laughing. And arguing on occasions. I remember me saying to him, 'I'll see you out of the Baseball Ground.' As if to say, 'You won't be selling me this time'." Daly turned out to be correct in this respect. When he was transferred by Derby to Coventry City in August 1980, Docherty had been gone for 14 months. Daly spent three seasons at Coventry and while he was there, Docherty, by now at Wolves, enquired about his services. "I was on the transfer list at Coventry," Daly recalls. "I used to go in practically every day to see if anybody had made any enquiries. I went into the receptionist and she said, 'Oh yes, Tommy Docherty's been on the phone enquiring about you at Wolves.' She didn't have a smile on her face at the time. If she'd had a smile on her face, she would have known about myself and Tommy Docherty. That's why I took it as being serious. Nothing actually happened in the end." Would he have been willing to hook up again with The Doc? "I suppose if it had been a serious offer … "

Leicester City, Birmingham City, Shrewsbury Town, Stoke City and Doncaster Rovers were his other berths. "I had a long, long time in football with various clubs," he says. "Luckily I never had to move terribly far. There was always a club that was very near that wanted me. I probably only had about three houses in all the clubs that I've had." He briefly tried management with non-League Telford United following his 1989 retirement. Daly: "That was like banging your head against a brick wall because as soon as you got a half-decent player you had to sell him … There didn't seem to be any ambition … " A report on the BBC's website in 2009 claimed that Daly "…is unable to work because of a back problem. Daly claims to have been promised a testimonial by the FAI but it never materialised."

"I've seen Tommy Docherty twice now since the years have gone by when he does his after-dinner speaking," says Daly. "The last time I was sat in a club and he was going out to the toilet. I didn't even know he was doing an after-dinner speak at this particular thing that I was in. I said, 'Hello boss.' I wouldn't dare call him Tommy. He looked [at me] and he went, 'Oh Jesus – Gerry. Hang on for a minute, I'm going out to the toilet', and he came back and he sat with me at the bar for 35 minutes. We've all got older, we've all mellowed, times go on." To such an extent that Daly says of the scheming behind Docherty's ejection of him from Old Trafford, "Never single him out for being the only one. It was rife in the game, that."

However, there seems a lingering sadness with Daly over the fact that his career at Old Trafford was terminated against his will. When it is suggested to him that his catalogue of mostly top-flight and/or noteworthy clubs marks a decent career, he replies, "Well, half-decent." Because leaving Manchester United can only be a step down? Daly: "Well it is. I've always said it and still maintain it to this day. If you're in love with a club and you get on really with the supporters … A player knows when the supporters like him or they dislike him. You can tell by their reactions. Even if you make a mistake, they don't have a go at you. The supporters were absolutely brilliant. Even now, I get Manchester United supporters writing to me. It's unbelievable the amount of mail that I get."

## RON DAVIES
**Manchester United games: 0 (10)**
**Manchester United goals: 0**
**Full international caps: 29**
Swapping George Graham for Welsh international Davies in November 1974 seems another nail in the coffin for Agnes Docherty's theory that her husband was Welshphobic, unless bringing him to Old Trafford only to grant him fewer than a dozen appearances – all of them as substitute – before despatching him to Arcadia Shepherds in South Africa on a free in March 1975 was an elaborately cruel joke by The Doc. Davies was born in Holywell, Flintshire, on May 25 1942. After leaving United, Davies played a handful of games for Millwall but most of the rest of his career was spent in the States. His first club in the NASL was Los Angeles Aztecs, where he has said he was signed on the recommendation

of their team member George Best. Davies later recalled an amusing conversation with the latter. Conversant with his long service with the Saints (Davies scored 153 goals in 277 appearances for Southampton over seven years), Best approached him with some news. "I remember him coming up to me at training one day and saying, 'You'll never believe what has happened – Southampton have beaten Manchester United in the FA Cup final'." Davies said. "I thought he was taking the piss."

Davies moved on to the Tampa Bay Rowdies and the Seattle Sounders. He then spent a decade coaching Stateside. Settled in a mobile home in America (he has dual citizenship), his battered body has recently undergone two hip replacements.

## WYN DAVIES
**Manchester United games: 16 (1)**
**Manchester United goals: 4**
**Full international caps: 34**

Though over 31 by the time he left United for Blackpool in June 1973, Davies would play League football for a further five years, turning out for Crystal Palace, Stockport County and Crewe Alexandra. Additionally, he played some games for Welsh League club Bangor City. He might even have played longer but for a knee injury. He moved to Bolton, working as a baker for the company Warburtons before retiring. Davies seems a naturally happy soul: BBC Wales/North West reported in May 2009 that he "has lots of pleasure in going for a walk with his dogs each day". Which makes it all the more remarkable that his interactions with Docherty have left him so bitter that he responded to an interview request for this book by stating in no uncertain terms that he had nothing whatsoever to say about Docherty.

## IAN DONALD
**Manchester United games: 6 (0)**
**Manchester United goals: 0**
**Full international caps: 0**

A 21-year-old full-back inherited by Docherty, Donald is perhaps not technically one of The Doc's Devils as he was not allowed to add to his half-dozen United appearances before Docherty released him to Patrick Thistle in January 1973 free of charge. Donald played only one League game for Partick and four for his next club Arbroath and there, at the age of 24, his professional footballing career ended. However, success awaited him in other avenues. His father Dick had been chairman of his hometown club Aberdeen and Ian followed in his footsteps in 1994, having been on the board since 1980. He was chairman for four years and retired as club director in 2004. Donald served on the council of the Scottish Football

Association and the Scottish Football League. He is chairman and managing director of JF Donald (Aberdeen Cinemas) Limited.

## TONY DUNNE
**Manchester United games: 534 (1)**
**Manchester United goals: 2**
**Full international caps: 33**

Born in Dublin on July 24 1941, the veteran European Cup-winning full-back and Republic of Ireland international was 32 when Docherty let him go on a free in the summer of 1973, but the man who had picked up every honour in club football that anybody cared about – League championship (twice), FA Cup and European Cup – was far from finished. Bolton Wanderers proceeded to enjoy the two-footed, speedy and composed presence of Dunne for six seasons, during which he racked up more than 200 appearances in all competitions and helped them take the 1978 Second Division championship. Almost paradoxically considering his long post-United afterlife at Bolton, though he had the usual stint for players of his generation in the NASL (Detroit Express), it was only for a dozen games. Dunne was Bolton's assistant manager for a couple of seasons following his 1979 retirement. His only term as manager proper occurred when he took charge at Norway's Steinkjer in 1982/83. He runs a golf driving range near Altrincham, Greater Manchester.

## PAUL EDWARDS
**Manchester United games: 66 (2)**
**Manchester United goals: 1**
**Full international caps: 0**

Born on October 7 1947 in Crompton, Lancashire, defender Edwards was again arguably not technically one of The Doc's Devils because he never got a game in the first team under the new manager before being sold to Oldham Athletic in March 1973 for £13,000–£15,000 following a loan period. Edwards was a member of Oldham's Third Division championship-winning side in 1973/74. He also played for Stockport County. He works for the parts department of a Manchester motor firm.

## JOHN FITZPATRICK
**Manchester United games: 141 (6)**
**Manchester United goals: 10**
**Full international caps: 0**

John Fitzpatrick – a fearsome defender the like of whom journalists tend to refer to as having more commitment than skill – had already played the last of his games for the Reds when

Docherty became manager, but that is probably more down to the arthritic knee condition that forced his retirement in July 1973 than The Doc being disinclined to make him one of his Devils. Born in Aberdeen on August 18 1946, Fitzpatrick runs a wine-importing business that straddles two cities in his native Scotland. He has an interesting footnote in United history: following the introduction of substitutes in soccer in 1965, he became the first United player to replace another during a game when he came on for Denis Law against Spurs in October of that year.

**PETER FLETCHER**
**Manchester United games: 2 (5)**
**Manchester United goals: 0**
**Full international caps: 0**
Docherty both blooded the striker who had signed to the club in 1969 as a boy and discarded him when he had to offer Hull something more than £170,000 for Stuart Pearson. Fletcher played 36 League games for Hull, where he notched up his first goal in professional soccer, one of five League goals with the club. Fletcher: "Terry Neill signed me and then he went. Then the manager that was there started playing the players that were there before me and making me sub quite a lot." He moved to Fourth Division Stockport County after a couple of seasons. After scoring 13 goals in 51 League games, Fletcher moved on to Huddersfield. "I had a decent run there," he says of 99 League matches during which he scored 37 goals. "We won the Fourth Division championship there as well. That was probably the most enjoyable period of my life." Unfortunately, he had to retire at 29. "My back finally went and I had to end up having a disc taken out which finished me career ... I was told that if I didn't give up I'd end up with a limp. I've not been involved in any coaching or managing. I had a young family to bring up. I was ill for five months on the sick, trying to recuperate to walk properly again and just get back normal mobility. A job came up with Stockport council, a security supervisor's position, in 1983 and I've been there ever since. It's a big difference. There's nothing like [football] – it must be one of the best careers anybody could ever have, especially now with the money they're earning." Fletcher, though, has memories that none of today's multi-millionaires will ever be able to boast: "When I first joined, 17, the changing room I went into, sat opposite Law and Best, Paddy Crerand, people like that." He adds, "And it's not done anything to me, not making any money. I've lived a happy life."

**ALAN FOGGON**
**Manchester United games: 0 (3)**
**Manchester United goals: 0**
**Full international caps: 0**
After his three substitute appearances and no starts, Docherty sold Foggon to Sunderland for reputedly £5,000 more than the £25,000 he paid for him (although some accounts

state £2,000 less). Some might suggest The Doc never gave Foggon a proper chance. However, he seems to have left with no hard feelings over a transfer that Docherty had crossed the Atlantic to secure, saying in 2009, "Tommy Docherty was fine, no problem, obviously good at his job and a lovely guy as well." Foggon never seemed to settle after his move, having brief spells at Sunderland, Southend United, Hartlepool United and a couple of American clubs. He was playing non-League football by the time he was 28. He divides his time between overseeing a security company and managing a pub in South Tyneside.

## ALEX FORSYTH
**Manchester United games: 116 (3)**
**Manchester United goals: 5**
**Full international caps: 10**

Alex Forsyth admits that had Docherty not been sacked, he would probably have asked for a transfer from Manchester United: "I'd have liked to have moved on to try and get first-team football again." If he was hoping that a new manager at Old Trafford might lead to his abilities being revaluated, he was in for a disappointment: "When Dave Sexton took over, he brought me in his office and said, 'Look, you're not in my future plans. Do you want to move on?' I said, 'Obviously I want to move on if I'm not in your plans'." Though Forsyth says, "I liked Dave Sexton. He talked to me very nicely. He was a perfect gentleman", he also avers, "Dave Sexton never gave me a chance at all. I don't know if he ever saw me play but I never played under him. [In fact, Forsyth made three starts and one substitute appearance during Sexton's tenure.] He said, 'I'll try and get you another club' and he phoned up Rangers. I went on loan there for a year." Following this loan period with the Scottish club that began in August 1978, Forsyth cannily engineered a proper transfer on a free basis the next season after United stated they wanted a prohibitive £30,000 for him: "I spoke to Dave Sexton and he told me to go to Martin Edwards. I said, 'Look, I've been down there six, seven years and I've never caused them any bother, been a good servant for them, any chance you can give me a free or anything like that?'"

Rangers were probably one of the few British clubs that would not have constituted a step down, ever the stigma attached to leaving Manchester United. "We went into Europe and beat Juventus," reflects Forsyth. "Okay, there wasn't a lot of money then but it wasn't a bad move. But in hindsight, I should maybe have moved ... into the Second Division in England or something like that. The Scottish game is always struggling, it's always 100 mile an hour. Different kettle of fish altogether ... Forest were interested in me. A few American teams were interested in me. Swedish teams."

Forsyth also played for Motherwell and Hamilton Academical (the "Accies"), retiring in 1985. Of his post-retirement career, Forsyth says, "I went back to Partick and coached the youth teams and all that for a couple of year and done alright with them." However, he "never really fancied" management. He runs a pub in his native Scotland.

## GEORGE GRAHAM
**Manchester United games: 44 (2)**
**Manchester United goals: 2**
**Full international caps: 12**

George Graham played 61 League games for Portsmouth and 44 for Crystal Palace before bringing the curtain down on his English football career. Naturally, he had his stint in America, turning out 17 times for California Surf.

Following his retirement, Graham moved first into coaching (he had Gordon Hill under his wing at QPR), then management. He spent three years bossing Millwall before taking the helm at the club with which he would always be far more associated than Manchester United, Arsenal. He was at Highbury from 1986 to 1995 and brought the Gunners great success, obtaining for them two League championships, two League Cups, the FA Cup and the Cup Winners' Cup. He was a surprisingly authoritarian manager considering the playboy image he had possessed as a player and considering the grievances he bore Docherty over his harsh treatment. Those inclined to view his managerial style as the height of hypocrisy were given further ammunition about his character when he was sacked by Arsenal after it emerged he had been given £425,000 by an agent involved in a transfer. He subsequently managed Leeds for a couple of seasons and then Tottenham Hotspur – much to the disgust of many Spurs fans who felt his "boring, boring Arsenal" style (to quote a terrace taunt) was the antithesis to the historical White Hart Lane flair. Though he won Spurs the League Cup, he was sacked in 2001 and has not had a management job since. He works as a pundit.

## BRIAN GREENHOFF
**Manchester United games: 268 (3)**
**Manchester United goals: 17**
**Full international caps: 18**

As with several of his ex-United charges, Docherty later expressed an interest in purchasing Brian Greenhoff when he was a manager of a different club. In this case, The Doc made an overture while boss at QPR. "He offered me far bigger wages than I was on at United and he offered me a nice little signing-on fee, but London just didn't interest me," says Greenhoff. "If I was going to go down there I'd have gone to West Ham. We went down and had a look, thinking, 'I just can't do it.' Wasn't for me. I'm a Northern lad and didn't want to move. Probably one of the reasons I went to Leeds is I'd no need to move out."

Brian Greenhoff's record-breaking (for the Reds) £350,000 transfer to Elland Road in August 1979 was deemed by some to be an ironic response to the way he had found himself marginalized at Old Trafford by ex-Elland Road man Gordon McQueen, though this theory is undermined by the fact that Sexton wanted him to stay. Greenhoff says of the Leeds move, "I didn't go to play centre-half, I went to play in midfield. I did play centre-half a few times and full-back, which was par for the course for me anyway 'cos I did that at United. It was alright, but it went pear-shaped in the end 'cos Allan Clarke was the manager and after having a really good first season with him, he just changed. It's weird. He left me out the first game when I'd played all pre-season, never told me why, and then said, 'Oh sorry, I was wrong,' put me back in. Then I think I got a bit of an injury and didn't get back in, then he just basically ignored me and that was it basically. It was just a matter of time when I could get out. I got released from me contract because they tried to sell about four, five or six of us at the time because they wanted to reduce the wage bill."

Not that staying at Elland Road would have necessarily made Greenhoff a happy man. Like so many ex-Old Traffords, he had begun to experience a feeling of inexplicable emptiness about his football career. Greenhoff: "People always say that the only way is down after being at United and I've got to say I do believe that. It is true. Once you've been there ... And I was fortunate, I was there for 11 years in all. It was a fantastic club. We were well looked after. The wages could have been better but I can't say a bad word against them."

After the Yorkshire club gave Brian a free transfer in 1982 following his 72 League games for them, the Greenhoff double-act was resuscitated when he joined his big brother at Rochdale. The elder Greenhoff became the Fourth Division club's player-manager, with his sibling one of his playing staff. Brian: "I got him the job 'cos I knew some of the board and they were getting rid of the manager so I just had a word with them ... I was basically just a player but I was the gofer. I used to go all games watching teams, doing this, doing that, and he used to go home. To be fair, our kid wasn't very good as a manager ... Looking back, when I got him the job, I should have took it, 'cos I could have dealt with the board far better than him. It's a small football club. We were literally ringing up every morning finding a place we had to train. And having to take money with us to pay for us to train ... We were without a contract, just worked for expenses ... It's not easy. And living where he lives, having to travel up every day ... He'd stop with me three or four nights a week. One time he even slept on the floor in his office. He couldn't handle it. He'd have been better as a coach somewhere ... I knew the board, I told him what they were like, but he couldn't handle them. He was always going to fall out with them and that's what happened." Though Brian was prepared to stay on at the club when his brother was dismissed after 16 games in charge, ("I played in Finland for a few months to get fitter, came back") he, too, walked out after an altercation over pay. The fact that Brian had turned down an alternative offer to play in Hong Kong ensured the experience left an ever more bitter taste in the mouth. He says, "We didn't get a contract so really I missed out on good wages in Hong Kong."

Greenhoff never really picked up the thread of his playing career from there: "I got offered a job back in South Africa. I didn't take it. I got offered to play in Malta, which I went twice and didn't play because my registration hadn't come through and the next time the referees went on strike. They only played every fortnight so I was three weeks without wages so I said, 'I can't be doing with this.' Then I tried to get a job in football. Nothing happened, so you've got to realise there's other things to do. Had a pub for about 12 months or more. We came out of that 'cos we'd got three young kids and were finding it difficult. Then I just did bits and bobs here and there and finished up about 11 years, 12 years with a sports wholesale company in Manchester." Brian subsequently lived in Spain for five-and-a-half years, ticking over on part-time jobs. Changing exchange rates meant he could no longer take advantage of the strength of the pound against the euro and he moved back to England at the end of 2009.

Sadly the two Greenhoff brothers who were once so close are now estranged. Brian says of Jimmy, "I haven't seen him for 17 years, something like that [i.e. since approximately 1992]. Not my problem, it's his problem. He made a decision that he didn't want us to be part of his life so we just respected that. Only he can tell you why he decided to do it 'cos he hasn't told us."

Those images of a tearful Greenhoff being consoled by Docherty after the 1976 Cup Final perfectly encapsulate the special relationship that the player had with The Doc. Greenhoff was one of those young men who felt that in Docherty they had something far closer to a mentor, even a father figure, than a football manager. Of Docherty as a manager, Brian Greenhoff says, "The best one I've played under because he was the best with me. He was fantastic with me, he was nothing but help. I'm one of the ones I'd never slag Tommy Docherty off but you'll get one or two more who don't like him. You speak to Willie Morgan, he'll ... tell you something that's not true to me 'cos I didn't think Tommy Docherty did anything wrong with Willie Morgan." As with so many of the players who look back with fondness on their spell serving under Docherty – ones who were almost invariably the younger players at the time – Greenhoff exhibits an almost pitiful refusal to see the bad side of The Doc in the face of not just direct, daily interaction but reams of subsequent written documentation. Asked about Docherty's apparent callousness in dispensing with players, he proffers a metaphorical shrug as he says, "I think every manager has got to be ruthless. If you don't want them you've got to get rid of them. The Denis [Law] one probably could have been handled a bit better ... "

## JIMMY GREENHOFF
**Manchester United games: 119 (4)**
**Manchester United goals: 36**
**Full international caps: 0**

The man who was already a veteran when Docherty took him to Manchester eventually racked up more than a century of United appearances. Not only that, but at the end of the 1978/79 season, he won the Manchester United Supporters Club Player of the Year award at the grand old age of 33. Even after Sexton gave him a free to Crewe Alexandra in December 1980, he still had quite a bit more football in him, albeit not at that Fourth Division club, where he made 11 League appearances: as well as racking up 81 appearances for Canadian side Toronto Blizzard, he played 48 League games for Port Vale and 16 for Rochdale. His brief stint as the latter club's player-manager was his only foray into management.

Life has not gone too well for Greenhoff Major in recent years. Not only has he fallen out with his brother, but in 2008 he told the *Daily Mail* that he had "lost everything" 12 years previously in a failed insurance venture: "My business, my house and almost my health. I worked in a warehouse for a while and the taunts were pretty bad. I hated it. It was rubbish, brutal." At the time of the *Mail* interview, he was working nights at a pharmaceutical company in Stoke. However, he refused to sell his FA Cup winner's medal and took solace from his wife, grandson and his memories, as well as corporate hospitality work at Old Trafford.

## CLIVE GRIFFITHS
**Manchester United games: 7 (0)**
**Manchester United goals: 0**
**Full international caps: 0**

Born in Pontypridd on January 22 1955, Clive Griffiths was a teenage central defender whom Docherty inherited at Old Trafford. He gave him a try, and furthermore one involving several starts – rather than substitutions – in a short space of time. Though he dropped him after the seven matches he granted him in the space of eight weeks, it wasn't until April 1976 that he offloaded him. Griffiths was loaned out to Plymouth in 1974/75. There seems to be some confusion as to the club to which he was subsequently given a free transfer, with most sources stating he was signed by Bill Foulkes's Chicago Sting in April 1976, even though he played for Tranmere Rovers in 1975/76. As well as Chicago Sting, Griffiths turned out for the Tulsa Roughnecks and appears to have settled Stateside, at one point holding down a directorship of the company International Soccer Camps.

## TONY GRIMSHAW
**Manchester United games: 0 (2)**
**Manchester United goals: 0**
**Full international caps: 0**

Born on December 8 1957, local lad and midfielder Grimshaw got a couple of substitute appearances in the Reds' first season back in Division One after relegation and was then never seen in the Football League again. A broken leg ended his football career. He tried to get back into the game with a loan spell in 1978/79 with Northern Ireland side Ballymena United but by 1979 had retired, though did play a few times for non-League Mossley.

## GORDON HILL
**Manchester United games: 133 (1)**
**Manchester United goals: 51**
**Full international caps: 6**

Though he would give good service to clubs both here and abroad for another decade, Gordon Hill's 'real' career – the one in which he was unhampered by physical conditions that prevented him playing at the peak of his abilities – ended on Wednesday August 30 1978. In a second-round League Cup tie for Derby against Leicester City, Hill had just scored what would turn out to be the only goal of the match when an awkward fall shattered his knee ligaments. "It was bad," he recalls. "It was career threatening. The surgeons said I may never play the game again. And that ain't easy to a 22, 23-year-old that's top of the tree." It was 18 months before he kicked a ball again in a competitive match. When he came back, he still had great skill, naturally, but something was gone. "It was pace," says Hill. "You know me, [what] I was renowned for ... give me a split, give me six inches and I was gone, the ball was in the back of the net." He also says his paucity of caps is down to this injury: "I lost my England place at Derby because of my knee. I'd just come off a European tour with Bobby Robson and [was] leading goal scorer and I was getting ready for the Nations Championship against Poland, so you could imagine how that was."

Hill left Derby in 1979. "I went to London because I was going through a divorce, so I went there for personal reasons and it happened to be QPR, which suited me down to the ground really." Not least because Docherty was currently the boss at Loftus Road. It seems a measure of the personal affection that Docherty had always had for Hill and the indulgence he had so often shown him that far from disdaining Hill for being a shadow of the player he once was – as he had done with so many of his charges who'd had bad injuries – Docherty redeployed Merlin so as to accommodate his restricted movement. "I started to settle down as a constructive midfielder," says Hill. "I could play a ball anywhere. You have to adjust. I started to do the bits and pieces in the defence and be the outlet, but I'd still get up and score. When I came to QPR there was Ian Gillard, Shanksie, Stan Bowles, quality players, and it was fantastic." Mention of the name of Stanley Bowles in conjunction with that of Gordon Hill will make many immediately observe that Rangers had 100% more of their fair quotient of nutters at this point. "But those two nutters could play," points out Hill. Terry Venables, Docherty's successor, did not seem to think so. "He came in and he just said he was going to bring in the younger players to re-create QPR," Hill recalls. "He said if there's a club out there, fine I'll help you. He said [it to] Tony Currie and Ian Gillard [too]. I was only about 28."

Hill moved to Canadian club Montreal Manic, who played in the NASL. "We played against all the teams, the Napolis and all that, in the Transatlantic cups, and Marseille put a bid in for me. We'd beaten them 2-0. I scored both goals and ripped them to pieces. I'd come back to what I wanted, but it's like the same old story: out of sight with England, out of mind." Hill recalls the Sammy McIlroy testimonial between the Doc's United and Atkinson's team as the occasion that led to Hill almost rejoining the Reds: "I remember The Doc turning round to Ron Atkinson and he said, 'That's who you should get back now, Hilly'."

Hill also played for American clubs New York Arrows, Kansas Comets, Tacoma Stars and Finland's HJK Helsinki. "Then I came back," he says. "I was about 33, 34 and I was living in Derby and I was looking for a club to finish me game over there. I said, 'Right, I've had a good career, I've been happy, I've reached the heights that I wanted. It was unfortunate I got an injury, but I've done whatever I can do.' So then I got a phone call from FC Twente in Holland. They said, 'Can we have a look?' So I went over and I had [a] one-week [trial] and two days afterwards they said to me, 'Listen, we'd like to sign you.' So I went over and played against Ajax and teams like that. Languages don't really mean much in football because your sign language is just as good and you pick up the little bits and pieces and the manager knows what you can do. I only wanted a season there. At the end of the season we played Ajax at their new stadium and we drew 1-1 and I had an absolute stormer, and Franz [Tyson] and Arnold [Muhren] said to me, 'Hey Gordon, are you coming back next year? You could play in this League for about three or four years.' I went, 'Yeah, but I'd like to finish on my own turf' and that was it and I came back." He rounded out his career at a non-League side with an old colleague: "I'd finished, I didn't want to know, I was about 36, and Stewie Pearson asked me to go to Northwich [Victoria] with him part-time, and I went, 'Yeah, that will be a bit of fun'."

Hill has ended up in Texas, a journey he relates with the sort of mangled syntax and stream-of-consciousness that so many of his fellow Doc's Devils found simultaneously amusing and infuriating: "I'd been back home in Manchester for close on eight years. I was a manager and director of football at Chester and there was no money so it was like kicking a dead horse. And then I took all my licences, all my badges and I went. I was working at Man U and doing TV for a lot of years, Sky, BBC, TV pundit, radio, match analysis, usual stuff, and then I was doing Manchester United hospitality because they got their new suites and everything. Yet someone said to me, 'Gordon, we're looking for some top-class coaches, would you be interested?' And I happened to have my green card, which allows me to live and work here. When we came out here, the weather was conducive to what we want. The youth leagues here. I got my own little club here." The name of his youth club rings a bell. "United FC was just a name I conjured, just popped out of the air, said, 'United FC – that'll do me.' We happen to play with the red and white and we happen to have a badge that looks like it."

Some of Hill's ex-colleagues might be shocked at the idea of him having the maturity to be a manager. "I studied very hard," says Hill. "I took my licences in Canada and now I've got in the pipeline a facility here that we're looking at putting up that will be about four to six millions dollars' worth. It will be a centre of excellence."

## JIM HOLTON
**Manchester United games: 69 (5)**
**Manchester United goals: 5**
**Full international caps: 15**
Following his transfer from United, Big Jim would only stay with Sunderland a year, moving on to Coventry in early 1977. There, he finally got into his groove again, playing with the Sky Blues for four years. However, injuries continued to dog him and he didn't even play a game for his last club, Sheffield Wednesday, before retiring at 30. Post-football, Holton ran a pub in Coventry but his life ended early, too, shockingly so: in October 1993, at the age of just 42, he died from a heart attack, leaving behind a wife and two children.

## STEWART HOUSTON
**Manchester United games: 248 (2)**
**Manchester United goals: 16**
**Full international caps: 1**
After missing his chance to obtain an FA Cup winner's medal in 1977, Stewart Houston's career never really recovered at United. When he regained fitness, the Docherty era of the

club was well and truly over and in Sexton's United he and Albiston were often vying for the same place in the team (although they did sometimes play alongside each other). "Dave was decent with me because he took me on a tour," Houston recalls. "They went away in the summer of that year and I wasn't anywhere near fit and he still took me on the tour. It was well into the autumn before I started making any progress." Houston points out, "Dave had seen me as a fit person as a young boy at 18, had the confidence to put me into the team at the time with Chelsea, and then seen me get an injury and go downhill. And the story actually repeats itself. So maybe he made an assumption somewhere along the line." However, he does admit, "I don't think anybody ever gets back to where they were before. We could all say 'Yes' quite easily, but I don't actually think physically and mentally they do. It's just a scar that you take on board. You don't actually really recover 100% from any big injury like that.

"My contract expired in 1980. Dave was still the manager and I was told at Christmas that they weren't going to renew the contract at the end of the season." Houston's move – on a free – was to Sheffield United. As he was still only 30, it wasn't too surprising then that he proceeded to rack up nearly a century of appearances for both Sheffield United and then Colchester United. Houston: "I had a decision to make – was I going to drop down? Which I did. I had three years of a wee bit of up and down at Sheffield and I continued on until I was nearly 36. I went to Colchester. The Colchester one took me on to the next step for the coaching. If somebody said to me at 17, 'You'll play till you're 36', I would have probably laughed. I know it's not at the highest level but I still enjoyed my time at Sheffield and I thoroughly enjoyed my time at Colchester."

Though Houston did not get to know George Graham well when their paths briefly crossed at Old Trafford, the two would become synonymous when Graham decided to employ him as his assistant manager at Arsenal. He and Graham were considered very much a team by the Gunners' fans during the very successful period in which they guided the club's fortunes. (Graham also later appointed him as his number two at Tottenham.) However, it has to be said that any assumption that Houston was capable of replicating that success on his own was disproven when he was appointed caretaker manager at Highbury following Graham's dismissal, and then again when subsequent manager Bruce Rioch was sacked. Houston: "In all walks of life, I think you find that the step from number two to number one's a small one on paper, but it's a huge one in terms of what you have to do." Houston also had stints as manager at QPR and coach at Walsall. He works as a scout for Arsenal.

Asked how he looks back at his two stints serving under Tommy Docherty, Houston says, "He gave me my start, which I have to be very grateful for and thankful for. He still showed confidence [in me] years later. I could see certain things and qualities in the man that I thoroughly like. There was nothing really bad about [him]. I just found some of his decisions at times a little bit strange. The biggest thing you can have as a coach or a manager is enthusiasm, and Tommy had loads of it."

## TOMMY JACKSON
**Manchester United games: 22 (1)**
**Manchester United goals: 0**
**Full international caps: 35**
The prosaic midfielder signed in the close season before the return to the top flight made the odd appearance in the final two years of Docherty's tenure. If this indicated a lack of enthusiasm by The Doc for Jackson, then Sexton was clearly completely uninterested, offloading Jackson to League of Ireland side Waterford in June 1978 on a free without having given him a game. Jackson was player-manager at Waterford, and has since been manager at several Irish sides, both north and south of the border.

## STEVE JAMES
**Manchester United games: 160 (1)**
**Manchester United goals: 4**
**Full international caps: 0**
Steve James' departure in January 1976 saw him drop down a division to sign for York City, for whom he turned out more than 100 times and would surely have racked up considerably more games for had not injury seen him sitting out the whole of the 1978/79 season. He subsequently played for non-League Kidderminster Harriers and Tipton Town.

## JIMMY KELLY
**Manchester United games: 0 (1)**
**Manchester United goals: 0**
**Full international caps: 0**
There would seem to be something of a conveyor belt for The Doc's rejects running from Old Trafford to Chicago Sting. Bill Foulkes picked up 19-year-old Kelly in April 1977 – initially on loan, then on a free – after the midfielder failed to get another game following his substitute appearance against Wolves at Christmas 1975. Kelly subsequently played for Los Angeles Aztecs, Tulsa Roughnecks and Toronto Blizzard. Since 1987, he has been men's soccer coach at College of DuPage, Illinois.

## BRIAN KIDD
**Manchester United games: 257 (9)**
**Manchester United goals: 70**
**Full international caps: 2**

As well as Arsenal, Manchester City, Everton and Bolton Wanderers, 'Kiddo' turned out for American clubs Atlantic Chiefs, Fort Lauderdale Strikers and Minnesota Kicks. On his retirement, Kidd served as Lou Macari's assistant at Swindon Town and then had management stints at Barrow and Preston North End. For those with a sense of poetry about footballing appointments, Kidd's engagement as Manchester United youth-team coach by Alex Ferguson in 1988 seemed wonderfully appropriate. The ascension of this Old Trafford legend to Ferguson's assistant three years later was even more appropriate, as was the fact that his arrival coincided with the return of United's title-winning abilities. He stayed in that post until 1998. Some understandably inferred that it was Kidd's influence that had brought the glory back to Old Trafford, one of those people apparently being Jack Walker, owner of Blackburn Rovers. Kidd departed to the latter club to see whether his assistant skills would translate well to a full management role at a top flight club. As with Stewart Houston's stint as full-blown Arsenal boss, it transpired they didn't: he failed to stop Blackburn being relegated to Division Two and was sacked when they were in danger of relegation to the Third Division. Kidd subsequently returned to assistant work for Leeds and Sven-Goran Eriksson's England. Prostate cancer necessitated he quit the latter post, but he subsequently worked as assistant manager for Sheffield United and Portsmouth. He is now a youth coach at Manchester City.

## DENIS LAW
**Manchester United games: 398 (6)**
**Manchester United goals: 237**
**Full international caps: 55**

Manchester City manager Tony Book was somewhat unsympathetic about the dilemma Law faced in his last club match. "I wasn't too fussed with United's relegation but Denis was distraught afterwards," he later wrote. "As far as I was concerned, Denis was a City player – we paid his wages and he had scored a great goal and that was the end of it." He also didn't feel able to find a place for Law in City's first team in the 1974/75 season, causing Law to conclude that it was time to announce his retirement, which he did on August 5 1974.

Law has admitted that it took him a long time to adjust to 'real life', not so much due to the loss of football, more because of the absence of the camaraderie of the dressing room. Surprisingly, though, this player who is considered by many the greatest ever to pull on a red shirt – he seems to outrank Best and Charlton in the eyes of long-term United followers – never passed on what he had learnt in the game by going into management. He admits he was too proud to train for a coaching badge, although his verdict of himself as "obstinate" seems harsh considering the absurdity of the notion of people who had none of his achievements in the game presuming to try to teach him about football. Instead he worked first as a carpet salesman, then in a similar salesman's job for ex-footballer Francis Lee's paper business. However, one of the all-time greats was inevitably going to be in-demand as a media pundit and he was able to build up commentary work on radio and television. From 1995 to 2006, that work sometimes saw him noting the quality of the performances of Arsenal's Dennis Bergkamp, which sublimely gifted striker was named after him (although Dutch authorities refused to let Bergkamp's parents spell his Christian name with one 'n' because it would look too similar to Denise). Law's lack of any Royal honour when much lesser players are thrown MBEs is mystifying.

**TED MacDOUGALL**
**Manchester United games: 18**
**Manchester United goals: 5**
**Full international caps: 7**
Ted MacDougall achieved prolific scoring rates at West Ham, Norwich, Southampton and in his second stint at Bournemouth. Some might claim that this proved Docherty's disdain for him irrational. However the caveat should be added that at four of his clubs (including York City and Bournemouth, pre-United), MacDougall was working in collaboration with fellow striker Phil Boyer, a long-standing, club-jumping partnership with a colleague attuned to his play that few footballers have enjoyed the privilege of. However, he banged them in consistently without Boyer's assistance as well, not least his three goals in his seven matches for Scotland. These matches for his country all took place in 1975 and his paucity of caps is a source of grievance to many Caledonians. Only in his short stint as player-coach for Blackpool at the end of his career did MacDougall fail to score consistently – indeed, at all. Subsequently, he played non-League football for Salisbury, Poole Town and Gosport Borough. He is now a youth team coach for the Atlanta Silverbacks in Georgia, USA.

Docherty would seem to have ultimately changed his mind about the player whom he admitted he had received more (presumably protesting) letters about than any of his other discards. MacDougall recalls that The Doc tried to sign him when he was managing South Melbourne a decade after they had worked together in Manchester. MacDougall: "I couldn't play for him because he thought he only had four overseas players and it turned out he had an extra one or something in the reserves that he didn't know about and he couldn't sign me in the end. But I was going to sign for him." He also says of their unhappy time together at Old Trafford, "I've met Tommy many times since then. Fine. I don't have a problem with him."

## JIM McCALLIOG
**Manchester United games:** 37 (1)
**Manchester United goals:** 7
**Full international caps:** 5

Following his settling of scores with Docherty by setting up Southampton's goal in the 1976 Cup Final, things did not go well for McCalliog and he departed the club the following season for – that club again – Chicago Sting. McCalliog: "Me and Willie [Morgan] went to Chicago Sting. I think the guy that was the owner at Chicago was very respectful of United's position in world football." McCalliog wasn't so respectful of Chicago Sting: "For me, it just wasn't what I wanted. It just wasn't the standard I wanted. Although the owner wanted me to go back, I wouldn't go back." He also played abroad for Norway's Lyn Oslo. He returned to English football with Lincoln City. He says, "All my clubs, from Chelsea, Wednesday, Wolves, Man U and Southampton, I thoroughly enjoyed all of it and at each place I've had quite a bit of success without winning a champions [medal]."

McCalliog recalls of The Doc, "He wanted me to go to Derby as a squad player. There was a guy there, right-back, he was the youth coach and I was going to share youth-coach duties with him. Probably about '79, '80 ... I didn't really want to share the youth-team duties, I thought that was encroaching a bit on somebody else so I didn't really want to be in that kind of situation."

McCalliog had a brief spell managing non-League Runcorn before embarking on a career as a publican, interrupted only by a stint as Halifax Town manager in 1990/91.

## DAVID McCREERY
**Manchester United games:** 57 (52)
**Manchester United goals:** 8
**Full international caps:** 67

Though he describes Sexton as a "lovely man", McCreery admits that his equanimity about being the perennial number 12 began to fray under The Doc's successor: "Dave offered me a contract and it was a case of I was in, I was out, I was in, I was out." 'Roadrunner' was sold to QPR – then managed by The Doc – in August 1979 after Docherty offered him a regular place in the starting line-up. McCreery tended to play in midfield at Loftus Road.

The almost obligatory NASL club on his CV is Tulsa Roughnecks, with whom he played in 1981 and 1982 after departing Terry Venables's QPR regime because the new manager had edged him aside in favour of imports from his old club Crystal Palace. McCreery: "After I played in the '82 World Cup, I was asked to sign for Real Sociedad because the Northern Ireland team did well, beating Spain and getting to the quarter-finals. I didn't sign and went back to the States. Newcastle phoned me up, Arthur Cox, and said, 'Do you want to come back home?' and I've been here ever since." At Newcastle United, he played alongside Kevin Keegan as the Tynesiders stormed their way back into the top flight.

Though he might be remembered as an integral part of The Doc's Devils, McCreery actually played most of his football at St. James's Park, clocking up 243 League appearances for Newcastle before moving north of the border to Heart of Midlothian in 1989. After a season with them, he played a season for Carlisle United. He then had short stints as player-manager of Carlisle (where he got the club to the Division Three play-offs) and Division Three's Hartlepool United. McCreery also played in the 1986 World Cup.

He bridged a move into business by acting as consultant for the newly formed Major League Soccer in the States and as European Consultant for Boca Juniors of Argentina. He is now a successful businessman. "I've got a welding company and a tooling company," he says.

## CHRIS McGRATH
**Manchester United games: 15 (19)**
**Manchester United goals: 1**
**Full international caps: 21**

McGrath made two starts and three substitute appearances in his partial season under Docherty, an inverted ratio that the statistics attest was sustained under Sexton. However, he couldn't really be categorised as a super-sub, scoring a solitary goal in his time at Old Trafford as well as demonstrating to most that his dribbling skills were often deployed to no purpose, something that put the misgivings about Gordon Hill in context. McGrath took the familiar rescue raft to the NASL, signing for Tulsa Roughnecks in February 1981 for £30,000. He did reasonably well for them, his 44 games involving no substitute appearances as well as the scoring of three goals. (He also scored four goals in his 21 Northern Ireland appearances.) However, the decline of the NASL necessitated another life raft destination. The one McGrath took was less familiar, but not unknown: Hong Kong soccer. He subsequently worked for GlaxoSmithKline.

**SAMMY McILROY**
**Manchester United games: 391 (28)**
**Manchester United goals: 71**
**Full international caps: 88**

"Very, very difficult to leave," says Super Sam of his departure from Old Trafford for Stoke City in February 1982 for £350,000 when he was 27. "It was a hasty decision to leave and I regret that, but it happens. After 13 years, it's part and parcel of you. It's in the blood." Despite his 13 years at Old Trafford under six different managers (including Busby and McGuinness, under whom he didn't get a game), McIlroy missed out, as did so many United players of his generation, on the League championship. "Second was the best I've done, runners-up to Liverpool," he laments. "I would have loved to have won a championship. Obviously the Second Division don't really count. To appear at three Wembley finals was good, but then only win one and lose two ... That's the only regret really – not winning a League championship."

After his 133 League games for Stoke, McIlroy had stints at Manchester City, Swedish club Orgryte, Bury, FC Moedling of Austria and Preston North End. He was player-coach at the latter club. Though he has yet to helm a top flight side, he has done well as a manager. After stints at non-League Northwich Victoria and Ashton United, he was boss at Macclesfield Town from 1993 to 2000, whom he transformed from non-Leaguers into Football League members. In 2000, he became manager of his national team, with whom, like McCreery, he had played in the 1982 and 1986 World Cup finals. Though he made a good start in his first year, form collapsed and the side failed to score any goals in 13 consecutive matches. He has subsequently managed at Stockport County and Morecambe. As with Macclesfield, he has gained the latter club entry to the Football League.

**LOU MACARI**
**Manchester United games: 374 (27)**
**Manchester United goals: 97**
**Full international caps: 24**

In the summer of 1984 – after a tremendous Old Trafford career and after having survived the regimes of both Sexton and (mostly) Atkinson – Lou Macari left United on a free transfer to become player-manager at Swindon Town. He transpired to be another rebellious footballer who turned into a surprisingly authoritarian boss. He took that club from the Fourth Division to the Second Division play-offs. Unsurprisingly, a club of greater stature – West Ham – came in for him, but though he took them to the League Cup semi-final he lasted only a season at Upton Park before resigning over a non-football issue. He was at Division Three's Birmingham City for an even shorter period, quitting after a row with the chairman, albeit not before obtaining them the Leyland DAF Trophy. He had two spells at Stoke City, which sandwiched an unhappy period managing his old club Celtic where he felt he was undermined (though he lost a legal case he brought against the club over his treatment). He did well at the Potteries, taking them up from the third tier (by now called Division Two) as champions and winning the Autoglass Trophy. He took over relegation-threatened Division One/second tier side Huddersfield Town in 2000, and although he wouldn't stop them going down was doing reasonably well in reviving their fortunes when his contract was not renewed.

Since then he has concentrated on punditry. He also owns (although does not run) Lou Macari's Chip Shop near the Old Trafford ground, having bought it in 1978. In 1999, Macari suffered the tragedy of one of his grown sons, Jonathan, committing suicide.

## MICK MARTIN
**Manchester United games: 36 (7)**
**Manchester United goals: 2**
**Full international caps: 52**
Following three seasons playing for West Brom, Martin was at Newcastle United for four years, played nearly 100 games for Vancouver Whitecaps, and had short spells at Cardiff City, Peterborough United, Rotherham United and Preston North End. (He could have gone to the latter club much sooner: Bobby Charlton unsuccessfully tried to sign him immediately upon becoming their manager.) Most reference books state Martin received 51 full international caps, but he insists it was 52. Says Martin, "I may not have been the greatest player ever, but to get 52 caps and to play over four, five-hundred games in your career, it takes a bit of doing ... I thoroughly enjoyed it, being part of Manchester United. It wasn't the biggest part or most successful part of the club's history, but to me I'd done what a lot of people would have liked to have done. I was good enough to do it and wished I [had] made a greater impression at Old Trafford, but football is not all that simple."

Of Docherty, Martin says, "If you were playing well and in good form and doing all the right things, you were flavour of the day. If you weren't playing so well and the team wasn't playing so well and you were losing games, you weren't spoken to or you were nodded to. But I will be ever grateful to Tommy Docherty for giving me the chance to come and play in England. We had our disagreements occasionally in the two-and-a-half years I was there and I felt that had I been a player who had came from an established club to Manchester United, I would have been able to handle myself better. But the fact that I was at Manchester United amongst all these stars, I thought to myself, 'Well, why should I be knocking on the door saying I should be in the team instead of him?' If I'd have come from, say, a Wolverhampton Wanderers or a

Notts Forest, I would have understood what it was about and stood up for myself a bit more. I just accepted things.

"At Newcastle, I was joint manager for a period of time while they were appointing a manager and I was a coach at Glasgow Celtic and Newcastle as well. ... I see Tom maybe two or three times a year when he's doing after-dinner speaking and we're the best of friends and I have nothing against Tommy other than that story which was the one that sealed my fate at Old Trafford. It's a long time ago now and I've met Tom on a variety occasions since then."

Martin is now a businessman. "I have a company I run myself," he says. "It's called Mick Martin Promotions and I supply companies nationally and locally with uniforms and corporate gifts and stuff that you give away, mugs and pens and key rings and all that stuff. Surviving. I'm still alive. That keeps me ticking over."

## WILLIE MORGAN
**Manchester United games: 293 (3)**
**Manchester United goals: 34**
**Full international caps: 21**
Post-Manchester United, Willie Morgan did pretty well for a supposedly one-eyed player. Following his brief, unhappy second stint with Burnley, he played 155 League matches for Bolton Wanderers before moving to Blackpool, taking in some North American clubs on the way, starting with – of course – Chicago Sting. Blackpool wanted him to renew his contract at the end of the 1981/82 season – hardly surprising, as his tally of four goals in 42 League games for them showed no slackening of his average – but he declined. Some mock Morgan for the way he has maintained his 70s feather-cut long past the point where it is remotely fashionable or seemly, but there is a brain beneath that antediluvian (and now grey) thatch. Upon his 1982 retirement, he retreated to the substantial house in Altrincham in which he had invested during his United days to embark on a post-football career involving punditry and – less obviously – a chain of launderettes and corporate hospitality.

## JIMMY NICHOLL
**Manchester United games: 235 (13)**
**Manchester United goals: 6**
**Full international caps: 73**
Asked if it might have been a bad thing to have become an FA Cup winner so young, Jimmy

Nicholl replies, "No, not at all. I'd hate the opposite – to lose and wait and wait. If you're at a club like Man United, you've a decent chance of achieving things and winning things but you just don't know how long you're going to be there. At that time, Liverpool and Notts Forest and Villa and all these boys [were] winning the League. It was hard to win the League. As much as it would have been great to do it, I never did. But two Cup Finals … It's when you get beat by Arsenal that you appreciate having won against Liverpool. Thank God for that – at least you've come away with something."

Nicholl's "decent chance of achieving things" disappeared when Dave Sexton was replaced by a man who had apparently even less confidence in him. Nicholl: "It didn't matter how many games I'd played under Tommy Docherty, Ron Atkinson turns round and says, 'Listen, I don't rate you, I'm bringing in John Gidman.' Right, fair enough. At least he was upfront and honest about it. You've got to take it on the chin and you just move on. I went to America. That was in the summer of '81. I went on loan to Sunderland for two or three months but I came back in March. I left in March '82." Of his new club Toronto Buzzard, to whom he was sold for £235,000, he says, "I didn't think for one moment I was going to end up there but at that time Northern Ireland were going to the World Cup in Spain '82 and I wasn't even playing for Man United reserves." Some English clubs had shown interest but United's high transfer-fee demands scuppered any domestic moves. Nicholl: "I had a three-year contract in America and in order to keep playing for Northern Ireland I would play in America six months in summer, six months in Britain in the winter. I played all year round."

After alternating between Canada and Sunderland, Nicholl went on to play for Glasgow Rangers (two spells), West Brom, Dunfermline Athletic and Raith Rovers. Does he agree with the proposition that any club after Manchester United is a downward move? "I think so. After that, the only time when you do get the feeling, the importance of being a big club, was when I was at Rangers, because you're expected to win every single game. When you're not at the big clubs, you don't have the same intensity." Nonetheless, he had a long career: "I played my last game when I was 39 for Raith Rovers. We'd already beaten Celtic in the Cup and our last game was in May at Partick Thistle's ground because we were ground-sharing. We played Hamilton and we got a point to win the League. We were going back up in the Premier League and I thought, 'That's it, that'll do me lovely. I've been hanging around too long now'."

Though he wasn't blind to The Doc's faults, Nicholl's memories of playing under Tommy Docherty were happy ones and he used them to help him in his management career. Nicholl: "I was player-manager at Raith Rovers, November '90 and we went full-time in the summer of '91. I said to them, 'I'm going to give you the most enjoyable time of my career, [which] was at Man

United with Tommy Doc. We had a certain way of working and a certain style of football and I'm going to give you the most enjoyable days that I had, providing you go about the job properly.' And as much as I enjoyed the years with Tommy Doc, some of my happiest years were with Raith Rovers because there was the same feeling. We were known as a team of young players and I was just copying the times that I enjoyed and the outlook and how you want your players to go out and enjoy and express themselves but still have that determination to win a game of football … What made an impression on me was Docherty's man-management with young players."

After a superb six-year stint with Raith Rovers in which the club won the Scottish League Cup and promotion to the Scottish Premier League as First Division champions, Nicholl was appointed manager of Millwall. He was less successful there, failing to prevent the club's relegation to Division Two. Following his dismissal, there was a bizarre interlude in his career in which he went to play for Bath City in 1997. Sent off during his first match, he never played for the club again. He returned to Raith Rovers that year but his two-year spell there was less successful than his first. Nicholl was caretaker manager of Dunfermline Athletic in November 1999 after having previously been assistant manager. In 2004, he and Dunfermline's new manager Jimmy Calderwood decamped to Aberdeen. In May 2009, after five years, Calderwood and the management team of which Nicholl was part left Aberdeen by "mutual consent" despite taking them into Europe. He was subsequently Calderwood's assistant at Kilmarnock before taking up the post of manager of Cowdenbeath.

## RAY O'BRIEN
**Manchester United games: 0**
**Manchester United goals: 0**
**Full international caps: 4**

O'Brien never got a game under The Doc after he brought him over from the League of Ireland in his first season at Old Trafford. Following his £40,000–£45,000 transfer to Notts County in December 1973, O'Brien made over 300 first-team appearances in his 10 years there and in the 1979/80 season managed the remarkable feat for a full-back of being the club's top scorer. He subsequently had short spells at Derby and non-League Boston United. He became assistant manager, then manager of that latter club. He subsequently managed other non-League clubs Corby Town and Arnold Town.

## TOMMY O'NEIL
**Manchester United games: 20 (0)**
**Manchester United goals: 0**
**Full international caps: 0**

Born in St. Helens on October 25 1952, full-back O'Neil was picked by Docherty for his first two games in charge, having been a regular under Frank O'Farrell. However, after that he was never seen in a red shirt again. A short loan to Blackpool in 1973 was followed by a free transfer to Third Division Southport, for whom he played just shy of 200 League games. He subsequently turned out for Tranmere Rovers and Halifax Town. Following the end of his League career, O'Neil continued in non-League football and as late as 1987 when fully halfway through his three-score-and-ten he was captain of the St Helens Town team that secured the FA Vase at Wembley. Post-retirement, O'Neil became a coach, a job that brought him back to Old Trafford, where he worked with the under-16s academy players. He died in 2006 from cancer, aged 53.

## STEVE PATERSON
**Manchester United games: 5 (5)**
**Manchester United goals: 0**
**Full international caps: 0**

The man reputedly nicknamed 'Pele' as a youngster for his precocious skills, who was earmarked to replace Jim Holton and whose United debut – aged 19 – was against no less a side than Ajax, turned out to have a non-starter of a career at Old Trafford. One is tempted to mischievously posit the reason as the fact that, post-Jim Holton, players of over six foot had no place in Docherty's United sides. In fact, an ankle injury, the departure of Docherty and the arrival of McQueen were what hindered the chances of the centre-half born in Elgin, Morayshire, on April 8 1958. He did try to revive his career elsewhere, but it was at clubs that were hardly household names like Hong Kong Rangers and Yomiuri of Japan. By the summer of 1980 (the year he failed a Sheffield Wednesday medical), his injury problems forced him into retirement. This utterly unprepossessing playing career, however, transpired to be a springboard to a highly successful career in management. Inverness Caledonian Thistle were at the time he took them over in 1995 not much better known than Hong Kong Rangers, but in his eight years there he transformed them from a Highland League side into a Scottish First Division club. Little wonder that giants Aberdeen swooped for his services in 2003.

In 2008, Paterson went into rehab for his gambling addiction, telling the media that his long-term illness had cost him his marriage and around £1m. (His stint in Japan had earned him a £40,000 pay-off that he blew within 48 hours at a race course.) His lack of success at Aberdeen was probably due to the heavy drinking in which he indulged to blot out the pain of his betting addiction. He was sacked in May 2004. The revelations about his addictions would seem to have hindered his subsequent managerial career, with him only having guided the fortunes of lowly clubs since.

**STUART PEARSON**
**Manchester United games: 179 (1)**
**Manchester United goals: 66**
**Full international caps: 15**

The arrival of Joe Jordan had put a question mark over the future of Stuart Pearson at Old Trafford. Although both he and Jimmy Greenhoff got the chance to partner the Leeds signing upfront, by the 1978/79 season Pearson had been reduced to making just two appearances, although knee problems that saw him endure three operations didn't help. He was transferred to West Ham in August 1979 after exactly five years at the club. (Stepney has said The Doc tried to sign him when he was Derby boss.) That Pearson, still just 30, had life left in him was demonstrated when he picked up an FA Cup winner's medal with the Hammers in 1980, which must have constituted a certain amount of sweet revenge considering Sexton's complete lack of honours at his former club. Pearson also finished as a League Cup runner-up and Second Division champion at Upton Park. "People say that when you leave Manchester United, the only way is down," he later said. "But I like to think I proved them wrong." However, three more knee operations reduced his appearances and eventually saw him retire from 'proper' football in 1982. After getting sick of people whispering about him when he signed on at the dole office, he had a spell owning a building firm. He made his way back into football by coaching at Stockport County in 1985. He served as manager of non-League Northwich Victoria in 1986 and was caretaker manager for West Brom in 1991, after a stint there as assistant manager. He was subsequently assistant manager at Bradford City from 1992 to 1994. He also ran a shop near Manchester that sold imported tiles.

Pearson now seems to be semi-retired, though he does travel over from his home in Spain to work as an Old Trafford match-day host. However, Pearson has disappeared of late from MUTV, United's official television channel on which several former Reds are employed as pundits and presenters. He was involved in controversy in 2002 when following a 3-1 Reds loss to Manchester City, he said on air, "I don't think I've seen a performance as bad as that for a long time – if I've ever seen one that bad before from a Manchester United team," and "Sir Alex is not getting it right in team selection or tactics. He has a lot to answer for." Ferguson was said to be so incensed at this criticism that he refused his usual pre-match interview with the channel at the next game.

## JIMMY RIMMER
**Manchester United games: 45 (1)**
**Manchester United goals: 0**
**Full international caps: 1**

After three years at Arsenal, during which he picked up an England cap, Rimmer moved on to Aston Villa, where he proceeded to have an Indian summer that took in a League championship medal (in stark contrast to the way his former colleagues at United were left barren in that department in this era) and a European Cup winner's medal. Rimmer is a popular football trivia question: "Which English goalkeeper won two European Cup winner's medals despite playing only a total of nine minutes of football?" Rimmer had a medal for being an unused substitute in the 1968 United victory and had to come off injured after nine minutes when Villa took the trophy in 1982. Following 229 League games for Villa, The Cat moved on to Swansea City, becoming their goalkeeping coach after his 1986 retirement, and serving as their caretaker manager in the 1995/96 season. After running a golf centre, he worked as a goalkeeping coach at China side Dalian Shide. He coaches in Canada.

## PADDY ROCHE
**Manchester United games: 53 (0)**
**Manchester United goals: 0**
**Full international caps: 8**

A trick of memory that afflicts many is the notion that after his disastrous spell in goal for United in November 1975 that may or may not have cost them the League championship, Paddy Roche was banished to the United reserves never to be seen again. In fact, he was at Old Trafford for a further seven years. Though he remained understudy to first Stepney and then Gary Bailey, he racked up a healthy half-century-plus of appearances for the Reds, a statistic that indicates that the loss of nerve many detected in him in that aforementioned disastrous month had been well and truly banished to history. Nonetheless, when Roche left United, he would not play top flight football again, moving first to Brentford in August 1982 for £15,000, then after 71 League games to Halifax Town, where he noticed up 198 appearances in the League. He has subsequently worked in coaching.

That for many Roche will only be remembered as a cartoon because of a handful of mistakes he made in a few matches is underlined by a claim in *The Guardian* in 1999 that Roche was, "now the butt of Tommy Docherty's after-dinner speech."

## DAVID SADLER

**Manchester United games: 328 (7)**

**Manchester United goals: 27**

**Full international caps: 4**

David Sadler had a hilariously lugubrious way of congratulating a team-mate on a goal, but he was no fool. Able to play in any outfield place but most comfortable as a centre-half, Sadler was perennially cool, collected and classy. He had a League championship medal, a European Cup winners' medal and a small but respectable collection of England caps to his name when Docherty took over at United. At this point – it is amazing to realise – this veteran who had made his debut at the club in August 1963 was still only 27. He was born in Yalding, Kent, on February 5 1946. The rumour that Martin Buchan heard that his knees were going may or may not have been based in fact but Sadler admits that his time served under The Doc was an "unhappy" period for him. Even so, Docherty didn't unload him for eight months despite fairly quickly dropping him from the first team. Sadler was reduced to two starts and one substitute appearance in the 1973/74 season. It can't only have been sentimentality that saw Bobby Charlton recruit his old colleague for Preston North End for £20,000–£25,000 in November 1973: Sadler would play more than 100 games for the club. Unfortunately, injuries caught up with him in 1977, forcing his retirement.

Sadler was a building-society branch manager in Hale, then worked for the Bobby Charlton Soccer Schools organisation. He now runs David Sadler Promotions, a corporate hospitality company, and contributes a column to the *Manchester Evening News*. He is secretary of the Association of Former Manchester United Players, an organisation which pools the skills and allure of ex-Reds for charity.

## CARLO SARTORI

**Manchester United games: 40 (16)**

**Manchester United goals: 6**

**Full international caps: 0**

United fans with long memories remember with some amusement Carlo Sartori, whose mixed parentage made him that rarest of beasts, a red-headed Italian. Though born in Caderzone near Turin on February 10 1948, he grew up in Collyhurst in Manchester and joined United as a schoolboy in 1963. A winger turned midfielder, despite his half-century of games (including substitute appearances) he never quite became a regular before Docherty inherited him. The Doc sold him to Bologna for £30,000-£45,000 within a month of his arrival without playing him. Sartori also played for Spal, Lecce, Rimini and Trento in the country of his birth. However, Manchester was evidently in his blood, too, and he moved back. He has a knife-sharpening business servicing hotels and restaurants.

## ARNOLD SIDEBOTTOM
**Manchester United games: 20 (0)**
**Manchester United goals: 0**
**Full international caps: 0**

Barnsley native Arnold Sidebottom was born on the same day (April 1 1954) as Gordon Hill, but the complete contrast of his slender footballing abilities with the sumptuous talent of Merlin is possibly the definitive repudiation of astrology. Though he got good notices for his debut in the match in which Bobby Charlton said goodbye to Old Trafford, it soon became apparent that Sidebottom was a mediocre centre-half at best. It's difficult to know, though, whether Sidebottom would consider his time at Old Trafford – or his soccer career *per se* – as a failure. As a successful cricketer, he may not have cared that Docherty gave him 20 starts before offloading him on a free to Huddersfield Town in January 1976, or that following 61 League games for that Fourth Division side and 21 for Halifax Town, his footballing days were over by the age of 25. He may also have been sanguine about his appearance at number five in a *Times Online* article in July 2007 which listed what purported to be the 50 worst players ever to appear in English football's top flight. His ex-schoolmate and cricketing and footballing colleague Brian Greenhoff says, "At the end of the day, he decided he was a better cricketer than footballer. And the lifestyle suited Arnie better. The last thing you want to do is be in cricket for about five months and then go back and play football, because a cricketer at that time had a good social life."

Sidebottom excelled as a fast bowler for Yorkshire and earned an international cap when he was picked for a 1985 Test match. He was already 31 by then and some are of the opinion that had it not been for both his soccer career and his participation in a South African tour that earned him a three-year international ban, he might have been called up far more often. Sidebottom's cricketing career extended right up to 1991. He is now a soccer and cricket coach at a Yorkshire school. His son Ryan has also received international cricketing call-ups.

## ALEX STEPNEY
**Manchester United games: 539 (0)**
**Manchester United goals: 2**
**Full international caps: 1**

With Alex Stepney maintaining his position in United's first team even with the arrival of Sexton, it almost seemed that the man who had held off the career Grim Reaper for so long could defy time indefinitely. However, Stepney lost his place to Roche three months into Sexton's first season, although was reinstated for the last six weeks. The season-ending away match at Wolves was Stepney's final appearance for the Reds. He then opted for a last big pay-day with the NASL's Dallas Tornado. Though he had publicly toyed with the idea of management in his 1978 autobiography after being inspired by his captaincy in reserve matches when he was dropped, he instead returned to playing, turning out for non-League club Altrincham. In a bizarre reversal of fortune, Stepney was succeeded in his short tenure there by John Connaughton, once his understudy at Old Trafford.

Stepney ran a pub and a transport business then worked for Manchester City as a goalkeeping coach. He is now an after-dinner speaker and football-themed radio-show host. He declined to be interviewed for this book, stating that what he would have to say about Docherty would be "too controversial".

## IAN STOREY-MOORE
**Manchester United games: 43**
**Manchester United goals: 12**
**Full international caps: 1**
Though he might have been injured out of the English game, Ian Storey-Moore's wingwork was still sufficient for the lesser demands of the NASL, so following his 'retirement', he became one of the first Manchester United men to fetch up at Chicago Sting. After one season there, Storey-Moore returned to his native land to player-manage non-League sides Shepshed Dynamo and Burton Albion. He also built up a betting shop business. He returned to Nottingham Forest, the club at which he had made his name, as chief scout in 1997. He now occupies the same position at Aston Villa.

## COLIN WALDRON
**Manchester United games: 4 (0)**
**Manchester United goals: 0**
**Full international caps: 0**
As well as the 20 League games Colin Waldron played for Sunderland upon his move there from Old Trafford, he also made 19 League appearances for Rochdale. Naturally, there were some NASL stints too, the defender turning out for Tulsa Roughnecks, Philadelphia Fury and Atlanta Chiefs. He bought a small betting shop and telephone betting business after hanging up his boots. It now claims to be one of the leading independent bookmakers in the Nelson, Lancashire, area. Says Waldron, "It was a disappointment that I hadn't given a good account of myself for [United]. If I'd have gone there and just genuinely played badly, understandable, but I wasn't given a chance because of the ill-health. That's a disappointment, but these things happen. I was just thrilled that I was given an insight into a big club. I'm glad I had the six months [sic] at Old Trafford because it opened my eyes and it was just nice to be under

Tommy Doc again. Got a lot of time for the fella. I still to this day see him and Mary, and two nicer people you wouldn't wish to meet."

**TONY YOUNG**
**Manchester United games: 79 (18)**
**Manchester United goals: 1**
**Full international caps: 0**

The man who Docherty admits he "messed about" in the 1973/74 season by moving him from position to position seemed to have felt somewhat more messed about by Docherty's typically disingenuous claims regarding his placement on the transfer list prior to his departure. That departure in January 1976 to Charlton Athletic on a free resulted in only 20 League games, but ones in which he scored the same number of goals he had in his 97 United appearances in all competitions. He moved to York City the following season – managed by Wilf McGuinness, who had known him ever since he signed for the Reds in 1968 as a 15-year-old – and scored twice for the club in 78 appearances before his retirement. But of course scoring was not his job, even if his actual job did seem ill-defined. As utility players tend to, he was caught between stools. Nonetheless, he helped keep United's goal-against record down to a more than respectable level in their relegation season, played alongside Law, Best, Charlton and Morgan and – before he left for the lower divisions – carved his name in the record books with his solitary goal against Chelsea in November 1973.

# APPENDIX II

# Results

## Matches played by Manchester United during Tommy Docherty's tenure as manager

NOTES

N = neutral ground; og = own goal

Friendlies not listed; Anglo-Italian Cup listed but not recognised as a competitive tournament

All league fixtures Football League Division One except for 1974/75 season, which are Football League Division Two

More than one attendance figure is listed where gates are in dispute

There were 22 clubs in Divisions 1 & 2 in the period covered

Own goals are listed last

## SEASON: 1972/73

| DATE | OPPONENTS | HOME or AWAY | COMPETITION | RESULT | SCORER(S) | ATTENDANCE | LEAGUE POS AFTER MATCH | NOTES |
|---|---|---|---|---|---|---|---|---|
| Sat 23 Dec | **Leeds United** | H | League | D 1-1 | MacDougall | 46,382 | 21 | |
| Team: | Stepney, O'Neil, Dunne, Law, Sadler, M Buchan, Morgan, MacDougall, Charlton, W Davies, Storey-Moore, | | | | | | | Used sub: Kidd |
| Tue 26 Dec | **Derby County** | A | League | L 1-3 | Moore | 35,093 | 22 | |
| Team: | Stepney, O'Neil, Dunne, Kidd, Sadler, M Buchan, Morgan, MacDougall, Charlton, W Davies, Storey-Moore, | | | | | | | Used sub: Young |
| Sat 06 Jan | **Arsenal** | A | League | L 1-3 | Kidd | 56,194 | 22 | Debuts of Forsyth and Graham |
| Team: | Stepney, Young, Forsyth, Graham, Sadler, M Buchan, Morgan, MacDougall, Charlton, Law, Storey-Moore | | | | | | | |
| Sat 13 Jan | **Wolverhampton Wanderers** | A | F.A. Cup 3rd round | L 0-1 | | 40,005 | | |
| Team: | Stepney, Forsyth, Dunne, Law, Sadler, M Buchan, Morgan, Kidd, Charlton, Law, Storey-Moore, | | | | | | | Used sub: Dunne |
| Sat 20 Jan | **West Ham United** | H | League | D 2-2 | Charlton (pen), Macari | 50,878 | 22 | |
| Team: | Stepney, Young, Forsyth, Law, Holton, M Buchan, Morgan, MacDougall, Charlton, Macari, Graham, | | | | | | | Used sub: W Davies |
| Wed 24 Jan | **Everton** | H | League | D 0-0 | | 58,970 | 21 | Debut of Martin |
| Team: | Stepney, Forsyth, Forsyth, Martin, Holton, M Buchan, Morgan, MacDougall, Charlton, Macari, Graham, | | | | | | | Used sub: Kidd |
| Sat 27 Jan | **Coventry City** | A | League | D 1-1 | Holton | 42,767 | 19 | |
| Team: | Stepney, Young, Forsyth, Graham, Holton, M Buchan, Morgan, MacDougall, Charlton, Macari, Martin | | | | | | | |
| Sat 10 Feb | **Wolverhampton Wanderers** | H | League | W 2-1 | Charlton 2 (1 pen) | 52,089 | 18 | |
| Team: | Stepney, Young, Forsyth, Graham, Holton, M Buchan, Morgan, MacDougall, Charlton, Macari, Martin | | | | | | | |
| Sat 17 Feb | **Ipswich Town** | A | League | L 1-4 | Macari | 31,918 | 21 | |
| Team: | Stepney, Forsyth, Dunne, Graham, Holton, M Buchan, Morgan, MacDougall, Charlton, Macari, Kidd | | | | | | | |
| Wed 21 Feb | **Florentina** | H | Ang-It Cup | D 1-1 | Holton | 23,951 | | |
| ??? Team: | Stepney, Dunne, Dunne, Graham, Holton, M Buchan, Martin, MacDougall, Charlton, Macari, Kidd | | | | | | | |
| Sat 03 Mar | **West Bromwich Albion** | H | League | W 2-1 | Macari, Kidd | 46,735 | 19 | |
| Team: | Stepney, Forsyth, Forsyth, Graham, James, M Buchan, Morgan, Kidd, Charlton, Macari, Storey-Moore, | | | | | | | Used sub: Martin |
| Sat 10 Mar | **Birmingham City** | A | League | L 1-3 | Macari | 51,278 | 20 | |
| Team: | Rimmer, Young, Forsyth, Graham, James, M Buchan, Morgan, Kidd, Charlton, Macari, Storey-Moore | | | | | | | |
| Sat 17 Mar | **Newcastle United** | H | League | W 2-1 | Holton, Martin | 48,426 | 18 | |
| Team: | Rimmer, Forsyth, Forsyth, Graham, Holton, M Buchan, Morgan, Kidd, Charlton, Macari, Martin, | | | | | | | Used sub: Martin |
| Wed 21 Mar | **Lazio** | A | Ang-It Cup | D 0-0 | | 52,834 | | |
| ??? Team: | James, James, James, Graham, Holton, M Buchan, Morgan, Kidd, Charlton, Macari, Martin | | | | | | | |
| Sat 24 Mar | **Tottenham Hotspur** | A | League | D 1-1 | Graham | 49,751 | 18 | |
| Team: | Rimmer, Young, James, Graham, Holton, M Buchan, Morgan, Kidd, Charlton, Macari, Martin, | | | | | | | Used sub: Martin |

| DATE | OPPONENTS | HOME or AWAY | COMPETITION | RESULT | SCORER(S) | ATTENDANCE | LEAGUE POS AFTER MATCH | NOTES |
|---|---|---|---|---|---|---|---|---|
| Sat 31 Mar | Southampton | A | League | W 2-0 | Charlton, Holton | 23,161 | 19 | Debut of Anderson |
| Team: | Rimmer, | Young, | James, | Graham, | Holton, | M Buchan, | Morgan, | Kidd, | Charlton, | Macari, | Martin, | Used sub: | Anderson |
| Wed 4 Apr | Bari | H | Ang-It Cup | H 3-1 | Law, Moore, Martin | 14,303 | | |
| Team: | ??? | | | | | | | | |
| Sat 07 Apr | Norwich City | H | League | W 1-0 | Martin | 48,593 | 19 | |
| Team: | Stepney, | Young, | James, | Graham, | Holton, | M Buchan, | Morgan, | Kidd, | Charlton, | Law, | Martin, | Used sub: | Anderson |
| Wed 11 Apr | Crystal Palace | H | League | W 2-0 | Morgan, Kidd | 46,895 | 18 | |
| Team: | Stepney, | Young, | James, | Graham, | Holton, | M Buchan, | Morgan, | Kidd, | Charlton, | Macari, | Martin, | Used sub: | Anderson |
| Sat 14 Apr | Stoke City | A | League | D 2-2 | Macari, og | 37,051 | 16 | Debut of Fletcher |
| Team: | Stepney, | Young, | James, | Graham, | Holton, | M Buchan, | Morgan, | Charlton, | Macari, | Martin, | | Used sub: | Fletcher |
| Wed 18 Apr | Leeds United | A | League | W 1-0 | Anderson | 45,450 | 12 | |
| Team: | Stepney, | Young, | James, | Graham, | Holton, | M Buchan, | Morgan, | Anderson, | Charlton, | Macari, | Martin, | Used sub: | Fletcher |
| Sat 21 Apr | Manchester City | H | League | D 0-0 | | 61,500 | 13 | |
| Team: | Stepney, | Young, | James, | Graham, | Holton, | M Buchan, | Morgan, | Kidd, | Charlton, | Macari, | Martin, | Used sub: | Anderson |
| Mon 23 Apr | Sheffield United | H | League | L 1-2 | Kidd | 57,280 | 15 | Debut of Sidebottom |
| Team: | Stepney, | Young, | Sidebottom, | Graham, | Holton, | M Buchan, | Morgan, | Kidd, | Charlton, | Macari, | Martin | |
| Sat 28 Apr | Chelsea | A | League | L 0-1 | | 44,184 | 18 | |
| Team: | Stepney, | Young, | Sidebottom, | Graham, | Holton, | M Buchan, | Morgan, | Kidd, | Charlton, | Macari, | Martin, | Used sub: | Anderson |
| Wed 2 May | Verona | A | Ang-It Cup | W 4-1 | Charlton (2), Fletcher, Olney | 8,168 | | |
| Team: | ??? | | | | | | | | |

# SEASON: 1973/74

| DATE | OPPONENTS | HOME or AWAY | COMPETITION | RESULT | SCORER(S) | ATTENDANCE | LEAGUE POS AFTER MATCH | NOTES |
|---|---|---|---|---|---|---|---|---|
| Sat 25 Aug | Arsenal | A | League | L 0-3 | | 51,501 | 17 | Debut of Daly |
| Team: | Stepney, | Young, | M Buchan, | Daly, | Holton, | James, | Morgan, | Anderson, | Macari, | Graham, | Martin, | Used sub: | McIlroy |
| Wed 29 Aug | Stoke City | H | League | W 1-0 | James | 43,614 | 15 | |
| Team: | Stepney, | Young, | M Buchan, | Martin, | Holton, | James, | Morgan, | Anderson, | Macari, | Graham, | McIlroy | |
| Sat 01 Sep | Queens Park Rangers | H | League | W 2-1 | Holton, McIlroy | 44,156 | 7 | |
| Team: | Stepney, | Young, | M Buchan, | Martin, | Holton, | James, | Morgan, | Anderson, | Macari, | Graham, | McIlroy, | Used sub: | Fletcher |
| Wed 05 Sep | Leicester City | A | League | L 0-1 | Sidebottom, | 29,152 | 13 | |
| Team: | Stepney, | Young, | M Buchan, | Daly, | Holton, | James, | Morgan, | Anderson, | Macari, | Graham, | McIlroy, | Used sub: | Fletcher |
| Team: | Stepney, | Young, | M Buchan, | Daly, | Holton, | | Morgan, | Anderson, | Kidd, | Graham, | McIlroy, | Used sub: | Martin |

| DATE | OPPONENTS | HOME or AWAY | COMPETITION | RESULT | SCORER(S) | ATTENDANCE | LEAGUE POS AFTER MATCH | NOTES | TEAM / USED SUB |
|---|---|---|---|---|---|---|---|---|---|
| Sat 08 Sep | Ipswich Town | A | League | L 1-2 | Anderson | 22,023 | 16 | Debut of B Greenhoff | **Team:** Stepney, Young, M Buchan, Daly, Sadler, B Greenhoff, Morgan, Anderson, Kidd, Graham, McIlroy, — *Used sub:* Macari |
| Wed 12 Sep | Leicester City | H | League | L 1-2 | Stepney (pen) | 40,793 | 20 | | **Team:** Stepney, M Buchan, Martin, Young, Holton, Sadler, Morgan, Anderson, Macari, Graham, McIlroy, |
| Sat 15 Sep | West Ham United | H | League | W 3-1 | Kidd (2) Moore | 44,757 | 14 | Debut of George Buchan | **Team:** Stepney, M Buchan, Young, Martin, Holton, Sadler, Morgan, Anderson, Kidd, Graham, Storey-Moore, — *Used sub:* G Buchan |
| Sat 22 Sep | Leeds United | A | League | D 0-0 | | 47,058 | 13 | | **Team:** Stepney, M Buchan, Young, B Greenhoff, Holton, Sadler, Morgan, Kidd, Anderson, Graham, Storey-Moore, |
| Sat 29 Sep | Liverpool | H | League | D 0-0 | | 53,882 | 14 | | **Team:** Stepney, M Buchan, Young, B Greenhoff, Holton, Sadler, Morgan, Anderson, Kidd, Graham, McIlroy, — *Used sub:* G Buchan |
| Sat 06 Oct | Wolverhampton Wanderers | A | League | L 1-2 | McIlroy | 32,962 | 17 | | **Team:** Stepney, M Buchan, Young, B Greenhoff, Holton, Sadler, Morgan, Anderson, Kidd, Graham, McIlroy, — *Used sub:* McIlroy |
| Mon 08 Oct | Middlesbrough | H | League Cup 2nd round | L 0-1 | | 23,906 | | **Team:** Stepney, M Buchan, Young, B Greenhoff, Holton, Sadler, Morgan, Anderson, Kidd, Graham, McIlroy, |
| Sat 13 Oct | Derby County | H | League | L 0-1 | | 43,724 | 18 | | **Team:** Stepney, M Buchan, Forsyth, B Greenhoff, Holton, Sadler, Morgan, Daly, Anderson, Graham, Kidd, — *Used sub:* McIlroy |
| Sat 20 Oct | Birmingham City | H | League | W 1-0 | Stepney (pen) | 48,937 | 16 | | **Team:** Stepney, Forsyth, Young, B Greenhoff, Holton, Sadler, Morgan, Anderson, Kidd, Graham, Best, — *Used sub:* G Buchan |
| Sat 27 Oct | Burnley | A | League | D 0-0 | | 31,796 | 16 | | **Team:** Stepney, M Buchan, Young, B Greenhoff, Holton, Sadler, Morgan, Kidd, Anderson, Graham, Best, |
| Sat 03 Nov | Chelsea | H | League | D 2-2 | Young, Greenhoff | 48,036 | 14 | Debut of Griffiths | **Team:** Stepney, M Buchan, Young, B Greenhoff, James, Griffiths, Morgan, Kidd, Graham, Macari, Best, — *Used sub:* Sadler |
| Sat 10 Nov | Tottenham Hotspur | A | League | L 1-2 | Best | 42,756 | 18 | | **Team:** Stepney, M Buchan, Young, B Greenhoff, James, Griffiths, Morgan, Macari, Kidd, Graham, Best, |
| Sat 17 Nov | Newcastle United | A | League | L 2-3 | Macari, Graham | 40,252 | 18 | | **Team:** Stepney, M Buchan, Young, B Greenhoff, Holton, James, Morgan, Kidd, Macari, Graham, Best, — *Used sub:* Martin |
| Sat 24 Nov | Norwich City | H | League | D 0-0 | | 36,338 | 18 | | **Team:** Stepney, M Buchan, Young, B Greenhoff, Holton, James, Morgan, Macari, Kidd, Graham, Best, — *Used sub:* Sadler |
| Sat 08 Dec | Southampton | H | League | D 0-0 | | 31,648 | 18 | | **Team:** Stepney, M Buchan, Forsyth, B Greenhoff, James, Griffiths, Morgan, Young, Kidd, McIlroy, Best, — *Used sub:* Fletcher |
| Sat 15 Dec | Coventry City | H | League | L 2-3 | Best, Morgan | 28,589 | 19 | | **Team:** Stepney, M Buchan, Forsyth, B Greenhoff, James, Griffiths, Morgan, Macari, Kidd, Young, Best, — *Used sub:* Martin |

| DATE | OPPONENTS | HOME or AWAY | COMPETITION | RESULT | SCORER(S) | ATTENDANCE | LEAGUE POS AFTER MATCH | NOTES |
|---|---|---|---|---|---|---|---|---|
| Sat 22 Dec | **Liverpool** | A | League | L 0-2 | | 40,420 | 19 | |
| Team: | Stepney, M Buchan, Young, Griffiths, B Greenhoff, Holton, Morgan, Macari, Kidd, Graham, Best. | | | | | | | Used sub: McIlroy |
| Wed 26 Dec | **Sheffield United** | H | League | L 1-2 | Sidebottom, Macari | 38,653 | 20 | |
| Team: | Stepney, Griffiths, B Greenhoff, Holton, Morgan, Macari, Kidd, Graham, Best. | | | | | | | |
| Sat 29 Dec | **Ipswich Town** | H | League | W 2-0 | McIlroy, Macari | 36,365 | 19 | |
| Team: | Stepney, Griffiths, Young, B Greenhoff, Holton, Morgan, Macari, McIlroy, Graham, Best. | | | | | | | Used sub: McIlroy |
| Tue 01 Jan | **Queens Park Rangers** | A | League | L 0-3 | | 32,339 | 20 | Debut of Houston |
| Team: | Stepney, Houston, B Greenhoff, Holton, Morgan, Macari, McIlroy, Graham, Best. | | | | | | | |
| Sat 05 Jan | **Plymouth Argyle** | H | F.A. Cup 3rd round | W 1-0 | Macari | 31,810 | | |
| Team: | Stepney, Forsyth, Houston, B Greenhoff, Holton, Morgan, Macari, Kidd, Graham, Martin. | | | | | | | |
| Sat 12 Jan | **West Ham United** | A | League | L 1-2 | McIlroy | 34,147 | 21 | |
| Team: | Stepney, Houston, B Greenhoff, Holton, Morgan, Macari, Kidd, Young, Graham. | | | | | | | Used sub: McIlroy |
| Sat 19 Jan | **Arsenal** | H | League | D 1-1 | James | 38,589 | 21 | |
| Team: | Stepney, Houston, B Greenhoff, Holton, Morgan, Macari, Kidd, Young, Graham. | | | | | | | Used sub: McIlroy |
| Sat 26 Jan | **Ipswich Town** | H | F.A. Cup 4th round | L 0-1 | James | 37,177 | | |
| Team: | Stepney, Forsyth, Houston, B Greenhoff, Holton, Morgan, Macari, McIlroy, Young, Martin. | | | | | | | |
| Sat 02 Feb | **Coventry City** | A | League | L 0-1 | James | 25,313 | 21 | |
| Team: | Stepney, Houston, B Greenhoff, Holton, Morgan, Macari, McIlroy, Kidd, Young. | | | | | | | Used sub: Kidd |
| Sat 09 Feb | **Leeds United** | H | League | L 0-2 | James | 60,025 | 22 | |
| Team: | Stepney, Houston, B Greenhoff, Holton, Morgan, Macari, McIlroy, Kidd, Young. | | | | | | | Used sub: Forsyth |
| Sat 16 Feb | **Derby County** | A | League | D 2-2 | Greenhoff, Houston | 29,987 | 21 | |
| Team: | Stepney, Forsyth, Houston, B Greenhoff, Holton, Morgan, Macari, Kidd, Young, Forsyth. | | | | | | | Used sub: McIlroy |
| Sat 23 Feb | **Wolverhampton Wanderers** | H | League | D 0-0 | | 39,260 | 21 | |
| Team: | Stepney, Houston, B Greenhoff, Holton, Morgan, Fletcher, Kidd, McIlroy, Macari. | | | | | | | Used sub: Daly |
| Sat 02 Mar | **Sheffield United** | A | League | W 1-0 | Macari | 29,203 | 21 | |
| Team: | Stepney, Houston, B Greenhoff, Holton, Morgan, Fletcher, Kidd, McIlroy, Martin. | | | | | | | Used sub: Daly |
| Wed 13 Mar | **Manchester City** | A | League | D 0-0 | | 51,331 | 21 | Debut of Bielby |
| Team: | Stepney, Houston, B Greenhoff, Holton, Morgan, Macari, Kidd, McIlroy, Daly, Bielby. | | | | | | | Used sub: Forsyth |
| Sat 16 Mar | **Birmingham City** | A | League | L 0-1 | M Buchan | 37,768 | 21 | Debut of McCalliog |
| Team: | Stepney, Houston, Martin, McCalliog, Morgan, Macari, B Greenhoff, Graham, Bielby. | | | | | | | Used sub: Graham |

| DATE | OPPONENTS | HOME or AWAY | COMPETITION | RESULT | SCORER(S) | ATTENDANCE | LEAGUE POS AFTER MATCH | NOTES |
|---|---|---|---|---|---|---|---|---|
| Sat 23 Mar | Tottenham Hotspur | H | League | L 0-1 | | 36,278 | 22 | Used sub: Bielby |
| Team: | Stepney, Forsyth, Houston, B Greenhoff, James, M Buchan, Morgan, McIlroy, Kidd, McCalliog, Daly | | | | | | | |
| Sat 30 Mar | Chelsea | A | League | W 3-1 | Morgan, McIlroy, Daly | 29,602 | 22 | Used sub: Bielby |
| Team: | Stepney, Forsyth, Houston, Daly, James, M Buchan, Morgan, McIlroy, McCalliog, Martin | | | | | | | |
| Wed 03 Apr | Burnley | H | League | D 3-3 | McIlroy, Forsyth, Holton | 33,336 | 21 | |
| Team: | Stepney, Forsyth, Houston, Daly, Holton, M Buchan, Morgan, McIlroy, McCalliog, Martin | | | | | | | |
| Sat 06 Apr | Norwich City | A | League | W 2-0 | Macari, Greenhoff | 28,223 | 21 | |
| Team: | Stepney, Forsyth, Houston, B Greenhoff, Holton, M Buchan, Morgan, Macari, McCalliog, McIlroy | | | | | | | |
| Sat 13 Apr | Newcastle United | H | League | W 1-0 | McCalliog | 44,751 | 21 | |
| Team: | Stepney, Forsyth, Houston, B Greenhoff, Holton, M Buchan, Morgan, Macari, McCalliog, Daly | | | | | | | |
| Mon 15 Apr | Everton | H | League | W 3-0 | McCalliog 2, Houston | 48,424 | 20 | |
| Team: | Stepney, Forsyth, Houston, B Greenhoff, Holton, M Buchan, Morgan, Macari, McCalliog, McIlroy | | | | | | | |
| Sat 20 Apr | Southampton | A | League | D 1-1 | McCalliog (pen) | 30,789 | 21 | Used sub: Martin |
| Team: | Stepney, Young, Houston, B Greenhoff, Holton, M Buchan, Morgan, Macari, McCalliog, Daly | | | | | | | |
| Tue 23 Apr | Everton | A | League | L 0-1 | | 46,093 | 21 | |
| Team: | Stepney, Young, Houston, B Greenhoff, Holton, M Buchan, Morgan, Macari, McCalliog, Daly | | | | | | | |
| Sat 27 Apr | Manchester City | H | League | L 0-1 | | 56,996 | 21 | |
| Team: | Stepney, Forsyth, Houston, B Greenhoff, Holton, M Buchan, Morgan, Macari, McCalliog, Daly | | | | | | | |
| Mon 29 Apr | Stoke City | A | League | L 0-1 | | 27,392 | 21 | |
| Team: | Stepney, Forsyth, Houston, B Greenhoff, Holton, M Buchan, Morgan, Macari, McCalliog, Martin | | | | | | | |

## SEASON: 1974/75

| DATE | OPPONENTS | HOME or AWAY | COMPETITION | RESULT | SCORER(S) | ATTENDANCE | LEAGUE POS AFTER MATCH | NOTES |
|---|---|---|---|---|---|---|---|---|
| Sat 17 Aug | Orient | A | League | W 2-0 | Morgan, Houston | 17,772 | 5 | Debut of Pearson |
| Team: | Stepney, Forsyth, Houston, B Greenhoff, Holton, M Buchan, Morgan, Macari, Pearson, McCalliog, Daly | | | | | | | |
| Sat 24 Aug | Millwall | H | League | W 4-0 | Pearson, Daly 3 (2 pens) | 44,756 | 6 | Used sub: McIlroy |
| Team: | Stepney, Forsyth, Houston, B Greenhoff, Holton, M Buchan, Morgan, Macari, Pearson, McCalliog, Daly | | | | | | | |
| Wed 28 Aug | Portsmouth | H | League | W 2-1 | Daly (pen), McIlroy | 42,547 | 2 | |
| Team: | Stepney, Forsyth, Houston, B Greenhoff, Holton, M Buchan, Morgan, McIlroy, Pearson, Martin, Daly | | | | | | | |

| | DATE | OPPONENTS | HOME or AWAY | COMPETITION | RESULT | SCORER(S) | ATTENDANCE | LEAGUE POS AFTER MATCH | NOTES | | | |
|---|---|---|---|---|---|---|---|---|---|---|---|---|
| | Sat 31 Aug | **Cardiff City** | A | League | W 1-0 | Daly (pen) | 22,344 | 1 | | | | |
| Team: | Stepney, | Forsyth, | Houston, | B Greenhoff, | Holton, | M Buchan, | Morgan, | McIlroy, | Pearson, | Martin, | Daly, | Used sub: Young |
| | Sat 07 Sep | **Nottingham Forest** | H | League | D 2-2 | Greenhoff, McIlroy | 40,671 | 1 | | | | |
| Team: | Stepney, | Forsyth, | Houston, | B Greenhoff, | Holton, | M Buchan, | Morgan, | McIlroy, | Pearson, | McCalliog, | Daly, | Used sub: Macari |
| | Wed 11 Sep | **Charlton Athletic** | H | League Cup 2nd round | W 5-1 | Macari (2), McIlroy, Houston, og | 21,616 | | | | | |
| Team: | Stepney, | Forsyth, | Houston, | Martin, | Holton, | M Buchan, | Morgan, | McIlroy, | Macari, | McCalliog, | Daly, | Used sub: Young |
| | Sat 14 Sep | **West Bromwich Albion** | A | League | D 1-1 | Pearson | 28,666 | 1 | | | | |
| Team: | Stepney, | Forsyth, | Houston, | B Greenhoff, | Holton, | M Buchan, | Morgan, | McIlroy, | Macari, | McCalliog, | Daly, | Used sub: B Greenhoff |
| | Mon 16 Sep | **Millwall** | A | League | W 1-0 | Daly (pen) | 16,988 | 1 | | | | |
| Team: | Stepney, | Forsyth, | Houston, | Martin, | Holton, | M Buchan, | Morgan, | McIlroy, | Macari, | McCalliog, | Daly, | Used sub: Young |
| | Sat 21 Sep | **Bristol Rovers** | H | League | W 2-0 | Greenhoff, og | 42,948 | 1 | | | | |
| Team: | Stepney, | Forsyth, | Houston, | B Greenhoff, | Holton, | M Buchan, | Morgan, | McIlroy, | Macari, | McCalliog, | Daly, | Used sub: Young |
| | Wed 25 Sep | **Bolton Wanderers** | H | League | W 3-0 | Macari, Houston, og | 47,084 | 1 | | | | |
| Team: | Stepney, | Forsyth, | Houston, | B Greenhoff, | Sidebottom, | M Buchan, | Morgan, | McIlroy, | Macari, | McCalliog, | Daly, | |
| | Sat 28 Sep | **Norwich City** | A | League | L 0-2 | | 24,586 | 1 | | | | |
| Team: | Stepney, | Forsyth, | Houston, | B Greenhoff, | Sidebottom, | M Buchan, | Morgan, | McIlroy, | Macari, | McCalliog, | Daly, | Used sub: Young |
| | Sat 05 Oct | **Fulham** | A | League | W 2-1 | Pearson 2 | 26,513 | 1 | | | | |
| Team: | Stepney, | Forsyth, | Houston, | B Greenhoff, | Holton, | M Buchan, | Morgan, | McIlroy, | Pearson, | McCalliog, | Daly, | Used sub: Macari |
| | Wed 09 Oct | **Manchester City** | H | League Cup 3rd round | W 1-0 | Daly (pen) | 55,159 | | Debut of Albiston | | | |
| Team: | Stepney, | Forsyth, | Albiston, | B Greenhoff, | Holton, | M Buchan, | Morgan, | McIlroy, | Pearson, | McCalliog, | Daly, | |
| | Sat 12 Oct | **Notts. County** | H | League | W 1-0 | M Buchan | 46,565 | 1 | | | | |
| Team: | Stepney, | Forsyth, | Houston, | B Greenhoff, | Holton, | M Buchan, | Morgan, | McIlroy, | Pearson, | McCalliog, | Daly, | Used sub: Macari |
| | Tue 15 Oct | **Portsmouth** | A | League | D 0-0 | | 25,608 | 1 | Debut of McCreery | | | |
| Team: | Stepney, | Forsyth, | Albiston, | B Greenhoff, | Holton, | M Buchan, | Morgan, | McIlroy, | Pearson, | McCalliog, | Macari, | Used sub: McCreery |
| | Sat 19 Oct | **Blackpool** | A | League | W 3-0 | Forsyth, Macari, McCalliog | 25370 or 22211 | | | | | |
| Team: | Stepney, | Forsyth, | Houston, | B Greenhoff, | Holton, | M Buchan, | Morgan, | McIlroy, | Macari, | McCalliog, | Daly, | Used sub: McCreery |
| | Sat 26 Oct | **Southampton** | H | League | W 1-0 | Pearson | 48,724 | 1 | | | | |
| Team: | Stepney, | Forsyth, | Houston, | B Greenhoff, | Holton, | M Buchan, | Morgan, | McIlroy, | Macari, | McCalliog, | Daly, | Used sub: Pearson |
| | Sat 02 Nov | **Oxford United** | H | League | W 4-0 | Pearson 3, Macari | 41,909 | 1 | | | | |
| Team: | Stepney, | Forsyth, | Houston, | B Greenhoff, | Sidebottom, | M Buchan, | Macari, | McIlroy, | Pearson, | McCalliog, | Daly, | Used sub: Morgan |

| | DATE | OPPONENTS | HOME or AWAY | COMPETITION | RESULT | SCORER(S) | ATTENDANCE | LEAGUE POS AFTER MATCH | NOTES | | | | |
|---|---|---|---|---|---|---|---|---|---|---|---|---|---|
| | Sat 09 Nov | Bristol City | A | League | L 0-1 | | 28,104 | 1 | | | | | |
| Team: | Stepney, | Forsyth, | Houston, | B Greenhoff, | Sidebottom, | M Buchan, | Macari, | McIlroy, | Pearson, | McCalliog, | Daly, | Used sub: | Graham |
| | Wed 13 Nov | Burnley | H | League Cup 4th round | W 3-2 | Macari 2, Morgan | 46,275 | | | | | | |
| Team: | Stepney, | Forsyth, | Houston, | B Greenhoff, | Sidebottom, | M Buchan, | Macari, | McIlroy, | Pearson, | McCalliog, | Daly, | Used sub: | Morgan |
| | Sat 16 Nov | Aston Villa | H | League | W 2-1 | Daly 2 (1 pen) | 55,615 | 1 | | | | | |
| Team: | Stepney, | Forsyth, | Houston, | Macari, | Sidebottom, | M Buchan, | Morgan, | McIlroy, | Pearson, | McCalliog, | Daly, | Used sub: | B Greenhoff |
| | Sat 23 Nov | Hull City | A | League | L 0-2 | | 23,287 | 1 | | | | | |
| Team: | Stepney, | Forsyth, | Houston, | Macari, | Sidebottom, | M Buchan, | Morgan, | McIlroy, | B Greenhoff, | McCalliog, | Daly, | | |
| | Sat 30 Nov | Sunderland | H | League | W 3-2 | Pearson, Morgan, McIlroy | 60,585 | 1 | Debut of R Davies | | | | |
| Team: | Stepney, | Forsyth, | Houston, | B Greenhoff, | Holton, | M Buchan, | Morgan, | McIlroy, | Pearson, | Macari, | Daly, | Used sub: | R Davies |
| | Wed 04 Dec | Middlesbrough | A | League Cup 5th round | D 0-0 | | 36,005 | | | | | | |
| Team: | Stepney, | Forsyth, | Houston, | B Greenhoff, | Holton, | M Buchan, | Morgan, | McIlroy, | Pearson, | Macari, | Daly, | Used sub: | Young |
| | Sat 07 Dec | Sheffield Wednesday | A | League | D 4-4 | Macari (2), Houston, McIlroy | 35,067 | 1 | | | | | |
| Team: | Stepney, | Forsyth, | Houston, | B Greenhoff, | Holton, | M Buchan, | Morgan, | McIlroy, | Pearson, | Macari, | Daly, | Used sub: | R Davies |
| | Sat 14 Dec | Orient | H | League | D 0-0 | | 41,200 | 1 | | | | | |
| Team: | Stepney, | Forsyth, | Houston, | B Greenhoff, | Sidebottom, | M Buchan, | Morgan, | McIlroy, | Pearson, | Macari, | Daly, | Used sub: | R Davies |
| | Wed 18 Dec | Middlesbrough | H | League Cup Fifth round replay | W 3-0 | Pearson, McIlroy, Macari | 49,501 | | | | | | |
| Team: | Stepney, | Young, | Houston, | B Greenhoff, | Sidebottom, | M Buchan, | Morgan, | McIlroy, | Pearson, | Macari, | Daly, | Used sub: | McCalliog |
| | Sat 21 Dec | York City | A | League | W 1-0 | Pearson | 15314 or 15567 | 1 | | | | | |
| Team: | Stepney, | Young, | Houston, | B Greenhoff, | Sidebottom, | M Buchan, | Morgan, | McIlroy, | Pearson, | Macari, | Daly, | Used sub: | R Davies |
| | Thu 26 Dec | West Bromwich Albion | H | League | W 2-1 | McIlroy, Daly (pen) | 51,104 | 1 | | | | | |
| Team: | Stepney, | Young, | Houston, | B Greenhoff, | Sidebottom, | M Buchan, | Morgan, | McIlroy, | Pearson, | Macari, | Daly, | Used sub: | R Davies |
| | Sat 28 Dec | Oldham Athletic | A | League | L 0-1 | | 26,356 | 1 | | | | | |
| Team: | Stepney, | Young, | Albiston, | B Greenhoff, | Sidebottom, | M Buchan, | Morgan, | McIlroy, | Pearson, | Macari, | Daly, | Used sub: | R Davies |
| | Sat 04 Jan | Walsall | H | F.A. Cup 3rd round | D 0-0 | | 43,353 | | | | | | |
| Team: | Stepney, | Young, | Houston, | B Greenhoff, | Sidebottom, | M Buchan, | Morgan, | McIlroy, | Pearson, | Macari, | Daly, | Used sub: | R Davies |

| DATE | OPPONENTS | HOME or AWAY | COMPETITION | RESULT | SCORER(S) | ATTENDANCE | LEAGUE POS AFTER MATCH | NOTES |
|---|---|---|---|---|---|---|---|---|
| Tue 07 Jan | **Walsall** | A | F.A. Cup 3rd round replay | L 2-3 after extra time | Daly (pen), McIlroy | 18,105 | | Used sub: R Davies |
| Team: | Stepney, Young, Houston, McCalliog, McIlroy, Pearson, Macari, Daly | | | | | | | |
| Sat 11 Jan | **Sheffield Wednesday** | H | League | W 2-0 | McCalliog 2 (1 pen) | 45,662 | 1 | Used sub: Daly |
| Team: | Stepney, Forsyth, Houston, B Greenhoff, James, M Buchan, Morgan, McIlroy, Pearson, Macari, McCalliog, Daly | | | | | | | |
| Wed 15 Jan | **Norwich City** | H | League Cup Semi final 1st leg | D 2-2 | Macari 2 | 58,010 | | |
| Team: | Stepney, Forsyth, Houston, B Greenhoff, James, Morgan, McIlroy, Daly, Macari, McCalliog | | | | | | | |
| Sat 18 Jan | **Sunderland** | A | League | D 0-0 | | 45,976 | 1 | Used sub: Young; Debut of Baldwin |
| Team: | Stepney, Forsyth, Houston, B Greenhoff, Morgan, McIlroy, Daly, Macari, McCalliog, Baldwin | | | | | | | |
| Wed 22 Jan | **Norwich City** | A | League Cup Semi final 2nd leg | L 0-1 Norwich City won 3-2 on aggregate | | 31,621 | | |
| Team: | Stepney, Forsyth, Houston, B Greenhoff, Morgan, McIlroy, Baldwin, Macari, McCalliog | | | | | | | |
| Sat 01 Feb | **Bristol City** | H | League | L 0-1 | | 47,118 | 1 | Used sub: Young |
| Team: | Stepney, Forsyth, Houston, B Greenhoff, James, M Buchan, Morgan, McIlroy, Daly, Macari, McCalliog | | | | | | | |
| Sat 08 Feb | **Oxford United** | A | League | L 0-1 | | 15,815 | 1 | Used sub: Young; Debut of Roche |
| Team: | Stepney, Forsyth, Houston, Daly, James, M Buchan, Morgan, McIlroy, Baldwin, Macari, McCalliog | | | | | | | |
| Sat 15 Feb | **Hull City** | H | League | W 2-0 | Houston, Pearson | 44,000 | 1 | Used sub: R Davies |
| Team: | Roche, Forsyth, Houston, B Greenhoff, James, M Buchan, Morgan, McIlroy, Pearson, Macari, Young | | | | | | | |
| Sat 22 Feb | **Aston Villa** | A | League | L 0-2 | | 40,353 | 1 | Used sub: R Davies |
| Team: | Roche, Forsyth, Houston, B Greenhoff, James, M Buchan, Young, McIlroy, Pearson, Macari, Martin | | | | | | | |
| Sat 01 Mar | **Cardiff City** | H | League | W 4-0 | Houston, Pearson, Macari, McIlroy | 43,601 | 1 | Debut of Coppell; Used sub: R Davies |
| Team: | Stepney, Forsyth, Houston, B Greenhoff, Sidebottom, M Buchan, Young, McIlroy, Pearson, Macari, Martin | | | | | | | |
| Sat 08 Mar | **Bolton Wanderers** | A | League | W 1-0 | Pearson | 38,152 | 1 | Used sub: Coppell |
| Team: | Stepney, Forsyth, Houston, B Greenhoff, James, M Buchan, Morgan, McIlroy, Pearson, Macari, Daly | | | | | | | |
| Sat 15 Mar | **Norwich City** | H | League | D 1-1 | Pearson | 56,202 | 1 | Used sub: Young |
| Team: | Stepney, Forsyth, Houston, B Greenhoff, James, M Buchan, Coppell, McIlroy, Pearson, Macari, Daly | | | | | | | |
| Sat 22 Mar | **Nottingham Forest** | A | League | W 1-0 | Daly | 22,000 | 1 | Used sub: Young |
| Team: | Stepney, Forsyth, Houston, B Greenhoff, James, M Buchan, Coppell, McIlroy, Pearson, Macari, Daly | | | | | | | |

| DATE | OPPONENTS | HOME or AWAY | COMPETITION | RESULT | SCORER(S) | ATTENDANCE | LEAGUE POS AFTER MATCH | NOTES |
|---|---|---|---|---|---|---|---|---|
| Fri 28 Mar | **Bristol Rovers** | A | League | D 1-1 | Macari | 19,000 | 1 | |
| Team: | Stepney, Forsyth, | Houston, | B Greenhoff, | James, | Coppell, Pearson, Macari, | Mcilroy, Daly, | | Used sub: Morgan |
| Sat 29 Mar | **York City** | H | League | W 2-1 | Macari, Morgan | 46,802 | 1 | |
| Team: | Stepney, Forsyth, | Houston, | Morgan, | B Greenhoff, | Coppell, Pearson, Macari, | Mcilroy, Daly, | | |
| Mon 31 Mar | **Oldham Athletic** | H | League | W 3-2 | Mcilroy, Macari, Coppell | 56,618 | 1 | |
| Team: | Stepney, Forsyth, | Houston, | Morgan, | B Greenhoff, | Coppell, Pearson, Macari, | Mcilroy, Daly, | | Used sub: Martin |
| Sat 05 Apr | **Southampton** | A | League | W 1-0 | Macari | 21,000 | 1 | Debut of Nicholl |
| Team: | Stepney, Forsyth, | Houston, | Young, | B Greenhoff, | Morgan, Pearson, Macari, | Mcilroy, Daly, | | Used sub: Nicholl |
| Sat 12 Apr | **Fulham** | H | League | W 1-0 | Daly | 52,971 | 1 | |
| Team: | Stepney, Forsyth, | Houston, | B Greenhoff, | James, | Coppell, Pearson, Macari, | Mcilroy, Daly, | | |
| Sat 19 Apr | **Notts. County** | A | League | D 2-2 | Houston, Greenhoff | 17,320 | 1 | |
| Team: | Stepney, Forsyth, | Houston, | B Greenhoff, | James, | Coppell, Pearson, Macari, | Mcilroy, Daly, | | |
| Sat 26 Apr | **Blackpool** | H | League | W 4-0 | Pearson 2, Macari, Greenhoff | 58,769 | 1 | |
| Team: | Stepney, Forsyth, | Houston, | B Greenhoff, | James, | Coppell, Pearson, Macari, | Mcilroy, Daly, | | |

## SEASON: 1975/76

| DATE | OPPONENTS | HOME or AWAY | COMPETITION | RESULT | SCORER(S) | ATTENDANCE | LEAGUE POS AFTER MATCH | NOTES |
|---|---|---|---|---|---|---|---|---|
| Sat 16 Aug | **Wolverhampton Wanderers** | A | League | W 2-0 | Macari 2 | 32,348 | 6 | |
| Team: | Stepney, Forsyth, | Houston, | Jackson, | B Greenhoff, | Coppell, Pearson, Macari, | Mcilroy, Daly, | | Used sub: Nicholl |
| Tue 19 Aug | **Birmingham City** | A | League | W 2-0 | Mcilroy 2 | 33,177 | 1 | |
| Team: | Stepney, Forsyth, | Houston, | Jackson, | B Greenhoff, | Coppell, McCreery, Macari, | Mcilroy, Daly, | | Used sub: Nicholl |
| Sat 23 Aug | **Sheffield United** | H | League | W 5-1 | Pearson 2, Mcilroy, Daly, Macari | 55,948 | 1 | |
| Team: | Stepney, Forsyth, | Houston, | Jackson, | B Greenhoff, | Coppell, Pearson, Macari, | Mcilroy, Daly, | | Used sub: Nicholl |
| Wed 27 Aug | **Coventry City** | H | League | D 1-1 | Pearson | 52,169 | 1 | |
| Team: | Stepney, Forsyth, | Houston, | Jackson, | B Greenhoff, | Coppell, Pearson, Macari, | Mcilroy, Daly, | | |
| Sat 30 Aug | **Stoke City** | A | League | W 1-0 | og | 33,092 | 1 | |
| Team: | Stepney, Forsyth, | Houston, | Jackson, | B Greenhoff, | Coppell, Pearson, Macari, | Mcilroy, Daly, | | |

| DATE | OPPONENTS | HOME or AWAY | COMPETITION | RESULT | SCORER(S) | ATTENDANCE | LEAGUE POS AFTER MATCH | NOTES |
|---|---|---|---|---|---|---|---|---|
| Sat 06 Sep | Tottenham Hotspur | H | League | W 3-2 | Daly 2 (1 pen), og | 51 641 | 1 | |
| Team: | Stepney, Nicholl, Houston, Jackson, B Greenhoff, Coppell, McIlroy, Pearson, Macari, Daly, | | | | | | | |
| Wed 10 Sep | Brentford | H | League Cup 2nd round | W 2-1 | Macari, McIlroy | 25286 | | Debut of Grimshaw / Grimshaw |
| Sat 13 Sep | Queens Park Rangers | A | League | L 0-1 | | 29237 | 1 | |
| Team: | Stepney, Nicholl, Albiston, Houston, Jackson, B Greenhoff, Coppell, McIlroy, Pearson, Macari, Daly, | | | | | | | Used sub: |
| Sat 20 Sep | Ipswich Town | H | League | W 1-0 | Houston | 50513 | 1 | Used sub: Young |
| Team: | Stepney, Nicholl, Houston, McCreery, Jackson, B Greenhoff, Coppell, McIlroy, Pearson, Macari, Daly | | | | | | | |
| Wed 24 Sep | Derby County | A | League | L 1-2 | Daly | 33 187 | 2 | |
| Team: | Stepney, Nicholl, Houston, McCreery, Jackson, B Greenhoff, Coppell, McIlroy, Pearson, Macari, Daly | | | | | | | |
| Sat 27 Sep | Manchester City | A | League | D 2-2 | McCreery, Macari | 46 931 | 3 | |
| Team: | Stepney, Nicholl, Houston, McCreery, Jackson, B Greenhoff, Coppell, McIlroy, Pearson, Macari, Daly | | | | | | | |
| Sat 04 Oct | Leicester City | H | League | D 0-0 | | 47878 | 1 | Used sub: McCreery |
| Team: | Stepney, Nicholl, Houston, Jackson, B Greenhoff, Coppell, McIlroy, Pearson, Macari, Daly, | | | | | | | |
| Wed 08 Oct | Aston Villa | A | League Cup 3rd round | W 2-1 | Macari, Coppell | 41 447 | | |
| Team: | Stepney, Nicholl, Houston, Jackson, B Greenhoff, Coppell, McIlroy, Pearson, Macari, Daly | | | | | | | |
| Sat 11 Oct | Leeds United | A | League | W 2-1 | McIlroy 2 | 40, 264 | 2 | Used sub: Grimshaw |
| Team: | Stepney, Nicholl, Houston, Jackson, B Greenhoff, Coppell, McIlroy, Pearson, Macari, Daly | | | | | | | |
| Sat 18 Oct | Arsenal | H | League | W 3-1 | Coppell 2, Pearson | 53 885 | 1 | |
| Team: | Stepney, Nicholl, Houston, Jackson, B Greenhoff, Coppell, McIlroy, Pearson, Macari, Daly | | | | | | | |
| Sat 25 Oct | West Ham United | A | League | L 1-2 | Macari | 38601 | 2 | Used sub: McCreery |
| Team: | Stepney, Nicholl, Houston, Jackson, B Greenhoff, Coppell, McIlroy, Pearson, Macari, Daly | | | | | | | |
| Sat 01 Nov | Norwich City | H | League | W 1-0 | Pearson | 50 587 | 1 | |
| Team: | Stepney, Nicholl, Houston, Jackson, B Greenhoff, Coppell, McIlroy, Pearson, Macari, Daly | | | | | | | |
| Sat 08 Nov | Liverpool | A | League | L 1-3 | Coppell | 49 137 | 5 | Used sub: McCreery |
| Team: | Stepney, Nicholl, Houston, Jackson, B Greenhoff, Coppell, McIlroy, Pearson, Macari, Daly | | | | | | | |
| Wed 12 Nov | Manchester City | A | League Cup 4th round | L 0-4 | | 50 182 | | |
| Team: | Roche, Nicholl, Houston, Jackson, B Greenhoff, Coppell, McIlroy, Pearson, Macari, Daly, | | | | | | | |
| Sat 15 Nov | Aston Villa | H | League | W 2-0 | Coppell, McIlroy | 51 682 | 3 | Debut of Hill / Used sub: McCreery |
| Team: | Roche, Nicholl, Houston, Daly, Coppell, McIlroy, Pearson, Macari, Hill, | | | | | | | |
| Sat 22 Nov | Arsenal | A | League | L 1-3 | Pearson | 40 102 | 5 | Used sub: McCreery |
| Team: | Roche, Nicholl, Houston, Daly, Coppell, McIlroy, Pearson, Macari, Hill, | | | | | | | |

| DATE | OPPONENTS | HOME or AWAY | COMPETITION | RESULT | SCORER(S) | ATTENDANCE | LEAGUE POS AFTER MATCH | NOTES | | | | |
|---|---|---|---|---|---|---|---|---|---|---|---|---|
| Sat 29 Nov | Newcastle United | H | League | W 1-0 | Daly | 52 624 | 4 | | | | | |
| Team: | Nicholl, | Houston, | Daly, | B Greenhoff, | M Buchan, | Coppell, | McIlroy, | Pearson, | Macari, | Hill, | Used sub: | McCreery |
| | Stepney, | | | | | | | | | | | |
| Sat 06 Dec | Middlesbrough | A | League | D 0-0 | | 32 454 | 4 | | | | | |
| Team: | Forsyth, | Houston, | Daly, | B Greenhoff, | M Buchan, | Coppell, | McIlroy, | Pearson, | Macari, | Hill, | Used sub: | Nicholl |
| | Stepney, | | | | | | | | | | | |
| Sat 13 Dec | Sheffield United | A | League | W 4-1 | Pearson 2, Hill, Macari | 31 741 | 4 | | | | | |
| Team: | Forsyth, | Houston, | Daly, | B Greenhoff, | M Buchan, | Coppell, | McIlroy, | Pearson, | Macari, | Hill, | Used sub: | McCreery |
| | Stepney, | | | | | | | | | | | |
| Sat 20 Dec | Wolverhampton Wanderers | H | League | W 1-0 | Hill | 44 269 | 2 | Debut of Kelly | | | | |
| Team: | Forsyth, | Houston, | Daly, | B Greenhoff, | M Buchan, | Coppell, | McIlroy, | Pearson, | Macari, | Hill, | Used sub: | Kelly |
| | Stepney, | | | | | | | | | | | |
| Tue 23 Dec | Everton | A | League | D 1-1 | Macari | 41732 | 1 | | | | | |
| Team: | Forsyth, | Houston, | Daly, | B Greenhoff, | M Buchan, | Coppell, | McIlroy, | Pearson, | Macari, | Hill, | | |
| | Stepney, | | | | | | | | | | | |
| Sat 27 Dec | Burnley | H | League | W 2-1 | McIlroy, Macari | 59726 | 2 | | | | | |
| Team: | Forsyth, | Houston, | Daly, | B Greenhoff, | M Buchan, | Coppell, | McIlroy, | Pearson, | Macari, | Hill, | Used sub: | McCreery |
| | Stepney, | | | | | | | | | | | |
| Sat 03 Jan | Oxford United | H | F.A. Cup 3rd round | W 2-1 | Daly (2 pens) | 41 082 | | | | | | |
| Team: | Forsyth, | Houston, | Daly, | B Greenhoff, | M Buchan, | Coppell, | McIlroy, | Pearson, | Macari, | Hill, | Used sub: | Nicholl |
| | Stepney, | | | | | | | | | | | |
| Sat 10 Jan | Queens Park Rangers | H | League | W 2-1 | Hill, McIlroy | 58312 | 1 | | | | | |
| Team: | Forsyth, | Houston, | Daly, | B Greenhoff, | M Buchan, | Coppell, | McIlroy, | Pearson, | Macari, | Hill, | | |
| | Stepney, | | | | | | | | | | | |
| Sat 17 Jan | Tottenham Hotspur | A | League | D 1-1 | Hill | 49 189 | 1 | | | | | |
| Team: | Forsyth, | Houston, | Daly, | B Greenhoff, | M Buchan, | Coppell, | McIlroy, | Pearson, | Macari, | Hill, | Used sub: | McCreery |
| | Stepney, | | | | | | | | | | | |
| Sat 24 Jan | Peterborough United | H | F.A. Cup 4th round | W 3-1 | Forsyth, McIlroy, Hill | 56 352 | | | | | | |
| Team: | Forsyth, | Houston, | Daly, | B Greenhoff, | M Buchan, | Coppell, | McIlroy, | Pearson, | Macari, | Hill, | Used sub: | |
| | Stepney, | | | | | | | | | | | |
| Sat 31 Jan | Birmingham City | H | League | W 3-1 | Forsyth, Macari, McIlroy | 50 726 | 1 | | | | | |
| Team: | Forsyth, | Houston, | Daly, | B Greenhoff, | M Buchan, | Coppell, | McIlroy, | Pearson, | Macari, | Hill, | Used sub: | McCreery |
| | Stepney, | | | | | | | | | | | |
| Sat 07 Feb | Coventry City | A | League | D 1-1 | Macari | 33 922 | 2 | | | | | |
| Team: | Forsyth, | Houston, | Daly, | B Greenhoff, | M Buchan, | Coppell, | McIlroy, | Pearson, | Macari, | Hill, | Used sub: | McCreery |
| | Stepney, | | | | | | | | | | | |
| Sat 14 Feb | Leicester City | A | F.A. Cup 5th round | W 2-1 | Macari, Daly | 34 000 | | | | | | |
| Team: | Forsyth, | Houston, | Daly, | B Greenhoff, | M Buchan, | Coppell, | McIlroy, | Pearson, | Macari, | Hill, | Used sub: | McCreery |
| | Stepney, | | | | | | | | | | | |
| Wed 18 Feb | Liverpool | H | League | D 0-0 | | 59 709 | 2 | | | | | |
| Team: | Forsyth, | Houston, | Daly, | B Greenhoff, | M Buchan, | Coppell, | McIlroy, | Pearson, | Macari, | Hill, | Used sub: | McCreery |
| | Stepney, | | | | | | | | | | | |

| DATE | OPPONENTS | HOME or AWAY | COMPETITION | RESULT | SCORER(S) | ATTENDANCE | LEAGUE POS AFTER MATCH | NOTES |
|---|---|---|---|---|---|---|---|---|
| Sat 21 Feb | Aston Villa | A | League | L 1-2 | Macari | 50 094 | 3 | Debut of Coyne |
| Team: | Stepney, | Forsyth, | Houston, | Daly, | B Greenhoff, | M Buchan, | Coppell, McIlroy, Pearson, Macari, Hill, | Used sub: Coyne |
| Wed 25 Feb | Derby County | H | League | D 1-1 | Pearson | 59 632 | 3 | |
| Team: | Stepney, | Forsyth, | Houston, | Daly, | B Greenhoff, | M Buchan, | Coppell, McIlroy, Pearson, Macari, Hill, | Used sub: McCreery |
| Sat 28 Feb | West Ham United | H | League | W 4-0 | Forsyth, Macari, McCreery, Pearson | 57 220 | 3 | |
| Team: | Stepney, | Forsyth, | Houston, | Daly, | B Greenhoff, | M Buchan, | Coppell, McIlroy, Pearson, Macari, Hill, | Used sub: McCreery |
| Sat 06 Mar | Wolverhampton Wanderers | H | F.A. Cup 6th round | D 1-1 | Daly | 59433 | | |
| Team: | Stepney, | Forsyth, | Houston, | Daly, | B Greenhoff, | M Buchan, | Coppell, McIlroy, Pearson, Macari, Hill | |
| Tue 09 Mar | Wolverhampton Wanderers | A | F.A. Cup 6th round replay | W 3-2 after extra time | Pearson, Greenhoff, McIlroy | 44373 | | |
| Team: | Stepney, | Forsyth, | Houston, | Daly, | B Greenhoff, | M Buchan, | Coppell, McIlroy, Pearson, Macari, Hill, | Used sub: Nicholl |
| Sat 13 Mar | Leeds United | H | League | W 3-2 | Houston, Pearson, Daly | 59 429 | 3 | |
| Team: | Stepney, | Forsyth, | Houston, | Daly, | B Greenhoff, | M Buchan, | Coppell, McIlroy, Pearson, McCreery, Hill | |
| Wed 17 Mar | Norwich City | A | League | D 1-1 | Hill | 27 782 | 2 | |
| Team: | Stepney, | Forsyth, | Houston, | Daly, | B Greenhoff, | M Buchan, | Coppell, McIlroy, Pearson, McCreery, Hill | |
| Sat 20 Mar | Newcastle United | A | League | W 4-3 | Pearson 2, 2 og | 41 427 | 2 | |
| Team: | Stepney, | Forsyth, | Houston, | Daly, | B Greenhoff, | M Buchan, | Coppell, McIlroy, Pearson, McCreery, Hill | |
| Sat 27 Mar | Middlesbrough | H | League | W 3-0 | Daly (pen), McCreery, Hill | 58527 | 2 | |
| Team: | Stepney, | Forsyth, | Houston, | Daly, | B Greenhoff, | M Buchan, | Coppell, McIlroy, Pearson, McCreery, Hill | |
| Sat 03 Apr | Derby County | N (Hillsbrough) | F.A. Cup semi-final | W 2-0 | Hill 2 | 55000 | | |
| Team: | Stepney, | Forsyth, | Houston, | Daly, | B Greenhoff, | M Buchan, | Coppell, McIlroy, Pearson, McCreery, Hill | |
| Sat 10 Apr | Ipswich Town | A | League | L 0-3 | | 34 889 | 3 | |
| Team: | Stepney, | Forsyth, | Houston, | Daly, | B Greenhoff, | M Buchan, | Coppell, McIlroy, Pearson, McCreery, Hill | |
| Sat 17 Apr | Everton | H | League | W 2-1 | McCreery, og | 61 879 | 3 | |
| Team: | Stepney, | Forsyth, | Houston, | Daly, | B Greenhoff, | M Buchan, | Coppell, McIlroy, Pearson, Macari, Hill, | Used sub: McCreery |
| Mon 19 Apr | Burnley | A | League | W 1-0 | Macari | 27418 | 3 | |
| Team: | Stepney, | Forsyth, | Houston, | Daly, | B Greenhoff, | M Buchan, | Coppell, McIlroy, Pearson, Macari, Hill, | Used sub: Jackson |
| Wed 21 Apr | Stoke City | H | League | L 0-1 | | 53 879 | 3 | |
| Team: | Stepney, | Forsyth, | Houston, | Daly, | B Greenhoff, | Jackson, | McCreery, McIlroy, McCreery, Macari, Hill, | Used sub: Nicholl |

| | DATE | OPPONENTS | HOME or AWAY | COMPETITION | RESULT | SCORER(S) | ATTENDANCE | LEAGUE POS AFTER MATCH | NOTES | | | | |
|---|---|---|---|---|---|---|---|---|---|---|---|---|---|
| | Sat 24 Apr | Leicester City | A | League | L 1-2 | Coyne | 31 053 | 3 | | | | | |
| Team: | Stepney, | Forsyth, | Houston, | Nicholl, | B Greenhoff, | M Buchan, | Jackson, | McCreery, | Coyne, | Macari, | Hill, | Used sub: | Albiston |
| | Sat 01 May | Southampton | N (Wembley) | F.A. Cup final | L 0-1 | | 100000 | | | | | | |
| Team: | Stepney, | Forsyth, | Houston, | Daly, | B Greenhoff, | M Buchan, | Coppell, | McIlroy, | Pearson, | Macari, | Hill, | Used sub: | McCreery |
| | Tue 04 May | Manchester City | H | League | W 2-0 | Hill, McIlroy | 59 528 | 3 | | | | | |
| Team: | Stepney, | Forsyth, | Houston, | Daly, | Albiston, | M Buchan, | Coppell, | McIlroy, | Pearson, | Jackson, | Hill, | Used sub: | McCreery |

# SEASON: 1976/77

| | DATE | OPPONENTS | HOME or AWAY | COMPETITION | RESULT | SCORER(S) | ATTENDANCE | LEAGUE POS AFTER MATCH | NOTES | | | | |
|---|---|---|---|---|---|---|---|---|---|---|---|---|---|
| | Sat 21 Aug | Birmingham City | H | League | D 2-2 | Coppell, Pearson | 58898 | 12 | Debut of Foggon | | | | |
| Team: | Stepney, | Nicholl, | Houston, | Daly, | B Greenhoff, | M Buchan, | Coppell, | McIlroy, | Pearson, | Macari, | Hill, | Used sub: | Foggon |
| | Tue 24 Aug | Coventry City | A | League | W 2-0 | Macari, Hill | 26775 | 3 | | | | | |
| Team: | Stepney, | Nicholl, | Houston, | Daly, | B Greenhoff, | M Buchan, | Coppell, | McIlroy, | Pearson, | Macari, | Hill | | |
| | Sat 28 Aug | Derby County | A | League | D 0-0 | | 34054 | 4 | | | | | |
| Team: | Stepney, | Nicholl, | Houston, | Daly, | B Greenhoff, | M Buchan, | Coppell, | McIlroy, | Pearson, | Macari, | Hill | | |
| | Wed 01 Sep | Tranmere Rovers | H | League Cup 2nd round | W 5-0 | Daly (2) Macari, Pearson, Hill | 37586 | | | | | | |
| Team: | Stepney, | Nicholl, | Houston, | Daly, | B Greenhoff, | M Buchan, | Coppell, | McIlroy, | Pearson, | Macari, | Hill | | |
| | Sat 04 Sep | Tottenham Hotspur | H | League | L 2-3 | Coppell. Pearson | 60723 | 8 | | | | | |
| Team: | Stepney, | Nicholl, | Houston, | Daly, | B Greenhoff, | M Buchan, | Coppell, | McIlroy, | Pearson, | Macari, | Hill, | Used sub: | McCreery |
| | Sat 11 Sep | Newcastle United | A | League | D 2-2 | Pearson, Greenhoff | 29642 | 8 | | | | | |
| Team: | Stepney, | Nicholl, | Houston, | Daly, | B Greenhoff, | M Buchan, | Coppell, | McIlroy, | Pearson, | Macari, | Hill, | Used sub: | McCreery |
| | Wed 15 Sep | Ajax | A | UEFA Cup 1st round, 1st leg | L 0-1 | | 25000 or 30000 | | | | | | |
| Team: | Stepney, | Nicholl, | Houston, | Daly, | B Greenhoff, | M Buchan, | Coppell, | McIlroy, | Pearson, | Macari, | Hill, | Used sub: | Foggon |
| | Sat 18 Sep | Middlesbrough | H | League | W 2-0 | Pearson, og | 56712 | 5 | | | | | |
| Team: | Stepney, | Nicholl, | Houston, | Daly, | B Greenhoff, | M Buchan, | Coppell, | McIlroy, | Pearson, | Macari, | Hill, | Used sub: | McCreery |
| | Wed 22 Sep | Sunderland | H | League Cup 3rd round | D 2-2 | Pearson, og | 46170 | | | | | | |
| Team: | Stepney, | Nicholl, | Houston, | Daly, | B Greenhoff, | M Buchan, | McCreery, | McIlroy, | Pearson, | Macari, | Hill, | Used sub: | Foggon |

| DATE | OPPONENTS | HOME or AWAY | COMPETITION | RESULT | SCORER(S) | ATTENDANCE | LEAGUE POS AFTER MATCH | NOTES |
|---|---|---|---|---|---|---|---|---|
| Sat 25 Sep | **Manchester City** | A | League | W 3-1 | Coppell, McCreery, Daly | 48861 | 3 | |
| Team: Stepney, | Nicholl, | Houston, | Daly, | B Greenhoff, | M Buchan, | McIlroy, | | Pearson, Macari, Hill, Used sub: McCreery |
| Wed 29 Sep | **Ajax** | H | UEFA Cup 1st round, 2nd leg | W 2-0 | Macari, McIlroy | 58918 | | Debut of Paterson |
| Team: Stepney, | Nicholl, | Houston, | Daly, | B Greenhoff, | M Buchan, | McIlroy, | | Pearson, Macari, Hill, Used subs: Albiston, Paterson |
| Sat 02 Oct | **Leeds United** | A | League | W 2-0 | Daly, Coppell | 44512 | 1 | |
| Team: Stepney, | Nicholl, | Houston, | Daly, | B Greenhoff, | M Buchan, | McIlroy, | | Pearson, Macari, Hill, Used sub: McCreery |
| Mon 04 Oct | **Sunderland** | A | League Cup 3rd round replay | D 2-2 after extra time | Greenhoff, Daly, pen | 30831 | | Debut of Waldron |
| Team: Stepney, | Nicholl, | Houston, | Daly, | Waldron, | M Buchan, | McIlroy, | | Pearson, Macari, Hill, Used sub: Albiston |
| Wed 06 Oct | **Sunderland** | H | League Cup 3rd round 2nd replay | W 1-0 | Greenhoff | 47689 | | |
| Team: Stepney, | Nicholl, | Houston, | Daly, | B Greenhoff, | M Buchan, | McIlroy, | | Pearson, Macari, Hill, Used sub: Albiston |
| Sat 16 Oct | **West Bromwich Albion** | A | League | L 0-4 | | 38037 | 8 | |
| Team: Stepney, | Nicholl, | Houston, | Daly, | B Greenhoff, | Waldron, | McIlroy, | | McCreery, Macari, Hill, Used sub: McCreery |
| Wed 20 Oct | **Juventus** | H | UEFA Cup 2nd round, 1st leg | W 1-0 | Hill | 59000 | | |
| Team: Stepney, | Nicholl, | Houston, | Daly, | B Greenhoff, | Houston, | McIlroy, | | McCreery, B Greenhoff, Macari, Hill, Used sub: McCreery |
| Sat 23 Oct | **Norwich City** | H | League | D 2-2 | Daly (pen), Hill | 54356 | 9 | Debut of McGrath |
| Team: Stepney, | Nicholl, | Albiston, | Daly, | B Greenhoff, | Waldron, | McIlroy, | | Pearson, Macari, Hill, Used sub: McGrath |
| Wed 27 Oct | **Newcastle United** | H | League Cup 4th round | W 7-2 | Hill (3), Houston, Pearson, Nicholl, Coppell | 52002 | | |
| Team: Stepney, | Nicholl, | Houston, | Daly, | B Greenhoff, | Houston, | McIlroy, | | Pearson, Macari, Hill, Used sub: McGrath |
| Sat 30 Oct | **Ipswich Town** | H | League | L 0-1 | Houston, | 57416 | 11 | |
| Team: Stepney, | Nicholl, | Albiston, | Daly, | B Greenhoff, | Houston, | McIlroy, | | Pearson, Macari, Hill, Used sub: McCreery |

| DATE | OPPONENTS | HOME or AWAY | COMPETITION | RESULT | SCORER(S) | ATTENDANCE | LEAGUE POS AFTER MATCH | NOTES | | | | Used sub(s) | |
|---|---|---|---|---|---|---|---|---|---|---|---|---|---|
| Wed 3 Nov | **Juventus** | A | UEFA Cup 2nd round, 2nd leg | L 0-3 | | 66632 | | | | | | Used subs: | McCreery, Paterson |
| Team: | Stepney, | Nicholl, | Albiston, | Daly, | | Coppell, | | Pearson, | Macari, | Hill, | | | |
| Sat 06 Nov | **Aston Villa** | A | League | L 2-3 | Pearson, Hill | 44789 | 14 | | | | | | |
| Team: | Stepney, | Nicholl, | Albiston, | Daly, | Houston, | McIlroy, | Pearson, | Macari, | Hill, | | | | |
| Wed 10 Nov | **Sunderland** | H | League | D 3-3 | Hill, Pearson, Greenhoff | 42685 | 15 | Debut of Clark | | | | Used sub: | Clark |
| Team: | Roche, | Albiston, | Houston, | Daly, | Coppell, | B Greenhoff, | Pearson, | Macari, | Hill, | | | | |
| Sat 20 Nov | **Leicester City** | A | League | D 1-1 | Daly (pen) | 27071 | 13 | Debut of J Greenhoff | | | | | |
| Team: | Stepney, | Nicholl, | Albiston, | Daly, | Coppell, | McIlroy, | Pearson, | J Greenhoff, | Hill, | | | | |
| Sat 27 Nov | **West Ham United** | H | League | L 0-2 | | 55366 | 15 | | | | | | |
| Team: | Stepney, | Forsyth, | Albiston, | Daly, | Coppell, | McIlroy, | Pearson, | J Greenhoff, | Hill, | | | | |
| Wed 01 Dec | **Everton** | H | League Cup 5th round | L 0-3 | | 57738 | | | | | | | |
| Team: | Stepney, | Forsyth, | Albiston, | Daly, | Paterson, | Coppell, | McIlroy, | Pearson, | J Greenhoff, | Hill, | | | |
| Sat 18 Dec | **Arsenal** | A | League | L 1-3 | McIlroy | 39572 | 17 | | | | | Used sub: | McCreery |
| Team: | Stepney, | Forsyth, | Houston, | McIlroy, | B Greenhoff, | McCreery, | J Greenhoff, | Pearson, | Macari, | Hill, | | | |
| Mon 27 Dec | **Everton** | H | League | W 4-0 | Pearson, Macari, Hill, J Greenhoff | 56786 | 15 | | | | | Used sub: | McGrath |
| Team: | Stepney, | Nicholl, | Houston, | McIlroy, | M Buchan, | Coppell, | J Greenhoff, | Pearson, | Macari, | Hill, | | | |
| Sat 01 Jan | **Aston Villa** | H | League | W 2-0 | Pearson (2) | 55446 | 13 | | | | | Used sub: | McCreery |
| Team: | Stepney, | Nicholl, | Houston, | McIlroy, | M Buchan, | Coppell, | J Greenhoff, | Pearson, | Macari, | Hill, | | | |
| Mon 03 Jan | **Ipswich Town** | A | League | L 1-2 | Pearson | 30105 | 14 | | | | | Used sub: | McCreery |
| Team: | Stepney, | Nicholl, | Albiston, | McIlroy, | M Buchan, | McCreery, | J Greenhoff, | Pearson, | Macari, | Hill, | | | |
| Sat 08 Jan | **Walsall** | H | F.A. Cup 3rd round | W 1-0 | Hill | 48870 | | | | | | Used sub: | McGrath |
| Team: | Stepney, | Nicholl, | Houston, | McIlroy, | M Buchan, | Coppell, | J Greenhoff, | Pearson, | Macari, | Hill, | | | |
| Sat 15 Jan | **Coventry City** | H | League | W 2-0 | Macari (2) | 46567 | 11 | | | | | Used sub: | Daly |
| Team: | Stepney, | Nicholl, | Houston, | McIlroy, | M Buchan, | Coppell, | J Greenhoff, | Pearson, | Macari, | Hill, | | | |
| Wed 19 Jan | **Bristol City** | H | League | W 2-1 | Pearson, B Greenhoff | 43051 | 9 | | | | | Used sub: | McCreery |
| Team: | Stepney, | Nicholl, | Houston, | McIlroy, | M Buchan, | Coppell, | J Greenhoff, | Pearson, | Macari, | Hill, | | | |

| DATE | OPPONENTS | HOME or AWAY | COMPETITION | RESULT | SCORER(S) | ATTENDANCE | LEAGUE POS AFTER MATCH | NOTES |
|---|---|---|---|---|---|---|---|---|
| Sat 22 Jan | Birmingham City | A | League | W 3-2 | Houston, J Greenhoff, Pearson | 35316 | 8 | |
| Team: | Stepney, | Houston, | McIlroy, | B Greenhoff, | Coppell, | J Greenhoff, | Pearson, Macari, Hill, | Nicholl, | Used sub: Daly |
| Sat 29 Jan | Queens Park Rangers | H | F.A. Cup 4th round | W 1-0 | Macari | 57422 | | |
| Team: | Stepney, | Houston, | McIlroy, | B Greenhoff, | Coppell, | J Greenhoff, | Pearson, Macari, Hill | Nicholl, | |
| Sat 05 Feb | Derby County | H | League | W 3-1 | Macari, Houston, og | 54044 | 7 | |
| Team: | Stepney, | Houston, | McIlroy, | B Greenhoff, | Coppell, | J Greenhoff, | Pearson, Macari, Daly | Nicholl, | |
| Sat 12 Feb | Tottenham Hotspur | A | League | W 3-1 | Macari, McIlroy, Hill | 45946 | 6 | |
| Team: | Stepney, | Houston, | McIlroy, | B Greenhoff, | Coppell, | J Greenhoff, | Pearson, Macari, Hill | Nicholl, | |
| Wed 16 Feb | Liverpool | H | League | D 0-0 | | 57487 | 6 | |
| Team: | Stepney, | Houston, | McIlroy, | B Greenhoff, | Coppell, | J Greenhoff, | Pearson, Macari, Hill | Nicholl, | |
| Sat 19 Feb | Newcastle United | H | League | W 3-1 | J Greenhoff (3) | 51828 | 4 | |
| Team: | Stepney, | Houston, | McIlroy, | B Greenhoff, | Coppell, | J Greenhoff, | Pearson, Macari, Hill, | Nicholl, | Used sub: Albiston |
| Sat 26 Feb | Southampton | A | F.A. Cup 5th round | D 2-2 | Macari, Hill | 29137 | | |
| Team: | Stepney, | Houston, | McIlroy, | B Greenhoff, | Coppell, | J Greenhoff, | Pearson, Macari, Hill, | Nicholl, | Used sub: McCreery |
| Sat 05 Mar | Manchester City | H | League | W 3-1 | Pearson, Hill, Coppell | 58595 | 4 | |
| Team: | Stepney, | Houston, | McIlroy, | B Greenhoff, | Coppell, | J Greenhoff, | Pearson, Macari, Hill, | Nicholl, | Used sub: McCreery |
| Tue 08 Mar | Southampton | H | F.A. Cup 5th round replay | W 2-1 | J Greenhoff (2) | 58103 | | |
| Team: | Stepney, | Houston, | McIlroy, | B Greenhoff, | Coppell, | J Greenhoff, | Pearson, Macari, Hill | Nicholl, | |
| Sat 12 Mar | Leeds United | H | League | W 1-0 | Coppell | 60612 | 4 | |
| Team: | Stepney, | Houston, | McIlroy, | B Greenhoff, | Coppell, | J Greenhoff, | Pearson, Macari, Hill, | Nicholl, | Used sub: McCreery |
| Sat 19 Mar | Aston Villa | H | F.A. Cup 6th round | W 2-1 | Houston, Macari | 57089 | | |
| Team: | Stepney, | Houston, | McIlroy, | B Greenhoff, | Coppell, | J Greenhoff, | Pearson, Macari, Hill, | Nicholl, | Used sub: McCreery |
| Wed 23 Mar | West Bromwich Albion | H | League | D 2-2 | Hill (pen) Coppell | 51053 | 5 | |
| Team: | Stepney, | Albiston, | McIlroy, | B Greenhoff, | Coppell, | J Greenhoff, | Pearson, Macari, Hill, | | |
| Sat 02 Apr | Norwich City | A | League | L 1-2 | og | 26125 | 6 | |
| Team: | Stepney, | Houston, | McIlroy, | B Greenhoff, | Coppell, | J Greenhoff, McCreery, | Macari, Hill, | Nicholl, | Used sub: McGrath |

| DATE | OPPONENTS | HOME or AWAY | COMPETITION | RESULT | SCORER(S) | ATTENDANCE | LEAGUE POS AFTER MATCH | NOTES | | | |
|---|---|---|---|---|---|---|---|---|---|---|---|
| Tue 05 Apr | Everton | A | League | W 2-1 | Hill (2) | 38216 | 6 | | | | |
| Team: | Stepney, | Houston, | Nicholl, | McIlroy, | B Greenhoff, | Coppell, | J Greenhoff, | Pearson, | Macari, | McCreery, | Hill, | Used sub: | Albiston |
| Sat 09 Apr | Stoke City | H | League | W 3-0 | Houston, Macari, Pearson | 53102 | 5 | | | | |
| Team: | Stepney, | Houston, | Nicholl, | McIlroy, | B Greenhoff, | Coppell, | J Greenhoff, | Pearson, | Macari, | Hill, | Used sub: | McCreery |
| Mon 11 Apr | Sunderland | A | League | L 1-2 | Hill (pen) | 38785 | 5 | | | | |
| Team: | Stepney, | Houston, | Nicholl, | McIlroy, | B Greenhoff, | Coppell, | McCreery, | Pearson, | Macari, | Hill, | Used sub: | Albiston |
| Sat 16 Apr | Leicester City | H | League | D 1-1 | J Greenhoff | 49161 | 5 | | | | |
| Team: | Stepney, | Albiston, | Nicholl, | McIlroy, | B Greenhoff, | Coppell, | J Greenhoff, | Pearson, | Macari, | McCreery, | Used sub: | Hill |
| Tue 19 Apr | Queens Park Rangers | A | League | L 0-4 | | 28848 | 5 | | | | |
| Team: | Stepney, | Albiston, | Nicholl, | McIlroy, | B Greenhoff, | Coppell, | J Greenhoff, | Pearson, | Macari, | McCreery, | Used sub: | Forsyth |
| Sat 23 Apr | Leeds United | N (Hillsbrough) | F.A. Cup semi-final | W 2-1 | J Greenhoff, Coppell | 55000 | | | | | |
| Team: | Stepney, | Houston, | Nicholl, | McIlroy, | B Greenhoff, | Coppell, | J Greenhoff, | Pearson, | Macari, | Hill | | |
| Tue 26 Apr | Middlesbrough | A | League | L 0-3 | | 22000 | 6 | | | | |
| Team: | Stepney, | Houston, | Nicholl, | McIlroy, | B Greenhoff, | Coppell, | J Greenhoff, | Pearson, | Macari, | Hill | | |
| Sat 30 Apr | Queens Park Rangers | H | League | W 1-0 | Macari | 50788 | 6 | | | | |
| Team: | Stepney, | Houston, | Nicholl, | McIlroy, | B Greenhoff, | Coppell, | J Greenhoff, | Pearson, | Macari, | Hill, | Used sub: | McCreery |
| Tue 03 May | Liverpool | A | League | L 0-1 | | 53046 | 6 | | | | |
| Team: | Stepney, | Houston, | Nicholl, | McIlroy, | B Greenhoff, | Coppell, | J Greenhoff, | Pearson, | Macari, | Hill, | Used sub: | McCreery |
| Sat 07 May | Bristol City | A | League | D 1-1 | Forsyth, Albiston | 32166 | 6 | | | | |
| Team: | Stepney, | Houston, | Nicholl, | Jackson, | B Greenhoff, | Coppell, | J Greenhoff (pen), | Pearson, | Macari, | Albiston, | Used sub: | McIlroy |
| Wed 11 May | Stoke City | A | League | D 3-3 | Hill (2), McCreery | 24632 | 6 | | | | |
| Team: | Stepney, | Albiston, | Nicholl, | McIlroy, | Jackson, | Coppell, | McCreery, | McGrath, | Macari, | Hill | | |
| Sat 14 May | Arsenal | H | League | W 3-2 | J Greenhoff, Macari, Hill | 53232 | 5 | | | | |
| Team: | Stepney, | Albiston, | Nicholl, | McIlroy, | B Greenhoff, | Coppell, | J Greenhoff, | Pearson, | Macari, | Hill, | Used sub: | McCreery |
| Mon 16 May | West Ham United | A | League | L 2-4 | Hill, Pearson | 29232 | 6 | | | | |
| Team: | Roche, | Albiston, | Nicholl, | McIlroy, | B Greenhoff, | Coppell, | J Greenhoff, | Pearson, | Macari, | Hill, | Used sub: | McCreery |
| Sat 21 May | Liverpool | N (Wembley) | F.A. Cup final | W 2-1 | Pearson, J Greenhoff | 100000 | | | | | |
| Team: | Stepney, | Albiston, | Nicholl, | McIlroy, | B Greenhoff, | Coppell, | J Greenhoff, | Pearson, | Macari, | Hill, | Used sub: | McCreery |

# Bibliography

## BOOKS

Best, George, *Best of Both Worlds* (Pelham, 1968)

Best, George; Lovejoy, Joe, *Bestie* (Pan, 1999)

Best, George; Wright, Geoffrey, *Where Do I Go from Here?* (Futura, 1982)

Book, Tony; Clayton, David, *Maine Man: The Tony Book Story*, (Mainstream Publishing, 2005)

Charlton, Bobby, *My Manchester United Years* (Headline, 2007)

Coppell, Steve, *Touch and Go* (Collins, 1985)

Crerand, Paddy, *Never Turn the Other Cheek* (HarperSport, 2007)

Crick, Michael; Smith, David, *Manchester United: The Betrayal of a Legend* (Pelham Books, 1989)

Docherty, Tommy, *The Doc: My Story – Hallowed Be Thy Game* (Headline Book Publishing, 2006)

Docherty, Tommy, *Call the Doc* (Hamlyn, 1981)

Docherty, Tommy, *Manchester United: The Quest for Glory* (Sidgwick & Jackson, 1991)

Docherty, Agnes; Docherty Tom, *Married to a Man of Two Halves* (John Blake Publishing, 2008)

Doherty, John; Ponting, Ivan, *The Insider's Guide to Manchester United* (Empire Publications, 2005)

Dunphy, Eamon, *Only a Game? The Diary of a Professional Footballer* (Penguin Books, 1987)

Endlar, Andrew, *Manchester United: The Complete Record* (Orion, 2007)

Graham, George, *The Glory and the Grief: The Life of George Graham* (Andre Deutsch, 1995)

Harding, John, *Behind the Glory: A History of the Professional Footballers Association* (Breedon Books Publishing Co, 2009)

Kelly, Stephen F., *Back Page United* (Aurora, 1990)

Kurt, Richard; Nickeas, Chris, *The Red Army Years: Manchester United in the 1970s* (Headline Book Publishing, 1997)

Law, Denis, *The King* (Bantam Press, 2003)

Law, Denis; Gubba, Ron, *Denis Law: An Autobiography* (Futura, 1980)

Macari, Lou, *United We Shall Not Be Moved* (Readers Union, 1977)

Macari, Lou, *Football, My Life* (Bantam Press, 2008)

McIlroy, Sammy, *Manchester United: My Team* (Readers Union, 1981)

Meek, David, *Manchester United Football Book No. 6* (Stanley Paul, 1971)

Meek, David, *Manchester United Football Book No. 7* (Stanley Paul, 1972)

Meek, David, *Manchester United Football Book No. 8* (Stanley Paul, 1973)

Meek, David, *Manchester United Football Book No. 9* (Stanley Paul, 1974)

Meek, David, *Manchester United Football Book No. 10* (Stanley Paul, 1975)

Meek, David, *Manchester United Football Book No. 11* (Stanley Paul, 1976)

Meek, David, *Manchester United Football Book No. 12* (Stanley Paul, 1977)

Meek, David, *Manchester United Football Book No. 13* (Hutchinson, 1978)

Mourant, Andrew, *The Essential History of Leeds United FC* (Headline Book Publishing, 2002)

Parkinson, Michael, *Best: An Intimate Biography* (Hutchinson, 1975)

Ponting, Ivan, *Manchester United: Player by Player* (Polar Print Group, 2002)

Ponting, Ivan, *Match of My Life – Manchester United* (Know the Score Books, 2007)

Stepney, Alex, *Alex Stepney* (Arthur Barker, 1978)

Tossell, David, *Playing for Uncle Sam: The Brits' Story of the North American Soccer League* (Mainstream Publishing, 2003)

White, Jim, *Always in the Running: Manchester United Dream Team* (Mainstream Publishing, 1996)

The Official Illustrated History Of Manchester United (Orion, 2006)

*Foul: A Compilation* (Simon & Schuster, 1987)

## WEBSITES

www.news.bbc.co.uk

www.european-football-statistics.co.uk

www.fchd.info

www.football-england.com

www.manchesterunited-mad.co.uk

www.redissue.co.uk

www.sevenpennynightmare.co.uk

www.soccer.mistral.co.uk

www.stretfordend.co.uk

www.wikipedia.org

www.youtube.com

## MAGAZINE

*Red News*

## NEWSPAPERS

Every national UK newspaper that existed in the period covered in this book was of great help for match reports and articles about off-field activities.

## VIDEO

*United in the 70s* (Manchester United)

## DVD

*Southampton vs Manchester United 1976 FA Cup Final* (ILC Sport)

*Manchester United vs Liverpool 1977 FA Cup Final* (ILC Sport)

*Manchester United The 70s* (Sanctuary Digital Entertainment)

# Other titles available from Cherry Red Books

*A Plugged In State Of Mind: The History of Electronic Music* Dave Henderson

*All The Young Dudes: Mott The Hoople & Ian Hunter* Campbell Devine

*Best Seat In The House: A Cock Sparrer Story* Steve Bruce

*Bittersweet: The Clifford T Ward Story* David Cartwright

*Block Buster! – The True Story of The Sweet* Dave Thompson

*Burning Britain: A History Of UK Punk 1980 To 1984* Ian Glasper

*Celebration Day: A Led Zeppelin Encyclopedia* Malcolm Dome and Jerry Ewing

*Children of the Revolution: The Glam Rock Encyclopedia* Dave Thompson

*Death To Trad Rock: The Post-Punk fanzine scene 1982-87* John Robb

*Deathrow: The Chronicles Of Psychobilly* Alan Wilson

*Embryo:- A Pink Floyd Chronology 1966-1971* Nick Hodges and Ian Priston

*Fucked By Rock (revised and expanded)* Mark Manning (aka Zodiac Mindwarp)

*Goodnight Jim Bob:On The Road With Carter USM* Jim Bob

*Good Times Bad Times - The Rolling Stones 1960-69* Terry Rawlings and Keith Badman

*Hells Bent On Rockin: A History Of Psychobilly* Craig Brackenbridge

*Independence Days - The Story Of UK Independent Record Labels* Alex Ogg

*Indie Hits 1980 – 1989* Barry Lazell

*Irish Folk, Trad And Blues: A Secret History* Colin Harper and Trevor Hodgett

*Johnny Thunders: In Cold Blood* Nina Antonia

*Kiss Me Neck – A Lee 'Scratch' Perry Discography* Jeremy Collingwood

*Music To Die For: The International Guide To Goth, Goth Metal, Horror Punk, Psychobilly etc*
 Mick Mercer

*No More Heroes: A Complete History Of UK Punk From 1976 To 1980* Alex Ogg

*Number One Songs In Heaven – The Sparks Story* Dave Thompson

*Our Music Is Red - With Purple Flashes: The Story Of The Creation* Sean Egan

*Prophets and Sages: The 101 Greatest Progressive Rock Albums* Mark Powell

*PWL: From The Factory Floor (expanded edition)* Phil Harding

OTHER TITLES AVAILABLE FROM CHERRY RED BOOKS

*Quite Naturally - The Small Faces* Keith Badman and Terry Rawlings

*Random Precision - Recording The Music Of Syd Barrett 1965-1974* David Parker

*Rockdetector: A To Zs of '80s Rock / Black Metal / Death Metal / Doom, Gothic & Stoner Metal / Power Metal and Thrash Metal* Garry Sharpe-Young

*Rockdetector: Black Sabbath – Never Say Die* Garry Sharpe-Young

*Rockdetector: Ozzy Osbourne* Garry Sharpe-Young

*Tamla Motown - The Stories Behind The Singles* Terry Wilson

*The Day The Country Died: A History Of Anarcho Punk 1980 To 1984* Ian Glasper

*The Legendary Joe Meek - The Telstar Man* John Repsch

*The Motorhead Collector's Guide* Mick Stevenson

*The Rolling Stones: Complete Recording Sessions 1962-2002* Martin Elliott

*The Secret Life Of A Teenage Punk Rocker: The Andy Blade Chronicles* Andy Blade

*Those Were The Days - The Beatles' Apple Organization* Stefan Grenados

*Trapped In A Scene: UK Hardcore 1985-89* Ian Glasper

*Truth... Rod Steward, Ron Wood And The Jeff Beck Group* Dave Thompson

*You're Wondering Now – The Specials from Conception to Reunion* Paul Williams


Please visit www.cherryredbooks.co.uk for further info and mail order

# Also by Sean Egan from Cherry Red Book

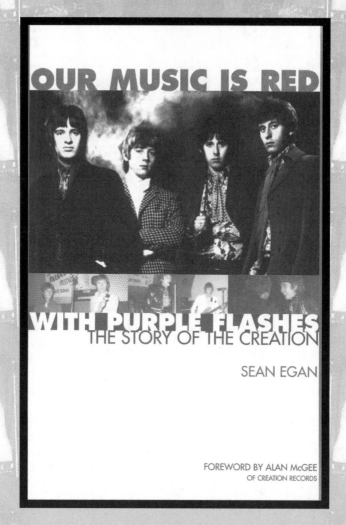

The life and times of the legendary 'Greatest Band You Never Heard Of'.
Explored in amazing detail, from their 1960s heyday through to their 1990s
reunion, and with a foreword by Mr Alan McGee of Creation Records, this
is the definitive account of a much loved band whose influence has spread
far and wide, despite their releasing only a clutch of singles and falling
between the cracks of the industry after a tantalisingly brief career.

**Includes photographs, complete discography and song-by-song analysis**

# CHERRY RED BOOKS

Here at Cherry Red Books we're always interested to hear of interesting titles looking for a publisher. Whether it's a new manuscript or an out of print or deleted title, please feel free to get in touch if you've written, or are aware of, a book you feel might be suitable.

books@cherryred.co.uk
www.cherryredbooks.co.uk
www.cherryred.co.uk

CHERRY RED BOOKS
A division of Cherry Red Records Ltd,
Power Road Studios
114 Power Road
London
W4 5PY

THE SONGS OF PORTSMOUTH FC

GOONER CLASSICS

GLORY – GLO
TOTTENHAM H

GLORY GLORY AYRSHIRE K

CHERRY RED RECORDS

**Cherry Red is an established authority on football related music (if we dare call it that!). Our catalogue features numerous individual titles, including:**

ABERDEEN FC & SUPPORTERS - COME ON YOU REDS
ARSENAL FC - HIGHBURY ANTHEMS: 18 GOONER CLASSICS
BIRMINGHAM FC & SUPPORTERS - SINGING THE BLUES
BURNLEY FC - CLARET COLLECTION
CARDIFF CITY FC - BLUEBIRDS: THE SONGS OF CARDIFF
CELTIC FC - SONGS OF CELTIC GREEN AND WHITE
CHELSEA FC - BLUE FLAG: A TRIBUTE TO CHELSEA
EVERTON FC - FOREVER EVERTON
HEARTS FC - HEARTS SONGS: 20 JAMBO CLASSICS
HIBERNIAN FC - GLORY GLORY TO THE HIBEES
IPSWICH TOWN FC - SINGING THE BLUES
KILMARNOCK FC - GLORY GLORY AYRSHIRE KILLIE
LIVERPOOL FC - THE KOP CHOIR
MIDDLESBOROUGH FC - BORO SONGS
NORWICH CITY FC - ON THE BALL CITY
RANGERS FC - FOLLOW FOLLOW: THE RANGERS ANTHEMS
SHEFFIELD WEDNESDAY FC - WE ARE THE OWLS
SOUTHAMPTON FC - SUPER SAINTS
SUNDERLAND AFC - MACKEM MUSIC
THIS IS ANFIELD - LIVERPOOLS GREATEST HITS
TOTTENHAM HOTSPUR FC - GLORY GLORY TOTTENHAM HOTSPUR
WE ARE TOTTENHAM - SPURS ANTHEMS
WEST HAM UNITED FC - FOREVER BLOWING BUBBLES
WOLVERHAMPTON WANDERERS FC - OLD GOLD ANTHEMS
VARIOUS ARTISTS - HAIL! HAIL! CELTIC
VARIOUS ARTISTS - BLUE MOON: TRIBUTE TO MAN CITY
VARIOUS ARTISTS - SCOTTISH WORLD CUP ANTHEMS
VARIOUS ARTISTS - BLUE ANTHEMS: SOUND OF RANGERS
VARIOUS ARTISTS - ALBION ANTHEMS
VARIOUS ARTISTS - THE SONGS OF CELTIC ANTHEMS 2
VARIOUS ARTISTS - PLAY UP POMPEY
VARIOUS ARTISTS - WALES, LAND OF MY FATHERS
VARIOUS ARTISTS - THE OFFICIAL BARMY ARMY COLLECTION

Spurs Anthems

**www.cherryred.co.uk**

THE SOUND OF